Slavery and the American West

MICHAEL A. MORRISON

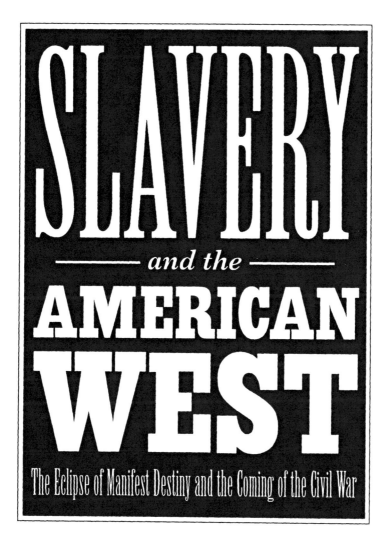

SLAVERY
—— and the ——
AMERICAN
WEST

The Eclipse of Manifest Destiny and the Coming of the Civil War

THE UNIVERSITY OF NORTH CAROLINA PRESS

CHAPEL HILL AND LONDON

The paper in this book meets the guidelines for permanence and
durability of the Committee on Production Guidelines for Book
Longevity of the Council on Library Resources.

Library of Congress Cataloging-in-Publication Data

Morrison, Michael A., 1948–

Slavery and the American West : the eclipse of manifest destiny and
the coming of the Civil War / by Michael A. Morrison.

p. cm.   Includes bibliographical references and index.

ISBN 0-8078-2319-8 (cloth: alk. paper)

ISBN 0-8078-4796-8 (pbk.: alk. paper)

1. United States—History—Civil War, 1861–1865—Causes. 2. United
States—Territorial expansion. 3. Slavery—United States—Extension
to the territories. 4. Sectionalism (United States). I. Title.

E415.7.M88   1997   96-23855

973.7′11—dc20   CIP

Portions of this work appeared earlier, in somewhat different form, in
"Westward the Curse of Empire: Texas Annexation and the Ameri-
can Whig Party," *Journal of the Early Republic* 10 (Summer 1990); "'New
Territory versus No Territory': The Whig Party and the Politics of
Western Expansion, 1846–1848," *Western Historical Quarterly* 23 (Febru-
ary 1992); and "Martin Van Buren, the Democracy, and the Partisan
Politics of Texas Annexation," *Journal of Southern History* 61 (November
1995), and are reprinted here with permission of the publishers.

cloth   06 05 04 03 02   5 4 3 2 1

paper   06 05 04 03 02   7 6 5 4 3

To my parents, for character

To my wife, for courage

Contents

Acknowledgments

A colleague and friend of mine once observed that to be a historian one must listen to the voices of the past in a loving and critical way, reflect upon those voices, and write them up. Although for me history was a celestial calling, I learned to listen and understand by adopting and, I trust, absorbing the professionalism of others. Bradford Perkins, a man of broad intellectual horizons and great personal dignity, encouraged me to examine old questions from new perspectives. Seeing this project through from first drafts to book manuscript, he has been at once encouraging, skeptical, tolerant, and good-humored. Brad always posed the most challenging questions, made prescient suggestions, and provided timely support whenever I faltered. Sidney Fine, a prodigious researcher and writer, set standards of conduct and accomplishments that are for me as inspiring as they are intimidating. A quintessential scholar, Sidney inspired in me a love of labor. Moreover, he made me aware that our students are a family, and I am lucky to be one of his. My greatest intellectual debt, one that I can never repay, is to J. Mills Thornton III. The spiritual father of this study, Mills has shaped and continues to mold my thinking in subtle and incalculable ways. His interest in, and enthusiasm for, my work are constant and critical sources of sustenance. Most important, Mills taught me how to hear and understand those voices from the past. Whatever value this book may have is owing to his guidance and inspiration.

My colleagues at Purdue, John L. Larson, Robert E. May, and Harold Woodman, have read various parts of the book and have freely offered incisive critiques. John J. Contreni, the head of my department, has been solicitous and supportive of a young scholar's spiritual and financial needs.

I have tried out my ideas in a variety of ways—formal and otherwise—on willing and long-suffering peers. John M. Belohlavek, Kinley J. Brauer, Daniel W. Crofts, Daniel Feller, Phyllis F. Field, Ralph D. Gray, Peter B. Knupfer, Stephen E. Maizlish, Craig M. Simpson, Fred Somkin, Harvey J. Strum, Eric H. Walther, and William Earl Weeks have all read, reacted to, and informed various sections of this work. William W. Freehling and Major L. Wilson have pored over larger portions of the manuscript and have challenged my assumptions in an encouraging and supportive manner. They are real gentlemen. Special mention goes to Peter S. Onuf and Lacy K. Ford Jr., who read the revised manuscript and provided me with clear, direct suggestions for its improvement. My debt to all of these professionals, and I use the term advisedly, is enormous for, as Sir Isaac Newton once put it, "If I have seen farther, it is by standing on the shoulders of others."

It has been said that money makes the world go around; it certainly is critical to research and writing. I had the very good fortune to be the American Historical Association's J. Franklin Jameson Fellow for 1990-91. The association's support was critical to the postdoctoral research that informs my work. A travel grant from the National Endowment for the Humanities allowed me, ever the Yankee, to pillage additional archives in the South. Grants from the Purdue Research Foundation and the School of Liberal Arts underwrote a summer and a semester of writing.

I would also like to thank the librarians and archivists at the manuscript depositories and public and university libraries where I did my research. To a person, they were helpful, courteous, and attentive. In particular, I would like to express my gratitude to David Wigdor and his colleagues at the Library of Congress. The library is a magnificent and unique resource, and the individuals who staff it are unequaled in their professionalism. Not to be outdone by federal largesse, the Southern Historical Collection is an equally invaluable resource for slave-state manuscripts. The staff there went out of their way to alert me to relevant collections. Thanks as well to Purdue's Interlibrary Loan Office which processed my many requests and put up with my pestering.

I am delighted beyond words that the University of North Carolina agreed to publish this book. Lewis Bateman, the press's executive editor, likes to say he was in on this project from the beginning. I would be a fool to deny it. Lewis has been as much a good friend as an interested editor. He was patient, encouraging, and understanding. I, like many others in the profession, owe him a lot.

Ron Maner, the managing editor for the book, has guided this tyro through the publication process with sage advice, warm support, and good humor.

Throughout, he has been attentive and solicitous, and for that I am much in his debt. Trudie Calvert edited the manuscript with the greatest care. Trudie saved me from a number of errors, idiotic and egregious, and at every turn her editorial input has improved the whole. Maria L. Drake, my partner in crime at the *Journal of the Early Republic*, provided critical technical and editorial assistance in the preparation of the manuscript. More important, she does not sweat visibly when I harass her with another computer problem. Montgomery Buell performed yeoman service checking the accuracy of the notes and bibliography.

Finally, family. My parents, Al and Joan Morrison, whose roots stretch from the Canadian prairies to the steel towns of western Pennsylvania, taught me the purpose and rewards of work and accomplishment. By example, they imbued their firstborn with a sense of responsibility to self and others. I love and revere them. My brothers and sisters continue to provide a warm, loving support system. Although they sometimes have lost track of my work ("Don't get mad, but what is it that you're writing about?" "You know, the Civil War—it was in all the papers!"), they have always taken great pride in my accomplishments—whatever they might have been.

My mother-in-law, Ellen Gabin, provided room, board, and psychological maintenance on my several research trips to New England. As for my sister-in-law, Jody, who was always good company, "Oh, how I wish that you were here again; just to see you and touch you with my hand."

Special mention and a heartfelt thank you go to my uncle, Bernard R. Morrison. A retired steelworker, he was my boon companion on a number of research trips. We share a love of history, an addiction to cribbage, the thrill of adventure on the open road, and rooms in some of the more exotic motels in America, including our favorite, the Snow White motel outside Richmond.

I will never admit, for I do not believe, that scholarship and teaching are mutually exclusive. Alas, scholarship and parenting are. Both my children, Natty and Katie, have lived with this book since they entered this vale of tears. Katie, who is the youngest at six, has always evinced a healthy skepticism of the historian's craft. Still, she has often sat quietly with me and colored in her "scientist's books" while I cranked microfilm and labored at the computer. Her very presence has lessened the solitude of my work. Older by four years and more philosophical, Natty has been more tolerant and appreciative—up to a point. Upon hearing about the contract he observed, "See dad, all that hard work paid off—[pregnant pause]—*now* can we go shoot hoops?" Both of my beautiful children have been constant reminders that there is indeed a delightful life beyond academe. I hope that when Natty and Katie get older they will not begrudge me the time spent on this work and will know that throughout I carried them in my heart.

This book would not have seen the light of day without the support of my wife, Nancy Felice Gabin, whose "love is the whole and more than all." Generous to a fault, she put aside her own important research to read, criticize, and edit the manuscript. Nancy played the role of single parent when I was away and tended to the needs of Natty and Katie when I was holed up in the study. Because she embodies and counsels patience and perseverance, she infused me with the strength to complete this work. Above all, Nancy's companionship provides the context for my life. Looking ahead to our lives together, I trust that "the way be long, full of adventures and experiences."

Slavery and the American West

Serious history is the critique of myths . . . not the embodiment of them.
Neither is it the destruction of myths. — C. Vann Woodward

I cannot tell how the truth may be;
I say the tale as 'twas said to me.
— Sir Walter Scott

Introduction

On October 13, 1859, three days before John Brown's raid on Harpers Ferry, a worried Democratic newspaper editor, Thomas B. Stevenson, wrote to diplomat and author William B. Reed about the Democracy and the nation's future. Stevenson, an ardent expansionist, urged Reed to write an article on the territorial question in such a way as to allay the persistent and, to Stevenson's mind, infernal wrangle over the slavery issue. There were far more important matters than slavery to be considered when addressing the question of federal power and policy respecting the territories, he claimed. "They are such, in my opinion, as seriously affect the future of the Union: whether it can be legitimately strengthened by expansion, and the proper modes and ends of providing our children happy destinies in the future." Although Stevenson wanted to seize upon the issue of expansion to divert the minds of the people, he despaired because demagogy seemed ascendant. "It is easy in the North to gain power by denouncing slavery's existence in the South, and as easy in the South to win favor by denouncing its northern opponents," Stevenson observed. "It is not, I fear, either the actual status or the actual settlement of the slavery question that the antagonistic agitators really wish to effect. It is the use they can make of it as it exists."[1] What Stevenson sensed but could not bring himself to accept was the eclipse of interparty debate between Democrats and Whigs over expansion by the regionally defined politics of the slavery extension issue. That transformation is the focus of this work.

The southern historian Charles Ramsdell once observed that no other event in American history has produced such a flood of controversial literature as the Civil War.[2] The earliest interpretations of the conflict focused on war guilt. Northern writers such as Henry Wilson, appealing to the moral absolutes of freedom and national unity, charged that secession was the result of a slavepower conspiracy that was intent on breaking up a Union it could not control. "By means illegitimate and indefensible," Wilson asserted, "reckless of principle and of consequences, a comparatively few men succeeded in dragooning whole States into the support of a policy the majority condemned, to following leaders the majority distrusted and most cordially disliked."[3]

Southern writers, in contrast, flatly denied that they had perpetrated any perfidy or wrong or had broken any sacred compact. To the contrary, apologists such as Alexander H. Stephens maintained that northern restrictionists, stung by their defeats in Congress, openly resorted to stirring up a sectional conflict "with a view to kindle a general war in the States, for the total abolition of slavery."[4] He and others contended that northern politicians and capitalists consolidated the numerical majority of their own section on the pretext of restricting the spread of slavery. Their real design was to destroy the rights of the southern states and subvert the Constitution in order to seize political power, exploit the slave states, and thereby promote their own wealth. Southern states withdrew from the Union to protect their people from destruction by a hostile majority.

Beginning in the last quarter of the nineteenth century and into the early twentieth, scholars such as James Ford Rhodes, Edward Channing, Frederick Jackson Turner, and John Bach McMaster identified slavery as the central—indeed virtually the only—cause of the Civil War. The North and South, alienated by irreconcilable differences over the institution—one detesting, the other embracing it—constituted two distinct nations living under a common constitution and government. "Two such divergent forms of society could not continue indefinitely to live side by side within the walls of one government," Channing observed, "even within the walls of so loosely constructed a system as that of the United States government under the Constitution." Riven by a moral issue, the free and slave states found themselves in an intractable disagreement over the continued existence—and extension—of the institution, which eventually exploded in an irrepressible conflict. Given the moral implications of this sectional conflict, Rhodes concluded, "it seemed well nigh impossible to hit upon the common ground of opinion which was a necessary antecedent to compromise."[5]

Progressive historians, especially Charles and Mary Beard, disregarded moral considerations and placed in opposition not slavery and liberty but agrarianism and capitalism, free trade and protection. The "dynamic thrust" of northern industrialization, the centralization of political and economic ties between the agricultural West and the industrial Northeast, "and the southward pressure of the capitalist glacier" were too powerful for slaveholders to resist: "The approaching triumph of machine industry, warned the planters of their ultimate subjection."[6] Sectional conflict, as the Beards had it, was a struggle over the distribution of wealth. Highly charged verbal disputes were simply "linguistic devices" that masked material conflict. Principles were rationalizations; power was real.

Subsequently in the 1940s and into the 1950s, revisionists like James G. Randall and Avery Craven, writing in the shadows of the great world wars, argued that the Civil War was a "repressible conflict"—a needless war—precipitated by a blundering generation of inept and demagogic politicians who inflamed public sentiment over irrelevant issues. "To see the period as it is," Randall concluded, "is to witness uninspired spectacles of prejudice, error, intolerance, and selfish grasping."[7] Small minorities, then, caused the war; the sections fought it.

Historians influenced by a concern for civil rights again emphasized the moral dimension of the sectional conflict over slavery. Arthur M. Schlesinger Jr. condemned revisionists for their "tendency to seek in optimistic sentimentalism an escape from the severe demands of moral decision." Schlesinger admitted that the territorial issue along with the fugitive slave law were critical to sectional tensions. But he maintained that it was the "moral issue of slavery . . . that gave the struggles . . . their significance."[8] In the 1960s, modernizationists defined the crisis as one that pitted the value systems of a northern industrial society against the South's agrarian, anticapitalist way of life. The most nuanced and sophisticated statement of this position is Eric Foner's study of free labor ideology and the unfolding of a political antislavery movement that glorified northern society and used it as a yardstick by which to measure the South's society and economics.[9]

Since the late 1960s, "new political historians" have contended that the sectional emphasis on the war's origins had created a false synthesis. Instead they have discounted the importance of slavery, the territories, and a national political agenda altogether. They contend that variables such as religious affiliation and ethnicity and issues like temperance, nativism, and anti-Catholicism shaped political alignments and determined voting behavior. The disruption of the Union and the Civil War, however, remain undeniable and bothersome facts. Some have contended that secessionists, most of whom were Democrats, feared the cultural hegemony of ascendant Republicans who wished to remake the world by purging it of its evils. Because these included slavery, southern defense of the institution is to be seen in the context of the traditional Democratic defense of pluralistic values.[10]

Clearly the complexity of factors—some obscure, others elusive, and all difficult to analyze quantitatively—continues to baffle and intrigue historians of the middle period. For more than a century, generations of historians working in shifts like coal miners have labored to unearth the real source and thus the true essence of sectional strife. Adding to their efforts, this book examines the relationship between the territorial issue and the origins of the American Civil War. The story is familiar; this telling is not. Lying at the intersection of political, diplomatic, and intellectual history, it explores the origin, force, and effect of expansion and western settlement on national politics in the 1840s and 1850s. The book is a narrative of political affairs. It does not, however, focus on party structure or political maneuvers. Those are better and more fully handled elsewhere.[11] Rather than retell events, the purpose here is to illuminate and analyze the principled conflicts over slavery extension. The debate between Democrats and Whigs over Texas in 1844 were based on economics and divided the parties along national lines. By 1860, the struggle over westward expansion and settlement issued in sectional alignments and a fragmented political system. This transformation is the story herein told.

In the spring of 1857, as Congress and settlers battled among and between themselves for control of Kansas, a Pittsburgh editor told his readers what no doubt they well knew. "The prevailing epidemic in this country is to 'go West,'" he observed. "Hardly a man can be found but desires to 'go West' either to speculate in lands for a time, or to settle there permanently." He knew, as did Americans North and South, that "cheap lands" and "soil and climate are the main attractions." In fact, western migration from the seventeenth century to the advent of the Texas question had proceeded in a cyclical fashion, advancing rapidly in boom times and lagging in periods of international crisis and economic depression. Nonetheless, the most vigorous, sustained era of expansion took place between 1790 and 1840 when Americans moved to the West at the astoundingly high rate of 2.47 percent per annum.[12]

Aggregate numbers are even more striking. From 1810 to 1860, Americans and European immigrants moved west steadily and in large numbers. Rates of population increase per decade in these years averaged 96 percent in the Old Northwest and 109 percent in the slaveholding Southwest. Put in other terms, the average population growth of the Old Northwest and the Southwest doubled every ten years. By 1860, the population of the Midwest (Iowa, Minnesota, Nebraska, Kansas, and the Dakota territory) surged to 988,000. From 1840 to 1860, the population of Iowa alone rose from 43,000 to 675,000, an increase of 1,470 percent. After the Oregon issue was resolved in 1846 and California and the Far West were acquired two years later, the number of settlers there swelled to nearly 600,000 by 1860.[13]

Pushed onto the frontier by overcrowding and soil exhaustion in the East, immigrants were also pulled to the West by the prospects of personal independence and upward mobility. Although per capita income in the Old Northwest and Southwest was somewhat lower than in the East, wealth on the frontier was more evenly distributed. More important, prospects for upward mobility and self-sufficiency were significant, regional variations notwithstanding. In the rural North and South, young tenant farmers could reasonably expect to own their own farms by the time they reached middle age. Households grew wealthier as their heads became older, and approximately two-thirds of antebellum households owned land.[14] Therefore, when John Tyler introduced the issue of territorial expansion into the national political dialogue in 1844 with Texas annexation, its appeal and force could not have been more resonant.

The first theme of the book is to root expansion and western settlement within the context of Jacksonian politics. Instructed by a political culture whose purpose was to realize and extend the basic republican tenets of equality and liberty, enthusiasts of Texas annexation understood the political power of territorial aggrandizement. Though traditionally viewed as a southern ploy to sectionalize parties, annexation of Texas, as Tyler knew, could be made the means of reorganizing a fragmented and fluid political system. Territorial expansion and settlement promised literally enlarging freedom over space by the extension of American institutions into the Southwest and to the Pacific coast. They also promised to ensure personal freedom by meeting the territorial needs of a nation of autonomous, self-reliant, footloose yeomen. Finally, Texas, then Oregon, promised to ameliorate class divisions and promote equality by providing the means of upward mobility through enhanced commercial opportunities and newly opened lands.

In their defense of widespread and rapid territorial growth, expansionists quoted chapter and verse from *Federalist* Number 10. Like James Madison, they believed that to "extend the sphere . . . you make it less probable that a majority of the whole will have a common motive to invade the rights of other citizens." This much expansionists had adopted from revolutionary republicanism. Yet they forgot or failed to comprehend that Madison premised his brief for a widespread republic on the recognition that liberty and equality—freedom and democracy—are fundamentally antagonistic. *Federalist* Number 10 said so explicitly.[15] By 1844, however, expansionists in both parties and in all sections insisted that they were interchangeable and mutually reinforcing. Therein lay the power of Tyler's initiative.

The desire to maintain and expand freedom accordingly gave significance and force to antebellum territorial aggrandizement. It propelled western migration. It also meant that the political source of the Civil War would come to be anchored in the meaning of national expansion. Thus a second theme of the book is to explain how specifically the territorial issue contributed to the fragmentation and sectionalization of the two-party system. For if the origin and essence of expansionism are rooted in Jacksonian political culture, then one must examine the breakup of Whiggery and the Democracy to account for the absence of widespread territorial growth in the 1850s. The territorial issue, as we shall see, was not an abstraction as the revisionists claim. Nor did its importance abate after the resolution of the Kansas crisis in 1858. Americans in both sections believed that their future and that of republican institutions everywhere were tied to the slave status of the territories.

The introduction of the Wilmot Proviso in 1846, which would have barred slavery from the Mexican cession, initiated the transition of interparty debate over expansion to the sectionalized politics of slavery extension. If Madison assumed that expansive republics "made it more difficult for all who feel [a common interest] to discover their own strength, and to act in unison with each other," he miscalculated badly.[16] The proviso posited an immutable battle between the North and South for control of the government and thus the ability to secure the fortunes of one or the other section. Although the final resolution of the problem was more than a decade away, the basic parameters of the sectional equation were articulated and defined in the late 1840s.

In a nation that abhorred dependency and repudiated inequality, slavery constituted an organizational metaphor that infused the sectional debate down to the secession of the South. Citizens of the free and slave states insisted that freedom as a symbol existed because slavery existed. Nahum Capen put it neatly: "Freedom is the condition of a living and self-sustaining principle, and slavery is a relative term, which indicates the degrees of its practical enjoyments. As one is advanced, the other is lessened."[17] As Capen perhaps understood, the meaning of slavery in the territorial issue must be read at a number of levels. As the nation addressed slavery's relevance to American society, it spoke to the present and the future. In short, were the institutions of the West, and for that matter future acquisitions, to resemble those of the North or South? The answer to this momentous question, it was believed, would determine the essence and ultimate destiny of the nation.

The surest way to secure the future, northerners asserted, was to plant the frontier with white, free labor. Slavery, they believed, retarded the progress of the nation, degraded white workers, and contravened the fundamental republican principles of liberty and equality. To them the essence of the territorial issue was whether the national government would be administered in the spirit of the revolutionary heritage or handed over to an aristocratic power. Southerners—slaveholders and nonslaveholders alike—replied that slavery promoted equality by meliorating class conflict and ensured liberty by making exploitation of white workers and independent agriculturists unnecessary. Northerners, of course, noted that restriction would affect only the slaveholders, not the poorer southerners. But if, as southerners believed, the northern free labor system generated hierarchy, oligarchy, conflict between capital and democracy, and relationships founded on economic dependency, inviting southerners to emigrate to such a society was to ask them to move to an alien, un-American world.

Inherent in the disruption of the second party system was the concomitant sectionalization of the inherited revolutionary political heritage. In a nation in which loyalties were first to the community, then to the state, the Revolution provided a common heritage to a diverse citizenry.[18] That experience shaped the outlook and was the language of Jacksonian America. This transformation forms the third theme of this book. Whereas the analysis of expansionism and the investigation of the territorial question take issue with the extant literature, a study of the changing nature of a nationally shared ideology fills a void in antebellum historiography. Michael Holt, Mills Thornton, William Gienapp, and Lacy Ford among others have affirmed the importance of a revolutionary ideology that both paid homage to, and was defined by, the tenets of liberty and equality.[19] They have also noted its relationship to political realignment in the 1850s. Nonetheless, historians have been slow to explore fully the manner in which this commonly shared heritage was modified.

Northern restrictionists contended that the Founding Fathers rebelled to defend their autonomy from the encroachments of a government hostile to their liberties and ambitions. Supporters of Wilmot's proviso were determined to perpetuate that legacy by defending the independence of western settlers against the pretensions and power of slaveholders. Denying that they acted aggressively, restrictionists claimed they were preserving the essence of the Revolution and the intent of the framers of the Constitution.

Southerners returned that the Revolution was to be understood as a defense of a minority's rights in a constitutional government. The revolutionaries resented their treatment as second-class citizens and rejected the oppression of inferiority by rising up and seceding from the empire. In their attack on slavery restriction, states'-rights southerners rejected the claims of provisoists that southern society was inferior. They dismissed out of hand any settlement to the territorial imbroglio that would relegate the slave states to a position of inferiority under the Constitution. They, too, were determined to live up to and live out their revolutionary heritage.

Democrats who attempted to define a middle ground between these extremes also drew on that same heritage. They concluded that the essence of the Revolution lay in the determination of colonists to manage their own affairs. Revolutionaries resented the intrusion of a distant, central government in the local affairs of the several colonies. The Founding Fathers had revolted against a Parliament that governed to promote its own interests against those of the colonists. These Democrats sought to preserve the autonomy of western settlers and their equality within the Union against the intrusions of Washington. Believing in the capacity of the people to manage their own lives, public and private, they determined to remove this matter of local concern from Congress and eliminate it from national political debate.

Each side in the territorial debate, therefore, believed it was defending and extending the legacy of the Revolution. None addressed, much less redressed, the basic inconsistency between individual freedom and democracy. All insisted that the defense of their liberties (to promote individual freedom, to carry their property to the commonly owned territories, or to govern themselves) would not—could not—come at the expense of the equality of any citizen or section. Their opponents begged to differ. Determined to pass down the revolutionary heritage unimpaired to the next generation but insensitive to its systemic assumptions, politicians and their constituents in both sections increasingly came to view each other as subversive and un-American.

After a thirteen-year struggle with Great Britain, revolutionaries declared themselves "one people" determined to break the "political bands . . . with another." After a fourteen-year battle over the territories, Republicans would claim in 1860 that the disruption of the Union did not result from "the democratic element in our politics. . . . It is the collision which has taken place between democracy on the one hand, and this foreign element and doubly aristocratical institution of negro slavery on the other." In the South, secessionists claimed that if they were engaged in a great civil war, "as well might we designate the Revolutionary war a civil war." Common to both, "the efforts of one portion of the people are concerned in throwing off a tyrannical and oppressive power, and the establishment of a form of government under which they can enjoy the rights and liberties which are the inalienable heritage of freemen."[20]

The American Civil War remains one of the two greatest events in the nation's history, the Revolution being the other. But as the late David Potter pointed out, whereas the body of historical knowledge has increased greatly, the historical profession cannot agree on a generally acceptable explanation for the cause of the war. Although this book differs in significant ways from the extant literature on the origins of the Civil War, it does bring a coherent and critical analysis to bear on each of the schools. Standing apart from the war guilt school, the weight of evidence in this study and others argues that there was no conscious conspiracy in either the free or slave states to deny the other a role in the government. This fact did not prevent both sections from operating on that assumption, however. Additionally, southerners, too, saw the sectional conflict as a question of freedom versus slavery. Finally, as we shall see, neither the North nor the South pursued a consistent position on states' rights. Northerners who supported the Wilmot Proviso and thus Congress's power to restrict the spread of slavery also maintained the power (or right) of a state to pass personal liberty laws. Southerners who adamantly endorsed nonintervention were, by 1859, ready to use the power of Congress to protect their property in the territories.

The unique culture interpretation implicitly denies the South's integration into Jacksonian America. This theory is incorrect. It underestimates the commonalities of language, religion, and especially political heritage. It evades the question whether regional social and cultural differences were great enough to promote the disruption of the Union. The war was not produced by the clash of different political cultures. Northerners and southerners shared a common—not disparate—revolutionary ideology and acted in ways that were intelligible to their constituencies and each other.

Was the Civil War, then, a crusade against slavery? On November 7, 1837, an antiabolition mob in Alton, Illinois, shot and killed Elijah Lovejoy, editor of an abolitionist newspaper. On November 6, 1860, Abraham Lincoln of Springfield, Illinois, was elected the first Republican president of the United States. The contrast is instructive. As the debate over slavery extension demonstrates, the focus on the institution of black slavery is too narrow. It underestimates the racism of antislavery activists and does not fully encompass the concept of slavery for nineteenth-century white Americans. Slavery was a graphic reminder to southerners of the reality of degradation, impoverishment, and despotism. It was also a mechanism, they contended, for encouraging independence and social mobility and a barrier against exploitation. In the North, slavery symbolized the negation of equality and democracy. So though I would agree with James Ford Rhodes that slavery caused the Civil War, I think it is necessary to explore that concept in its broadest context. Failure to do so renders the history of race relations in post–Civil War America a non sequitur.

This book raises serious objections to the progressive interpretations. By the 1850s, both sections were industrializing (though the South lagged behind the North) and Democrats—Young Americans—in both the free and slave states were becoming less antagonistic toward industrialization and commercial expansion. Agriculturists in both sections were anxious and saw the fate of the territories as critical to their own well-being. Put another way, if the true divisions in America were economic, it would have been possible—indeed necessary—to have dealt with the red herring of slavery extension so that congressmen and their constituents could return to the real conflict between capital and democracy. And, finally, the conflict over the territories suggests the animating effect of principles and ideology. That is, inherited revolutionary values were axiomatic and controlling.

As this book contends, the territorial issue was not an abstraction—a conflict, as revisionists claimed, over "an imaginary Negro in an impossible place." Rather, it was central to political life in the 1850s. Politicians in both sections, in all parties, were responding to the anxieties and aspirations of the citizenry. John Tyler, Henry Clay, William Lowndes Yancey, Stephen Douglas, Jefferson Davis, William H. Seward, Robert Barnwell Rhett, and Abraham Lincoln all conceived of their work as principled, responsible, noble. Admittedly, politicians and politics created the Civil War. But they were doing what they were supposed to do. By defining and articulating a new cause, first expansion and then the slavery issue, they were in essence representing the popular will through the manipulation of a powerful symbol. Given the importance of this crisis, war could have been avoided only if men like Lincoln and Yancey had taken actions that they would have regarded as ignoble, immoral, and cowardly.

Contrary to the view of the ethnoculturalists, this study argues that the issues of expansion and slavery extension were critical to the destruction of Whiggery, the resonance of the Republican and fire-eater appeals, the disruption of the Democracy, the election of Lincoln, and the secession of the South. Without minimizing the disorganizing effect of ethnocultural conflict, it was, in the words of Sherlock Holmes, the dog that failed to bark in the nighttime.

The methodology employed in the book is traditional; the study is based on multiarchival manuscript research as well as a close reading of a wide array of official, printed primary, and periodical sources. It asserts the important interplay of belief and behavior. Throughout, the mental world of the actors and the intellectual context for each group's viewpoint are recreated by assessing the meaning and importance of these events from the moment of their occurrence. History, as one of my mentors has often observed, is experienced forward; it is written backward. We know what the outcome is; our actors do not. This study, therefore, attempts to present the public and private discourse of antebellum Americans as it bore meaning in their minds. But though the study assumes the legitimacy of each faction's argument, it does not follow that they are endorsed. Understanding the importance of slavery to southern society is not to legitimize that heinous institution. Pointing out the deep-seated racism among antislavery northerners constitutes no brief for colonization.

These partisan arguments are also expressed generally in members' own words. This technique calls to my mind the observation made by one waspish historian that as writers his colleagues were at their peak when quoting. No doubt that is true here. But scholars also tend when bringing coherency to a topic to absorb the viewpoint of one of the groups of historical actors. They then unconsciously use it as the standard to judge all who invoke alternate values or opposing causes. The inevitable result is to dismiss the fundamental axioms upon which other groups and actors operated and thus to divest their actions of the internal logic they possess. Some reflect reality and act accordingly; others do not and act irrationally.[21] Therefore, some are right; others are wrong. This is history badly written.

Still, certain voices are silent here: women and African Americans. Their absence in manuscript and primary sources is notable. But it has been said that absence of evidence is not evidence of absence. Thanks to the efforts of historians of women and African Americans, we know that there were parallel political discourses that turned on the same questions of liberty and equality. These studies challenge the concept of a common, hegemonic voice that spoke for or defined American society in the middle period. Quite purposefully, these groups carved out a separate space for themselves in an environment traditionally appropriated by the literate and powerful.

Yet the gendered and racialized language that structured the political debates of the 1840s and 1850s is striking: the quotations in the book demonstrate as much. It is also suggestive. The legacy of this constricted understanding of political rights and freedoms has resonated throughout post–Civil War America. The first battles fought by minorities and women were for inclusion—political, social, and economic. They insisted upon their equal entitlement to that selfsame revolutionary legacy. More important, since the 1960s radical civil rights and feminist activists have attempted to force twentieth-century Americans to confront the basic antagonism between liberty and equality that antebellum whites ignored. As Mills Thornton has recognized, radical civil rights activists "asked Americans at large to reject the meaning of America as it had been fundamentally understood since the War of 1812, to pronounce it fundamentally flawed, and to recover the long-lost analytical framework of the Founding Fathers." They did not. Similarly, Nancy Cott, writing on the feminist movement, points out that "arguments for women's advancement were grouped around two poles—two logically opposing poles . . . 'sameness' and 'difference.'" Feminism, as Cott points out, "is nothing if not paradoxical."[22] In light of these observations, if, as

Shelby Foote put it, the Civil War was a "defining moment," one can only respond, "Alas!"

In the end, this book examines the change of American attitudes over time toward expansion and destiny. By extension, a close examination of the territorial dispute—on the participants' own terms—incorporates the South into the bumptious nationalism of Jacksonian America. It provides a new perspective on the political culture of the 1840s and 1850s by parsing the variant strands of antislavery activism, the essence of popular sovereignty, the origin of the Kansas-Nebraska Act, the layered meanings of slavery, and the multiple, actuating viewpoints of antebellum Americans on their history and the problematic nature of republican government. The purpose generally is to explore and assess the ideological framework of these familiar issues in a manner calculated to give a fuller and more complete understanding of the real essence of the sectional conflict. If we may imagine the territorial issue as a tributary flowing into a torrent that is rushing toward a vast ocean, we may say that the stream, though charted, remains unexplored. Plumbing the dark waters of this issue adds needed refinements to the maps of antebellum history.

I have said it! the thunder is flashing the lightning is crashing! already there's an earthquake in Dominora. Full soon will old Bello discover that his diabolical machinations against this ineffable land must soon come to naught. Who dare not declare, that we are not invincible? I repeat it, we are. Ha! ha! Audacious Bello must bite the dust! Hair by Hair, we will trail his gory gray beard at the end of our spears! Ha! ha!
— Herman Melville, *Mardi and a Voyage Tither*

Here is a party to contend with — with only two measures — Free Trade and Texas; and this last a stolen one, for it was John Tyler's hobby, all saddled and bridled, and ready to be mounted, when Polk stepped in and poked him from his seat, and set off for Texas on the hobby himself — *not the first man by a good many who has gone to Texas on a stolen horse.*
— *Weekly Register and North Carolina Gazette*

John Tyler's Hobby

Territorial Expansion and Jacksonian Politics

"The question of the annexation of Texas," Ralph Waldo Emerson confided to his journal, "is one of those which look very differently to the centuries and to the years. It is very certain that the strong British race which have now overrun so much of this continent, must also overrun that tract, & Mexico & Oregon also, and in the course of ages be of small import by what particular occasions & methods it was done. . . . It is a measure that goes not by right nor by wisdom but by feeling."[1] As Emerson understood, national destiny, mixed motives, controversial means, and, most important, the sheer force of expansion together gave meaning and transcendent significance to the Texas issue and the Oregon question in the latter years of John Tyler's administration.

Tyler first introduced the question of annexation into Congress in the spring of 1844, and it swept all before it in the fall presidential campaign. The larger and more powerful question of territorial expansion subordinated though did not obliterate established issues that traditionally had divided the Whig and Democratic Parties—the Bank of the United States, a protective tariff, and internal improvements. "On a subject of such magnitude," one group of New Englanders declared, "involving as it does the present and future glory & interest of our common country, we consider all other questions merged & party lines & the dictation of leaders obliterated." The editor of the *New Orleans Morning Herald* agreed: "The subject of annexation is the all absorbing question with us and that in refference to it all former party lines will be abolished—at least to a great extent."[2]

Tyler's treaty introduced formally and permanently a new issue into the American political system: territorial expansion. More powerful symbolically than the Bank of the United States or protective tariff, Texas annexation and then Oregon embraced the ideals of liberty and personal emancipation that gave substance to the feeling of boundlessness of the 1840s. As such, territorial aggrandizement drew upon the ideological essence of both political parties. At the same time, it spoke to the fervent nationalism of the 1840s, shared in equal measure by the North and the South.[3]

The question of annexation had been left in abeyance since Andrew Jackson's presidency. Jackson had hoped to acquire Texas as an "essential component of his dream of empire." Mexican hostility, the maladroit machinations of an American diplomat, and the Texas revolution itself, however, had combined to thwart his ambition. After Texas proclaimed its independence, the threat of war with Mexico, charges of presidential complicity in the revolt, the possible growth of sectional tensions, and Jackson's unwillingness to jeopardize Martin Van Buren's election reinforced his growing caution. Continued agitation in and out of Texas for annexation and mounting evidence of widespread American support for expansion persuaded the Senate to recommend formal recognition of the republic on March 1, 1837. Although still wary, Jackson acceded to Congress's initiative. Now convinced that Texas had become "an independent power," he appointed Alcée La Branche of Louisiana as chargé to Texas two days later.[4]

There the matter stood when Martin Van Buren assumed the presidency. Van Buren, who had only reluctantly acquiesced in recognition, would go no further. Preoccupied with a depression, he believed that annexation would strain a Union seriously distracted by severe financial problems and rising agitation over slavery. Not wholly opposed to expansion, Van Buren, nevertheless, was unwilling to endanger the harmony of the Democratic Party and the passage of his economic program by making Texas annexation an administration objective.[5]

Although two presidents had rejected annexation, it was never far off the stage of public affairs. Behind the scenes, investments in Texan bonds and speculation in its lands worked to strengthen the connection between the two republics. Also, as the depression continued, flight to Texas provided some emigrants relief from the entrapment of liens and debts. "To all intents and purposes," one southern paper observed in 1844, "Texas has been the Botany Bay of the United States for the last eight years." As the links between the two republics drew tighter, British overtures to Texas, public and private, raised with growing urgency the question of annexation. By 1841, when John Tyler succeeded to the presidency, investments, speculation, migration, and reviving public interest again made the fate of Texas a national concern.[6]

In Tyler, supporters of Texas found an expansionist of the first rank. In 1832 he had maintained that the destiny of America was to expand to the Pacific, "walking on the waves of the mighty deep . . . overturning the strong places of despotism, and restoring man to his lost rights." As president, Tyler noted with approval continued immigration into the Pacific Northwest. He urged Congress to extend the laws of the United States to that distant region to protect Americans there and to give "a wider and more extensive spread to the principles of civil and religious liberty." In the progress of time, he later predicted, "the inestimable principles of civil liberty will be enjoyed by millions yet unborn and the great benefits of our government be extended to now distant and uninhabited regions."[7]

Expanding the area of freedom was not the only string in Tyler's bow, however. He was eager to open, penetrate, and enlarge American markets overseas and to compete with Great Britain for commercial empire. As early as June 1842, for example, John Quincy Adams reported that Tyler had "his eye fixed upon China, and would avail himself of any favorable opportunity to commence a negotiation with the [Chinese] empire." The Treaty of Wanghia of 1844, which provided for freer trade between the two countries, nearly put the president "in an ecstasy." This treaty, he later claimed, not only expanded American markets in China but was the "nest egg" for opening trade with Japan. Tyler also sent agents to the Sandwich Islands to protect commercial interests there, and he pushed unsuccessfully for freer trade between the United States and the German Zollverein.[8]

Evidence suggests that the president committed himself to Texas annexation in the earliest days of his presidency. After Tyler's veto of a third bill to recharter the Bank of the United States, he broke with Clay and was banished from the Whig Party. By the late fall of 1841, Tyler looked to Texas as a means to restore lost prestige and popularity. Without a party and having only a "corporal's guard" in Congress, "his Accidency" had to introduce into the political order a new element that would appeal to, rather than divide, Whigs and Democrats; speak to the problems of a lingering depression; and direct attention away from his embarrassment with Henry Clay. Texas, it seemed, was the answer to his prayers. After years of maneuvering, the Texas government and the administration signed a treaty of annexation in early April 1844. Tyler sent it along to the Senate later that month.[9]

In an atmosphere charged with political ambition and ideological conviction, the Senate deliberated the merits of Tyler's treaty and territorial expansion generally in a series of highly charged speeches. Expansion west appealed especially to Democrats North and South, who looked to an ever-enlarging frontier to preserve and maintain individual liberty. Most immediately, the addition of Texas to the Union promised to extend the area of freedom by spreading American institutions farther into the Southwest. At a deeper level, however, Democrats believed that western expansion was a necessary and practical requisite of individual freedom and republican government. Personal liberty, they would say, was incompatible with overcrowding, exhausted lands, and wage slavery. Compression engendered extremes of wealth and poverty and would bring on "those evils so prevalent in other countries." Pent up, seduced by effete refinements or hedged in by the prerogatives of others, "man . . . becomes enervated and predisposed to be enslaved by vicious habits or dependent from circumstances."[10] Individual liberty, they concluded, was a function of an expansive republic.

Democrats believed that agriculturists, by their nature and circumstances, were less given to the headlong pursuit of private interests at the expense of the public good. They looked to independent yeomen "as the great and perennial fountain of that Republican Spirit which is to maintain and perpetuate our free institutions." The party's enthusiasm for the acquisition of new territory, cheap western land prices, and preemption rights spoke to a political agenda, first articulated by Thomas Jefferson, that fused territorial aggrandizement and settlement with agrarian egalitarianism into an ever-expanding empire of republican liberty. The principles of cohesion that bound Americans together and made possible the Union were the love of "liberty itself for its own reward" and the guarantee of personal autonomy by a limited government. "Distance and climate can have no influence on this bond," the *Democratic Review* alleged; "it is wholly independent of them."[11]

Concentration, land exhaustion, wage slavery, and entrapment were, in the view of Democrats, the deepest and darkest threats to personal autonomy and republican government. Dangers to liberty seemed especially acute in a nation slowly emerging from the serious and dislocating depression produced by the Panic of 1837. The lingering effects of economic stagnation and a decline in frontier settlement could have been hardly more significant in the Texas debate. "Our population has become comparatively dense; our new lands are exhausted," one reviewer noted. "We are separating more and more, capital and labor, and have the beginnings of a constantly increasing *operative* class, unknown to our fathers, doomed always to be dependent on employment by the class who represent the capital of the country, for the means of subsistence." Personal autonomy and true freedom, then, depended on "the creation of land owners not land lords. . . . [with] ownership in himself and not a master." George Bancroft, an ardent supporter of Texas annexation, concluded that every enlargement of the Union had made concentration and entrapment more difficult and, as a result, had strengthened, not weakened, the Union.[12]

In this context, the annexation of Texas and the addition of thousands of square miles of territory to the Union addressed the single most important prerequisite of republican freedom. One supporter of Tyler's treaty argued that personal dignity and happiness were dependent more on the cheapness and fertility of land, of which Texas had an abundance, than on any other circumstance. "With this there can be no slavery; and without it, there can be no freedom," he maintained. "Dependent upon no one for employment . . . the industrious Farmer . . . feels that he is a freeman. He owes no tribute, and knows no servility. . . . Why do people emigrate to new and fertile regions, if not for this very purpose?" Gauging the effect of annexation on a depressed economy, another ventured that the impact of cheap territory in the West "would be to invite a large number of individuals who had settled in the eastern cities, who were half-starved and dependent on those who employed them, to go to the West, where with little funds, they could secure a small farm on which to subsist and . . . get rid of that feeling of dependence which made them slaves." Closing the circle, another predicted that if the United States annexed Texas, "many a poor man that has been a renter for half a life time will be able to become a land holder very soon. . . . To all such the annexation of Texas is a measure of vital importance."[13]

Casting their nets widely, proponents of annexation broadened the appeal of Texas to attract manufacturers, merchants, and those engaged in the carrying trade. Levi Woodbury of New Hampshire contended that expansion was neither a western, southern, nor party question but one that affected Americans everywhere. Texas would open to agriculture more fertile soils and congenial climates. It would furnish wider home markets for manufacturers, new articles for commerce, and additional rivers and bays for the free navigation of western steamers. Indeed, expansionists linked Texas to broad commercial expansion that looked beyond, though it did not exclude, domestic consumers. Some believed Texas the first essential link to the Pacific and, consequently, Asian commerce. If this were to occur, commerce of the Far East and the islands of the Pacific would then meet that of the Mississippi Valley. This junction, annexationists claimed, "would revolutionize the commercial world and make the Mississippi the corner of trade." Considered in all its ramifications for agriculture, manufacturing, and commerce, the ratification of Tyler's treaty, a southern editor observed, "would be an epoch in American history, second only to the adoption of the Federal Constitution by the states."[14]

If personal autonomy and national economic growth were the functions of territorial aggrandizement, the federate nature of the American Union at once embodied the ideal of republican freedom and made possible the widest expansion. "There is no instance on record of equal rights and privileges extending throughout a land, however large, which did not secure it against internal disruption," Tyler's *Daily Madisonian* declared. William Wilkins, Tyler's secretary of war, maintained that the perpetuation of a federated Union and the diminution of the threat of consolidation and concentration of federal power were consequences of the nation's expansion. "In a confederation of great extent," he observed, "threats of disunion . . . carry no threats of alarm, and can never instill in the most traitorous bosom any hopes of success. . . . The bonds of connexion have strengthened with the increase of territory." Instructed by James Madison's *Federalist* Number 10, Wilkins and other annexationists such as New York congressman Chesselden Ellis believed that expansion "augments the power against which the spirit of disunion must contend whenever it awakes. It multiplies counteracting interests and lessens the danger of its influence." Sidney Breese of Illinois took this argument to its logical conclusion. He concluded in his support of annexation that "if the action of Congress is confined to its proper functions, and each state permitted to exercise its own undoubted powers, no reasonable bounds can be assigned to the proper extension of this confederacy."[15]

Opponents argued that the addition of Texas to an already expansive republic would produce unbearable sectional strains on the bonds of Union. The *Madisonian* replied that separation was not a consequence of growth but of inequality. The more extensive our system of confederated states, James Buchanan maintained, "the greater will be the strength and security of the Union because the more dependent will the several parts be upon the whole, and the whole upon the several parts." In a like vein, a pro-Texas meeting in Fauquier County, Virginia, concluded that bringing Texas into the Union, "with her markets, and immense accessions to commerce, agriculture and navigation—binding our people together by the ties of common interest," would enhance the nation's representative and federated system of government and diminish any untoward centrifugal tendencies.[16]

Democrats, then, placed Texas in the context of a familiar past unfolding into a certain future. Continuing emigration west, they argued, "produces that life and that energy which animates the American mind, and which literally makes us so extraordinary a race of people." Since growth was the sine qua non of an exceptionalist American character, the annexation of Texas was both desirable and inevitable. Buchanan thus viewed annexation not as an end but as an episode of a longer historical process. The United States's destiny, he said, was to inherit North America. "For this reason it is, that the Almighty has implanted in the very nature of our people that spirit of progress, and that desire to roam abroad and seek new homes and new fields of enterprise, which characterizes them above all other nations. . . . This spirit cannot be repressed." With decidedly less enthusiasm, an Illinois Whig declared with some asperity that "the old pioneers want [annexation] because they always want some place to drift to. . . . Texas is the hobby of all the western papers."[17]

By spring, when Tyler sent the treaty of annexation to the Senate, others, too, had concluded that the Texas issue was fast becoming "the general topic of discussion in all circles." According to this source, there appeared little difference of opinion "as to the justice, policy and absolute necessity of adding Texas to the Union." Although Whigs initially were inclined to ignore the issue, Tyler's initiative forced the party to respond. Earlier Henry Clay had contended that it was not right "to allow Mr. Tyler, for his own selfish purposes, to introduce an exciting topic, and add to the other subjects of contention which exist in the country." Despite having denounced the cession of American claims to Texas earlier in his career, Clay was disturbed by the disruptive effect annexation would have on the integrity of, and balance of interests within, the Union and his own presidential prospects.[18]

Confident in his ability to treat the Texas issue in such a way as to reconcile almost all Whigs to his position, Clay came out against immediate annexation in his Raleigh letter of April 1844. Sensing no evidence of broad, public support, he opposed the acquisition of Texas, encumbered as it was with the prospect of war with Mexico. Clay's position, informed by the logic of his American System, was that political leaders should seek to consolidate, improve, and harmonize the nation as it was; they should not chase a chimera that would be inevitably attended with discord and dissatisfaction. Clay concluded that Congress ought to pause a bit, develop the federal territory in hand, and augment the nation's strength, power, and greatness through material and moral enhancement. If, however, increased population demanded further territory, Americans "need entertain no apprehensions but that it will be acquired by means, it is to be hoped, fair, honorable and constitutional."[19]

Clay's letter was the view halloo for antiannexationists in and out of Congress. Opponents of Texas reinforced Clay's calculated political position with the substance of guiding Whig principles. In the process, they threw into relief more than simple differences between the two parties over territorial expansion. Whigs understood how Texas annexation complemented the Democracy's view of the Union, and they did not like it. They rejected the inevitable conflict between capital and democracy that was implicit in the annexationist argument. They denied the adventitious consequences of a widely dispersed population. They repudiated the assertion that expansive republics made possible and secured equality and free government. In their dissent, Whigs articulated an alternative version of Jacksonian society. And in their opposition to annexation, Whigs proposed a very different vision of a developing empire.

A pattern of progress, revealed by their reading of history, constituted the matrix that gave shape and meaning to Whigs' opposition and coherence to their hopes for the nation's future. "The world is not a treadmill, struggling to keep its place," the *American Review* claimed. "[Nations] are [moving] forward to some goal. . . . No one can doubt there is a law of progress working steadily and uniformly." In contrast to Democrats, who conceived of the work of the Constitution's framers as complete, needing only application, Whigs looked to build upon the achievements of their forefathers. Henry Clay, for example, viewed the work of the revolutionary fathers as a point of departure for the growth of civilization in America. Succeeding generations, he observed, "have accomplished much in advancing the growth, the power, and the greatness of this nation. . . . Let us recollect that we have . . . far higher duties . . . to perform toward our country, toward posterity, and toward the world."[20]

Whigs consistently argued that progress was being frustrated by Democrats "who wish the present to be the future, who are satisfied with the good now in possession. . . . They labor with tremendous, perverted powers to destroy what others build, to invert the upward movement of their generation, and to roll back the tide of improvement." Charles Sumner conceded that to enjoy the freedom secured by the Revolution was a "most precious treasure; but to enjoy it without transmitting it to the next generation, and without adding to it yourselves, this is the height of imbecility."[21]

Beneath this faith in progress lay two common assumptions: that society must order and direct change and that progress encompassed personal and material development. "Action is an inevitable condition of liberty," one Whig explained. Yet, he warned, Americans should not confuse unrestrained liberty with true freedom. Progress and change should not degenerate "into wild and fitful restlessness. . . . [They should] be harmonized, directed and concentrated into healthful, beneficial MOVEMENT." To be truly free and to progress, it was necessary "to act within the limits of conscience and the law;

for to violate conscience is to lose internal, and to violate law, external liberty." The chief threat to freedom, it again followed, was the Democracy, who "despairing of their own improvement . . . devote the energies which they should have employed for their own good to the injury of others."[22]

The marrow of Whig political ideology was harmony, enterprise, and uplift. "It is a truth most trite, but not the less important," Daniel Webster proclaimed, "that the great interests of society are mingled. The commercial— the agricultural—the manufacturing pursuits of individuals are entwined . . . and must flourish together or fade together." Party members idealized America as a naturally harmonious society free of class interests and antagonisms. Whigs like Webster, Clay, Alexander H. Stephens, and William H. Seward accordingly looked to economic growth and the diffusion of property and capital to preclude social conflict. More important, in a positive sense, economic growth and diversification would perforce uplift the individual and enrich the meaning of American civilization. In a rather didactic letter to William Cabell Rives, Abbott Lawrence outlined the noneconomic benefits of industry. "You will find, very soon," Lawrence observed, "that a desire for knowledge will be created; more education, more intellectual cultivation, will be desired by those engaged in the mechanical departments. . . . The sphere of labor must be enlarged, diversified, if you would bring out the energies of your people." Thus an American Whig was an individual "who believed that the primary object of all political institutions ought to be '*to consult the greatest good to the greatest number*' . . . [and was] always ready to promote civilization."[23]

To guarantee the creation of a virtuous citizenry, Whigs argued that government must represent accurately and promote the various social and economic interests of the nation to foster harmony and balance among them. "In free elective systems," Webster observed, "political society exists and coheres . . . not by super incumbent pressure on its several parts, but by the internal and mutual attraction of those parts; by the assimilation of interests and feelings; by a sense of common country, common political family, common character, fortune and destiny."[24] Accordingly, Whigs looked to the agency of the federal government to meliorate potential economic and sectional tensions and to foster domestic peace, prosperity, and progress. This, they concluded, would generate orderly and productive interaction within the government by fusing private and public interests.

National progress, then, implied expanded opportunities and an extension of personal liberty. Like those who supported Texas, Whigs, too, talked of expanding freedom. Indeed, Jacksonian Americans as a people were acutely aware of the unique mission of the American republic. Edward Everett proclaimed that "liberty is the lesson, which we are appointed to teach." To this extent, all Americans of the Jacksonian era agreed. Yet Democrats, most of whom supported annexation, desired to widen the area in which American government and institutions operated. For Whigs, however, the extension of liberty meant primarily its augmentation over the years within the United States. Senator Alexander Barrow of Louisiana asked annexationists if they intended "to announce to the world that we consider this government such a paragon of perfection and such a paradise of purity and happiness that we are ready . . . to invite all nations to come under our pale?" Far better, Barrow held, to extend equality and protection to the lives, liberty, and property of Americans and "to elevate them in the scale of intelligence and morality."[25]

Whig opposition to rapid expansion, and to Texas in particular, is best viewed in the light of these beliefs. If their reading of history illuminated the brightest hopes for the nation's progress, a careful examination of imperial powers from ancient Rome to tsarist Russia was equally illuminating. "In all the past, history has presented one uniform truth," claimed a Whig dissident. "Governments must be oppressive somewhat in proportion to their extent." Opponents of Texas believed that, like the Caesars of Rome, annexation- ists betrayed a hunger for power and an unquenchable thirst for territorial aggrandizement. "Once begin it, and *where* will it end?" they asked. "Shall we *ever* have territory enough for ambition, though we have enough for our wants?" "The true vocation of this great republic," the *American Review* pro- claimed, "is not aggrandizement but national growth."[26]

Indictments of Texas were also specific and to the point. "We could not . . . incorporate Texas into the Union without involving the United States in war with Mexico," Henry Clay observed, "and, I suppose, nobody would think it wise or proper to engage in war with Mexico for the acquisition of Texas." The *New York Tribune*, noting the popularity of annexation, feared that Clay supposed wrong. "Our country has been nearly thirty years at peace," it declared. "She is now enjoying a very general and obviously growing pros- perity. But she has thousands of restless spirits, who have an aversion to the dull ways of steady industry—who sigh for the license and chances of war." To Whigs, annexation symbolized moral declension and signaled an indefensible break with established principles that had shaped foreign policy since Washington's presidency. They maintained that to the supporters of annexation "our treaty stipulations were nothing . . . our published prin- ciple of non-intervention, nothing; our past history, nothing; the public law of nations, nothing; the opinion of the world, *nothing*."[27]

If international disgrace dismayed Whigs, annexation's effect on the Union alarmed them. Whigs believed that republics by their nature were held together by intangible bonds rather than force; the party therefore rooted its main attack on Texas in a defense of the mutuality of social and economic interests and a common feeling of national identity. Vermont's legislature, for example, resolved that annexation "would directly tend to weaken the bonds of our Union, by multiplying the various and conflicting interests of its members, and diminishing its power to foster and protect them." With each boundary extension, another antiannexationist asserted, "we go on weakening the feeling of nationality, until at last we break into fragments." As the binding ties of nationalism and mutual interest were thus attenuated, selfishness, prejudice, and fragmentation would grow. The Union, this New England Whig predicted, "would soon break asunder or vanish by its own diffusiveness."[28]

Dilating on that aspect of the annexationist argument that stressed agrarian freedom and anticonsolidation, Whigs saw expansion as but another appeal, however powerful, calculated to pander to the prejudices of the laboring classes to ensure Democratic ascendancy. Viewing divisions over the Texas issue in the light of partisan conflict, Whigs alleged that Democratic support for annexation was, like the Loco position on the bank and tariff, "to array, in most unnatural hostility, the poor against the rich—the laborer against the employer—the mechanic against the merchant—the farmer against the manufacturer."[29] Party members denounced the acquisition of Texas as a measure that would produce dependency, depopulation of the East, concentrated landholdings, and, as a result, class conflict.

New England protectionists, not surprisingly, charged that annexation would have the effect of strengthening "the voices of the free trade system." Therefore, it would "open our ports . . . close the doors of our factories . . . [and] render us dependent on foreign countries for the most common and essential fabrics." In a similar vein, Louisiana's Senator Barrow noted that annexation would render his state's production of cotton, sugar, and rice unprofitable. He, among others, doubted the common sense and fiscal sanity of proannexation farmers who were already suffering from overproduction and low prices. Nor could that specious Texan market, about which the Democrats spoke so glowingly, offset the untoward effects of free trade and agricultural surpluses. Whigs accurately pointed out that customers of this new market would, in fact, be emigrants from the older states, and thus consumers "will not be increased more than by remaining where they now are."[30]

Eastern Whigs especially deplored this rush west in what they sneered was a never-ending quest for "an *El Dorado*, where everything is to be gained and nothing can be lost." Senator Jacob Miller of New Jersey cautioned that as territorial expansion would lead ultimately to the founding of an American empire, "it becomes the small states to be somewhat jealous . . . for fear that we might be left behind like rotten boroughs in this majestic march after universal dominion." Others pointed out that as a result of this depopulation, land in the East was becoming "impoverished to improve the lands of the West." Consequently, property ownership in the older states was concentrated increasingly in fewer hands.[31]

Southern Whigs also rued the deleterious economic effect of annexation. They predicted that the newly annexed lands would attract thousands of southerners, especially slave owners. As they abandoned the settled areas of the Southeast, these emigrants would leave behind lands desolated by squalor and debt. Tennessee's Spencer Jarnagin maintained that "in the great tract thus abandoned by much of its proprietary, and more of its laboring population, lands must of course sink prodigiously in value. . . . On a diminished population and depreciated property, [public] debt . . . will fall with a terrible weight of taxes; and these will operate to induce fresh migration into a new country whose debt has been assumed." To southerners inclined to doubt Jarnagin's argument, the *Columbus Enquirer* noted that the experience of Georgia's older counties was suggestive. Already depopulated by westward migration, these devalued lands were concentrated in the hands of a few large barons, and "the country looks more like the abode of ghosts than the habituation of human beings." Texas, it concluded, "will produce the same effect on us."[32]

Beyond the conflict between the East and West, Whigs apprehended that annexation would also increase tension between the free and slave states. Northern Whigs—particularly in New England, New York, and the Western Reserve—feared that the addition of Texas would give an unwelcome and unnecessary advantage "to one section of the Union to represent and extend property." Disclaiming political abolitionism, opponents of slavery extension charged that those who would urge expansion on sectional grounds, such as Tyler's secretary of state John C. Calhoun, placed the issue not on a broad platform that sustained equally the interests of the entire Union but on a narrow, insupportable plank of political and economic self-interest. William Henry Seward denounced annexation as a Democratic Party measure intended to divide Whigs and, more ominously, to place slavery "henceforth and forever among the elements of political action in the Republic." Southern Whigs, too, denounced this unprincipled manipulation of the slavery question to gain a partisan advantage. The whole annexation movement, Alexander Stephens groused, was "a miserable political humbug got up as a ruse to divide and distract the Whig party at the South."[33]

Quite naturally, southern antiannexationists condemned northerners who based their opposition to Texas on sectional, antislavery grounds alone. This, one Georgia Whig contended, branded the South as "outlaws, as it were, from the government, when benefits might fall to our lot from its action." It also implied, as one historian has argued, "that the nation was not a whole, that the expansion of the South and the expansion of the nation were not one and the same thing." Although assumptions of sectional equality and assertions of southern rights cut across party lines in the South on the Texas issue, Whig antiannexationists rejected their opponents' argument that expansion would strengthen slavery. Informed by the Whig belief in integration, development, and material progress, southern anti-Texas activists maintained that too rapid an extension of the institution would ruin the older states and weaken slavery everywhere. Looking to the palladium of state government and, even more, to the guarantees of the Constitution, Whigs like John Berrien and Alexander Barrow repudiated the claim that the expansion of slavery into the West was a necessary part of extending the area of freedom. The safest, surest, and most legitimate means of extending freedom, Barrow countered, was "for our government to observe with religious fidelity its obligations foreign and domestic." [34]

Despite the portentous implications of free-state opposition to annexation, Texas neither created nor defined slavery agitation. It was but one, albeit a prominent, thread in the antiannexationist tapestry. Yet as the *American Review* declared, "Slavery is but an incident to our original condition and present frame of government, and, be the period longer or shorter, will, in the course of events, have an end." [35] In 1844, therefore, Whigs viewed the institution as one of several issues that still divided Americans. Henry Clay, among others, believed that through the course of time Americans would come together in a harmonious Union, and under those circumstances, expansion could be given its head. For although the most conservative Whigs argued for permanently restricted boundaries (the crankier New England types no doubt pining in their hearts for the Atlantic and the Hudson River), others like Seward and Stephens proclaimed themselves favorable to expansion if accomplished honorably, constitutionally, and without jeopardy to the Union.

This attitude, in fact, is the essence of Clay's much criticized Alabama letters of July 1844. In a later private letter to William C. Rives, Clay looked to the day the South would support a protective tariff. Then, he predicted, northern attacks on slavery would abate, "and it is possible that a condition of the public mind may ensue, which would reconcile all parts of our country to the annexation of Texas." Clay believed that as economic pursuits were harmonized and sectional differences ameliorated through the agency of an integrated market economy, the perpetuation and enhancement of the Union would be secured. Under these conditions, controlled expansion served the public interest. Senator Jacob Miller of New Jersey advised his colleagues that when the country was "still more knit together by the labor of the citizens from the north to the south, and from the east to the west," it could then safely continue the westward course of empire. [36] With growing national resources and new internal markets fostering development and strengthening the bonds of interdependence, freedom would expand simultaneously over space and through time.

Whigs therefore apprehended that a Democratic empire premised on unchecked territorial aggrandizement would subvert the evolution of American civilization by pitting economic self-interest against the common weal. Henry C. Carey, a Whig economist, later asserted, "The more the dispersion, the greater are the profits of speculators, and the greater is their power to procure, from needy members of Congress, further grants of the public domain, and further legislation tending to compel the closing of mills and furnaces—thus producing greater dispersive tendencies, and larger profits." As the population grew increasingly nomadic, he argued, there would develop an innate dislike for peaceful pursuits. The natural resources of the nation would dissipate. The abilities of its citizens would remain undeveloped. The republic would stand condemned to a state of fragmentation and declension. Like the Democratic argument, the Whig perspective on the connection between Texas and slavery was complex. Beyond the obvious expansion of the institution itself, party members held that annexation also would have the effect of promoting widespread bondage by enslaving millions to the degraded conditions of a primitive, colonial economy. Territorial growth, then, was problematic. Unbridled, it promised "demoralization, slavery, and barbarism." Harnessed, expansion could enhance the freedom and liberties of all Americans in an unfolding empire.[37]

Fearing that premature and rapid expansion would preclude progress and promote degeneration, party members stood solidly against Tyler's treaty of annexation. On June 8, 1844, a handful of free-soil Democrats joined Whigs in killing the measure 16 to 35.[38] Fears of war and slavery agitation undoubtedly played a significant role in its rejection. These factors, however, were but part of a larger constellation of issues, beliefs, and assumptions that shaped and illuminated the debate. The perceived effect of Texas on the future of republican government, though, made certain that expansion would become a principal issue in the 1844 canvass.

Even though Democrats controlled Congress, the party's prospects in the approaching campaign were at best unclear. A series of losses and alarmingly narrow victories in state elections in late 1843 and early 1844 were enough in the minds of some to "rouse the Democracy if not to a sense of their danger, to the fact now rendered certain that we are to have a hard contest in 1844." Even in Van Buren's New York, one observer warned that the party was "in a bad way." Many abhorred "the too frequent bickerings and jealousies" that paralyzed the Democracy. Others cautioned that while Whig state organizations had improved, Democrats "remained stationary," and their leaders were "too idle and too thoughtless." An Alabama editor feared that within his state, there was "no distinct point for reunion" among the many elements within the party. William Cullen Bryant's *Evening Post* complained that recent Democratic losses in the state merely demonstrated "how loosely it is organized, and with how little mutual understanding its different portions have acted."[39]

Divisions in the party ran toward the Byzantine. Presidential hopefuls John Calhoun, Lewis Cass, Richard M. Johnson, and James Buchanan spun webs of alliances throughout the Union that functioned as rivals to each state's Van Buren wing. In New England, for example, Calhoun forces promoted Levi Woodbury's favorite-son candidacy. Cass supporters in Buchanan's Pennsylvania included Governor David Porter, George M. Dallas, Richard Rush, and Charles J. Ingersoll. Johnson, Kentucky's happy warrior, boomed the Oregon question in the Old Northwest, weakening Cass. All these shifting alliances were enhanced and exacerbated by the pyrotechnic politics of loose and informal state organizations.[40]

None of this fractiousness denies the deep personal enmity between Calhoun and Van Buren. Opposition to Van Buren, however, did not issue from personal animosity, ambition, or party structure alone. For instance, hostility to the former president in the West was a function not of personal politics and ad hominem attacks but rather of policy differences within the state parties over money and banks. Van Buren's evasive position on the tariff estranged protectionist supporters of Cass and Buchanan. Southern Van Burenites found Calhoun's position on protection too extreme, but the waffling of their free-state allies on the tariff also astonished and dismayed them. The array of positions within the party on internal improvements and fiscal policy placed all candidates, but especially the vulnerable Van Buren, in a withering crossfire so long as the Democrats struck solely to economic issues.[41]

Whig victories and Democratic divisiveness, Cave Johnson observed, served only to increase dissatisfaction and encourage despondency among party members. Similar gloom abounded nationwide. With only a modest amount of hyperbole, an Indiana House member warned Van Buren that though the Whigs were wholly united in his state, the Democracy was riven by factionalism, and party members were openly voicing discontent. Closer to home, a correspondent told Van Buren that national and local issues prostrated the New York Democracy. In Virginia, Thomas Ritchie declared that he had never seen the party "in so much danger. We are breaking up into factions." This factionalism facilitated a Whig victory in spring state elections and as one observer had it "struck (the [D]emocratic members of Congress) with panic."[42]

Congressional Democrats had good reason to panic. Fragmentation of state organizations reflected intraparty conflict in Congress over a variety of issues debated in the late session. Sectional tensions abounded. Silas Wright lamented that the House seemed to have become solely absorbed by an acrimonious—if abstract—debate over the gag rule. "We do not yet seem to approach a state of organization, or of action," he complained to Van Buren. A western Democratic alliance with eastern Whigs in support of two river and harbor bills infuriated southern representatives and engendered still more partisan confusion. Western Locos, for their part, were restive and dissatisfied with the evasive course pursued by New York Democrats (and coincidentally, Van Buren supporters) on the tariff. As Congress neared adjournment, Cave Johnson observed that many Senate and House Democrats were "greatly disheartened—almost without hope. . . . Many of us feel so much disgraced by the conduct of our party here that we think that we will be serving the country most effectually, by separating us as soon as possible."[43]

Democratic divisiveness did nothing to strengthen the hand, increase the popularity, or enhance the prospects of the party's leading presidential candidate. Although Van Buren had secured a majority of pledged state representatives to the Baltimore convention and had successfully beaten back John C. Calhoun's challenge to his party leadership, one shrewd Whig concluded that he had "seen his culminating point & is now rapidly on the decline." Even early support for Van Buren in the *Washington Globe* was less than enthusiastic. "The Democracy has never permitted one of its illustrious men to be stricken down in its service, without lifting him up, if his fall was not justly attributable to his own fault," Frank Blair wrote. Blair contended that there was no need to introduce a new name "to induce the people to right themselves, and bring retributive justice on those at whose hands the public morals, and interests, and institutions suffered so much."[44]

Perhaps. Yet Van Buren could neither stem the growing factionalism within his party nor prevent the discontented from supporting rival presidential and expansionist-minded hopefuls. Though by spring Calhoun's candidacy faded, formidable "Young Democratic" rivals remained openly in the field. The *Globe* admonished Loco newspapers for supporting, or at least assessing the merits of, other candidates and thus increasing party dissension and creating ill-will among its leadership. While praising Van Buren for having so many and such distinguished rivals, Blair ridiculed "the organs of those strange Democrats" that were incessantly "weakening the influence and deprecating the character of Mr. Van Buren."[45]

Not that anti–Van Buren Democrats thought that the task was particularly difficult. A Boston Loco noted that Van Buren had gained the presidency on Andrew Jackson's popularity and lost it with all the government's patronage to sustain him. "He was never really a popular candidate," he sniffed, "and there is nothing & never was anything really great or noble about him."

Quite before Texas derailed Van Buren's campaign bandwagon, Whigs relished the prospect of his candidacy. Robert P. Letcher sarcastically observed in January that he feared Van Buren's "ability to *stand up*"—much less make an effective run for the presidency. He wrote that Van Buren was "like Baillie Peyton's steer, which was so poor and weak it had to be *held up* to be shot." A month later, Willie P. Mangum claimed that Whigs, fearing the popularity of a compromise candidate, were avoiding all cooperation with Van Buren's unfriendly colleagues in Congress. Knowing well that the former president was no daisy, Mangum hooted, "If we cannot beat Mr. Van Buren, we can beat no one."[46]

On April 27, only five days after Tyler had sent his treaty to the Senate, Van Buren came out against annexation in a closely reasoned argument published in the *Washington Globe*. Deciding to risk the nomination and election rather than jeopardize his vision of the nation's future, Van Buren declared annexation to be inexpedient as long as Mexico opposed it. He would, however, support it if Texas and Mexico resolved the question of war and a majority of Americans and senators were favorable to annexation.[47]

Those northern Democrats like John Fairfield who opposed annexation and feared its widespread appeal applauded Van Buren's position, hoping that it would put a check on the growing enthusiasm for Texas in the free states. Similarly, a Pennsylvania party member informed Frank Blair that, before the *Globe* made public Van Buren's position, the rank and file in that state had worked themselves "into a pretty hot Texas fever," but they would not yet surrender their support for him on that account. Other supporters regretted its timing, for they had hoped that public hostility to antiannexationists would be brought to bear on Whig antiannexationists, not Van Buren. A Hoosier Democrat, pointing out the general enthusiasm for Texas in Indiana, proclaimed himself "mortified" at Van Buren's letter and warned the former president that it "has had a dreadful effect."[48]

Not unreasonably, supporters of Van Buren wondered why anti-Texas sentiment produced so much less dissent within the ranks of Whigs, even in the South. Like most historians, they cast the Texas issue in sectional terms and consequently ascribed the origin of the issue and the subsequent hostility to Van Buren to slave-state pretensions. If Van Burenites, northern Whigs, and their historians concluded that the primary effect of annexation was to spread slavery, other antebellum Democrats in the free and slave states maintained that westward expansion was an opportunity—an obligation—to extend the freedom inherent in American institutions. A Virginia Democrat noted that "by this Union [with Texas] we take the surest means of fortifying . . . the greatest defenses of liberty, and securing the perpetuity of our glorious institutions." One supporter claimed that extending the boundaries within which American institutions operated had been the "doctrine" of the Founding Fathers. "Is freedom [now] so valueless," he asked, "that it has become a crime and a dishonor to extend it to other countries? Is it so circumscribed in its operation that we cannot extend it to others without losing it ourselves?" The Whig answer, of course, had been yes. Thomas Gilmer rebutted the slur. "Our Union has no danger to apprehend from those who believe that its genius is expansive and progressive, but from those who think the limits of the United States are already too large and the principles of 1776 too old fashioned for this fastidious age." A Pennsylvania editor maintained simply that territorial aggrandizement and the "consequent extension of the area of freedom, must, at all events, forever constitute a popular theme with a republican people."[49]

Andrew Jackson, voicing the opinion of many Democrats, was "filled with regret" by Van Buren's position. Party members North and South, expecting Van Buren's support, professed to be "all in confusion, distraction & despair." Looking upon this issue as "a question of patriotism and of country," many of his erstwhile supporters found themselves "rather in low spirits" and expressed a determination not to vote for Van Buren in any event. To counteract the letter's effect on the public mind and to neutralize the capital that Van Buren's rivals could make of it, an Iowa Democrat implored the former vice-president to write another letter strongly endorsing the reoccupation of Oregon.[50]

On the eve of the convention, Amos Kendall wrote Van Buren a long, gloomy letter spelling out the defections (and by implication the defects) among the former president's supporters. All, he noted, "have caught the parrot note—'*he cannot be elected.*'" His nomination now opposed by annexationists as well as personal enemies, Van Buren was repudiated by the Democrats at the Baltimore convention in June. If, as Calhoun wished and historians have supposed, Van Buren's Hammet letter was the occasion of his overthrow, Democrats in Baltimore, some of them Van Buren supporters, understood that it was the means, not the cause, of his demise. Noting the factionalism that had grown steadily for a decade within the party and increasingly so since 1840, Cave Johnson claimed that by 1844 the "*disease [was] beyond remedy.*" Much of the factional opposition to Van Buren "was erected before the Texas question—but now it is all attributed to it." A disappointed Tennessee supporter claimed that "a rabid desire to get more land brought the whole mass to a decision at once in favor of [annexation]." A friendly Virginian complained that he and others had been caught unawares by the popularity and importance of the Texas question among the citizens of Richmond. Although the spring state election (which the Democrats lost) had turned exclusively on federal politics, he observed that "in that more vital struggle in November next, we shall in addition to these issues be compelled to meet this new and mighty question of Texas annexation."[51]

The party turned instead to another Jackson protégé, James K. Polk of Tennessee. Polk, a man with few enemies and known to be an enthusiastic supporter of Texas, ran on a platform that called for the "re-annexation" of Texas and the "re-occupation" of Oregon and, for good measure, an ambiguous tariff plank calculated to appeal both to merchants and to farmers.[52]

The force of expansion in the canvass was obvious. Despite the danger that Texas might disrupt Democratic unity by shearing off the party's Van Buren wing, most Democrats saw expansion into the Southwest and Northwest as the "*great and new element* which has entered into this momentous contest, and which by *its superior importance, is enough of itself, to determine the vote of every freeman.*" Given the centrality of the issue and solid Whig opposition, some like George Bancroft believed that "re-annexation" and "re-occupation" together constituted the dividing line between parties much as the bank and tariff had done in past elections and promoted unity, not divisiveness, among the rank and file and between sections. Whigs, he explained, "advocating centralization, must wish & have ever wished to narrow our territory; [Democrats] with States Rights, know no limit to the possible extent of the Federal Union."[53]

Expansionists argued with some accuracy that the explosiveness and power of the issue caught antiannexationists unexpectedly and they were attempting to defuse this situation by reducing Texas to a question of party or section. Ever intent on putting their own advantage ahead of national interests, so the proannexationists claimed, this class of politician had "deserted the sure and stable foundations on which the framers of the Constitution rested the prosperity of the country, — they have sought to place it upon the shifting sources of a temporary and ephemeral expediency, — on schemes, 'the Cynthia of the minute.'" The time will come, the *Richmond Enquirer* darkly warned, "when the opponents of this treaty will deeply deplore the sacrifice of Texas on the altar of *party.*"[54]

Especially offensive and threatening were antiannexationists' efforts to galvanize opposition by arguing that slaveholding Texas was basically a southern, not a national, question. To claim as opponents did that the measure ought to be opposed precisely because it ensured the safety of slavery seemed to deny that the national government had any obligation to protect the property and guarantee the well-being of a large number of its citizens. Levi Woodbury admitted that the treaty presented a fortunate and timely occasion to enforce better the guarantees of the Constitution by promoting domestic tranquillity in the South and Southwest. The property and institutions of the South, he maintained, were secured by that instrument as well as by legislative and judicial decisions, "and so must they continue to be, till the compromises of the constitution are wantonly violated, or the Union dissolved." Denying that any real patriot would distinguish between the social rights and institutions of the country, George McDuffie declared, "We ask you to give us nothing; we only ask you to protect the property we have."[55]

More important than defaulting on constitutional obligations, antislavery opposition cast the South in an adversarial role, denying it not only the equal protection of the government but a shared nationalism. When they implied that the security and safety of one section of the country jeopardized the republic as a whole, opponents, expansionists argued, denied the legitimacy of the South's partnership and equality within the Union. By waging a relentless war against southern institutions "and making those Institutions the avowed ground of objection to a political Union with those who in every other respect are bone of our bone and flesh of our flesh," antiannexationists, from the perspective of annexationists, were in reality sectionalists who little valued the Union and held in low esteem a large portion of their fellow countrymen. Has it come to this, asked McDuffie, "that a man who feels himself to be a free citizen of these United States dare not even *speak* of his rights, and of the obligations of this government to protect them against every danger, direct or indirect, open or disguised, from whatever quarter it may come?" "A more stinging insult," he concluded, "could not be offered to a free people."[56]

Democrats easily and naturally wove Oregon into their campaign. As annexationists had already pointed out in the annexation debate, "the march of empire is Westward." American settlers had been flowing into the Northwest in increasing numbers since 1842; by 1845 more than five thousand had migrated there. Although control of the territory was still a matter of contention between the United States and Great Britain, the security of the emigrants, growing disputes over landownership, and increased national interest in the fate of Oregon required a permanent solution. Any idea of arresting migration seemed as futile as it was undesirable. "You might as well attempt to turn the waters of the Missouri river back upon its source in the Rocky mountains," David Rice Atchison of Missouri suggested.[57]

Oregon's importance to a future American empire on the Pacific neatly dovetailed with the market expansion theme developed by Texas annexationists. Representative John A. McClernand of Illinois, speaking to western agriculturists and eastern merchants alike, argued that possession of the mouth of the Columbia River was essential to trade with China and the Sandwich Islands. Operating from a new commercial emporium there, aggressive entrepreneurs would bring these accessible markets within the scope of American commerce. Besides functioning as an outlet for the West's agricultural surplus, China and the Sandwich Islands would also ensure a steady market for manufacturers and in the bargain secure the fur trade of the Northwest. Raising their voices in agreement, Ohio expansionists demanded that American sovereignty be extended over the territory and that the United States "build up cities in that fertile country on the Pacific, and on the only ports we have opening towards the East Indies—the richest trade in the world." [58]

In an election year, Oregon's political value and natural relationship to Texas were obvious and exploitable. South Carolina's Francis Pickens advised Secretary of State John Calhoun to take the highest grounds on the Oregon question. Stung by antislavery opposition to Texas, Pickens claimed that Oregon was "the only question where we of the South have nothing to lose. It gives us the sympathy of the nonslaveholding states of the North-West and separates them from the Middle and Northern states." Unhappily for Pickens, some northerners persisted in the charge that southern congressmen were extorting northern support for Texas by holding Oregon hostage. In essence, they complained, the South said to the free states, "unless you help us take what is not ours, we will oppose you in taking yours." In contrast, a northeastern expansionist, no less calculating than Pickens, suggested that the Texas question be made "a bridge over which we are to bring our own 'territory' in." [59]

Oregon provided an additional stimulus to growing expansionist enthusiasm, and it conveniently offered something to those sectionalists who argued that Texas was a southern question. Crass manipulation is too circumscribed a view of the annexationists' motives: it fails to comprehend the force and broad attraction of westward expansion within Jacksonian political culture. Taken together, Texas and Oregon raised a popular outcry against British influence on the continent and, more important, to the American Whigs who did their bidding. Drawing parallels to Federalist opposition to the Louisiana purchase, the *Globe* reminded its readers that the opposition had ever been hostile to the welfare of the masses. "The spread of the republic is the spread of democracy," Blair claimed, "and blasts the hopes of those who would make stockjobbers, manufacturing companies, incorporations wielding money influence, the animating principle of government." [60]

Oregon, then, was at once an extension and a reflection of the appeal of annexation. Bringing Texas into the Union was not an end but, in expansionist thinking, part of an ongoing process of physical growth and commercial enhancement. Expansion, an Illinois congressman maintained, constituted "the condition of our national existence." It was also the heart of the Democratic appeal in the campaign. [61]

As expected, the Whigs ran Clay. He and the Whig leadership wished rather than hoped that the older established economic questions were not entirely obscured by the territorial issue. Yet, unable to quiet the agitation for expansion and intimidated by its growing popularity, party members sullenly concluded that Texas cast a long and dark shadow across their presidential aspirations. Cursing the darkness, they damned their opponents for appropriating this "*new issue*" and making it the "sole hobby of the party, *fons et origo*, of their political creed. In this one principle, or no principle, the party have submerged every other." Despite their own conviction that the Locos' enthusiasm for Texas was a measure of Democratic political bankruptcy and desperation, Whigs like Robert Winthrop maintained all along that "Mr. Clay's friends are afraid of the question, & therefore desire to shake off all allusion to it."[62]

Whig apprehension was not misplaced. As the campaign progressed, Democrats attuned to politics at the state and local levels sensed that the appeal of territorial expansion transcended party limits. A Michigan Democrat considered Texas, and to a lesser extent the tariff, "the leading and primary questions." The older established issues, he observed, "are considered so far settled as to be of lesser interest." He added that expansion "is now looked upon as important, not only as tending to promote the welfare of the whole country, but as the question, that is to save the Democratic party from defeat in the coming contest, if anything can." Another northwestern Democrat had already claimed that in his state, Whigs, too, "will go the [Texas] question with a perfect rush."[63]

As momentum for expansion appeared to build, Whigs found it increasingly difficult to restructure the campaign debate along established lines. At the risk of party unity, northern Whigs resorted to antislavery attacks on Texas in hope of neutralizing the issue in the free states. An Ohio editor informed his readers that, since slavery symbolized a political power, annexation could not for a moment be entertained. "It enlarges representation on a basis, and *by a qualification*, ANTI-REPUBLICAN in all its features," he maintained. "It gives to PROPERTY in one section of the Union, a power denied to it in the other." The *Albany Evening Journal* asserted that the Texas movement "originated among Southern politicians, with a view to secure a permanent preponderance of Slave interests and influence in the Government."[64]

Clearly this line of attack was unthinkable to slave-state Whigs. In the South, antiannexationists stood by Clay's moderate position on Texas. A Georgia Whig concluded that "taking as the party ground the position in favor of that measure when the country requires it, and when it can be properly affected [*sic*], we have thought the safest ground, on which to meet the usual feeling of our people for the acquisition of land." Similarly, a Virginia antiannexationist conceded, "The Whigs, while they desire to obtain Texas, are very anxious to feel justified in adopting Mr. Clay's view of postponing its acquisition."[65]

Yet other slave-state party members expected the worst. "The public mind is excited," one warned Clay. "Men are confederated together in appeals to the very worst passions of our nature, and the public mind is feverish, and unstable." William Payne of Virginia reported to William C. Rives that some Whigs, "a few bright and industrious ones," were dissatisfied with the party's opposition to annexation. "On this Texas question there really seems to be in many minds a spirit of infatuation prevailing," Payne observed. "They appear to think that honor, prosperity, happiness & even the very salvation of the United States depended on the immediate acquisition of Texas." A glum Mississippi Whig agreed. "*Poke & Texas*, that's the thing," he snapped, "it goes like wild-fire with the folks as kant rede, nor don't git no papers."[66]

With a calculating eye to the force of expansion, Alexander H. Everett predicted confidently in October that "the Texas question operating directly on the people, & sweeping them along with it . . . broke down one of the two prominent candidates at Baltimore and, to all appearances, will break down the other at the polls." And so it did. In a close contest, Polk carried the election by 170 electoral votes to 105. He won a narrow plurality of 38,367 popular votes out of more than 2.7 million cast, thereby becoming the second president to win without a majority.[67]

In the election, the Liberty Party secured 2.3 percent of the ballots cast, increasing its popular vote from 6,225 in 1840 to 61,999 in 1844. Historians generally attribute its gains and a significant upsurge in Democratic support in the slave states to the sectional nature of the Texas issue. A more careful examination of the vote throughout the North raises serious reservations about this long-held assumption. In every free state except Rhode Island in which the total vote in 1844 exceeded that of 1840, Democratic increases outpaced those of the Whigs, often markedly. Further, if every Liberty Party vote was added to Whig numbers, Democrats still enjoyed comfortable, usually formidable, margins of increase. Throughout the free states the Democracy added 116,997 votes to its 1840 total. Whigs added but 10,595. In New England, where the vote decreased by 4,732 votes, the Democrats added 219 to their 1840 total. In the Middle Atlantic states of New York, New Jersey, and Pennsylvania, Democrats captured slightly over 55 percent of the additional ballots. And in the Old Northwest, they won 69 percent of the 89,170 new votes.[68]

At the county level, Democrats increased their hold in every section including New England. The party added 107 Democratically controlled counties to its 1840 figures. Whigs lost control of 86 counties. In 21 newly created counties, Democrats captured all 3 in Pennsylvania, the only new one in Ohio, 2 of 3 in Indiana, and 8 of 12 in Illinois. The Whigs managed to capture the sole new counties in New Jersey and in Michigan. Democrats held majorities in seven free states, while the Whigs controlled six. And in five states where the party held a majority of counties in 1840 — New York, Michigan, Ohio, Indiana, and Illinois — it seized a majority in 1844.[69]

A look at the South is equally instructive. There the Whigs held their own. Although they got beat up rather severely in Alabama and North Carolina (a state they held for Clay) in every other slave state except Tennessee the party increased its totals over 1840. If Texas was a sectional issue wholly removed from a broader economic context, the party responsible for the defeat of Tyler's treaty should have been annihilated.[70]

Without minimizing the efficacy of the issue in the slave states, widespread Democratic gains in the North and Northwest indicate that party members understood expansion to be consistent with the ideological premises of the Democracy and placed the reannexation of Texas and reoccupation of Oregon within the context of their established programs. Whig competitiveness in the South, however, shows that the issue of Texas was contested not on sectional grounds but on competing visions defined by party and persuasion of governance, progress, and empire.

Claiming that this outcome was "perfectly astounding," one staggered Whig groaned, "The storm is over, and we the people of the United States have been shipwrecked." Surveying the wreckage of their campaign, many Whigs believed that agitation for expansion "did more to beat us than anything." George Prentice maintained that the contest turned simply on whether Texas should be annexed and all of Oregon seized. "Mr. Clay," he concluded, "represented anti-annexation and Mr. Polk was ardent in favor of annexation. It so happened that a majority of the people were anxious for the bringing of Texas into our confederacy and so they voted." An Alabama planter and supporter of Clay concurred. "I [have] been among the common people & I live with them & talk to them," he informed Alexander Stephens. "I know their views and how they do talk & there [sic] reasons for voting for Polk. ¼ of the vote in the Dist went for him on account of Texas. They say the poor man can get lands cheap & all this sort of talk if Texas is anext." One acerbic observer snarled that "for anyone now to say that the Texas question had no influence on the Presidential election only makes a fool or an ass of himself."[71]

"The Fate of the Union is now decided," the *Vicksburg Whig* keened, "and the Texas humbug was made the hobby on which [Polk] should ride into power." Only time would tell "whether the great principles laid down by the patriots of the Revolution are to be carried out, or whether the principles set forth by new aspirants for office and political demagogues are to prevail." The test was not long in coming. As Congress began its session in December, dispirited Whigs listened to Tyler's last annual message urging that annexation be effected by a joint congressional resolution rather than by a treaty. A handful of Whigs in the West and South persuaded themselves that they were "too much of a Republican" to see annexation thwarted, "or rather not to see the will of the majority prevail." The astute Joseph Peyton pointed out that no one, not even Clay, "ever took ground against annexation at the proper time & on proper principles." Even antislavery opponents of Texas read the election as a mandate for annexation "if it can be done constitutionally, with proper regard for all interests of the country, and the rights of Mexico."[72] Once blind, these Whigs could now see that annexation by treaty, bill, or joint resolution was constitutional and imperative. Congress, they now assumed, would execute the will of the people.

In the House, debate centered on a joint resolution that was largely a recapitulation of the rejected treaty's terms. After a rehash of all the old arguments and a welter of confusing resolutions aimed at answering the constitutional scruples of opponents, the House voted on January 25, 1845, by a margin of 120 to 98, to adopt a resolution introduced by Milton Brown, a Tennessee Whig, to admit Texas as a state. As added balm to soothe the consciences of the more honorable, the boundary dispute between Texas and Mexico was postponed for later arbitration, and Texas was left to handle itself the problem of its debts and public lands. In an ambiguous trade-off between slavery extensionists and antislavery men, the resolution allowed Texas to split itself later into several states, and slavery was forbidden in the portion of the territory north of the Missouri Compromise line.[73]

After the Senate Foreign Relations Committee rejected the House proposal, annexationist senators renewed their efforts to have Texas brought into the Union. In a revision of an earlier bill to renegotiate the treaty, Thomas Hart Benton of Missouri introduced a proposal that appropriated $100,000 for renewed negotiations with Texas, without any mention of Mexico's consent. As in the House debate, this provided the occasion for senators to review at length the old established positions, break some ground on the constitutionality of annexation by joint resolution, and in the process search for the common ground of compromise. A majority in both houses finally agreed to a proposal by Robert J. Walker of Mississippi that empowered the president to offer Texas the choice of the terms in the joint resolution of annexation or the negotiation of a new treaty of annexation. The deadlock was broken when every Democratic senator and three Whigs voted for Walker's amendment. The House concurred the following day by a wider margin than it had passed its own resolution.[74]

Passage of the joint resolution reflected and reinforced growing public support for annexation. Although most annexationists assumed that President-elect Polk would carry out the proposal, on the last night of his administration Tyler, vindicated, and persuaded by his vanity as much as by the blandishments of pro-Texas men in his own cabinet, ordered the American chargé in Texas, Andrew Jackson Donelson, to present the House resolution to the Texas government at once.[75]

Andrew Jackson hailed annexation as a "great and important national act" which embodied "the wishes of the great majority of the people of this union." Others saw annexation "as settling the question that the Anglo Saxon race . . . are destined to be finally united in one vast union." Here in the Western Hemisphere, they concluded, "this wonderful race is to end in the establishment of the mightiest empire the world has seen." Perhaps more to the point, sensitive observers saw it "as the triumph of republican energy" and "the triumph of free minds." The issue had thus been met, victory won, and the god Terminus destroyed. "Well you will see how slick we have annexed Texas," a jubilant New Hampshire Democrat wrote, "and thus [got] rid of one matter that may distract Polk's administration."[76] The ascendancy of republican freedom was, they believed, secure in a rising American empire.

—black it
stood as night,
Fierce as ten furies, terrible as hell,
And shook a dreadful dart; what
seemed his head
The likeness of a kingly crown had on.
Satan was now at hand.
— John Milton, *Paradise Lost* II

We owe it to our ancestors to preserve entire those rights, which they have delivered to our care: we owe it to posterity, not to suffer their dearest inheritance to be destroyed.
— *Letters of Junius*, No. 20, August 8, 1769

Milton's Devil

Slavery Restriction and the
Revolutionary Heritage, 1820–1846

On the oppressive Saturday morning of August 8, 1846, the first session of the Twenty-ninth Congress began fitfully to round up and complete its unfinished business. Adjournment was set for noon the following Monday; in fact, some congressmen already had left for home. Around midday, amid the end-of-session confusion, Speaker John W. Davis laid before the House a message from James K. Polk in which the president expressed his sincere desire to terminate the two-month-old war with Mexico "by a peace just and honorable to both parties." The chief difficulty, he apprehended, would be a satisfactory adjustment of the boundary line between the two republics. Polk therefore requested an appropriation of $2 million "to pay a fair equivalent for any concessions which may be made by Mexico." [1]

In this eleventh-hour message, Polk finally made public his administration's objectives that previously had been expressed only privately. As early as the fall of 1845 he had begun to pressure Mexico to cede Upper California and New Mexico to the United States in exchange for a satisfactory adjustment of the Texas boundary, the surrender of American claims against Mexico, and an appropriately large douceur. Later, in a private meeting with Thomas Hart Benton, Polk remarked that the American people would never permit Mexico's western provinces to pass into the possession of Great Britain. He claimed to have "California & the fine bay of San Francisco as much in view as Oregon." Although Polk preferred to realize this grandiose scheme for territorial expansion by peaceful coercion or purchase, he did not shrink from the opportunity that the Mexican conflict presented. In the opening days of the war, the president made clear first to his cabinet and then to select supporters in Congress his determination to acquire California, New Mexico, and, perhaps, some of the northern provinces of Mexico as indemnity for outstanding American claims against that government. Territorial cession, he asserted, also would defray the cost of a war "which that power by her long and continued wrongs and injuries had forced us to wage."[2]

Fearing a premature disclosure of these objectives, Polk initially attempted in a secret executive session of the Senate to secure an appropriation to negotiate such a treaty. Because this plan failed in the face of Whig opposition, the president was forced to make his intentions a matter of record when he renewed his request in early August. He stayed his hand, however, until the eve of adjournment to minimize anticipated Whig protests. Despite the lateness of the hour, Democratic floor leaders adroitly maneuvered an agreement through the House on Saturday afternoon to take up the appropriation that evening. To ensure a vote, the chair limited debate to two hours and held each representative to ten minutes of comments.[3]

As the sweltering afternoon gave way to a sultry evening, representatives unenthusiastically straggled in from the dinner recess to take up Polk's request. Subdued by the weather, dinner, and some by alcohol, they resolved themselves into the Committee of the Whole and began deliberation on a bill presented by James I. McKay of North Carolina appropriating $2 million "to enable the President to conclude a treaty of peace with the Republic of Mexico, to be used by him in the event that said treaty . . . shall call for the expenditure of the same, or any part thereof."[4]

Whigs immediately attacked. They strongly suspected that Polk had provoked war with Mexico to seize what he could not buy. So far opponents could refuse to support the war effort and deny appropriations for the army only at the hazard of their party's future political ascendancy. Polk's August 8 message at last made his dark purposes clear and, they believed, left the president open to the charge that he had involved the nation in a war of aggression and conquest. Hugh White of New York called the conflict with Mexico "unnecessary, uncalled for, and wholly unjustifiable." The $2 million, he argued, was not to buy peace but rather to pay for ill-gotten territory. White, who further suggested that the administration's real object was to extend the area of slavery, challenged Democrats to restrict the institution from any newly acquired lands. Following White, Robert Winthrop of Massachusetts flayed the president and stated that he, too, "was uncompromisingly opposed to extending the slaveholding territory of the Union." The next two speakers, Pennsylvania's Joseph Ingersoll and Kentucky's Henry Grider, both Whigs, hailed "the rainbow of peace" and affirmed their support of the bill.[5]

The chair then recognized David Wilmot, a portly first-term Democrat from northeastern Pennsylvania. As Wilmot took the floor, more than a hundred spectators, including Major General Winfield Scott, who was leaning on the bar, listened with an air of expectancy. Wilmot, a loyal supporter of the administration, took issue with those who claimed this was an unnecessary war, a war of conquest. He regretted Polk's secretiveness; yet Wilmot believed the president's actions both necessary and proper. He now trusted that Polk was sincerely ready to negotiate an honorable peace. To assure that end, this little-known Democrat, adopting the language of the Northwest Ordinance, offered an amendment to McKay's appropriation bill: "That, as an express and fundamental condition to the acquisition of any territory from the Republic of Mexico . . . neither slavery nor involuntary servitude shall ever exist in any part of said territory, except for crime, whereof the party shall be first duly convicted." As the *Boston Whig* presciently observed, this amendment, the Wilmot Proviso, "brought to a head the great question which is about to divide the American people."[6]

Actually, Wilmot's proposal intensified but did not immediately reorient the lines of debate. Cabinet members hurried to the House to hear a succession of speakers use their allotted ten minutes to comment on the expediency of McKay's bill and the relevance of the proposed amendment. The expiration of the time designated for debate cut short rising emotions. As the House moved to vote, Indiana's William Wick, a Democrat, offered a substitute for Wilmot's proviso. In it, Wick proposed to extend the Missouri Compromise line of 36°30' to any new territory acquired from Mexico. His proposal was voted down 54 to 89, and, returning to Wilmot's original amendment, the House passed it, 83 to 64. A Kentucky Democrat, William Tibbats, then moved to table the entire bill rather than vote the $2 million with the obnoxious proviso attached. This maneuver was rejected in an ominously sectional vote, 78 to 94. The bill was then passed.[7]

The Senate took up the $2 million bill the following Monday, just an hour before the scheduled adjournment. The administration's plan was to strike

Wilmot's amendment, pass the appropriation, and return it to the House with just enough time to pass the bill without the restriction. Unhappily, this strategy ran afoul of Senator John Davis of Massachusetts. Quite to the contrary, he intended to speak on the measure until there would be only enough time left in the session for the Senate to swallow hard and accept the appropriation with the proviso attached. Unfortunately for Davis but also for Polk, the senator was unaware of an eight-minute difference between the clocks in the Senate and the House. Davis was still expounding on the merits of the proviso when an exasperated Dixon Lewis of Alabama informed him that it was needless to continue; the House had adjourned. Polk had been denied his money, and the free-soil revolt had been halted as quickly as it had begun.[8]

A disappointed Polk thought the amendment "mischievous & foolish. . . . What connection slavery had with making peace with Mexico it is difficult to conceive." Along with Polk, scholars have long noted the critical role that the proviso played in fomenting sectional tensions. They have infused an air of inevitability into the sectional struggle over slavery restriction, claiming that it widened an existing and immutable rift between the North and South and demonstrated the extent to which "the opposing camps were ready to fight even when little or nothing was at stake." Historians of the antebellum South contend that slavery — narrowly defined in institutional terms — largely if not exclusively informed and shaped southern politics.[9] By extension, they imply that the essence of southern Democratic thought was both sectional in nature and outside American political culture. By reasoning backward from the failure of Wilmot's initiative to preclude a conflict over the territories and to prevent sectional and partisan rifts, the literature casts northerners as irrational extremists and southerners as adversaries both of the Union and of the fundamental premises of the Democracy.

Wilmot's revolt against the administration suggested a serious though not yet widespread split within the Democratic Party. Wilmot spoke for a group of antislavery northern Democrats who were themselves raw over insensitive treatment by the administration, disgruntled with the seeming dominance of the party's southern wing, and troubled about a southern president's plan for newly acquired territory. The Walker Tariff of 1846, which significantly reduced rates, alienated protectionist Democrats from the North and East. John M. Niles, a Connecticut Democrat, grumbled that it was "an act to bring down the free labor of the North, and try to bring up the slave labor of the cotton planters & tobacco growers of the South." Polk's veto of a popular river and harbor bill angered western Democrats. Both the tariff and the veto were the occasion of angry speeches (and, at times, broken party ranks) on the floor of Congress.[10] The party's fissures so evident in the last years of the Tyler presidency had resurfaced.

Even more portentous than conflicting economic views, built-up resentment over too severe party discipline and the insensitivity of its leadership was the perceived southern tilt of Polk's administration. The repudiation of Martin Van Buren in 1844, alleged to be the work of southern Democrats who opposed his position on Texas, had left his supporters irritated and suspicious. Van Buren's friends were temporarily but not completely reconciled to Polk's nomination when the convention balanced expansion into the Southwest with a demand for the reoccupation of Oregon. After Congress brought Texas safely into the Union, Van Burenites, especially in the West, expected Polk to make good on his—and the party's—claim to all of Oregon. When, however, a month after the Mexican War had broken out, Polk sent the Senate a treaty dividing the territory between Great Britain and the United States, the split within the party widened. Democrats favoring the 54°40' line were apoplectic. "Our Rights to Oregon have been shamefully compromised," charged the *Cleveland Plain Dealer*, "not so much to avoid war as to permanently fix the boundaries of free territory. . . . We are hemmed in with the parallel of 49 and British slavery on the North, and Mason & Dixon's line with African slavery on the South. It is time lovers of freedom should unite in opposing the common enemy by fixing bounds to their aggression." After Walker's tariff passed with solid southern support the following July, many northern party members finally concluded that narrow, sectional objectives were subverting the principles of the Democracy. The time had come, one Van Burenite concluded, for northern Democrats to make a stand.[11] It was against this background of discontent and mistrust that Wilmot, Preston King, Jacob Brinkerhoff, and other free-soil Democrats staged their revolt.

Eric Foner has astutely pointed out that although resentment and alienation lurked behind the proviso, northern Democrats supported it as a means to allay growing opposition in the free states to the Mexican conflict and prospective expansion. Wilmot's proviso, the *Ohio Statesman* declared, "is our *declaration of independence* from southern dictation, arrogance, and misrule." This was not hyperbole, nor was the analogy misplaced. Free-soil Democrats alleged that the proviso, like the Declaration of Independence, was essentially a conservative document. By adapting the language of the Northwest Ordinance, Wilmot was simply restating what he and other free-soilers believed to be widely acknowledged first principles: free territory had been and would continue to be consecrated to the spread of human freedom. Like the Revolution, moreover, their revolt, so free-soilers maintained, was essentially defensive in nature and intent. Free-soil Democrats opposed neither the war nor any territorial cession that might come from it. Nor did they wish to widen or make permanent the breach in their party. By supporting the proviso, Wilmot, King, and the rest intended to assure their constituents that the administration did not wage war to extend the area of slavery and wished, in the process, to restore the party to its historical function of moderating sectional antagonisms. Proponents of restriction, then, viewed Wilmot's amendment, perhaps myopically, not as a challenge to the South but as a defensive action aimed at ending discord within the party by returning it to its original purpose. More to the point, they also hoped that support for the amendment would unify northern Democrats who faced rising antislavery sentiment at home.[12]

This line of reasoning, though, evinces a tendency to absorb the viewpoints of free-soil Democrats and uses it as the standard to judge the slave-state response. Consequently, it perforce fails to integrate the South into the nation's political culture. A closer look at the choice of imagery and historical logic employed by restrictionists and southern Democrats suggests that the battle over Wilmot's proviso was not produced by the clash of different political cultures. Informed by their understanding of the meaning of 1776 and the intent of the revolutionary generation, southern statesmen, too, intended to live up to and live out the legacy of their unique heritage. Thus northerners and southerners shared a common—not disparate—revolutionary heritage and ideology and acted in ways that were intelligible to their constituents and each other.

The issue of slavery restriction, of course, had already been raised. John C. Calhoun and others had insisted just two years before that Texas be added to the Union to ensure the safety and expansion of the South's peculiar institution. Conscience Whigs and abolitionists opposed annexation for precisely the same reason. In spite of the bitterness of those arguments, the larger question of territorial growth overshadowed the question of slavery extension. Grounding the Texas question on traditional party principles, northern Locos criticized those of the Calhoun stripe for discussing the Texas issue "as if its chief merits rested on local grounds." Southern Democrats heatedly and repeatedly attacked northern antiannexationists who insisted that Texas be solely considered—and rejected—as a sectional question. They were also equally disposed to castigate fire-eaters who threatened disunion if Polk lost. Yet rapid expansion ran counter to Whigs' faith in national progress. Annexation of Texas and Oregon threatened to undermine the evolution of an integrated market-based economy and society that the party idealized and nurtured. Inasmuch as views on expansion were shaped by traditional ideological differences between Democrats and Whigs, established party lines broadly defined and safely contained antislavery arguments.[13]

The instance, therefore, that appears on the surface to have been most directly comparable was the Missouri debate of 1819–20. It would seem that the issue at hand then, too, was the spread of slavery into the West. The upshot in that case was also the threatening, albeit temporary, sectionalization of congressional debate over the question of restriction. At first glance, the lineaments of the Missouri Compromise appear to foreshadow and to a certain extent to define the later free-soil crisis. A closer examination, however, of the constitutional logic and actuating principles of the Federalist-Republican debate and a comparison with those of the free-soil argument reveal significant and ominous differences. The Missouri debate engaged the advocates of two variant types of freedom, each of which rested upon a definition of the future shape and power of the federal government. The free-soil conflict, in contrast, had the effect of pitting North against South for the right to expand and control the government. Whereas the ideological differences apparent in the Missouri debate extended into the Jacksonian, or second party system, the free-soil revolt disrupted, then displaced those party divisions altogether.[14]

On February 13, 1819, the House of Representatives resolved itself into the Committee of the Whole to consider statehood enabling bills for the territories of Missouri and Alabama. The Missouri bill was taken up first, and in the course of the House's review of the legislation, James Tallmadge Jr. of New York offered an amendment providing that the federal government ban the further entry of slaves into Missouri and all the remaining territory of the Louisiana Purchase. In addition, it ordered that, after Missouri's admission, all children born to slaves there be made free at the age of twenty-five. The debate precipitated by Tallmadge's amendment produced a deadlock in Congress. Twice the House passed the Missouri bill with the restriction only to have the amendment struck out by the Senate. The bill was finally tabled when the session expired.[15]

Judging by their arguments, members of Congress saw more at stake than the provisions of the Missouri bill alone. Most immediately, the sectional balance of power within the Union hinged on the outcome. More important, though, the terms of Missouri's admission would set a precedent for other, and presumably numerous, states hatched from the remaining Louisiana territory. Passage of the Missouri bill with Tallmadge's amendment would mean that the federal government claimed the power to restrict or expand slavery as it deemed necessary to promote the general welfare. This obviously implied a vast accretion and centralization of power in the hands of Congress at the expense of liberty on the periphery. If, to the contrary, Congress admitted Missouri without restriction, it would seemingly deny Washington the power to touch the existence of slavery in the states and check the encroachment of federal power at the expense of states' rights.[16]

As members of Congress peered at the landscape of the future, their vision was illuminated not only by the brightest hopes for the nation's progress but by the lights of the American past as well. Those who supported restriction, Federalists for the most part, believed in a steady improvement in the human estate. They looked to the agency of the federal government to promote this general welfare through the course of time. Critical to this view was the Federalists' understanding of their constitutional past. Harrison Gray Otis of Massachusetts believed that absolute self-government was an original right of the citizens of the first thirteen states alone. Having exercised that right when they "breathed the breath of life" into the federal Constitution, they thus rendered it physically impossible for the inhabitants of new territories and new states to be placed in the same relationship to the Union as that of inhabitants of the older states. The citizens of the old thirteen, he explained, "are the sources of power, and the Constitution the reservoir; in the other [case], the people of the United States are the fountain, whence must issue the streams destined to irrigate and fertilize the ceded territories, and Congress, as their agents, may and ought to prescribe the course and direction, and erect the mound and the dykes which a regard to the common welfare may demand."[17]

Their reading of history described a Union created by the original thirteen states that, once called into being, took on a life and purpose of its own. No mere agent of the states, the federal government was endowed with sovereignty, a unique character, and a will. The nature of the Union was protean and perforce changed as the nation expanded across the continent. It was, therefore, increasingly incumbent upon the federal government to impose order and direction on growth, to assure that the change would bring positive results. As a consequence, the relationship between the individuals of new states and Washington was continually being altered.

The restrictionists' idea of the Union incorporated a distinction between old states and new ones like Missouri. Jonathan Roberts, a supporter of the Tallmadge amendment, thought the Missouri question a simple one. Shall a territory, he asked, foreign to that which composed the parties to the Constitution, be admitted on any terms it desired, even though they might be harmful to the nation's political and social well-being? Difficulty, he argued, resulted from the wrongheaded assumption that Congress should bring these "entire new members" into the Union unrestricted, on an equal footing with the original states. In Missouri's case, that would mean that the original compromises of the Constitution regarding slavery would necessarily be extended beyond the "original limits" of the nation. This idea restrictionists rejected. These concessions, Rufus King pointed out, were part of a settlement among the thirteen states; "the considerations arising out of their actual condition, their past connexion, and the obligation which all felt to promote a reformation in the federal government, were particular to the time and parties." Therefore, he concluded, the three-fifths compromise and fugitive slave clause did not apply automatically to new states that Congress might admit to the Union. This was especially so for territory acquired after the original states ratified the Constitution. Although Congress extended these agreements to the western territories of states that were themselves original parties to the Constitution, states carved from the Louisiana Purchase had no similar claim. "As this acquisition was made at the common expense," King argued, "it is very fairly urged that the advantages to be derived from it should also be common." [18]

To King and other Federalists, promoting the general welfare to assure the upward progress of the nation was a preeminent obligation of the federal government. First, as Otis observed, Congress represented not only the equality and sovereignty of the states but, more important, the unity of their interests. Also, as a sovereign entity, the government of the Union, though limited in powers, was supreme in its proper sphere of action. To promote the general welfare in an ever-expanding nation required decisions of no small moment when the federal government brought new states under the aegis of the Union. Because the nature of the Union evolved over time, "the quality and character" of the new states, Lemuel Shaw claimed, would be crucial in determining the nation's future. Thus in 1819 it was not Missouri alone that ought to be the sole consideration of Congress. As Prentiss Mellen reminded the Senate, "We are then by our decision, preparing evils or blessings for an extensive country and for posterity." [19]

King, Tallmadge, and others based their restrictionist arguments on a broad mandate derived from the general welfare clause and their claims as to the limited nature of the Constitution's compromises on slavery. Consequently, they rejected the assertion that the Constitution circumscribed Congress's ability to limit the extension of slavery. Could it be, John Taylor wondered, that "the supreme legislature has no power to provide rules and regulations for ameliorating the condition of the future ages?" Why, the Constitution plainly authorized the enactment of whatever law Congress might deem conducive to the general welfare of the country. Congress had the power to admit or reject the admission of new states as it saw fit. Taylor argued it was therefore logical to conclude that Congress also had "the power of prescribing such conditions of admission as may be judged reasonable." No derogation of the status of the new state was implied. If Missouri accepted the condition of restriction, upon its admission it would be bound by the compact and the Constitution in the same manner as Ohio and the other states of the Old Northwest. [20]

After having established the right of Congress to prescribe conditions for admission of new states, Tallmadge's supporters argued that limiting the spread of slavery would guarantee progress and enhance the nation's greatness. Arguments on the expediency of restricting slavery provided the occasions for wide-ranging, at times severe, criticisms of the institution. If colored by the rhetoric of indignation, these indictments were political in nature and essentially amoral in content. Although there was no single perspective, collectively these views focused on one central thesis: that the extension of slavery would retard progress and inhibit security, liberty, and the general good.

King suggested that the criteria for admitting new states were the extension of the principles of free government, equalizing public burdens, and consolidating the power of the Union. Failure to restrict slavery's spread, he and others maintained, would frustrate these ends. Given what they alleged to be the feudal nature of slave society, new states admitted with slavery would thereby be denied a truly republican form of government. Slave labor, "very prejudicial to agricultural improvements," would impoverish millions of acres of virgin land and in the bargain exclude "the poore and more laborious classes of society." Finally, to extend slavery to the western reaches of the United States would bring into contact with foreign powers "a weak frontier and the degraded instruments of intrigue and revolution." If slavery were confined to its present limits, however, "the principles of freedom [will] be extended and strengthened, [and] an exposed and important frontier will present a barrier, which will check and keep back foreign assailants."[21]

Extension of slavery into the West would also injure the older states of the North by enlarging the area in which the three-fifths compromise operated. The equality of rights and the equality of burden were vital principles in the theory of American government, King explained. Nonetheless, the extension of this disproportionate advantage, King concluded, "would be unjust and odious. The States whose power would be abridged, and whose burdens would be increased by the measure, cannot be expected to consent to it." In a like vein, Prentiss Mellen maintained that "this balance, this equality, will be destroyed, should the [three-fifths compromise] be extended beyond the Mississippi to an immense country beyond the range ever in contemplation of the Convention."[22]

"Freedom and slavery are the parties which stand this day before the Senate," King declared. "Upon its decision the empire of one or the other will be established." With an eye to enhancing the quality of life and expanding the capacities of men in an evolving Union, King, Otis, Mellen, and other Federalists linked the fate of the nation to Missouri and the West. Congress's decision on the issue of slavery restriction would, they concluded, affect the future progress of America. Immediately, it would determine whether Missouri would be a land of highly cultivated farms, populated by "a neat, blooming, animated peasantry," or one of plantations overrun by weeds and inhabited by "squalid, slow motion blacks." More important was what it would say about the federal government's commitment to circumscribe the area of slavery, removing or at least limiting one of the evils of American society. Looking far into the future, they held that the precedent established by Missouri's admission would decide the status of slavery in the development of an expansive American empire and the unfolding of the national character. "Those whom we shall authorize to set in motion the machine of free government beyond the Mississippi, will, in many respects, decide the destiny of millions," one Federalist asserted. "Our votes this day will determine whether the high destinies of this region, and of these generations, shall be fulfilled."[23]

Marshaling their forces for a counterattack, orthodox Republicans from the South viewed the struggle over restriction as but the most recent battle in a protracted and bitter war. The assault on the South's peculiar institution was, of course, as menacing as it was insulting. Southerners placed the Missouri crisis in historical context. They contended that it was, at bottom, another Federalist measure, like Alexander Hamilton's national bank or protective tariff, to promote the unconstitutional consolidation of power in the federal government. William Plumer Jr. of New Hampshire wrote his father, "Besides this business of Missouri, [southern congressmen] say that the General Government is every year setting up new claims & pretensions—They mention the establishment of the Bank; the jurisdiction assumed . . . by the Supreme Court; & many other encroachments, as they deem them, of the Government generally."[24] Despite threats of secession, southern Republicans primarily were intent on denying any additional power to the federal government. Although the terrain of the battlefield was different, they found the strategy of previous encounters instructive. Blowing the dust off battle plans drawn up by Jefferson and Madison twenty-some years earlier, these cavaliers sallied forth to engage what they thought to be a well-known enemy.

Southern Republicans parried the Federalist thrust, first, by affirming the timeless, unchanging nature of the Union. In their view of history, the states were originally sovereign, without any limitation. Unable to protect themselves singly, the old thirteen entered into a Union to defend the republic against foreign violence. In doing so, the states surrendered no power to manage domestic concerns; indeed, the security of that power was one of the great objects of the Union. Hence the Constitution and Union, as Maryland's William Pinkney observed, were "*means* not an *end*." Accordingly, Republicans rejected out of hand the Federalist concept of a Union imbued with sovereignty and purpose. The Constitution, Pinkney went on, was a common compact for mutual defense and established a "Union *inter pares*." The addition of new states neither recreated nor transformed the nature of the Union; it simply enlarged the Union's scope of operation. Southerners rejected the Federalists' argument that the federal government was obliged to direct and control westward expansion to secure the Union's stability and permanence. They maintained instead that "the strength of this Union must depend on the sameness of the political institutions, and the equality of the rights which are secured to the States which compose it." Otherwise, "the end is sacrificed to the means."[25]

Southern Republicans defended the integrity of a Union of equal, sovereign states. Fear and jealousy, not wisdom and principle, animated restrictionists, they charged. Alarmed at the diminution of their own political power, eastern Federalists would subvert the Constitution and pervert the Union to serve their selfish, narrow ends. Opponents of the Tallmadge amendment predicted that restriction would transform a Union of equals, "*inter pares*," to one of "*disparaties*, between giants and a dwarf, between power and feebleness, between full proportioned sovereignties and a miserable image of power." Shorn of one branch of her sovereignty, Missouri would be forever fixed with "the badge of inequality and degradation." No, Congress could not prescribe conditions that would reduce the sovereignty of a state. Missouri must be admitted as "a State with all such sovereignty as belongs to the original parties; and it must be into *this Union* that you are to admit it, not into a Union of your own dictating, formed . . . by qualifications and new compacts, altering its charter and effect."[26]

As a creature of all the states, new and old, the Union was naturally and immutably extended when citizens moved across the continent. These "hardy sons of the West" carried within them the genius and capacity for self-government that made a viable nation of independent communities. Republicans denounced the paternalism and arrogance of those who would control new states like dependent colonies in a despotic empire. Federalists could hardly expect that the inhabitants of Missouri, infused with the same spirit of independence that animated the heroes and patriots of the Revolution, would tamely submit to an infringement of their right of self-government and equality within the Union. Such submissions and humiliation might be expected from the slaves of an Eastern despot, Freeman Walker of Georgia scoffed. "But to expect such submission from the free born sons of America, upon whose birth the genius of liberty smiled, who have been nursed in the lap of independence, and grown to manhood warmed and animated by the genial influence of our happy Constitution is to expect that which reason and nature forbid. 'Tis to expect from freemen the conduct of slaves." The issue raised by the Tallmadge amendment was not the prohibition of slavery, the *Missouri Gazette* reminded its readers. It was, rather, more fundamental and foreboding. "Bear in mind, fellow citizens, that the question now before us is . . . whether we will meanly abandon our rights and suffer any earthly power to dictate the terms of our Constitution."[27]

Federalists claimed that Congress had the power to restrict or allow the expansion of slavery as it deemed expedient. And James Madison conceded that the clause granting Congress jurisdiction over the common territory was "of a ductile character." Madison concluded, however, that it "cannot well be extended beyond a power over the Territory as property." The federal government had no authority to restrict slavery in the admission of a new state. Madison and other Republicans deemed the basic issue of the Missouri crisis to be the growth of unchecked authority and tyranny of the central government. What they consistently guarded against was the exercise of power against a minority "who are defenceless against it; who cannot check it, or contribute to check it in its exercise." If Congress may arrogate to itself the authority to regulate the domestic institutions of the states, one Republican observed, "who shall stay its hand or prescribe its limits?"[28]

The doctrine of strict construction did not preclude tensions between northern and southern Republicans. Northerners were equally adept at using a narrowly interpreted Constitution and—like Federalists and southern Republicans—invoking the imagery of the Revolution in their case often to defend restriction. Drawing on the tenets of the Declaration of Independence, they described a Union consecrated to the promotion of individual liberty and equality. Federalists contended that the womb of time held the improvement of the human condition. Northern Republicans, however, held that the animating principle of the Union was individual freedom and, by extension, that the Constitution was an antislavery document. It followed that as Congress extended the Constitution over new territories and states, it brought to them the blessings of freedom, not the entailed curse of bondage.[29]

Although the tension between the two wings of the Jeffersonian party presaged the free-soil revolt of 1846, it was muted in the face of a common enemy during the Missouri conflict. Republicans believed that the war over restriction was at bottom a disingenuous attempt to resuscitate the Federalist Party. It was not the love of liberty, humanity, or religion that lay behind northern opposition to slavery, Charles Pinckney scoffed. "It is the love of power and the never ceasing wish to regain the honors and the offices of government." Faction and party spirit laid the groundwork; envy and fear shaped the crisis. All were calculated "to blast the fair fame, both of the dead, and the living; and cause Tyranny, like Milton's devil, 'to grin horrible, a ghastly smile.'" More threatening than the apparition of the dead were parties founded on local distinctions. If antislavery were to dominate the agenda of the new party, free- and slave-state divisions would replace the old partisan conflicts between Federalists and Republicans. Although the former might have the semblance of legitimacy, Jefferson claimed, it was clearly calculated to give Federalists ascendancy "by debauching their old opponents to a coalition with them." The prospect of sectional parties, concurred Madison, was to be dreaded.[30]

The summer and fall following adjournment did little to diminish sectional antagonisms. When the first session of the Sixteenth Congress met in December, the battles of the previous spring were soon rejoined. Debates traversed familiar ground, and intellectual engagement degenerated into a rehash of established charges and defenses. The logistics of compromise were complicated because the District of Maine was also applying for statehood. Ironically, however, it also made agreement, or rather trade-off, on Missouri possible. "Equality is equality," Henry Clay argued, "and if it is right to make the restriction of slavery the condition of the admission of Missouri, it is equally just to make the admission of Missouri the condition of that of Maine." The Senate linked the two enabling bills and voted to admit Maine as a free state and Missouri without restriction. Senator Jesse B. Thomas of Illinois enlarged the compromise by an amendment to ban slavery in the remaining Louisiana Purchase north of 36°30'. The House at first rejected the Maine-Missouri bill, then the Thomas amendment, and again approved a Missouri bill with restriction. Once more, Congress deadlocked. Eventually, weariness, anxiety, and the deft manipulations of Clay fashioned a compromise. On March 2, 1820, the House agreed to strike restriction and concur in a Senate bill admitting Missouri as a slave state with the Thomas amendment attached.[31]

"The settlement of the Missouri question I think a happy thing," Clay remarked, "yet there are some persons on both sides of the question dissatisfied with it." Sensitive to the nuances of public opinion, the Speaker of the House perhaps understood that the Compromise of 1820 fell a good deal short of a comprehensive settlement of the slavery extension issue. Southern Republicans, it was true, had carried their major objective: Congress's right to impose slavery restriction on a state was denied. Considered in other particulars, the Missouri settlement also reflected a consensus among a Republican majority on the nature of the Union and the restricted powers of the federal government. Strict construction and the equality of states had been sustained; the various slavery provisions of the Constitution were extended to new states; and the irrelevance of congressionally imposed territorial restrictions to a state's authority over the institution was conceded. Yet in this last instance, compromise essentially meant postponement, and the two are not the same. Consensus among Republicans in 1820 on the constitutional issues before them spoke less to the question of slavery restriction in the territories than to the proper relation of federal and state power. At the core of the 1819–20 debates were variant interpretations of the future shape of the national government, the nature and fate of the Union of states, and the means best suited to secure the liberties of the periphery against the power of the center. Considered from this perspective, territorial restriction was a secondary issue; indeed, it was the means by which to reach compromise. If, however, future antislavery conflicts focused on congressional authority over the common territory, not on the authority of the states over their domestic institutions, then restriction would put the cohesiveness of the Republican phalanx to a sterner test. Were that territorial question posed, John C. Calhoun brooded, "no one can calculate the consequences."[32]

After the lapse of twenty-six years, James K. Polk may be forgiven for having been unmindful of Calhoun's warning. With the Oregon imbroglio recently resolved, the war going well, and California in revolt against Mexico, the president was eager to realize his plans for a continental empire. In conversations with his cabinet and members of both parties, Polk modestly indicated that he would be satisfied with the acquisition of New Mexico and the Californias. In return for the cession of Mexico's northern provinces, the United States would pay liberally, assume the debts of American claimants, and bear the expenses of the war. Dismayed but undaunted by the skirmishing over the proviso of the previous session, Polk still found it politic to forswear more southerly territory so as to give no occasion for renewed agitation of the question of restriction. Accordingly, in December 1846 Polk asserted in his second annual message that although the government had not waged war to conquer, an honorable peace required ample indemnity for combat expenses and injured American citizens. The president thus recommended that Congress again take up his appropriation request so that he could use the $2 million (later $3 million) to buy this indemnity. Congress obliged, and on January 4, 1847, Preston King of New York moved that Wilmot's proviso be attached to the $3 million bill.[33]

If Polk may be excused for having paid little heed to Calhoun, who was always full of dark foreboding, he and other expansionists might have taken greater pains to understand the summer's free-soil revolt. It is true that from 1820 to 1846 antislavery sentiment in the North had been limited by a matrix of constitutional obligations. Racism and veneration of the Union — a union with slaveholders — precluded any direct attack on the institution in the South. Northerners' opposition to slavery, however, had not diminished in those years, nor was their commitment to freedom any less. If Congress skirted the issue by admitting Texas as a slave state, the prospect of acquiring an enormous cession of territory from Mexico made further evasion impossible. Time and again Americans had pointed to the importance of the West to the destinies of the nation, and the fate of the territories seemed likely to determine the fate of the republic. Gideon Welles expressed the hope "that soil which is now free may remain so, and that free labor there may never be impaired by the introduction of slaves." As the sectional antagonisms became explicit, free-soil Democrats argued that Congress had the power and an obligation to ensure that slavery would not follow the American flag into areas now free. As one Democratic restrictionist put it, "The question is not whether black men are to be made free . . . but whether white men are to remain free." [34]

Although conscience Whigs united with rebellious Democrats to restrict slavery, a strict, rather than broad, construction of the Constitution informed the free-soil argument. The Democratic attack on slavery expansion contemplated no new powers for Congress, no reinterpretation of the Constitution, no assault on the institution in the South. "I am content," one New York Democrat pledged, "to leave slavery where the Constitution has left it." Restrictionists held slavery to be solely a creature of local law, wholly within the purview of southern states, protected but limited in its scope of operation. As a local institution it could not be extended to territories already free without positive legislation by Congress. This, they argued, was legally impossible. Speaking for many, Salmon P. Chase maintained that nowhere did the Constitution recognize slavery "as a national institution, to be upheld by national law." In all places under the exclusive jurisdiction of Congress, he concluded, "Slavery is Constitutionally impossible." As the free-soilers understood it, the question was not whether slavery should exist unmolested. For instance, David Wilmot claimed, it was "whether it shall be carried to new and distant regions, now free, where the footprint of a slave cannot be found." If northerners failed to defend the Constitution from the latitudinarian assaults of proslavery southerners, Wilmot concluded, "We are cowards, slaves, and deserve to have the manacles fastened upon our own limbs." [35]

Insofar as free-soilers desired to hew closely and narrowly to the Constitution's slavery provisions and no more, they could proclaim that their intent was to restore the nation to its pristine mission: the spread of individual freedom. Believing that the character of the Mexican territories was by law and by nature free, restrictionists understood what they regarded as the attempt by southerners to extend slavery into the far West to be in contravention of the Constitution and subversive of the purpose of the Union. Hence in the eyes of free-soilers, the dangers and ramifications of the antiproviso movement were far more ominous than had been those of the Missouri crisis or the Texas debate. Slavery existed in both. "The question is now in a shape it never before has and never before could have assumed," Silas Wright observed. "To contend that Congress should introduce, or engraft, slavery upon territory now free, is to ask the people of the Union to consider and treat slavery as a positive benefit and blessing to be diffused and extended by the action of Congress." This, free-soilers concluded, signaled a direct attack on the essence of freedom that lay at the core of American civilization. Freedom, one northerner later observed, "is the rule, by the law of Nature; Slavery is the exception by the law of force; By the same laws, Freedom is universal; Slavery is local. Freedom is general; slavery is particular."[36] Imbued with this ontological and emotional content, the proviso debate assumed an importance that overshadowed the ostensible and practical question of slave migration into the West.

Unflagging commitment to a Constitution and a timeless Union dedicated to the principle of human freedom differentiated Democratic free-soilers from other antislavery activists such as abolitionists and conscience Whigs. Abolitionists of the William Lloyd Garrison stripe contended that the Constitution was inherently evil and the Union "imperfect, oppressive, monstrous." Whereas free-soilers venerated the principles and work of the Founding Fathers, Garrison thought the Constitution a nullity, "a most bloody and Heaven-daring arrangement . . . according to the law of God." It followed that the Union, but another name for the Constitution, was "founded in unrighteousness and cemented in blood." Calling for a separation of free from slave states, Garrison dismissed the Liberty Party as "unprincipled . . . insidious, and . . . dangerous." The free-soil movement indicated progress. Still he claimed that it was the duty of all genuine antislavery activists "to show them and all others, that there is a higher position to be obtained by them." Garrison's higher law, framed "in the name of God and humanity," required "a dissolution of our blood-cemented, atheistical Union."[37]

If Garrisonians considered the Constitution to be a pact with Satan, Whigs, like Federalists before them, saw it as a blessed document to be used to promote the general welfare. Antislavery elements in the party's northern wing, like Senator William Upham of Vermont, looked to restriction to promote the interests and existing order of the nation through the years ahead. Broadly interpreting congressional power over the territories, northern Whigs came to support restriction for reasons different from those of free-soilers. Whereas the latter saw the proviso as a reaffirmation of limited government, a rededication of the government to the national purpose, and a remedy for northern opposition to the war, antislavery Whigs viewed restriction as a positive act by Congress to foster the public weal through reform and, more important, as a way to hoist the Democrats with their own petard, thereby ending the war. "Now is the time for us [Whigs] to '*progress*' in our antislavery," a House Whig urged. "Nor should our action be *negative*. We ought to take *affirmative* action." Convinced that the South was determined to expand and believing the war to be an administration plot to further its cause, antislavery Whigs looked to the proviso as a tactic to bring the war to an end. Dash the hope that more slave territory will be acquired, Pennsylvania's Andrew Stewart predicted, "and you at once put an end to the war, by defeating its object."[38]

Free-soil Democrats stood apart ideologically from both abolitionists and antislavery Whigs. Although, as Major Wilson has pointed out, free-soilers shared Garrison's absolutism and the Whig concept of Union and liberty, they saw the Constitution as an antislavery document and the proviso as a return to the first principles of the founders. Dismissing Garrison's position that the Constitution was inherently evil, free-soilers maintained that, however flawed, it was intended "to establish the National Government and Policy upon such principles as would bring about, at length, the desired results of Universal Freedom." They alleged that the entire history of the nation was a tribute to, and an unqualified endorsement of, human freedom. In the Declaration of Independence, "for the first time in the history of the world, was the doctrine of the inalienable RIGHT of every man to life, liberty, and the pursuit of happiness, solemnly proclaimed as THE BASIS OF A NATIONAL POLITICAL FAITH." From the assembling of the First Continental Congress to the final organization of the government under the Constitution, "the American government was antislavery in its character and policy," Chase insisted. "The deliverance of our country from the curse & crime of slavery *through the Constitution* is the great, glorious & practicable object of the True Democracy."[39]

Free-soilers cast themselves as the spiritual heirs of their revolutionary forebears. In their view, the American Revolution was an inevitable and climactic battle between despotism and freedom, between aristocratic and democratic principles. The founders claimed no new or peculiar rights; they only demanded security in the enjoyment of rights of all English citizens. In creating the Union, they confided in a general doctrine of equal rights and endeavored to establish a national government upon such principles as would bring about the desired result of universal freedom. As defenders of liberty against the encroachments of slavery, free-soilers refought the battles of their fathers. Their purpose was "to carry forward and perfect the great work of individual, social, and civil elevation which our fathers nobly began." Indeed, free-soilers avowed themselves in their first principles to be "the same party as that which in 1776, rallied around the Declaration of Independence. . . . The same party as that which, in 1787, formed our own federal Constitution."[40] Like the revolutionaries, free-soilers claimed for themselves no new rights, no exclusive privileges. Their duty and their purpose were to rescue the government from the control of slaveholders, to harmonize its practical administration with the provisions of the Constitution and the underlying principles of the Union.

Time and again, free-soilers declared that Washington, Madison, Jefferson, and the forefathers believed slavery to be inconsistent with the other institutions of the Union. They avowedly and from the bottom of their hearts sought its extinction. Expecting slavery to "run out," they agreed to the compromises of the Constitution only to provide a decent interval in which the institution could die. The Ordinance of 1787, the end of the slave trade, and the ban on slavery north of 36°30' in the Louisiana territory evinced a determination by the revolutionary generation to realize the principles of the Declaration of Independence. Over time, however, as slavery became entrenched in the cotton states, southerners gradually found themselves at war with the sentiments and organic law of the government. They gradually abandoned the faith of their fathers. A moral and political incubus upon the body of the South, slavery contributed to the general declension that blighted the slaveholding states. By the 1840s the activating principle of the Union had become a nullity in the South. "I never yet saw a slaveholder, who drank in the idea of human equality," Gerrit Smith declared. "No slaveholder can drink it in & remain a slaveholder."[41] Now southerners were boldly threatening to thrust the institution into yet larger tracts of newly acquired territory and, in the process, subvert the mission and the character of the nation.

More to the point, free-soilers claimed, territorial acquisitions and pro-slavery aggrandizement were giving a preponderance to the South and, by way of the three-fifths compromise, allowing an aristocracy of slaveholding southerners to control the government. Because of this fear, the crisis precipitated by the proposed proviso seemed to the free-soilers to reshape the existing political terrain. It was not, in their opinion, like the older struggles over the bank, the tariff, or even the Missouri crisis, which had been defined by conflicting ideas of the powers of the federal government and, consequently, the future shape of the Union. And they ridiculed Whigs for ignoring this great question, talking instead about "making a dam across some stream & erecting thereon factories, for the *boys and girls to make things in*" or fretting over "the fall of molasses." The territorial issue was nothing less than "a question whether, in the government of the country, [the free states] shall be borne down by the influence of . . . slaveholding aristocratic institutions, that have not in them the first element of Democracy."[42] Cast in the light of the Revolution, the specter of slavery extension seemed a reincarnation of the ancient struggle between slavery and freedom, aristocracy and democracy, for the right to expand and, more important, to control the government. Slavery restrictionists therefore concluded that the territorial issue was both a new and an old one. It contained within it the seed of sectionalism and the ominous possibility that in the future, parties and the nation would be divided along geographical lines. Yet the proviso was also the traditional,

American position of the Declaration of Independence: a reaffirmation of the nation's commitment to individual freedom.

Imagine the surprise of southern representatives to learn that they were benighted enemies of freedom. Long accustomed to the attacks of degenerate Whigs, Democrats from the slaveholding states now saw to their consternation that Wilmot's proposition was an "apple of discord" that was breeding ill-will and dividing the ranks of their party. First into the breech was an ally of Calhoun, Armistead Burt of South Carolina. In January 1847 he moved to amend a bill organizing the territory of Oregon that excluded slavery by applying to it the Ordinance of 1787. Instead, Burt proposed to declare the territory free because it lay north of 36°30'. Burt's amendment seemed to suggest that a similar proposition to divide the anticipated Mexican cession might be acceptable to the South. The amendment, however, was defeated by a sectional vote, and prospects for compromise correspondingly dimmed. They were nearly eclipsed altogether when, in February, Calhoun stepped forward and introduced into the Senate a series of resolutions that, taken together, denied Congress the right to prevent citizens from taking their slaves into the territories. Basing his argument on the Fifth Amendment, which prohibited Congress from depriving any person of liberty or property without due process of law, Calhoun defined the extreme southern position on the territorial question.[43]

Speaking for states'-rights Democrats throughout the South, James Henry Hammond declared, "The South venerates the Constitution and is prepared to stand by it forever, *such as it came from the hands of our fathers.*"[44] Southerners, like free-soilers, rested their position on the provisions of the Constitution, making no new claims for exclusive rights or privileges. Individual freedom may have been the operative principle of the free-soilers' Union, but for Calhounites, at least as fundamental a principle was the equality and inviolability of state sovereignty. The mechanism of the Constitution, they claimed, forever defined the general government. As the common agent of all the sovereign states, the federal government was limited in power by the Constitution, the guarantor of individual rights and property. It was this common agency, moreover, that was used by the states to spread their dominion over the whole of the continent. As it did so, the federal government was strictly bound to observe the compromises struck by the framers and embodied in the Constitution.

Ironically, Calhoun and his supporters agreed with free-soilers that Congress had limited power over slavery. Restrictionists used this narrow interpretation of the Constitution to deny the federal government the ability to establish purely local institutions in the public domain. Southerners, however, interposed the doctrine of strict construction to disclaim the right of

Congress to appropriate territory to the exclusion of any citizen or section. To say the least, Calhounites considered free-soil Democrats latitudinarians; to say the most, they thought the proviso an ideological monstrosity. Here was the old Federalist idea of a supreme national government, a consolidated despotism. Such apostasy they could not abide. No, concluded Robert Barnwell Rhett, all provisions of the Constitution, or none, extended over territory acquired. It was right that the Union expand, one Alabamian insisted; but as it did, Americans might "well infer a contemplated expansion of all its institutions."[45]

To the skeleton of Calhoun's strict construction, others added the sinew and flesh of states' rights and sectional comity. Following Calhoun's lead, they declared that the territories belonged "to the several states of this union, as their joint and common property, in which each and all have equal rights." The proposed acquisitions from Mexico were acquired by the blood and treasure of the entire nation. The proviso, if implemented, would prevent the slaveholding states from enjoying the full benefits of territory so dearly paid for. Where, Kentucky's John Tibbats asked, "is the justice in excluding the South from territory for which they are now fighting shoulder to shoulder with our northern brethren?" He knew the answer. The denigration of the equality of states was justice denied. A Mississippi editor agreed. He maintained, "The territory which *we must and will retain* out of the regions swept by our banner, is either to be attached to the whole confederacy, and be free alike to the South, North and West, or called *Wilmot*, or surrendered to Mexico."[46]

Some claimed to hear in the clamor of southern objections the faint echo of the Missouri struggle. The common chord that at first hearing resonated in the two crises was a restrictionist assault on the basic American tenet of equality. But if the Federalist attack had been on the rights of the sovereign states, southerners maintained that Wilmot's proviso subverted the equality of an entire section. This, thought Supreme Court justice Peter V. Daniel, was fraught with dangers greater than any calculation of mere political influence or profit. Restriction, the Virginian maintained, "pretends to an insulting exclusiveness . . . which says in effect to the Southern man, Avaunt! You are not my equal, and hence are to be excluded as carrying a moral taint with you." Free-soilers insisted that restriction affected only slaveholders, and even they could move to the territories if they left their slaves behind. Southerners saw it differently. As a Montgomery editor put it, restriction was an admission "that a free citizen of Massachusetts was a better man and entitled to more privileges than a free citizen of Alabama." How galling to be the inferior not only to the Tappans, Garrisons, Wilmots, and Kings but to the foreign immigrant who "never struck one blow or paid one cent of the expense for its acquisition [and] may move unmolested into its domain & live there in peace with all his household goods." Meanwhile, the sons of the patriots of the Revolution "shall be ignominiously expelled from its bosom, if they venture to carry with them the property inherited from their ancestors & guaranteed by the Constitution." Should we submit, one slaveholder observed, "we are far worse slaves than our vassals."[47]

This was no mere argument of logic-chopping slaveholders. As any schoolchild knew, the history of the Revolution was one of a struggle by British colonists against the oppression of inferiority. Although the provocation was "of trivial, practical oppression," resistance was based on defense of a principle and "the consequent facilities of future exactions to their utter ruin." The trials and perils of that contest inculcated in those patriots one truth above all others, Virginia's James Seddon explained. "The least concession of inferiority in position or rights—the smallest provision in the framing or working of a government, by which the interests or property of one part of the people are to be less conserved or more prejudicially operated upon than those of another . . . would afford the opening, and be made the pretext and means of encroachments and inroads, until superiority, riches, and domination would become the arrogated possession of the favored portion, and degradation, impoverishment, and subjection, the bitter lot of the latter."[48] As residents of slaveholding states, many of whom were slaveholders themselves, opponents of restriction were uncomfortably familiar with the reality of degradation, impoverishment, and subjection. The warning and historical legacy of the War for Independence thus had, for southerners, an especial and ominous resonance.

As southerners read the Constitution by the lights of the Revolution, they saw in it a spirit of compromise, not isolated to the few specific paragraphs on slavery but breathing throughout the entire instrument. That spirit of compromise, Howell Cobb reminded northerners, "recognized the existence of these sectional interests. The object was to guard them, to protect them, to make the one a check upon the other." And it was just those beliefs in compromise and justice, William Giles concurred, "which gave being, and which have ever since given life and vitality, to the Constitution." The question now posed by the proviso was whether the guarantees of the Constitution were sufficient to protect a minority. Experience had shown, Waddy Thompson observed, that honest differences of opinion existed over "the bank, the tariff, and the internal improvement powers, of the national government." But as to the power to prohibit the emigration of slaveholders and their property to the West, "the usurpation is at once so flagrant, so insulting, and so dangerous, that I do not hesitate to say that its practical exercise will be, in effect, the abrogation of the Constitution and all the securities which it gives for the public liberty." It was, he sadly concluded, "a slander upon our fathers to say it is such a Government which they left us."[49]

The proviso, then, not only marked an abandonment of the principles of the Revolution and an abrogation of the Constitution but signaled as well the beginning of another epochal struggle between a tyrannical majority and an abused minority. "The South is a minority, a weakening minority, by the rightful and natural observation of things," a southern Democrat observed. "She, therefore, cannot injure the North. They alone have the weapon of aggression in their hands." As the past informed the present, so, too, history made the future clear. Excluded from the territories, surrounded by free states, the South was to be fixed, limited, forever. Calhoun and others brooded upon this fate. "The Government, sir, will be entirely in the hands of the non-slaveholding States—overwhelmingly. . . . We shall be at the entire mercy of the non-slaveholding States. Can we look to their justice and regard for our interests?" Apparently not, for as one Virginian predicted, should the principle of the proviso be engrafted upon federal legislation, "for the fraternal bond that has hitherto connected us, you will have substituted the chain of despotism."[50] Taken to this entirely logical conclusion, the defense of slavery as an institution and of slaves as property was transcended and eclipsed by a more fundamental concern: defense of white minority rights and interests in a republican government. In the fight against the proviso, the premise and promise of the Union hung in the balance.

The choices of imagery and historical logic employed by southerners and free-soilers suggest the minatory nature of this ideological deadlock. Major Wilson has shown how northern restrictionists viewed the struggle over the territories as an irrepressible conflict between the two halves of the monism of liberty and slavery. As they cast their argument, northern Democrats carefully noted the ominous similarities between the danger presented by a grasping despotism, Great Britain, and an expansive, aggressive slavocracy. Common to both was the intractable struggle between freedom and despotism that had been launched by the American experiment. Destiny, the nation's manifest destiny, required "that young Liberty may march boldly and safely onward, till she has wrested the last sceptre of dominion from the iron hand of grey-headed Despotism." It must be added that southerners, too, understood the proviso conflict in the same elemental terms. In language that drew on the historic tyranny of the British government, opponents of the proviso evoked images of overweening despotic majorities enslaving minorities and degrading republican institutions. Free-soilers, they argued, were calling upon the United States government to array itself upon the part of the strength of the Union against the weaknesses of the Union. Claims for such despotic power, one Virginian observed, were and always had been "better suited to the precincts of Westminster Abbey than to the Hall of Representatives in the United States."[51]

The most threatening implications of this debate remained unstated and seemingly unacknowledged. By the Jacksonian era, the notion that liberty and equality were interchangeable and reinforcing had not just jelled; it had ossified. Jacksonians aped the language but had not internalized the assumptions that informed the political culture of the early republic. If James Madison and others had known, Jacksonian Democrats appeared to have forgotten that freedom and democracy—liberty and democracy—are inherently antagonistic. In their brief for expansion in 1844, for example, they insisted that Texas and Oregon would simultaneously ensure individual liberty and promote equality of condition. Yet the arguments for and against restriction reveal the essential conflict between these principles. Restrictionists contended that a reaffirmation of the national commitment to freedom demanded that the social and economic institutions of one-half of the Union be prohibited from the common territories. As southerners had it, the freedom of antislavery northerners to inhabit and enjoy the territories could come only at the expense of denying the equal rights of the slave states. For all the appeals of free-soilers to individual liberty and southern demands for sectional equality, neither side saw the inconsistency, much less the antagonism, between the two concepts. They had acquired the rhetoric of the Revolution without absorbing its internal logic.[52]

Although some Whigs and a smaller number of Democrats wanted to extend the Missouri Compromise line of 36°30' to the new territories, mutual concession proved difficult. "This is a matter entirely of *feeling*, and not *pecuniary interest*, with the South," declared a Texas Democrat. "*Principle* is dearer to us than *interest*." In like manner, the *Brooklyn Daily Eagle* held that there could be no halfway work in the matter of slavery in the new territory: "We must either have it there, or have it not." As the rhetoric of Jeffersonian democracy became increasingly couched in the idiom of sectionalism and vitiated by false assumptions and analytical solecisms, deadlock over national expansion loomed. Free-soilers looked to the proviso to allay the fears of antislavery expansionists. In fact, restriction threatened to divide the forces committed to territorial growth in the face of a Whig Party that appeared united in its opposition to the war and its fruits. Perhaps the greatest evil of the proviso, the *New Orleans Daily Picayune* contended, was that it "curses in advance all subsequent accretions of territory with a restriction unknown to the Constitution or to any State new in the Union. . . . Could such a proposition as this be made except as a 'firebrand'—as [a] humbug?"[53] Perhaps; but few Democrats, North or South, could deny the portent of the restrictionist debate for the coherency, ideological and political, of their party.

Enough of them, however, were willing to postpone the denouement. Despite the terrific pummeling members of his party were administering to each other, President Polk refused to admit any connection between the slavery question and the "practical business" of appropriating $3 million. Having ridden the hobby of Texas to the White House, Polk was quick to see others mounting the hobby of slavery to secure the coming presidential election. Alas, he concluded, the agitators rode a Trojan horse. "The Federalists [Whigs] are delighted to see such a question agitated," Polk moaned, "because it divides and distracts the Democratic party and increases their prospects of coming into power. . . . I deplore this state of things." So did other Democrats. Though an avowed opponent of slavery extension, the *Harrisburg Democratic Union* warned that if the party allowed itself to be diverted or, worse, permanently divided by the proviso, "the result will establish our defeat, and place our civil and political rights in subjection to Federal thralldom."[54]

The apparition of sectionalism haunted the Democracy, especially in the North, where the party split over the proviso. It was not that antiproviso northern Democrats refused to take a position against slavery. Massachusetts's Robert Rantoul, for instance, thanked his God that slavery was sectional and liberty national. But until the 1850s, Rantoul and some other northern Democrats never considered slavery extension the most important threat to the principle of limited, constitutional government. Less concerned with reforming distant states and territories, Rantoul for one believed Massachusetts itself needed change, so bank- and corporation-ridden had it become. Also, love for the Union and an abiding respect for the states' rights upon which it was based inhibited any permanent rupture with the southern wing of the party. Indeed, Democrats like Polk, Rantoul, Michigan's John Chipman, and Illinois's Sidney Breese thought the proviso actuated by sickly philanthropy and, in addition, deeply threatening to the safety and permanence of the Union.[55]

In the end, however acrimonious the debate, almost all Democrats in both sections still saw more binding the party together than dividing it. Jefferson Davis, for example, acknowledged that extensive defections had occurred among northern Democrats. He confidently predicted, however, that enough good feeling existed to sustain the hope "that as a party they will show themselves worthy of the ancient appellation, the natural allies of the South, and will meet us upon just Constitutional ground." The crisis of war would ensure cooperation, many concluded. Believing the patriotism of northern Democrats equal to that of the South, the *Mississippian* could not bring itself to doubt "that in this struggle, so big with consequences to the Union and mankind, they would still be true." Michigan's Lewis Cass reminded his party's free-soil rebels that the Democratic commitment to expansion far outweighed in importance any abstract division over slavery extension. Fearing that such a division would ultimately bring the war to an ignominious end, Cass warned that "the eyes of Europe are upon us. Nothing worse can happen to us, than to stop ingloriously. . . . We want almost unlimited power of expansion."[56]

The need for party unity, the exigencies of war, and a fundamental desire to expand the boundaries of the nation persuaded a handful of northern Democrats in Congress to vote to put off the issue of slavery extension until territory was acquired. Indiana's Edward Hannegan asked fellow Democrats, "Why, Sir, endeavor to kindle a flame on either side about this matter now? Will it not be time enough to make laws for the territory, and to prescribe its municipal regulations, when we possess it?" Some, like Thomas Hart Benton, concluded that the wings of the party were at loggerheads about nothing because Mexican law already prohibited slavery in New Mexico and California. Others, President Polk for example, doubted whether slavery could or would be extended to these provinces. Following an old recipe for preparation and cooking of fish, most Senate Democrats therefore decided first to catch their fish. With some members impatient and a few asleep, the Senate finally called for a vote on Polk's request. On March 1, 1847, it voted 21 to 31 to reject the proviso and passed the $3 million appropriation, 29 to 24. Two days later, the House, in Committee of the Whole, inserted the proviso, and then, when the bill was reported, removed it. Representatives finally passed the $3 million appropriation without restriction, 115 to 81.[57]

Polk finally had his $3 million, but the issues raised by the proviso had not been resolved. It is too much to argue that the congressional struggle of early 1847 presented a serious constitutional crisis or a bona fide threat to the Union. Nor was it at bottom an extension of the earlier debates over Missouri and Texas. The latter were contests between parties with variant concepts of freedom, involving the power of the federal government to shape the Union according to those concepts. The proviso debate posited an immutable battle between North and South to control the government and thus to secure the fortunes of the one or the other section of the Union. Although the final resolution of the conflict was more than a decade away, the basic parameters of that sectional equation were articulated and defined in the spring of 1847. As one observer later put it, the debate "afforded the ground upon which the battle of the giants was to be waged," as "the consecration of the territory of the United States to freedom became from that day a rallying cry for every shade of anti-slavery sentiment." Yet, as the Twenty-ninth Congress wearily adjourned, its members only vaguely sensed the future. Left to brood on the meaning of the clash over the proviso, only a few apprehended the breakup of the old party organization. In any event, for once, all could agree with that Jeremiah John C. Calhoun when he observed, "Our difficulty *within*, will commence with the termination of those with Mexico."[58]

For besides all those inestimable favors which he received from her at the hands of her celestial daughters, the *Virtues*, she threw over him her own magic mantle of *character*. And it was this that immortalized Washington. By inspiring his countrymen with the profoundest veneration for him as the *best of men*, it naturally smoothed his way to supreme command. —Mason L. Weems, *The Life of Washington*

The truth is General Taylor has long since fixed his eyes on Gen. Washington as the model of all that was great and good; he has studied his character thoroughly, and I doubt if there will be an incident of Washington's life, with which he is not familiar.
—"A Louisiana Whig" to the *Daily National Intelligencer*

Washington Redux

The Whig Party and the
Politics of Slavery, 1846–1848

The Mexican-American War was a year and a half old in the winter of 1848 and in the field things had gone well for President Polk's administration. The United States effectively controlled New Mexico and Upper California. From the spring to the fall of 1847 American troops had won a series of victories at Buena Vista, Vera Cruz, Cerro Gordo, Contreras, Churubusco, Molino del Rey, and Chapultepec. Finally, on the morning of September 14, forces commanded by Winfield Scott entered and occupied the capital of Mexico City. Yet for all the military victories, Polk had failed to achieve peace. In the late fall the war ground to a halt and negotiations with a divided Mexican government faltered. At home, frustration with an enemy allegedly too stupid or too stubborn to conclude a just peace led to demands in the press and Congress for the annexation of most or all of Mexico. Abroad, war-weary soldiers were inspired and invigorated by this crescendo of public enthu-siasm. James Russell Lowell's imaginary private echoed those homegrown expansionist sentiments, with Lowell's Whig gloss, when he observed:

> An' here we air ascrougin' 'em out o' thir own dominions,
> Ashelterin' 'em, ez Caleb sez, under our own eagle's pinions,
> . . . Wal, it doos seem a curus way, but then hooraw fer Jackson!
> It must be right, fer Caleb sez it's reg'lar Anglosaxon.[1]

An often choleric Polk became increasingly irritated at Mexico's refusal to cede New Mexico and the Californias as part of an overdue treaty of peace. As fall turned to winter, the president's territorial ambitions grew. Although his enlarging horizons were no match for the most extreme expan-sionists in his party (including members of his cabinet), they did come to encompass Mexican departments south of New Mexico and the Californias. Anticipating a protracted war and a higher price for peace, in his third an-nual message in December 1847 the president called upon Congress to raise additional regiments to serve in Mexico. He warned darkly that if the enemy stubbornly prolonged the war, the United States "must continue to occupy her country with our troops, taking full measure of indemnity into our own hands, and must enforce the terms which our honor demands."[2]

Despite these swelling though ill-defined objectives, events were rapidly worsening for the president at home and abroad. In October, Polk had re-called his peace emissary, Nicholas Trist, primarily because he and his cabi-net were convinced that Mexico neither intended to bargain in good faith nor, at bottom, wanted peace. Worse, Trist had shown an alarming willing-ness to accept greatly curtailed cessions as a basis for an accord. But rather than returning to Washington, Trist sent a condescending and (to Polk) in-furiating sixty-five-page letter in which he asserted that he still could reach an accord with Mexico. Thus, Trist concluded, it was his moral duty to ignore the recall and remain in Mexico as a private citizen to continue negotiations.[3]

As Polk was left to reflect on the character and parentage of insolent, headstrong State Department clerks, his sangfroid was upset further by grow-ing public and congressional opposition to the war. Chancellor James Kent, for example, condemned Polk's aggression as "causeless & wicked & unjust." Worse, Kent feared, "the acquisition of [a] large Mexican Territory would ruin us & destroy our Institutions. . . . No people pretending to be enlight-ened & civilized were ever before governed by a Set of drivelers & profligate demagogues." As casualties and military expenditures continued to mount, a disgusted Maryland farmer wondered, "How long shall our patience be abused by being told that this war is necessary either for the good or the honor of the country?" Throughout December 1847 and January 1848, Whig after Whig offered resolutions in Congress demanding to know exactly where and how the war had begun, calling for the withdrawal of American troops, rejecting territorial acquisitions, and requesting all relevant correspondence relating to the peace negotiations. Blistered in a series of speeches on the floor of the Senate and House for his duplicitous and inept conduct of the war and spiritedly defended by party regulars, Polk watched the Thirtieth Congress quickly degenerate into a furious melee.[4]

On the afternoon of February 2, 1848, the president complied with one of the Whig resolutions and sent to the Senate correspondence relating to the stalled negotiations. That evening, Polk had a long, discursive conversation with a fellow Democrat and chairman of the Senate Foreign Relations Committee, Ohio's William Allen. Mindful of the unhappy events that were closing in on him thick and fast, he shared with Allen his views on Congress, the future prosecution of the war, and the treachery of Trist. As their conversation came to a close, Polk and Allen agreed that Trist was a scoundrel, and both condemned him in unqualified terms. At the same time this discussion was taking place in the White House, a small, dignified ceremony was being held in the village of Guadalupe Hidalgo outside Mexico City. A little before dusk, citizen Trist met with commissioners of the Mexican government to sign a treaty ending the Mexican-American War. By the terms of the agreement, Mexico gave up all claims to Texas above the Rio Grande and ceded New Mexico and Upper California. In return for the cession of 619,000 square miles of territory, the United States agreed to pay Mexico $15 million and assume the claims of American citizens against that government up to $3.25 million. Later that night, Trist dispatched his friend and confidant, journalist James L. Freaner, to Washington with three copies of the treaty.[5]

After a hasty journey by steamer and coach, Freaner rode into the capital on Saturday evening, February 19, and delivered the treaty to the house of Secretary of State James Buchanan. At about nine o'clock, Buchanan brought it to the White House. Polk gave the document a cursory reading that night and critically examined it in all its particulars the following day. He convened a special meeting of the cabinet Sunday evening. After an inconclusive exchange of views (laced with de rigeur condemnations of Trist), the president felt compelled to postpone a final decision on whether to submit the treaty to the Senate for ratification until Monday noon. Clearly, Trist's handiwork had placed Polk on the horns of a dilemma. True, the terms of the treaty conformed generally to his original instructions to Trist, and the ceded territory included the administration's major goals. Also, the price tag for peace did not exceed the amount both he and Buchanan had been willing to pay. The problem for Polk, however, was that his own territorial ambitions and those of a large and vocal segment of his party now went beyond the cession of New Mexico and Upper California. The Mexican army had been routed, its government was in disarray, the force of expansionism at home was intense, and Mexico seemed ripe for plucking.[6]

For all Polk's indecisiveness, the decision had already been made for him. The president conceded as much at Monday's cabinet meeting. He told the members that he intended to submit the treaty for ratification, recommending only minor revisions. Polk acknowledged that although present conditions in Mexico perhaps warranted a larger cession, the treaty did conform in the main to Trist's instructions. More important, however, were the likely consequences of rejection. The Whig Party, Polk claimed, was fully arrayed against the administration and unremitting in its attacks on the war. If he were now to reject a treaty made on his own stated terms, the president anticipated that Congress would grant neither men nor money for the war. Enthusiasm alone could not sustain the army, and American forces, "constantly wasting and diminishing in numbers," would probably have to be withdrawn. As a result, New Mexico and Upper California would be lost. If, then, the Whigs should succeed in carrying the fall's presidential election, the country forever would "loose [sic] all the great advantages secured by this Treaty." Therefore, against his party's inclinations but not his better judgment, Polk readied the treaty for the Senate's consideration.[7]

However much the president may have felt compelled to acknowledge his antiwar critics and submit the treaty, it did not signal a victory for the Whig Party. Initially cautious in their opposition, Whigs gradually became more emboldened, more critical, more obstreperous. As they found their spine, party members added layer upon layer of condemnation so that, taken as a whole, the Whig critique became a reflection and extension of a collective view of good—or perhaps more accurately, bad—government and national progress. It was also more. Opposition to the war, and, significantly, to the acquisition of large tracts of foreign territory was an honest, though futile, effort to force the divisive slavery question out of American politics. Most recently and ominously introduced by the Wilmot Proviso, the issue of slavery extension threatened to sectionalize party organizations and to rend the Union. The disruption of their party disturbed Whigs; the possible dissolution of the Union frightened them. Ironically, antipathy to the proviso provided them with a broad common ground upon which they could shift from reluctant acquiescence to outright opposition to Polk's policies. Defined by the logic of their argument, slavery restriction (or extension, depending on the view) was interwoven with the nature and objects of the war. Opposing the former, Whigs were increasingly compelled to oppose the latter, for in the balance hung the unity of the party, the safety of republican government, and the preservation of the Union.

The first skirmish came at the very onset of the war, a clash over the administration bill introduced into Congress on May 11, 1846, authorizing the president to accept the services of volunteers to defend the nation against Mexico. In his message accompanying the request, Polk asserted that war "exists by the act of Mexico herself, [and] we are called on by every consideration of duty and patriotism to vindicate with decision the honor, the rights, and the interests of our country." To make certain that there would be a roll call consensus on this claim, the House Committee on Military Affairs added a preamble to the bill which again stated that war existed "by the act of the Republic of Mexico." House Whigs had little time to fret over their dilemma of either endorsing this view or rejecting the bill with its obnoxious preamble and thus endangering the safety of American troops on the Rio Grande. The Democratic majority severely circumscribed debate. The leadership also prevented Whigs from carefully examining voluminous documents that accompanied the message and purported to support the president's claim. Administration supporters forced a vote on the measure that day. Despite the hue and cry of (unrecognized) Whig dissidents, the chair ordered the roll to be called, and the bill passed 174 to 14. In the Senate, unlike the House, voices of Whig opposition led by John M. Clayton, John J. Crittenden, and John M. Berrien were distinctly heard, although what they had to say was unclear. Support for a vulnerable army in the field and a desire by some to chastise Mexico obscured Whig hostility to the underlying premises and objectives of Polk's policy. With their antiwar sentiments foundering in a sea of ambiguity, Senate Whigs were saved the embarrassment of further obfuscations by another hastily called vote at which time the administration's request passed 40 to 2.[8]

Reluctant support was both pragmatic and principled. For congressmen who viewed history as didactic, Whigs found the lessons of Federalist opposition to Madison's war instructive. One New England critic pointed out that the war against Great Britain was mainly a war of defense; in that contest Federalist dissent was ill-advised. But now, he went on, "we are . . . the invaders, driving the people of another nation from their homes." Hence Polk's policy was odious. Still, with an eye to the future after a hasty glance backward, John McLean advised against withholding supplies. Although openly and consistently condemnatory of Polk, McLean nonetheless contended that to impede the war effort, as had the Federalists, "would be suicidal. Whilst it will destroy us, it can never bring the war to an end. . . . Such a position taken by the Whigs, as a party, overthrows all our hopes for reform, and of a coming triumph."[9]

Haunting fears and political designs on the White House, however, do not explain fully the party's initial unenthusiastic yet consistent support of the bulk of Congress's war measures. Whigs such as Daniel Webster and Daniel D. Barnard hazarded splits within their party by rejecting the suggestions of extreme antiwar members that opposition be without quarter. However distasteful the war and reprehensible its authors, Webster, Barnard, and others held that the duty of a true statesman was to stand by the nation and its forces. "We support the country," Barnard wrote, "though we do not support the administration; we support the war, though we condemn those who have brought us into it." Whigs saw themselves motivated by principle, not the slaves of public opinion. They believed that by coupling intelligent, rational dissent with a patriotic support of American troops, the party would articulate and reaffirm the basic premises of republican government. More important, they would gain the respect and admiration of the nation. "The true policy of the patriot is to give all *proper* supplies to carry on the war," advised a North Carolina Whig. "It will make no factious opposition to the Administration, when the Whigs oppose everything and propose nothing. The people will not then put confidence in them, [even] when they rightfully oppose measures."[10]

A reluctant endorsement of Polk's policy did not preclude the development of a sustained and articulate indictment of the war: it invited one. A House Whig maintained that, of course, the true party policy was to give aid necessary to conclude this unhappy war. But, he added, "*never* for a *moment* cease holding Polk up to utter execration for sending the army to the Rio Grande to provoke hostilities." Having been maneuvered by the commander in chief into supporting his actions as well as his views, embarrassed Whigs in Congress and out tried to outflank Polk by condemning him and damning his objectives. They first laid siege to the war message and bill that threw the onus of commencement upon Mexico. This thesis, one Whig spat, was "a vile attempt to cover up the grossest act of usurpation and aggression by the President known to the history of the country." The remote cause of the war, he contended, was the annexation of Texas; the immediate cause was Polk's decision to occupy the disputed territory between the Nueces and the Rio Grande Rivers. Daniel Tilden, an Ohio Whig, asserted that the president's defense of the extreme boundary claim was intended to enrich Texas land speculators. Now that war had been declared, jobbing and corruption would increase because a door had thus been opened to the partisans of the administration for speculation in jobs, contracts, and the sale of old ships."[11]

Especially disturbing was that Congress had never declared war: it had merely acquiesced in the war's existence. This was at best unwise; at worst, it was unconstitutional. Garrett Davis of Kentucky reminded House members that to make war was the most fearful power exerted by human government. Realizing this, the Founding Fathers entrusted to the president "the national shield," but the sword—the war power—was deposited with Congress. Yet, he asked, what was now the case? "The constitutional war power has not spoken its fiat—[and the president] takes it upon himself to make war with Mexico, and deigns not to consult Congress, although it is holding daily sessions in his immediate presence." Executive usurpation of congressional authority, a Georgia dissident shrilled, "strikes a blow at the vitals of the Constitution . . . violates the fundamental principles of republicanism . . . erects the standard of the one-man power." It also established a dangerous precedent. If ambition, not law, bound a president, he might "establish a monarchy, or any other form, at his discretion." [12]

The attack on Polk's usurpation went beyond partisan considerations. It represented a deep-seated fear among Whigs, as among the framers of the Constitution, of a domineering executive who threatened to upset the checks and balances safeguarding the government. This belief that Polk was conspiring to exploit the war to arrogate power to himself and to distribute its spoils among the Democratic rank and file was neither surprising to Whigs, whose origins as a party lay in their opposition to the perceived executive abuses of Andrew Jackson, nor extreme to a political organization that took its name from British country politicians. All executives in all ages tended to constitute in themselves the government and to regard all opposition as treasonable, Davis cautioned. That Polk would attempt to minimize congressional involvement in the conduct of the war was to be expected for, as one critic noted, "to an usurper, an independent legislature is a very inconvenient thing." This vindication of a constitutional balance among the branches initially structured the Whig critique of the war. It also provided them with their first line of defense. Senator Berrien, speaking for a majority of congressional dissidents, held that "if the mere act of declaring war . . . did not create a military dictator . . . [then] the power to prosecute the war . . . belongs, and belongs exclusively, to Congress." [13]

But to control the war's course party members were forced to confront its territorial objectives. Whereas some of the surlier New Englanders yearned for permanently restricted boundaries, others, convinced of the efficacy of states' rights and the elasticity of the federal system, often leaned perilously close to toppling into the blathering expansionism of spreadeagle Democrats. Party members as diverse as William H. Seward and Alexander H. Stephens viewed territorial aggrandizement as a way to promote national liberation and personal upward mobility through market expansion. For example, growing interest in the commerce of the Pacific and the peaceful settlement of the Oregon imbroglio kindled enthusiasm for the addition to the Union of Upper California with its fine bay of San Francisco. As a means to an enhanced American carrying trade in Asia, the acquisition of a Pacific port would strengthen the nation's maritime power and, by extension, promote the economic independence envisioned by the party's American System. Sensitive to the issue of slavery extension raised by Wilmot's proviso, these expansionist Whigs noted that San Francisco lay north of 36°30' and therefore assumed that this "terrible question" would be given the go by.[14]

Yet, however intoxicated they might be by the bumptious nationalism of the mid-1840s, Whigs stopped short of swallowing whole the Democratic elixir of rapid, widespread territorial expansion. Even as they coveted California, indeed because they coveted it, divisions arose within the party over the pace of growth and the extent of territory desired. There were men such as Henry Hilliard of Alabama who were convinced beyond a doubt of the efficacy of states' rights. They believed that the federal system was so elastic "that it may be extended over any space, great or small." Others, more cautious and inclined toward the consolidation of government and the integration of society, were content for the nonce to concentrate on the great work of building up and sustaining Oregon before adding more territory on the Pacific. All agreed, whatever their position, that whenever and wherever expansion came, it must be peaceful, must proceed gradually with the consent of the governed, and, of course, must be accomplished without violation of Whig constitutional principles.[15]

Whiggish views on territorial growth fashioned and made specific the general indictment of the administration's expansionist program. Taking the measure of this most "absurd & senseless war," William Cabell Rives thought that he understood why lately the government had added thousands of square miles "to the boundless wastes we already hold." Territorial aggrandizement, he judged, "seems to be the vulgar prize of ambition for every whipster whom chance [read: Tyler] or caprice [Polk] raises to the Presidency." Such pretensions, he held, degraded the presidency, dangerously expanded the powers of government, and, most important, corrupted the republican virtues that were the essence of the Union. Time and again, Whigs contended that expansion pursued as an end in itself was inconsistent with the spirit of American institutions. Where, Senator James Morehead asked, "did the genius of the Constitution permit the adoption of such a course?" Wars of conquest, wars that aped the European practice of dismembering neighboring sovereignties, begot "an aggressive spirit and a disposition to tyrannize over the weak, which ought not by any means be fostered in a Republic."[16]

Morehead, Davis, Berrien, William Brownlow, and others believed that Polk waged war for "the conquest . . . of territory which is not ours." The administration might prate about security, indemnity, and honor, but, the *National Intelligencer* countered, "The spirit of conquest, of dominion, of aggrandizement, is at the bottom of this war." The spectacle of a republican government embarking on a career of aggressive expansion was an affront to Whigs who stressed the virtues of discipline, self-control, and leadership by example. "Instead of being considered the conservative head of a great system of American republics, we are likely to be looked upon as rapacious, grasping, and unscrupulous conquerors," Maryland's James Pearce lamented.[17]

Whigs apprehended that this "career of conquests" would not only degrade the nation's honor but also undermine the social basis of republican government. Seduced by the glory of military triumphs, Americans appeared ready "to abandon the fertile fields of powerful industry, to follow the slippery and blood stained path which leads to extended empire." Looking to the future progress of the nation, Whigs contended that a widespread, dispersed population would promote declension. A New England dissident complained, "What do men know of the great national, commercial, international interests who are brought up in the backwoods & whose extent of vision is limited to the forest around him." Even the more ardent friends of expansion like Alexander Stephens were troubled. "No principle is more dangerous to us, than that of compelling other nations to adopt our form of government," he warned. "No instance is to be found upon record of any republic having ever entered upon such a hazardous crusade, which did not end in the subversion of its own liberties and the ultimate enslavement of its own people."[18]

Having inherited a taste — as opposed to a talent — for expansionist designs, by late 1846 Whigs found that their appetite for distant acquisitions had diminished considerably. As ever larger chunks of Mexican territory became entrapped in the maw of the American army, dissidents fretted over the prospect of ruling remote provinces in the Southwest and on the Pacific. Once swallowed, what will you do with them, Berrien asked. "Will you govern them as *subject provinces*? You will find no warrant for this in the Constitution of the United States," he asserted. Stephens, a fellow Georgian, concurred. "Will you make a Sicily of [California], and place it under the praetorship of a Verres, to extract tribute from the inhabitants . . . and make a Bombay of [New Mexico], and place it under the rule of a Hastings, who, by grinding oppression, shall cause annual streams of treasure to flow into your coffers?" The governance of these distant provinces, of course, would fall to governors, secretaries, district attorneys, and judges — all appointed by the executive. "What a presentation day there will be at the White House when all these officers attend to kiss hands and take leave, on their departure for their distant posts," John Bell sneered.[19]

Imperial rule, it also followed, implied the conquest and governance of a hostile population. This in itself marked a fundamental violation of the most basic tenet of representative government: consent of the governed. A Hoosier Whig declared that the United States could not extend its laws over the inhabitants of Mexican provinces against their consent without denigrating the principle of freedom upon which American institutions are based. "We cease to be republicans in principle the very moment we force upon those people our form of government against their will," Edward McGaughey asserted. By degrading themselves, Americans degraded those whom they would uplift. "Teach the people to disregard these great principles of natural right . . . and you teach them not only to enslave others, but to enslave themselves. This Government can only exist in its present form, while the people adhere to and love its principles for their own intrinsic worth."[20]

These noble concerns had a hard edge, however. Whigs believed that governments embodied "the moral sense of the race." Fundamental laws and institutional arrangements, therefore, reflected the distinctive society and culture of each nation; they were not readily adaptable. McGaughey himself was careful to point out that Mexicans had shown by their dissensions and revolutions that they were incapable of submitting to, much less of appreciating, a republican government. Obedience to law would never come, he ventured, "unless an armed force is present at all times to enforce submission through fear." Nor was that the worst. Acquisition of foreign lands naturally meant the incorporation of alien races. Annexation of "Mexican provinces . . . filled with a population, not only degraded, but of every possible shade and variety" thus presented Americans with an unpalatable problem. "Either all these people with colors as various as the rainbow, must be placed on an equality with each other, and with us, or they must be reduced to servitude." If they were not enslaved, soon "representatives of ignorance & barbarism" would infest the halls of Congress. Having no sympathy with the great mass of Americans, neither knowing their interests nor regarding them if they did, these "mongrel races" would hold in their power the American birthright of republican government. In that event, a northern Whig groaned, they "will change the whole character of our institutions." The forms of the republic might be preserved, another ventured; "but, as it was with Rome, the forms may survive after the spirit of republicanism shall have passed away." In such a case, another colleague sighed, the Union would be "an entity changed and hardly worth preserving."[21]

Whigs now openly—and in contempt of public opinion—rejected forcible expansion and a too rapid growth of territory. Years before, Daniel Webster had advised Americans, "Our augmentation is by growth, not by acquisition; by internal development, not by external accession." With Webster's dictum in mind, James Pearce argued that expansion often weakened a nation. Its powers diminished by dispersion, its burdens correspondingly increased, and free government imperiled by large standing armies, an overextended nation risked its eternal glory for temporary greatness. Instead, Pearce counseled restraint. "To make a nation great, prosperous and happy, it should be compacted, well peopled, well educated, blessed with the sound and prudent legislation of peace, improved and adorned by all that art and utility can furnish for its benefit and embellishment." Looking around them, many Whigs saw a nation sufficient to these ends. "Here surely is a field wide enough for all our restless spirit of enterprise," one observed. "Here is an arena for the display of every civil and social virtue." [22]

Just when the Whigs' expansionist horizons became increasingly enshrouded in uncertainty and caution, Wilmot's thunderbolt illuminated the dangerous landscape of a prospective Mexican cession. To many party members the slavery issue appeared to foreshadow the creation of sectional political organizations, which threatened the bonds of the Union. A Massachusetts Whig doubted if any national party could be kept permanently together if the issue of slavery were introduced into the political system. "Are not matters coming to such an issue as will inevitably alienate one portion from the other," he wondered. "I try to avert my eye from such a prospect—but is it not looming up in the mist—dark and portentous?" More threatening than the creation of geographical parties was the consequence of such distinctions. "As long as our party distinctions are founded on abstract principles, and measures of internal policy, they never will divide the Union," another said. He cautioned that should geography define party lines, "you at once strike a fatal blow at the integrity of this Union." Hence most Whigs concluded that the slavery issue could not be sidestepped as some hoped. A national crisis was at hand, an Indiana Whig declared, "a crisis in the history of our republic of no ordinary character." To escape required wisdom, prudence, patriotism, and much forbearance. Even at that, he worried, "I fear our work will founder or be wrecked in the present storm. . . . I pray to God to deliver us." [23]

In the apparent absence of divine guidance, the party's initial response to Wilmot's initiative was confused. Some northern Whigs believed that the proviso would prove to be a litmus test on Democratic war aims and therefore the party should not suppress it. For expansionist Democrats to argue that the present was not the time to prescribe conditions to any possible cession and in so doing prevent a vigorous prosecution of the war was both disingenuous and, ironically, revealing. Washington Hunt responded that this was neither more nor less than to say that "unless the majority in one section will yield to the minority in the other, the Government will be unable to carry on the war." Pass the proviso, Robert Winthrop recommended; "cut off, by one and the same stroke, all idea both of the extension of slavery and the extension of territory." To these antislavery Whigs, frustrating the purpose of the war meant peace. End the hope of slavery extension, one northern dissident argued, "and you at once put an end to the war by defeating its object."[24]

Even if passage of the proviso failed to end the war or prevent a large-scale Mexican cession, antislavery Whigs looked to it as a reform measure calculated to uplift and improve American society. Slavery, they affirmed, weakened the power and efficacy of the government and, worse, inhibited its ability to defend and protect the United States from foreign aggression. Its effect on the economy and society was hardly less great. Discouraging productive industry, inhibiting the emigration of whites and retarding the settlement of the West, and blighting the land wherever it was extended, slavery would always tend "to destroy the springs of industry, and consequently to diminish the annual products of the country."[25]

Antislavery Whigs like James Dixon and William Upham looked to the federal government to enhance the quality of life and to promote the nation's welfare. They concluded that the national legislature was morally bound to restrict the peculiar institution. As an inherited evil, slavery was exclusively a question of state jurisdiction. To this extent the power of the federal government over it was limited. Yet as Maine's Luther Severance argued, the patriots of the Revolution never intended to extend slavery, much less to have the federal government promote its expansion. The question now thrust upon the American people was "whether the powers of their government shall continue to be exercised for the great and glorious purpose for which that government was instituted, of '*securing* the BLESSING of liberty to ourselves *and our* POSTERITY.'" Distinct from the Democracy's strict construction, free-soil argument, antislavery Whigs viewed restriction as a positive act of reform implemented by a federal government whose raison d'être was to promote the expansion of individual liberty and moral uplift. "The question," a Whig restrictionist commented, "is not one of constitutional authority, but of general policy, involving considerations of public good and national harmony."[26]

Southern Whigs expected but did not welcome this antislavery attack. Casting themselves as the ablest defenders of southern rights and the Constitution—the shield of those rights—paladins like Stephens, Berrien, Pearce, and Hilliard drew on revolutionary principles that were a heritage as much as their convictions. Restriction, they admitted, had not yet injured the South. The call to arms, therefore, was not to throw off oppression but to defend an abstract right. The Founding Fathers had done as much when they shouldered their muskets in defense of the fundamental propositions of republican government, one argued. We Whigs of the South, they noted with pride, "have not lost all chivalrous spirit as to permit a principle equally important to fall to the ground without notice." Believing that the animating principle of the Union and the general spirit of the Constitution was equality, states'-rights Whigs (like southern Democrats) denounced any restriction that would inhibit migration of southerners into jointly owned territory. Such a breach of faith between the sections and with the past, they feared, would "destroy the great principle of equality between the States, which lies at the foundation of the Constitution, and ultimately break up the Confederacy itself."[27]

However portentous the intonations of these alarms, they were at bottom fiercely Unionist. Unable to agree on how the animating principles of the republic—liberty and equality—were to be applied to any western cession, Whigs recognized the sinister nature of this deadlock. For all their insight, however, they were unwilling to meet the problem head-on. Instead, the party tacked in another direction. Acutely sensible as they were of the fundamental threat posed by the still unresolved slavery issue, party members attempted to render powerless the inherent divisiveness of expansion by giving agitators nothing upon which to act. Already disturbed by the effects of a far-flung empire on American civilization and republican government, Senator Berrien informed his colleagues that the acquisition of territory would bring before them, "with accumulated force, a question which now menaces the permanence of the Union." Faced with asserting "at whatever the hazard, our rights, and the rights of our constituents," or of adhering to the Union "by submitting to this inequality of distribution in the acquisitions of our common territory," Berrien concluded that the safety of the South demanded opposition to any acquisition of territory whatever. This appeal, he said, "is not merely to southern Senators, but to American Senators from whatever quarter of this Union they may come. The appeal is to them to exclude from the national councils this dire question." Accordingly, in early February 1847, Berrien offered an amendment to the administration's $3 million appropriation bill declaring it "to be the true intent and meaning of Congress in making this appropriation, that the war with Mexico ought not to be prosecuted by this Government with any view to the dismemberment of that republic."[28]

At first blush Berrien's proposal appears to be an evasion of responsibility, if not reality. William C. Rives, no friend of the war, looked with concern on the amendment, thinking it both premature and by nature divisive. Yet in early February the string of military victories that would take American troops to the halls of Montezuma had not occurred. Also, their indictment of Polk's usurpations and machinations constitutionally and morally obliged antiwar Whigs to determine the war's objectives. Tennessee's Merideth Gentry warned his fellow representatives that if they failed to perform the constitutional duties that properly belonged to Congress by limiting executive discretion in the prosecution of the war, "the day is not distant when it will require all the virtue, intelligence, and patriotism of the country, to preserve the Union, and save the public liberty."[29] Berrien's motion was, then, first an effort to put the party, and with luck the Senate, on record as opposed to a rapid and expansive acquisition of foreign lands and mongrel races.

More important, however, the amendment's supporters wished to force the slavery issue introduced by the proviso out of national politics to preserve the integrity of the party system, the Constitution, and the Union. Bloated empires, scattered settlements, and alien peoples attenuated the bonds of Union; slavery agitation promised to cut them asunder. It will not do to argue the inevitability of expansion and of the sectional crisis and thus, by extension, the unreal nature of Berrien's motion. Judged by their convictions, Whigs who supported the no-territory proposition fancied themselves realists and patriots of the first rank, determined to resolve this most critical issue. It would indeed be a poor victory, one Kentucky Whig remarked, "after having carried our arms to the Pacific, if the acquisition of territory, which should be the result of that proceeding, should have the effect of creating internal discord, and destroying the institutions of this country." "He must be blind to the signs of the times," Gentry observed, "who does not perceive that there is a fixed and almost universal determination in the Northern States not to acquiesce in the further extension of territory without attaching the [proviso]." If this was the present temper of the nation, or at least half of it, prospects for the future were dark. Angrily fixing his one good eye on expansionist Democrats sitting across the aisle, Senator Reverdy Johnson thundered that there was but one way to obviate this certain crisis of Union: "It was by keeping the question out."[30]

In the weeks following the introduction of Berrien's motion, moderate northern Whigs rallied to the no-territory proposition. Ohio's Thomas Corwin at once made himself the darling of antislavery Whigs and the scourge of the administration with a fierce denunciation of the war. His basic intent was often lost in the sanguinary excesses of Corwin's rhetoric and for a time obscure to antislavery Whigs. We of the North, he observed in his remarks, cannot consent that the South shall carry slavery where it does not now exist. Could Congress expect, Corwin went on, that southerners should expend their blood and treasure in the acquisition of territory and then willingly forgo the right to carry their slaves there and to inhabit these new lands if they pleased to do so? To persist, under these circumstances, in a war of expansion would seem to be nothing less than to foster purposely and irresponsibly "internal commotion." This, shouted the angry Corwin, was "treason, treason to the Union, treason to the dearest interests, the loftiest aspirations, the most cherished hopes of our constituents." Rising to the occasion, Corwin implored his fellow senators to abandon all idea of acquiring territory as an object of this war. "Let us close forever," he urged, "the approaches of internal feud and so return to the ancient concord and the old ways of national prosperity and permanent glory."[31]

Antislavery Whigs reacted warmly to Corwin's speech. But what dissidents in the Northeast and Western Reserve failed to understand, at least right away, was that Corwin's endorsement of Berrien's amendment and his indictment of the administration's policy were designed to heal—not widen—the breach between the party's northern and southern wings and, more significantly, to neutralize—not accentuate—the slavery extension issue. "I still cling to the belief," Corwin wrote, "that the Whig party only can save us a government worth saving, and I fear disunion in that party as much as dismemberment of the States." Throughout the summer and fall Corwin repeatedly attacked abolitionists and antislavery Whigs while consistently endorsing the no-territory strategy. He publicly denounced the proviso as a "dangerous question" and demanded that the administration formally and immediately renounce any cession of territory from Mexico as a prerequisite of peace. Although Corwin remained popular with a large segment of Ohio Whigs, his moderation undermined the support of Liberty Party leaders and antislavery Whigs who once looked to him as a possible presidential candidate. Restrictionists such as Joshua Giddings and Charles Francis Adams charged that attacks on the proviso pleased proslavery propagandists and that a no-territory position delivered the Whig Party into the hands of the South. Consequently, they moved further away from the conservative mainstream by rejecting all such sham solutions to the slavery issue.[32]

However admirable the position and righteous the cause of the antislavery Whigs, a majority of northern party moderates nonetheless endorsed Berrien's resolutions. Understanding the intent of the proviso perhaps better than did men like Giddings and Adams, the *Scioto Gazette* declared that Wilmot's proposal "admitted the principle that it was right to wrest territory from Mexico. That of Berrien expressly denied that right. That of Wilmot was narrow and sectional, compared with the other—while that of Berrien would have the tendency to unite all good men, of all sections and all parties, against dismembering Mexico, under any pretence whatever." Caleb Smith, a Whig representative from Indiana, could agree with Giddings that the slave question would admit of no compromise. Like Berrien, he believed that "the only ground of safety—the only ground which will secure the peace and harmony of the country—is to keep the territory, with all·distracting questions connected with it out of the Union." As the bitterness engendered by

Wilmot's proviso grew, revealing divisions within their party, congressional Whigs closed ranks to drive the slavery issue from the field. An Ohio Whig claimed that opposition to the acquisition of territory, at once a broader and more elevated position than simple antiwar dissent, was a moral high ground upon which all statesmen could stand together.[33]

Berrien's resolutions were eventually voted down although all but one Whig, Henry Johnson of Louisiana, voted in support of them. By exactly the same vote, the Whigs opposed the administration's $3 million appropriation bill. In the aftermath of defeat Daniel Webster sadly remarked that the question of slavery extension "might have been settled here this night, and settled finally and forever." Now, looking to the future, Webster declared that the opinion of the party's majority remained unchanged. "In their judgment it is due the best interests of the country, to its safety, to peace and harmony, and to the well-being of the Constitution, to declare at once, to proclaim now, that we desire no new States, nor territory to form new States out of, as the end of conquest."[34]

To a majority of Democrats Webster's comments were plainly twaddle. Reluctant to believe that a great event had small causes, Democratic expansionists became increasingly convinced throughout the latter half of 1847 that the war must be the outcome of profound forces. "The principles of free government are destined to progress and extend, and in due time they will be diffused all over Mexico," declared the *Nashville Union*. The *Philadelphia Public Ledger* similarly believed that the success of Winfield Scott and Zachary Taylor in Mexico "would seem to indicate, that the hand of Providence is directing our destiny, without regard to the policy of man." Similar loose talk about providential intervention led others to divine that the Almighty was really grasping at all of Mexico—and perhaps beyond. Expansion was the great movement of the age, the *Democratic Review* announced. The *Review* concluded that until Americans occupied every acre of the North American empire, "the foundation of the future empire shall not have been laid." This boast, if it be one, was not at all extravagant, Robert J. Walker affirmed. "Altho its fulfillment is distant—it is quite certain. The advance towards it is rapid."[35]

By the late fall of 1847, the American public, led by the Democratic Party, became more rabid in its demand that the United States annex all or most of Mexico. As it gathered for its first session in December, the Thirtieth Congress listened to a long, vituperative, and predictable message from Polk in which the president contemptuously rejected the Whig doctrine of no territory. To take such a position, he argued, was to proclaim publicly that "our country was wrong . . . [and that the war] was unjust and should be abandoned." There was slim chance of that, Polk declared: territorial cession was now the sine qua non of any peace settlement. We must have, he claimed, "indemnity for the past and security for the future." To first-term Illinois Whig representative Abraham Lincoln, the war part of the president's message was "like the half insane mumbling of a fevered dream." To other dissidents, however, Polk's demands—even if deranged—signaled a transformation of the war itself. Having formerly disavowed any intention of conquest, the administration now desired to wage a war of "subjugation" as distinct from the acquisition of one or two Mexican departments. To grant Polk's request that Congress provide him with an additional ten regiments and a loan of about $18.5 million was "to enter on a new war; and the tendency was, the entire annihilation of Mexico." Democrats tell us that the force of circumstances compels us to go forward, to coerce a continental empire, John Bell groused; they call it destiny. Bell thought it "political death."[36]

Whigs in Congress and elsewhere had their own ideas about the nation's destiny, although it was no longer so manifest. Daniel Webster thought it impudent that the "poor worms of earth could pretend to understand and explain the purposes of the Deity." Away with this cant about "divine mission" and "manifest destiny," of warrants from the Most High "to civilize, and christianize, and democratize our sister republics at the mouth of a cannon," New York's William Duer exclaimed. "I turn from Polk to Washington . . . [and] there I find patriotism surrounded, hallowed, adorned, by truth, justice, humanity." Moderate antiwar dissidents turned predictably and, given the inflamed state of public opinion in early 1848, one may say in some desperation, to the fundamental intent of the fathers as they understood it. The founders' purpose, a New Englander explained, was so to direct "our Government as to develop our resources and encourage domestic industry, improve the means of intercourse and education, advance our agriculture, commerce, and manufactures, improve our laws and their administration, and thus make us a homogeneous people, all elevated and adorned with taste and refinement becoming members of a *glorious republic*." Renewed articulations of the basic purpose of the Union were, in 1848, a positive alternative vision of manifest destiny. Both were premised on the no-territory position. And, the *Boston Courier* noted confidently, Washington if alive would unquestionably affirm the Whig position.[37]

Sadly for the Whigs, Washington had long since passed to his reward, and in any case, by early 1848 it was highly unlikely that even he could have sold the party's no-territory argument to a majority of Americans. Themselves undoubtedly influenced by the expansionist fervor to acquire all Mexico, some antiwar dissidents began to waffle, talking again about one or two ports on the Pacific and, among the more sanguine, of the extension of territories by honorable means. Nevertheless, as a party they continued to thrash Polk in public and private and to fight a rear-guard action against his expansionist policies.

As a consequence, when the president submitted Trist's peace treaty to the Senate on February 23, he presented the party with an unpleasant choice. They might reject it and perhaps as a result prolong the war, enhancing the all-Mexico movement. Or the Senate might accept the treaty with its large territorial cession and in the bargain run the risk that the slavery issue might become inextricably woven into national politics. As the Senate sat in executive session, Webster sought to postpone this dilemma by submitting a resolution that recommended that Polk appoint another commissioner to negotiate a new treaty. On the motion of another Whig, North Carolina's Willie P. Mangum, it was ordered to lie on the table. In the end, Whigs found that their powerful, effective antiwar campaign left them with precious little room for maneuver. As one southerner put it, the issue was "between the continuance of an expensive & unfortunate war & a *bad* treaty—the people want peace." No Whig paper was fiercer in its denunciation of the war and its objectives or more explicit in its distaste for the treaty than the *New York Tribune*. It, too, admitted that a flawed settlement was better than an "aimless and endless foreign war. . . . Let us have peace, no matter if the adjuncts are revolting." [38]

As the Senate continued deliberation, both expansionists and antiwar Whigs expressed their disapproval of the treaty. Both a motion to amend the pact to include more territory and another to delete all acquisitions were defeated. For the most ardent dissidents, the war had turned out ill, in the end. But that is the ill nature of wars, to end always in less than had been hoped. The fact is that most Whigs regarded the question of additional territory settled by Trist's agreement. Rejecting the treaty, Representative Andrew Fulton declared, "would only subject us to the necessity hereafter of taking more; of the two evils therefore, I choose the least." And indeed, so did the party. On March 10, the Senate ratified the treaty thirty-eight to fourteen with seven Whigs joining seven expansionist Democrats in dissent. Fourteen antiwar Whigs voted for it. The irony appears to have been lost on Polk, among others, that although he reluctantly submitted what he thought to be a too modest treaty for fear that failure to do so would result in the loss of all the territory that had been gained, most antiwar Whigs accepted it with an equally heavy heart to prevent an even larger cession. We Whigs have fallen on evil times, Fulton brooded. "Although the blood of our citizens shall cease to flow in further prosecution of the war . . . yet the consequences which are to follow . . . must in a great degree impair our institutions." With the slavery issue now afoot in earnest, this Virginian concluded, "the future is pregnant with evil." [39]

Fulton realized that ratification transformed what was once an abstract connection between slavery expansion and a possible Mexican cession into an undeniable and portentous question. Wilmot and Calhoun had already suggested the extreme solutions. Yet as the problem of territorial organization became real and then pressing, moderates in both parties began to search for middle ground. On the day Wilmot introduced his proviso, Indiana's William Wick had offered a substitute amendment that would have extended the Missouri Compromise line of 36°30' through any new territory. Although the House rejected Wick's proposal and similar amendments to the $3 million and Oregon territorial bills, the idea of territorial division persisted as a compromise solution. Polk, Buchanan, Stephen Douglas, and a majority of southern Democrats all rallied to its support.[40]

Many found this approach as uncomfortably unambiguous as those of Wilmot and Calhoun, however. For these moderates, Daniel S. Dickinson's idea of local self-determination, or, as it would become known, popular sovereignty, held promise. Northern and southern members of Congress hinted at it as an alternative in 1846 and 1847, but not until the presidential hopeful Lewis Cass made it his hobby was popular sovereignty put clearly before the people. As he delineated the doctrine in his "Nicholson letter" of December 1847, Cass refused to take an explicit stand on Congress's power to regulate slavery in the territories. Rather he contended that even if such power existed, it ought not to be exercised. Congressional leadership, he argued, "should be limited to the creation of popular governments and the necessary provision for their eventual admission into the Union; leaving in the meantime to the people inhabiting them to regulate their own internal concerns in their own way." As a good Jacksonian Democrat, Cass closed with a democratic appeal: if Congress "leave to the people who will be affected by this question, to adjust it upon their own responsibility and in their own manner . . . we shall render another tribute to the original principles of our government and furnish another guarantee of its permanence and prosperity." Because popular sovereignty endorsed the fundamental principle of self-government, its appeal was powerful. Of more immediate importance, Cass's doctrine also held out the twin and seemingly paradoxical advantages of resolving the territorial issue and postponing its denouement. For although popular sovereignty proposed to remove this vexing question from Congress, Cass was as silent as the dumbest oracle on the precise stage of territorial development at which inhabitants were to regulate slavery.[41]

Faced with four possible solutions, some clear, others ambiguous, and all supported and attacked with vehemence, Congress predictably found itself deadlocked over territorial organization in the spring and summer of 1848.

Violent speeches, threats, challenges to duels, logic chopping, and artful ob-fuscations spoke to the burden that slavery imposed on the parties and the country. Both were being fragmented and sectionalized. Perhaps nowhere was this strain more apparent than in the Whig Party. Whereas moderate Democrats in both sections could take temporary refuge in the convenient ambiguity of Cass's doctrine of self-determination, Whigs as a party looked traditionally to the federal government to shape and direct the nation's growth. These territories are our common heritage, a Western Reserve Whig contended; we want them to prosper and grow. We also know that slavery "paralyzes the prosperity and retards the advancement of the land, and the community that are subject to its influence. . . . We do not want it to pre-vail in any country where [the federal government has] a proprietorship." To say, as Calhoun had, that federal governance carried slavery into the ter-ritories of the United States implied that "whenever [the American] flag is planted, there is planted with it an irrepealable law of bondage." New York's William Duer concluded that northern Whigs heralded another creed and honored a different heritage than Calhoun. Our flag, he asserted, "was first unfolded under the declaration of the natural and unalienable right of man to liberty."[42]

These attitudes, widespread among northern Whigs, seemed to one Ken-tuckian to be "pharisaical—blessing themselves that they are better than others. . . . I ask you if it be not [an] arrogant assumption on your part to pre-scribe institutions for other people?" Alexander Stephens asserted that the fruits of the late war belonged to all the people of the nation, to the South as well as the North. "Any legislation by Congress," he argued, "which would exclude slavery would be in direct violation of the rights of Southern people to an equal participation in them and an open derogation of that equality between the States of the South and the North." Still unable to agree as to how Congress was to apply the animating principles of the republic—liberty and equality—to the territories, the party was unable to reach an accord or a common strategy on the organization of the Mexican cession. Whigs were also troubled about the precedent an adjustment would set for the future; their concern further inhibited compromise. As one North Carolina Whig claimed, "We have as great a right to acquire territory as any nation or re-public in the world, and the only restraint on our rule is that which arises from our own convictions as to what is right and proper." A settlement ad-verse to southern rights would in the future "force the South to choose the least of these ruinous evils—a submission to the oppressive legislation on the subject of slavery, an adoption of emancipation measures, or a secession from the Union." As if by way of reply, Vermont's Samuel Phelps hoped that the Senate "should yet be consistent enough to refuse to extend the evil of slavery to whatever territory may fall into our hands." Thus was the past tied to the present crisis and bound to future glory.[43]

As they listened with dismay to the invectives and reproofs that were rapidly becoming the substance of political discourse, the sectional wings of the party chafed under the friction. "The people of the Union," one Whig restrictionist wrote, "are now involved in a great and overshadowing issue more pregnant for more good or evil in its vast results than any that ever agitated this continent." North Carolina's David Outlaw observed with some irritation that "day after day the evils of slavery—its sin—its evils moral, social and political are paraded for our entertainment by men who know nothing of our actual condition, or of the practical bearings of the question which they attempt to discuss. It tries a man's patience, not a little." Just as it had during the war, party cohesiveness weakened and sectional harmony declined as congressional Whigs groped for a consensus on their revolutionary birthright. Inasmuch as Democrats, too, followed their consciences and indulged their prejudices, the first session of the Thirtieth Congress failed to reach an agreement on the ceded lands of the West. True, a bill to organize the Oregon territory without slavery was passed in the session's closing hours. The middle ground still proved elusive; other compromises failed. The Mexican cession remained unorganized and Congress adjourned in ill temper, at odds, and at sea.[44]

That year's presidential canvass illustrated both the fears and the hopes of Whigs. Democrats nominated Cass and offered a cryptic platform that endorsed the "principles and compromises of the Constitution." The Nicholson letter, however, clearly put Cass and his party on the side of nonintervention. Frustrated Whigs went for the throat. First they trashed the candidate. Cass, they scoffed, "has always been . . . an irresolute man, who, if he had an opinion on a doubtful question, did not exactly know what it was." Once a Federalist, now a Democrat, "he has been a synchophant to power, a parasite to demagogues, a mercenary spoils hunter." He was a "HERO *without a battle*, a STATESMAN *without a measure of public good*." Not satisfied with ad hominem attacks, Whigs assailed the cruel joke woven into the Democracy's campaign. Nonintervention, they mocked, was a "poor effort to hoodwink and bamboozle the people of the Southern States." They charged that Cass, who had "boxed every point of the political compass," was a "trimming politician who has been on both sides of this [territorial] question." Whigs, especially in the South, charged that he was "ultra in all things that may flatter the passions or the prejudices of those whose support he thinks may bear him to the Presidential chair." A Cass administration, they concluded, "will be a virtual license to increasing corruption, and a sanction to all the ruinous measures which until now the rulers of the country have never dared to enforce."[45]

Damning Cass may have made Whigs feel better, but it fell a great deal short of resolving their quandary. Convinced that a crisis of the Union was at hand greater than that which had menaced the nation during the war years, the canvass presented Whigs with a challenge and an opportunity. In one way, to be sure, this contest was like all others. The election would determine "whether the policy and principles of the government as established by the great fathers of the Republic and confirmed by the Revolution . . . shall be restored to their first purity." By the summer of 1848, however, party Nestors were convinced that they were entering into a new, more threatening world, one that bore little resemblance to the known. "Nothing is talked of—but Slavery—free territory—& the Wilmot Proviso," an Illinois Whig observed. "It seems as if old things would pass away & all things become new." Seeking their bearings, party members tacked first toward the beacon of their party organization. Here, too, the ill wind of slavery threatened to drive them on the shoals. The territorial issue, a Mississippian declared, "was likely . . . to upturn both parties." Both were "surrounded with difficulties, threatening their very existence, and it will depend in a great degree upon the course which they shape for themselves . . . whether the old party lines are maintained." Stated simply, the danger facing the party—and the Union—was, as it had been during the war, the introduction of a new, pernicious political division founded on sectional distinctions. As one western editor viewed it, "The agitation of the [slavery] question . . . seems inevitably tending to the production of that most dreadful result."[46]

Disoriented at first by this new polestar, Whigs again undertook to mitigate slavery agitation. Henry Clay shrewdly observed that the retrocession of New Mexico and California was not "practicable." Consequently, the slavery question "should long remain unsettled and the existing excitement and agitation should continue and increase." Some Whigs went beyond contemplating the obvious and did what they could to ignore the slavery issue, but without success. Others attacked the Democrats for parenting the proviso (as they did in both sections) or for being under the thumb of slavery expansionists (as they did in the North). This may have won points for Whigs at home but hardly served to lessen the salience of the issue. The plight of Whig moderates in 1848 suggests a person being sucked down by mire. Ignoring their situation, struggling against it, or wishing that they were not trapped as they slowly went under, all produced the same result: disaster. And yet they were not without hope or prospects. For most would still agree with Florida's E. Carrington Cabell that for all its troubles, the Whig Party "embraced in its comprehensive view the whole country. It is not influenced by a narrow, contracted sectional party."[47]

Their identity imperiled by the territorial issue, Whigs now availed themselves of a helping hand to extricate the party from the mire of the slavery issue and raise the country above the muck of sectional antagonisms. For the presidency they nominated Zachary Taylor, a man with no established party identification, no clear political views, but with a very distinct image. The "Hero of Buena Vista," many predicted, "would be carried into [the presidency] upon the full tide of patriotic feeling, and would be free to labor for the general good." Although a general and a military hero, he was "essentially democratic in nature." Hence, as the candidate of a party often maligned for its aristocratic pretensions, Taylor held immense appeal to Whigs and even Democrats. In an unwittingly revealing compliment, Joseph Baldwin effused, "There is something sublime in the simplicity—the unaffected, child like simplicity of this pure and heroic old Soldier." He was at once "honest and heroic," "brave and modest." His "great simplicity of character, nobility of purpose, soundness of judgment, and good, hard, practical common sense" made him "a man for the times." A disconsolate Hoosier Democrat noted, "Men, women and children are rising up in his favor." "I hear of many democrats who will vote for Gen'l Taylor," a North Carolina Whig gleefully exclaimed, "and of no Whigs who will vote for Cass." Surveying the canvass, a more calculating and pragmatic Abraham Lincoln concluded, "We cannot elect any other whig. . . . [But with Taylor] we can . . . make great inroads among the rank and file of the democrats."[48]

Lincoln's crass assessment of Taylor's candidacy is largely beside the point. In the midst of a sectional crisis that evinced a declension of national purpose, the party turned to a Washingtonesque figure whose force of character and patriotism would overcome sectional partisan divisions. A Clay supporter who voted for Taylor at the Whig convention observed that, like Washington and Jackson, the general had "*daguerreotyped* himself upon the popular heart." Indeed, Taylor's tenuous and recent affiliation with the party only enhanced his connection to Washington and the fathers. Democrats, who believed and feared every aspect of Taylor's mythical standing, might ridicule the general for never having held an elected office and for lacking political experience. Whigs were quick to point out that neither was Washington a politician. Nevertheless, "our fathers wisely thought that Gen. Washington . . . by the greatness of his achievements, the moderation and firmness he everywhere manifested . . . might be safely entrusted with the destinies of a country which his valor had preserved." So, too, it was said of Taylor. The *Scioto Gazette* insisted that the public was convinced "that Gen. Taylor is a Whig of the Washington school—a man of great wisdom, stern integrity, inflexible virtue, [and] pure patriotism." With a character that "equals Cincinnatus" and a sense of patriotism "that of Marcus Curtius," Taylor "if called on to administer the government, would, in the station of President, render him second to no man who has been elevated to that exalted preeminence, save our WASHINGTON."[49]

Somewhat paradoxically, Whigs claimed that their candidate was the choice of the people, not a party. "I admire him because he is not an ultra party man," a Kentucky Whig asserted. "Parties are not necessary to the country. Washington had no party—Monroe may be said to have had no party." Public affection, not "wire pulling friends," secured the general's nomination. Now, party members bragged, " 'caucus dictation and convention discipline' will for once since the days of Washington be stripped of power." Taylor's platform—none—was "Washington's platform. . . . There is where Washington stood more than sixty years ago!" Unencumbered with the antirepublican pretensions of party juntos, Taylor would be free to pursue the public interest. Georgia's Robert Toombs, an early booster of the general, assured his Whig colleagues "that, without any embarrassing connection with the past, he will administer the Government within the old well-defined Republican landmarks. Washington, Jefferson, and Madison, are his avowed models." With Taylor's election, Abbott Lawrence predicted, "the Dark Ages of corruption and misrule which have so long held sway will vanish—before the upright and enlightened measures of a Whig administration—and Republicanism."[50]

Of course, other campaigns and other candidates had made similar claims to this cherished ancestry. Whigs, though, purposefully cloaked Taylor's candidacy in the imagery and rhetoric of the Revolution. They understood that the significance of the nomination lay less in the merits of Taylor himself than in the patriotic response he evoked. This desired effect came through his close association in the public mind with the revered memory of Washington and his generation. There is about General Taylor, a South Carolinian wrote, something more "*classic*, Spartan, or rather Roman, *Catonian* . . . than any public man we have had since Washington." Like Washington, Taylor was celebrated not for a character that was unique but because he exemplified the essential qualities, moral and intellectual, shared by the entire revolutionary generation. Robert Winthrop believed that, as a paragon of virtues of which all Americans claimed a share, Taylor through the sheer force of his personality would summon from the nation's history the spirit that should pervade all patriotic hearts. "As an honest man of spotless character, sterling integrity, strong sense, indomitable courage, tried patriotism, and just principles, he has far higher claims upon us all."[51]

The close identification of Taylor with Washington that Whigs assiduously planted in the public mind had another, larger purpose. Washington himself was associated "with a time of patriotic war, a time when geographical, political, and social differences came closest to being submerged under a sense of national unity." Now Whigs expressed a desire to "see the times of Washington, Monroe, and the younger Adams return, when the government was administered for the benefit of the country not of a faction." Quite naturally, as the 1848 canvass unfolded, these longings to restore "the era of good feelings" centered on Washington's proclaimed spiritual heir. Early on, the general's brother Joseph counseled that his apolitical reputation would redound to his—and the country's—advantage. "Should you be called to the presidency," he wrote, "you would *be* and act *only* as President of the nation and *not* of a party." Seargent Prentiss later declared that Taylor "does not belong to us Whigs. . . . He will be the President as he has been the leader of our armies—not of a party or a class, but of the whole people." It would be a glorious spectacle to see such a man called to the presidency, Henry Hilliard affirmed. "He rises far above party; he looks into the open Constitution for his guide; men of all creeds welcome him, and invoke God's blessing upon him in his great task." Whigs presumed that, as president, Taylor would be a man above sections, parties, and cliques, at once embodying and executing the public will. Thus it was that John Clayton could argue, with guile perhaps but certainly without irony, that "every man who occupies Democratic ground may vote for General Taylor without degrading or disgracing himself, because General Taylor admits the will of the majority ought to govern, and every Democrat admits the same."[52]

Taylor's aura and his nonpartisanship allowed the candidate and the party both to transcend and evade the territorial issue in the canvass. With any other Whig candidate—Clay, McLean, or Webster—Democratic politicians desiring to get on the sunny side of the proviso issue "could, at least, do enough, to make capital of [it] in the canvass: with old Zach they could not." With some insight, Sergeant Prentiss observed to the Louisiana Whig state convention that the Democracy was divided. There were the "wild radicals, whose devotion to liberty runs into licentiousness," and the more familiar "selfish demagogues who are looking to their own interests." As the party lurched between the extremes, the "Government, instead of remaining Republican, has departed so widely therefrom, as to exhibit in many of its features the lineaments of monarchy." In contrast, there stood Taylor. Occupying the "broader and better ground" of the Constitution, he was "not committed to this particular measure [read: Wilmot Proviso] or that, in such a way as to have his freedom of judgment or action shackled." Scorning their opponents' charge that the general had "neither compass nor rudder," Whigs insisted that Taylor "will bring back our Republican Institutions to their purity." One self-satisfied Maryland editor resolved that he for one would be delighted to see "*E Pluribus Unum*" rather than "*To the Victor go the spoils*" guide the next administration.[53]

With no record and a broad commitment to the Constitution and Union, Taylor, or more precisely his advocates, also were able to run different campaigns in both sections. In the slave states, Whigs claimed that northern fanatics would have defeated any other nominee. Southerners declared that Cass and the Free-Soil candidate, Martin Van Buren, were both "pledged to pursue a policy which will equally deprive us of our rights" and that nonintervention in particular was "a piece of paltry trickery to gain southern votes." Taylor, in contrast, "will not bow his neck to the yoke of pledges to be made President, when no other pledge is required by his country than fidelity to the Constitution and the Laws." Southerners asserted that the general was "conservative" and "utterly opposed to the radical notions of many of the leaders of the Locofoco party." Having graduated from the "school of Washington," Taylor, they affirmed, "will give a just and liberal construction to the Constitution."[54]

In the free states, Whigs extolled Taylor as a "Whig, who places his country above his party." They gathered corroborating scraps of evidence such as his approval of an article printed in the *Cincinnati Signal* critical of slavery extension. They noted with pride that the general accepted the nomination of New Jersey Whigs "who nominated him on expressly the ground that he was opposed to . . . increasing the preponderancy of the slave power." Taylor's free-state advocates insisted that although the general was a slaveholder, he would "oppose any scheme intended to give preponderance to any portion of the Union [and] sustain our great national interests."[55]

To dilate on these equivocal claims, however, underestimates Whiggery's larger hope for a Taylor presidency. Southerners like James Gadsden and John Bell and northerners like Truman Smith assumed that by justice, moderation, and firmness, Taylor might stay the tide of fanaticism. Above all, however, his supporters believed that the general's transcendent qualities would give sectional agitators nothing upon which to act. Smith, writing for the Whig Executive Committee, advised his colleagues to "enter into no controversy with any on the subject of free soil, for controversy is what agitation desires. The assurance that the whole country will be safe in the hands of Gen'l Taylor is enough for us." Politically astute and not a little disingenuous, this advice was defined by an honest and romantic belief in Taylor's integrity and an abiding faith in the virtue of the American people. Taylor, they contended, "bows to the will of the people as expressed through their representatives." Whigs obviously presumed that the will of the nation would become manifest in any territorial accord reached by the statesmen who represented them. Following the implications of this rather peculiar brand of popular sovereignty, Whigs as diverse as Washington Hunt and Merideth Gentry were satisfied that the party finally had come to grips with the slavery issue. They contented themselves that as president Old Zach would "leave all legislative questions to the decision of Congress." That decision, they believed, would be inspired by renewed patriotism and defined by national—not sectional—considerations.[56]

Confidence in Taylor's administration of government was a function of the party's long-standing opposition to the presidential veto and belief in cabinet government. This faith, not surprisingly, defined one of the Whigs' strongest attacks on Cass during the campaign. With Tyler's vetoes and Polk's usurpations fresh in their minds, many argued that the canvass posed the question "whether all the power—the power of the purse and sword, the power of peace and war—was to be exercised by the President; whether, with the *veto power* in his hands, exercising legislative as well as executive power, he was to become supreme in this country . . . and Congress and the people were to dwindle into perfect insignificance." General Cass and his party "talk about 'Jeffersonian Democracy,'" a Pennsylvania Whig hooted. "Why, sir, they go for the VETO *power*, the great conservative power of *putting down* the will of the people, and *putting up* the will of the president." Harkening again to the party's theme of regeneration, the *Vicksburg Whig* pointed out that on the issues of executive power and presidential veto, Taylor stood "precisely on the ground on which Thomas Jefferson originally made a party difference with John Adams." As some Whigs busied themselves counting the number of vetoes in the administrations of Washington, Adams, and Jefferson (by most accounts, just two), others assured the faithful that the general took a narrow view of the veto power and "has given no pledges to check or thwart the will of the people."[57]

Informed repeatedly by their Democratic opponents that Cass would veto the Wilmot Proviso if it were enacted, northern Whigs such as Lincoln maintained stoutly that they preferred "a candidate who, like General Taylor, will allow the people to have their own way regardless of his private opinion." Taylor's free-state supporters acknowledged that they did not know exactly what the general would do on the proviso. They were confident, however, that "a patriot and statesman, who has the good of this country at heart, and is determined to endeavor to discharge his duty faithfully and honestly, under the Constitution ought not to pledge himself . . . [to] veto any particular measure that Congress might adopt."[58]

Southern Whigs would not doubt their candidate on this question. They believed that as a southerner and a slaveholder he could be trusted on questions concerning the rights of the South. Yet the essence of southern support of Taylor, like that of the North, evinced an abiding faith in the wisdom and patriotism of the statesmen who led their party. Robert Toombs stated confidently that "the Whigs do not fear to trust those measures which they deem important to the public welfare to the uncontrolled judgment of the people, speaking through their constitutional agents for legislation." Virginia's Thomas Flournoy admitted that "there is much difference of opinion as to the powers of the Federal Government over the Territories." He held, nevertheless, that the slavery question "will be considered and acted upon in a spirit of patriotism; the recollections of the past and the bright hopes for the future will not be disregarded. . . . The memories of our fathers will not be forgotten." Speaking for all Whigs North and South, Flournoy concluded that his party had "a deep attachment for this Union, and . . . they will preserve it." [59]

Willing to trust in Taylor and, even more, in themselves, Whigs rejected Cass's solution to the territorial imbroglio. In their minds, popular sovereignty was tantamount to ignoring and frustrating the public's will on this matter. A Taylor supporter from Ohio asserted that as representatives of the people who know their wants, Congress was obligated "to redress their grievances, to protect their just rights, to guard the public interests, to legislate for their best interests, public and private, as we deem best, and as the true interests of the country demand." Whigs in 1848 demanded that Congress must untie the Gordian knot of slavery restriction. As one New Englander put it, "The power of Congress to legislate on this subject is unquestionable, and the duty is as clear as the right. A vast majority of the people demand the exercise of this power, and the popular will must and will be obeyed." Even states'-rights Whigs such as Hilliard, Stephens, and Toombs concurred in believing "that the whole power over the Territories originally rests in Congress is clear and satisfactory." Who, they wondered, but an abstractionist or a political mountebank like Cass would have the folly to maintain that Congress had the authority to acquire territory but no right to govern or control it? Using the Mexican War as a test case, an incredulous Charles Hudson parsed the logic of this "strange doctrine." "We may, as we have, commence a war of conquest, expend millions of money, and sacrifice thousands of lives and . . . pay fifteen millions more for the worthless provinces of Mexico; and after this territory is acquired at an immense cost, lo and behold, the very authors of this war and conquest discover that we cannot govern the territory we have obtained!" The very statement of Cass's case, he spat in disgust, "furnishes its best refutation." [60]

Although there was a consensus on congressional authority, the sectional wings of the party differed sharply over the extent of that power. Few northern Whigs disagreed with Hilliard when he maintained that Congress had exclusive but not unlimited power. Most antislavery activists, though, believed that the Constitution clearly spelled out those limits, and nowhere did they discover any restriction on the ability of Congress to prohibit the extension of slavery into the territories. For all that, no Whig was inclined to leave the resolution of this critical problem to the people of the territory. Southern Whigs were especially adamant in their opposition. We oppose General Cass's doctrines, Toombs declared, "because they surrender our principles and submit our rights to our ignorant, imbecile, conquered slaves." Where is there a "more dangerous and degrading doctrine," another southerner asked, "than citizens of a territory—black, white and yellow—have a right to regulate this matter and settle the question against the privileges and interests of the South?" Southern Whigs saw no difference between a congressional restriction on slavery extension and one that originated in the territories. "The mode by which you defeat our rights is wholly immaterial to us," Toombs contended. "The slaveholding States hold that this right exists nowhere."[61]

United in their contempt, Whigs opposed Cass's doctrine (or, in the context of the election campaign, his hobby) for very different reasons. Antislavery Whigs held that it was an abnegation of federal power and, worse, of congressional responsibility. "I look upon the election of General Cass as perfectly fatal to all the hopes of the friends of free soil," one exclaimed. "His election seals the doom of all the friends of freedom in this country for this and the next generation." Slave-state Whigs viewed popular sovereignty as but another, more insidious means of abridging the rights of the South. There was, however, something about Cass's solution that all could equally fear. Coupled as it was to an aggressive foreign policy, popular sovereignty carried within it the seeds of unlimited expansion. Cass's doctrine proposed to remove the greatest restraint on expansion by neutralizing and postponing the territorial crisis. Whigs apprehended the worst. "If we shall get safely out of this difficulty, have we, in the policy of the Democratic party, any security for the future?" Virginia's Flournoy asked. Undoubtedly not, for he and others concluded that "it is in the frequent recurrence of this question that there is danger to the country. It will come with accumulated difficulties and dangers upon every extension of our limits." Given the disturbed and agitated state of the nation, William Rives urged that it was doubly important in this election to "rescue the country from the hands of Loco Foco charlatanism." Toombs likewise appealed to his countrymen: "Let us unite and throw overboard the authors of this mischief, and elect our candidate. His wisdom and firmness, his lofty character and unsullied purity, will be a tower of strength to prudent and conciliatory counsels."[62]

The persuasiveness of the rhetoric of the Taylor campaign speaks to the resonance that his campaign had with a public whose self-confidence had been shaken. Troubled by the sectional antagonisms engendered by the territorial issue, Whigs and Democrats now supported a candidate whose essence reaffirmed the genius of their revolutionary heritage. With a reinvigorated sense of national purpose, Taylor enthusiasts again expressed their faith in the didactic nature of the American experience. The election of 1848 was ultimately less a referendum on territorial solutions than a reaffirmation of the idea of mission. Presented with two possible answers to the territorial crisis—Cass's popular sovereignty pragmatism and the proviso absolutism encompassed by the newly organized northern Free-Soil Party—a majority of Americans rejected both. They elected instead a man with no established political views and the weakest of ties to the party that nominated him. The Whig ticket was given electoral majorities in the North and the South and received 98 percent of the party's percent of the 1844 vote. Taylor carried four states that Clay had lost in 1844, and in the critical Middle Atlantic area he ran more than twelve thousand votes ahead of Clay despite an almost fourteen-thousand-vote drop in New York. Taylor received 98 percent of Clay's totals in the free states, carried the border states with a larger plurality than had Clay, and swept four of seven Deep South states. In some districts, Taylor ran better than the elected Whig candidate for Congress.[63]

By invoking and calling forth the spirit of the revolutionary fathers, Zachary Taylor transcended his personal shortcomings, his party's disorganization, and the sectionalism that plagued the nation. The quintessence of his candidacy, of his character, of all that he represented affirmed the moral continuity of the American people with their birthright. Despite its power, Taylor's appeal was a dangerous one because by 1848 that revolutionary national spirit had become sectionalized. For the moment, however, the romantic impulses of an earlier age prevailed over the reality of a nation in deadlock. Taylor, gratified by the confidence manifested in his honesty, truthfulness, and integrity, had already expressed his determination to rule over the people and their destiny in a disinterested manner "never surpassed & rarely equaled since the days of the Father of his country." Yet as he and Congress turned again to the problem of territorial organization, faint but worried voices could be heard whispering in the background, "Either the North or the South has been cheated by the election of Zachary Taylor."[64]

And the Lord said: "Truly they are one people and they all have the same language. This is the beginning of what they will do. Hereafter they will not be restrained from anything which they determine to do. Let us go down and confuse their languages so that they will not understand one another's speech."—Gen. 11:6–8

While I am still alive, I shall never be in such slavery, as to forgo my own kindred or forget the laws of our forefathers. —Flavius Josephus

Tower of Babel

Social Ideology and the Crisis of
Territorial Organization, 1849–1850

On Thursday afternoon, January 28, 1848, a drenched and mud-splattered rider entered John Sutter's fort at New Helvetia, California. James W. Marshall, Sutter's partner, had traveled two days in a driving rain from their sawmill on the south fork of the American River. Now standing dripping wet in Sutter's office, a visibly agitated Marshall abruptly asked his partner for a private interview. After they had adjourned to an adjoining empty room, Marshall pulled a white cotton rag from his pocket and unwrapped a one-ounce glass vial. Emptying its contents into his hand, Marshall held it before Sutter's eyes and said, "I believe this is gold." Sutter learned that Marshall had found the yellow particles four days earlier while inspecting the trailrace of their mill. After making various tests on the metal, Marshall had decided to ride to New Helvetia to ask Sutter to determine if these pebbles and grains were indeed gold. The two men now made additional tests. Finally, after consulting the *Encyclopedia Americana*, Sutter satisfied himself that Marshall's find was genuine. He ventured that the specimens were of twenty-three-carat purity, at least. "I believe," he told Marshall, "that this is the finest kind of gold."[1]

Of course, neither man had any idea, yet, of the importance of this find. Eager not to disclose the news until construction of the as yet unfinished sawmill was complete, Sutter received a promise from his artisans to say nothing of Marshall's discovery for six weeks. Word got out, however, and "spread like magic." By May, gold mania had reached San Francisco. Soon schoolteachers, mechanics, lawyers, ministers, editors, merchants, gamblers, storekeepers, sheriffs, housewives, and children began a wild scramble to reach the mines around Sutter's fort. Sailors deserted their ships as soon as they anchored in San Francisco Bay. Army volunteers fled their posts to join in the hunt. In the summer of 1848, according to one estimate, three-fourths of the houses in San Francisco were abandoned. Real estate fell in value from 50 to 75 percent. Meanwhile, in the countryside ranches were deserted, wheat remained unharvested, mills lay idle, and livestock roamed at will. "A complete revolution in the ordinary state of affairs is taking place," Thomas O. Larkin wrote.[2]

Although for a time obscured by the heated presidential canvass, gold fever began to spread slowly east in late 1848. In October and November, symptoms of California gold frenzy erupted in Washington, Baltimore, New York, New Orleans, Louisville, Pittsburgh, and Indianapolis. The *Philadelphia Public Ledger* declared in December that gold delirium had become an epidemic in that city as well as New York. In Boston, the disease was "rising to fever heat," and those infected were reportedly "starting off for California by the dozen, the score, and the hundred, hardly allowing themselves time to pull on their boots, and put bread and cheese in their pockets." The Second Coming could not have generated more excitement than the interest in California gold, the *Anti-Slavery Standard* lamented.[3]

As emigrants from all sections swarmed by land and sea to San Francisco, the military governor of California strongly urged Washington, in August 1848, to give the territory a suitable government as soon as possible. That month, however, a deadlocked Congress adjourned, leaving the whole Mexican cession unorganized. The question of the extension of slavery into the newly acquired territories lay at the core of the impasse. Arguments for and against slavery restriction were of many different types and echoed discordantly the rhythms of Democratic and Whig motets. Beneath the cacophony, however, appeals made by antislavery northerners and southern rights representatives had an internal logic and consistency. Separately and together, they extended and reflected the most deeply held beliefs about historical truths, the nature of Jacksonian society, and political realities. Although the same may be said of the expansionist debates of 1844, the congressional stalemate of 1848–50 differed in significant ways. The dialogue four years earlier united parties nationally. That is, differences between northern Democrats and Whigs over Texas and Oregon paralleled those among their southern colleagues. The territorial debates of 1848–50, however, exposed the salience of the single institution that separated the North and South: slavery. Of course, slavery had previously and heatedly entered congressional and public discourse. Nonetheless, the deadlock over the Mexican cession forced Congress and the public to address the relevance of slavery to the nation's future and assess Washington's obligation to determine it. As legislators moved from objections to specific proposals to general discussions of the territorial issue, arguments for and against restriction indicated that the institution and the broader concept of slavery were intimately bound to the social ideology of both sections.

Although specific solutions to the crisis remained elusive and partisanship remained high, debates on the organization of the cession had the paradoxical effect of uniting elements of both parties in the North and South. Principles that had once seemed to divide them—liberty and equality—now brought Whigs and Democrats together in their analysis of the territorial question. Northern Whigs supported Wilmot's proviso, arguing that the spread of slavery would impede the progress of the nation and its citizenry over time. Free-soil Democrats argued that slavery inhibited individual liberty and the spread of free labor. In the South, Whigs saw slavery as a means of upward mobility and therefore opposed its restriction. Their Democratic opponents believed it to be the first line of defense against the exploitation of nonslaveholding whites. They, too, opposed limiting slavery's expansion.

As they took measure of their sectional opponents, free- and slave-state legislators beheld antagonists not simply hostile to the institutions of their section but deviant from the American way of life. Returning to a major theme of Jacksonian politics, each side satisfied itself that the other was controlled by an aristocracy of wealth hostile to the interests of average Americans. Northerners argued that planters, whom they likened to the Tories of the Revolution, had a political, social, and cultural stranglehold on the South. Contemptuous of nonslaveholding whites, they scorned their aspirations. Southerners, Whigs as well as Democrats, contended that the free-labor system of the North built up an oligarchy of industrialists and bankers who, like their Federalist ancestors, scorned their workers' welfare and ambitions. Although more suggestive than explicit, the sectional arguments fashioned in and out of Congress in 1848–50 painted portraits of adversaries who embraced opinions and social ideologies that were un-American. Therefore, asking their constituents to migrate to a territory defined by the other, alien section posed a Hobson's choice: it was no choice at all. It was precisely this ominous possibility that gave the territorial issue its salience.

Adding to this babble of voices, moderate Democrats charged that these extremists in both sections betrayed a disdain for the intelligence and rights of territorial citizens. Restrictionists and southern rights' radicals would intervene in the internal affairs of the territories, one to prohibit, the other to protect slavery. Both smacked of congressional despotism and would undermine the freedom of Americans to determine their institutions for themselves. Intervention of either stripe contravened the equality of territorial residents in the Union. From this third perspective, the proposals of Wilmot and Calhoun were as foreign to the genius of American government as the worst excesses of European despotism. One embraced Federalism, the other Toryism. Both engendered inferiority and inequality. Both restriction and slavery extension were premised on a strong national government that paralleled though did not exactly resemble the claims made by advocates of a national bank, protective tariffs, and federally funded internal improvements. Moderates' argument for popular sovereignty reflected the Democracy's long-held belief in the genius not of government as such but of the American people. In their attack on intervention, these Democrats led yet another charge on the royalists who seemed to dominate the sectional extremes in Congress.

While Congress remained paralyzed, disruption and discontent continued to grow in California throughout the fall of 1848. President Polk fretted that disgruntled settlers would seize the initiative and establish an independent republic. In October he dispatched an agent to California to assure the citizens there that the American people would not abandon them. Polk expressed his deepest regrets that Congress had not provided them with a territorial government. For now, he had nothing but promises and hope to offer. The president assured these "bold and patriotic citizens" that when Congress reconvened he would urge it "in the strongest possible terms" to organize the territories and would use every effort consistent with his duty "to ensure its accomplishment." Until then, Polk asked the people of California "to live peaceably and quietly" under the de facto government that had been operating since the end of the war.[4]

This was something that the citizens of California were unwilling to do. As the Thirtieth Congress gathered in Washington for its second session in December, agitation for a civil government continued to spread throughout California. In his last annual message, a worried Polk declared that the existing condition of California and New Mexico "imperiously demands that Congress should, at its present session, organize territorial governments over them." Admitting that the reason for the failure of the previous session's efforts was well known, the president held that the question of slavery extension was "believed to be rather abstract than practical." Nonetheless, he conceded that it did involve a principle of equality of rights of the several states and that those could not be disregarded. Guided by the Democratic beacon of strict construction, Polk now charted a course for Congress to follow. He maintained that in organizing territorial governments, the Constitution imposed no duty on Congress to legislate on the subject of slavery. Indeed, its power to do so was in serious question. Let Congress, therefore, abstain from interfering with the slavery issue and the people of the territories would be free "to adjust it as they may think proper when they apply for admission as States into the Union." Polk assured Congress that he was still willing to accept an extension of the Missouri Compromise line or, alternatively, some form of the stillborn Clayton compromise (which would have referred the slavery question to the territory's federal courts, with an appeal to the Supreme Court) as expedient solutions to the territorial question. Still, he concluded that if this was "an original question it might well be insisted on that the principle of non-interference is the true doctrine."[5]

Polk was eager to organize the Mexican cession to prevent a revolution in California and to reduce sectional animosities. Others were willing to give the territorial question the go by altogether. The day before Polk's message was delivered to Congress, Senator Stephen A. Douglas informed his colleagues that he intended to introduce a statehood bill for California. Accordingly, on December 11, Douglas laid before the Senate a proposal to admit the entire Mexican cession as a single state. Echoing Polk, he declared in support of his measure that a revolution had taken place in that country that required its organization. Douglas candidly admitted that he despaired that any territorial bill would pass at the existing session "for reasons which may be apparent to all of us, as three different bills presented for that purpose have already been rejected." Hence Douglas proposed to bypass the stumbling block of the proviso and meet the pressing needs of California by organizing it as a state.[6]

Polk, among others, supported the measure. In the main, however, the response to Douglas's bill was unenthusiastic. Although the bill allowed Congress the right later to create additional states from the territory that lay east of the Sierra Nevada, many still thought the area too unwieldy and the whole idea impracticable. The fiercest opposition, though, came from free-soilers and Calhounites. Joshua Giddings declared that Douglas's maneuver was "one of the grossest frauds ever perpetrated upon a free people." He and other antislavery northerners would accept no settlement short of the "absolute, unconditional, and uncompromising proviso." For their part, southern rights supporters, especially those of the Calhoun stripe, charged that the California bill was simply the proviso by a different name. They held that inasmuch as the effect, if not the intent, of immediate statehood would be to exclude slavery, it was "a matter of little importance . . . practically, how we are deprived of the common conquest and purchase." Statehood, one Georgian stated flatly, was "a substantial yielding of the question by us and a practical triumph of the fanatics. The Southern people . . . are not willing to give up the substance for the shadow." [7]

Whigs, particularly those who favored a moderate congressional settlement of the territorial issue, hardly could have been encouraged by the opposition to Douglas's bill. Granted, his proposal at best was innovative, at worst farfetched. Still, the intransigence of free-soilers and Calhoun's supporters seemed to indicate that extremists in both sections, pursuing their own agenda, would provide formidable opposition to any comprehensive settlement. "Giddings & his crew . . . would destroy every interest of the country and destroy the Union itself to build up their party," a Hoosier Whig complained. On the other side, Georgia's Robert Toombs ventured that John C. Calhoun's effort in the winter of 1849 to join southern Whigs and southern Democrats into a united front in Congress was "a bold strike to disorganize Southern Whigs and either to destroy Genl Taylor in advance or compel him to throw himself in the hands of a large section of the democracy at the South." [8]

Believing that northern free-soilers were united with many southern Democrats in an effort "to break up [Taylor's] forces before he gets on the field," a number of Whigs hoped to settle the slavery question before his inauguration. Despite the promise of Taylor and the hopes for his administration, simple faith in the uplifting effect of the general's force of character was not a practical solution for the territorial deadlock. To save Taylor this embarrassment and possibly to rescue his administration, William B. Preston, a Virginia Whig, introduced a California statehood bill in the House of Representatives on February 7, 1849. Closely resembling Douglas's measure, the bill would make the entire Mexican cession into a single state. And like Douglas, Preston would settle the slavery question on the basis of congressional noninterference. The territorial issue "has been called the great question of the age," Preston asserted. "I will attempt to try it by the great principle of the age." By renouncing the exercise of territorial authority and jurisdiction, the bill eschewed an "arbitrary and tyrannical power—this power of making governments here for a people abroad." If there is anything great and venerable in our past, he declared, "it is [the conviction of the Founding Fathers] that a foreign government, not further from us on that shore than our friends in California are on the other, could not and ought not, upon every principle upon which our Constitution and Government are formed, control and direct our legislation." Thus Preston's bill, which recognized "the great principle of popular supremacy and popular government," was but "the spirit of the Revolution . . . the spirit of our institutions." Its great merit, therefore, was "that it is a bill under which neither party is victorious, and neither party overcomes. *It is no compromise at all.*" Most important, "*the bill now offered and gives finality to the question.*"[9]

Preston's approach to statehood was attractive to apprehensive Whigs, and it enjoyed some bipartisan support. For example, John J. Crittenden advised Senator John M. Clayton that he doubted that Congress could resolve the slavery question by direct action. "Let it settle itself," he suggested, "by admitting those territories as States at the earliest practicable period." Whigs such as Charles S. Morehead of Kentucky were willing to place themselves by Preston's side "upon the high ground of popular sovereignty." Across the aisle, Democrat James McDowell believed that both Douglas's and Preston's bills furnished "an honorable and common ground upon which our conflicting opinions on the subject of that measure may be mutually given up, and our national difficulties about it suitably and finally disposed of."[10]

Unhappily for Preston and his supporters, most southern Democrats and northern free-soilers remained unconvinced. Mississippi's Albert Gallatin Brown sardonically congratulated his Whig colleague that he was "at last so near on the 'Cass platform.'" Hopkins Holsey was less amused. Douglas's and Preston's bills, he scoffed, were "founded upon a mere quibble." Opponents also argued that the people of those territories were "unprepared to take [the] position as citizens of a sovereign State in the Confederacy." With unconfined glee, Democrats quoted at length from Whig speeches made during the war in which dissidents had charged that the degraded citizens of California and New Mexico had "no notions of our institutions, or of any free institutions." Democrats blandly asked the Whig supporters of California statehood whether such a people ought to give laws to those territories and thus "shape and mold their institutions for the present, and possibly for all time."[11]

Antislavery northerners, many of them Whigs and all of them preferring the Wilmot Proviso, attacked Preston's bill as a southern scheme to allow slavery to enter the cession. Ostensibly to guard against that catastrophe, but more likely to scuttle California statehood, free-soilers proposed amendments to the bill that explicitly prohibited slavery in the newly created state. Approved by a close 91 to 87 vote, slavery restriction effectively torpedoed Preston's bill. California statehood, now blown up by the proviso, failed to receive a single aye vote in the House and sank without a trace.[12]

Meanwhile, in the Senate, Douglas's bill lay dead in the water. As it drifted toward adjournment, Congress made a final attempt to provide temporary governments for California and New Mexico, with retention of Mexican laws, by amending the civil appropriations bill. This last struggle over territorial legislation stormed during all-night sessions of Congress on the weekend of March 3–4. Several grossly intoxicated senators exchanged insults, threats, and punches. Some southern Democrats threatened to cut out the hearts of their northern colleagues if they refused to vote for the amendment. As dawn broke on the morning of March 4, members at last regained their senses and some their sobriety. In a close, fetid Capitol, first the House and then the Senate defeated this last attempt to organize the cession. As the gavel fell at seven o'clock that morning, Congress adjourned, exhausted and still at sea. It had failed again to agree on a common set of principles on which to anchor a territorial settlement. "Never in my life . . . have I felt more sorely oppressed with doubt and despondency, or considered the Union more in danger," Henry S. Foote mourned. "Had we been able to effect last winter some fair and fraternal compromise on the question of *slavery in territories*, as at one time was confidently expected, there would have been little in the vista of the future to sadden the heart or alarm the fears of the patriot." [13]

The following day, March 5, Zachary Taylor took the oath of office. To weary members of Congress who looked to the new president to chart a course around the breakers of sectionalism, his inaugural address had precious little to offer. Promising (again) to follow the Constitution and the examples of earlier presidents in the discharge of his duties, Taylor (again) declared his determination "to maintain to the extent of my ability the Government in its original purity and to adopt as the basis of my public policy those great republican doctrines which constitute the strength of our national existence." Moving from the familiar to the implausible, the president concluded by stating that he would look with confidence to the enlightened patriotism of Congress "to adopt such measures of conciliation as may harmonize conflicting interests and tend to perpetuate that Union which should be the paramount object of our hopes and affections." Taylor's speech was notable for the absence of any proposed solution to the territorial storm. The address, one observer sniffed, "was remarkable only for its brevity, simplicity, good idiomatic English, and the absence of great promises in high sounding phrases." A North Carolinian groaned that Taylor's ambiguous position on the territories was about the worst he could occupy. "I think the *Adm*[inistration] would have been stronger by taking *either* side than it will be taking *neither*." From March to July Taylor made no speeches on the territories. "That the administration is now amidst rocks, shoals, and whirlpools no one, I think, can be so blind himself as not to see," a disillusioned Whig journalist wrote. [14]

Many began to suspect that the Hero of Buena Vista had feet of clay. Taylor, one critic sighed, "is not considered so rough as had been expected,—unluckily, too, he is not found to be half as ready." But in fact, the president was already on the move. Always the general, Taylor took firm and decisive action to end the territorial crisis. In the spring, two of his closest advisers, Crittenden and Clayton, now secretary of state, had argued that his administration should renew the commitment to California statehood. The slavery question, Crittenden observed, "is the only really formidable obstacle in the way of the administration, & it can only be effectively removed by the admission of California into the Union as a state." He advised the secretary that statehood "ought to be regarded as the *great object* of the administration, and its accomplishment sought with all its policy and energy." [15]

Clayton and Taylor agreed. Not willing to risk further delay, Taylor decided to maneuver around another possible stalemate over an enabling act for California. Instead, he would present Congress with a fait accompli. That spring, the president dispatched Thomas Butler King of Georgia to California as his special agent. Publicly, his mission was to inspect the mail steamship lines to that region and to examine a route for a transisthmian railroad. Privately, King, "fully possessed of the President's views," was to assure Californians of Taylor's concern for their welfare and of his desire to protect them "in the formation of any government, republican in its character, hereafter to be submitted to Congress, which shall be the result of their . . . deliberate choice." King was cautioned that this spontaneous move for statehood must originate with the citizens themselves. Nevertheless, he could "with propriety suggest to the people of California the adoption of measures best calculated to give them effect." [16]

When King left Washington, Clayton assured Crittenden that "as to California . . . everything is done as you wish." The state, he predicted, "will be admitted free and Whig." When Taylor's emissary reached San Francisco on June 4, he discovered that on the previous day, General Bennet Riley, the military governor of California, had issued a proclamation calling for a constitutional convention to organize a state government. King, assisted by Riley and General Persifor F. Smith, commander of the Pacific Division, began to scout northern California for recruits to the constitutional convention. Received "as a sort of deliverer," King informed Clayton that "the feeling among all classes in favor of forming a State Government soon became . . . universal and strong. . . . We are now on the high road to success." In accordance with Riley's June 3 proclamation, delegates to the constitutional convention met in Monterey on September 3. They soon fashioned a constitution that drew on the fundamental law of Iowa and New York. As Clayton had predicted, it embodied a clear prohibition of slavery. The state constitution was ratified by a wide margin in November, and the new civil government assumed power from the military authorities the following month.[17]

The president completed his flanking maneuver by urging the same solution on the citizens of New Mexico. Like Californians, the citizens of New Mexico had been agitating for a civil government since the signing of the Treaty of Guadalupe Hidalgo. Prominent citizens of New Mexico met in September 1849 to consider the problem of creating a civil government. The delegates eventually adopted a territorial constitution, petitioned Congress for territorial status, and elected a governor and a delegate to Congress. Between the conclusion of the fall convention and the opening of the Thirty-first Congress, Taylor decided to encourage New Mexicans to follow the example of California. The people of New Mexico did not draft and adopt a state constitution until May 1850, however. By then, the stalemate between the administration and Congress was complete.[18]

If not fully implemented, Taylor's strategy for resolving the territorial crisis was in motion by November 1849. The president was unable to press his solution on Congress because the House was deadlocked over the selection of a Speaker. With a nearly even balance between the Whigs and Democrats and each party split along sectional lines, the House spent day after day in fruitless balloting. For forty, fifty, then sixty ballots the contest continued. Day after day the Senate met only to adjourn, while in the House a parade of Whigs made vitriolic speeches that heightened tensions and shortened tempers. William Duer of New York charged Virginia's Richard K. Meade with disunionism. Meade denied it. Duer called him a liar. In the background, colleagues yelled, "Shoot him! Shoot him!" "Where is your bowie knife?" Some members were pained by such scenes; others laughed. None could deny that feelings on all sides were raw. "No one can say how soon we may be involved in the dangers & calamities of disunion," one northern Whig mused. "The house is not yet organized & parties are becoming inflamed." At last on December 22, after the parties agreed to abide by a plurality decision, House members elected Howell Cobb, a Georgia Democrat, on the sixty-third ballot by a majority of 3 votes of the 201 cast.[19]

To this factious Congress Taylor now submitted his territorial initiative. In his first annual message, he stated that the citizens of California soon would apply to Congress for admission to the Union as a state. Taylor recommended that Congress quickly approve California's request and that of New Mexico when it, too, should present itself for admission. "With a view of maintaining the harmony and tranquillity so dear to all," Taylor enjoined members of Congress to "abstain from the introduction of those exciting topics of a sectional character which have hitherto provided painful apprehensions in the public mind." The president further clarified his position on

January 23, 1850, in a special message to the Senate. Taylor declared that he was motivated by an earnest desire to lift Congress above its bitter and angry divisions. Organizing the territories necessarily provoked discussions on slavery. But, he maintained, no one would deny that every state had the right to regulate its municipal laws and domestic institutions.[20]

In essence, Taylor asked Congress to take no new action on the territorial issue, allowing the people of the West to assume the initiative. With the dust kicked up by the bitter speakership struggle just now settling, a few southern Whigs conceded that the president's approach had a certain innate appeal. Admittedly, his solution dodged the contested issue of the South's right to carry slaves into the commonly held territories. More important, it was certain to prevent the adoption of a measure that in its application threatened to confine slavery forever within its existing limits. Moderate northern Whigs greeted it with general approbation though their support, too, was often tepid and qualified. Frankly admitting that he was "somewhat puzzled what to do about the slavery question," Robert Winthrop believed that Taylor's course was certainly open to objections. Yet he conceded reluctantly, "it is certain that we can do no better." Nonetheless, many antislavery Whigs remained wary of expedient solutions. Indiana's Schuyler Colfax, for example, would not accede to Taylor's request for nonaction "until the North had in the House passed & repassed the Proviso as evidence, earnest and emphatic, that Territory coming to us free, shall not be cursed with the withering blight of slavery." Admit California as she is, Thomas Corwin argued; that was safe. But, "keep N. Mexico free from bad habits . . . [by] providing that she shall not take to putting yokes on the necks of other people black or white."[21]

Although, as Colfax pointed out, no Whig wished to assume a position of hostility to the administration, still the professed policy of the party's northern wing was to do "all in their power to extend the Wilmot Proviso over all the territories of the United States." To them, Taylor's initiative smacked of backsliding. Compromising principles, restrictionists protested, would not gain northern Whigs the support of their southern colleagues and would forfeit them the goodwill of honest free-soilers. Taylor's plan was also dangerous. Minimally, it left the outstanding issue between the North and the South "where it was. It leaves it open to future discussion, but gets rid of the prohibition of slavery." This was to play the South's game. If the cession remained unorganized or even in a territorial state long enough, slavery eventually would "get such a foothold that when they came to ask admission as states, they will come in as slave states. It is a positive gain therefore to the South to get all the territory they can organized as a territory without the Wilmot Proviso." Ironically, inaction would ultimately convert the national government "into an instrument for the propagation of slavery without limit and without restraint."[22]

Such sentiments were not without their effect on Whiggery's southern wing. Legislators like Robert Toombs angrily concluded that "there was a strong and nearly unanimous disposition on the part of Northern Whig members to interpolate the old Whig creed with Free-Soil opinions. . . . I found them, with but few exceptions, pledged and determined to engraft the Wilmot Proviso upon Territorial bills." Largely for this reason, southern Whigs placed little value on the president's solution. If, on the one hand, Congress admitted California as a state without any mention of the proviso, slave-state Whigs predicted that frustrated and enraged free-soilers would dismember Texas, award the disputed territory to New Mexico, then organize it with a specific prohibition of slavery. Restrictionists, on the other hand, would hail efforts to conciliate the North by allowing California and New Mexico to enter the Union as free states as an antislavery triumph. This, southerners argued, would increase, not abate, northern attacks on the South. Worse, Thomas Clingman declared, "should we give way, California, Oregon, New Mexico, Deseret, and Minnesota will come into the Union in less than five years. . . . With immense controlling majorities in both [Houses], will they not at once, by act of Congress abolish slavery in the States?" Consequently, many of Taylor's southern allies complained that his proposal "is just no plan at all. It leaves ample material for the ultras North and South to keep up the agitation of the slavery question, so dangerous to the slave interest, and so dangerous to the Union." Better, Clingman suggested, to settle the question conclusively at the present session.[23]

If states'-rights Whigs considered the president's leadership maladroit and his plan specious, southern Democrats charged that his actions were purposefully harmful to the South. Giving substance to the fears of antislavery northerners, southern rights adherents advocated delay. Slave labor, they held, was admirably suited to gold mining; therefore, there were no natural limits to the institution in California. Now Washington had interfered in the affairs of that country and encouraged the settlers there to adopt a constitution excluding slavery. It was, David Yulee protested, an effective mode "of sealing our exclusion from these territories, before our emigrants have had time to reach their destination and establish their due influence in the direction of affairs there." California statehood was worse than the Wilmot Proviso, Calhoun warned. "What the latter proposes to do openly the former is intended to do covertly and fraudulently." In Taylor's scheme, popular forms disguised the evil. The intent was "to thwart and defeat that resistance and opposition which might be successfully brought to bear against it in the other."[24]

In early January 1850, Robert Winthrop noted apprehensively "that matters begin to look a little serious. They certainly will be worse before they are better." He was right. On January 17, Senator James M. Mason of Virginia introduced a new and more stringent fugitive slave bill. New York's William H. Seward proposed an amendment giving those alleged to be fugitive slaves the right to a jury trial and the writ of habeas corpus. Henry S. Foote of Mississippi offered a bill to organize California, New Mexico, and Deseret into territories without reference to slavery. Thomas Hart Benton introduced another measure that gave Texas $15 million to pay off its public debt in exchange for a cession of two hundred thousand square miles to the United States. Clingman flatly denied Congress's power to adjudicate the Texas boundary issue in any fashion and suggested that if the North continued its aggression, southern congressmen might block all legislation in the House. The slavery question, one northerner remarked, entered into every discussion. "Indeed it is the point on which the whole government turns." Amid the confusion, rancor, and threats of disunion, President Taylor remained stolidly confident about his plan for the territories. Despite the widening rift within his party and the unruly scenes in Congress, the Hero of Buena Vista remained "calm, collected and determined." Others, more alarmed at the sectional cannonades that were exploding around the general's position, were less charitable about his leadership. Taylor, claimed one of the disenchanted, was "an honest, plain, unpretending old man but about as fit to be President as any New England farmer."[25] The mutiny had begun.

In mid-January Henry Clay decided to wrest the initiative from the president, his former rival for the Whig presidential nomination, by proposing a comprehensive alternative to the administration's policy. Now seventy-two, in feeble health, but supremely confident of his talents, Clay laid his compromise proposal before the Senate on January 29. Its purpose, stated in the preamble to the resolutions, was "to settle and adjust amicably all existing questions of controversy . . . arising out of the institution of slavery, upon a fair, equitable, and just basis." This was to be accomplished by admitting California as a free state; providing territorial governments for the rest of the Mexican cession without restrictions as to slavery; assuming Texas's public debt in exchange for its yielding in the boundary dispute with New Mexico; abolishing the slave trade, but not slavery, in the District of Columbia; and enacting a more rigorous fugitive slave law.[26] Although the first wave of opposition to Clay's plan came from the South, it opened to mixed reviews. An Indiana Democrat asserted that Hoosiers throughout the state favored the compromise, inasmuch as it would defeat "the madness of the North and the treason of the South." Similarly, David Outlaw, a North Carolina Whig, praised Clay for pursuing a course that was national, patriotic, and conservative. "I wish most sincerely he were now the President of the United States," Outlaw stated. Edward Everett, however, looked askance at Clay's efforts. The compromise, he groused, "can please nobody. If adopted it would bind nobody." A southern Whig editor complained that Clay failed to understand that "times have changed, the spirit of forbearance [in the South] . . . has given way to the belief that premeditated and intentional wrong shall [have to] cease before peace can be restored to a distracted country."[27]

Congress debated the merits of one or another aspect of Clay's proposal for more than six months. Provisoists and states'-rights southerners in their opposition fashioned arguments that would be developed fully in the coming years. Their themes seemed perhaps allegorical to a majority of Americans in 1850; only events of the decade would give substance to them. This is not to say that their prophecies were either self-fulfilling or inevitable. For the moment, however, their imagery and, indeed, their fears were already sufficiently persuasive to array most legislators against a comprehensive settlement of the territorial issue. The spirit of their struggle suggests as well the extent to which sectional divisions had begun to eclipse established political differences.

The sheer size of the contested territory imbued the debate with an added sense of urgency. The cession, all agreed, consisted of "the seats of new States, the cradles of new commonwealths, and the nurseries . . . of new Republican empires." Antislavery activists contended that Providence had committed the task of molding Americans' institutions and thus shaping their destinies into the hands of Congress. All history and all examples had shown that "as a State begins to settle, and continues to settle, during its territorial existence, so will be its destiny as a State." If inhabited by a free population, it would go on to be a free state; if it commenced with slavery, the territory would be condemned to degradation and thralldom. Thus, because it was establishing the rudiments of society in the cession, Congress in effect was "determining the servitude of many generations." On Congress's action, free-soilers proclaimed, "hang the liberties of a country as large as this Confederacy was when it was formed. . . . On its determination hang also the hopes of this republic."[28]

The surest way to secure the future, free-soilers asserted, was "to plant the frontier with a free population. That is the remedy, and there is no other which can be effectual." By paying homage as they did to the "worthy, unpretending, intelligent, independent" laborers of the free states, restrictionists celebrated northern society as they envisioned it. Thaddeus Stevens declared that "the middling class who own the soil, and work it with their own hands, are the main support of every free government." In the North, the individual who labors, "who makes the best of the advantages he may possess . . . who strives continually to progress . . . is the favored individual." All men in the free states "are, or at least claim to be equal—not in talent or advantages, but in rights and privileges." Insofar as labor was elevated and made honorable, individuals came to believe that they had within themselves "the ability to procure . . . the wants of life without depending upon another for them." Autonomous farmers and mechanics concentrated their efforts on developing the resources and advancing the prosperity of the nation. They built schoolhouses, churches, and villages; put up manufacturing establishments; constructed railroads; and developed the free states in every way. "We believe that the cultivation of the intellect—the advancement of public morals—are the true sources of happiness," an Ohio Whig declared. It seemed axiomatic that free labor on free soil was "the only mode of maintaining a republican government."[29]

Northern restrictionists apprehended that the extension of slavery into the Mexican cession would inhibit northern migration to the territories. The reason was clear. "Where slavery exists," they declared, "the labor of the white man is in danger of being degraded." They asserted that in the South, non-slaveholding whites "are among the poorest in the world . . . [and] in the slave districts far worse than the slaves." Inasmuch as white laborers in the South were debased with the slave, they were excluded from the society of the slaveholder. Forced to associate "with the colored population . . . they feel that they are degraded and despised; and their minds and conduct generally conform to their conduct." With "a puny, sickly appearance" and degraded to a condition "which the slaves themselves need not envy," the nonslaveholding class in the South was "the most worthless and miserable of mankind." Even the dullest discovered eventually "that all hope of bettering their lot is denied them, so long as the reigning order of things continues." In a few instances, their antagonism led white mechanics to demand legislative enactments "prohibiting slaves from engaging in such pursuits as will bring their labor in competition with them." More often, however, "the active and enterprising, born in it, fly away." The institution, as anyone could see, "has always been at war with the rights of free labor." Consequently, free-soilers denied the charge that political antislavery was merely an abstract sentiment for them, irrelevant to their personal interests. The existence of slavery in the territories, they countered, "would be an insuperable bar to the emigration of the laborers of the free States." For, stated simply, "free labor requires free soil."[30]

Little imagination was required to gauge the future of American civilization if slavery were spread over the territories. The sad example of the South furnished an all too clear vision of its probable effect. William Sackett, a New York Whig, came straight to the point: "A high state of civilization, slavery, and prosperity, are utterly incompatible; they never did, and never will exist together." Slavery, Montgomery Blair contended, "retards the growth and prosperity of communities, impairs enterprises and paralyses the industry of a people and impedes the diffusion of knowledge amongst them, to say nothing of the aristocratic tendencies and the degeneration it attaches to labor." Another restrictionist explained that although the institution made "the master too proud to labor, and thus renders him comparatively useless to himself, and to society," it also rendered the enslaved "unskillful, listless, feeble, leasing, indolent, truculent and perfidious." The truth, commented the *American Farmer*, was that "one white laborer at the North performs more than any two slaves at the South." Antislavery northerners concluded simply that the institution "was debasing to the individual and to the State."[31] Its extension, they avowed, was opposed to the best interests and the welfare of the country.

Just as threatening, the institution contravened the fundamental principles of freedom and democracy. "Republicanism founded upon slavery is the purest and most exclusive form of aristocracy," the *American Review* proclaimed. Because a slave economy created a small number of large landholders, free-soilers considered the institution "a monopoly, subversive of the just rights of the free laborers." In contrast to the North, where productive property was diverted and divided into thousands of channels, declared Henry Bennett, "the slave interest and slave property is peculiar; wherever it goes it is *the* great controlling interest, and, like Aaron's rod, 'swallows up' all others." In the South, Blair charged, "all political power and social consideration [are] in the hands of the slaveholders, who are occupied, like the English aristocracy, almost exclusively with political affairs and amusements." Like their British Tory counterparts, southern slaveholders intended "to make the laboring class a degraded class, and to deprive them of all power and consideration in the country, which inevitably subjects them to oppression." Drawing on analogies closer to home, an Ohio Whig argued that "the old Bank of the United States with all its branches, and officers, and dependents . . . would be an adversary quite insignificant and harmless, compared with the one which the friends of free soil now have to encounter." Blair added, "Like the small number who were interested in the profits of the Banking System, [slaveholders] have been able by combination to control the government for years."[32]

As the free-soilers defined the essence of the territorial issue, it was "whether this Government shall be administered in the spirit that gave it birth, or whether the sufferings and trials of the Revolution shall have been endured in vain . . . [and] this Government become an Aristocracy, based on slave property, and slave representation." The grand design of government was to secure justice and the blessings of liberty to all. "Slavery in principle and in practice conflicts with this design," a New England Whig stated. "It neither secures justice nor the blessings of liberty. It subverts and destroys them." Realizing this great, if sad, truth, Senator John Clarke asserted, the fathers intended that slavery was to be "hedged in, girdled round, pent up." Yet from the time that the foundations of the government were laid, an aristocracy based on and bound together by property in slaves and, alas, "by the political power which the Constitution has deposited in their hands . . . [has been] opposed to the temper and spirit of our institutions."[33]

Able to wield all political power in states and territories where the institution held sway, this aristocracy, according to free-soilers, gradually and inexorably increased the scope of its domain. "The purchases of Louisiana in 1803, and Florida in 1819, and the annexation of Texas in 1845 . . . are so many instances of the aggressions of the slave power, which has managed to extend the curses, and crimes, and cruelties of slavery, by its last consummated plot, more than five hundred thousand square miles," a Pennsylvania Whig exclaimed. William Bennett pointed out, "Instead of the gradual but certain extinguishment of slavery . . . we find that the slave States have held the sway and ascendancy in the National Government, from almost the first exercise of its power." All the while contravening "the great truths of the Declaration of Independence," slaveholders, emboldened and arrogant, no longer "content with that share of influence and power given them by the Constitution, demand the absolute control of this Government." What could be more despotic, Democrat David Wilmot asked his colleagues? "To dictate what Congress might, and what it might not do," he stated, "would be to change this Government . . . into an absolute monarchy."[34]

Now, in 1850, slaveholders resolved to force the institution into the free territories of the cession. Accepting the susceptibility of humans to corruption and their lust for aggrandizement, restrictionists rejected the claims of more moderate northerners such as Daniel Webster that the institution was "confined by natural law to certain parallels of latitude." Slavery, one of them rejoined, "is singularly cosmopolitan in its habits. The offspring of pride and lust and avarice, it is indigenous to the world." Natural limits arguments were "*all apocryphal*," a New Mexican wrote in disgust. "I do not believe there is one intelligent man in a hundred here who believes it." Indeed, one observer claimed that there was a great plot afoot in New Mexico to create proslavery sentiment "to secure the admission of slavery in that Territory" and from there "*to extend its dominions if found necessary to Tierra Del Fuego.*" Such charges did not seem fantastic. Free-soilers had heard southern members of Congress assert that but for the antislavery agitation, slaveholders would have carried their slaves to the mines of California in such numbers that they would have made it a slaveholding state. Salmon P. Chase therefore warned his antislavery colleagues on both sides of the aisle, "Let us take care that we do not deceive ourselves, or mislead others. Neither soil, nor climate, nor physical formation, nor degrees of latitude, will exclude slavery from any country." The entire history of the Union, he concluded, was alarming testimony to the truth that there was not "a degree of latitude beyond which slavery has not gone, [nor] any . . . country to which it has not, at some time, found access."[35]

In the unfolding sectional conflict, free-soilers considered the North the aggrieved party. "I charge the *South* with aggressing upon the *North* by every addition of slave territory since the adoption of the Constitution," a northern Democrat thundered. The South, Schuyler Colfax charged, "not satisfied with having all the Government in its hands, Presidential, Cabinet, Diplomatic, Judicial & Senatorial, all except the House, begin to rave and swear and threaten." It insists that the slavery question "be settled now at the tap of the drum." It demands that "the North shall give bail for her future good conduct, or she will 'devote all she has, all she is,' to the settlement of the question by violence, even to the division of the Union." Northern opponents to slavery drew one ineluctable conclusion: "The object of the South is manifest—she is determined to rule this nation in all time to come." If the influence of the federal government were not "kept actively and perpetually on the side of freedom," they cautioned, northerners "are as certain to find the power of government sliding into the hands of those opposed to your free institutions, as you are to find any result whatsoever." We have arrived at a point from which we cannot retreat, David Wilmot asserted. "*We must go forward.* To step back—to cower under these threats, is base dishonor—a virtual surrender of our rights and the rights of free men whose representatives we are." Daniel King cried, "When the people shall, in the power of their might, declare that there shall be no more slave territory, they will have extinguished [the slaveholder's] insatiable lust for acquisition."[36]

Because the extension of slavery was "a wrong done to humanity—to the rights of humanity, to the friends of humanity," free-soilers denied that its restriction was, as southerners charged, oppressive and iniquitous. "So long as we act for the promotion of that which is morally right," Ohio's Lewis D. Campbell retorted, "we cannot aggress." Free-soilers, therefore, rejected compromise on the territorial question. "Is it the business of Congress to strike a balance between slavery and freedom?" a Pennsylvania Whig asked. "Are we here, as if for no other purpose than to see that freedom has no advantages?" The emphatic answer was no. There could be no harmony between the "absolute right of freedom" and the "absolute wrong" of slavery, Sackett explained. The Wilmot Proviso, one Hoosier representative declared, was "the very life blood of freedom." It was, added Kingsley Bingham of Michigan, "the great idea" that the founders embraced "in the earlier and better days of this Republic." Turning to the southern members of the House, Connecticut's Thomas Butler stated finally, "We stand where our fathers and their fathers stood—we abide by their principles."[37]

Perhaps they did, responded southern congressmen, but not likely. To their mind the northern commitment to antislavery was, as Henry Clay had suggested, simply "an abstraction, a sentiment—a sentiment . . . of humanity and philanthropy." Conveniently for free-soilers, it was, too, "a sentiment without danger, a sentiment without hazard, a sentiment without sacrifice, without peril, without loss." Those southerners less charitable and less interested in compromise argued that free-soilers were motivated by "fanatical prejudice, or fanciful notions of the abstract fitness of things." Northerners, a Virginia Whig charged, knew nothing of the realities of the institution, nothing of the strong attachment of the master to the slave, nothing of the feeling, education, and habits that bound the southern states to slave labor. To southerners, an Alabama Democrat stated, slavery was "a vital reality, an essential principle of their very organism, and indissolubly interwoven into the very framework of their being." How could anyone claim, another asked, that it was no contravention of southern sensibilities, to say nothing of their rights, to compel slaveholders "to part with the great mass of [their] movable property before emigrating, or not to emigrate at all?" Such terms, a Maryland Whig asserted, "destroy the independence of private judgment, morals and religion; they admit the right of government to prescribe by law what is right and what is wrong."[38]

At best a mere expression of sentiment for northerners, the issue of slavery restriction was for southerners "a question of our very existence." If, Senator David Yulee added, slavery was confined and, as a result, the population of the South became too great for subsistence or comfort, only two results would follow. "Either the black race must be sent out free, as emigrants, at the cost of the structure and habits of our society, or the whites must . . . emigrate, leaving in the end the graves of their sires to be trodden under the heel of the African." As southern rights advocates in both parties agreed, this implied that freed slaves could not live together as equals with whites. Such a thing was forbidden "by the recollection of their former relative position . . . [and] by the laws of God and Nature." Thus yet another and more horrible prospect loomed as a result of restriction. "The success of abolition [read: restriction] will throw the two races into a fearful conflict—a conflict which admits of no compromise but death—no quarter but in the grave—no termination but its extinction." Clay asked northerners to imagine the unspeakable terror. "Behold," he cried, "that dwelling-house now wrapped in flames. Listen, sir, to the rafters and the beams which fall in succession, amid the crash; and the flames ascending higher and higher as they tumble down. Behold those women and children who are flying from the calamitous scene, and with their shrieks and lamentations imploring the aid of High Heaven." According to Clay, however lurid, such scenes were neither exaggerated nor farfetched. "The conflagration which I have described is raging in the slave States," he informed northerners, "produced . . . from the inevitable tendency of the measures which you have adopted, and which others have carried far beyond what you have wished."[39]

Slavery, southerners informed their free-soil opponents, degraded neither the black nor the white nonslaveholder. No man, Alabama's David Hubbard countered, "owning negroes, would be allowed to live in a southern State, who suffered his slaves to perish for food, clothing, or shelter. . . . The negroes are housed, clothed and waited on in sickness; in addition to this, abundance of good food. . . . Can you say as much for the cities where you have the profits of hired labor in plenty? You know you cannot." Hubbard claimed that his nonslaveholding constituents benefited the most from the institution. "With us, none but a black man will be a waiter, a servant, and obey orders; a white man will not do it; he feels above it; and therefore all upright white citizens are placed upon an equal footing as freemen. . . . With us it is color and race which gives distinction; with you it is wealth." Hubbard's colleague Williamson R. W. Cobb bragged, "Many of my constituents are these who labor and do not own slaves, and who not only associate with the best slaveholders, but are considered equal in society to the man who owns his hundreds." Southern Democrats were not alone in stressing the meliorating effect of slavery on the presumed inevitable conflict between capital and democracy. Slave-state Whigs, as was their wont, assumed a harmony of interests between the two classes. William Alston, an Alabama Whig, assured restrictionists that "the poor white man, although not interested in the value of this property . . . has too much good sense . . . to aid you in such mad schemes. . . . The poor man will never consent to be degraded to either social or political equality with the emancipated slave . . . and well knows that while his want of means would fix him to the soil, the rich man could go where he pleased."[40]

Southerners contended that slavery, by meliorating class conflict and promoting white equality, enhanced the dignity and well-being of nonslaveholders. One Virginian boasted that in the South "the white laborer is exalted by the fact, that the slave is subordinate to him—ready to ease him off the more menial manipulations." Rather than being employed in degrading tasks, nonslaveholders "are made mechanics, artisans, farmers, &c, and the change in the kind of employment is favorable to increased wages." Citing statistics that showed wages in the slave states to be 25 percent higher than in the North, Missouri's James Green boasted, "Labor is rewarded South better than it is North." Feeling solicitous for his obtuse free-state colleagues, Virginia's Richard K. Meade patiently explained to them the importance of these facts. Slaves felt—and accepted—their natural inferiority, he remarked. Representative Meade tellingly observed that the white man "feels his equality, and is ever disposed to assert it. His condition he attributes to the wrongs of society, and longs to avenge them. . . . The black horse that we are riding is a docile and willing animal—the white one you have saddled is restive and impatient. . . . beware!" Before dumbfounded northerners could gather their wits, tongues, and statistics to reply, Representative E. Carrington Cabell seized the ultimate moral high ground for the South. "We daily hear northern gentlemen complaining of the undue influence of the South, in the affairs of this Confederacy," he sneered. "This does not proceed from the force of numbers, but from the *moral power of slavery*. Nowhere is there so pure a spirit of freedom and true republicanism as with us. . . . Nowhere is there so much *individual happiness*, as among the southern people."[41]

Southern rights legislators brought the territorial issue to the homes and hearths of their nonslaveholding constituents by linking restriction to the constituents' future progress—or degradation. The essential point raised by the proviso, congressmen argued, was whether slavery "shall be confined to a limited space, to the destruction of the people, or whether it shall be permitted to diffuse itself over a wide surface . . . and disseminate its advantages." William Colcock of South Carolina assured skeptical northerners that southern white laborers "understand the question well. . . . They will never consent to elevate the negro to an equality with themselves; and, thus, while they reject your sympathies, they know and despise your purpose." Never, southerners claimed, would nonslaveholders quit their own egalitarian society to migrate to territories shaped in the free-labor image of the North. The system of free labor, David Hubbard spat in disgust, made whites "paupers and then criminals, reducing them so low in morals that they regard neither right nor wrong." Virginia's Thomas Averett warned darkly that if northerners "look at home, they will see better reason to fear and tremble at the prospect of strife between classes in their own section of the Union, than to glory . . . in the supposed weakness of the South." In the free states, observed one Kentuckian, "mobs. . . . antirenters &c are frequent now & must increase." Every day, William Colquhoun chimed, "the most respectable farmers of the Northern and free states are moving to Virginia to avoid the overgrown masses of pauperism which exists under the false reforms of the red Republican and socialist."[42]

Nonslaveholders, then, understood their representatives when they charged that "the Wilmot Proviso is a declaration of war against the south." For the nonslaveholder, his liberties, his rights, and his way of life were in imminent danger. "Abolitionism is no longer confined to a few fanatics, but is at the heart of a great political organization," Jefferson Davis claimed.

"From every point of view [its] attitude is the same, always that of grasping of political power." History has shown, he averred, "the tendency of power to corrupt rather than purify the heart. The progress of assumption and aggression [has] advanc[ed] by equal step with the increase of sectional power." In the full confidence of their numbers, Democratic and Whig restrictionists speciously appealed to the majority principle "to use the authority of Congress, for the destruction of Slavery in the United States." In palmier days, a Georgia Democrat noted, a persecuted minority could point to the provisions of the Constitution "and demand of the majority, too often arrogant in its strength, 'thus far mayest thou go, but no further.'" Now, Senator Andrew P. Butler observed sadly, the South had not the power to enforce it. He added, "I do not see what avail the Constitution is, if the majority can give it construction." None, replied Butler's colleague James L. Orr; it then became a nullity. "If the will of the majority is absolute," he explained, "it is the strong against the weak—the law of force which existed between individuals before Government was instituted." If the North persisted in such pretensions, Orr concluded, "it requires no spirit of prophesy to foresee that it must end in disunion."[43]

Orr was no Cassandra. As citizens of slaveholding states, southerners knew the reality of slavery and hence were terrified at the prospect of their own enslavement. Once the proviso breached the redoubt of strict construction, Davis asked, "can anyone believe that the local rights of the slaveholding states will be respected[?]" No, replied Benjamin Yancey, the plan was clear: "The doctrine of the North now is to carve out of the Territories none but free states—to acquire the complete supremacy in the Government." Should that day ever come, Georgia's John Berrien wrote, "slavery will then exist in a double aspect—the African and his owner will both be slaves. The former, will as now, be the slave of his owner—but that owner in all matters within the sphere of federal jurisdiction, will be the doomed thrall of those, with whom he associated on the basis of equal rights." With this vision before him, a defiant David Hubbard exclaimed to free-soilers, "We [do not] intend to permit you to place us in shackles, with a view to force us to abolish [slavery] in the future, or to increase your sectional power for such objects."[44]

Thralldom, of course, implied degradation of status. For that reason, restriction had the effect of destroying egalitarianism within the slaveholding states while subverting the equality of the South within the Union. The territories, a Mississippian claimed, were the common property of all the states. "To exclude the property of the people of the Southern States," he contended, "is in effect to exclude those people, and appropriate the country to the Northern States." Would the Founding Fathers "say this is justice—this is the equality upon which our Union and Constitution were based?" Pushed to his emotional limit, Richard Meade sprang to his feet in the House to defend his section. "The North goad us with abuse, throw fire-brands in our dwellings. . . . Bestowing upon us the epithets of slave-drivers, bloody tyrants, and dealers in human flesh. Why, sir, there is not a man from the South who, if he be a man, does not at times find his attachment to this Union giving way under a disgust of their associations here so redolent of abuse, vulgarity and malignity." Beyond assaults on their dignity and pride, southerners apprehended that the consequent inequality would change and irrevocably alter the essence of the Union. If Congress denied the South access to the territories, Thomas Clingman told his constituents, "it is obvious that the character of our political system would be essentially changed; so that the Government, instead of being that of the whole Union, would have been converted into a mere machine, for the advancement of the northern section." William Lowndes cautioned New York's John King, "You must not think that you can hold the South united to the North as Poland is to Russia, or as poor Ireland is to England."[45]

All southerners concurred that "Union without equality, will enslave us." Most agreed that northern free-soilers were morally bankrupt; the repeated passage of the proviso in the House was proof of that. Constitutional arguments against such tyranny seemed of little avail. "Power," Representative Daniel Wallace said, "is never restrained by written laws." From this point of view, R. M. T. Hunter concluded, "it becomes all-important for us to claim . . . the right to settle and colonize the vacant territory of the United States. . . . If the South could preserve the same political weight which she has hitherto enjoyed—if she could retain even that which she now possesses— she would have the power in the Government to protect herself within the Constitution and Union." Give us our rights under the Constitution, Davis demanded. "We are content to take our chance, as our fathers did, for the maintenance of position in the Union. . . . We believe in the merits of our own institutions, we are willing to trust in time and fair opportunity for the working out of our own salvation." If, however, Congress "*make distinctions to their* [southerners'] *disadvantage*," the duty of southerners was clear, Alexander Stephens claimed. "No people . . . who deserve the name freemen, will continue their allegiance to any Government which arrays itself not only against their property, but against their social and civil organization."[46]

Stephens's threat made the deadlock in Congress complete. Most northern Whigs still clung to Taylor's initiative. Their southern colleagues, however, thought it conceded all to the North. Although many slave-state Democrats supported Clay's proposal, a significant number of them such as Calhoun and Davis contended that it, like Taylor's plan, was a fraud, and an insidious one at that. All the while, free-soilers and southern rights advocates agitated the slavery question in an effective, if dangerous, manner. They carefully shaped and articulated appeals for and against restriction that resonated with the most deeply held convictions and most basic interests of their constituents. At this juncture, moderate Democrats dove into the maelstrom to guide Congress between the Scylla of restriction and the Charybdis of disunion. Challenged by free-soil defectors from northern ranks and harassed by extreme southern rights colleagues, beleaguered moderates, mostly but not exclusively from the North, sought to fashion a compromise that would be distinctively Democratic and, more important, would throw overboard party extremists in both sections. They decided that by recasting Clay's blueprint for the territories to include the Democratic principle of popular sovereignty, the party would calm the storm of fanaticism that threatened to sink the Democracy and wreck the Union.[47]

William Marcy confided to his diary that "politicians have the abstract right to commit suicide if they only kill themselves—They have no right if thereby they injure their friends." Marcy, no doubt, harbored murderous feelings toward the Barnburners in his own party. Nevertheless, rather than engage in the character assassination of extremists within the Democracy, he and other moderates began to lay the foundation for a settlement by blaming Whigs for the crisis of Union. First on their list of indictments was the moral bankruptcy of the opposition. A northwest Democrat charged with some accuracy that the existing difficulties grew out of the preceding presidential canvass. Taylor, he argued, was represented at the North "as unfavorable to the extension of slavery—as being favorable to the Proviso, or at least not being opposed to it"[48]

If Taylor's campaign had been a hoax on the electorate, northern Whig support of the proviso was no mere humbug. Many Democrats would have agreed with Henry Marie Brackenridge that "the malignant, fanatical abolitionist" liked the proviso because it was a calculated insult to the South. Whig endorsement, however, suggested another, darker motive. "The doctrine of the Wilmot proviso presupposes that Congress has the power to do everything, not expressly forbidden," Indiana's Willis Gorman contended, "instead of the republican doctrine, that Congress can exercise no power not expressly granted . . . and that all power not expressly granted to the General Government is reserved to the States respectively, *or to the people*." Such an assertion of power, another Democratic representative claimed, "is in violation of the theory and genius of our institutions—is the very essence of despotism." Moses Hoagland of Ohio reminded the House that if Congress "possesses no power to charter a bank for the West, under the pretence of regulating the currency, or a protective tariff for the North, under the specious pretext of protecting northern industry . . . [then, likewise] the power to legislate on the subject of slavery is not conferred upon us by that instrument." Hoagland's colleague David Disney took his argument to its logical conclusion. "The sovereignty of the people, acting through and in their local organizations, is the only power which can establish for each its own peculiar laws," he asserted. "On this distinction hangs the nation's safety."[49]

As moderate Democrats sought a way out of the territorial vortex, they, like free-soilers and southern rights supporters, looked to the heritage of the Revolution for inspiration. The party journal, the *United States Magazine and Democratic Review*, explained that despite the variety of colonial governments, "the leading principle at bottom was the sovereignty of the people. . . . If imperial authority of the mother government was acknowledged in general matters, the necessities, the wants and the wishes of the people governed in local legislation." Thus the essence of the Revolution, Indiana's Cyrus Dunham declared, lay in the charge leveled at Great Britain by the fathers "that she sought to govern these colonies, not according to the wishes and interests of the colonies, but for her own benefit." "We were always freemen," a Tennessee Democrat exclaimed, "and never declared our liberty, but our Independence, which means simply freedom from British rule. . . . Our revolution was not prosecuted to change the social, moral or civil condition of the people of these colonies, but to transfer their allegiance from the English Crown to themselves." The right of self-government, Dunham declared finally, was "that great principle which lies at the foundation of republican liberty—the principle declared by our revolutionary fathers, and sealed with their blood."[50]

Once enshrined by the revolutionary struggle, Stephen A. Douglas argued, self-government became the principle upon which our republican system was founded. The genius of the Constitution, the *Review* contended, was that it was able to reconcile "the old diversified forms of government, the incongruities of religious bickerings, and the clashings of material interests" by adhering to the principle of self-government and "acknowledging the people as the only source of power." Unfortunately for the republic and its people, some political leaders of the early national period "from a strange predilection entertained for the British form of Government . . . aimed at strengthening the arm of the General Government at the expense of the states." The Democratic Party, observed the *Pittsburgh Morning Post*, "entertained opinions diametrically opposite—they looked upon the Union as limited in its design . . . and to be strictly confined to the exercise of those powers expressly delegated by the Constitution."[51]

Americans of the Jacksonian era would have concurred, in the main, with Moses Hoagland when he argued that "every departure from principle must necessarily produce its penalty." Certainly Cyrus Dunham did. "Sir, the great error which has brought this difficulty upon us and which now prevents its settlement, is, that we have forgotten and have violated, and still seek to violate that great principle . . . [of] the right of the governed to have their government administered to their own wishes." William Richardson of Illinois appealed to his disputatious colleagues in the House, "Come to the Democratic policy, the policy of that party which has carried this Government gloriously and triumphantly through all the difficulties and dangers that have threatened it in times gone by." This was no mere partisan cant. Time and again moderate Democrats reminded party members that the doctrine of the Founding Fathers was that "the people are the fountain of all power and the source of all authority—that they have instituted governments for their own ends—that they have a right to establish and modify their government at will." Only by revivifying this basic principle, by hewing closely to the fundamental premises of the Democracy, Dunham assured the disgruntled, shall Congress "find the thread which shall guide us from this labyrinth in which we are involved, and which threatens destruction to us." [52]

By arguing that the people of the territories had the capacity and the right to manage their own affairs free from outside manipulation, these Democrats insisted upon the settlers' equality within the Union. Daniel Dickinson told a Tammany Hall audience that history had shown that "there always has been and, there always will be, a strong repugnance on the part of freemen to have their domestic affairs controlled by those who are not chosen by themselves." Noting that the distance from London to the colonies approximated that from Washington to the territories of the cession, Democrats spun out the comparison by equating the situation of the fathers to that of the western settlers. "When we make laws for them," claimed John Savage of Tennessee, "they are not their laws—they are not represented here; we assert over them a right, for the claiming of which by Great Britain all the blood of the Revolution was shed." A Western Reserve Democrat contended that just as the revolutionaries were bound to the empire by natural rights, constitutional liberties, and common law, so, too, the allegiance of western settlers was not to some distant governmental body but rather "to the organic law of the country to which it belongs." Taking a middle position between the defenders of southern rights who argued that the territories were the common property of the states and the free-soil claim that the federal government exercised a trusteeship over the cession, Democrats stated flatly, and to their minds conclusively, that the public lands belonged to the people. They added inevitably, "Whenever Congress will assume the attitude and settle down upon the firm basis of non-intervention, thereby acknowledging the right and the capacity of the people to govern themselves, this sectional agitation will cease." [53]

This happy state of affairs, of course, never came to pass. Historians looking at the Kansas fiasco and the sectional animosity it engendered have generally pooh-poohed popular sovereignty as a humbug, a fraud, a hoax. That it failed no one would deny. Nor, as we shall see, was there any consensus as to its practical application or even its meaning. Yet to dismiss the concept and the values it embraced as bankrupt is, one could argue, to assume in effect the position of either a free-soiler or a fire-eater. That is, by viewing the appeal of these moderates backward from the secession crisis of 1860, historians, among others, have been drawn ineluctably to ask, Who could ever have believed that popular sovereignty would work? This, at least, is to misconstrue the essence of popular sovereignty; at worst, it misses the point altogether. Perhaps the more interesting and fruitful question to pose is, Why did its advocates expect it to succeed?

At bottom, popular sovereignty rested on a historic, enduring, and deeply held belief in the capacity of the American people not only to govern themselves but to do what was right. "I have an abiding confidence in the intelligence and integrity of the people," one northern Democrat trumpeted, "in their ability for self-government—in their ability to examine and decide for themselves all questions which may arise in the administration of their Government." Democrats acknowledged—indeed, they insisted—that the Union encompassed a welter of conflicting opinions, feelings, prejudices, and factions. But they vehemently asked free-soilers, "Shall we fear to trust [the people of the territories] with their own interests?" Confidence in the people, they declared, was "the basis of republican liberty everywhere, and wherever that trust is most implicit, there freedom is most perfect." Their trust was grounded on a faith in the virtue and innate goodness of most American citizens. George Bancroft, for example, proclaimed that "truth is a social spirit; her home is in the breast of the people, in the heart of the race." Consequently, by giving power to the whole people, "you gain the nearest expression of the law of God, the voice of conscience, the oracle of universal reason." If the Whig appeal in the 1848 campaign was quintessentially an abiding belief in a great leader's integrity and his ability to raise the American people above their sectional antagonisms, the attraction of popular sovereignty reflected a continuing faith in the libertarian tenets that defined the Democracy and in the capacity of the people for self-government. To suppose otherwise, Cyrus Dunham maintained, to suppose that the people of the territories "cannot and will not pursue the path of right and virtue, that they cannot discover, secure, and protect their own interest and happiness, is . . . a position which will find no advocates with the real Democracy of this country."[54]

Neither faith nor romantic convictions, however, could obscure the dangerous divisions between the sections about the practical application of popular sovereignty. Some northern Democrats assumed that until the people of the territories acted on the subject of slavery, Mexican laws that prohibited the institution remained in force. Equally comforting was the widespread conviction that "a deep moral prejudice against the institution of slavery pervades amongst the people at the North." Lewis Cass asserted that the territorial inhabitant, invigorated by the bracing atmosphere of the frontier environment, would come to possess "those elements of enterprise, of progress, and of improvement" that had always proven the safest and most effective barriers to slavery.[55]

Free-state Democrats gathered that there were other, larger forces at work that made popular sovereignty essentially antislavery in its effect. Like the provisoists, they embraced the superiority of northern society and a free-labor economy. Yet they declared that the free-soilers exaggerated the danger of slavery extension. "We cannot help believing," one northern editor wrote, "that the man who does not see that slavery must certainly give way to the rapidly accumulating population and force of white labor, as the natives of the forest and savage life have had to recede before the tread of the white man, has observed the progress of the times to but little advantage." This position went beyond the natural limits argument made by Whigs such as Webster and Clay; here, soil and climate determined the outcome. Moderate Democrats were satisfied that even in lands and environments compatible with the institution, "the energies of free labor will cultivate it, to the entire exclusion of the slaves." The South, they declared, could not alter the natural course of events and thus would always be at a disadvantage in unfettered competition.[56]

No doubt southern Democrats even beyond Calhoun's circle thought such an idea piffle. They welcomed—demanded—the chance to compete. "We do not ask Congress to express an opinion in relation to the decrees of nature, or say that slavery shall be planted in any of the Territories of the United States," Jefferson Davis told the Senate. "We only claim that we shall be permitted to have the benefit of an experiment, that we may have . . . an opportunity to be heard in the determination of their permanent institutions." Viewed in this light, southerners were not expressing a willingness to lock arms with northern Democrats and walk down the entire road to territorial self-government. Popular sovereignty meant congressional nonintervention, period. An exasperated southern congressman informed doubtful northerners that to allow the territorial legislatures to legislate on the subject of slavery would be to confer on them a much larger power than was possessed by the federal government. Such a claim, southern rights Democrats declared, was more than specious: it "must belong to the right of revolution, the right to take the territory of the United States, and appropriate it to themselves."[57]

Moderate Democrats may have been disheartened by this parting of the ways, but they were undeterred. Amid a jabber of voices in the House and Senate, in the face of a deadlock between supporters of the administration's proposal and congressional compromisers, beset by acrimonious disputes over the precise meaning of local self-determination, moderate Democrats, under the deft leadership of Stephen Douglas, struggled to shape a settlement. In February, at the initiative of Mississippi's Henry Foote, Clay's separate proposals were packaged together into a single bill. Free California was harnessed to territorial organization without the Wilmot Proviso. Non-interference was written into the bills for New Mexico and Utah. The gap between the sections was bridged (or glossed over) by extending the Constitution over all territories and allowing for appeals on the slavery question to the Supreme Court. Mexican law was thus invalidated, private property was protected, and the federal courts were given jurisdiction over the constitutionality of all territorial legislation, including any laws bearing on slavery. In a series of bewildering maneuvers, however, opponents separated the territorial bills from the package in late summer and, despite the most heroic efforts of its supporters, extremists defeated Clay's compromise.[58]

On July 9, as debate raged in Congress, Zachary Taylor departed this life as unexpectedly as he had entered into public notice. Fortunately for the nation, the more flexible Millard Fillmore assumed the presidency. Heartened undoubtedly by the mysterious and providential workings of the Almighty, Douglas resurrected Clay's newly Democratized proposal and took the field. Having learned that there was no majority in Congress that favored a comprehensive adjustment of the territorial issue, Douglas decided to bring the measures up one at a time. This way, those who favored one or another part of the compromise as an individual proposition would with the advocates of general compromise form majorities for each, and all could be enacted. Riding herd over the large minority that favored a congressional resolution, Douglas maneuvered the separate bills through the House and Senate in August and early September. When at last the House passed the California and Utah bills, the tensions and animosities of the summer gave way to raucous celebration. "All look upon the question as settled and no fears are felt in relation to the movements in either the North or South," wrote one Washingtonian. "The successful are rejoicing, the neutrals have all joined the winning side, and the defeated are silent."[59]

The next morning many of the more enthusiastic winners were laid low by a variety of ailments: headaches, heat prostration, overindulgence in fruit. A more sober-minded observer might have awakened to an even harsher reality. For all the loose talk of compromise, there was never a common vision of, much less a fundamental agreement to, a comprehensive sectional adjustment. Extremists, North and South, together constituted a majority in Congress. None of the bills obtained clear favorable majorities from both sections. The voting strength of one section repeatedly was brought to bear against the strength of the other. The central problem of territorial organization, of course, had been resolved on the basis of nonintervention. Yet, while Douglas was telling his constituents that the settlement recognized the right of the people to regulate "their own internal concerns and domestic institutions in their own way," Robert Toombs was informing Georgians that the wrong of 1820 had been righted and that the right of the people of any state to hold slaves in the common territories was recognized. Beneath the Compromise of 1850, the sectionalization of the Jacksonian political system continued.[60]

As the groggy revelers finally returned to their seats in the Senate and House, they may have had their suspicions. But they also had their hopes. Moderate Democrats could take comfort in the knowledge that their solution of the territorial problem had been written into law. "It is a great source of honest congratulation to the Democratic party, that the great issues which it has made in previous contests, have been decided in its favor by the recent action of Congress," the *Illinois State Register* asserted. "The doctrine on nonintervention in the territories . . . so ferociously assailed by the entire federal party, has now completely triumphed." What made the victory specially significant, the editor noted, was "that it has been gained by the aid of Clay, Webster and the other leading Whigs." In New York, William Marcy hailed the triumph of a resolution that "stood on old democratic ground." The continuing validity of those principles, he alleged with satisfaction, had attracted renegade free-soil Democrats back into the party's ranks. What is more important, it had also caused numerous Whigs to defect from the black flag of antislavery Whiggery and to adopt the doctrine of nonintervention. None of this was lost on the politically astute Douglas. The experience of 1850 had made manifest to him again the efficacy and transcendent force of the basic premises of the Democracy. With one eye on the distracted ranks of the Whigs and the other on the coming presidential election, Douglas reminded the faithful, "We have, gentlemen, important duties and high responsibilities devolving upon us, which demand the immediate organization, union, and consequent success of the democratic party." As party members busied themselves in preparation for the canvass, they paused to reflect on past triumphs and future prospects. The lessons seemed obvious; the course appeared clear. A party victory was certain, an Arkansas Democrat gushed, "with Douglas and Cuba inscribed on our flag, as in 1844 we had Polk, Dallas, and Texas."[61]

Strong Bellerophon hastened,
      slipped the soothing bridle over the cheeks
of winged Pegasus, and rode him
in maneuvers of war, mounted
in full bronze. . . .
          He killed
Chimaira, breathing fire, and the Solymo;
His fall I won't recount, but Pegasus
entered Olympus and Zeus' ancient stable.
        —Pindar, *Olympian* XIII

Ef a feller don't make every aidge cut, he's in the background directly. —Johnson J.
Hooper, *Adventures of Captain Simon Suggs, Late of the Tallapoosa Volunteers*

Of Pegasus and Bellerophon

Popular Sovereignty, Stephen A. Douglas, and the Origins of the Kansas-Nebraska Act

On a rainy June 11, 1852, Benjamin Pierce decided to write to his mother, Jane. He was visiting his Aunt Mary in Andover, Massachusetts, and that afternoon his cousin Edward had brought news from Boston "that Father is a candidate for the Presidency." Knowing his mother's aversion to politics and to the capital in particular, Bennie added, "I hope he won't be elected for I should not like to be at Washington and I know you would not either." Unhappily for Bennie and his mother, the fates were against them. Franklin Pierce carried all but four states in the fall election, winning the electoral college 254 to 42. His margin of victory in the popular vote was less impressive (1,601,474 to the Whig candidate Winfield Scott's 1,386,580). Still, the Democracy controlled 1,100 counties nationwide, the Whigs but 434. For the first time since 1836, Democrats carried Delaware, Florida, Maryland,

and New Jersey.[1] Along with his father, mother, and a host of congressional Democrats, little Bennie was headed for Washington.

After spending the Christmas holidays in Massachusetts, the Pierce family prepared to return to Concord to arrange the move. Before their departure, a friend asked Bennie what he thought about living in the White House. Pierce's only son reportedly replied, "I don't know about going to live there at all. I would rather go out to live on a farm." As the family headed back home on January 6, the front axle of their railroad car broke outside Andover. The engine dragged the car for a distance down the rails, then the coupling between the engine and passenger car gave way. The Pierces' car spun violently sideways, ran off the track, and plunged down a twelve-foot embankment. As the passenger car first lurched, Pierce put his arms around his wife sitting next to him. He then bent forward to catch Bennie, who had been sitting in front on a side seat next to the door. At first thinking the boy unhurt, Pierce removed Bennie's cap only to discover that a sharp object had taken off the top of his son's head, exposing the brain and killing him instantly.[2]

Pierce's wife, who earlier had fainted upon hearing of her husband's nomination, went to pieces. Believing that God had taken Bennie so that the president-elect would have no distraction during his administration, she never recovered from the loss. Returning to Concord, Jane Pierce did not move to Washington until late 1853. She never attended White House dinners and spent a great deal of time dressed in black, grieving in private, and writing letters to her dead son. Pierce, crushed by the loss of Bennie and damning himself for his ambition, assumed the presidency with little enthusiasm and diminished confidence. His inauguration was less than auspicious. Vice-President-elect William R. King, dying of tuberculosis in Cuba, took the oath of office there. He was dead in three months. Pierce, wary of God's wrath, affirmed rather than swore to uphold the Constitution.[3] Never forceful, always seeking approbation, and often given to moodiness, President Pierce now had to overcome the rampant factionalism within his party and end the Democracy's drift in a sea of voter apathy. Worse, in less than a year, a disgruntled party rival would confront the amiable and sometimes besotted Pierce with the most serious challenge to his presidency, the Democracy, and the Union.

On the surface, the years between the passage of the Compromise of 1850 and Pierce's election appear to have been a period of stability. The territorial and statehood bills, to be sure, removed all the outstanding territorial issues from Congress. But sectional hostilities clearly did not go away. Worse perhaps for the Jacksonian political system, the desire of the wings of the two parties to get on the right side of the finality issue furthered, rather than retarded, the process of sectionalization and fragmentation. As early as October 1850, a Maryland observer wrote, "The divisions between the two parties now are . . . merely artificial & for the most part personal." Six months later, as the corrosive debate over finality, southern rights, northern recreancy, resistance, submission, and agitation continued to eat away at the bonds of the Democracy and Whiggery, a North Carolina Whig ruefully concluded that "there is but little party feeling manifested as between the old parties."[4]

Amid the ongoing fragmentation of the Jacksonian political system and in the absence of effective presidential leadership, Stephen A. Douglas took it upon himself to reassert his party's basic tenets and, in the bargain, reinvigorate the Democracy. He combined westward expansion, internal improvements, and popular sovereignty into a program that issued in the Kansas-Nebraska Act. Nearly all extant interpretations of the Civil War emphasize the effect of Douglas's initiative on the growth of sectionalism and, concomitantly, the disruption of the Jacksonian political system. By focusing on the bill's origin and authorship, however, the literature often ignores its intent. The tendency has been to dismiss the fundamental axioms upon which Douglas operated. A closer look at the bill's essence as it bore meaning in his mind shows why he and other supporters of the Nebraska bill believed it necessary, or rational, to pursue this course of action. Simply put, self-government, or popular sovereignty, a principle they believed had been embodied in the compromise, ratified by Pierce's overwhelming victory, and seemed to be working in Utah and New Mexico, was to be ridden by Douglas and the party to new heights of personal and national glory.

"The slavery agitation I hope is now and forever put to rest," wrote William Marcy in the fall of 1850. Like millions of Americans, Marcy was heartily tired of the sectional acrimony that had grown steadily since 1846. He, like they, "rejoiced . . . that the agitating & dangerous questions were settled, without saying they were settled in the best possible way." Whatever his reservations, Marcy wished that the compromise would "be regarded as a finality." Marcy was far too astute a politician, however, to believe that the territorial crisis of 1848–50 would recede without leaving its impression on the political landscape. In the privacy of his diary, he considered the effect of the compromise on the old party organizations. The Whigs (née Federalists, as Marcy had it) had generally been out of power since 1801. Their few successes had been the result of accidental causes. As unscrupulous men, he asserted, they naturally resorted to expedients to sustain the party and occasionally to prevail over their opponents. Lately, the disorganized condition of the Democracy brought on by the machinations of Martin Van Buren offered the Whigs an opportunity. "The Whigs greatly rejoiced at our divisions as well they might for they reaped a rich harvest by it," Marcy contended. "Slavery agitation was just the thing that scheming politicians thought a source of popularity." Determined to avail themselves of this hobby, northern Whigs "labored to their utmost to prevent the settlement of the disturbing questions which had arisen on the subject." Arrayed against them, Democrats and a large minority of Whigs eventually prevailed, and the compromise bills were passed. The settlement, Marcy observed, "is generally well received by the Democratic party in the free states where the attempt to organize a free soil party had failed; but it is likely to lay the foundation of a serious division among the Whigs."[5]

If, as we shall see, Marcy misconstrued the effect of the compromise on his party, he did gauge well the difficulties of the Whigs. President Fillmore in his message to Congress in December 1850 proclaimed the measures "final and irrevocable" and recommended that the legislation be regarded as "a final settlement" of the territorial issue. Antislavery Whigs contemptuously rejected the president's advice. They charged that the administration and its supporters "propose[d] to walk away from the main body of the Whig party, simply exchanging the Whig principles of non-extension and non-aggression of slavery for a new cookoo [sic] song of 'Union and the Constitution' re-arranged and set to music by a few restless and uneasy politicians." The truth, Horace Mann declared, is that "the Slave Power of the South & the Money Power of the North have struck hands." Dismayed by the subversion of principle by self-interest, these dissidents were positively disgusted by popular support for the compromise. "Really there is something painful in the contemplation of the willingness of our people to be humbugged," Hamilton Fish snorted. "But so long as the people like it, it will be done."[6]

If the compromise was a humbug, the idea of finality was a seditious fraud. "The whole battle against slavery is yet before us," a Vermont free-soiler warned. "The past has witnessed only skirmishes. And yet the antislavery men are subsiding, like children, overcome with sleep, into a drowsy indifference to the portents of the future." Antislavery activists despaired that the easy habits of established party affiliations would pave the way for more craven compromises. "There never was so much need of contending against the slave power as now," Mann declared. "We must see that we have Congresses that will stand their ground; & therefore the antislavery principle must not be suffered to sleep."[7]

The more moderate Edward Everett countered that continuing antislavery agitation "tends to disunion, civil war, & a murderous struggle between the races," whereas strict adherence to the measures "until time has softened the asperities of feeling, which formerly influenced the minds of the Extremes of our country, will tend more to the preservation of our Constitutional Union, than any other course of conduct." Equally disdainful of free-soil agitators and states'-rights demagogues, Whig moderates looked askance at extremist attacks that "would rend asunder the bonds of union which have hitherto raised us to an unprecedented state of prosperity, and set at naught the Constitution and laws on which our Fathers laid the foundations of the Republic." Webster reminded those opposed to the compromise that "we have grown, flourished, and prospered under [the Constitution], with a degree of rapidity, unequalled in the history of the World. . . . Are we of this generation," he added, "so derelict, have so little of the blood of our revolutionary fathers coursing through our veins, that we cannot preserve what they achieved?" Finality, another New Englander agreed, was the platform upon which all Whigs could—and must—unite.[8]

Southern Whigs thought some planks of the compromise platform were weak; others were rotten. Yet these Whigs, too, embraced the settlement. Many expressed confidence in northern good faith. The intrinsic merits of each provision were less important to southern Whigs than the fact that their passage gave hope for an end to sectional hostilities. "The crisis thro' which we have passed has been a most trying and painful one," William Cabell Rives remarked. "There is one development which has resulted from the late crisis that is, in itself, a compensation for all the painful agitations. . . . It is the strong & unshaken attachment it has disclosed in the body of the people almost everywhere to the Union."[9] More to the point, Whigs would realize the promise of the party's victory in 1848: adjustment would leave the South in peace.

For all the talk about finality, quiescence, and sectional goodwill, southern Whigs never lessened their commitment to southern rights. Indeed, many viewed the compromise measures as a vindication of those rights. Robert Toombs of Georgia, for example, believed that the territorial bills for Utah and New Mexico "contained all [the South] did demand; and I supported them in conformity with the deliberate and frequently expressed opinions of an overwhelming majority of the people of the South." Unionists pointed out that the bills had gone further to support southern rights than merely defeating the Wilmot Proviso: they had clearly recognized the principles of noninterference and self-determination. A North Carolina Whig even took solace that the admission of California as a free state meant that "this is the doctrine contended for by those who opposed the Missouri restriction—this is the only safe doctrine of the South. . . . It is what Southern Statesmen have always contended for."[10]

By taking the "southern rights with peace" ground, as one historian has put it, slave-state Whigs outflanked the more intransigent Democratic states'-rights advocates (whom they portrayed as cryptosecessionists) and thus were able to sustain themselves throughout the South. The viability of the national organization was another matter, however. The internecine struggles of the preceding two years left many southern Whigs embittered toward the northern wing of the party—and not a little vindictive. "Seward and his faction, are disposed to apparent peace, and are secretly asking for quarter," a North Carolina Whig wrote. "I think we should not be content with that, although they are observing a cowardly silence, but should eject them, from place, and strip them of the influence of office." Repeated attempts in Congress to endorse the compromise as a finality (which had worked so well for Whigs within the South) failed to unite the party. Rather, their cumulative effect exacerbated the tensions between the party's two wings. The party looked toward the 1852 election with dimming hopes. "There will be no national Whig convention," Alexander Stephens predicted. "And I trust there will be no Whig organization kept up." [11]

Despite Marcy's sanguine assessment, the Democracy fared only somewhat better than the Whigs in 1851–52. Here, too, sectionalization and disorganization within the ranks were evident. Many slave-state Democrats "look[ed] with distrust on the compromise as too facile on the subject of southern rights. They feel as if their rights had been sacrificed, from indifference [*sic*] in some and for the want of a better firmness in others." The South, one alarmed Virginian contended, instead of meeting the free-soil challenge in a firm and fearless maintenance of the southern rights position, had saved nothing but its skin. "Our former greatness; our former hatred of oppression and wrong . . . is *all* gone. We not only acquiesce but glory in our degradation." Albert Gallatin Brown asserted that in reality the best friend of the Union "is he who stands boldly up and demands equal justice for every state and for all sections." [12]

In particular, southern Democrats thought the admission of California to be a "wrong & a great fraud on the South." The greatest violation of the Constitution, Langdon Cheves explained, was "to employ the use of its forms to violate its spirit. . . . The admission of California was expressly with a view to destroy [slave] property in the territory; and to make it instrumental in destroying slavery within all the States." Nor did the territorial bills offer the South hope. Jefferson Davis informed his Mississippi constituents that Congress's refusal to repeal the Mexican laws excluding slavery effectively deprived southerners of their territory. "It was dedicated to free-soil," he asserted. What had been gained? Precious little, these Locos declared. "Give me my negro fugitive, & I will allow you to kick me out of my own domain, [and] to tell me to stand aside, for 'I am holier than thou.' . . . Can degradation go further?" [13] Some believed it could.

One Mississippian declared that "the question that absorbs all others . . . is 'Union or Disunion.'" A careful observer would have known better. The extreme states'-rights ranks divided between those who advocated separate state action on secession and others who sought to defer action in the hope of cooperating with other secessionist states later. Still other southern rights Democrats contended that disunion and violence posed greater threats to the South than did northern hostility. They advocated less drastic remedies such as the development of southern manufacturing and economic nonintercourse with the free states. A larger number of moderate Democrats North and South were willing to trust in each other and, even more, in the healing effects of the compromise. "In the repudiation of the Wilmot Proviso, and the enforcement of the Constitutional obligation to deliver up fugitive slaves," Georgia's Howell Cobb asserted, "the North have given practical evidence of their intention to stand, in good faith, by the Constitutional Union of their fathers—recognizing and enforcing all the rights guaranteed by that solemn compact to their brethren of the South." Realizing that the compromise was "a hard measure for the South," James Buchanan advised Democrats throughout the nation to "yield it a generous support, upon the principle that however it may be regarded in either quarter, it would be suicidal to jeopard our blessed Union for such a cause & for measures, in their nature, irrevocable."[14]

As the integrity and coherence of parties became less distinct, the Fillmore administration and Congress found it increasingly difficult to hold a middle line or a national position on national affairs. The effect was that sectional conflict and recrimination cropped up at odd times and on peculiar issues. Territorial expansion, for example, which as a political issue had once helped define the parties, was now a complex and frustrating problem for Fillmore. Although dormant, manifest destiny was not dead. In particular, filibustering expeditions to Cuba in 1850 and 1851 led by Narciso López, a Venezuelan by birth, resuscitated the issue of territorial expansion. Taylor and, after his death, Fillmore attempted to suppress the filibustering efforts of the irrepressible López. Attacks from all quarters on the administrations' position were not long in coming. Fillmore's opposition to filibuster, argued one southern editor, had little to do with national honor and less with international comity. Contrasting Daniel Webster's defense of a filibustering expedition to Canada in 1838 with his silence on López, the *Arkansas Gazette* asserted that "the only evasion, that we can conceive of, of decisive and plain language is that Canada was FREE SOIL while Cuba is slaveholding country. 'Ay, there's the rub.'"[15]

Support for annexation in the South was less than López's enthusiasts believed, however. Filibustering was piracy and filibusters were dogs, William Brownlow exclaimed. Northerners, too, objected to López's antics. Yet, unlike Fillmore, they were less concerned with peace and honor than with the motives and character of the filibusters. López's supporters, a northern Democrat charged, were the "ignorant, conceited young men of the South, knowing little beyond their plantations and courthouses, and inflated through their habit of commanding Negroes with inordinate self importance." The idea that such a movement would extend the area of freedom was at best improbable, at worst immoral. The *Philadelphia Public Ledger*, once a leading advocate of expansion, sneered, "For this purpose they would invade Cuba, rescue it from that oppressive Spanish rule which looks forward to the extinction of slavery, and make it a bright star in the Southern Confederacy, brilliant with the lustre of that peculiar institution which secures universal freedom by interminable bondage."[16]

Objections to expansion generally reflected a diminished sense of national confidence and a sensitivity to residual sectional tensions. Looking inward, the *Ohio Statesman* argued that with Cuba "we get another chance to quarrel and wrangle about slavery, to the neglect of all the legitimate and pressing business of Congress." Many southerners, too, were genuinely glad that Spain had put down the filibusters. Whatever the value of Cuba, the *Columbus Enquirer* concluded, "for our own part we would not give ten years of peace and prosperity of this glorious country for ten such islands."[17] Although manifest destiny was not in eclipse, to a growing number of Americans in 1851 expansion no longer appeared to promote automatically the ideals of liberty and emancipation. Cuba, clearly, was not Texas; López was no Sam Houston. Caution and introspection began to overshadow the sense of boundlessness of the previous decade.

In a similar vein, whereas Americans saw in the European revolutions of 1848 the dawn of a political millennium, they were more tentative and divided when the Hungarian patriot Louis Kossuth visited the United States three years later. In 1842 Americans boomed that "the rotten and antiquated foundations of every despotic and exclusive institution of the Old World . . . only await a coming shock to crumble into ruin." Unhappily, the revolutions of 1848 degenerated into class struggles, spread socialism, and culminated in despotic repression. "Republics," concluded one New England author, "cannot grow on the soil of Europe; at least, not republics in the sense we give to that word. There is no nourishment for them in the present condition or past history of the nations there." Change ran uphill in the Old World, a Jacksonian Democrat sighed: "The disease of Europe is the unequal division of Property, the poverty of the masses; the excessive Taxation consequent on accumulated debts; and great hereditary establishments, all acting on a surplus population. No change in the form or spirit of Governments can cure these evils."[18]

True, the North and South received Citizen Kossuth enthusiastically.

European revolutionary movements, however, had lost much of their earlier attraction. John Bell asserted that revolutionary ultraisms "have brought obloquy upon the very name of republicanism throughout Europe." The central problem, as John Appleton of Maine saw it, was that European republicans advocated a wrongheaded progress that "like the fabled Phaeton, seizes the reins with passion, drives madly off the course, and nearly ingulfs the world in darkness."[19]

Appleton's criticism spoke to an anxiety felt by many Americans that the "*bloomerism* of politics" that plagued Europe now infected the body politic of the United States. A Maine Democrat, for instance, decried "Freesoilerism, Federalism, Temperance, and all the other isms that have tended to operate against the stability of our institutions." A Georgia Whig feared that "new ideas of republican government are sought to be infused in the minds of our people by the teachings of European revolutionists." Already there were "the Mormon . . . and Mrs. Bloomer . . . the 'spiritual rappers' and 'the harmonial circles' who profess to hold communion with the dead . . . women's rights conventions, peace congresses, and republicans, fourierites, grahamites, anti renters, strikers, female doctors, prize fighters, communists, screamers and heaven knows what, not to mention the Millerites who are determining by arithmetic when the world and its mad men and women will be burnt up." In fact, another Georgian predicted, should the conservative Washington be called from his grave (presumably through the efforts of a harmonial circle), "thousands of men and women . . . would vote him the most unmitigated humbug on earth. . . . They would consider him simply as a curious specimen of antiquity."[20]

Southerners, in particular, watched with alarm attempts by free-soilers to exploit the message and propaganda value of Kossuth. To some, the man might have possessed "the purity of a Washington, the sagacity of Jefferson." Others, having discovered ruefully that the late Zachary Taylor fell a great deal short of those pristine ideals, refused to be deceived so quickly again. William Brownlow, still raw over the Taylor fraud, grunted that history would write Kossuth down "not among the Heroes, but rather among the *Humbugs*, of which the nineteenth century has been so prolific." With perhaps greater insight, William Dawson of Georgia contrasted Kossuth's visit with that of the Marquis de Lafayette in 1824. "Lafayette, when he came to this country," Dawson remarked, "was received in a manner which was justifiable on the part of the Government of that day, because he was connected with the Revolution which gave us the liberties we now enjoy." What connection, he asked contemptuously, did the magnificent Magyar have with our past or with the nation's republican institutions? The comparison was instructive. Dawson's disdain for ersatz heroes radiated a concern felt by many Americans in the

1850s that increasingly the nation was unable either to recapture the spirit or to agree on the essence of their Revolution. First engendered by the proviso debates and exacerbated by the territorial crisis, the fear now was that "in a very few years more not a link will remain of that magic chain which connects the present with the past era of our country." Taylor could not summon forth the spirit of Washington. Kossuth evoked no images of Lafayette.[21]

To be sure, neither Fillmore's refusal to wink at the antics of López nor Kossuth's failure to induce Congress to go to war with the Habsburgs constitutes anything like a watershed. The idea of any meaningful intervention in Europe, to say nothing of military adventurism, was the perihelion of Young American hyperbole. Expansion, as the 1852 campaign would presently indicate, still had political currency. Nevertheless, as the nation turned its attention to the coming canvass, it was distinctly less self-assured. The political vicissitudes and fragmentation that attended the compromise, a realization that the fruits of manifest destiny were hard to digest, and a growing sense of declension were all undercurrents that eroded the optimism of the 1840s. To many the cant of Young America seemed worn. And if Stephen Douglas and others still spoke of sustaining Democracy so as "to triumph upon its old issues," many northerners and southerners remained to be persuaded that the established positions that separated the parties were either viable or relevant.[22]

In February 1852, at the same moment when thousands of Cincinnatians were cheering Louis Kossuth, a worried southern Democrat remarked, "The country was never more unsettled than at present & there never was a time when we needed more a firmer and manly president who by a life time[']s service had [so] identified himself with Democratic Principles, that he would not be tempted to do some new or strange things of doubtful propriety to render him popular." Democrats were already groping their way toward principled consensus and, they hoped, to organizational coherence. One obstacle at least had been removed. The slavery issue that had alienated free-soilers and fire-eaters and strained relations among moderates was no longer an overtly divisive political question. Off-year congressional elections in 1850 and 1851 demonstrated the public's general acceptance of the compromise. Barnburners and southern rights Democrats, realizing the political dangers of resistance, straggled back into the party's ranks.[23]

Having avoided open disruption, the Democracy now skirted Unionist finality. As southern Whigs, Fillmore supporters, and slave-state Union Democrats pressed the question in Congress, moderate party members repudiated their maneuvers as "unwise, mischievous, and out of place." Noting that the country acquiesced in the compromise measures, Stephen Douglas charged correctly that inasmuch as the compromise was intended to remove the vexed question of slavery from politics, the finality men now were be-coming, ironically, sectional agitators. "I am heartily sick of the controversy," he claimed. John Floyd, a New York Democrat, assured friends of the com-promise in the House that slavery agitation could not be allayed "by making [finality] a political question, to be bandied by politicians, and to be deter-mined one way or the other, as may best suit the purposes of the hour, or to be made a fulcrum to hoist third-rate politicians into notice." Douglas simi-larly rejected the idea of a new party organized on that basis. "The Demo-cratic party is as good a Union party as I want," he averred.[24]

Turning their backs on finality, northern and southern Democrats wended their way to a common ground by a path that seems now obscured. Floyd of New York pointed the way. "If this cause [of sectional melioration] could be left to the great mass of Democratic voters," he told his House colleagues, "there would be one universal response: 'Pursue the plain, beaten path of safety and success—stake not the interests of a whole people on an issue of doubtful experiment—the principles of a national party like the Constitu-tion itself must be such as to embrace all, from the extreme North to the extreme South.'" The farther Floyd and his colleagues moved away from the territorial settlement of 1850, the less they focused on the legislation itself. From the vantage point of 1852, the compromise measures appeared to them to be an endorsement of established Democratic orthodoxy. That is, from their perspective the dynamic elements of the 1848–50 crisis were not pro- or antislavery as such but consolidation versus limited government. Douglas, the architect of the settlement, observed that "the necessity for confining the federal government clearly within the limits of its legitimate functions . . . and for a strict observance of every provision of our constituents—state and national—has never been rendered more manifest than by our recent ex-perience." A Florida Democrat reflecting on the territorial crisis asserted, "What does the history of the past three years prove, but that the might of the majority is to be the rule of right as soon as it can be sufficiently con-centrated." An Arkansas editor was compelled to remind a people who felt increasingly removed from their own political heritage that "under the doc-trine of consolidation by constructive usurpation, all virtue, all purity is lost. The government becomes wholly corrupt . . . and at length . . . degener-ates into a minister of vengeance and oppression against all who oppose and denounce its usurpations." In light of the excitement of the last three years, a northern Democrat concluded that "our safety lies . . . in administering our Government faithfully, according to the design of its founders and never permitting its accurate adjustment of powers to be disturbed."[25]

Moderate Democrats looked at the compromise in a way that Unionists did not. "The principles of the Democratic party are coeval with the existence of our Government, and . . . there is nothing to add, or subtract therefrom," Junius Hillyer of Georgia explained. Strict construction and states' rights "are the great principles of the party, and they induce the support of many distinct and separate *measures*." The specific measures of the Democracy, he pointed out, could not be coeval with its existence. What did Jefferson know of the subtreasury or Madison of the annexation of Texas? What did the Founding Fathers know of the organization of Utah and New Mexico? Yet, Hillyer observed, "these measures came upon the country, and it was necessary that the Democratic party should take action upon them. This is the true doctrine—that whenever a measure arises, national in its character, it is the duty of the Democratic party to take sides upon that measure in accordance *with its principles*, and to go wherever its principles carry it." The compromise is not entitled to be dignified by political creed, Maine's John Appleton chimed. "I concur with the gentleman from Georgia . . . that it is not even a political principle. It is only the fruit of certain old and established Democratic principles, applied to a serious exigency in affairs." Arthur P. Bagby of Alabama and a supporter of the compromise closed the circle. "Democratic principles, the Constitution and the Union must flourish and triumph together," he claimed, "or they must fall and perish together."[26]

By the eve of the canvass, the moderates' position had fully developed. Explicitly, consolidation of power, especially in the federal government, posed the greatest threat to individual liberty. The core of the Democracy's orthodoxy was strict construction of the Constitution and states' rights. The acquisition of territory in 1848—itself a function of party principles—raised for the first time since 1819 the question of congressional power over a local institution. The Compromise of 1850 reaffirmed a federal government of limited powers. Stated positively and simply, it endorsed the primacy of local autonomy. Because it embodied traditional principles, the legislation was not a finality or an end in itself: Congress applied fundamental axioms to an exigency. Democrats proclaimed—one would scarcely say they proved—that finality, if there was one, applied to the efficacy and vitality of the party's creed. To antislavery Whigs and to Unionists the logic was mixed. To the mind of a party out of power it was unanswerable. A southern rights Democrat assured Marcy that the present tenor of public opinion in the slave states was "to trust rather the *National Democratic party* than to the present Whig leaders at the North."[27] Hence Marcy and other moderates deduced that all the party need do in the coming canvass was to return to the broad ground of Jacksonian orthodoxy.

In the spring of 1852, Linn Boyd, Speaker of the House, proclaimed that there was no longer any danger of a dissolution of the Union. On the contrary, he declared, "the danger is, that, in the future, as in the past, each conflict involving the question of the 'Union' will but facilitate the constant accumulation & consolladation [*sic*] of its power at the expense of the States." Having reduced the crisis of 1850 to the familiar threat of centralization, office-hungry Democrats now turned on the avatars of consolidation. Andrew Jackson Donelson, editor of the *Washington Union*, informed revelers at a Democratic banquet that institutions built on any other foundation than local autonomy "*produce only centralization and despotism. Here lies the secret of our American liberty. . . . It is municipal freedom, local independence and States rights* which constitute the only safe democracy." Strong governments and the absence of municipal rights, argued another Democrat, "mean in Austria, *absolutism*—here it means *consolidation*. The old fashioned Democrat Republicans of 1798–'99 had been, and their successors are now, the saviors of public liberties and of the Union."[28]

As was their wont, Democrats again looked to expansion to preserve and extend liberty. In the bargain, they hoped to make issue with the Whigs. Party members blistered the Taylor and Fillmore administrations for neglecting the diplomacy of annexation. The corpulent Lewis Cass, who in the throes of enthusiasm would tear off his collar, coat, and vest and harangue audiences in his shirtsleeves, found other, more tasteful ways of demonstrating that he was not an old fogey. Cass maintained that just as the Democracy's principles had been coeval with the Union, every expansion of national boundaries that gave substance to those tenets had been made by men and measures of the party. Following Cass's polemical lead, Stephen Douglas reminded listeners that each addition of territory was "strenuously opposed by our political opponents on principle—they taking the ground distinctly that our territory is already too large for any one system of government." Nathaniel P. Banks dredged up one of the better-known Democratic chestnuts when he told a Philadelphia audience, "We are now, almost for the first time, standing at that point of our history, where we may witness beyond our own borders, a universal recognition of the ennobling theories of the Declaration, and of the possibility of perpetuating free institutions upon that basis. We no longer have doubts of its expansive power."[29]

While Democrats tried to achieve harmony with well-known set pieces, Whigs blended the counterpoints of the compromise and sectional agitation into a dismal coda for the party. Throughout 1851 and 1852, southern Whigs continued to press the northern wing for a blanket endorsement of the compromise. North Carolina's David Outlaw suggested that free-state support for the measures would "make the Whig party a national and conservative party, and keep it . . . upon principles broad enough, and upon a basis comprehensive enough, to embrace every portion of this great republic, and the interests of every portion." Alexander Stephens added that party members must reconstruct their organization on sound American constitutional principles; it must become "a party that shall drive from its ranks every man tainted with Abolition or 'higher law' heresies—a party formed upon those controlling issues which present the paramount questions of the day."[30]

Unhappily, free-state support of Winfield Scott's candidacy in 1852 confirmed the party's bankruptcy to most southern Whigs. Having just supported one man-above-faction candidate, slave-state party members, sadder and wiser, decided not to tie their fortunes to another nonentity. "As he now stands before the country," William Brownlow hooted, "he is the man of all men, for rallying under a common standard, all the fragments, all the shades and stripes, of Anti-Slavery and Native-Americanism in the North." Worse, unlike Fillmore, who had signed and endorsed the compromise, Scott maintained a cagey silence on finality. In fairness, Old Fuss and Feathers had few options in a party so deeply riven. To southerners, however, his reticence spoke to efforts by antislavery Whigs to capture control of the party to make it work for a "higher law." Christopher Williams, a Tennessee Whig, taunted northern party members, "Is there a cheat in contemplation? Do you intend a fraud? Which section is to be cheated—the North or the South? How is this? Frankness, candor, courage—moral courage as well as physical courage—are the attributes of a noble hero! How can he remain silent *under existing circumstances*? How can he repress his patriotic impulses?"[31]

In arguments strikingly similar to those made during the territorial crisis, southern Whigs contended that they constituted "a very decided minority of their party in this Union; that its true power and acknowledged strength lies in the North; and that it is to the sentiments of Northern Whigs we can alone look for a true exposition of that policy which must give tone and character to the Whig party of the Union." When, therefore, antislavery Whigs decided "to leave the Compromise question open for future agitation," the beleaguered minority became determined "to either nominate a person openly and avowedly in favor of the Compromise, or to pass a resolution acquiescing in it as a measure of the Whig creed."[32] Increasingly, slave-state Whigs looked to the latter. Finality was, in the first place, good politics; it was also more. Southerners knew that minority rights in the party, as well as the Union, would be abridged unless there was an expressed recognition of constitutional guarantees.

Antislavery Whigs bristled at what appeared to be another self-serving demand made by arrogant slaveholders. Truman Smith, one of the Young Indian architects of the Taylor campaign, informed a southern colleague that, in the North, party members "are willing to put forward the old Whig issues—on them we stand a chance to beat our opponents but on the plan of these hot heads, *never!*" Wishing the whole territorial question "to sink quietly & forever into oblivion," northern Whigs thought that "the South should take Scott as he is without sectional pledges." They apprehended that southern Whigs opposed Scott "because he is not sectionalized—not pledged to interpose the Arm of the Executive influence in *their* favor should legislation come. The objection in fact is because he is *national* as well as *Whig*. They would unWhig the Whig party." By the eve of the convention, even moderates such as John Davis had concluded that the party's southern wing "cannot be restored to common sense."[33]

Acrimony and distrust boded ill for Whiggery. Slave-state members insisted that the platform be drafted before the nomination and that convention delegates endorse the compromise as a final settlement, "in principle and sentiment." It was, and it did. Scott was then nominated on the fifty-third ballot, receiving 142 northern and only 17 slave-state votes. If each wing was aware of, but insensitive to, the political difficulties of its erstwhile ally, even the most obtuse knew that "the limits of the Whig party must not be divided by a geographical line, but must be coextensive with the bounds of the Union, or the party is not worth preserving." Scott's grudging and muted support of the platform served only to worsen the party's split. Feeling that a tyrannical majority had imposed a sectional candidate on them, southern men huffed that they were not "satisfied . . . that the influences which surround the nominee of the Whig party are in unison with the principles for which we contend—principles above and beyond party ties. We *are* satisfied that those principles would be better secured by the success of the nominee of the Democratic party." With that Parthian shot, nine southern congressmen, including the Young Indians Stephens and Toombs, fled the party. During the canvass, other prominent renegades like Brownlow, Waddy Thompson, and Kenneth Rayner followed them into opposition. Meanwhile, antislavery Whigs who found the platform unpalatable trooped off to join unrepentant Democrats in support of the Free-Soil candidate, John Parker Hale.[34]

Despite the sectional rift within the Whig Party and the loose talk by Locos about Young America, the 1852 canvass, in significant ways, conjured up images of earlier campaigns. Having hitched municipal freedom and individual liberty to the star of expansion, Democrats now needed a president who would drive "the chariot of the sun, so as to give light to all the earth." Although no Helios, Franklin Pierce was another Young Hickory. And like Polk, he was a dark-horse candidate with sound principles and a minimum of enemies. For their part, Whigs—the faithful and the lapsed—saw their fears of 1848 materialize: Democrats coupled popular sovereignty to an aggressive foreign policy. Democrats were again plotting unlimited expansion.[35]

Nonetheless, the 1852 campaign differed markedly from both the 1844 and 1848 races. In 1844, expansion helped save a divided party. In 1852, anticonsolidation (or rather federate freedom) and expansion could not paper over all the cracks that had appeared in the Democracy. Tension between "hards" and "softs" in the North and states'-rights advocates and Unionists in the South continued to plague the party. Indeed, factionalism in New York was so pronounced that campaign contributions dried up; the party there was forced to borrow its way through the canvass. Managers in both parties found public enthusiasm at a low ebb. Traditional economic issues, like the bank and the tariff, had lost much of their salience. On others, such as internal improvements, a large portion of the Democratic Party, in particular Young Americans, occupied a position similar to that of the Whigs. Spread-eagle foreign policy, although colorful, rang hollow. Both major parties were committed to the compromise with varying degrees of enthusiasm; slavery as a political issue was for the moment dead. In some desperation, northern Whigs flirted with nativism as a fillip for the party's fortunes, only to see their situation made worse.[36]

Retrospective voting analysis has confirmed what contemporaries only sensed: the malaise of the Jacksonian party system. True, the total vote was higher than in 1848, and no one could deny that Pierce had won a great victory in the electoral college. The popular vote tells another, more ominous story. Factionalism still weakened the Democracy. Of 3 million votes cast, Pierce's advantage was 53,190 or 1.6 percent. Even in the South, Democrats gained only 35,000 votes and over three-quarters (or 27,000 voters) of these came from Virginia's expanded electorate. The Whig vote in the Northeast declined, but the party increased its totals in the Midwest. Most significant, as measured against the number of eligible voters, turnout sank to its lowest level since 1836. Not until 1904 would the percentage of turnout again be as low. Despite rapid population growth, turnout dropped absolutely in some states. Between 1848 and 1852, nonvoters rose from 33 to 64 percent in Alabama, from 11 to 54 percent in Mississippi, and from 51 to 54 percent in Louisiana. In the Old Northwest, the Democratic vote in 1852 declined by one-sixth from 1848, the Whig by one-eleventh, and the Free-Soil by nearly 50 percent.[37]

Burdened by his fecklessness and distracted by his son's death, Pierce could resuscitate neither Democratic unity nor public support. The president at first tried to use the glue of patronage and cabinet appointments to cement the party's cracks. Trying to placate all factions, Pierce pleased none. The president, observed one southerner, "seems to have determined to avow and act upon the principles of the Compromise Union men, and distribute the patronage among the fire-eaters and free-soilers." An unpopular administration found itself unable to impose discipline upon the party. A Connecticut Democrat lamented, "There is not that healthy state of feeling here that I wish there was—there is not that eagerness to defend the Administration policy which is so necessary to Administration success." Equally disquieting to moderates was that in a period of social change, economic prosperity, and sectional quiescence, traditional lines of party division were blurred. "We lack . . . for issues," Democrats worried, "the real grounds of difference upon important political questions no longer correspond with party lines. The progressive Whig is nearer in sentiment to the radical Democrat than the radical Democrat is to the 'fogy' of his own party; *vice versa*." Americans increasingly viewed their parties with skepticism. Apathy and alienation were the result. Voter turnout continued to decrease in state and local elections in 1853.[38]

Despite (or, more accurately, because of) Democratic dominance in the Thirty-third Congress, party activism and solidarity were at a low ebb. At the opening of the first session, Stephen Douglas concluded that the Democracy was "in a distracted condition & it requires all our wisdom, freedom & energy to consolidate its power and perpetuate its principles." The rank and file condemned Pierce's "hesitancy, timidity, [and] irresolution." They warned that unless the president "marks out a sound line of national policy, and makes it known to the country by unmistakable *action*," the administration was headed toward "total failure."[39]

In the absence of effective presidential leadership, Douglas and other congressional Democrats took it upon themselves to reassert party orthodoxy and, they trusted, to revivify the Democracy. As early as 1844, Douglas had expressed a desire to organize that area of the Louisiana Purchase west of Iowa and Missouri. A decade later, rising foreign immigration and westward migration increased the pressure on Congress to provide for an orderly settlement of the territory. To that end, Senator Augustus Dodge of Iowa introduced a bill in December 1853 to organize the Nebraska territory.[40]

Douglas, chairman of the Senate's Committee on Territories, thus was presented with an opportunity and a challenge. As a leader of an emerging group within the Democratic Party that stressed both expansion and internal improvements, he naturally would champion the organization, surveying, and development of new territories. As a railroad booster, he considered personal gain. By seizing the initiative from Pierce, Douglas could settle old scores with a president who had ignored him and his supporters. Above all, if he could gain southern support for a Nebraska bill and at the same time make issue with the consolidationist Whigs, Douglas would be the progenitor of a program that would restore order to the Democracy, slay the chimera of Unionist Whiggery, and ensure his own ascendancy.

Douglas accordingly reported his Nebraska bill to the Senate on January 4, 1854. It was a vastly different bill than that presented by Dodge. Douglas's measure greatly increased the size of the territory to be organized to encompass the entire unorganized area of the Louisiana Purchase from north of 36°30' to the Canadian border. Furthermore and most critically, despite the Missouri Compromise's ban on slavery in the Louisiana Purchase (of which the Nebraska territory was a part), states eventually formed out of the territory could allow or prohibit slavery as they wished.[41]

Supporters of Douglas's Nebraska bill defended it as a measure that would check the drift toward the consolidation of power in the general government. "Our chief source of safety is found in the doctrine of the inviolability of states rights," an Illinois editor declared. "When these shall be successfully invaded we may look for the obliteration of state boundaries, speedy consolidation and an ultimate destruction of our beautiful and almost perfect system of government." What, however, did states' rights have to do with the Nebraska Territory? "All that we enjoy as a state, we should concede to others, and what the states enjoy they should be willing to confer also on the territories," he rejoined, "there should be no partiality." Contending that Douglas's plan "carries out the Democratic principle to its fullest extent," the *Missouri Republican* warned its readers that if Congress had the power either to dictate the terms on which a state might enter the Union or to prescribe and proscribe local institutions for the territories, "pray tell us where that power begins and where it is to end?"[42]

Iowa's Dodge then dropped the other shoe. Those who attack the bill, he asserted, "I cannot but regard as federalists or monarchists at heart. . . . Never was there a question which revived more thoroughly the distinctive differences between federalism and democracy, State rights and consolidation, than does the 'Nebraska-Kansas' bill." Representative Willis Allen mocked the faithlessness of the opposition. "Do they doubt the intelligence of the people? Do they doubt that they are competent to decide what is best for their own interests? . . . The truth is, these gentlemen are afraid of the people, and so are the party to which they belong." If the popular will cannot be trusted, the *Cleveland Plain Dealer* clucked, "we might as well lapse into absolutism at once, and blot from our history our disastrous republican record."[43]

Nebraska Democrats hoped to mix expansion and local autonomy into an antidote for a party system afflicted with malaise. Popular sovereignty was in a way a homeopathic cure for a nation plagued by self-doubt and disillusion. Indiana's William English said of the prescription, "At last, sir, the great and vital question at issue is, whether the people of the Territories shall be left to settle for themselves the institutions under which they are to live; and even this question may be narrowed down to the isolated question whether a man, because he happens to live in a Territory, is less worthy of being trusted with all the rights and privileges of an American freeman than his more fortunate brother who happens to live in a State." Asserting that the people of the territories had as much intelligence, wisdom, and ability as the citizens of the states, Senator Richard Brodhead of Pennsylvania affirmed that the Nebraska bill was "based on the great principle which lays at the foundation of our Government, to wit: the right and the ability of the people to govern themselves."[44]

Of course, they knew well that the extension of slavery had done much to cause the disease. Trusting, however, in the underlying resilience and vigor of the patient, they asserted, "Who has a better right to settle this question than the hardy pioneer who subdues the wilderness and changes the forest into cultivated fields, who substitutes the neigh of the horse, and the bleating and lowing of the herds, for the howl of the wolf, the scream of the panther, and the growl of the more ferocious beasts of these western wilds." Proponents of the Nebraska bill called to those "who regard the welfare of the bold and fearless pioneer, not to shackle him with illiberal and oppressive laws, but let him go forth to the western wilds, in full dignity of his manhood, and the rich enjoyment of his freedom." To contend for anything less, they cried, was "to virtually deny the Republican doctrine of the sovereignty of the citizen, and his ability for self-government."[45]

Supporters of Douglas's measure believed this fundamental tenet had given shape and definition to the 1850 measures. The Nebraska bill was, therefore, in the view of its proponents, less an extension of those laws than a reaffirmation of their actuating principle. Edmund Burke, a New Hampshire Democrat, heartily endorsed Douglas's initiative, noting that the senator was "not disposed to treat the principles of the late Compromise Acts, as nullities, mere expedients to escape the peril of the moment." Like other supporters, Burke saw the underlying premises of the 1850 statehood and territorial bills "as practical things to be sacredly observed whenever occasions arise which demand their practical application." The Nebraska bill "assumes what cannot be controverted," the *Washington Union* stated flatly, "that the great principles of the compromise of 1850, so far as the question of slavery in the new territories is involved, was the recognition of the doctrine of congressional nonintervention." This being true, the *Union* deduced that "it must be apparent that its introduction into the Nebraska bill is no more than giving permanency and perpetuation to that compromise." In fact, added the *Richmond Enquirer*, the South accepted the compromise and pronounced it acceptable "because, in all future cases, it would lead to an easy and constitutional adjustment of the question of slavery; and for this reason it was called a *final adjustment of the whole issue of slavery in the territories.*"[46]

Although free-soilers gagged on this assertion, evidence suggests that the *Enquirer's* argument, if not wise, was credible. "Instead of being in opposition to the Baltimore platform, the Nebraska bill is in strict accordance with it,"

OF PEGASUS AND BELLEROPHON

the *Illinois State Register* contended. Douglas "embodied in his bill the known views and sentiments of this party, as expressed in the national convention and laid down in the national platform." A Tennessee Whig who supported Douglas's proposal had the audacity to scold anti-Nebraska Democrats who had argued that the settlement of 1850 had no bearing on the case at hand. "Did they imagine they would never be called upon to organize another Territory?" he scoffed. Another Whig convert argued that he construed finality only in one sense: the compromise "could not be a finality in any other sense than in that of an actual acknowledgment of the fundamental *principle* on which all our territorial governments should be organized," he declared. To say that these organizing principles applied solely to the territories of the cession, exclaimed John C. Breckinridge, was to reveal to the South and to the nation that they had gained "only a deceitful truce, a suspension of hostilities; the suppression of the symptom, not the eradication of the disease."[47]

Supporters of the Nebraska Act noted that the framers of the 1850 compromise considered and rejected the Missouri line. "It was not until the North, in repeated instances, had satisfied the South that the Missouri Compromise was not to be applied to Mexican acquisitions," one claimed, "that the South threw itself back on her original rights and insisted . . . that the principle of non intervention . . . should be carried out, and hence its application to Utah and New Mexico." Frederick Stanton, a Tennessee Democrat, developed the logic of this argument. To extend a geographical line or, more exactly, to extend slavery restriction south of it, "you mete out a different measure of freedom to the two communities; and in doing so, you disregard a fundamental principle of republican government, viz.: that which requires the law to be general and uniform, not partial and special."[48]

Popular sovereignty as it applied to Nebraska and Kansas, it followed, was a necessary but insufficient remedy. "Congress must learn & know that it is not her will but the will of the People, that must rule in this Government," an Indiana Democrat argued. "If our people are capable of Self-Government, I cannot see why they are not just as capable on the N[orth] as on the S[outh] of a certain line." Stanton now made the home thrust. "Sir, every consideration or consistency, uniformity, equality, constitutional obligation—all require that we should disregard the restriction of 1820, and remove it from our path, in the performance of our duty, in organizing any and every Territory of the United States."[49]

The most logical and persuasive argument to make for the repeal of the 36°30' line was that if it remained, popular sovereignty was meaningless. An often made but more vulnerable claim was that its abrogation "was intended to remove all room for doubt as to the true meaning and operation of the Compromise of 1850." Whatever the case, repeal had a deep resonance among southern political leaders. Archibald Dixon, who brought intense pressure to bear upon Douglas to amend the Nebraska bill to include the repeal of the Missouri line, asserted that restriction "tramples the great doctrine of equality of States and of citizens underfoot, and tears asunder the chart upon which the liberty of the people is written." Given the acrimony of the territorial debates and lingering sectional hostility, Henry Breckinridge observed that "if in passing bills to organize Nebraska and Kansas, Congress should refuse to abrogate or repeal it . . . the people of the South will feel with twofold keenness the mark of inferiority put on them in 1820." [50]

Denying that any practical abundance would accrue to slaveholders as the result of its repeal, southerners demanded an end to restriction "because a great principle is involved—and is there nothing in principle?" Repeal of the Missouri restriction was not to discriminate in the South's favor: it was to restore the slaveholding states to equality within the Union. Strike down the equality of the states, the *Charleston Mercury* stated, and "you have those who rule [northerners] against those are ruled [southerners]—imperial domination and a colonial subjection." Repeal of the Missouri restriction was more than a syllogistic quibble. Indeed, when the Nebraska bill was finally amended to include an explicit abrogation of the 36°30' line, it at once became something larger than even Douglas had first intended. "This is the last, final struggle between the sections of the Union," one southerner declared, "a struggle in which there will be no compromise, and in which there should be no compromise. The principles contained within this bill are just and correct within themselves, just to all sections of the Union." [51]

Despite all that came to pass, supporters of the amended bill viewed it as part of a larger, ongoing political process that was expanding the liberties of American citizens. "Every step we have taken is a step toward republican liberty in the government of the Territories," Indiana's Cyrus Dunham told the House. "The antiquated systems of the Old World have not yet been thoroughly eradicated, and will not be by this bill; yet it makes an onward stride to the accomplishment of that great object." [52] Without a doubt, Douglas and other key proponents of the bill were motivated by considerations of personal, financial, and partisan gain. Still, neither Douglas nor his southern allies wanted to exacerbate or make inexorable the rifts within the Democracy. Rather, they wished to return it to its original purpose. That is, they and others supported the Nebraska bill as a way to revitalize the Democracy's heritage, as they understood it, and thus viewed it as a means to allay the debilitating sectionalism that had grown since 1846.

Self-government, Douglas held, was "the principle in defense of which the battles of the revolution were fought. It is the principle to which all our free institutions owe their existence, and upon which our entire republican system rests." It was no accident that he and others dubbed the opposition "British Toryism." A Maine Democrat reminded the bill's opponents that "the sovereignty of the people, their right to rule in political affairs, was first proclaimed to the startled ears of the Old World by our own Declaration of Independence. The tenacity with which our forefathers clung to this doctrine is written in the blood and the carnage, the suffering and the self-denial of the American Revolution." The revolutionary fathers felt keenly the grievances of restriction; "they had been oppressed and trodden underfoot by British legislation without representation in Parliament." Now, Nebraska supporters asked, were their sons so recreant, so unmindful of that legacy that they would persist in a like wrong of restriction that might end "in consequences most disastrous to our common well-being, and the hopes of mankind?"[53]

Defense of individual liberties and of limited government did not end with the Revolution. As Douglas pointed out, these principles were "recognized and affirmed in the Constitution and bill of rights of every state in this Union as the cornerstone in the temple of our liberties." Hence the question as framed by the bill's supporters addressed the nature and character of the nation's polity. "If the Federal Government is sovereign," South Carolina's Lawrence Keitt posited, "then the Constitution is abdicated, and we are enslaved by an irresponsible public despotism." But if strict construction and states' rights were in accordance with the theory of American government, then it followed that "popular sovereignty . . . is to our political system what the Sun is to the universe."[54]

If it was democratic to let the people of the territories control their own lives, then popular sovereignty was "the true Democratic doctrine, and the only doctrine that can give all portions of the U[nited] S[tates] equal justice upon this question." Howell Cobb maintained that if Douglas's views offered in defense of the bill "did not reflect the feelings and principles of the national democracy—then I have not understood them." To reject the bill, to abandon the principle of self-determination, the *Mississippian* asserted, "would be to discard a cardinal article in the Democratic creed. Indeed, it would be rejecting the very cornerstone on which the superstructure rests. Without it, there could be no national organization." Northern Democrats, too, were quick to assure their constituents that the principles embedded in Douglas's bill were both conservative and correct. Nonintervention, a Hoosier Democrat explained, "is no interpolation upon the Democratic creed. In one shape or another, it is as old as the creed itself." The aggrandizement of federal power and strict construction, he claimed, "was the leading division between the Federal and Republican parties, is to some extent an issue between the parties of the present day, and is certainly involved in the bill now under consideration." Put simply, the Nebraska bill was "the old square toed democratic platform upon which all true democrats have always stood & *must continue to stand*."[55]

Thus the issue Nebraskaites hoped to make with the bill's opponents was not slavery extension versus slavery restriction but a more familiar one. A Pennsylvania Democrat charged, "There has been that steady, unyielding determination on the part of the minority in Congress generally to resist everything which looks toward the establishment of Territories, the erection of new States, or the extension of the area of freedom. We meet the same determination here in the bill that has been reported in this Congress." William Marcy had pointed out four years earlier that these higher-law advocates often stooped to specious expedients like slavery agitation to sustain themselves. Now Douglas and others moved to neutralize such tactics. Missouri's Samuel Treat contended that Federalists first raised slavery restriction "as a mere pretext to resuscitate themselves politically." Treat added that it was telling that the same illegitimate dogma had been "blazoned on every Free Soil banner during the last six or seven years." What Whiggery really opposed, the *Pittsburgh Morning Post* insinuated, was not the loss of free territory but the loss of their hobby. "Pass the bill," Maine's Moses McDonald advised the House; "give the people of the Territories the right to determine for themselves the question, whether they will tolerate slavery or not, and the question becomes local. No longer will there be any inducements, and most certainly no propriety, in discussing the question at the North, or in non-slaveholding communities."[56]

Looking toward a brighter future, a young Kentucky farmer gave voice to the tested axioms that he believed lay at the heart of Douglas's policy. Writing to Senator Breckinridge in support of the Nebraska bill, he observed that "the Democratic party is founded upon the sole ground of truth and reason. It speaks to the honesty and intelligence of mankind." He asserted that the party's principles, embracing the inestimable republican heritage of the Revolution, had ever looked to the elevation of mankind. "It is these facts," the young man concluded hopefully, "that render [the Democracy's principles] so congenial to the feelings of a republican people causing them to spread in every direction, and evidencing to the world that they are best adopted to the welfare of mankind and the maintenance of a free and enlightened government."[57]

The ferocity of the free-soil attack on the Nebraska bill suggests the extent to which this romantic vision, which had given force and meaning to expansionism in the 1840s, had become eclipsed by the slavery extension issue in the 1850s. Opponents first charged that the ostensible motive for organizing Kansas and Nebraska was a deception. There were lands aplenty in existing states and territories suitable for settlement. Antislavery critics, however, did accept the assertion that the Nebraska bill was a Democratic measure and a test of party orthodoxy. But what a heresy it now embraced. "To spread and extend slavery, enlarge its borders, to increase its power, to remove all obstacles in the way of its onward march, is the modern test of Democracy," Representative Aaron Harlan declared. "The barricades and bars heretofore erected to obstruct the progress of slavery are to be broken down, and a great highway is to be opened up to facilitate its progress by the passage of this bill." [58]

Individuals who lied about their motives and beliefs were liable to spread other self-serving falsehoods as well. A northern Democrat contended that the legislative history of territorial organization proved "the individuality, the exclusiveness of each, and everyone of these slavery compromises—that they were never dependent one upon the other." Taking direct aim on Douglas, he fired: "The legislation of 1850 embodied no principle. It was an expedient." Curiously, other opponents of slavery extension took a very different view of the 1850 measures but came to the same condemnatory conclusion. "The compromise measures of 1850 were not destructive," one publicist argued, "they constituted a new bond, a new *compact*, in its moral force between the free and the slave states." New York's John Dix pointed out in agreement that the essence of the compact for the North was repose from slavery agitation. "The Nebraska bill violates this understanding and disturbs this repose," he charged. Noninterference, therefore, applied solely to the territories of the Mexican cession; the Missouri restriction related exclusively to the Louisiana Purchase. The claim that one superseded the other, cried a northern editor, was "the hellish spawn of demagoguism and partisanship." [59]

For nearly thirty years, opponents of the Democracy had argued that demagoguery had been the coin of the Loco realm. Demagogic pandering in this case took the form of that greatest of humbugs, popular sovereignty. It was, to antislavery Democrats and Whigs, at once an absurdity and a frightfully dangerous policy. "This idea of 'squatter sovereignty' is a burlesque on our whole system of states rights and state sovereignty," Gideon Welles complained. Charles Upham, a Massachusetts Whig, declared that the people of Kansas and Nebraska "are to be kept under the imperial hand of the Executive. He is to appoint by the advice and consent of the Senate acting as his privy council, their governors, judges, marshals, and other officers." Completing this line of argument, the *Albany Evening Journal* asserted that the sovereignty embodied in Douglas's bill was a swindle. "In this particular there is no more 'popular sovereignty' in that bill than was conceded to this government in the days of its colonial dependence," the *Journal* declared. "The 'Home Government' holds the veto power in its own hands. . . . Kansas and Nebraska . . . are mere dependencies." [60]

Paradoxically, free-soilers, fearing the extension of slavery, also protested that squatter sovereignty left the settlers with too little direction. At the very least, Douglas's bill placed "slavery and freedom on equal terms, and proclaims that freedom and oppression are looked on with equal favor by the people of the United States." Giving voice to his long-held prejudices and, as well, to the caution and doubts of the new decade, Edward Everett was unwilling to trust in the wisdom of those settlers. Slavery, quite simply, was too portentous an issue to be left to the people. Anti-Nebraska legislators denied—derided—the argument that natural obstacles would bar slavery from the territories. Nor, they concluded, could settlers there keep it out. A Massachusetts Whig, neatly skewering his strict-constructionist opponents with their own principles, informed his House colleagues, "The argument denies the right of Congress to prohibit slavery in the Territories, and of course it follows that if Congress has not the power to prohibit slavery from being carried into a Territory, it cannot confer upon a Territorial legislature the power to prohibit it." The real right of self-government recognized in the Nebraska bill, ventured an Ohio Whig, was "the power to establish the despotism of slavery."[61]

To the minds of free-soilers, then, the bill's pretense of popular sovereignty was worse than a "palpable cheat." It was to be the means by which slavery would be engrafted on the territories. In the race to control the territories, they predicted, the slaveholders from Missouri and adjacent slave states would be the first into the area. It mattered little how many, for, as anti-Nebraska dissidents repeatedly pointed out, "the effect of slave labor is always to cheapen, degrade, and exclude free labor." Nor did slaveholders need to come in large numbers to seize control of the territorial government. A beachhead—an opening—was all that slaveholders needed. "It is because Slavery can be carried into Nebraska, and because it *will be* carried there," the *Albany Evening Journal* cautioned, "that the advocates of that Institution so tenaciously insist upon [the bill's] enactment." Believing that, as Preston King explained, "the character of the Territories will certainly determine the character of the State," antislavery northerners resigned themselves to a renewed contest, initiated by the South, "for the ascendancy of slavery over freedom."[62]

Slaveholders had denied this, of course. Free-soilers, however, knew that truth was often a stranger to conspirators. "Why do they then so earnestly and consistently strive to break down the barriers to the progress of Slavery?" they asked. The answer was as clear as the plotters were odious. "The slaveholding states desire to secure for themselves an absolute ascendancy in the Federal Councils, so that they can shape all the legislation of the country, and make it subservient to the interests of Slavery instead of freedom." This latest aggression, according to one Hoosier Democrat, was part of an alarmingly familiar pattern. As he and other free-soilers placed the Nebraska bill in the context of events stretching back a decade, they came to an unpleasant but inevitable conclusion. The Nebraska bill, they argued, was only "one of a series of measures. Slavery is being nationalized—existing everywhere except where prohibited by State laws."[63]

The tragic and telling irony of the Nebraska bill is that both its supporters and detractors saw the abrogation of the Missouri line as a corollary to popular sovereignty. To slave-state Democrats and Douglas's northern supporters, it meant the elimination of an invidious measure that for more than thirty years had denied the South both its constitutional rights and its equality within the Union. It symbolized, therefore, the beginning of a kind of sectional restoration and, adventitiously, a return to the animating premises of the Constitution. To antislavery northerners, its repeal represented something else. "We arraign this bill as a gross violation of a sacred pledge," free-soil Democrats charged, and "as a criminal betrayal of precious rights; as part and parcel of an atrocious plot to exclude from a vast unoccupied region, immigrants from the old world and free laborers from our own states, and convert it into a dreary region of despotism, inhabited by masters and slaves." Contrary to Douglas's expectations and southern hopes, the Nebraska bill symbolized to a growing number of northerners a marked acceleration in the deterioration of free government. "The land marks of Freedom planted in 1820 are taken up in 1854," they mourned, "this is 'progress'—& this is '*modern* democracy.' . . . The Spirit of Liberty now lies low, smitten down and wounded. Sectionalism & slavery propagandism, & party subservience, are in ascendant." Aggrieved northerners enjoined slave-state aggressors to give the country repose. "Leave our [territory] to us," they cried, "do not violate our solemn compact in an attempt to snatch it from us." Hoisting southerners with their own rhetorical petard, the bill's opponents told them, " '*All we ask of you is to be let alone.*' "[64]

The bill's opponents claimed to "be acting only on the defensive." Nebraska critics looked with alarm and contempt at the dangerous attempts by the bill's supporters to pervert and appropriate the revolutionary legacy for their own base purposes. They rejected out of hand Democratic and southern arguments that drew on analogies to the colonies, the spirit of the fathers, the Constitution, or the essence of Union. "The Colonies, were distant, outside dependencies, with no prospect of a union or fusion with the old country," Israel Washburn of Maine argued. "Here, the Territories are integral parts of the American Union, soon to take their place as sovereign States in this great sisterhood of Republics. In the meantime—during their minority, they are to be looked after, cherished and protected by the General Government." Frank

Blair contended that whereas the Declaration of Independence asserted the rights of liberty and humanity, "the Kansas act would spread [slavery] over the continent; and to effect it, establishes a new system of politics and morals for the democratic party, for which it is prescribed as a test."[65]

Casting themselves as conservatives in the sense that their position hewed to the policies and intent of the fathers, antislavery Democrats and Whigs were especially quick to point out that the nation began its life by stating its belief in the universal truths of liberty and equality and, having sustained those convictions by arms, had, in less than eighty years, assumed "an attitude of conquest and dominion, with the avowed design . . . of extending and perpetuating a system of human slavery over whatever of territory it may require." A northern Democrat expressed despair at the depths to which his party and his country had sunk. He wrote with some shame that "Washington, Jefferson, Madison, Munroe [sic] & Jackson would disdain to mock the nation with a proposition to abrogate the guards established by the founders of our republic against the extension of slavery, and submit the grave question of slavery or freedom to the discussion of a few trancient [sic] traders & squatters."[66]

Douglas's greatest miscalculation was his conviction that popular sovereignty (and the repeal of the Missouri line) would eliminate slavery agitation from Congress and, consequently, be the means by which the nation could continue its westward course of empire. Sadly for Douglas, many Democrats and nearly all northern Whigs were coming to the conclusion that it was delusive to hope for a final settlement of the slave controversy. "*Politicians* may now pretend that at length the controversy is finally disposed of," sighed one disillusioned northerner, "but I fear it is like the Hydra—every time you strike from it a head, two grow out to supply its place." Do you of the South, William Seward asked, "see any signs that we are becoming indifferent to freedom? . . . The slavery agitation which you deprecate so much, is an eternal struggle between conservatism and progress, between truth and error, between right and wrong." The final vote on the Nebraska bill, one publicist deduced, "will decide, as far as human foresight can reach . . . whether free soil shall be protected any where, from the all-grasping encroachments of our Southern masters."[67]

An increasing number of free-soil Whigs and Democrats cast the events of the preceding decade as the unfolding of a plot to subvert the fundamental liberties upon which the Union was founded. If Texas annexation was once viewed as a demagogue's hobby, if Calhoun's reading of the Constitution was mistaken, if the attempts to extend slavery into the West were evil, the Nebraska bill now infused them with a new, more ominous meaning. In all the compromising from 1820 to 1850 and in all the Union saving, another antislavery man added, "the demands of the slave interest have never been satisfied, agitation quieted, or harmony promoted. . . . For myself I am sick of all this temporising [*sic*] policy." So, indeed, were thousands of other northerners. Only one conclusion could be drawn from the facts, they argued. "There is now no middle ground between slavery and freedom. We must fight now or be slaves. . . . It is for [northerners] to decide which they will have, *all slavery and no freedom, or all freedom and no slavery*."[68]

Wounded by this withering antislavery fusillade, moderate northern Democrats maneuvered to what they thought was safer ground. Answering his critics, William English asserted, "In voting for this bill, I do not vote to extend slavery. I do not vote to give it legal existence where it is not. The people of the Territories will never adopt this institution." Pennsylvania senator Richard Brodhead concurred with English's letter-of-the-law logic. "We are not asked to give protection to property in slaves," he declared, "or say that the local Legislature shall not pass laws on the subject of slavery." A somewhat bolder Nebraska supporter believed "that all sensible men will . . . acquiesce in the principle of the Nebraska bill, as one placing all sections on the same footing and giving the prizes of new States to those most active in fair competition." Thus all was safe. "Freedom can forever outrun slavery," boasted a Pittsburgh editor; "emigration from the free states is an infinitely more easy and rapid process than emigration from slave States." Others looked beyond foot speed and movable property to the sense of the nation — and the times. Noting that both houses of Congress as well as public opinion were against slavery, they maintained that the limits of slavery were set. It was not just that Kansas and Nebraska would be free states, moderates contended; this was too narrow, too crass a view of freedom. The settlers there would not only be free from slavery "but free to manage their own local affairs, as of right they should be. . . . What democrat will say that the principle of self-government shall not prevail?" Entitled to the last word, Douglas asked why free-soilers did "not state the matter truly, and say that it opens the country to *freedom* by leaving the people *perfectly free* to do as they please?"[69]

Douglas's amended Nebraska bill, which organized two territories — Kansas and Nebraska — and which declared that the Missouri Compromise "was superseded by the principles of the legislation of 1850, commonly called the compromise measures and is hereby declared inoperative and void," passed the Senate on March 3 by a 37 to 14 vote. Although Senate passage was no easy matter, the battle in the House was more intense. A filibuster led by Lewis D. Campbell, an Ohio free-soiler, nearly provoked the House into a war of more than words. Campbell, joined by other antislavery northerners, exchanged insults and invectives with southerners, neither side giving quarter. Weapons were brandished on the floor of the House. Finally, bumptiousness gave way to violence. Henry A. Edmundson, a Virginia Democrat, well oiled and well armed, had to be restrained from making a violent attack on Campbell. Only after the sergeant at arms arrested him, debate was cut off, and the House adjourned did the melee subside. Worn down by exhaustion as much as by sheer numbers, Nebraska critics eventually were overcome. Under the adroit leadership of Alexander Stephens, a Georgia Whig, Douglas's bill passed the House, 113 to 100. "Nebraska is through the House," the diminutive Stephens wrote. "Glory enough for one day." Ominously for the other Little Giant, northern Democrats split 44 to 44 on the bill while southern Democrats and Whigs favored it by a 69 to 9 margin. Every northern Whig opposed it.[70] In a tragically curious way, Douglas's plan had in part succeeded.

"The crime is committed," thundered the *Albany Evening Journal.* "The work of MONROE, and MADISON, and JEFFERSON, is undone. The wall they erected to guard the domain of Liberty, is flung down by the Lords of an American Congress, and Slavery crawls like a slimey reptile over the ruins, to defile a second Eden." There was but one lesson to be learned from this free-soil defeat, a determined New Englander concluded. "There can never be another contract, compact, or compromise with slavery by the friends of freedom." The North, observed a Hoosier free-soiler, "while willing to observe all constitutional guarantees of the institution . . . will yield no further to its aggression. Slavery may live as long as its supporters want it, where it now is, but it can't anywhere else."[71]

Douglas, who would soon travel home to Illinois by the light of his own burning effigy, boasted that he was undeterred by the violent insults of northern Whigs and abolitionists. "The storm will soon spend its fury and the people of the North will sustain the measure when they come to understand it," he wrote Howell Cobb. "In the meantime our Southern friends have only to stand firm and leave us of the North to fight the great battle. . . . The great principle of self government is at stake, and surely the people of this country are never going to decide that the principle upon which our whole republican system rests is vicious and wrong."[72]

Douglas was correct. The principle of self-government was, indeed, at stake. As the congressional elections of 1854 and 1855 would show, Douglas's optimism was unwarranted, his partisan agenda miscalculated. Because he was a party leader shaped and informed by the Jacksonian political culture, he understood that he had to identify the fears and give voice to the prejudices of the electorate. As their paladin, he had to assist in bringing their aggregate power to bear on institutions and individuals that threatened the public weal and, in particular, their individual liberties. Douglas correctly sensed the ongoing degeneration of the Jacksonian party system. His belief in self-government was not misguided. If his confidence in the efficacy of expansion and federate freedom as an antidote for declension was a logical extension of that belief, the same could not be said for hundreds of thousands of northern Democrats and Whigs. True, they, along with Douglas, were aware of the malaise and restiveness that beset the nation following the compromise. Yet, unlike him, they viewed expansion as unsettling, not reinvigorating. More significantly, they considered popular sovereignty (joined as it was to a repeal of the Missouri Compromise) not as a national reaffirmation of an actuating principle of republicanism but as a provocative and hostile initiative that jeopardized rather than enhanced public liberties.

Of course, Whigs had said the same of Texas annexation. Yet a decade later, partisan demagoguery had a decided sectional cast. Many Whigs and Democrats who had once opposed each other on the issue of national expansion now stood together in hostility to the expansion and enhancement of the slavepower. Thus Douglas's tragedy was less that he was insensitive to the moral repugnance of slavery, for so, too, were many who opposed the Nebraska Act. Rather, it was his inability to recognize that the territorial crisis that followed the Mexican cession had burned a swath across the political landscape and separated the nation from the ebullient nationalism of the mid-1840s. Time had passed, and sectional hostility had dimmed the confidence of an earlier age.

Douglas's remedy for the political fragmentation of the early 1850s exacerbated the sense of declension. The off-year election returns of 1854–55 suggest the extent to which Douglas's agenda seemed radical and, hence, unacceptable to the northern electorate. In Pennsylvania, the Democratic governor, who had won by eight thousand votes in 1851, lost by thirty-seven thousand in 1854. Twenty-one anti-Nebraska representatives were sent to Congress as opposed to four Douglas supporters. Every congressional district in Ohio and all but two in Indiana sent Nebraska opponents to Congress. In New England the Democracy was completely vanquished. Every New York Democrat who voted for the bill was defeated. Anti-Nebraska candidates carried every congressional district in Maine. In Pierce's New Hampshire, John P. Hale, his bête noire, was returned to the Senate. In all, only seven of the forty-four northern Democrats who voted for the Nebraska bill saved their seats. From 1854 to 1855 the northern Democracy saved but twenty-five of ninety-one seats. By contrast, it lost only four of sixty-seven in the slave states.[73]

Speaking to a Chicago audience in the aftermath, Douglas told them, "Let us be of good cheer, all is well. Though the heavens are partially overcast, the clouds are passing away." Later that November, more than seventeen hundred Missourians crossed the border into Kansas to cast fraudulent votes in a territorial election. That month, Secretary of State William Marcy, who four years earlier expressed his hope that slavery agitation was put to rest, learned that all nine New York congressmen who voted for the Nebraska Act were turned out of office.[74] The pattering rain of an approaching storm had begun.

Men's convictions as to the Truth, or what they receive as the truth . . . depend entirely upon their understanding of the facts. Convictions are always sincere.
—Alexander H. Stephens, *A Constitutional View of the Late War between the States*

Where justice is denied, where poverty is enforced, and where any one class is made to feel that society is in an organized conspiracy to suppress, rob, and degrade them, neither persons nor property will be safe. —Frederick Douglass

A House Dividing

The Conspiracy Thesis
Joined and Defined

A decade later, while imprisoned in Fort Warren federal prison on George's Island in Boston Harbor, Alexander Stephens, the former vice-president of the Confederacy, recalled a distant day in the summer of 1855 when he stood before the House of Representatives. Speaking on the affairs of Kansas, Stephens, then a representative from Georgia, used the occasion to address charges made by Ohio's Lewis D. Campbell. Two days earlier Campbell, a former Whig and recent convert to the nativist American Party, had declared that the passage of the Nebraska bill was the cause of all the troubles in Kansas Territory and the country. Stephens retorted belligerently that the problems of Kansas and of the nation were the result of "the mischievous designs and reckless purposes of those who, in their efforts to defeat the quiet and peaceful purposes of that bill, have been engaged in their unholy work of attempting to get up a civil war in the country." These malcontents, he went on, had for years been endeavoring to produce a sectional conflict by disregarding the equality of the states and the sacred obligations of the Constitution that bound them together. Consequently, free-soil clamor about bleeding Kansas arose "much more from a desire and hope of exciting by it sectional hate and alienation of one portion of the Union from the other, than from any wish to have even 'free Kansas' admitted to the Union." Their ultimate object, Stephens concluded, "is not so much to get another state added to the Union, as it is to use the question [of Kansas] to produce a severance of those States now united."[1]

In the solitude of his cell, Stephens returned to these themes in a number of fictive conversations with an old Georgian lawyer friend that he wrote down in his diary. After his parole in 1865, the former vice-president developed these sketchy dialogues into a two-volume apologia explaining the South's policy in connection with the sectional crisis and its secession from the Union. *A Constitutional View of the Late War between the States* is a series of imaginary colloquies between Stephens and three fictitious Unionists—a radical Republican, a conservative Republican, and a war Democrat. Judge Bynum, the radical Republican, is Stephens's bête noire and foil. Throughout, the judge maintains that the turmoil that culminated in the war of rebellion was the product of slavepower ambition. By their strength, menaces, and threats, he claims, the slaveholding states carried through the Missouri Compromise, the annexation of Texas, and the compromise measures of 1850 "with the sole object of strengthening their power, of extending their peculiar Institution." And, the judge asks pointedly, "Did they not afterwards, in 1854, when strong enough, openly repudiate this Compromise, as well as the solemn Compact entered into on the admission of Missouri? Did they not then repeal the prohibition of Slavery over the whole North-Western Territory, which was the condition upon which Missouri was admitted; and by this act desecrate to human bondage soil, which by this Compact had been forever consecrated to human liberty?" Judge Bynum rounds out his indictment by concluding, "I think it can be made clearly to appear that from the beginning this Slave Power by insinuating itself craftily with the interests of subservient allies of the North . . . has all along looked to nothing but the perpetuation of its dominion."[2]

Asking Stephens not to take personal offense, Judge Bynum assured his host that these views were founded on "the impregnable position of Truth, Justice and Right." To this, the waspish master of Liberty Hall returns, "Our ideas of Truth, Justice and Right, in political as well as social matters, and all the relations of life, depend very much on circumstances. This seems to be owing partly to the infirmities of human nature. There ought, however, to be no difference between intelligent minds as to Truth, which rests simply and entirely on matters of fact." As Stephens weaves his defense of the South, it appears that truth—and the facts—have changed not at all since that distant summer's day. Stephens informs the judge that after the North refused to compromise on an equitable division of the Mexican cession, Congress decided to abandon the principle (and the wrong) of restriction altogether in the 1850 settlement. The Nebraska Act, therefore, merely executed in good faith the organizational principle of noninterference that Congress had agreed to and established in 1850. "There was no aggression in it on the part of the South," he states matter-of-factly. "There was no 'perfidy' or 'breach of Compact' or 'wrong,' perpetrated by anybody in securing its accomplishment." Restrictionists, stung by their defeats in Congress, then stirred up a bloody conflict in Kansas "to kindle a general war in the States, for the total abolition of slavery." The judge, staggered by these and collateral arguments, soon falls into a low state of mind. To maintain his courage at one point, he rejects his host's offer of lemonade for "something a little stronger." Deflated and demoralized, Bynum, a teetotaler, glumly sighs, "I guess it wouldn't hurt me much." Finally, after the former vice-president develops his unanswerable (and interminable) rebuttal in 1,455 pages (exclusive of indexes), Judge Bynum's argument collapses under the weight of its own inherent and incurable infamy.[3]

Stories of conspiracies against public liberties, real or bogus, stretch back to the days of Gog and Magog. Most historians, however, have rejected the judge's view of this discourse and have proved to be much more resistant than Bynum to Stephens's logic. The conflicting views of the judge's slavepower thesis and his host's abolitionist conspiracy seem antediluvian today. Historical evidence reveals no conscious conspiracy in either the free or slave states to deny the other a role in government. This fact did not prevent political leaders and constituents in both sections from operating on that assumption, however.

By the mid-1850s, there was widespread disagreement between parties and between sections over the nature of the threat to republican government and to the ideological heritage it embraced. As we have seen, moderate Democrats couched their defense of the Nebraska Act and of popular sovereignty in terms of their understanding of the revolutionary heritage. Republicans, using the same language, drew a wholly different conclusion. Slave-state Democrats, no less than Republicans and the northern Democracy, linked their message to a defense of republican government. They believed that this legacy was just as much their birthright as that of their antislavery opponents. Like the judge and his colleagues, southerners, too, saw the sectional conflict as a question of freedom versus slavery.

Both sections would develop fully the conspiracy thesis during the Union crisis of 1860–61. The South's understanding of the territorial issue's role in national politics, however, and its portentous response to the growth of the Republican Party were already apparent by 1856. Its reaction to this sectional party and, as it appeared to them, the Republicans' self-aggrandizing agenda, escalated the territorial controversy in that canvass to a crisis of Union. A series of subsequent events—the *Dred Scott* decision, the Lecompton fiasco, the Freeport doctrine, demands for a federal slave code, the rupture of the Democracy, and Lincoln's election—each linked to the territorial question would only provide evidence for the conspiracy theses so resonant with the judge and Mr. Stephens and which became apparent in the Buchanan-Frémont-Fillmore contest.

At the time when Stephens was replying to Lewis Campbell, three of his House colleagues were concluding their investigation into the troubled affairs of Kansas. Writing for the majority, William A. Howard of Michigan concluded that "it cannot be doubted that if its [Kansas's] condition as a free Territory had been left undisturbed by Congress, its settlement would have been rapid, peaceful and prosperous." Once the Missouri restriction was removed, however, "the aspect of affairs entirely changed. The whole country was agitated by the reopening of a controversy which conservative men in different sections hoped had been settled in every State and Territory *by some law* beyond the danger of repeal. The excitement which has always accompanied the discussion of the slavery question was greatly increased by the hope on the one hand, of extending slavery into a region from which it had been excluded by law; and on the other, by a sense of wrong done by what was regarded as a dishonor of a national compact."[4]

Refusing to concur in this allegation, Howard's fellow committee member Mordecai Oliver of Missouri affirmed in a minority report "what he believes to be the truth of the matter." All the difficulties in Kansas from its organization down to 1856 were to be found, he contended, "in the various organizations of members of Congress, and in the northern and eastern States, with the avowed purpose of colonizing the Territory with persons of antislavery Sentiments, to the end of making Kansas a free State." Unable, however, to elect a free-soil legislature, "the antislavery party in the Territory of Kansas, in a fit of desperation, determined to set themselves up in opposition to, and in resistance of, the laws passed by the Kansas legislature, and to resist then to a 'bloody issue,' if necessary to their defeat and utter subversion." Free-soil emigrants were determined to pursue these ends, Oliver concluded, "even should such resistance result in the subversion of the government of the Territory, and to the peril of the Union itself."[5]

Although Howard and Oliver drew different conclusions from the same evidence, they were sincerely convinced that the semblance of constitutional government, law, and order had wilted on the dusty plains of Kansas. Without minimizing the importance of the frequent and violent quarrels over land titles in that unhappy territory, politics there came to embrace the same controversy over slavery extension so lately heard in Congress. Even before the passage of the Nebraska bill, Eli Thayer of Massachusetts obtained a state charter incorporating the Emigrant Aid Company to send antislavery migrants to Kansas. Though the number of immigrants dispatched to the territory by Thayer and other northern aid societies was small and the number of permanent settlers fewer yet, their presence alarmed and provoked proslavery forces in Missouri. When, therefore, Governor Andrew Reeder called for the election of a territorial legislature in March 1855, thousands of Missourians crossed into Kansas to cast fraudulent ballots. Reeder allowed the election to stand save in a few districts where the vote was challenged. A proslavery legislature elected by illegal votes then met and passed a Draconian slave code. Understandably, free-soil settlers refused to accept the legitimacy of this government and its laws. In the summer of 1855 they drafted a free-state constitution and ratified it in December. The following January they elected a governor and legislature, and in March this shadow government convened in Topeka.[6]

Beyond making a mockery of self-government, the political turmoil in Kansas had the effect of dividing the settlers into warring camps. Free-state immigrants considered the proslavery legislature fraudulent and its laws repugnant to the idea of local self-determination on the question of slavery. Proslavery forces regarded the Topeka movement as illegitimate, even revolutionary. Sadly but not surprisingly, both sides began to arm. To be sure, the violence in Kansas was less than was reported. Yet a series of sometimes violent encounters between the two sides from November 1855 to May 1856 convinced Howard, Oliver, and the nation that popular sovereignty was very much in jeopardy in Kansas. Bushwhacking, intimidation, the return of "border ruffians" from Missouri, the sack of Lawrence, and John Brown's murder and mutilation of five innocent settlers near Pottawatomie Creek — all enhanced by colorful and creative reporting — seemed proof that a civil war had begun in Kansas.[7]

Governor Wilson Shannon, who replaced Reeder, called upon President Pierce to allow him the use of federal troops stationed in Kansas to restore order. Although events in that unhappy territory had reached a fork, Pierce followed a middle road. Desperate to make popular sovereignty work, the Democratic president denied Shannon's request. "It is not the duty of the President of the United States to volunteer interposition by force to preserve the purity of elections, either in State or territory," he declared lamely. Pierce committed himself instead to support the laws of Kansas and to uphold the proslavery government against the rebellious free-soil movement.[8]

While a weak president was relying on executive authority and his powers of persuasion to quell violence, Congress proved equally ineffective. William Seward introduced a proposal to admit Kansas as a free state under the Topeka constitution. Robert Toombs countered with a bill to hold a new registration of voters in Kansas in preparation for an election of delegates to a state constitutional convention. For all the inflammatory displays that these bills engendered (including the caning of Massachusetts senator Charles Sumner by Representative Preston Brooks of South Carolina), neither contributed to any settlement of the Kansas imbroglio. Seward's measure was never voted on. Toombs's more moderate proposal passed the Senate in July 1856, only to die in the House.[9]

Despite ample evidence suggesting that the failure of popular sovereignty in Kansas was, in a sense, the failure of the people to govern themselves, pro-Nebraska Democrats (those who survived the electoral slaughters of 1854 and 1855) and moderate southern former Whigs still were convinced that their formula could yield a solution to the territorial problem. Toombs, among others, asserted, "We have put the Territory of Kansas exactly where it was when we bought it from France, exactly where Jefferson put it by his territorial laws; exactly where it was in 1820 . . . where New Mexico was; where Utah was . . . where every State of the Union was, so far as the question of slavery was concerned." The frauds and violence there, Ohio's John McLean added, "do not belong to our system, and they should be rebuked and punished by the national power." Similarly, a Cleveland Democrat, proclaiming himself hostile to all things that did not harmonize with the democratic principle of self-determination, equally condemned brute violence and higher law obstructionism. "The one, as well as the other, is anti-republican."[10]

Nebraska adherents claimed that the measure was equitable and wise and its principles at one with "the natural working of our form of government." Then, as the *Cleveland Plain Dealer* suggested, "the evil will be charged, not to the bill itself, but to the malign influences which prevent the execution of it." A Pittsburgh Democrat agreed. "There was nothing in the nature of the new territorial bill to bring this result," he averred. The sole cause of the disturbances there "may be traced to the conduct of certain ultraists who, not content with managing their own affairs, must take to regulate the internal policy of their neighbors." In truth, however, these busybodies neither had nor sought any other interest in Kansas except for "keeping alive the slavery question and making political capital of its ingredients."[11]

While pro-Nebraska Democrats scrupulously included the Missouri "border ruffians" in their indictment, they understandably singled out northern Republicans as the primary instigators. Those legislators, claimed a suspicious Virginia Democrat, "made 'pretended shew' of opposition to [the] Kansas bill in order to maneuver the South into support." The intent of this great free-soil victory, he reasoned, was to convert "Kansas into a great hotbed to hatch Presidents to bring home to a *section* all the fruits of the Federal Government." Senator Stephen A. Douglas of Illinois concurred with the gist of his argument. He railed at the free-soil opposition across the aisle: "We believe that you organised all the difficulties, and are justly responsible for the consequences. . . . We believe there never would have been any trouble in Kansas but for your efforts, and they were for political objects." Their immediate object was to keep the slavery question before Congress and the nation to unite the masses and the disaffected. Should popular sovereignty fail in Kansas, "an exclusive sectional party against the organization of which we were so often warned by the fathers of the republic . . . [would] crush out the only national party in the country—the democracy."[12]

Stubborn Democratic defense of popular sovereignty provoked amazement and amusement on the other side of the aisle. Conviction and political realities, however, led pro-Nebraska representatives to conclude that popular sovereignty was the best safeguard of freedom and the fiercest opponent of slavery. If northern Democrats considered it an effective, constitutional method of limiting the spread of the South's peculiar institution, all party members would agree that popular sovereignty embraced a larger, more fundamental freedom. The party's defense of noninterference was part of the anticonsolidationist impulse that Democrats everywhere and always embraced. Benjamin F. Hallett reminded a meeting of Massachusetts Democrats that despite Republican slanders, nonintervention "is simply the fundamental doctrine of democratic institutions, *the right of self-government*." A doctrine so long regarded as sound in theory and fact and applied to the territories reflected "unlimited confidence in the power of the truth," the *Cleveland Plain Dealer* declared.[13]

Because popular sovereignty was the American idea, Democrats rejected with heat any suggestion that the Nebraska formula was an unsuccessful experiment. "What, sir, the idea which lies at the very basis of American freedom throughout all the States a failure!" exploded Senator Charles Stuart of Michigan. "That principle an experiment which was born, so far as this country is concerned, with the Revolution, which is so resplendent this day as to command the admiration of the civilized world!" Howell Cobb of Georgia asked a New Hampshire crowd if in seeking a satisfactory solution to the slavery issue, it had ever occurred to them to reflect on the causes of the Revolution. Oppressed and wronged by a distant Parliament legislating on their rights and welfare, the fathers thought they were capable of managing their affairs. "The important lesson taught by the American Revolution is the right and the capacity of the people to decide for themselves the nature and the character of the institutions under which they shall live," Cobb asserted. Appealing to their patriotism, he asked his audience to sustain popular sovereignty in Kansas and thereby "not only preserve the principle [of self-government] in name and form, but live up to it in spirit and truth." [14]

From this historical perspective, Democrats considered free-soil opposition not merely obstructionist but subversive. Benjamin Hallett warned that congressional interference in Kansas was only the first step. The next position "for the fusion party to adopt was that the Constitution did not authorize slavery anywhere, and therefore, we had a right under the Constitution to abolish it in all the States! And further, if that was not good doctrine, then they would put down the Constitution and dissolve the Union!" In like vein, Cobb told New Hampshire Democrats that the question was not whether slavery was right or wrong, a blessing or a curse. It was, rather, whether the tenets of American civilization were valid. The individual who subverts the doctrine of popular sovereignty "wars upon the principle of self-government and the constitution of his country." Noninterference "sanctioned by the wisdom of our fathers . . . presents a common ground upon which all true men of every State and section can stand harmoniously together," Cobb insisted. "It compromises no principle and sacrifices no interest. It is the doctrine of a common constitution; let it be defended by a united people." [15]

To members of the newly formed Republican Party, this was ridiculous if not insane. Popular sovereignty had not provided a common ground but a battleground. Since Congress passed the Nebraska Act, Senator Henry Wilson charged, "Kansas has been twice or thrice invaded. Houses have been burned, cities have been sacked, people have been robbed, plundered, murdered;—they have been arrested on their way to the territory, disarmed, and turned back to their old homes." Those northerners who remained in the territory groaned under a despotic, illegal legislature. Benjamin Wade of Ohio suspected that a Democratic president intended to use the executive arm of the national government to sustain a territorial administration "used to prostrate men, women and children in the territory of Kansas, to burn, rob and destroy the American citizen, despoil him of his rights, and drive him from his settlement." This is the condition to which the pro-Nebraska advocates have brought the country, he cried. "In four short years this prosperous Republic, the pride and glory of the world, has come down to the robbery, rape, arson and murder of its own citizens."[16]

Republicans assured northerners that the Kansas civil war was no distant, isolated, or unique incident. The contest in Kansas was a metaphor for—an extension of—the conflict between the free and slave societies. Slavery advocates imposed laws on free-state settlers ("the flower of the industrial classes of New England, the North, and the West") that robbed them of their rights and degraded them into a condition of abject humiliation. Henry Wilson insisted, "Freedom of speech and freedom of the press were cloven down. Trial by jury was made a mockery. . . . The people of Kansas were bound hand and foot—reduced to the pitiable condition of conquered menials of the slave power." Andrew Eliot of Massachusetts had written in 1765 that when tyranny is abroad, "submission is a crime." Perhaps mindful of this injunction, the *New York Times* advised northerners of the settlers' obligation. "The provocation of our forefathers to Revolution was trifling with that which these Kansas settlers have experienced," it asserted. "If the settlers in Kansas do not resist the enforcement of such laws *to the last extremity* . . . and [are unwilling] to spill the last drop of blood rather than thus be degraded and conquered, they are unworthy of their name and descent."[17]

As they had in 1848, 1850, and 1854, restrictionists again charged that popular sovereignty was "one of the grandest humbugs ever concocted by the Democratic Party." Foreign ruffians' enslavement of free-soil colonists, the *Albany Evening Journal* pointed out sarcastically, "was not only a violation of every principle of Republicanism, but an abrogation of the principle of 'squatter sovereignty.'" Richard Yates, an anti-Nebraska congressman from Illinois, contended that in territorial Kansas, "self-government means not, that one class of people may govern themselves, but that they shall have control of others." This Democratic doctrine, he claimed, "is no less than a denial of the first principles of justice, right and humanity."[18]

Popular sovereignty was more than a violation of the principle of self-government. Disorder in Kansas was a warning sign "that the Slaveholding interests will omit nothing that may be necessary to secure the practical advantages sought by the repeal of the Missouri Compromise—the extension of the *political power* of slavery over the whole Territory of the United States." Of course, Republicans would not minimize the particular crime of Kansas, "where citizens of a common country are fighting with each other for the introduction or exclusion of human servitude." What anti-Nebraska forces added, though, was that Kansas had become the most immediate and visible event in a broad assault on public liberties. In the Senate, Benjamin Wade lashed out at the slavepower "felt in every corner of the Republic." It was an oligarchy, he warned, "which reigns and domineers over four fifths of the people of the South; which rules them with a rod of iron; which gags the press; which restrains the liberty of speech."[19]

Similar charges had been made before—and often. In 1855 and 1856 Republicans were alarmed by the naked arrogance and rapid progress of this tyranny. "In Kansas, in Washington, everywhere, [the slaveholding oligarchy] exhibit the same intolerance, the same hatred of freedom, of courage and manhood," the *Cincinnati Gazette* complained. "Everywhere they seek to trample the weak under foot. They cannot tolerate free speech anywhere. . . . Every Free State man must feel that the slave oligarchy must be crushed or his own freedom must be given up." Two months before Preston Brooks caned him into senselessness, Charles Sumner confessed to editor Henry Raymond that he was lathering for a scrap with the slavepower. Clearly, he wrote, "at this moment Kansas is the inevitable point. In protecting this Territory against tyranny we are driven to battle with tyrants, who are the oligarchs of slavery." Although other Republicans never felt the sting of Brooks's gutta-percha cane, nevertheless they too believed themselves badly used by an arrogant slavepower. "For more than ten years the measures of the Federal Government have been directed mainly to the increase of the Slave States," a convention of New York Republicans complained. "One measure has followed upon another, each bolder than the last, until we have violence ruling in the Federal Capitol, and civil war raging in the Territories."[20]

In 1776, colonial writers had similarly ascribed the distresses and complaints of the American people to an overweening, arbitrary power that dominated absolutely the king, Lords, and Commons. In 1856, an Ohio Republican, Timothy Day, likewise complained to a friend that slaveholders considered northerners "to be their natural enemies, and in many instances as their inferiors. The education of a life has taught them to command and be obeyed." Lust for power and self-aggrandizement in their private lives made slaveholders tyrants in public office. Today, the *New York Times* flared, they control the executive branch "and wield it without justice, or conscience, or shame." The slave states also dominated the Senate "to extinguish all the independent power of the popular branch of the legislature." Although the foundation of American government was republican, the *Albany Evening Journal* declared, "the superstructure that has grown up, or been built upon this foundation, is of a totally different order. . . . From Republican we have become Oligarchic. . . . The American Union from self-government, has steadily degenerated into a government of the many by the few."[21]

The political domination of slaveholders undermined the principles of free government and menaced constitutional checks and balances. Widespread corruption in the South made their ascendancy possible. Charles Eliot Norton, for example, observed during a sightseeing trip through the slave states "that the farther you go towards the South the more absolutely do shiftlessness and careless indifference take the place of energy and active precaution and skilful arrangement." Social degeneracy, it followed, festered in the dissipated condition of the slave-state population. The all-absorbing ambition of slaveholders was for wealth because "it is the inherited proceeds of unrequited toil which give the highest social position." To be a poor white was a byword and a reproach, one Republican publicist argued. "Slavery crushes those who are neither slaveholders or slaves. The poor white is too proud to associate with negroes, his superiors too proud to associate with him; . . . with a hopeless prospect for himself and children, there is absolutely no sphere for him but to labor for the supply of his own animal wants, despised and dejected." The effect of slavery then was, as Norton observed, "to deaden the moral feelings and to obscure the intellects of masters" and to degrade the nonslaveholders into abject poverty. Neither, it was clear, "will . . . be vigilant in self-government."[22]

Republicans maintained that in every southern state, "the slave holders wield the whole political power,—make just such laws as their own interests require or their own prejudices dictate, and hold the whole body of the white population in a condition of political subserviency quite as absolute as that of their slaves!" Because they controlled all or nearly all the property in the South, members of the aristocracy "act as a united body in all matters of business and politics that affect their interests as slaveholders." Before the collapse of the second party system, the critique of the South tended to divide along partisan lines. Antislavery Whigs had criticized the slave-based, one-crop culture of the South that prevented the rise of the yeomanry. Free-soil Democrats had complained that the slave states "legislate for the benefit of *capital*, and against *men*," thus exploiting the nonslaveholding white.[23] After the passage of the Kansas-Nebraska bill, these partisan differences blurred and then were merged.

As antislavery Whigs and Democrats merged in a single Republican Party, they moved away from specific indictments of the institution itself. Instead, Republicans used slavery to define broadly the meaning and limits of freedom not only within the North's free-labor economy but, more important, within the nation's republican political state. In the South, Ephraim Squier claimed, the rigid European class system was well defined and immutable. Fixed institutions, he warned, whether European or southern, led to "the permanent establishment of a privileged and titled aristocracy [and to] assumptions and encroachments which power—imperious and selfish power, made from time to time upon the rights and privileges of mankind." Here Squier only restated what revolutionaries such as Jonathan Mayhew had made explicit a century earlier. "Power is of a grasping, encroaching nature," Mayhew had pointed out in 1766. It "aims at extending itself and operating according to mere *will* wherever it meets with no balance, check, control, or opposition of any kind."[24]

The connection between power and slavery (and, for that matter, slaveholding) was clear in the minds of Republicans. So, too, was the argument that liberty and individual rights were the victims of power. By drawing on this long-held and deeply felt belief, antislavery activists had little trouble persuading the converts that there was a broad-based threat to northern freedom. Railroad baron John Murray Forbes admonished a South Carolinian that the masses "can be roused upon two points, their nation's interests and their own prejudices; and if there is anything in this country fixed, it is the prejudice against aught which has even the appearance of aristocracy." Republican leaders incessantly contrasted the slaveholders' dominance of the South with the alleged universality of political privileges in the North. The conclusion was obvious. Patriotism and virtue coexist with free white men, they averred, because "the mechanism of the State is not merely for classes, or for property, but for the great interests of the whole and true interests of the individual."[25]

The conclusion drawn in 1856, as in 1776, 1800, 1828, and 1844, was that a seditious oligarchy menaced the balance of power within the national government. However calculated, this argument meant that the animating principles of equality and liberty that echoed discordantly in the struggles of the Revolution, Jefferson's Revolution of 1800, and the Jacksonian political system would reverberate through the appeal of the Republican Party and thus resound with a public deeply steeped in this historical and intellectual tradition. Gideon Welles pointed out that twenty years earlier the slave states championed states' rights to defeat the monster bank and an iniquitous protective tariff. "But matters are now reversed," he concluded. "The Slave States are engaging in National schemes and centralizing measures to fortify and extend their great interest." Southerners used states'-rights arguments in defense of slavery "as long as they were its protection, and overthrown the moment they became its barrier," a New York Republican held. "Slavery no longer asked toleration of Freedom. It no longer even claimed equality with it. It assumed the Republic in the stead." The imminent danger, Forbes suggested, was that the North might soon "wake up to find itself bound through corruption and fraud to the will of the aristocratic minority."[26]

To most Republicans, a slavepower conspiracy had assumed a specific shape by 1856 and, equally significant, its aggressive designs were developing in identifiable, coordinated, and inexorable phases. From the Louisiana Purchase to the Kansas debacle, the litany of the slavepower's advances had become part of the Republican canon. Only the acquisition of new territory in the 1840s, first the admission of Texas and then the Mexican cession, brought the North and South into open, direct, and immutable conflict. From the Democracy's first flirtation with territorial aggrandizement to the latest agonies in Kansas, events demonstrated "the marks of concert of action and of a deliberate plan. The actors on the plains of Kansas . . . have been only the tools of men who saw the end from the beginning," Henry Raymond observed. "This so-called Democratic party," the *Albany Evening Journal* sputtered, "may be regarded as the organized Barbarism of this country. . . . The party which sustains, and is sustained by Slavery, Rowdyism and Ignorance, is everywhere easily recognized."[27]

So, apparently, were its aspirations. To hear Republicans tell it, the slavepower, operating through a debauched Democracy, had become thoroughly intoxicated by its power. Now its expansionist thirsts were insatiable. Most immediately, Forbes maintained, southerners were aiming to create enough new slave states "to give them a majority in the Senate which would then become practically a House of Lords, with a veto on all legislation and with a claim to a large share of the patronage of the government." This "open contest for supremacy," one Republican would later declare, was merely a gambit. "The Slave-power," he explained, "by trying to carry slavery into Kansas by force, showed the ultimate design of cutting the free States, with a line of slave states to the Canada line, from all possible extension toward the great West and Mexico." Nor was this all. Forbes warned his friend J. Hamilton Cowper of South Carolina that "the conviction is being daily forced upon the North that the designs of the South do not stop with introducing slavery into our own territories." The issue to be decided, he asserted, "is whether the whole power of the confederacy shall be exercised for buying or conquering all the islands north of Panama for the mere extension of your institution."[28]

With these warnings in mind, Richard Yates told a sympathetic audience, "Our struggle is not for a party measure—for the triumph of a Bank or Tarriff [*sic*], but for measures and principles which strike at the vitality of liberty itself, at the foundation of free institutions—they are nothing more nor less than whether the great principles of the Declaration of Independence and of free Gov[ernment] shall be maintained." Yates's statement is instructive. Historians have noted that conspiracy paradigms not only arrange events into recognizable patterns and attribute them to the design of agents: they also point to possible solutions. Throughout the nation's history the assumption has been general that American institutions are good and its citizens virtuous. Threats to liberty therefore issue from moral declension and are attributed to a calculating minority. The remedy to slavepower incursions, as Yates implied, was to urge the American people not to question but to revitalize their institutions. And in fact, the persuasiveness—the pervasiveness—of a conspiracy argument raised the Republican appeal from abstruse constitutional debates and the mundane world of political strategies to the ethereal heights of a regenerative creed.[29]

"The Union," James Shepherd Pike asserted, "was made to subserve the cause of liberty." Now, he added, slave-state activists and their doughface allies were perverting it to the pestilent uses of human bondage. "This perversion of the purposes of Government," Pike warned, "if not arrested, must work its downfall." Henry Wilson claimed that if the Democrats imagined that "anything . . . can be done . . . to make peace in this country between the great contending powers of freedom upon the one side, and slavery upon the other, they are greatly mistaken; they do not comprehend the vastness and extent of the issues." A Pennsylvania Republican did understand. What we need, he argued, "is [to] form a united stand by the North placing fidelity to the Constitution and Freedom ahead of partisan gain." Salmon Chase informed a wildly enthusiastic gathering of Ohio Republicans that the slavepower had subverted the original policy of the Fathers to limit slavery. "We simply demand its restoration," he cried. "Where they stood, I stand. What they felt, I feel. What they labored to accomplish, I labor."[30]

Like every American politician stretching back to the pristine Washington, Republicans carefully, purposefully, identified their position with the revolutionary generation. We Republicans, Benjamin Wade declared, "stand upon the Declaration of Independence, which met the approbation of the men who molded our Constitution. . . . I ask no man to go further than the fathers of our Constitution have gone. Within the pale of the United States, I claim that all is freedom." Historians, nonetheless, continue to point out that the ideological heritage of that era—republicanism—had evolved (or devolved) since 1776 or 1787. Changing attitudes sheared republicanism of its moral dimension, its assumption that a natural aristocracy would perceive the general good more clearly than could the masses, its antiparty bias, its anticommercial bent (at least for most Americans), and the historic connection between property and full citizenship. Republicanism over the years had become less coherent, more protean.[31] Speaking the language of republicanism, the Republican Party justified its cause. Embracing the basic principles of liberty and equality, which Americans at mid-century understood to be the premises of a democratic polity, Republicans legitimated their organization. If it failed or was unable to recognize the inherent tension between the two or the inconsistencies in its message, Republican leaders did appreciate the power of the party's appeal.

The first half of their argument was essentially didactic: the fragility of republics, the danger of power, conspiracies against liberties. As Sumner, Wade, and Chase suggested, however, their revolutionary analogies were meant to transcend a specific era or event. They embraced an ideological heritage that the party pledged itself to protect and defend. To Democratic and southern charges that their party was sectional and hence subversive, Republicans effectively countered that its animating ideology embraced a legacy "which is at least noble and elevating; it is an idea which draws in its train virtue, goodness, and all the charities of life—all that makes earth a home of improvement and happiness." The function of our party, Sumner observed, was "to guard those great principles which the Union was established to secure."[32]

By linking their message with the historical causes of the Revolution as well as with its presumed ideological legacy, a party that existed almost exclusively in one half of the Union claimed in good conscience that it was a national party. When both the didactic and prescriptive aspects of its ideology were combined, they produced a sense of immediatism that bordered on hysteria in the Republican appeal. "We are now at a turning point, a crisis in the history of the American people," Richard Yates cried. "The question now rises before us—a present question, not to be avoided but to be met—whether slavery is to be nationalized. . . . The triumph of the slave interest now, is its triumph forever." The monistic nature of this argument was as unmistakable as it was powerful. "I recognize no equality, in moral right or political expediency, between slavery and freedom," William Henry Seward explained. "I hold the one to be decidedly good and the other to be positively bad." An Illinois Republican implored every patriot to eschew further compromise. "I see no chance of neutrality on the subject," he declared. "Slavery demands more room—more *scope and verge*. Shall she have it? The answer must be yea or nay."[33]

This sense of crisis and immediacy had the effect of heightening the importance of the territorial struggle. Most recently in Kansas, "hostilities between the Democratic principle, and the aristocratic element of slave labor society, have transcended debate, and the contests of Politics." Benjamin Wade worried that slavery would be established not only in Kansas but in every territory if not in every state of the Union. These concerns, stated so extremely, deepened the North's stake in Kansas. "It appears to me," a Pennsylvania Republican observed, "not only *necessary*, in the ordinary acceptation of the word, but absolutely *indispensable*, to success, that the Commonalty [*sic*]—the humbler class of labourers—male and female, have [the territorial issue] brought home to them—that this is, emphatically, *their* cause." William Cullen Bryant warned a meeting of New York City Republicans that if the North abandoned Kansas and its antislavery immigrants "we shall be justly branded as cold-hearted, selfish, and cowardly. No nation in the history of the world was ever so faithless to the obligations of humanity as to be indifferent to the fate of the colonists it had planted." [34]

Moving from general principles to specific programs proved to be more difficult, however. The first territorial policy deduced from these premises and assumptions was the restoration of the Missouri line. This was the demand of party moderates. In reaction to the unfolding crisis in Kansas and their own growing slavepower phobia, other Republicans took a more advanced (and to the South a more menacing) position. Kansas's troubles imparted a fresh aspect to the slavery question. The slavepower exhibited new characteristics, new traits of temper, and new modes of conduct. "It was seen to be faithless as well as ambitious," the *New York Times* noted, "treacherous as well as grasping. It revealed a new necessity for withstanding its aggression, lest it should achieve the predominance it seeks." Now more than ever, an Indiana party member maintained, the North must "stand by the Declaration of Independence in letter & Spirit." New York's Hamilton Fish took this argument to its logical conclusion. To oppose the admission of any territory "*except as a Free State*," he declared, "is a Conservative and Constitutional position — moreover it is just." If the Congress would adhere to the policy of no more slave states, Salmon Chase wrote, it would restore the republic "to its original policy, will renew her strength & move forward in the fulfillment of her sublime mission, with the applause of all the patriotic & all the good. Talia saecla, cunite." [35]

Rallying to the cause of Kansas meant sustaining the free-soil population there. Other party members (and some Democrats) claimed without any apparent irony that it was the duty of the federal government to intervene in Kansas so that noninterference could work. Most Republicans were blunt in their condemnation of noninterference and asserted to the contrary that true self-government was expressed through Congress. Henry Wilson told Robert Toombs, "Our position is, that this Government has the right to govern the Territories of the United States; that the will of the American people, expressed through Congress, shall be the law for the territories during their territorial existence." All were convinced that the manifest destiny of Kansas — and the West — was to be free. "We are for free Kansas," the *Illinois State Journal* declared simply, "because we are for free white men." [36]

So, too, were southerners. They, no less than Republicans, were obsessed with the fate of free government in the territories. Those slave-state observers closest to Kansas charged that northern reports of atrocities in the territorial elections were "merely imaginary — a moral mirage seen only from the standpoint of those who occupy fanatical positions, and who presume to judge others by a code of their own, dignified as the 'higher law.'" The proslavery victory, they claimed with a straight face, resulted from the desertion of the Massachusetts Emigrant Aid Company's rank and file, who either settled in the Old Northwest or gave up in Kansas. Having failed at the ballot box, abolitionists (as they were routinely called) proposed to ignore the legal government, disobey the laws enacted for the good of the citizens, and introduce anarchy and confusion throughout the limits of the territory. A confidant of John M. Clayton informed the Delaware senator that even if violence and improprieties surfaced in the elections, the proslavery legislature had "at least the semblance of Legality." The Topeka government, however, was "a body totally destitute of a single attribute of legitimacy." Between the two evils, he declared, "I cannot help believing, that the evils arising from the irregularities of the first election would be far less than would result from recognizing the acts of a body which never had any legal existence & which commenced its career if not by resorting to violence, at least by threatening to sustain its position by carrying matters to a 'bloody issue.'"[37]

Like northern Democrats and Republicans, slave-state legislators, too, despaired that the turmoil in Kansas "speaks of a deplorable state of society in a country which boasts the dominion of law as the supreme power in the Republic, and holds itself up to the world as the successful example of the capacity of the people for self government." Southerners, though, believed that free-soil fanatics in the North were unwilling to let civilization flow in its normal course and would not allow natural laws to determine territorial institutions. Migration to Kansas from Arkansas and Missouri was obvious, one southern editor contended. But "it was contrary to nature, common sense and common policy, that emigration from Massachusetts should pass through the more fertile Northwest, to settle in that distant Territory." Free-soil sympathizers, another concluded, "proceeded to forestall the South, and exclude its institutions by their aid society." Success in that distant territory would strengthen Republican numbers in Congress. "The question of equality even now settled against us will be followed by that of existence, and the South[,] a hopeless minority, will fall farther and farther back into a position of dependency and weakness," the *Charleston Mercury* cautioned.[38]

Southern Democrats knew that Republicans would insist minimally on the restoration of the iniquitous Missouri line, and they did. But when Henry Wilson for one informed southern senators that he would never vote to admit Kansas as a slave state, Senator David Reid of North Carolina asked his colleagues if Wilson's position "does . . . not violate every principle of the Constitution of the United States? Does he not violate every principle of free government?" Reid's associate Senator Asa Biggs claimed that Republicans were "tired of the Constitution which was formed by our pure and revolutionary ancestors. . . . *Now* every plan is resorted to evade its sanctions, and to embarrass its action, with the hope of crushing out an institution which they, in their intensified philanthropy, suppose wrong." Success for Republicans apparently meant terror for the South. Again, states'-rights southerners asserted that the growth of the Republican Party was in essence the ascendancy of a sectional spirit that would brand all southern states as "outlaws" and "make them aliens to a government which is yet to administer their most vital interest." The exclusionist movement was "inspired by the genius of discord, and the meaning is that the free and slave states shall not live together in peace after the manner of our Fathers."[39]

Formation of a sectional party was not unexpected. Since the late eighteenth century, many southerners argued, northerners representing the moneyed interests of that section had seen in the slave states a great producing agent. These conspirators, they contended, "sought to reverse the laws of nature, and make produce the great slave of manufactures." From the Alien and Sedition Acts through the Hartford Convention to the Bank War, these agents repeatedly promoted inequality among persons and classes. Since the onset of the Wilmot Proviso struggle they had exploited antislavery sentiment to further their ends, for, as Lucius Q. C. Lamar declared, "the step was easy to an inequality between communities and states." If the South should succumb to this assault on states' rights, he cautioned, "the white line might be distinctly drawn around her, and a servile government constituted to rule, not protect her."[40]

The rapid growth of the Republican Party after 1854 clearly proved that the South's position had become precarious. For decades these quasi-abolitionists had rowed to their objective with muffled oars, soothing the suspicions of the South while contriving to avoid an open and irreparable break. Now they appeared to hold sway over northern public opinion. Worse, the conspirators converted that sentiment into political power, "and for the first time in the history of the country, [abolitionism] exerts a negative control at least over the legislative department of the government." If Republicans captured the presidency with all its patronage, a South Carolinian predicted, the slave states would be "reduced to a state of colonial vassalage, stripped of power in the Federal Government, confined to the strictly tropical regions." Then, with the South "subservient to the direction of the master section, the North might live and fatten at our expense."[41]

From these premises, others drew specific conclusions about the nature of Republican political power. Edmund Ruffin, for example, declared that the party drew its strength from the "very ignorant . . . or unprincipled or debased and vicious individuals—who also because of their poverty, have but little interest in the . . . welfare of their country." The bleak irony of being enslaved to a section that embodied inequality and degradation was not lost on

A HOUSE DIVIDING

slaveholders. The sacred, natural, and paternal social system of the South, James Henry Hammond concluded, was being "superseded by the modern *artificial* money power system in which [men] are all subject to the dominion of capital—a monster without a heart—cold, stern, arithmetical." Cutting to the heart of the issue, Andrew Johnson informed Tennessee Democrats that the North opposed the South's institutions because free-state entrepreneurs had discovered that white slavery was cheaper. "Such, gentlemen, is the position of those who oppose our institution—standing by the side of Great Britain, with her iron-heel upon the necks of seventeen millions of laborers at home, and fifty four million abroad." "Free society," the *Richmond Enquirer* stated flatly, "is a decided failure."[42]

The conviction that sectional politics was the function of a debased, undemocratic society implied that republican government was best preserved in and diffused throughout the slave states. In part, this belief reflected an assumption of cultural superiority. "Certain duties, necessary in the regimen of society, are antagonistic to mental culture," Lawrence Keitt of South Carolina explained. "Therefore that civilization is highest which rescues the improving and ruling race from their performance—alias the South through slavery." Edmund Ruffin bragged that the superior domestic manners and refinement of southern society was owing to the institution of African slavery, "which, by confining the drudgery and brutalizing effects of continued toil, or menial service to the inferior race . . . gives to the superior race leisure and other means to improve mind, taste and manners." In the North, where entire families labored, there might be a general accumulation of wealth. Nevertheless, Ruffin observed sadly, "such a population, of necessity must be . . . rude in manners, and greatly deficient in refinement of feeling and cultivation of mental and social qualities."[43]

Invidious distinctions were more than the booming of Cavalier culture. Hershel V. Johnson wrote the editor of the *Philadelphia North American* that white laborers in the South were treated with more respect than workers in the free states. "So far from degrading and enslaving them," Johnson asserted, slaveholders "would delight to see them rising day by day in thrift, intelligence and moral worth." Having black slaves, the *Richmond Enquirer* noted, the South repudiated the idea that white workers must be exploited. "We would keep the white citizen far, far above the black slave," the *Enquirer* explained. Slavery not only ameliorated class distinctions; it also constituted an economic system in which the whims of the marketplace did not dictate social relations. "Slavery is the poor man's best Government," Georgia's governor Joseph E. Brown declared. "Among us the poor white laborer is respected as an equal. . . . He belongs to the only true aristocracy, the race of white men." Because slavery (and the subordination of blacks) was therefore the foundation of white equality and freedom, Andrew Johnson concluded, "our institution instead of being antagonistical to Democracy is in perfect harmony with it."[44]

For all its benefits—social, economic, political—slavery was a constant reminder of the realities of thralldom. As such, it connected two normally antagonistic groups—up-country yeomen and slaveholders—in opposition to the Republican Party. In a slaveholding republic, states'-rights southerners argued, "the white looks upon liberty as the privilege of his color, the government particularly his own, himself its sovereign. He watches it with the jealous eye of a monarch." Considered in light of increasing sectional hostilities, the belief in a free-soil conspiracy against republican government gave a new meaning to these claims. Liberty and equality for whites, allegedly disappearing in the free states, were best guaranteed in a slave society. The cause of the South was thus transformed. In 1850 it had been the defense of slavery; in 1856 it was a crusade to vindicate and sustain the political heritage of the Revolution. The *Charleston Mercury* told its readers that slavery was essential to republican nationality.

> But for the stern and unflinching vindication of the rights of white men by the independent citizens of the slaveholding states, whom power could not intimidate, capital buy, or money crush, this Confederacy would have long since merged into a central despotism. . . . The Bank monopoly on the one hand, the manufacturing monopoly on the other, combining with the large monarchical element . . . would have been able to effect this, but for the steady manly opposition of the Southern people. . . . It was in slavery that the conservative element of republicanism was found, to overcome this reactionary movement towards the annihilation of individual liberty and dignity and State sovereignty.

An increasing number of southerners could concur with the editor of the *Mercury* when he concluded that it was only the slave states "who can hereafter maintain a safe and honorable Union and enjoy rational liberty."[45]

The ascendancy of a sectional party and free over slave states portended more than exploitation. A plainly alarmed correspondent of Clement Claiborne Clay told the Alabama senator, "Sir, I believe you can find no place in ancient or modern history of the world, where a people lost their country without loseing [*sic*] their *Liberty*." Like all descendants of the revolutionary generation, states'-rights southerners recognized that the viability of republican institutions "presume[s] that the voters in a free government, who select their representatives to rule them, are sufficiently virtuous and intelligent to select the wisest and the best men." If, however, the people are ignorant and depraved, the *Mercury* claimed, "they would not want a just government, but a government under which they could rob and steal."[46]

In 1855 and 1856 this constellation of premises, beliefs, assumptions, and convictions translated into an uncompromising defense of congressional non-interference and states' rights. With Congress deadlocked over Kansas, southerners considered that the proper basis for compromise between conflicting claims was congressional restraint. This, they argued, was not only fair and reasonable; it was the only constitutional solution. Politically, nonintervention was also a logical extension of the Democracy's attack on centralization. A pro-Nebraska southerner informed Mississippi's John A. Quitman, "My dear General, I deneigh any mans wright under the constitution to ask [territorial settlers] wether they wish to apply as a slave state, that is their business and not mine, and I have no wright to dictate to them what they shall have or what they shall not have." At its deepest level, however, democracy constituted the basis of free government. Limiting the powers of Washington and leaving municipal and local interests to the citizens of the several states was "the only basis on which a confederacy can long survive."[47]

The wholly logical deduction from this position was that Republican demands for either a restoration of the discriminatory Missouri line or, worse, a complete prohibition of slavery in the territories subverted the origins and purposes of the Union by denying equality among states and the liberty of slaveholders to take their property into the commonly owned territories. Virginia governor Henry A. Wise declared that Congress, heeding Washington's injunction not to recognize geographic lines in politics, passed the Nebraska bill and restored the nation "to *status quo ante* 1819, '20 where Washington and Hancock, Adams and Jefferson, Virginia and Massachusetts, and the old thirteen stood. It brought us back to the Constitution." As a result, the *Richmond Enquirer* observed, the repeal of the Missouri restriction had the added corrective effect of "relieving the South of an odious brand of inferiority, and restoring us to an equality of right and dignity in the confederacy. . . . a triumph of no inconsiderable consequence." Toombs pointedly warned Senate Republicans, "We have asked for nothing but equality and justice to the South; it has been granted by an American Congress; it is for the constituency to reject or approve the act, and thereby hangs the thread of the republic."[48]

The 1856 campaign stretched that thread to its breaking point. The Democracy endorsed the Nebraska legislation while maintaining convenient ambiguity on the power of territorial legislatures to prohibit slavery. By wide margins, convention delegates also adopted an aggressive, expansionist foreign policy. The party pinned its hopes on an old wheelhorse, James Buchanan of Pennsylvania. John C. Breckinridge of Kentucky was made the nominee for vice-president. Southern Democrats had preferred Franklin Pierce, then Stephen Douglas. When both failed to become the presidential nominee, they supported Mississippi's John A. Quitman for vice-president. The man southerners and the party settled for to head their ticket was plodding, available, orthodox, and from a crucial northern state. Buchanan, minister to Great Britain for the preceding four years, was mercifully free from all Nebraska taint. In short, he was viable in the North and acceptable to the South. Some even argued that his age (sixty-five) and his stodginess had merit. That is, he appeared to embody the claim that the Democracy was the nation's true conservative party.[49]

As viewed by the Democrats, the election of 1856 was more than a referendum on the success of the Nebraska solution. They reiterated their claim that the Republicans used the act as a pretext for attacking the principle of democracy. Again, these Democrats asked whether the citizens of the several states would "now refuse, to the people of the Territories the rights your noble sires demanded of the Crown, and won by their blood—thus placing yourself in opposition to the right of self-government in the Territories, thereby occupying the very position towards the Territories that George III did to the colonies?" Indeed, the Democracy looked beyond the immediate crisis in Kansas and declared that the nation's problems could be traced to the neglect of the party's fundamental principles. The greatest folly of government, Ohio's Clement Vallandigham asserted, was the attempt to "square our political institutions and our legislation by mere abstract, theoretical, and mathematically exact, but impracticable truths."[50]

For three decades Democrats opposed any circumscription of individual liberties by external forces or institutions. The bank, Henry Clay, Daniel Webster, and the Whig Party had all passed into the shades, however. Still, the *Cleveland Plain Dealer* averred that the battle against Republican restriction was the same "that has ever existed between the democratic and anti-democratic parties in this country. It was the doctrine of HAMILTON and the elder ADAMS that the people were not capable of self-government, and therefore should not be trusted with power. JEFFERSON held differently; and here political parties sprang up, dividing on the principle of popular sovereignty." Drawing a clear line between the Democratic territorial policy and that of the Republicans, the *Plain Dealer* situated the Nebraska formula in these long-established differences. "We go for *encouraging* freedom in the Territories by donating lands in small parcels to actual settlers, and favoring emigration thither of the oppressed of all the nations without regard to birth or creed," it held. "Then we give to *the people* of said Territories the right to determine the character of their own institutions." Robert J. Walker, soon to be governor of Kansas, warned the party faithful that if the Democracy's principles were broken down, "We will all then stand amid the ruins of the irrevocable past. . . . The books will be opened, and the despots [will] pronounce our sentence, the doom of our race as they believe, self government is a bloody and delusive phantom."[51]

Just as revealing as the Democracy's defense of its principles was the party's definition of, and attack on, the Republican movement. In 1854 Democrats observed with some contempt and perhaps a little concern that "a Fusion, Free Soil, and Abolition conglomeration of opposition has taken [Whiggery's] place, which, blending all the isms and one-ideans [sic] of this free thinking or political freebooting community, promises to give us plenty of business for some time to come." And so it did. A year later, in 1855, southern Democrats observed with alarm that in the North, parties divided between a sectional organization "made up of isms, infidelities, superstitions and heresies on the one side, and the old, well-tried, successful and conservative Democratic party on the other."[52]

By 1856 Democrats North and South likened the antislavery movement to a black hole that swallowed up other issues such as temperance and nativism. The *Illinois State Register* claimed that former Whigs, "having more love for power and office, than for principle or consistency, united . . . with the entire abolition horde." In like vein, the *New Orleans Daily Picayune*, noting the disparate and hostile "isms" that made up the Republican Party, concluded that it was logical and inevitable that they would fuse on a single, sectional issue. Elements of the party, it explained, "are types of ultraism, which, antagonistic in all other points, harmonize in [a] phrenzy [sic] of hatred to Southern institutions and enmity to Southern claims of equality under the constitution." Simply to say that antislavery was the glue that held these disparate reform movements together misses the point. William Cabell Rives conceded the power of Know-Nothingism throughout the nation. He added, however, that "the antislavery feeling is, at present, so predominant in all New-England that neither 'know nothings' nor any other political party or portion of society sufficiently numerous to make itself felt there, is exempt from it."[53]

Democrats believed that the Republican Party had transformed Jacksonian political dialogue. A Florida Democrat maintained, "It is a momentous issue. The South must meet it." Andrew Stevenson, a Virginia Democrat, attacked slavery agitation because it had caused established party divisions to fall before a sectional and geographical combination. This lamentable development, he cried, was "that monstrous evil against which the warning voice of Washington was so signally raised. . . . The times [are] of great peril and danger to all that is dear to the country. . . . They have no parallel in its annals!" Of course, the Democracy had always blathered on in the same hyperbolic way in every election since 1828. Yet whereas "their points of difference were confined to the principles on which the Government might be administered with most benefit and advantage to the common weal," the case was now different. A wholly sectional party was contesting for the presidency, the *New Orleans Daily Picayune* declared, "on the basis of avowed and unrelenting hostility to the domestic institutions and equal constitutional rights of the Southern States." Secretary of State William Marcy concluded that the 1856 contest involved much more than the rise or fall of a party. The triumph of the Republican ticket would try the strength of the bonds of Union. "The experiment is full of danger which I am loathe to see made," he commented ruefully.[54]

The Democracy first tried to neutralize the Republican appeal with racebaiting. One Pittsburgh editor declared, "To elevate the African race in this country to complete equality of political and economic condition with the white man, is the one aim of the [Republican] party." Democrats charged that Republicans dangerously manipulated antislavery sentiment to reap political advantage. Excitement of the slave question seemed to be the very lifeblood of the Republican Party. Take this away, a Democratic publicist ventured, "and there remains to them only a few minor and kindred topics, by the agitation of which they cannot hope to secure position and notoriety."[55]

A much more evocative argument was the Democracy's appeal to a citizen's love of the Union and attachment to the party. Robert J. Walker reminded Democrats that northern voters composed the Republican Party and that its doctrine was not only sectional, aggressive, and belligerent but revolutionary. In contrast, Democrats crowed, "Our position is with the great conservative party of the day. The party that has ever stood true to its principles. It is a national party." Its fundamental tenets were states' rights and self-government. When those doctrines have been rigidly and faithfully applied, one party member pointed out, "no aggressions have been made by the General Government on either the rights of the States or the liberty of the people." Even former Whigs, like North Carolina's Daniel Barringer, admitted that on the territorial question, the Democracy occupied the conservative, constitutional, and national ground. "It is the only party now in existence, which can meet together—discuss and adopt principles and resolves on the 'subject' of the same or even similar character *in every land and in all sections of the country.*"[56]

For the moment, the Democratic message was upbeat and familiar. "The only party in the country at the present time which can set up a pretense of nationality is the Democratic party," the *Nashville Union* asserted. "There is nothing wonderful in this, to those who believe that no party can permanently exist save as the representatives of sound and national principles." Senator John B. Weller of California told an audience of New Hampshire

Democrats that the Constitution, administered on Democratic principles, had made Americans a great and prosperous people. The nation had expanded. Commerce had grown. Arts and sciences had progressed. "Hold on, then, to the Union," he begged; "secure to each State the full, free, and undisturbed enjoyment of its constitutional rights, and our republican institutions shall continue to dispense the blessings of liberty to millions upon millions yet unborn."[57]

That is how it was to play within Democratic ranks. Republicans, however, hooted that "there is no enthusiasm for Buchanan which has its origins in the hearts of the people." A more telling blow was the charge that Buchanan, indeed all the old leaders of the northern Democracy, had closed ranks with the aristocratic oligarchy of the slave states. Party members further pointed out that even if Buchanan embraced democratic principles, the Democratic platform compelled him to continue the pro-southern course of the Pierce administration in Kansas. "The 'squatter sovereignty' hobby and the "non-intervention' dodge," one party member snorted, "holds together at the present time two wings of the black Democracy."[58]

In June 1856 Republican delegates met at the Music Fund Hall in Philadelphia. Save for internal improvements, they omitted the economic questions that had shaped Jacksonian politics. Focusing on the sectional issue, the platform asserted that the fathers had committed the nation to an antislavery policy. It denied Congress, territorial legislatures, or "associations of individuals" the authority to give legal sanction to slavery in the territories. The platform asserted that Washington had sovereign power over the territories and that it was Congress's right and duty to prohibit the extension of slavery. In an appeal to nativists and immigrants alike, the party called on all those who agreed with the platform's antislavery principles, however they might disagree on other questions, to support the national ticket. The delegates nominated John C. Frémont for president and a former Whig, William Dayton of New Jersey, for vice-president.[59]

Responding to the Democratic claim that they were sectionalists and antidemocratic radicals, Republicans answered tu quoque. The Democratic Party, they asserted during the canvass, "has no basis but in the oligarchy of the South—we might well call it the BLACK OLIGARCHY." Hannibal Hamlin of Maine charged that his former party's sole criterion for admission to its ranks was support for slavery. "It has no other issue," he declared; "that is the standard by which it measures everything and every man!!! Beautiful Democracy!!! I did not learn my principles, and shall not practice, in that school." Henry Raymond argued that only the Locos advocated subversive and revolutionary principles. Buchanan, Douglas, and the rest had abandoned strict constitutional construction; had moved from conserving a Union dedicated to freedom to dissolving it for the sake of slavery; had broken solemn compromises to practice fraud, perjury, and wrong; and had degenerated from civilization to barbarism. It is, he contended, "a progression moving with accelerated velocity away from the faith and practice of the fathers." A Hoosier Republican closed the circle when he maintained, "Liberty and the rights of Freedom and the Free North are only secondary objects in [the Democracy's] view of the true intent and meaning of the sacred charter of American Liberty." Democratic policy, he argued, "subverts and overthrows the great fundamental doctrine of our institutions, viz: that the majority shall govern."[60]

Republicans fashioned a national campaign that sought to appeal to the widest spectrum of anti-Democratic groups. The first step was to convince the northern public that the slavepower controlled the Democracy and that the entire party was recreant to the principles of the Revolution. Accordingly, Republicans warned free-state voters that the nation was "fast falling backwards toward a kingly government—towards an aristocracy founded on slavery such as the world never saw." Abraham Lincoln lamented that the spirit that animated the fathers "has itself become extinct, with the *occasion* and the *men* of the Revolution. . . . The fourth of July has not quite dwindled away; it is still a great day—*for burning fire crackers*!!!" Josiah Quincy of Massachusetts feared that there was no longer any life left in the revolutionary heritage. "The palsy of death rests on the spirit of freedom in the so-called Free States."[61]

Expanding on and exploiting these sentiments, Republicans urged voters to restore the nation to its original purpose. James Shepherd Pike, writing in the *New York Daily Tribune*, informed his readers, "If we cannot, as a nation, agree to go back to the position of the founders of the Government . . . and administer Government in the interest of universal Freedom . . . the longer continuance of the existing Union is a political impossibility." In a dramatic call to arms, Hamlin told a gathering of Boston Republicans that the 1856 canvass was "a time for men of all classes to rally to the standard and preserve the institutions of freedom bequeathed by your fathers." An Ohio Republican ventured to Benjamin Wade that the election would mark "the beginning of the second 'American Revolution'—the North is the band struggling for freedom—the South is the despotic power which wishes to enslave the North." The ineluctable conclusion to be drawn from the party's regenerative appeal was, Horace Greeley deduced, that "the Republican movement is defensive not aggressive; conservative of freedom . . . and its success will be, not a consummation but a glorious beginning."[62]

Without denying the strength of nativism or the importance of Know-Nothing support, Republicans were able to define the issues of the 1856 election in such a way as to eclipse (though not obliterate) cultural concerns. Aided by events in Kansas, the Republican organization emerged as the dominant party in the North by stressing its committed opposition to the slavepower. The party assumed that the goal of the black oligarchy was to make slavery "FOREVER THE CONTROLLING ELEMENT OF OUR GOVERNMENT." Consequently, Henry Wilson told the Republican convention that the object of the party was "to overthrow the Slave Power of the country, now organized in the Democratic party of the country." Although the platform emphasized the power and duty of Congress to restrict slavery, the *Albany Evening Journal* declared, "in purpose and in spirit it is a second Declaration of Independence, and as such, after accomplishing its immediate mission, it will be transmitted to future generations as the CHART by which we were guided through a great and triumphant Political Reformation."[63]

The absolutist nature of the 1856 struggle is indicated by the Republican claim (a mirror image of that of the Democrats) that the stakes of the campaign were the maintenance of republican government. Republicans became increasingly convinced that "the breach between the North and South is becoming wider and the distinctive features that have marked great political parties are becoming less & less visible." Hamlin likewise agreed that the only issue facing the republic is "whether liberty and the Union or slavery and the Union, shall be characteristic of our government." Thurlow Weed had already pointed out to New York Republicans that adjustment could settle finance and taxation questions. Issues of civil or religious proscription would expire eventually. "But so long as there is a Foot of Free Soil owned by the Union," he contended, "or a Slaveholder who covers it, so long will there be questions of Freedom and Slavery." It was no longer a mere question of slavery extension or free soil, another Republican argued, "but of Liberty and Republicanism on one side, and 'Divine Right' and Despotism on the other."[64]

Southern rights Democrats heartily concurred. The election of Frémont on a sectional, antislavery platform, they maintained, would exclude the South from all share in the executive branch. If slavery was now made "by a *coup d'etat* the ground of banishment from the Federal Executive," the *Richmond Enquirer* cried, "we [must] complain of a test, which, in violation of the Constitution, excludes us permanently from Government, and subverts its fundamental principles. We complain that the Government is revolutionized." Slave-state politicians denied that "a free government [can] exist controlled by a section. . . . It is an utter impossibility, at war with the plainest dictates of reason and common sense." Whatever sense the South might have of its rights, a Carolina editor maintained, it would be fettered by the power of the absolute majority to vote it down. To submit to the election of Frémont, the *Enquirer* concluded, "would be to acknowledge ourselves as a conquered province, and to invite the victors to despoil us of all our remaining rights and property."[65]

The wholly logical conclusion to be deduced from this southern rights response to the 1856 Republican campaign was that Frémont's election would signal an end to the Union of the fathers. R. M. T. Hunter warned a New York audience that to administer the government on Republican principles and in conformity with its platform "would be virtually to dissolve the Union, because it has excluded the South from all benefit of the Constitution." The *North Carolina Standard* declared that even if the administration made no overt or direct attack on the South, the Union could not be administered nor could it exist on sectional grounds. "No true or decent Southern man would accept office under him," it exclaimed, "and our people would never submit to have their post offices, customs houses and the like, filled with Frémont's Yankee abolitionists." The life of the Union, of course, was the Constitution. Daniel Barringer, a southern Whig who took the field for Buchanan, asserted that the South loved the Union, but the Union under the Constitution. "She will not tamely submit to be put under the political ban—and live in the Union in a condition of colonial vassalage and dependence," he declared.[66]

Throughout the campaign, southerners talked openly of the possibility of secession. Some continued to believe that the threat of secession by a united South would lead northerners to rebuke a sectional party. Other southern Democrats moved beyond browbeating. Frémont's election, they contended, would seem to prove that the northern mind was thoroughly imbued with its supposed supremacy and stubbornly bent upon pursuing its own sectional ideas. In that case, secession would be a guarantee for the future and a means by which republican government might be preserved. Make no mistake, southern rights advocates asserted; the South is loyal to the Union "but she will not sacrifice all that is valuable—property, self-respect & social happiness upon its altar."[67]

Precisely because the South did cherish the Union, states'-rights activists were compelled to remind southerners that "the Federal Union is not a god—it is a human institution." It was formed, they averred, to benefit the people who made it. "So long as it answers the ends of its creation, it should be and will be carefully preserved," one Alabamian claimed. "When it fails those ends, it should be discarded." Those southerners who were willing to contemplate secession denied repeatedly that it would be a deathblow to republican government and, thus, "that the interests of other nations following in our footsteps, would be irrevocably ruined." It was the substance, not the shadow, of liberty that was to be regarded, the *Richmond Enquirer* would later claim: "The Union is only the corporeal clay containing the soul of liberty.

Let the Constitution be perverted and prostituted, and we would willingly admit, that self-government is not a fact but a failure. Dissever the Union rather than disregard the genius of our institutions, and that section that separates sooner than submit, carries with it, and will ever retain, the vital principles of our government." Simply put, should a sectional party triumph and thereby force the slave states to secede, "the North would be the violator of government, the South its protector."[68]

Although the logic of secession was advanced in 1856, the case against the North was not yet conclusive. Pierce appeared to be taking a neutral course in Kansas. Buchanan's nomination was a disappointment to the president's supporters in the South, but discerning states'-rights advocates conceded that it was "a ticket for the Union Wing of the Southern Democracy, such as Houston, Cobb of Georgia, *et id omne genus*." The most hopeful had always asserted that "the Democracy of the North is intelligent, patriotic and faithful to the Union and the Constitution." Still, like their northern colleagues, southern Democrats admitted in 1856 that differences existed over the exact meaning of popular sovereignty. Yet they trusted that reason would triumph in Kansas and expected "that the Courts of law as constituted in that Territory, and above all that the Supreme Court of the United States would [not] respect a subsequent law of the territory, interfering with rights which have accrued under the provisions of the act of Congress." Whatever their suspicions and concerns, none could deny that against the "monstrous combination" of Republicanism, "the Democracy of the North, and the Democracy alone, opposed a bold front, and proclaim eternal war." So, for the moment, it was "consoling to reflect that the Democratic party in every State of the Union, stands like a break water, resisting the onsweeping tide of fanaticism and folly."[69]

The usually cautious James Buchanan informed Virginia's John Y. Mason that he was confident of election. But, he warned, "if this should be accomplished by the votes of the Southern States united with Pennsylvania & New Jersey alone, it might only be the beginning of the end." The Democratic ticket took every southern state except for Maryland but carried only the five free states of Pennsylvania, New Jersey, Douglas's Illinois, Indiana, and California. Frémont won eleven northern states — all of them except for Ohio were farther north than Buchanan's twenty — and 114 electoral votes. If Pennsylvania and either Illinois or Indiana had gone for Frémont, the Republicans would have triumphed in their first presidential contest. Equally ominous was that, although Buchanan had 59 percent of the electors, he polled only 45 percent of the popular vote. Frémont polled 33 percent, and Millard Fillmore, the Know-Nothing candidate, 21 percent. Frémont and

Buchanan, however, captured 86 percent of the free-state vote. Fillmore, the nativist candidate, did not carry a single northern state and finished second in only one, California. In contrast, in the South, where the American ticket was seen as a Unionist movement, it received at least 40 percent of the vote in ten of the slave states.[70]

Putting the best face on the results, Tennessee's Andrew Johnson exalted that the American people "have Shown their Capacity for Self Government more conclusively in this election than at a[n]y time heretofore—It has not been a triumph of a man; but of principle over faction and Sectionalism." William Marcy, however, who would be dead within a year, wrote to George Bancroft that "uncertainty and gloom" clouded the future of politics. Arguing that hatred for slavery was deep-seated in the North, a southern rights Democrat said that the settlement of the territorial question had been postponed and that "the fight has yet to come off." Republicans, disappointed by defeat but heartened by the party's rapid advance, remained firm in their conviction that as long as slavery continued to exist it would be aggressive. And as long as the slavepower continued its own aggrandizement, they would continue to argue, it would "require such a party as the Republican [one] always in the field to resist its overall strides. . . . The war is *not over*: it is only just begun."[71]

James Buchanan's inauguration was held on March 4, 1857, a perfect spring day. The inaugural parade began at noon and started off down Pennsylvania Avenue. It was delayed slightly when the arrangements committee discovered that, through an oversight, it had forgotten to pick up President Pierce at the Willard Hotel. Finally, after twenty minutes, the committee fetched the president, and he joined the president-elect in his four-horse barouche. When they reached the Capitol, the group gathered first in the Senate Chamber, where Vice-President Breckinridge took the oath of office. Afterward, the dignitaries adjourned to the stand in front of the east portico. There Buchanan met with Chief Justice Roger B. Taney, and the two had a brief chat. Then the president-elect delivered his inaugural address. He viewed his victory as an endorsement of man's capacity for self-rule. Buchanan congratulated Congress for similarly adopting the simple principle that the majority shall govern the settlement of the territorial issue. He admitted that there was some difference of opinion as to the moment when the people of the territories could decide this question for themselves. But, he added, it was "a matter of but little practical importance. Besides, it is a judicial question, which legitimately belongs to the Supreme Court. . . . To their decision, in common with all good citizens, I shall cheerfully submit, whatever this may be." Once this question had been laid to rest, Buchanan concluded, "may we not, then, hope that the long agitation on this subject is approaching its end, and that the geographical parties to which it has given birth, so much dreaded by the Father of his Country, will speedily become extinct?"[72] Chief Justice Taney then swore in James Buchanan as the nation's chief executive. Twenty-eight years would pass before another Democrat would be sworn in as president.

Oh, that deceit should steal such gentle shapes,
And with a virtuous vizard hide foul guile.
—Shakespeare, *Richard III*

When people expect to get "something for nothing" they are sure to be cheated, and
generally deserve to be. —Phineas T. Barnum, *Struggles and Triumphs*

To the Egress

Humbug and the Disruption
of the Democracy

The sun broke clear and bright over Washington on the morning of March 6,
1857. Throughout the capital, Democrats were still recuperating from eat-
ing the five hundred gallons of oysters, eight hundred chickens, one hundred gallons of ice cream, and unlimited quantities of venison, beef, turkey,
pheasants, ham, and lobster served at James Buchanan's inaugural ball. As
subdued party members attempted to shake off the effects of these powerful aliments, the United States Supreme Court convened in the dim, cool
basement of the Capitol. At precisely eleven o'clock, a procession of black-
robed justices following the uncertain gait of Chief Justice Roger B. Taney
marched into the chamber. Taney, tall, thin, bent, with deeply furrowed features and a waxy complexion, began reading the Court's decision in the case
of *Dred Scott* v. *Sandford*. He spoke in a reedy voice until half past one, by

which time his words had become a whisper. As the remaining justices read their separate concurring opinions, the spectators, who included Secretary of State Lewis Cass, former attorney general Caleb Cushing, and Senators John J. Crittenden and Henry Wilson, drifted away. By late afternoon news of the decision was spreading throughout the North. The Court, reports read, had nationalized slavery. It had repudiated the power of Congress to outlaw slavery in the territories. Popular sovereignty, Republican editors claimed, had been dealt a crippling, perhaps fatal, blow. The triumph of the slave-power appeared complete.[1]

However electrifying the decision, it was not unexpected. The case had been wending its way through the federal court system since May 1854. Buchanan said in his inaugural address that he would cheerfully submit to the Court's decision. The president, who was aware of the nature of the ruling, expected that "an expression of the court on this troublesome question" would allay sectional tensions, destroy the Republican Party, and ensure harmony within the Democracy.[2] The decision unleashed sectional passions and provided Republicans with conclusive proof of the existence of a slave-power conspiracy.

Because the unhappy story of the Buchanan administration is the story also of the disruption of the Democracy, most historians have tended to draw a line from the *Dred Scott* decision to the blowup of the party in 1860. By stressing the theoretical contradiction between Taney's opinion that territorial legislatures could not prohibit slavery and the northern version of popular sovereignty, historians have underestimated the consensus within the party regarding the Court's decision. They have overemphasized its effect on sectional differences over the meaning of noninterference. Initially, at least, *Dred Scott* had a much greater effect on the Republican belief in a slavepower conspiracy than it did on sectional divisions within the Democracy. The Republican attack on the case had the effect of uniting the Democracy behind the Court. A conservative New York editor asserted that *Dred Scott* "dissipates the mist in which we have been enveloped for years; it exposes in all their deformities the slavery heresies by which we have been disturbed for more than a half a century."[3]

Although both wings of the party initially applauded the Court's decision, extreme states'-rights southerners remained wary. They had little confidence that a single court case could put down antislavery politics at the North. At the point when these slave-state Democrats began to wonder if the guarantees of the decision might prove illusory, the struggle over the Lecompton Constitution demonstrated what little support southerners could expect from the northern wing of their party. Put in other terms, the Lecompton fiasco proved to them that their alliance with northern Locos was a trap and that popular sovereignty was a hoax. Northern Democrats, in contrast, left the battlefield bloodied and convinced that the slave states were willing to resort to trickery and fraud to gain a sectional advantage.

As southern Democrats saw it, the status of Kansas as a free or slave state was less important than the principle of state equality. Because the history of the middle period is written backward from 1860, historians remain as skeptical of their argument today as Republicans then were. Yet Lecompton Democrats also knew that the slave population in Kansas was small. They realized that the viability of the institution there was problematic. If, then, the Lecompton question is viewed forward from the perspective of 1854, their analysis does not appear so farfetched. And it was this analysis of the issues involved in the struggle over Kansas statehood that proved fatal to comity within the party. When Douglas split with the administration over Lecompton, extreme states'-rights Democrats concluded that their alliance with the northern wing was a sham. Lecompton, not *Dred Scott*, was the beginning of the end for the Democracy.

On the heels of that debacle, Douglas's Freeport dodge and John Brown's raid on Harpers Ferry convinced southern fire-eaters that they must confront black Republicanism directly. As one southerner put it, stale arguments commanded no new listeners, and compromises and adjustments "seem to be alike distasteful to both sections." Humbuggery must stop. Thus on the eve of the 1860 nominating convention, southern senators insisted that Congress and the Democracy state positively that the national government would intervene if necessary to protect slavery in the territories. Douglas Democrats were quick to point out the incongruity of such a demand by the advocates of states' rights and limited government. Historians have followed their lead. Slave-state senators, however, believed their demand to be necessary, consistent with the Constitution and Democratic principles, and a function of a government whose purpose was to protect property rights. If this bold declaration of the Democracy's principles meant discarding Douglas, so much the better. In the aftermath of Lecompton and Douglas's shuffling at Freeport, his opponents had come to the conclusion that his brand of popular sovereignty was "like 'Radway's Ready Relief,' a cure 'for all the ills that the flesh is heir to.' It is not only a panacea, but like the cap of Fortunatas, it will make all rich who wear it."[4] Thus it was less *Dred Scott* than events in Kansas, Illinois, Virginia, and within the Democratic Senate caucus that proved fatal to the unity of the Democracy.

To Republicans, it was no coincidence that Scott's case had been introduced into the federal court system the same year that the Kansas-Nebraska Act passed. The slavepower "planned to inaugurate on the 4th of March, 1857, a Federal combination of influences in behalf of slavery, that should include the Executive power, the legislative power and the Judicial power of the Republic," the *Albany Evening Journal* argued. "To this end the appeal of the case of Dred Scott had been prepared." In Buchanan's inaugural, Senator William H. Seward observed, the president cheerfully pledged his submission to the Court's final and authoritative decision, while the chief justice and his associates remained attentive—and silent. On the following day, Seward sneered, "the judges without even changing their own silken robes for courtiers' gowns," paid their respects to the president. "Doubtlessly," the senator from New York claimed, "the President received them as graciously as Charles I did the Judges who had, at his instance, subverted the statutes of English liberty." On March 6, the oligarchs apparently achieved their grand object: the *Dred Scott* decision transformed free territories into "one great slave pen."[5]

Republicans mounted an intense, vituperative attack on the Court's southern members. They especially vilified Taney, a former slaveholder from Maryland. Once they had aroused the suspicions and the passions of the North, party members then denied flatly that the decision was binding. They claimed that once the majority had decided that Scott, either as a black or as a slave, had no recourse to the federal courts, the Court resolved the question before it. Republicans like Senator Hannibal Hamlin charged that the Court "had no more authority to decide a political question for us, than we had to decide a judicial question for them. . . . We make the laws, they interpret them." By circumventing the decision, Republicans were able to attack the intent of the Court, ignore Taney's circumscriptions of congressional power, and assert that they were defending the nation's institutions, not subverting them. Senator William Pitt Fessenden informed his colleagues that he did not attack the decision for the Court had made none. "My belief is, my position is, that that very opinion, if carried into practice, undermines the institutions of the country," he warned.[6]

Fessenden's comment is suggestive. On the one hand, Republicans denied the force of the decision by alleging that the Court took up a political issue and ruled on a question not properly before it. On the other, it was precisely because the Court attempted to exceed its authority that the decision appeared so threatening. By using the Constitution to protect property created by state and municipal law, one Republican argued, the Supreme Court "has changed the Constitution of the United States in a most material point. It has given to that instrument a character which was not designed by its Framers, known or suspected by the People who adopted it." Thus the positions assumed by the majority were "palpable perversions of the views of the Fathers of the Republic," the *Ohio State Journal* concluded. Previously, antislavery northerners had vied in political combat with states'-rights southerners for the right to control the government. *Dred Scott*, most now believed, had taken the struggle into a new phase. "Are we to accept, without question, these new readings of the Constitution," William Cullen Bryant asked, "to admit that the Constitution was never before rightly understood, even by those who framed it — to consent that hereafter it shall be the slaveholders' instead of the freemen's Constitution? Never! Never!"[7]

The first crisis of Buchanan's administration was, for Republicans, a denouement. Abraham Lincoln suggested to an audience in Springfield, Illinois, that "when we see a lot of framed timbers different portions of which we know have been gotten out at different times and places and by different workmen — Stephen, Franklin, Roger and James, for instance — and we see these timbers joined together . . . in *such* a case we find it impossible to not *believe* that Stephen and Franklin and Roger and James all understood one another from the beginning, and all worked upon a common *plan* or *draft* drawn up before the first lick was struck." Eschewing metaphors for historical reconstruction, a Pennsylvania editor informed his readers that seventy years before, the Ordinance of 1787 hemmed in slavery. Thirty years earlier southerners rubbed out part of that line by opening up slavery south of 36°30'. In 1854 Democrats erased the line altogether. Now, he claimed, "they turn humbly to [the slaveholder], hat in hand, and say, 'Go where you please; the land is all yours, the National flag shall protect you, and the National troops shoot down who ever resists you.' This is the Dred Scott Decision."[8]

For all its inherent dangers to Republicans, the *Dred Scott* decision had its advantages. It proved that the South's defense of states' rights was so much tomfoolery. Gideon Welles, a former Democrat, charged that states'-rights southerners who historically opposed a strong national government had reversed their position. "They are now the centralists," Welles exclaimed. "When their interests and their principles are in conflict, they take care of their interests, and would nationalize it, at the expense of those principles they have hitherto expressed." Senator James R. Doolittle extended Welles's argument, declaring that since the Constitution of the United States was the paramount law of every state, if it recognized "slaves as property, as horses are property, no state Constitution or State law can abolish it, or prohibit its introduction."[9]

The Court's decision, an Illinois Republican declared, "puts an end to the hypocrisy of those who, while supporting Mr. Buchanan, pretend to oppose the spread of slavery. . . . That neither the territories nor Congress have any power over slavery is the doctrine of the day, professed by those who call themselves Democrats, and who are in fact the tools of a provincial oligarchy." Buchanan, elected on a platform of noninterference, pledged that his administration would carry out the principles of the Constitution as expounded by the Court. Taney and his coconspirators then judged that the "Constitution *ex proprio vigore* carries slavery into every portion of the federal territory." It was wonderful irony. By declaring that Congress had no power to prohibit slavery, one Ohio editor reasoned, the Court in reality decided "that the people of the territories have no power, through their legislature or otherwise, to pass laws restricting or prohibiting slavery therein." Hence a decision conceived in chicanery, steeped in fraud, and designed to cheat northerners of their rights effectively placed popular sovereignty in conflict with the Constitution. This Democratic hoax, the *Illinois State Journal* blithely declared, "is stricken down, acknowledged to be a humbug, which has had its day, and is now laid aside, as useless, in the political garret."[10]

Republican hopes notwithstanding, initially both free- and slave-state Democrats heartily endorsed the Court's decision. Regarding *Dred Scott* as the authoritative and final settlement of sectional issues, the *Illinois State Register* hailed it as "the greatest political boon which has been vouchsafed to us since the founding of the Republic." Party members in both sections bragged that *Dred Scott* "fully and completely vindicates and sustains the Democratic party in the patriotism and wisdom of its course throughout the entire history of slavery agitation." A Pennsylvania Democrat predicted that inasmuch as the Court had laid the question of slavery in the territories to rest, "there is nothing, so far as the slavery question is concerned, about which the national democracy can possibly differ."[11]

In contrast to the internal strains evinced in 1848, 1850, and 1854, the Democracy understood the decision to be an endorsement of the principles that sustained the party in those heated debates. Most immediately *Dred Scott* validated the maligned Kansas-Nebraska Act. As party members viewed it, the Court put to rest antislavery claptrap about violations of sacred compacts by deciding that the Missouri restriction had always been unconstitutional and, therefore, void. "Its repeal, then, by the Nebraska bill, was a harmless act, proper in itself, and, in fact, changing no existing law," a Pittsburgh Democrat observed. At a more fundamental level, the Court also appeared to endorse the Democracy's solution of noninterference in the territorial issue. Far from being a fraud and a firebrand as Republicans had charged, the *Louisville Daily Journal* contended, *Dred Scott* left no doubt that the states to be formed out of the territories would determine for themselves the status of slavery. Hence the decision left the slavery question "with the only proper tribunal to decide upon its existence or nonexistence within a given boundary": the people of the several states.[12]

For Democrats, the decision endorsed principles that they had championed since the age of Jackson. One Alabama Democrat understood the Court's decision to be another check against the unwarranted and unconstitutional centralization of power in the federal government. "From the idea of the character of the Federal and State Government, have sprung an antagonism to a United States Bank, a Protective Tariff, Internal Improvements by the General Government and a host of other dangerous measures," he wrote. "To it we owe the Kansas Nebraska Act and the recent decision of the Supreme Court." That the decision embraced the axiomatic truths of state equality and the equal rights of the citizens of the various states especially satisfied southern Democrats. Inasmuch as *Dred Scott* recognized slaves as property and the right of the master to property in slaves, it followed that there was no longer any doubt that the power of Congress over the territories was limited; in no way could the federal government contravene the right of the free and slave states to joint occupancy. This did not imply any special right, privilege, or advantage to the slave states. It simply embodied the premise of equality and the promise of open competition. The North, one states'-rights southerner acknowledged, "will always roll on its own axis west along its own latitude a stream of emigration which the South cannot possibly equal, so that it would appear impossible for the South to people States as rapidly as the North." [13]

As this observation suggests, the South did not consider the decision to be sectionally biased, aggressive, or revolutionary. Moderates in the slave states congratulated the Supreme Court for enacting this bulwark—not establishing an advanced position—of southern rights. The *Nashville Union* observed that, as a conservative statement of fundamental rights, *Dred Scott* meant that "now every Department of the Government has sanctioned our views, and the principles of the Kansas Nebraska Act has [*sic*] been recognized by a majority of Congress, a Northern President and Northern Judges of the Supreme Court." Even fire-eaters were content to observe with some sarcasm that as so-called disunionists they had neither disturbed the law, intruded novelties upon the country, nor sought to break up established principles. "We have been simply a step in advance of the highest tribunals in the country, in declaring what was the law of the land, and seeking honestly and faithfully to enforce it," the *Charleston Mercury* gloated. [14]

Democrats North and South hailed *Dred Scott* as a triumph of nationalism. "*Sectionalism* has been rebuked, and abolitionism has been staggered and stunned," a Virginia Democrat cheered. In a call to arms, the *Cleveland Plain Dealer* added, "The conservative, intelligent good sense of the people . . . will ultimately triumph over those who now profess to be ready to raise the standard of revolution." Senator William Bigler told embattled Pennsylvania Democrats that the Court "swept away the entire stock in trade of the Republican agitators. . . . Their long cherished business of agitation is gone—gone forever." Speaking for all southerners, the *New Orleans Picayune* maintained that *Dred Scott* "puts the whole basis of the Black Republican organization under the ban of law, stamps its designs as hostile to the Constitution, and forms a basis upon which all conservative men of the Union can unite for the maintenance of the Constitution as it is and the Union as it is."[15]

Democratic Party leaders and editors asserted that "the people who revere the Constitution and the laws . . . will hail the decision with satisfaction" and therefore must regard *Dred Scott* as the "authoritative and final settlement of grievous sectional issues." Adherence to *Dred Scott* consequently became a test of sectional goodwill. A southern rights advocate claimed that "there is no duty now but obedience." Continued dissent "*is revolutionary in its character*," the *Nashville Union* thundered. "There is no longer any pretense to cover treason." Looking askance at the sectional politics that had riven Congress and the nation for more than a decade, the *Louisville Daily Journal* expressed the wish that the decision would "mark the beginning of a revolution in the politics of the country."[16]

As early as June 1857, however, Stephen Douglas declared openly his belief that irrespective of the Court's decision and Taney's obiter dictum, slavery could not exist in a territory against the wishes of the citizens there. Douglas conceded that the *Dred Scott* decision clearly guaranteed the right of a master to take his slaves into a territory. The right, however, was "barren and worthless" unless public sentiment supported it and "unless sustained, protected and enforced by appropriate police regulations and local legislation." Southern Democrats such as Samuel Smith of Tennessee and James L. Orr of South Carolina had already said as much. The *Washington Union*, which would later attempt to read the Illinois senator out of the party, praised Douglas's speech for its "lucid statements, vigorous thoughts, and powerful arguments."[17]

Perhaps taking note of these arguments, extreme states'-rights southerners were quick to suggest that the South's high expectations for the efficacy of *Dred Scott* in the territories would prove delusive. A North Carolina editor reminded his readers that northerners had unsound principles and as a people were excitable. Another slave-state citizen who refused to be hoodwinked pointed out that the South had never lacked for legal and constitutional barriers to fanaticism. "The Northern mind is intent upon compassing sectional predominance, and the subversion of the South under her dominion," he cautioned. Drawing on these and like beliefs, this dissident complained, "The attempt to deceive ourselves—to allow ourselves to be deceived is weak." Southerners, therefore, were ambivalent about the effect of *Dred Scott*. All believed its principles conservative. Some cautiously predicted a return to party unity and sectional goodwill. More than a few, however, admitted that agitation against slavery would continue. In that event, one southern Democrat declared, "the people of the South will be in the condition of our Revolutionary Fathers. . . . They could neither appeal to a violated Constitution or a crushed judiciary."[18]

The struggle over Kansas statehood substantiated these fears. The history of the Lecompton Constitution is as suggestive as it is painful. Just before Franklin Pierce left office, the proslavery legislature in Kansas called for the election of delegates to a convention that would frame a state constitution. Buchanan, hoping to make popular sovereignty work and wishing to remove the territorial question as a bone of sectional contention, sent Robert J. Walker to the territory as governor. Walker was to impose order and to secure an impartial and fair election. Instead, he alarmed slave-state settlers with what many considered his free and easygoing attitude toward the free-state settlers in Kansas. Walker then infuriated southerners with loose talk about an "isothermal" line north of which slavery could not exist. Finally, he altogether discredited himself in the eyes of the South by seeming to dictate the terms of Kansas's admission to the Union. In his inaugural address, Walker asserted that "in no contingency will Congress admit Kansas as a slave state or a free state, unless a majority of the people of Kansas shall first have fairly and freely decided this question for themselves by a direct vote on the adoption of the Constitution, excluding fraud and violence."[19]

Southerners were apoplectic. "*We are betrayed*," one Georgian exploded. "Our victory is turned to ashes on our lips." Walker's seeming coziness with the Topeka agitators, the "twaddle" about natural limits to slavery, and his interference in the internal affairs of Kansas reportedly raised "the devil all over the South." Because many believed that the president knew of and approved Walker's actions, he, too, came under fire. "Buchanan has a finger in the fire, for his deuced cunning," South Carolina's Lawrence Keitt wrote. "Bring in Kansas as a slave State, and the Northern Democracy goes to the devil—therefore she must come in as a free state—and at the same time the South be blinded—We have a political Mephistopheles—only a worse rascal—an ingrained knave." If, thanks to Walker and Buchanan, Kansas were to be admitted as a free state, Thomas W. Thomas foresaw that southern Democracy would stand condemned in the eyes of her people.[20]

As it turned out, Kansas did present itself for admission as a slave state. Claiming that the voting procedure was a fraud, free-state settlers refused to participate in elections in June to the constitutional convention. Although the proslavery delegates to the convention did not represent the free-soil sentiments of a majority of the settlers, their election was legal. At the urging of Governor Walker, free-state voters then participated in the territorial elections in October and won control of the legislature. The Lecompton delegates, furious at Walker's intervention and egged on to new excesses by an emissary of slave-state forces within the administration, drafted a proslavery constitution. Instead of submitting the entire document to the voters as Walker had demanded, the delegates offered settlers the option of voting for a constitution "with slavery" or one "without slavery." If they voted "without slavery," it meant an end to the importation of slaves into Kansas. In either case, those slaves already in the territory (and their descendants) would remain. Kansas would be a slave state in either case.[21]

Buchanan maintained that the actions of the convention were strictly legal. He now declared that submission of the slavery question alone conformed to an earlier pledge to "stand or fall" on the right of the people to vote on the constitution. In his first annual message in December 1857, he asserted that the actions of the Lecompton convention complied with the letter and spirit of the Kansas-Nebraska Act. He warned free-soil forces in the territory that if they failed to vote on the constitution, "this will be their own voluntary act and they alone will be responsible for the consequences." The president believed that bringing the territories in as states as quickly as possible would end sectional quarreling over territorial rights. Disclaiming any sectional or partisan advantage in that event, Buchanan contended that Kansas had occupied too much of the public's attention for too long. Free-state voters in Kansas were unmoved. Again charging voting fraud and convinced that the partial submission was a hoax, they stayed at home. To no one's surprise, the Lecompton Constitution "with slavery" was carried by a vote of 10,226 to 138.[22]

After hearing the president's message, renegade northern Democrats began deserting their chief. The floor manager of the Compromise of 1850 and the architect of the Kansas-Nebraska Act, Senator Stephen A. Douglas, led the rebellion. When the clerk completed reading Buchanan's message, Douglas jumped to his feet to dissent from the president's comments on Kansas. He broke altogether with the administration over the Lecompton Constitution in a long, heated speech the following day. The Illinois senator flatly denied that submission of the slavery question alone complied with the intent and meaning of the Kansas-Nebraska Act. Worse, Douglas complained, the Lecompton swindle was a gross violation of Democratic practice; it smacked of deceit. "We aroused the patriotism of the country and carried the election [of 1856] in defense of that great principle, which allowed all white men to form and regulate their domestic institutions to suit themselves," he reminded his Democratic colleagues. Warming to the task, Douglas roasted the former proslavery Kansas legislature for exceeding its authority. He hotly rejected the assertion that the Lecompton convention had the power and authority to establish a state government. Above all, he excoriated the delegates and the administration for attempting to force this constitution on the people of Kansas against their will. "Is that the mode in which I am called upon to carry out the principle of self government and popular sovereignty in the territories?" Douglas asked Lecomptonites. "What are you to gain by it? . . . Neither the North nor the South has the right to gain sectional advantage by trickery or fraud." Not for the last time Douglas declared that he did not care whether slavery "is voted down or voted up in Kansas." Dismissing the constitution as the product of "trickery and juggle," he sat down.[23]

Southern Democrats replied with spirit to Douglas's charges. They declared that the people of Kansas had decided to hold a convention to frame a state constitution. The legislature duly called the convention. It required no enabling act. Remembering that the people of California had required no law authorizing them to call a convention in 1849, a Mississippi representative asked, "Are we of the South to be made to see California hurried into the Union against all law and all precedent *because she is a free state* and Kansas subjected to the rigors of the inquisition because she *has a chance* of being a slave state?" Senator William Sebastian of Arkansas didactically instructed his free-state colleagues that American forms of government were representative republics, not popular democracies. Lecompton, therefore, "is the work of the people in their sovereign capacity." This being so, an Alabama Democrat maintained that Congress had only the right to inquire whether the convention had been fairly elected and if its proceedings were in accordance with organic law. Then its sole responsibility was to determine whether the constitution was republican. To do otherwise, Virginia's R. M. T. Hunter declared, "would be to deny [Kansas] equality with other States in the Union."[24]

Southern Democrats expended much time, energy, air, and newspaper print on briefs for the Lecompton Constitution. The fact that the convention delegates were on the whole ignoble and their action outrageous made these heroic efforts necessary. Many states'-rights southerners, inclined to follow Hunter's lead, appeared troubled. "There has been to [*sic*] much of time spent, & of noise made: & so many other issues collateral to the main question that the Southern mind has been distracted," one complained. Alexander Stephens, too, maintained that all the opponents and many of the supporters of the Lecompton Constitution had overlooked the main issue by directing their attention simply to the propriety of submitting the entire document for ratification. The debate, he insisted, "brings up the old Missouri question — the right that is, or power of Congress to impose conditions or restrictions upon the new States in the formation of their Constitutions."[25]

A Tennessee Democrat who viewed the struggle in the same terms maintained that the slave states did not advocate the principles of the Kansas-

Nebraska Act because the act conveyed on them a special advantage. On the contrary, he argued, "they were incorporated in good faith into the Democratic creed because . . . the Kansas law was founded upon the great idea [self-government] upon which the superstructure of our government rests." Senator Hunter of Virginia reminded a constituent that to establish and defend the equal rights of states and the right of local self-determination, "the Democratic party has submitted to losses and sacrifices, which could only have been justified by the successful accomplishment of a great object." The southern position on Lecompton, therefore, was deduced from both abstract principles and loyalty to the party creed. Thus the pro-Lecompton *Louisville Courier* could claim in good faith, "Our position would have been the same if the Constitution now presented had been a free soil document."[26]

Southern Democrats concluded that for Congress to obtrude itself into the territory would be "a flagrant violation of the very spirit of the Kansas-Nebraska Act." Mississippi Democrat Albert G. Brown asked Nebraska dissidents in his own party, "What becomes of this boasted doctrine that the people are allowed, in the name of popular sovereignty, to organize their domestic affairs in their own way, if you are to interpose at every point to tell them what they shall and shall not do, and not only what they shall do, but when and how they shall do it?" Thus contrary to Douglas's opinion (and the weight of historical judgment), southern Democrats concluded that the Lecompton Constitution was a logical deduction from—not an aberration from—the Kansas-Nebraska Act. (Republicans heartily agreed.) Brown admonished his northern colleagues that in 1856 every member of the Cincinnati convention, its nominees, and the party throughout the Union stood on the same platform all during the campaign: "That Kansas was to be admitted . . . with or without slavery, as her people should determine . . . when she came to form her State constitution." To those who now charged "trickery and juggle," Alexander Stephens replied, "If *tricksters* were the authors of [Lecompton], they [the Democratic Party] were the *tricksters' backers.*"[27]

Slave-state Democrats in and out of Congress expressed the hope that "the 'sober second thought' of a more mature consideration" would deter their northern allies from following Douglas into rebellion. Congressional interference, commented one rather unobservant senator, "would be to transfer the discords of Kansas to the Halls of Congress, and make national issues out of Kansas quarrels." Most important, if northerners rejected the Lecompton Constitution, they would not only abridge the equality of states but also deny to the South its equal rights on a historically vital point. The free states would declare, Senator Hunter wrote, "that the most valuable of the advantages which flow from Territorial acquisition are to be confined exclusively to ourselves and to be denied to another."[28]

Northern Democrats were divided. A few, like Senator William Bigler of Pennsylvania and Representative Graham Fitch of Indiana, believed that if Congress admitted Kansas as a state, slavery agitation would be localized and sectional tensions allayed. Most free-state party members, however, were furious at Buchanan and southern Democrats. "The Democrats ought to yield the President all the support they consistently can, but something is due to the feelings and opinions of the people throughout the North," a Hoosier Democrat complained. Northern Locos observed, rightly, that the Lecompton Constitution "is more or less tainted with fraud, and its schedule, which dictates the terms of its submission to the people is redolent with trickery." Ohio's William S. Groesbeck demanded that his southern friends not force Lecompton on the free states: "Let it be executed." The real fear, of course, was that if northern Democrats did not kill Lecompton, it would kill them. A supporter cautioned Indiana representative John G. Davis, "I believe every man—North or South—who votes for 'Lecompton' will be repudiated by his constituents." [29]

Anti-Lecompton Democrats took great pains to detail the various swindles and irregularities swirling around the Lecompton convention. Taking issue with President Buchanan, they contended that the semblance of legality should not be confused with honesty. Party members also scoffed at Buchanan's suggestion that if Kansans were unhappy with the constitution, they might amend it after statehood had been granted. But like their southern counterparts, free-state Democrats considered these issues peripheral. "'Majorities must rule' . . . was tried by our forefathers and found entirely *adequate*," an Ohio Democrat maintained. "The people of Kansas have not been left *perfectly free* to regulate their domestic institutions in their own way." Lecompton, one declared, was "a gross outrage upon the very principles upon which the American Revolution was fought." Stephen Douglas, now in open revolt against the administration, stated that Lecompton "should be repudiated by every Democrat who cherishes the time-honored principle of his part, and is determined, in good faith, to carry out the doctrine of self-government and popular sovereignty." [30]

Whereas slave-state Democrats based their defense of Lecompton on the complementary principles of the equality and inviolability of state sovereignty, free-state dissidents believed that support for the constitution would revolutionize the genius of American government. That governments derived their power from the consent of the governed, Gideon Welles maintained, was "as self-evident a truth in 1857 as it was in 1776." To abandon this principle now "would be to surrender the cornerstone of our whole political system." If Kansas were admitted, a new doctrine would be introduced into our political system, Douglas cautioned. It would mean that "organic law is not to be the embodiment of popular will; that the wishes of the people have nothing to do with the provisions of their Constitution; that Congress may put any instrument on them it pleases." A careful reading of Douglas's objection suggests a tragic irony. Southern Democrats had frequently and forcefully argued that congressional interference in Kansas would tend toward, if not constitute, centralization and tyranny. Free-state Locos opposed the constitution for precisely the same reason. Charles Stuart of Michigan warned pro-Lecompton southerners that imposing Lecompton on the people of Kansas against their will was tyrannical and rested on an assumption of despotic power by the national government. Welles denounced Lecompton as "more arbitrary and more centralizing than any measure ever proposed since the adoption of the federal constitution."[31]

The Republicans, one anti-Nebraska Loco maintained, "are anxious that the Union, Day Book, Bigler & Buckhannon recent doctrine may prevail & repudiate Squatter Sovereignty & establish the doctrin that the president & Congress Shall govern the territorys which is a party of republican Creed, the same doctrin repudiates States rights." Should either of these forms of the same centralizing heresy prevail, he ventured, it "will madden the whole Democrating Northwest to a fury." A Pennsylvania editor therefore warned the administration and pro-Lecompton southerners to stand by the Kansas-Nebraska Act and the Cincinnati platform. "The Democratic party, if it wishes to maintain the confidence of the people[,] must stand by its promises," he argued. "And in this case, when they were so unequivocal and fair, particularly should they be held sacred." Rank-and-file party members applauded dissidents for hewing to historic Democratic principles of strict construction, limited government, and local self-determination. Douglas, in particular, was congratulated for his "stand upon the principles of self government and true democracy as announced by Jefferson and expounded by Jackson." Although their numbers in the free states were dwindling, Democrats continued to assert that popular sovereignty "derives all its real strength and popularity by the substitution of the will of the people immediately interested, for the will of Congress."[32]

While admitting their own precarious situation in the free states, northern Democrats cautioned pro-Lecompton southerners that a party division was even more dangerous to the interests of the South. It subverted the best and surest guarantee of southern institutions: the Democracy. Southern Democrats agreed that a united party was the last best hope of the confederacy. Slave-state representatives bristled at the suggestion that they were subverting the Democracy or the Union. An Alabama editor, however, added that the Democracy could be preserved only "by a rigid adherence, in practice as well as reflection, to the principles of its common creed and the pledges of its alliance."[33]

Repeatedly denying any desire to enforce a new orthodoxy upon any Democrat, party members in the slave states expressed "disappointment in our cooperators who favor the Douglas heresy of radical mobocracy." South Carolina's James H. Hammond told his colleagues in the Senate that Douglas's principles "would lead us directly into populous sovereignty, not popular sovereignty." The latter, he explained, was the sovereignty "of a legal, constitutional ballot box. . . . The voice of the people . . . is the voice of God; but when it is outside of that, it is the voice of a demon, the doctrine of the reign of terror." Mississippi's Albert G. Brown understood the northern Democracy's position to be "the Dorr rule, or the Brigham Young rule, or the Jim Lane rule," an "appeal to the masses without law." Mindful of growing Republican popularity in the North, they prophesied that if now with Douglas's help Lecompton was rejected and the rebels sustained, "it will establish a principle which may be carried out to the utter destruction of all popular government."[34]

All objections raised against Lecompton were "smoke and dust," the *Charleston Mercury* claimed. "It is only an old stratagem used . . . to blind the people of the South, and divert attention away from the occupation of an advanced position towards securing Southern subjection and Northern rule." Despite loose talk about southern frauds and blighted faith, Senator Hunter concluded that antagonism to Lecompton must either be because opponents "desire to keep the question open for political purposes, or else because they are unwilling to admit, even for a moment, any State which tolerates slavery by its Constitution."[35]

Notice that Hunter said "even for a moment." Disgruntled southern Democrats concluded with alarm that Lecompton's defeat would also demonstrate the pervasiveness of antislavery sentiment in the free states. Because most southerners believed that Kansas would never remain a slave state, the Lecompton battle was a practical test of the uncompromising Republican position of "no more slave states." That is, precisely because slavery's hold in the territory was so tenuous, Congress's refusal to admit Kansas would indicate the extent to which antislavery mania had grown in the free states. "The truth which has been concealed . . . has become apparent to all of us," Louisiana's Judah P. Benjamin maintained; "Kansas shall never be admitted as a slaveholding State . . . not even . . . if the whole people of the territory should establish a Constitution recognizing that institution." Even if Kansas was admitted with the Lecompton Constitution, the *Richmond Enquirer* asserted, no one entertained the notion that slavery would ever flourish there. "It is, therefore, the great principle of equality for which we are contending."[36]

Lecompton supporters in the South charged that Douglas flinched and "in an emergency abandoned his principles." The South would be opposed to Douglas and his followers forever, the *Louisville Courier* declared, "not so much because the South desire Kansas should be a slave State, as on account of the great principle set forth in the Kansas-Nebraska act, which has been violated and most shamefully set at naught." Clearly, since vindication of states' rights and southern equality was at stake in the Lecompton struggle, dissent—and dissimulation—were intolerable. An Alabama Democrat stated that support for Lecompton should be "the great test and touchstone which will put an end to all doubts and suspicions as to the sincerity of the Northern Democracy in supporting the Cincinnati platform."[37]

Alienated northern Democrats retorted that southern intransigence would prove disastrous to Kansas, the party, and the country. Admitting Kansas would not extinguish slavery agitation, they claimed; it would pour fuel on the fire. Party leaders in the free states admitted reluctantly that, previously, good Democrats in both sections had been permitted to hold and express such opinions on the territorial issue as they might deem proper without affecting their party standing. Even at that, they groused, "we have had to swallow many things which were disgraceful to us, for the sake of preserving the first great principle of democratic unity." Northern Locos were now asked to forfeit their entire heritage to battle "for the will of the minority over the expressed will of the majority." A Pennsylvania Democrat admonished his southern friends not to allow their fanatical devotion to the institution of slavery to "carry them to the extent of this, impugning the honesty of our motives, and the sincerity of our purposes." Destroy confidence between the party's sectional wings, he declared with some heat, "and you destroy the Union."[38]

Republicans basked in the glow of these Democratic pyrotechnics. "It is as clear as noonday, to even the most blinded party optics, that the 'great fundamental principle' of the Nebraska Bill was a 'great fundamental lie,'" one party leader chortled. William Fessenden suggested that the Democracy might discover that their "blighted faith" originated in the Kansas-Nebraska Act itself, not in the rascality of the Lecompton delegates. Zachariah Chandler suspected that enthralled northern Democrats could not, and imperious southerners would not, fulfill the promise of the Kansas-Nebraska Act. The Democracy, he and other party members declared, had never and did not yet believe in popular sovereignty. Not that anyone should have been surprised. A Pennsylvania Republican pointed out that since its inception, the Democracy had twisted the Constitution into every conceivable shape on every possible occasion so that an "issue may be raised . . . or a President elected." Since the Kansas-Nebraska Act in particular, Senator Lyman Trumbull claimed, the party "has been changing its position . . . almost from day to day."[39]

In this age of humbug, Republicans had little difficulty persuading northerners that in the Lecompton affair things were not always as they seemed. This was not a question of the admission of a state, New York's Preston King declared, nor was it largely or exclusively an issue of local self-determination. Lecompton revealed that "the organization of the Democratic party has fallen irretrievably under the control of nullifiers and slave propagandists." Buchanan's message on Kansas, Henry Wilson averred, was "a complete and absolute public surrender by the President of the United States to the principles, the doctrines, the policy, and the sentiments of the slaveholding propagandists of this country." In 1854, the slavepower made the Kansas-Nebraska Act a test of Democratic Party loyalty. Another test was to be made of Lecompton. Republicans cried that even Douglas, the wizard who had conjured up the act, was now transformed into a black Republican in the southern imagination. "No matter though his whole life has been devoted to the interests of slavery," Wilson boo-hooed, "if he pauses now, if he refuses to allow slavery to triumph by palpable frauds he is to be crushed . . . and to be read out of the Democratic party." Entertainment value aside, Douglas's martyrdom had its merits. It meant, William H. Seward maintained, that the Democracy "by the creeds of their party, are the recognized defenders and only defenders, of slavery in the Union."[40]

By early 1858, the wings of the Democracy were firing salvos at each other and Republicans were lobbing shells in from the outside. President Buchanan, nevertheless, pressed grimly ahead. Offers of jobs, bribes, dinner parties, alcohol, and the incomparable lures of female pulchritude were all employed (with little effect) to ram Lecompton through the two houses. As members questioned each other's integrity, morals, and family history, Congress slowly degenerated into an armed battlefield. The most spectacular melee occurred in the House on an early morning in February. When Republican Galusha Grow infiltrated the Democratic camp to palaver with anti-Lecompton northerners, Lawrence Keitt, stretched out between two seats, ordered him to leave. Grow replied hotly that it was a free House and he was a free man; he went where he pleased. Keitt, who had been asleep, grabbed Grow by the throat, initiating a fistfight that involved more than thirty members of the House. Some drunken members jumped on top of their desks and shrieked that members should stop fighting. The battle royal ended when Elihu Washburne of Illinois inadvertently knocked off William Barksdale's wig. The Mississippi representative was angry not only because few knew he wore one but also because his hairpiece was being trampled under the feet of the combatants. In his haste to retrieve his dignity, he snatched the wig up but put it on inside out, "much to the amusement of the spectators." Amid howls of laughter, the fray came to an end.[41] By this point most congressmen suspected, if the president did not, that the Senate and the House were deadlocked.

Lecompton did pass the Senate, but rebellious northern Democrats joined Republicans to prevent it from carrying in the House. In a face-saving maneuver worthy of P. T. Barnum, the administration devised a compromise that was even more preposterous than Lecompton. Known as the English bill, it offered Kansans prompt admission into the Union under Lecompton if they would accept a reduced grant of public lands to their new state. If voters insisted on the larger grant requested by the Lecompton convention, then Kansas would remain a territory until its population was equal to the number required for one representative in the House. The bill required Kansas to hold a referendum on the land grant question. Southerners bravely argued that this was not resubmission. It simply was intended to settle the one question of public lands, just as the earlier vote in Kansas on Lecompton settled the issue of slavery. Nor, they asserted, did it imply an expansion of congressional power. Speaking for an embarrassed administration to skeptical southerners, the *Washington Union* asserted that the English bill "had the merit of still recognizing the Lecompton instrument as the *legally* and *regularly* ordained constitution of Kansas."[42]

An Illinois Republican blurted, "This project is the biggest swindle yet." Senator John P. Hale contended "that if Kansas has population enough to qualify her for admission into the Union as a slave State, she has enough to qualify her for admission as a free State, if there is anything in the doctrine of the equality of States." Because the English bill's only option was to admit Kansas as a slave state, Senator Benjamin F. Wade dismissed the compromise as "trickery" and a "fraud." An exasperated William Seward told the bill's supporters that "the use of equivocation, or the double *entendre*, is an act of immorality in legislation, deserving of severe censure."[43]

Across the aisle, Douglas the heretic was agog. "It has been argued in one portion of the Union that this is a submission of the Constitution, and in another portion it is not," he pointed out. "We are to be told that submission is popular sovereignty in one section, and submission in another section is not popular sovereignty." Such duplicity, an Illinois Democrat asserted, "is discreditable legislation to say the least of it." A Douglas ally, Charles Stuart of Michigan, predicted that if the administration insisted on trickery, "the honest heart of the whole Republic will, involuntarily, revolt at it." The proposition, Stuart stated flatly, was unworthy of the sons of the revolutionary generation.[44]

While Douglas and Stuart stood firm, other anti-Lecompton Democrats wavered. On April 30, the English bill cleared the Senate 31 to 22 and the House 112 to 103. At the passage of the bill in the spring, some southern Democrats expressed relief to be "rid of this vexed question." Influential and extreme elements within the party's southern wing, however, were disgusted. Buchanan's "does not come up to my idea of a Southern Rights Administration," Alabama's William F. Samford complained. "We cannot accept the issues of this Administration and make the battle of 1860 upon them. . . . Depend on it, *defeat*—disastrous—ruinous, awaits us if we make this Administration the standard and watchword of the Democracy!"[45]

Samford's desire to make "open, plain issues with the Black Republicans, without any nonsense about 'Squatter Sovereignty' among them,"[46] was facilitated by three events that arose between 1858 and the spring of 1860: the Lincoln-Douglas debates, John Brown's raid on Harpers Ferry, and Senate Democrats' advocacy of Jefferson Davis's resolutions endorsing positive protection. The first, the Lincoln-Douglas debates, has been examined often, in depth, and with insight. Thus the exchanges may be quickly summarized. This dialogue, however, is important for several reasons. It illustrates the attempt by northern leaders in both parties to get on the right side of the slavery issue through appeals to America's republican heritage. By extension, the debates also reveal divisions between northern and southern Democrats and between Republicans and states'-rights southerners over the essence of that heritage. Finally, Douglas's plaintive argument and Lincoln's resonant appeal suggest the extent to which the idea of federative freedom that had given a decided impetus to territorial expansion in the late 1840s was in eclipse a decade later.

Throughout the debates, the aggressive Douglas denounced the sectional politics of the Republican Party. He repeatedly maintained that the Founding Fathers, recognizing the diversity of interests and institutions of the nation, established a Union on the fundamental right of each state "to do as it pleases, without meddling with its neighbors." Limited government and the inviolability of states' rights—the essence of federative freedom—had ever been the animating principles of the Democracy. The Compromise of 1850 embraced them, the Kansas-Nebraska Act wrote them into law, and the *Dred Scott* decision reaffirmed the right of each state to settle local questions. It mattered not, Douglas held, what the Supreme Court might in the future decide on the abstract question of the right of territorial legislatures to prohibit slavery; popular sovereignty was secure. Still trusting in the intuitive good sense of public opinion, Senator Douglas pointed out in the Freeport debate "that slavery cannot exist a day or an hour anywhere, unless it is supported by local police regulations." Therefore, he denounced the unnecessary agitation of the slavery issue. It impeded territorial expansion, slowed the spread of free institutions, and prevented the nation from realizing its manifest destiny. "Why cannot this nation exist forever divided into free and slave States as our fathers made it?" Douglas asked. Just act on the republican ideals of local self-determination and the equality of states, he enjoined, "and this Union will not only live forever, but it will extend and expand until it covers the whole continent, and make this confederacy one grand ocean-bound republic."[47]

That was precisely the source of the present difficulties, Lincoln replied. Certainly diversity of interests, occupations, and productions were bonds of Union. Slavery, however, had ever been an apple of discord and an element of division. Peace existed when slavery was limited to its present bounds. "Whenever there has been an effort to spread it," he exclaimed, "there has been agitation and resistance." Lincoln deduced that Douglas's plea to return to the principles of the fathers was a lie and worse. The policy of the founders was to limit the spread of slavery into new territories already free, he maintained. "But Judge Douglas and his friends have broken up that policy and placed it on a new basis by which it is to become national and perpetual." The *Dred Scott* decision, of course, greatly aided the conspiracy. Sadly for Douglas, Lincoln observed, the Court had also "*squatted* his Squatter Sovereignty out." The Freeport humbug, he asserted, merely maintained the pretense of local self-determination. There was vigor enough in slavery and malevolence aplenty among the slavepower to ensure that the institution would be grafted onto the territories, legislative inaction or hostility notwithstanding. Contemptuous of Douglas's sidestep, Lincoln (like Samford of Alabama) hoped that the slavery issue could be distinctly made "and all extraneous matter thrown out so that men can fairly see the real difference between the parties."[48]

Lincoln concluded that the difference between Douglas and himself—between northern Democrats and Republicans—did not involve the question of states' rights or any desire to make invidious distinctions between the rights of the citizens of the several states. The issue, he stated, was the preservation of republican institutions—the eternal struggle between the two principles of right and wrong. He scoffed at the notion that popular sovereignty in any form could end slavery agitation. And the idea that the Kansas settlement had stopped it, Lincoln thought insane. "There is no way of putting an end to the slavery agitation amongst us but to put it back upon the basis where our fathers put it," he advised. "Restrict it forever to the old States where it now exists." New territories, Lincoln demanded, must be preserved in such a condition "that white men may find [a] home . . . where they can settle upon some new soil and better their condition in life."[49]

To southerners disappointed with a doughface president, Douglas's apostasy and Lincoln's heresies, though alarming, were hardly novel. Taken together with Lecompton, however, the Freeport doctrine and the Republican restrictionist position evinced a widespread antislavery consensus in the free states. Mindful of persistent debates over slavery in the territories, Thomas Stevenson warned on the eve of the presidential canvass that fiery speeches reflected "the *ill-will* & *animosities*" existing between the sections. Antislavery sentiment had been given voice in 1787, 1789, 1820, and 1850, he observed. Then, however, "patriots lived in the North . . . who had the power over their constituents . . . but these men have gone —!" Denying that Republicans stood for any American principle, southern Democrats denounced the party as "a faction," which was "great in numbers, strong in the ignorant prejudices of the northern masses, [and] led by farseeing and unprincipled leaders."[50] As for the Douglas Democracy, plus ultra.

The loss of Kansas, Douglas's Freeport revisionism, and Republican restriction were most portentous and offensive to those in the slave states who envisioned southern rights as a collection of privileges and constitutional guarantees calculated to ensure the equality of that minority section within the Union. Yet it must be remembered that the position of moderate slave-state Democrats was that the fundamental southern right was the right to be left alone. John Brown's attack on Harpers Ferry raised serious doubts whether even this modest demand was now possible. To be sure, the Senate investigating committee chaired by Senator James M. Mason of Virginia found that Brown was not connected formally to any political party. But though southerners believed Brown to be a fanatic, they declared that his enterprise could only be considered "as an effort by some of his own followers to put to the test the Seward theory of an 'irrepressible conflict.'" To Republican suggestions that Brown's attack was a natural outgrowth of violence fomented by the slavepower in Kansas, Senator James Chesnut of South Carolina replied that it resulted from "the miserable, intermeddling, nefarious spirit of many of the people of our associate States with [a] matter that concerns them not."[51]

Southerners were repelled by, but could understand, the actions of a person they considered insane. What stunned public opinion was evidence of the support provided Brown by New England reformers, the so-called Secret Six. The majority report concluded that "with such elements at work, unchecked by law and not rebuked but encouraged by public opinion, with money freely contributed and placed in irresponsible hands, it may be easily seen how this expedition to excite servile war in one of the States of the

Union was got up." Looking ahead to next year's presidential election, a Mississippi Democrat admitted that a Republican administration would not directly promote servile war in the slave states. Not that it would have to. "The very fact of the inauguration of the party, would unchain the spirit of fanaticism and encourage it to the committal of the wildest excesses."[52]

Widespread support for Brown in the free states posed an even graver question. John C. Rutherfoord, for many years chairman of the Virginia state Democratic Party, believed that only a change in sentiment in the free states could preserve southern rights and maintain the Union. Acknowledging that "public opinion is king," Rutherfoord asserted that northern antislavery prejudice had led to a "nullification of a constitutional compact for the security of our property; the denial of our equal rights in the territories; the insecurity of our property in the states; the unfriendly action of the federal government; the hostile legislation of Northern states; and even the bloody invasion of our soil."[53]

A logical but none too comforting deduction from Rutherfoord's observation was that the free-state Democracy was "powerless to arrest the growing fanaticism and aggressive predominance of the North." Senator Alfred Iverson of Georgia pointed out that the repeated desertions of voters into the antislavery Republican Party drained away Democrats' political strength. The remaining corporal's guard, he acidly observed, was craven. They were afraid to denounce Brown "because they know when they do this they will run counter to the public feeling of their States, and must die the political death themselves." James H. Taylor went a step further and declared that northern "conservatism itself is rotten in the core." A more restrained Iverson scorned Douglas and his followers for claiming to embrace the principles of the founders, but it was not "the old Republicanism of our fathers . . . the Republicanism of Jefferson and of Madison and of Jackson."[54]

Southern response to Union meetings in the free states engendered by Brown's raid, therefore, was underwhelming. Some thought them "fashionable with the weak, the timid, the vacillating." That they were necessary at all indicated "the strength and formidableness of the fanatical current which they are designed to arrest." Others warned that Unionism was a sham and that the proceedings "were all for southern consumption." Noting the lack of conservatism evinced at the polls in the North, slave-state Democrats warned their constituents not "to be made the dupes of Union loving *professions*." Fear of being lulled and tricked again moderated the southern response. So, too, did the realization that Unionism appeared to have a very different meaning in the North. Free-state Unionists were "perpetually shrieking imprecations upon all who venture to breathe a hint of the possibility of a dissolution of the Union," a Texas editor observed. "They would have the Union just so long as they can with impunity harass the South . . . just so long as the Southern sheep quietly suffers its wool to be plucked by Northern sharers [*sic*]."[55]

Northern sympathy for Brown placed anti-Lecompton defections and the Freeport heresy in perspective. It also explained, though of course for southerners it did not justify, the equivocal behavior of free-state Democrats on southern rights. The raid, moreover, evinced clearly that Republican Party members were intent on "the conquest of the South." The Harpers Ferry raid therefore belied an often made Republican claim. "While they are professing to observe the rights of the southern States, and say that they do not intend to interfere with slavery in any State of this Union," Iverson exclaimed, "they are endeavoring by every possible means in their power to strengthen the antislavery sentiment in the northern states, and . . . to break down the institution of slavery by fair means or foul means."[56]

The terror that swept the South after Harpers Ferry lent emotional and intellectual credence to fire-eaters' long-held belief in an abolitionist conspiracy. In late November 1859, the *Baltimore Sun* traced the shift in southern public opinion. At first, the raid was regarded as "the act of a mere crazy, old fool. People never dreamed that it was the fruit and matured result . . . of a long and deliberately prepared plan." Brown's actions, a North Carolina Democrat maintained, proved that "nothing seems too monstrous for the credulity of a large portion of the Northern people."[57]

Radical southern rights proponents were delighted. External events now appeared to justify the pessimism and warnings that they had expressed since at least 1850. Though not as radical as most papers, the *Richmond Whig* exulted that "the Harpers Ferry invasion has advanced the cause of disunion, more than any other event that has happened since the formation of the Government; it has rallied to that standard men who formerly looked upon it [disunion] with horror." Disconsolate southern moderates agreed. One editor claimed that before Harpers Ferry talk of secession had all but died out. The raid and northern public approbation of it, however, "have shaken and disrupted all regard for the Union."[58]

By the winter of 1859–60, Democratic extremists in the slave states frankly refused to believe that "a *majority* bitterly hostile to slavery in its every aspect—moral, political and social—will prove willing to protect *a minority* who are struggling on the one issue of its perpetuity and extension." Believing as he did that a fanatical majority would afford "*partial*" and "*temporary*" protection to southern rights, John Williams of Montgomery advised Clement Claiborne Clay, "*The minority must then rely on themselves.*" A Kentucky Democrat asserted that all southern politicians known to him opposed any interference with slavery in the territories. They were, he claimed, "absolutely *afraid* . . . of their own [political] standing in case they are found sympathising with moderate northern views in regard to restriction."[59]

Nevertheless, Lecompton, John Brown's raid, and the undeniable rift in the Democracy produced neither a southern convention nor, as some hoped, secession. Now, however, Republicanism and abolitionism became a distinction without a difference. Southerners everywhere reiterated their belief that Republican ascendancy would subvert the equality of the states and pervert the essence of the Union. Senator James Chesnut warned that the Union must not become a badge of servitude. "We will sunder the Union, pull it to pieces," he vowed, "before we will submit to be crushed by a Government which is our own as well as yours." Alabama's Clement Claiborne Clay asked his colleagues across the aisle whether they thought that the South would endure the burdens of the government while being denied its benefits. If so, Clay said, shaking his head, "you must think us unworthy of the freedom which was purchased by the blood of our sires as well as yours." Far from the fray in Congress, a "plain" North Carolina farmer and "a fervid Union man" wrote that he was willing to risk the chances of every evil that might arise from disunion, "sooner than submit any longer to Northern insolence and Northern outrage."[60]

As an increasing number of southerners began to doubt the efficacy of the Union to ensure their rights, congressional Democrats in Washington tried to hammer out an agreement on party principles and policies. The center of debate was positive protection. The apparent uselessness of *Dred Scott*, Lecompton's defeat, Douglas's defection, and free-state malice exhibited by Brown's raid led southern Democrats to look to the federal government for redress. On February 2, 1860, Jefferson Davis of Mississippi introduced in the Senate resolutions asserting that it was the duty of the federal government to provide the necessary protection of slave property—as of all property—in the common territories. "If experience should at any time prove that the judiciary does not possess power to insure adequate protection," one resolution read, "it will then become the duty of Congress to supply such deficiency."[61]

In defense of this proposal, southern senators charged that Republicans were hiding behind the theory of states' rights to justify the passage of personal liberty laws, which were in clear violation of the Constitution. In the territories, moreover, nonintervention had become a "siren's song." Davis complained that it was "a thing shadowy and fleeting, changing its color as often as a chameleon. . . . It has been woven into a delusive gauze thrown over the public mind, and presented as an obligation to stand still . . . to do nothing; to prove faithless to the trust that [Congress] hold[s] at the hands of the people of the States." Southerners used up more than their metaphors denouncing northern aggressors. You see what delay had produced, Senator Albert G. Brown thundered to northern Democrats; still you ask us to wait. "What I demand is protection—that protection which you admit we are entitled to by the Constitution. Give it to us now; do it at once." [62]

Davis's logic assumed that territorial legislatures were the creatures of Congress. Territorial legislation, he and others contended, must conform to the Constitution and be subordinate to Congress, which alone represented the will of the owners of the territories. If, then, any territory refuses to protect my slave property, Brown told the Senate, it is my duty, my right, to come here and say to you, "Senators: this Territorial legislature is your creature. You breathed it into existence. . . . Your creature is denying to me rights guaranteed . . . by the sacred charter of our liberties as expounded by the highest judicial tribunal in the land." What I now ask, Brown added, is "whether you will grant me that protection." [63]

By 1860, Douglas had backed away from his "unfriendly legislation" position. He and his supporters now maintained that such an eventuality posed a judicial, not a legislative, question. Southerners, however, pointed out that, in the first place, nonaction could not be brought before the Supreme Court. Furthermore, Douglas's argument assumed the ineffectiveness of a Court decision upholding the legality of slavery in areas where the people were hostile to the institution. Obviously, Brown concluded, nonaction "would as effectively exclude us as positive action." [64]

Although northerners remained unpersuaded, southern Democrats continued to assert that Davis's measures provided for the protection of slaves as property, not protection of the institution. "The monstrous proposition that the Constitution of the United States establishes slavery has never been advocated by us," Senator Louis T. Wigfall declared. "Slavery is a political institution." From Wigfall's perspective, the slave code was neither another test of party fealty nor an embroidery on states' rights. It simply demanded the enforcement of constitutional obligations, the last line of defense for minorities. Noting the growing disparity of power between the free and slave states, an Alabama Democrat stated that it was "absurd to rely on the majority giving *ample protection* to the minority—the protection in such cases will never be *full*—allways [*sic*] *partial* and most generally *temporary*." A slave code, then, would reaffirm that this was a Union "*inter pares.*" [65]

Davis, Brown, and others believed that the resolutions reaffirmed Congress's traditional protection of settlers' property. "I ask no slave code, no horse code, no machine code," Davis told the Senate. "I ask the Senate, to declare great truths today, and for all time to come, to bring back the popular judgment to the standard of the Constitution." Southern Democrats scoffed at the suggestion that, as crypto-disunionists, they were trying to interpolate new doctrines into the Constitution or into the party creed. Davis rooted his resolutions in that fundamental compact as well as the traditional American defense of property rights. It was a measure of the extremism of northern antislavery opinion, he held, that opposing senators branded them as radicals for simply demanding a recognition of constitutional rights. "We fight to preserve the Constitution," Senator Judah P. Benjamin maintained, "and, in so doing, fight to preserve the Union."[66]

Northern Democrats and especially Douglas, who had built his political life around popular sovereignty, heatedly rejected the suggestion that they had misled anyone on the principles of popular sovereignty. They then counterattacked. Those who made war on party members for holding the same principles as they themselves had held in 1850, 1852, 1854, and 1856 "should frankly avow [their] change," Douglas declared. Southerners, he exclaimed, were constantly shifting their position and altering their principles to suit their needs. They were for noninterference when the people of the territories wanted slavery. "But the moment the people say that they do not want it, and will not have it, then Congress must intervene and force the institution on an unwilling people." Southern duplicity had a high cost, Michigan's Charles Stuart exclaimed. Despite the correctness of the party creed, the northern Democracy had been cut down at the polls and "not because an argument could be made against the doctrines of the party," he asserted, "but because our opponents . . . could point to southern statesmen and politicians advocating principles at war with the creed of the party; and claim that that was the intention of the party, and not the platform itself."[67]

The congressional intervention required by Davis's resolutions "is the doctrine of the Tories of the Revolution," claimed Douglas. "Am I now to be called upon to enforce that same odious doctrine on the people of a Territory, against their consent?" Douglas claimed the mantle of Washington, Adams, and Jefferson. By defending the principles of the Kansas-Nebraska Act, he told the Senate, "I am asserting, on behalf of the people of the Territories, just those rights which our fathers demanded for themselves against the claim of Great Britain." Douglas, George Pugh, Charles Stuart, and Henry Payne, rooting their principles in the revolutionary heritage, assumed the middle ground between Republican sectionalism and southern extremism. "There is no difference in principle between intervention North and intervention South," the Illinois senator declared. "Each denies the right of self-government to the people of the Territory over their internal and domestic concerns. Each appeals to the passions, the prejudices, and the ambition of his own section, against the peace and harmony of the whole country."

In a final appeal to his southern rights colleagues, Stuart asked them to remember the wisdom of the fathers and the older members of the party: cease agitating the slavery question; remove it from political discourse.[68]

Never, southern Democrats replied. It would be foolish to deny that personal hostilities and political advantages were not a consideration in this struggle; many did not. The *Nashville Union* stated it flatly. Nonetheless, southern rights Democrats like Judah Benjamin believed that the party could no longer be sustained on "a basis of plunder or of spoils." Constitutional obligations transcended party compromises. Government, resting as it did on popular consent and public opinion, "was not formed to deceive the people and to manage them by men in office," Jefferson Davis asserted. "We should derive our opinions from the people. . . . To know what their opinion is, it is necessary that we should pronounce, in unmistakable language what we ourselves mean." If the Democracy cannot unite on principle, he concluded, the sooner it is disrupted the better.[69]

A Senate Democratic caucus eventually adopted a modified version of the Davis resolution. Although the proposal was introduced on March 1, no vote was taken.[70] Even though the modified resolutions fell short of Brown's demand for a slave code, compromise did nothing to bridge the chasm within the party. Douglas's supporters claimed that the resolutions had no binding force on the Democracy and rebuked the Senate for its "tyranny and usurpation." They argued that the caucus had acted in contempt of public opinion and that it intended to dictate to rather than represent their constituents. Douglas's backers also condemned southern and administration Democrats for attempting to revive the congressional caucus system, now dead some thirty-six years, which had recognized the pretensions of John Quincy Adams over the legitimate claims of Andrew Jackson to the presidency. Drawing on Jackson's 1824 campaign theme, Douglasites adopted his role as an outsider opposing Washington wire-pullers and adapted it to the mood of their anti-Washington constituents. "These senators have lived so long about Washington that they have forgotten the mighty masses of this country," one southerner asserted. "They forgot that they are to represent public opinion, and not to undertake to dictate to it. There never was a time when people were less disposed to listen to politicians."[71]

Proponents of the amended resolutions rejoined that critics complained "because it is their habit to censure every good movement of the Democratic party—every movement which has for its object the declaration of principles promotive of the best interests of the country." They conceded that the Democracy was divided and distracted. Yet they also maintained that the principles agreed on in caucus were "sound—eminently sound" and that "Democratic champions from every section of the Republic" endorsed them.

Little wonder, then, that the resolutions did not suit "that class of political tricksters" who seemed concerned solely with "devising the best means to elect Douglas, and give the offices to its clique instead of defining great constitutional rights." The *New York Daily News* forecasted "the beginning of a healthier public opinion with the masses of our party—the commencement of a regathering within our old landmarks—the treading again of old paths and the sitting down upon the old platform." At all hazards, a Mississippi editor demanded, the upcoming Charleston nominating convention must affirm the vital principles of the caucus resolutions and leave no doubt "as to the true meaning of the Democratic creed."[72]

Now determined to confront and settle the territorial issue in the upcoming presidential canvass, the extreme wing of the southern Democracy was fully arrayed against the candidacy of the apostate Douglas. In the fall of 1859 John B. Floyd, Buchanan's secretary of war, already had written the president that his contacts in the South considered Douglas to be nothing less than a traitor. By winter, slave-state opponents believed his brand of popular sovereignty to be pure sophistry and "objectionable in principle." Given the widespread electoral weakness of northern Democrats, they scouted the notion of Douglas's availability as a candidate. Douglas, they jeered, was supported solely by a "miserable horde of political jobbers, bankrupt politicians and peripatetic gasometers." Mindful of the effect of a Republican victory on their rights in the territories and within the Union generally, fire-eaters concluded that Douglas's certain defeat November next was simply too dear a cost "for the favor conferred upon the multitude of wire workers, office-seekers, and plunderers" who composed his retinue.[73]

Administration supporters in the free states also came out openly against Douglas. Their opposition reflected the many fault lines that had grown since 1857 and now ran through the party nationally. John Appleton observed that in New England, "Douglasism" was "more an appearance than a reality. . . . The wiser politicians regard him as unsafe & do not like to risk the chances with him." Although the senator fared better in delegate nominating conventions in the Old Northwest, administration dissidents there grumbled that "false & deceitful men" wielding official influence betrayed the president. Free-state opposition to Douglas was more than a function of presidential patronage. Party members complained that he and other anti-Lecompton Democrats had leagued with black Republicans, and the effect, if not the intent, was to weaken the Democracy throughout the North. Isaac Cook therefore advised administration officials to state in blunt language "that there can be no compromise between the party, or any of its organizations, or representatives, and Mr. Douglas." With a keen grasp of the obvious, a Maine editor nonetheless fretted that Democratic factionalism, not the Republican

Party, posed the greatest danger in 1860. Still, even he recommended neither compromise nor conciliation, while denouncing Douglas's "personal ambition, misrepresentation and malice."[74]

Opposition to Douglas within the party was intense, implacable, personal, and generally reflective of Democratic fragmentation. So, too, had it been in 1844 with Martin Van Buren. Then the party had rallied around its animating principles to revivify the organization and make issue with Whigs over expansion. Now, expansion into the West and the acquisition of new territories were problematic and disorganizing. Many believed that the party evinced "a marked degeneracy" and that too much attention focused on availability, too little on the party's doctrines. Whereas the Democrats had come out boldly with an expansionist platform in 1844, party members admitted that recent state resolutions and national platforms were "too often intended to conceal, rather than express, opinions—to deceive and mislead the public, rather than work out a course to be pursued in the event of success." A Kentucky Democrat found such dissimulation "humiliating." Accordingly, the *Memphis Daily Avalanche* predicted that a Douglas victory in 1860 "would be the victory of an *expediency*—a compromise at once dishonoring and insulting to the South." It reasonably pointed out, "If the principles of our platform are *true*, they cannot admit of a compromise with antagonistic systems without losing their verity." The party must select candidates "with reference to measures and principles," Douglas's opponents demanded, "measures and principles must not be deflected, changed or abandoned to suit men."[75]

Thus to northern Democrats' plea that no new tests be imposed on the party, Douglas's opponents replied that popular sovereignty northern-style was a "cowardly dodge" guaranteed to make the Democracy "a party of the past, and not of the present." Far from interpolating new creeds, they maintained that the territorial question "has a right and wrong side." A Kentucky Democrat asked, "Is it no longer progress, even so far as to apply the principles upon which [the party] is based to measures affecting the welfare of the country, as they arise?" Likewise, a Tennessee party member condemned past compromises on the territorial issue because they neither quieted agitation nor halted northern aggressions. Instead he demanded from the North *"a restoration of the Constitutional rights, of which she has rob[b]ed the South, and a restoration of that equilibrium of political power which originally was incorporated into the government by the fathers of the republic."*[76]

Douglas Democrats could not—and did not—deny the growing impotence of the party in the free states. They were equally certain, though, that in 1860 "the burden of the battle falls on the North." Some, mindful of their weakness and sensitive to the growth of "the spirit of disunion" in the free states, feared that southern Democrats were daily losing confidence in the party's ability to preserve the ligaments of Union. Others concluded that the Democracy's commitment to "principles in regard to slavery at war with all we have fought for during the last six years" depleted their ranks. All Douglasites complained that a "corrupt Administration is too big a load for us at present to carry." An Indiana Democrat proclaimed party dissidents "SCAMPS" and their actions "disreputable," "disgusting in the extreme," and "basely dishonest."[77]

The Douglas wing could and did demand sympathy if not empathy from southern colleagues. Even Franklin Pierce complained that slave-state Democrats had no idea of the state of public opinion in the North. Accordingly, he maintained that "full justice" had not been given free-state Democrats. He and other northerners found it "humiliating" to be told that they were no better than black Republicans. "Fighting *the battles of the South*," John Cain of Vermont observed, had devastated, and in some states nearly obliterated, the party in the North. Cain exclaimed to a southern colleague, "For humanity's sake, do not ask us . . . to be shot down by Republican fanatics armed to the teeth in fighting for your 'niggers' and then to be tauntingly told we are in a minority."[78]

Douglas Democrats charged that some southern party members had become "too exacting." They claimed that the entire history of the party was proof of, and a tribute to, the northern wing's fidelity to the constitutional rights of the slave states. Any new litmus test, such as positive protection (or, rather, congressional intervention) was not only "pointless . . . unstatesmanlike and unpatriotic," but "fatal" to the northern Democracy. No northerner, claimed a Northwest Democrat, could stand a moment on that doctrine. If intervention by Washington be connected to the party, he ventured, "we shall be kept subject to black republican rule at home, merely to enable our southern friends to claim the abstract right to carry slavery where the people don['t] want it."[79]

His southern supporters warned Douglas that the "rabid tone, and rampant action" of fire-eaters had first alarmed and then alienated their constituents from the party's northern wing. For their part, northern Democrats retorted that they were "fast becoming bitterly offended at the language and conduct of their southern allies." Proclaiming, though hardly proving, their constancy on popular sovereignty, the Douglas wing in both sections accused the administration and its supporters of trimming. Representative William Wick of Indiana wrote R. M. T. Hunter that all southerners including fire-eaters had gloried in nonintervention in 1856. Wick claimed that in his state and elsewhere in the Old Northwest, "Our people are thoroughly indoctrinated into the dogma, or Truth above stated, and to change our ground is to break up and destroy the Dem[ocratic] party *with us*." Without an unequivocal endorsement of popular sovereignty in the party's presidential platform, another Hoosier declared, "we may as well quit and save our credit."[80]

Douglasites in the North urged "the joint efforts of all national men working in unison and harmony" to defeat the common enemy. Yet their calls for comity and intraparty cooperation were not unqualified. "While ready to answer all just expectations, from the South," one northerner wrote, the free-state wing was "not prepared for absolute self-stultification." This meant to northerners, just as it did to dissidents, measures not men. Douglas himself advocated "a bold, honest platform, avowing our principles in unequivocal language." This call to arms resonated deeply with Douglas's supporters convinced as they were that "non-intervention was acknowledged by all Democrats North and South in 1856 to be the true policy of the national Democratic party." Popular sovereignty, they concluded, "has become part of our nature, and we cannot, and will not support any other doctrine."[81]

On the eve of the Charleston convention, an editor in the Douglas wing of the party expressed his determination to go to South Carolina "to oppose sectionalism South as well as North." He was heartily tired of being beaten up by clubs put into Republican hands by southern extremists who "foment discord and preach disunion in the Democracy." He declared himself "sick of living in a minority country, in States which once were, and now naturally are Democratic." Six days later, while northern delegates were wending their way to South Carolina, the *Charleston Mercury* denounced the South's "timid and faithless expedient of concession to [northern] encroachments." The Democratic Party, "now overthrown by Centralism and Consolidation," was, in its opinion, "dead. It exists now only as a powerful faction." Refusing to bend to the "false pretenders to Democracy in the North," the *Mercury* called upon southern delegates to come to Charleston "to rebuild the Democratic party."[82] A divided America and a crippled Democracy now lurched toward the denouement.

> Modern politics is, at bottom, a struggle not of men but of forces. — Henry Adams

> Democracy is the theory that the common people know what they want, and deserve to get it good and hard. — H. L. Mencken

The Eclipse of Manifest Destiny and the Disruption of the Second Party System

On Wednesday morning, April 18, 1860, August Belmont bid his wife, Caroline, and their children good-bye and left his stately Fifth Avenue home for a pier on the Hudson River. There he would board the steamship *Nashville* that would take him and the other New York delegates to the Democratic nominating convention in Charleston, South Carolina. The delegates, accompanied by a bevy of amiable businesswomen, boarded the *Nashville* in high spirits and with high hopes. As he stood at the rail looking down at a large group of well-wishers on the dock, Belmont, too, was confident. The recognized Douglas man in the New York delegation, he anticipated a hard-fought but ultimately victorious battle with administration forces and disgruntled southern Democrats. Giving in to the exhilaration of the moment, Belmont and the delegates stood laughing and waving their handkerchiefs at supporters on the pier. Catching their exuberance, the crowd, which included Fernando Wood and other supporters of the Buchanan administration, began to pelt the departing steamboat with oranges. One of the oranges sailed through the railing and hit the dignified Belmont in the groin. As the *Nashville* slipped out of New York harbor, the leader of the Douglas delegation had to be helped below deck to recover.[1]

Although Belmont could not have known it then, this blow below the belt was an omen. Perhaps he would come to view it as a metaphor for the experience of the whole northern Douglas contingent at Charleston. Housed in overcrowded, fetid rooms, victimized by price-gouging and sweltering in temperatures that ranged around 100°, northern delegates went into the convention with enough strength to shape the platform but, thanks to the party's two-thirds rule, not enough to secure Douglas's nomination without southern support. They were opposed by a contingent of southern rights delegates, led by William L. Yancey of Alabama, who had come to the convention determined to throw over the Illinois senator and to extract from the convention an open acceptance of the South's equality in the Union. Yancey represented a group of fire-eaters who were convinced that sectional equality could no longer be gained by halting northern aggressions or even solely by acknowledging the right of slaveholders to enter the territories. Yancey did not go to Charleston to disrupt the Democracy. He and other fire-eaters were adamant, however, that it should be the means for securing southern rights. The party must clearly avow a program that would restore to the minority section its rights and its equality. Corrupt bargains and strategic dissimulation on principles would have to cease.[2]

They did. Unable to agree on men or measures in Charleston, the Democracy divided. When the convention adopted a minority platform endorsing noninterference, delegations mainly from the Lower South withdrew. The remaining delegates adjourned, agreeing to reconvene two months later in Baltimore. By then, two other parties had taken the field. Republicans nominated the obscure but safe Abraham Lincoln; he stood on the platform of slavery restriction. Conservatives put up John Bell and stood by the Constitution and the Union. Reassembling in June, the Democracy found itself still divided. National Democrats ran Stephen Douglas and hewed to noninterference. Southern Democrats and supporters of the Buchanan administration put forward a platform endorsing *Dred Scott* and a federal slave code. Vice-President John C. Breckinridge was their nominee. By the summer of 1860, the disruption of the Jacksonian party system was complete.

Though portentous, political fragmentation was hardly unique. There were four presidential candidates in 1824 and 1832; Martin Van Buren defeated four Whig presidential contenders in 1836. What caused the breakdown in 1860 or what it meant remains elusive, however. Not that there is a shortage of explanations. Sectional conspiracies, moral differences over slavery, economic conflicts (practical and principled), inept politicians, cultural differences, and the democratic process itself have alternately been argued. The public and private discourse of the campaign indicates that the election turned largely on a single point: the future of slavery in the West. Although the territorial imbroglio was largely responsible for the minatory politics of 1860, its relationship to the crisis is complex. Expansion, introduced into the political system by Tyler in 1844, raised the issue of slavery extension. Unlike economic divisions that were interparty, the agitation of this issue over the next decade and a half divided Americans along sectional lines. By 1860, it had raised the real prospect of a sectional president.

The effect of the territorial question on the dynamics of the 1860 canvass proved determinative. First, there was no common vision of, no nationally acceptable solution to, the territorial issue. Second and as a consequence, no political party could exist effectively as a national unit. Third, moderation in one section was perceived as extremism in the other; indeed, parties within the same section perceived each other as dangerous extremists. Finally, the sectional politics of Lincoln and Breckinridge eclipsed, though they did not wholly displace, the established but attenuated Democratic and Whig policies represented by Douglas and Bell respectively. A survey of the four campaigns will illustrate these points.

In an address to the Mississippi legislature in November 1859, Albert Gallatin Brown had declared that he was not hopeful about the party's prospects at Charleston. Brown predicted that there would be "attempts to hoodwink us with fair promises and expressions of kind regard." Northern delegates would force the South to yield on this point and that. Still the party platform would consist of "apocryphal sentences strung together, meaning everything . . . or nothing, just as one chooses." Two months before the convention, an administration editor in Belmont's New York pointed out that divisions within the party, resulting from "a misunderstanding and misconception of our principles," had led inevitably to the decimation of northern Democrats. These critics concluded that the most important function of the Charleston convention was to bring the party back "within its ancient landmarks, and [replace] it firmly upon its original and true platform of principles." Brown asserted that if the events of the Buchanan presidency revealed nothing else, they demonstrated that a party platform with Janus-like northern and southern faces encouraged the desertion of free-state voters and betrayed the South. "Scorning *policy*," a Tennessee Democrat likewise advised, "the Democracy of the nation must boldly and unequivocally enunciate its ancient creed."[3]

Certainly, southern Douglasites agreed with fire-eaters that "eternal vigilance . . . [was] the price of our principles and sovereignty." Yet if they were sympathetic to a South united, these slave-state Democrats differed from Yancey, Rhett, and other dissenters in significant ways. They contended that extremists — and extreme demands — stimulated sectional tensions and thus jeopardized the most effective guarantee of southern rights: the Union. Amid growing demands for positive protection of slavery in the territories, southern Douglasites, trusting in constitutional guarantees, "only asked to be let alone." Looking ahead to the convention, L. M. Stone asked the Alabama senate to reject dire threats, impracticable demands, and personal attacks on northern delegates. He invited Alabamians "in good faith, [to] meet in convention our Democratic friends from every section of the Union . . . who would . . . cooperate with us in our effort to maintain our equality in the Union."[4]

There was slim chance of that. At the end of the first week of the convention, a deadlocked committee on resolutions presented three platforms to the delegates. The majority report, supported by the slave states plus California and Oregon, upheld the *Dred Scott* decision in denying the power of Congress or territorial legislatures to abolish or prohibit slavery or in any way impair the right of property in slaves in the territories. It also hedged in the direction of a congressional slave code by stating that it was the duty of the federal government "to protect when necessary, the rights of persons and property on the high seas, in the Territories, or wherever its constitutional authority extended." The resolutions also called for the acquisition of Cuba, the enforcement of the federal slave law, and the construction of a Pacific railroad. A minority report, offered by Douglas's supporters, concurred in these last three planks. On the territorial question it stood by the Cincinnati formula of congressional noninterference with slavery in the territories despite subsequent developments. The minority acknowledged that there were differences within the party over the nature and extent of the powers of a territorial legislature over slavery. They therefore promised (again) to abide by any future decision of the Supreme Court on that question. Benjamin F. Butler offered a third compromise resolution that simply reaffirmed the Cincinnati platform without alteration.[5]

Speaking in support of the majority report, William W. Avery of North Carolina declared that the Lecompton struggle had convinced southern Democrats that, should popular sovereignty again be adopted by the party, it "would be as dangerous and subversive of their rights as the adoption of the principle of congressional intervention or prohibition." Other southern rights Democrats declared that Douglas's Freeport heresy made it imperative that the party present the public with a true and unequivocal interpretation of its creed. To those who argued that breaking with the Cincinnati platform violated good faith, Mississippi's William Barksdale replied, "It is still more discreditable to persist in propagating a political falsehood at the expense of the rights of sovereign States and the Constitution itself."[6]

Free-state Democrats were already faring poorly with the northern electorate; throwing over popular sovereignty northern-style for *Dred Scott* and a slave code was unthinkable. Yet from the perspective of Yancey and other southern rights extremists, there was an internal logic in what otherwise appears to be an irrational expectation. The affairs of the Buchanan administration had demonstrated to more observers than just fire-eaters that antislavery sentiment was predominant at the North. The rights of the minority section were not only abused, fire-eaters claimed; they were abandoned. "Ours is the property invaded," Yancey told northern Democrats; "ours are the institutions which are at stake; ours is the property that is to be destroyed." The supposed gains of the South—the Kansas-Nebraska Act, the *Dred Scott* decision, the Lecompton Constitution—had proved largely illusory and temporary. Formerly there had been no apparent conflict between devotion to party principles and policies and a commitment to southern rights. Now it appeared that a misunderstanding, purposeful or otherwise, of the party's creed in the North had come to involve "consequences deeply affecting the interests of the slaveholding members of the Confederacy." As a consequence, the majority section, relying on its numerical strength, no longer looked to the Constitution "to see in what the minority was to be respected, and how it was to be protected."[7]

That may be, Senator George Pugh of Ohio replied, but the majority report was a corruption of the fundamental purpose of the party to construe the Constitution strictly and to deny Washington all doubtful powers. No, sir, he cried, I shall not arm the federal government with such "an imperial, arbitrary, complete power." A slave code, he averred, "is contrary to the principles of the Constitution; it is contrary to the faith of the fathers; it is in violation of the reserved rights of the States, and in violation of the rights of the people of the territory." Henry B. Payne, Pugh's friend from Ohio, reminded southerners that the Democracy endorsed noninterference first because it was just but also to remove the slavery issue from Congress, eliminating it from political discourse. The northern mind "has become thoroughly imbued with this great doctrine," Payne argued. To abandon that position, he concluded, would be attended by the overthrow of the Democratic Party in the North.[8]

Douglas had enough strength at Charleston to block the proposed southern platform. By a vote of 165 to 138 the minority report was substituted for the majority one. According to binding instructions and prior arrangement, delegations from Alabama, Mississippi, Louisiana, South Carolina, Florida, and Texas and some members of the Delaware and Arkansas delegations thereupon walked out of the convention. Georgia and the remaining Arkansas delegates withdrew the next day. D. C. Glen, a Mississippi delegate, told the convention as he withdrew that the southern states came not to dictate but to settle on common principles. "We came as equal members of a common Confederacy, simply to ask you to acknowledge our equal rights within that Confederacy." A Louisiana dissident asked northern delegates if it was fair or possible to run a two-faced campaign. "Are we not divided," he said, "and divided in such a manner that we can never be reconciled, because we are divided on principle?"[9]

Having won the battle, Douglas now proceeded to lose the war. Caleb Cushing, the convention president and a Buchanan man, ruled that the winning candidate had to secure a two-thirds majority of the total number of delegates, not of the delegates present and voting. Although Douglas did have the support of two-thirds of the rump convention, Cushing's ruling prevented his nomination. Douglas's supporters, however, foiled Cushing by arranging for the convention to adjourn.[10]

Opposition to the bolters was both practical and principled. Northern Democrats, conceding that the original platform might carry the South, warned that it also would "keep the North everlastingly in the chains of Black Republicanism." A Louisiana Democrat also pointed out that dictation to the convention by a minority of states contravened the party's fundamental commitment to majority rule. A Missouri editor added that the bolters' "rule or ruin" policy not only broke with party usages but was "at war with the very theory and genius of our system of government." A party was a "*body political*," one northerner maintained; "its existence implied *union* and *organization*." Majority will must govern the party, he concluded, for if an unsympathetic minority ruled, the Democracy would become "a *farce*."[11]

Political calculations and procedures notwithstanding, the central thrust of the bolters' movement struck deeper at the core of the party's orthodoxy: limited government and self-rule. Douglas's ally John Forney declared that "the agents of the disunion party" had tried unsuccessfully to drive the Democracy "from its ancient faith, a thousand times renewed." Southern Douglasites concurred but took a different tack. They claimed that the South, following John C. Calhoun's lead, had become unified on nonintervention. With this doctrine the Democracy had controlled the national government and ruled the nation's destiny. "But Alas! a new light has recently sprung upon us," a Tennessee editor lamented, "a light which is destined to bring back upon us the troublesome times of old . . . and the hitherto united South is sundered in twain!"[12]

Reminiscent of John Adams's comment that the Intolerable Acts had ripped the mask off British conspirators, Douglas Democrats maintained that the withdrawal of the southern delegates plainly revealed their underlying purpose. The bolters came to Charleston, they claimed, "to make, a pretence for a quarrel and a secession." With their strategy long premeditated and prepared, the seceders would have rejected all attempts at accommodation. Some Douglas Democrats believed their intent was to force "their peculiar tenets" onto the party; others concluded that the effect was the disruption of the Democracy and the dissolution of the Union. In either case, all agreed that "the designs of the seceders are so unveiled in all their nakedness, that the people must choose between a cordial support for sound Democratic principles, or disunion."[13]

If, as Hershel Johnson assumed, the disruption of the Democracy foreshadowed disunion, others were more hopeful. J. L. Foster, editor of the *Dover Gazette*, wrote Douglas that however much he regretted the bolt, "it is far better to have that, then [*sic*] the eternal disgrace of abandoning our principles, and dying a traitor death in the end." In a plaintive letter to the *Montgomery Daily Confederate*, a rural Alabama Democrat declared that the revolutionary struggle of 1776 had been rejoined. The contest now as then was "whether a few politicians shall rule this government, or will the people claim their sovereign power." Himself the son of a "Revolutionary sire," he like all Alabamians was proud of his state and, like most, satisfied with "the Union as it is." And like every other citizen of his state, he was determined to pass that revolutionary heritage to the next generation. "I almost cease to live for myself," he claimed. "I live for my children and grand children, and those who come after me. I seek no place—I want no power. I want our government preserved in her purity to the latest generations."[14]

Looking ahead to the proposed Baltimore convention in June, Douglas's supporters demanded without irony that the people rise up against the politicians, especially members of the Senate caucus who interjected positive protection into the convention. Responding to this call, an Indianapolis editor promised that should Senators Jesse Bright and Graham Fitch—each of whom vowed political death to Douglas—return home to Indiana, rank-and-file Democrats would whale them mightily to soften their arrogance and cleanse them of such infamous ideas. At the very least, he claimed, the two would "breath[e] a different political atmosphere from that which surrounds Washington. . . . They will find that the honest yeomanry care but little, if anything, about the petty squabbles of this man, of the disappointed ambition of this man, or the defeated aspirations of another." In Ohio, a leading Democrat noted that the long and frequent absence of members of Congress from their constituents made them a poor judge of popular will. Remembering the Senate's support of the Bank of the United States in 1832, he contended that "the most undemocratic branch of the American government" more often than not had been arrayed "on the side of power and prejudice against the people."[15]

When the Democratic delegates reconvened at Baltimore on June 18, Douglas's managers were able to seat contested Douglas delegations from the bolting states. When pro-Yancey supporters were denied seats, the Virginia, North Carolina, and Tennessee delegations, half of the Maryland, California, and Oregon delegates, and most of the Kentucky, Missouri, and Arkansas Democrats trooped out. Although Douglas did not have two-thirds of the full vote after two ballots, the convention adopted a resolution declaring him unanimously nominated. The Baltimore convention then nominated Benjamin Fitzpatrick of Alabama for vice-president. When Fitzpatrick declined the nomination, the Democratic National Committee chose Hershel V. Johnson of Georgia to replace him. Douglas's nomination, his supporters claimed, was illustrative of the power of popular sovereignty writ large. "The nomination of Mr. Douglas was not the victory of an individual," the *Boston Herald* proclaimed; "it was a triumph of the people over the politicians."[16]

The bolters and their sympathizers begged to differ. They bitterly condemned "the dark empire of the Black Douglas men . . . the hungry pack from the free soil kennel." It was Douglas, not those who seceded from the convention, that "compelled every man to an unconditional submission to his construction [of popular sovereignty] or to fight him." They contended that the Douglas wing had high-handedly torn down the party's landmarks, subverted sectional comity, and attempted to dictate the platform and the candidates. All of this was undertaken "to foist that *one man* upon the Convention." Writing from Kentucky in the aftermath of the Charleston debacle, former vice-president Richard M. Johnson claimed that the prospect of a Douglas nomination on the Cincinnati platform was the worst of all possibilities. "I *do* not see how I could stomach the former," he maintained, "& the latter is awful to contemplate."[17]

Admittedly, personal hostilities lay at the heart of the attacks on Douglas. Yet as Robert Toombs claimed, "There is a right and a wrong to the controversy for all that." The most immediate wrong appeared to be political suicide. The *Mississippian* averred that submission to the demands of a minority of the party "would have been as fatal to the vitality of the Democratic party, as a party of principle, and as the defender of Southern rights and interests, as submission to Black Republican domination would be fatal to the equality of the South in the Union and under the Constitution." This view found sympathizers in the free states as well. A Cleveland Democrat insisted that southern voters would vote only for a candidate "who speaks the Democratic sentiment of the country." The inference was clear: Douglas did not. Thus the logic of the bolt. "With Mr. Douglas, and the Protean doctrines, ever changing, ever new, that he has advocated for these three years past," he maintained, the seceders "feared that it would be impossible to make headway against the torrent of ridicule which would be heaped upon them — impossible to combat the heresies that candidate has promulgated."[18]

Southern bolters argued that slave-state delegations, asking for equality, had insisted only on their constitutional rights. The convention, one northern ally pointed out, placed "expediency in the foreground as that most likely to snatch immediate favors." Defenders congratulated bolters for their firm stand and urged them to make no concession. Despite popular perceptions that the Charleston brawl disgraced the party, a South Carolina editor declared that the disruption of the convention revealed that the Democracy was still "the only national party that has ever dared to meet at all the consolidation party of the Union. . . . They go forth with an appeal not to a section, but to the entire Union." A New Jersey Democrat held that the adjournment of the convention did not signal failure, but it "further demonstrates that there is virtue remaining in the Democratic party, and that the national organization is yet too impregnable to be broken down at the will or beck of any clique of politicians."[19]

By arraying themselves against the South, Douglas Democrats appeared to cave in to northern fanaticism. Thus to stigmatize the seceders as disunionists for simply insisting on their political equality was more than disingenuous: it was perverse. "We can assure the Union-croaking [Douglasites] that the dangers to the Union are not to be found in the South, but in the North," a Memphis Democrat countered. Seeing no practical difference between the discriminatory intent of Republican restriction and the equally discriminatory effect of Douglas's squatter sovereignty, a New Jersey Democrat declared that it would be creditable to the honesty of the free-state electorate if they chose the former's "bold, honest and unspoken platform of sectionalism."[20]

Yancey and other dissidents had agreed to meet in Richmond on June 11. There they voted to wait to see what happened at the reconvened Democratic convention. After the disruption at Baltimore, the new bolters and delegations from the states that had been denied reseating met with the Yanceyites to nominate Vice-President John C. Breckinridge and Senator Joseph Lane of Oregon to head their ticket. Calling themselves Constitutional Democrats, the party ran on a platform calling for congressional protection of slavery in the territories. At precisely the same time that Douglas Democrats were declaring themselves glad to be rid of the disorganizing elements in the party, his opponents were proclaiming the Democracy "purified and nationalized. . . . It has sloughed off these corrupting elements which have for some time distracted it and which have invited the attacks and criticism of its enemies." [21]

Principled differences over the territorial issue, proving to be too much of a strain for the party, tore one of the last remaining ligaments of national cohesion. Asserting that Breckinridge Democrats could have no honorable communion or political intercourse with the Douglas wing, a Kentucky editor flatly declared that the two sides were irreconcilably divided on the subject of slavery in the territories. As it was "the only question entering this canvass," he claimed, "any fusion, or union, or cooperation between them, would be fusion, or union, or cooperation for the spoils, at the sacrifice of principle." [22] The Democracy was formally and finally divided.

The Republican Party rushed into the breach. The lessons of the Charleston blowup were both predictable and instructive. Most immediately, secession of the Yanceyites demonstrated the "radical, aggressive progress . . . the claims of slavery have made during the last four years." Put in partisan terms, Republican observers considered the disruption a natural result of extreme demands imposed on the Democracy by "dictatorial . . . ultra Southern politicos." They attributed the inflexible course pursued by the Douglas wing to the state of northern public opinion. Born into a political world in which politicians gave voice to the fears and aspirations of their constituents, Republicans concluded that northern Democrats "have at length become aware that, in their efforts to avoid the Scylla of southern discontent, they were now in manifest danger of being completely swamped by the Charybdis of Northern indignation." This being so, an Indiana Republican maintained, "The dirt eater of the North and the fire-eater of the South, have parted their foul partnership of shame and treason." With the assembled wisdom of the Democracy brawling over platforms, personages, and policies, another held, no northerner could avoid the conclusion that the party had not a single principle that would be acceptable to the electorate. [23]

Republican critics asserted that the Democracy's demise issued less from principled disagreement over policy than from widespread corruption. Republicans deduced that the American system of government was not inherently flawed: the party controlling it was—and deeply. Twenty years earlier, Whigs had made the same charges. And as a New York Republican now observed, "In all ages, and under all forms of government, rogues have existed and climbed into public places." Yet in the changed and sectionally charged political atmosphere of 1860, the slavepower—not the money power—was the font of misrule. "Take any policy [read: slaveholding] that aims at injustice," a Hoosier observed, "and its inevitable result will be corruption. It *must* bribe, and lie, and intimidate. It has no other resources."[24]

If sectional rather than class-specific forces now caused corruption in the Democracy, Republicans plausibly argued that the party of Jackson was no more. Appealing to a disgruntled Democratic rank and file, Republicans claimed that northerners in particular "have been compelled to abandon one after another of their landmarks, and go whether so ever the Southern helmsmen guide the ship. They are obliged to consent to principles which they once looked on with abhorrence, or else they must be read out of the party." Maintaining the name while abandoning the substance of Jeffersonian Democracy, the party in 1860 more closely resembled Federalism. Republicans held that the underlying agenda of slave-state Democrats in 1860 was to reduce the working class "to such a condition of poverty and dependence, that they will not dare resist any oppression which may be imposed on them by those who own the property of the country."[25] Jacksonians once stood for the sovereignty of the people; now they upheld the domination of an oligarchy. They had preached equal rights; Democrats now sustained individual wrongs. Democrats formerly championed labor over capital; in 1860 at least half of the party, including many in the North, insisted that capital had a right to own labor. They once insisted on limited government to preserve individual rights; Senate Democrats now endorsed expanded legislative powers to deny territorial inhabitants self-government.

From these observations and assumptions, Republicans reasoned that the abyss of years separating 1860 from 1828 could hardly have greater significance. Noting that more than thirty years had passed since Jackson addressed his first Congress, the *New York Evening Post* maintained that the great questions of his day — banking, the currency, internal improvements, even territorial expansion — had been "either settled or forgotten, or thrust out of sight by the great present question of the extension or repression of slavery." "Graver issues now divide the people," a Wisconsin party member ventured. "Great principles, greatly allied to the very existence of free institutions, are involved in this campaign." One Chicago Republican put it simply: "The great political questions dividing the contending parties, have all been merged in the one of *human* slavery." Party members did not deny that other measures of public reform and improvement were at stake. They insisted, however, that their implementation depended "for their success upon the settlement of that engrossing [that is, territorial] question."[26]

Viewed from the Republican perspective, the election was a referendum on free versus slave labor in the territories. Despite their hostility to slavery as a social and moral evil, party leaders and editors believed — they demanded — that "the more effectual cause through which the back of the Democracy was [to be] broken, was the political encroachments of slavery." Plainly put, "The party which favors the preservation of the territories for the white settler, that takes ground against the extension of slavery, that does not wish to extend niggerdom and niggers, is certainly the white man's party." Dropping the other shoe, this Republican editor judged that "persons who oppose this party must be the nigger or black party." An Illinois Republican proudly observed that his party had never endorsed civil rights for African Americans much less equality of the races. Indeed, another Republican editor pointed out, "In whatever State negro suffrage is allowed, the law was passed either by Whigs or Democrats."[27]

For all the claims that new circumstances obliterated old issues, a common thread nonetheless ran from the Age of Jackson to the political crisis of 1860. The canvass again posed the question as to which party "pursues the policy best calculated to promote the interests of American laborers." Now, however, oppression of free labor had become regionally and racially specific. Republicans believed that separating the territorial issue from the discussion and determination of all public measures was neither desirable nor possible. The party resolved to seize, agitate, and resolve this question that "will not go down." Some Americans might wish to ignore it, keep still, or claim that it was an abstraction, a New England editor stated. But he went on, "Still it will return and force itself on you . . . for it is a subject upon which the policy of this government must be determined. . . . We must be ready to determine whether the extension of free labor or the propagandism of slavery is to be the result of our progress."[28]

Meeting in Chicago, Republicans passed over the preconvention favorite, William H. Seward, for the undistinguished but respected Abraham Lincoln. To some, Seward's talk of an "irrepressible conflict" seemed radical; hence his candidacy appeared to jeopardize the party's chances in the lower Midwest. More ardent antislavery forces, however, were disturbed about his late unsoundness on the slavery question—his favorable opinion of Douglas, a passive attitude toward popular sovereignty, his vote to admit Oregon with a Jim Crow constitution, and recent conciliatory statements on the South. Lincoln, by contrast, was sound on the slavery question, though not radical. Nominated on the third ballot, he ran on a platform that called for a homestead act, a protective tariff, and full observance of immigrants' rights. But antislavery was the core of the party's appeal: the platform denounced popular sovereignty as a fraud; it opposed any effort to reopen the slave trade; and it denied Congress or the territorial legislatures the power to legalize slavery in the territories. Although the antislavery resolutions were a toned-down version of the 1856 platform, the party still pledged to prohibit the extension of slavery outside the states where it existed.[29]

The entry of yet a fourth party into the 1860 campaign indicates the extent to which the territorial issue had fragmented the Jacksonian political system. Condemning Democrats and Republicans alike for disregarding matters of public welfare, conservative former Whigs and Know-Nothings repudiated the other parties' apparent determination to agitate the slavery question to further selfish, partisan ends. Calling on "the conservative, Union-loving masses of the people," they expressed confidence that "a majority of both sections prefer the Union as it is, the Constitution unchanged, the laws enforced, and the courts respected, to either the agitation of this sectional issue, or a dissolution of the government." Unionists like every other party in the field pledged their duty and patriotism "to hand . . . down . . . the priceless heritage of our fathers . . . unimpaired to our posterity."[30]

Unionists in both sections agreed that the issue of slavery extension had no connection with the national interest. Edward Everett claimed that "its *systematic agitation*" in Congress promoted extremism at the South. William C. Rives declared the territorial issue to be "settled, once for all, by the Constitution." The question of slavery in the West, another asserted, seemed "more appropriate to the realm of political metaphysics than the domain of practical legislation." He repudiated the "theories" of Democrats and Republicans alike as "equally defective and equally untenable in point of constitutional law, as interpreted by the fathers and founders of the Government."[31]

Because partisan self-interest caused the sectional crisis and no party had an effective solution, Unionists such as Everett and Rives saw little hope that a new party with a practicable answer to an imaginary problem would provide a remedy for the nation's ills. They and other conservatives therefore called for "a revival of fraternal regard between the North and South, a willingness to discriminate in both Sections of the Country between the violent words and deeds of a few extremists and the mass of right-thinking and right-feeling citizens." One Georgian moaned that for better than twenty-five years the spirit of the Revolution—mutual forbearance, concession, and fraternity—had given way gradually to radicalism, innovation, restlessness, and intolerance. With the passing of the revolutionary generation, substantive debate on matters of public policy disappeared. As one Unionist lamented, "This has been the cause of our woes!" Appealing to "true-hearted lovers of the Union everywhere," these conservatives wished rather than hoped "to bring back the times when parties were divided upon banks, tariffs, internal improvements, foreign relations, and other legitimate subjects of national legislation."[32]

On Washington's birthday, these conservatives and their adherents young and old called for all Union-lovers to meet on May 9 in Baltimore. Once assembled, they formed the Constitutional Union Party. Party members were determined to remove the slavery issue from politics. They instead stressed the development of the nation's resources, the maintenance of an honorable peace with the world, and, above all, respect for states' rights and devotion to the Union. Remembering the successful Whig strategy of 1840 and 1848, the party decided not to adopt a platform. Experience had demonstrated, they observed, that platforms adopted by partisan conventions "mislead and deceive the people," thereby encouraging the growth of sectional parties. The only political principle that the party recognized was "the Constitution of the Country, the Union of the States, and the Enforcement of the laws." With no Washingtonesque figure to lead the nation out of the wilderness, the party selected the ancient and colorless John Bell of Tennessee from a collection of old and uninspiring pretenders. They then added the somewhat less ancient but equally uninspiring Edward Everett of Massachusetts to the ticket. With warmed-over Whig principles and shopworn strategies, the two former Whigs tottered off into the fray.[33]

Throughout the campaign Democrats and Republicans repeatedly insisted that the territorial question was paramount. Douglas's defenders therefore insisted that the sole question of the presidential campaign focused on "the great battle of Popular Sovereignty or the rights of the people against congressional despotism." The locus of this contest did not center on the bank, a tariff, or internal improvements. Rather the interventionist policies of the "Disunionists of the South" and "the *Abolition* wing of the Republican party" constituted "the elements of disunion and anarchy [that] are prominent on the political horizon." Northern Democrats demanded that Douglas adhere unequivocally to nonintervention and its commitment of limited government. "Names are nothing, Principles are eternal," an Indiana farmer claimed. "The Democratic party must turn over a new leaf, in favor of economy, honesty in public affairs, and vindicate the right of people . . . or defeat is certain and deserved."[34]

In the context of the altered political environment of 1860, Douglas Democrats calculated that if the territorial question engendered new political equations, its ideological parameters remained constant. As one Ohio party member had already put it, "The question is one which must subsist as long as that of the 'Dividing line between federal and local authority'—and when is that question to disappear!" If consolidationists had ever constituted the "Anti-Democratic party," the current fallout within the Democracy revealed "a painful illustration how far the once distinctive lines of Democracy and Federalism have been effaced by the prevailing sectional controversy." The struggle at Charleston had been "between right and wrong, between principle and venality, and in short, between the true democracy of the country and the disguised but most dangerous forms of old federalism." Douglasites concluded that the Breckinridge platform "is pure Federalism. More than Federalism. It is Toryism."[35]

Having dispatched their consolidationist enemies to the south, Douglas Democrats trained their fire on northern interventionists. They remembered that Whiggery once advocated a strong national government to promote simultaneously the fortunes of the wealthy and the party. In so doing, it had condemned the Democracy for advocating mobocracy and preaching an irrepressible conflict between capital and labor. It was to no avail. When these issues wore out, so too did Whiggery. Without an organization, former party members hit upon a single issue—slavery extension—that was "not merely predominant, but alone, inviting the prejudices, provoking the passions, arousing the enthusiasm of the people." Exploiting the "hatred and disgust which white labor entertains for the black," Republicans were ironically the purveyors of a new form of class warfare. "The sections are brought face to face, as the opposites in the great battle between capital and labor," a Michigan editor declared. "It makes the slavery agitation endless, because it assumes that slavery in the South is antagonistic to labor at the North. . . . It is the willful array of the sections against each other for eternity."[36]

Lincoln's party might prattle on about free labor and free men, but the Douglas campaign scoffed at the idea that their opponents—"these negro sympathizers"—had any intention of implementing these doctrines among northern white workers. Returning to a familiar Democratic theme, party leaders noted widespread, obvious, and endemic conflict between capital and labor in the free states. In New York and New England, where Republicans were particularly strong, editors claimed that antislavery activists turned a blind eye to the "Pandora's box of social degradation and misery" there and were "deaf to the cries of distress from the down-trodden millions . . . doomed to a servitude more galling, a bondage equally degrading and more oppressive, than that of African slavery." Under Jackson, Democrats closed ranks against a class-based money power with a specific economic agenda. Now led by Douglas, they opposed an assortment "of old line Whigs, old Democrats and old Liberty men, holding different ideas upon the subject of protection, banks [and] internal improvements." Republicans' only hope, claimed a Wisconsin Democrat, lay "in shaking up the drowsy nigger . . . make him dance, jump Jim Crow, and cut up didoes generally—do anything, in fact, to keep Sambo continually before the people." Without "the lucky nigger question," he taunted, "they would be no where." Denouncing alleged Republican endeavors to promote racial equality as "preposterous and fraught with danger," northern Democrats reminded voters that "this government was made by white men, and for the benefit of white men."[37]

Believing that slavery had reached or nearly reached its natural limits,

Douglasites assumed that Republican hostility to the institution "must be as it exists in the [southern] States." Vain it surely was for Lincoln, Seward, and Chase to deny the intent or violent effect of their irrepressible conflict theory. Equally ludicrous was their claim that they struggled merely to settle the territorial issue and thus to calm inflamed sectional tensions. "They are fighting for permanent power," an Ohio Democrat declared, "and to reach and abolish slavery where it is, not where it is not. . . . It is that bold object, which inspires its masses with enthusiasm, imparts to them life and vigor, and makes their march so defiant." Sidestepping the immorality of slavery and falling back on the party's long-standing commitment to limited government, Democrats proposed "to leave that question where the constitution has left it, and where it has been regulated with great satisfaction for over seventy years." They concluded that this canvass was the "time that white people, however humble their calling, should be made to appreciate their own rights under a government made by white fathers and intended for white descendants."[38]

"Between abolitionism and disunion," a Vermont Democrat wrote Douglas, "the country is in a terrible condition." Douglas's allies in the free and slave states agreed that Republicans and Breckinridge Democrats "both are driving at the same end and . . . both are morally traitors." Party names— Republican and Constitutional Democrat—were as disingenuous as they were inappropriate. In disregard of popular government and the Constitution both pledged to intervene in and manipulate the internal affairs of the territories. "It makes no difference which way for the time being, we intervene," a Vermont editor observed; "the principle is the thing." Douglas concurred. He told a Petersburg, Virginia, rally that interventionists North and South harmonized on principles. They alike proclaimed congressional control and derided self-government. Appealing to the pride, prejudice, and passions of their respective sections, northern abolitionists and southern disunionists "are just as indispensable to each other as the two blades of a pair of shears," Douglas held. "Both of these parties turn on a common pivot— that of intervention by Congress, and cut in opposite directions."[39]

Northern Democrats constantly reminded their constituents that it was absurd to think that disunionism was confined to the fire-eaters. "Breckinridge claims larger privileges for the South than any other candidate for President; yet Yancey, Keitt & Co. go far beyond Breckinridge in their sectionalism," a Pittsburgh editor told his readers. "On the other hand," he added, "Lincoln carries his sectional views as far as the farthest of his dusky supporters." Speaking of policy, Douglasites claimed that if Congress could protect slavery in the territories with a slave code, it could similarly prohibit slavery with a free code. Convinced that intervention of either stripe meant disunion, Douglas told his followers that there was no hope for the Union "except by a faithful and rigid adherence to the doctrine of *non Intervention by Congress* with Slavery in the Territories."[40]

Electoral considerations notwithstanding, larger assumptions informed Douglas Democrats' commitment to nonintervention. Deduced from first—and, as they insisted, correct—principles, popular sovereignty, as Douglas Democrats conceived it, also constituted the conservative middle ground between the extremes of northern and southern interventionists. Even after the Charleston fiasco, Douglas's friends declared themselves "not discouraged. . . . We look forward and expect to see a union at Baltimore that will sustain popular sovereignty to the end of time as our fathers started this government on that glorious plan." Although they bravely maintained that nonintervention had "stood the barking of dogs & the howling of wolves [and] may yet stand the bleating of an ass," supporters also warned Douglas that "if your Doctrine falls with it must come the pillars of this Government."[41]

Whereas Jackson, Van Buren, and Polk had "fought against the doctrine of protection to native manufactures," Douglas now battled "the theory of Congressional protection to slavery [that] is the last and worst development of Federalism." A Louisville Democrat proclaimed that supporters of the Douglas-Johnson ticket stood "on the only national ground to be occupied." Inroads made against self-government in the territories, another warned, "are to be made the field for the first experiment against the liberties of the people." Should congressional interference be legislated as public policy, he ventured, "does anyone believe that this first usurpation of power will be the last?" Believing self-government to be safe for the whole country, Douglas Democrats openly professed an enduring, romantic "faith in the honesty of the masses. . . . They are true. . . . They mean to be true. They will be true. The 'rights' of no State or section will ever suffer intentionally at their hands." Should voters sustain Douglas, thereby reaffirming the nation's commitment to self-government for all, a Kansas farmer predicted, the country "will cease to be disturbed and disgraced." The faithful still clung to the belief that as always "Democracy and popular freedom are synonymous. . . . The mission of the Democracy . . . is to pull down aristocratic pretensions . . . to inaugurate principles of popular suffrage . . . and to preserve government from partizan bias and influences."[42]

Douglas Democrats understood their beliefs to be consistent with the revolutionary experience. In the Revolutionary War Americans exploded the idea that citizens derive their political power from the government, Douglas maintained. In the crucible of that conflict, "the principle of popular sovereignty was born," he said. "We hold, therefore, that the citizen does not derive power from Congress, for he has already derived it from Almighty

God." The power of this argument lay less in its historical accuracy than in its resonance with the public's sense of the American experience. Noting that nonintervention was "deeply rooted in the hearts of the American people," a Pennsylvania Democrat asserted that the principle was "a doctrine based upon the true philosophy of politics, and must eventually prevail." The prospect that it would not and that as a result the republican experiment would fail was unthinkable. William A. Richardson, speaking for Americans North and South, told a meeting of Douglas Democrats, "This Government is all the heritage that I received from my father; it is the only patrimony I expect to transfer to my children. I would rather give it to my boys as my father gave it to me . . . than bestow upon them all the mines of California."[43]

At precisely the moment when Douglas Democrats were making this plea, fire-eaters and their allies were proclaiming that the party of Jackson was no more. Robert Toombs explained to a fellow Georgian that, up to this time, the party had affirmed the principle of congressional nonintervention with slavery. But, he claimed, this doctrine in no way implied the right to intervention against slavery by the settlers on the public domain. That was the heretical belief of the party's minority, Toombs explained. "They desire to interpolate the party creed with it—to make it its rule of action." The so-called ultimatum of the South, the *Mercury* acidly observed, was simply the policy of equal protection in the territories and the equality of the South within the Union.[44]

Breckinridge Democrats excoriated Douglas's supporters in the slave states as "a set of hatless, shoeless, characterless political nondescripts . . . caring more for the accomplishment of their own purposes than for the permanence of our free institutions and libert[ies] of the people." The greed and duplicity of Douglas's southern wing had put Bell and Everett "on track" and "inspired the Black Republicans with confidence," they believed. Breckinridge's boosters asserted that the Little Giant's southern adherents proffered voters a "Union humbug [that] will live just long enough to defile the stupid old dotards who will fondle it." In fact, a Mississippi Democrat rejoined, these latitudinarians were willing "to place slavery under the ban of the Government and to accept for their own section a condition of inequality and degradation in the Union."[45]

Constitutional Unionists fared the same. Evasive, equivocating, and, above all, old, they were deemed "old fogies"—"the ghost of the old Whig party . . . [whose] dead bones still rattle to the breeze, with its fingers ever pointing to the condemned issues of a national bank—a high tariff—and an unpatriotic record . . . kept visible by the blue light of Federalism." Breckinridge supporters fumed that southern Unionists were "pursuing a suicidal course . . . that can only tend to complicate and embarrass the action of the South."

Like Douglas Democrats, Bell's supporters were "posted at the street corners of every town and village, crying out *disunion*, not knowing, poor simpletons! that their own party . . . invite[s] aggression by seeking to destroy the only conservative and resistive element at the South." Unionist submission, they cried, was but "pusillanimity. It is un-American, and unworthy of a resting place in the heart of a freeman." They regarded Bell's supporters "in the same light in which the true friends of American independence were wont to regard those who pled for the continuation of British rule on this continent."[46]

Constitutional Union opposition in the slave states sobered Breckinridge Democrats. The prospect of a Douglas victory alarmed them. But the idea that Lincoln could win struck Breckinridge's supporters with genuine horror. A Republican triumph would evince unchecked and uncontrollable antislavery prejudice in the free states and be "a declaration by the North of an unalterable determination to deprive the South of those rights guaranteed by the Constitution." This southern slaveholder put the prospect in familiar terms. A Republican victory, he pronounced, would be a declaration that "we should submit to [the] degrading vassalage of abolition rule without remedy." The nomination of an undistinguished, one-term congressman underscored these assumptions. Seward, they believed, at least had talent and ambition. Lincoln, however, was "an illiterate partizan . . . without talents, without education, possessed only of his inveterate hostility to slavery and his openly avowed predilections for negro equality." With only prejudice and fanaticism to recommend him to the party, Lincoln—"a slab-sided, rail-splitting Illinois politician"—was no less an irrepressible conflict candidate than Seward. Should he be elected, a North Carolina Democrat warned, it "will go far to confirm . . . that in fact secession would only be a form—that already we are two people."[47]

As one Tennessee Democrat had earlier put it, Republican policies (and by extension, Republican Party supporters) "deny and oppose every principle which the South deems essential to the preservation of her Constitutional rights, [and] stamp our institutions with the brand of infamy." More generally, others charged that Republicans held the working class in contempt and were hostile to its well-being. In the North, Breckinridge troops battled a familiar if disguised foe. They claimed that Whiggery was the controlling element within this sectional party. "By securing a triumph over the Democratic party and centralizing and increasing the power of the General Government," a New York editor predicted, "the Old Whig nucleus will be enabled to carry out all their long cherished ideas of exclusive and partial legislation." Insisting that "everything about their principles and purposes is Negrescent," Breckinridge's northern allies maintained that the Old Whig schemes of monopolies and restrictions, though hidden, were to be brought forward at the moment of Lincoln's victory. To ensure that end, they charged, Republican managers "guarded every step to the ballot box, and *compelled* [workers] to vote those [abolition] tickets, on penalty of dismissal from employment."[48]

Surveying the campaign battlefield, Constitutional Democrats surmised that they faced the combined forces of sectional prejudice and a party that was alien and un-American. For Breckinridge and his supporters to be bested would ensure northern ascendancy in the territories and cast "a bleak clime" over the slave states. Crowded poorhouses, impoverished labor, exploited women driven to crime and vice, rural poverty, and unremitting conflict between capital and labor would be the lot of a subjugated South. Victorious Republicans, so they believed, would insist that southerners give up their independence and privileges "and assume the places of the white slaves at the North. . . . So it will be forever. There will be two classes—the master and the slave."[49]

Long-standing Democratic fear of, and opposition to, minority tyranny and class-biased legislation had undergone a significant shift in the slave states by 1860. As recently as the 1844 canvass, party members North and South denounced an aristocratic, urban-based money power in the free and slave states opposed to expansion and favoring "a splendid consolidated government." Then they had charged that Whigs "threatened to dissolve the Union" unless the United States succumbed "to the pretensions and ascendancy of British power." Having been beaten on the old, economic agenda of class legislation, the Democracy's opponents gradually abandoned direct advocacy of it. They now pursued their consolidationist ends by circuitous but no less threatening means. The *Richmond Enquirer* claimed, "The real issue of this canvass is not union or disunion. . . . The effort on the part of the State Rights Democracy is to limit and restrain the power of this Federal agent. . . . It is nothing but the old contest between the friends of centralized, concentrated powers . . . and the advocates of separate, distinct, conservative powers."[50]

Accordingly, the Breckinridge campaign positioned itself between the mob rule of squatter sovereignty and the congressional despotism of Republicans. "Douglas Republicans," one put it succinctly, were "no better than Black Republicans." To him, that is, so-called Union Democrats differed from Republicans only as to who held the power to exclude the South from the territories. The distinction had no practical difference: "Both acknowledge the theory or false premise of antislavery, viz: that negro subordination . . . cannot exist without positive enactment . . . hence that it is not a thing in nature, but unnatural, and if so, it must be wrong." Administration supporters in the free states echoed these fears, warning that Lincoln's election would eventuate in a reckless, unconstitutional attack on slavery with "fatal consequences" for commerce, industry, and the Union. Looking over their other shoulder, they proclaimed that Douglas's doctrine of "unfriendly legislation" effectively "would do more to hand over the Territories to the agents of the New England Aid Society than any other doctrine ever broached." In either case, the *Louisville Courier* averred, both Douglas and Lincoln would "wrest the Constitution from its true intent and meaning." The editor concluded that upon the "vital" territorial question, "two of the three parties are necessarily wrong."[51] Perceptive readers required little imagination to conclude which party was right.

Taking measure of Republican restriction and squatter sovereignty, Breckinridge managers informed southerners, "By the one, we are to be throttled and robbed—by the other chloroformed and swindled." They made it clear that the party preferred the former to the latter. Douglas, they scorned, made "insidious, instead of open war upon the South." Like the Constitutional Unionists, Douglas Democrats wished to avoid the issue and thus "have nothing to do with this battle." If Constitutional Democrats detested the "abominable heresies" of Republicans, they nonetheless recommended that the South follow their strategic lead. "As blatantly as they vaunt their unconstitutional, revolutionary 'irrepressible conflict,'" one advised, "let us, with equal boldness, proclaim the true principles of the Constitution as adjudicated by the Supreme Court."[52]

Breckinridge's supporters' ears burned with the charge that they were disunionists. Nobody, they answered, wanted disunion. But these Democrats added that the Union "should not be maintained at the cost of the independence and equity of the States." Nor, they went on, should disunion "be avoided at the expense of the honor and the rights of the citizens of a whole section." In other words, the "*form* of union, without the spirit of justice and equality to give it soul" was not worth preserving. Breckinridge told a rally at Ashland that the great question of the canvass was southerners' equal rights in the territories and, by extension, the equality of the South in the confederacy. Asserting his policies to be constitutional, Breckinridge reasoned that his platform could not be sectional. "They cannot be abstract, minute or unimportant, for they concern the honor and equity of the States of this broad Union." With equality and justice to every state, "there will be no disunionists in any section," the *Richmond Enquirer* prophesied, "but a denial of the benefits and equality designed by the Constitution, will make disunionists in every section."[53]

Put in reductive terms, southern rights Democrats maintained that "the question, *the issue*, in this canvass is purely and simply one of state rights and state equality." Stating the obvious—the old line between parties on economic issues was dead—a Vicksburg editor declared that the "momentous question" to be settled now, once and forever, was "the fate of the Union and the preservation of the rights of one section of the noble heritage of our fore-fathers." Condemning "party hacks and political mountebanks" who sacri-ficed principles for expediency, supporters of Breckinridge refused to dodge, postpone, or ignore the territorial issue. They knew, if others had forgotten, that constitutional guarantees were above compromise and that equality of rights was absolute. "There is no Union," one observed, "but a Union based upon principles of mutual rights and benefits."[54]

The ineluctable conclusion drawn from this premise was that those who would abridge these rights were "the *real disunionists* as they are contributing to the advance of a policy which must inevitably lead to a dissolution of the Union or cause the people of the South to occupy in our federal relations the position of *uncivilized, immoral inferiors.*" Viewing the Union as they did, "*not as an end,* but as a means," southern rights Democrats of the Breckinridge stripe denied that the Revolution was fought "for this *Federal Union,* but for the inde-pendence and rights of the citizens of the thirteen colonies." Each element of the opposition appeared ready to forfeit that inheritance. If restrictionist Re-publicans successfully disregarded those ends, then "the creature [the federal government] [would acquire] the right to dictate to the creator [the states]." To those who insisted that the intent of Douglas's alternative of noninterven-tion would preclude this evil and preserve the Union, the Breckinridge camp returned that it threatened property rights and abridged equality and was, therefore, "revolutionary" and would strike "at the foundation of all govern-ment." They also denounced southern Unionists' devotion to the absolute of an indissoluble Union, which "continued to divide the South" and was "all affected for party success." Their northern allies agreed. Destroy the equality of the states, the *Hartford Weekly Times* ventured, "and that very day the Re-public will be on the direct road to ruin. Indeed, the Confederation must be broken up so soon as the Equality of the States is sacrificed."[55]

Rejecting the assertion that their platform was immoderate, unconstitu-tional, and disunionist, Breckinridge's supporters sniffed that "to stigmatize reform as revolution, is always the tyrant's expedient to suppress resistance to his usurpations." A defiant Virginian, believing that Breckinridge's election would end sectional agitation, urged slave-state voters to rally to the party "whether to save the Union, or to unite the South—the first depends on the last." The ticket concurred. Joe Lane warned, "Compromises of Constitu-tional principles [were] ever dangerous." He claimed that the Breckinridge platform "embodies . . . the only means of stopping sectional agitation by securing to all equality and constitutional rights, the denial of which has led to the present unhappy condition of public affairs." Writing from his home in Kentucky, John Breckinridge observed that throughout the nation's history politicians and their constituents found it necessary to stop and "solemnly assert the true character of this Government." That had happened in 1800 and was true again in 1860. "It is intended now to assert and establish the equality of the States as the only basis of peace," he maintained. "When this object, so national, so constitutional, so just, shall be accomplished, the last cloud will disappear from the American sky."[56]

The less hopeful in the party were more gloomy. Yancey warned an audience at the Cooper Institute in New York that "the very moment [the southern states'] equality is destroyed in the government under the constitution, then, in my opinion, it becomes the duty of the state to protect its people by interposing its reserved rights between the acts of the general government and its people." William Porcher Miles cautioned fellow Democrat and historian George Bancroft that in the event of a Republican victory, the same patriotic spirit and desire for self-government that Bancroft attributed to his state's revolutionaries "would actuate the good people of Carolina in 1861 as had moved their fore-fathers in 1776." In Mississippi, the *Vicksburg Sun* reminded its readers what they already knew: the preservation of the Union was secondary to the liberties it was designed to protect. "To preserve the Constitution in its purity," it declared, "to transmit its blessings to our children and our children's children, should be the primary object of patriotic desire, and not the mere preservation of a Union when its soul is fled."[57]

Suggestive of the thrust of the canvass, Republicans agreed with the Breckinridge wing on three crucial points. First, the territorial issue transcended the great questions of political economy that once divided the contending parties. More precisely, they "have all been merged into the one of *human* slavery." Republicans would also concur with fire-eaters that Douglas's brand of popular sovereignty was "new fangled . . . a doctrine of modern birth, and unknown to the fathers." The perversion of popular sovereignty ensued from a misunderstanding of the past. "The Fathers of the Republic intended to exclude Slavery from the Territories," a New Yorker claimed. Nonintervention, he pointed out with only modest exaggeration, "resulted . . . in the extension of slavery from the RIO GRANDE to the Gulf of California, and up to the 88th degree of latitude. . . . It seeks to undermine the freedom of the territories by stealth."[58]

Finally, Republicans agreed with the Breckinridge wing that the cure for sectional politics was, paradoxically perhaps, agitation. They ridiculed those Constitutional Unionists who pined for "the halcyon days of general reconciliation. . . . They forget that the very safeguard of democracy is agitation." Party leaders dismissed Douglas as "a political hermaphrodite [and] a giant of the neuter gender." The dodges "now promoted by the Shamocratic party must be abandoned," they insisted. Like Breckinridge's supporters Republicans held that since "the Triumphs of Despotism come through diplomacy . . . the day of concessions and compromises for temporary peace is past, North as well as South." "Agitation," the *Albany Evening Journal* freely admitted, "must continue and increase in intensity until the question is settled one way or the other."[59]

Republicans no less than Democrats demanded that the government be restored to its original purpose. Conceivably, Breckinridge, Yancey, and Rhett might have agreed with Moses Davis of Wisconsin when he earlier lamented that "the Union which our fathers formed seventy years ago is not the Union of today. The landmarks of that compact are fast becoming obliterated, and the sons of the Revolutionary fathers are becoming *slaves* or *masters*." Another Wisconsin Republican, Timothy Howe, added that the principles of the party were neither novel nor revolutionary but "coeval with the Constitution, and were avowed by all its makers." This fire-eaters would have considered infamous if not deranged. Still, Orville Hickman Browning persisted that Republican doctrines were "the same that were consecrated upon every battlefield of the Revolution—the same that were hallowed by the first patriot blood that was shed upon the plains of Lexington and the summit of Bunker Hill, and that secured . . . our patriot sires . . . their great and final triumph." David Wilmot exhorted delegates to the 1860 Republican convention that it was the party's mission "to restore this government to its original policy, and place it again in that rank upon which our fathers organized and brought it into existence." What was oppressive or heretical about the principle of freedom in the territories? a New York editor asked. "In this direction, WASHINGTON and JEFFERSON went as far, if not farther, than LINCOLN or SEWARD; and the Republicans of 1798 were far more emphatic in their words and works, than the Republicans of 1860."[60]

Some dated the degradation of the Democracy to 1845, when the annexation of Texas made American government "subservient to slavery." Others pointed to the Kansas-Nebraska Act, when the opposition "took a new shoot, not veering off from the course laid down by the founders of the government, but wheeling squarely around and going straight backwards." All concurred that "the Democratic platform of '52 was more proslavery than that of '48, and that of '56 exceeded that of '52." Charleston, Baltimore, and Richmond merely carried out the process. Another Republican and former Whig put it somewhat differently. He claimed that southern hostility to Whig economic programs such as the tariff, internal improvements, and distribution of the sales of public lands became embodied in the Democracy's platform when northern Locos, "for peace in the party and place in the government," acquiesced to southern demands. Northern cravenness, he concluded, "prepared the way for the Compromise of 1850, for the Kansas and Nebraska Act of

1854, for the Dred Scott decision, and for the threats of disunion openly expressed in 1856, and repeated now defiantly."[61]

Throughout the free states, Republicans followed this analysis. They claimed that Democratic policies consistently tended "to degrade free labor [and] to give the slave power the control of the government." Northern Democrats, one asserted, were like British Tories who "were so impressed with the majesty of the existing Government that they were prepared to submit to whatever law Parliament might prescribe, and stand by the throne forever." The "lordly masters" of the South who now governed the party constituted "a social and political hierarchy just as exclusive as any that exists in the monarchies of Europe." Like their foreign counterparts, the sectional, controlling influence in the Democracy was "ever ready to ridicule and thwart the efforts of laborers and mechanics to obtain a just compensation for labor." If the Revolution meant anything, Republicans concluded, it was "to relieve free born *labor* of the oppressive burdens which . . . under a tyrannical Parliament had been steadily accumulating on that labor."[62]

Republicans cautioned voters that, as a sectional and aristocratic party, "the Democratic party are pledged to a system of slavery extension . . . and when carried out to its logical conclusions . . . will spread slavery over every foot of soil, both State and territorial, over which the flag of our common country moves." The opposition, to be sure, was split. According to one source, however, the difference between the Douglas and Breckinridge factions was merely one of means, not ends. One looked to Congress, the other to "Presidents, Judges, Soldiers, and mobs" to extend the institution. The issue of the election, then, was manifest—if the nation's future was not. Carl Schurz put it succinctly. The electorate had to choose between "a consolidated political despotism on one side and a liberal enlightened progressive government on the other."[63]

Consistently avowing that slavery restriction was the only safe, honorable, and consistent policy for the government to pursue, Republicans, like both wings of the Democracy, nudged their way onto the middle ground. "For both the abolitionists and the southern fire eaters I have the same political contempt," one Wisconsin voter spat. Distancing themselves as well from the more extreme in their ranks, party members condemned alike claims to laws "*higher* than the Constitution of the United States" and "the organization of marauding expeditions in any of the States to attack the people or the institutions of neighboring states." Neither interventionist nor disunionist, the Republican Party took "the true conservative ground between the slavery abolition of the North on the one hand, and the Southern slavery extension on the other."[64]

Republican restrictionists pronounced that they opposed "innovations, novel doctrines and new fangled theories." They were the true conservatives. Despite popular prejudice to the contrary, the image of conservatives as old, wealthy, declensionist, and apolitical misrepresented reality. A true conservative, one party member ventured, "acts and acts vigorously . . . [and] was a friend to safe and sure progress and reform." The *Boston Daily Journal* claimed that an enlightened conservative was "one who, being satisfied with our form of government, would endeavor to preserve it in its purity and efficacy . . . leaning ever in the direction of experience, moderation, the welfare of all sections, and the permanent public peace." Contrast this with the "plan" of Constitutional Unionists, a New Jersey Republican suggested. "The Union party does nothing, proposes nothing," he jeered. "It pretends to take the Constitution for a guide, and so does every other party." A New York editor drove home his point: the whole subject of debate among the leading parties in 1860 turned precisely on the meaning of constitutional principles. "It is therefore a petty subterfuge," he twitted, "to say that one is in favor of these principles, when no particular principles are indicated or explained." [65]

Claiming that Constitutional Unionists could do no good but aware that they might do Republicans much harm, party managers warned their rank and file that increased support for Bell and Everett diminished the chances of success of those like themselves who wished to preserve the Union. They said phooey to the "Bell-Everett junto," claiming that these warmed-over Whigs were the descendants of a "silk-stocking" Federalist gentry "who sell principles and dry goods." They ridiculed the ticket as "too milk-and-water-ish." Unionists assumed that the country was in a crisis, a Boston editor growled, "but they don't wish to say what the trouble is, nor how we can get out of it. . . . With no platform, no openly dedicated purposes, [Bell and Everett] come to solicit votes for which they can give no reason. . . . They shut their eyes, and ring their bells." [66]

"The only true Union party in the country is the Republican." This might seem an extravagant claim for an organization whose existence even in the Upper South was precarious and problematic. They argued, however, that the weakness of the Republican Party in the slave states was proportional to the South's lack of commitment to republicanism. "Republicanism teaches that the nationality of a party must be decided by the principles it advocates," a Hoosier claimed. "Nationality is a steady adherence to the policy of the founders of the Republic." Simon Cameron claimed that throughout the Union, all who labored with their hands and wished to make labor respectable instinctively would support the Republican Party. He and others commiserated that "poor whites, the crackers [and] the sand-hillers" were "the most pitiable victims of the slave system." Still, a Delaware Republican tellingly complained that thousands of poor white southerners who did not own a slave or ever expected to were ever "ready to denounce their neighbors as abolitionists, if they do not subscribe to all the dogmas of . . . this Juggernaut which the Locofocos have set upon this land." Despite this reality, party leaders clung to the belief that Lincoln's election would expose the fault lines in the South, "breaking up the sheer despotism which the slaveholders of the South now exercise over the non-slaveholding whites."[67] It was a conviction that they would hold for a very long time.

Republicans maintained that they occupied more than the middle ground; they also were situated on the moral high ground. They dismissed the claim made by Democrats in both wings that Lincoln's election posed any threat to the Union. "There is not an item in the Republican platform indicative of hostility to the South," replied an Ohio restrictionist, "and there are no utterances by those who would shape the policy of the party, if it should come into possession of power, that would authorize any alarm as to its intentions." He admitted that the party did contain its share of "rash and extreme men." Yet as a party, Republicans "are for non-intervention by Government with the subject [of slavery]—against any attempted abolition of slavery by Government." He therefore reasoned that the South would not be called on "in any offensive or degrading sense to submit. There can be no dishonor and no terror in acquiescing in the inauguration of a President constitutionally elected, and in his administration, under the Constitution of the Federal Government." A Philadelphia editor reminded voters in eastern Pennsylvania that larger considerations transcended party success. "If these efforts [at intimidation] should succeed," he admonished, "we should consider this a poor country indeed, and that our citizens were unworthy of the liberties they enjoy. . . . They would be really lower than the Slaves of the South." A western colleague agreed that the issue was simply whether northern voters would "maintain, intact, the privileges secured to them by the Fathers of the Republic, or will they basely yield them at the bidding of a southern oligarchy—?"[68]

For Republicans no less than Breckinridge Democrats, the 1860 election was a defining moment in the nation's history. "We have not so effectively demonstrated the superiority of self-government," the *Indianapolis Daily Journal* worried. "The government is not what it used to be or was meant to be. The whole land is full of fraud, of corruption, of demoralization." In Illinois, Orville Browning predicted that if either Douglas or, worse, Breckinridge carried the day, slavery extension "will work a revolution in this nation which will change the entire structure of this government [and] subvert every principle upon which our fathers based it." Knowing as well as the revolutionary generation that "'power is always stealing from the hands of the many to the few,'" Browning declared that "all the political power of the government would, ultimately, concentrate in the hands of an aristocracy." A Portsmouth

Republican agreed. "The struggle for political ascendancy now pending, is a clear struggle between liberty and slavery," he alleged. "The strife is sectional, and it is a mere dodge to deny it."[69]

Members of the Constitutional Union Party looked with dismay on these and similar assertions. They condemned with equal vehemence northern Democrats, who despite the threat of disunion would acquiesce in Lincoln's election, and fire-eaters, whose agitation of the territorial issue had "set in motion the oar of Bla.k Republicanism." The party's reaction to the Charleston miscarriage only reinforced their sense of declension. "There is neither harmony, nor unity of creed, or even profession any longer among the unterrified Democracy," William Brownlow wrote. "The old party, as organized by Jackson, has gone to wreck. It is now but a bundle of corrupt factions furiously contending for mastery." With insight, one party member in Georgia declared that the party's breakup resulted from its "equivocal position upon the great question of our day and time—the question of slavery in the Territories." To his credit he realized the deeper significance of the Democracy's disruption. Perhaps this Georgian reveled in the Democracy's comeuppance; but he also knew there was "a special antagonism on principle which cannot be compromised without a sacrifice of honor, and at the same time a sacrifice *all prospect of success* for either wing."[70]

The breakup of the Democracy posed a challenge and an opportunity to Unionists. The widespread antislavery sentiment of the North they regarded as axiomatic; so, too, the moral bankruptcy of a Democracy that always had pandered "to any and every new thing, to every *ism*, and every devilish contrivance, which the leaders supposed would benefit the party temporarily." Adding these two truisms together, Unionists—especially in the South—deduced that the Douglas wing could never contest with Lincoln "*except by becoming equally odious, and equally dangerous* to the peace of the country, and the perpetuity of our institutions." Put in other words, Douglasites "could only defeat the Republicans by proving themselves *better* Freesoilers than the Republicans." Prospects in the South were equally bleak. There Democrats had ever "lived and kept themselves in power by this villainous [slavery] agitation."[71]

The Democracy's disruption proved to William Cabell Rives at least that in this election year no national party could be built on sectional issues. In that there was some hope, and the faithful offered up hosannas. Edward Everett believed that "in this general breaking up, a great many people will be glad to take refuge in a third Constitutional party." A Georgia Unionist concluded without a hint of irony that the Democracy's dismemberment was essential to the preservation of the Union. The corruption equally evident in Washington and Charleston "is sufficient instigation for the conservative elements of the country to come together and by a mutual action, to remedy the evil spoken of." A New Orleans conservative anticipated that voters would not hang on to "the wreck of the old Democratic party" that was "entirely 'played out.'" They would realize that Constitutional Unionists were the only national party. "They stand with cool composure," he boasted, "confident of their strength and rejoicing in the belief that their course is daily gaining the favor and affections of the people."[72]

Reinvigorated by these hopes, party members stepped up their attack on sectional politics. Before Charleston, Daniel D. Barnard observed that Democrats and Republicans "with nothing really between them but the question of slavery" desperately warred on one another not for principle but for "mastery in the government." The triumph of either on these means and with that end "would be a national calamity." Despite Brownlow's earlier claim that the territorial issue was "the great question of the day," Unionists paradoxically insisted that the nation divided on the "immaterial" question of territorial legislation that demagogues used "to distract the popular mind." A Unionist convention in Massachusetts resolved that there was no issue before the country demanding the maintenance of a party "which from necessity must be sectional." Others similarly discerned no pressing demand "on the score of population" for the unorganized territories. They wished that the problem would go away and trusted that "all fair-minded citizens" would soon be satisfied the territorial dispute was "more imaginary than real, more abstract than practical."[73]

As the canvass took shape in the minds of Constitutional Unionists, territorial sovereignty, slavery extension, and its restriction were irrelevant: "The question is *whether the Union will endure*." Despite southern Unionists' insistence that Lincoln's election was insufficient grounds for secession, John Bell warned that the Union could not survive a sectional president. In Illinois, John J. Crittenden ridiculed what he called "contingency Union men" [read: Breckinridge Democrats] who went for the Union only under certain conditions. Brownlow saw plainly a "*conspiracy* against this Union . . . to revolutionize the Government, and to establish upon its ruins a Southern confederacy." Unionists trusted that "those who are for renouncing this controversy, in which neither party has an actual stake, will act with the party which declares itself in favor of a cessation of the slavery question, for the Union, the Constitution, and the Enforcement of the Laws."[74]

Conservatives therefore set for themselves the Herculean task of slaying the hydra-headed monster of squatter sovereignty, mobocracy, restrictionist fanaticism, and southern disunion. Monster politicians fed on corruption and were themselves corrupt. Public affairs, Unionists exclaimed, were "in the hands of thieves, robbers and scoundrels, who are a disgrace to the age we live in." The popular will was "broken down, overwhelmed, strangled by cajolery, fraud and force." Instead of government of and by the people, Washington was "rapidly becoming a government of the few, and those the most debased and unscrupulous in the land." Like good Whigs they assumed that the interests of the masses were the same. Unionists not surprisingly called for "an inseparable union between the farmers, mechanics, laborers and honest men of the country to oppose [corruption] at the ballot box." Crittenden believed that his party would embrace an array of partisans. Old Whigs would naturally adhere. Conservative Democrats who left their party after the Kansas-Nebraska Act would find a home. Nativists who had been active "in the endeavor to establish an intermediate power" between the contending parties would realize their goal. And that "mass of quiet unobtrusive citizens, who have always shunned the turmoil of political life" would heed the Unionist clarion call. As a Georgia Unionist asserted, it would be "truly a Union party, standing on the middle ground between the extremists of each section, rebuking the fanaticism of the North and the ultraism of the South."[75]

Although they considered themselves unique, Constitutional Unionists, like every other party in the field, positioned themselves between the corrupt and the fanatic. "*Extremes are always dangerous*," the *Southern Watchman* declared, "*extremes are nearly always wrong! There is a happy medium, which is always safe, and generally right!*" And again like every other party in 1860, these happy mediums resolved "to learn our lessons of duty from the great fountains of instruction bequeathed to us in the examples and the recorded wisdom of the Fathers of the Republic." Everett urged that party leaders ape the Republican practice of drawing analogies between 1776 and 1860. Though that war opposed foreign aggression, he admitted, "the comparison *must* be made. . . . We have the blood of Patrick Henry on our side—His clarion voice called on our Fathers to throw off the yoke of oppression & . . . to preserve in all their strength the sacred bonds of Union." Unionists recalled Washington's warning about "the proscriptive spirit of party, and more especially of sectional politics." Pronouncing a southern confederacy an "impossibility" and a confederation of Gulf states "the most diminutive of humbugs," a Tuscaloosa editor reminded his conservative readers that "the Union is the priceless heritage of our fathers . . . and unless we are recreant to every principle of duty and patriotism, we will hand it down unimpaired to our posterity."[76] Such convictions were hardly new; they were, however, very powerful.

Constitutional Unionists ran a Janus-faced campaign to slay the hydra. Drawing on the admonitions of Washington and the rhetoric of Clay and Webster, northern Unionists denounced the possible triumph of higher-law politics over the constitutional rights of the South. If they believed Douglas a scoundrel, free-state conservatives could abide him—minimally. Lincoln's defeat was imperative. Everett frankly admitted that he preferred the election of Douglas and Johnson "on the simple ground that they both have warm supporters in the non-slaveholding states, as well as in the South." Giving voice to southern dread, Everett stated the apparent: "No sane man can, I think, suppose that the Republican party will ever gain a foothold in the slaveholding states. . . . If Messrs. Lincoln and Hamlin are elected it will be by a purely sectional vote." In a tactical non sequitur, he urged Washington Hunt to promote a union with either sectional wing of the Democracy in New York "on any terms consistent with personal honor."[77]

In the South Bell's supporters attempted to outflank Breckinridge by supporting southern rights and the Union. They defended Bell's record on slavery as "sound, constitutional, Southern, and natural." Slave-state Unionists assured voters that Bell and his platform "can be accepted with honor, self-respect and safety by every citizen of the Republic not bent on mischief." Little was said of Everett. Taking aim at Douglas and Lincoln, a Georgia Unionist affirmed that if either squatter sovereignty or restriction prevailed in November, "then we are no longer equals in the Union our fathers formed, and we would . . . counsel always no submission to either." At the same time and quite consistently, southern Unionists ridiculed Democratic fire-eaters who for a decade cried that the South's institutions and the Union were endangered but whose policies jeopardized both. Summing up the conservative argument, the *Savannah Republican* declared, "*The South is resolved, firmly and unalterably, and by the unanimous voice of all her citizens, never to submit to another federal discrimination against her on account of her institutions.*" Defining southern conservatism in practical terms, it insisted that the price of Union was the fugitive slave law, *Dred Scott*, and repeal of northern personal liberty laws.[78]

Extolling the inestimable virtues and benefits of the Union, the *Vicksburg Whig* claimed that the mission of the party in both sections was "to preserve our Nationality . . . to oppose the reckless and insane schemes of Northern fanatics and Southern extremists, to restore harmony and fraternal concord to our distracted country." Above all else, the paper insisted, we must "preserve the glorious institutions of our fathers, through all coming time."[79] These were noble sentiments without a doubt, but they were expressed by every other party in the campaign. The strength of the party's appeal—adherence to the Constitution and maintenance of the Union—was ironically its weakness. By the middle of 1860, the meaning of the Constitution was very much in debate. So, too, was the nature and purpose of the Union. There was no consensus on these issues. The resonant sectional appeals of the Republicans and Breckinridge Democrats spoke to the futility of the Unionist campaign.

As the election unfolded, it was apparent that there was no common vision of how to deal with the territorial issue. Popular sovereignty, positive protection, restriction, and enforcement of the laws each reflected a fragmented, sectionalized political system. That the system was coming apart, however, was a positive statement that the parties were functioning exactly as they were supposed to: representing the people. Douglas and Bell appealed to those in the electorate who either wished to remove the slavery issue from national politics or to avoid it altogether. Unhappily, the central tendency of the campaign ran against them. Lincoln and Breckinridge wanted to seize the issue, to agitate it, to resolve it. Moderate dissenters in both sections notwithstanding, sectional politics replaced, indeed made antiquated, established appeals for the expansion of freedom over space or for the liberation of individuals through time. As Lincoln squared off against Douglas in the North and Breckinridge faced Bell in the South, the sad truth was that the territorial issue, to a great extent, had polarized the Jacksonian political system along sectional lines.

In late summer, an again discomforted August Belmont wrote Douglas that fund-raising efforts had met and would continue to meet with little success "unless we can give our merchants & politicians some *assurance* of *success*. . . . There is at present an apathy & indifference, of which it is difficult to form an idea—the opinion has gained ground, that nothing can prevent the election of Lincoln." Two weeks later, Miles Taylor bluntly told Douglas that he had to win the Maine election to give the South hope. Douglas did not. Others complained that the party's general committee in Washington suddenly had short arms and deep pockets and that the financial resources made available to the Democracy's foot soldiers "does not amount to a drop in the bucket." Aware that the drift of the campaign ran against Douglas, the *Cincinnati Daily Enquirer* feared the worst. "A blindness, dark and terrible seems to rest upon the minds of large bodies of our country men," it fumed. "The ship of state is madly rushing on to the breakers of destruction, yet they are unaware of it—or if conscious, they put no hand to save it."[80]

Save it moderates could not. A series of Republican victories throughout the free states in the fall demoralized Democrats and Unionists North and South. Republican victories in Pennsylvania and Indiana in October appalled Breckinridge's supporters. With the defeat of conservative forces (conservative at least in contrast to Republicans), one claimed, "the boasted nationality of Bell and Douglas has received a death blow." Northern Democrats' ability to protect southern institutions proved to be "a myth which promises no relief." Douglas's slave-state supporters were no less despondent. Regarding a Republican sweep as inevitable, a Georgia Democrat considered any further discussion of fusion between the wings in the slave states useless "because we need *thirty-two northern electoral votes*, which all the South combined can't make." Thinking back to April, the *Louisville Democrat* concluded that the result of Charleston was "the triumph of the Black Republican party."[81]

So it was. By the evening of November 6, Lincoln's election was clear. He received approximately 1,865,000, or nearly two-fifths of the votes cast. Lincoln won every free state, only losing three of New Jersey's seven electoral votes. If all the opposition votes in the northern states were combined, Lincoln would have carried them all save Oregon, California, and New Jersey and still won the election. Besides the three electoral votes in New Jersey, Douglas carried only Missouri, and that slimly over Bell. Breckinridge took eleven southern states though he held majorities in only four. Bell won in Virginia, Kentucky, and Tennessee.[82] Lincoln's victory genuinely reflected irreconcilable divisions in the American electorate.

Three days later, a triumphant but sobered Lyman Trumball wrote his House colleague Benjamin Wade that "with power comes responsibility." The success of a Republican administration, he believed, depended on Lincoln "firmly carrying out the principles on which he has been elected, without pandering to cliques or factions from any quarter." Bravely and somewhat defiantly, Trumbull concluded by observing, "I have no fears of secession. No just cause will be given for such a cause." That very day a Richmond editor declared that "the sectional game has been fairly played out in the North." In the election of Lincoln the northern masses had given their "solemn sanction and its political power to the antislavery policy of the Black Republicans." Northern conservatism he considered "idle canvass prattle." The federal government, he presumed, "is in the hands of the avowed enemies of one entire section." Six weeks later, while Lincoln remained at home preparing for his presidency and Trumbull and other members of Congress looked ahead to the holiday season, word reached Springfield and Washington that South Carolina had seceded from the Union.[83] The game was afoot in earnest.

The tree of liberty must be refreshed from time to time with the blood of patriots
and tyrants. It is the natural manure.
— Thomas Jefferson to William Stevens Smith, November 13, 1787

The preservation of the sacred fire of liberty and the destiny of the republican model of
government, are justly considered as deeply, perhaps as finally staked, on the experiment
entrusted to the hands of the American people. — George Washington, *First Inaugural*, 1789

Conclusion
We Stand Where Our Fathers Stood

The gloom at the White House on January 1, 1861, was unmistakable. Three
days earlier, on Saturday, December 29, Secretary of War John B. Floyd of
Virginia had tendered his resignation from the cabinet in an insulting letter
to President James Buchanan. On a miserable, blustery sabbath, while the
president dallied over the secretary's initiative, he turned his attention to the
insolent demand made by South Carolina that the government turn over federal property in that "republic." After some prodding and Jeremiah Black's
threat to resign from the cabinet if the president did not take a firm stance,
Buchanan boldly decided that he would never abandon Fort Sumter. The
government would defend it "against hostile attacks from whatever quarter
they may come." The next day, New Year's Eve, he accepted Floyd's resignation in ill humor and without regret. Before retiring that evening, Buchanan
ordered troops, munitions, and supplies to Charleston Harbor. At the president's New Year's Day reception, irate southerners, raw over Buchanan's
decision to hold on to Fort Sumter, brazenly sported the blue cockade of secession. To a man, they refused to acknowledge Buchanan or shake his hand
as they passed down the reception line. The Old Public Functionary weath-
ered their insolence without complaint. By now he was used to abuse.[1]

Hostility and poor manners were not confined to Washington politics as
usual; they were illustrative of a nation divided. On the day that Floyd

252

resigned, a Mississippi Democrat and delegate to the state's secession convention expressed his determination to press for disunion. Writing to Joseph Holt, who would replace Floyd as secretary of war, he insisted that a final settlement of the territorial question and the slavery issue generally "must be made in some way *now*." He would brook no delay. Discussions of slavery in Congress must end. Attempts to restrict or interfere with it had to cease. Northerners should "in good faith render up all fugitives and accord to us our slave property[,] equal rights and security in the Territories." Without these guarantees, he asserted, "we must give up the Union. . . . I can see no way of escaping it." At the same time that Buchanan was suffering through his embarrassment at the reception, a New Orleans Democrat wrote to him advising that he let the southern states secede peacefully. Coercion, he claimed, "would result in the ruin of liberty in the western world."[2]

Much farther north, a Providence Republican took measure of secessionist movements in the Lower South. He observed that the "New Year opens upon increasing liberty in the Old World, and upon treason, disorder, and peril to free constitutional government in the New World. . . . How can we contemplate our present position without mingled shame and indignation[?]" An exasperated Illinois Republican reminded a by now less sanguine Lyman Trumbull that the history of humankind was the story of the struggle between freedom and despotism. He therefore urged that Congress adopt no expedient to quiet "the howlings of enraged oligarchs or the fears of trembling conservatives." Republicans like himself had labored too long and too hard to surrender now. "If our principles are worth contending for, they are worth insisting upon," he counseled. "*Progress* not *retrograde* should still and can be the watchword of Americans." Back in Providence, however, a disillusioned Democrat condemned Trumbull, Lincoln, and other Republicans for placing their party's creed above and before the Union. All still preached the "irrepressible conflict." If that was indeed the case, he snapped, "perhaps it may as well cease to exist at once."[3]

If not instant and at once, secession of the cotton states was not long in coming. Mississippi, Florida, Alabama, Georgia, and Louisiana left the Union by the end of the month. Texas seceded on February 1. Despite the apparent momentum of disunion, the contest had waxed warm between those who believed in immediate secession by the separate states and opponents who urged that the slave states act in concert. Accordingly, campaigns to elect delegates to secession conventions were everywhere hotly contested; the outcome in each was in doubt and sometimes controversial. (Sam Houston, for example, refused to convene the Texas legislature; a self-appointed committee instead called for the election of delegates to the state's secession convention.) Throughout the Lower South the margin of victory for "immediatists" was less than fire-eaters hoped but also less than moderates feared. In the Upper South, which yet remained in the Union, the disunionists' position was even more precarious.[4]

Interpretations of the fire-eaters' success in early 1861 (however limited) run from hagiographic to caustic, idealized to judgmental.[5] Yet the wonder is that they succeeded at all. Free-state politicians and voters consistently and roundly condemned them as traitors. No overt action precipitated their actions. In Washington, Buchanan, despite a slight stiffening of the spine, made no move to coerce South Carolina back into the Union. Throughout the secession winter he dithered. Lincoln remained in Springfield. Congressional Republicans disavowed abolition, claiming that they were the "white man's" party. Their one idea—restriction—affected only slaveholders, for whom southern yeomanry had evinced little affection and much hostility. Southern Unionists and Douglas Democrats vigorously opposed immediate and separate secession in the slave states. They agreed with fire-eaters that the South must defend its rights; however, the two warred over the wisdom and efficacy of disunion. Immediatists had to preach in and convert legislatures in which planters were a distinct minority of the elect. They made their case out of doors to a population of which roughly three-fourths owned not a single slave.

Yet the fire-eaters carried the day. But how? The chestnut of planter hegemony and its concomitant, the false consciousness of the nonslaveholding yeomanry who fought their war, will not do. Statistics and the history of antebellum southern politics demonstrate the falsity of the first assumption. Recent state studies also suggest that the yeomanry profited from a kind of political inflation: their power was all out of proportion to their net worth.[6] As for the fire-eaters themselves, their inflammatory rhetoric and political maneuvering were real enough.[7] And the case has often been made that no politician has ever gone bankrupt underestimating the intelligence of the voting public. Historians have long deliberated whether disunionists were deranged, personally ambitious, or liars. A little of each, perhaps.

These propositions are, however, beside the point. Ambition helps to explain why the radical states'-rights southerners used the opportunity of Lincoln's election to press for secession. To insist that principles alone motivated them strains credulity. The important question, usually begged, is why fire-eaters believed it necessary—or rational—to formulate a particular justification for disunion and pursue a specific course of action. In other words, they had to structure their argument for disunion within the assumptions and beliefs of Jacksonian political culture in order to legitimize a course of action that otherwise would be considered treacherous. Not surprisingly, they focused on the twin principles that structured and gave meaning to American political culture: equality and liberty. Put in other words, they contended that the Republican triumph abridged the equal rights of the South in the Union and the freedoms that inhered to self-government.

Since 1846, southern politicians, at least most of them, had defined the territorial question in terms of the South's equal rights in the Union. The southern response assumed that restriction had the effect of denying true equality to slave-state settlers in the territories, repudiating the constitutional guarantees of the South, and branding all southerners as moral inferiors. If evidence of northern perfidy was lacking earlier on, southern rights radicals insisted that this was the salient issue in the 1860. Defined in these terms, Lincoln's election was unacceptable. On the eve of his resignation from Buchanan's cabinet, Howell Cobb told the voters of Georgia that Lincoln's election brought to the South "the solemn judgment of a majority of the people of every Northern State . . . in favor of doctrines and principles violative of her constitutional rights . . . [and] destructive of her equality in the Union." Moderates agreed. An Arkansas Unionist, noting the conspicuous failure of the Bell-Everett ticket in the free states, proclaimed the government "denationalized" and suggested that continued chatter about northern conservatism be dismissed as idle and delusive. Back in Washington, as he prepared to withdraw from the U.S. Senate, Jefferson Davis told his Republican colleagues, "Your platform . . . denies us equality. Your votes refuse to recognize our domestic institutions . . . [and] our property which was guarded by the Constitution. You refuse us that equality without which we should be degraded if we remained in the Union."[8]

To be sure, no one denied the strict constitutionality of Lincoln's election. That was never the issue. James Henry Hammond recommended that South Carolina secede "not because Mr. Lincoln is elected President—for that ordinarily we would care little—but because of these insupportable invasions of all our rights . . . we feel convinced that the policy which will be inaugurated with Mr. Lincoln's election [will be] the policy of 'irrepressible conflict.'" As Jefferson Davis had it, Lincoln's election signaled the triumph of a majority over the constitutional rights of a minority. Nearly two weeks after his state's decision to secede, Davis told the Senate, "It has been a conviction of pressing necessity, it has been a belief that we are to be deprived in the Union of the rights which our fathers bequeathed to us, which brought Mississippi to her present decision." Senator Clement Claiborne Clay of Alabama believed the Republican platform departed from the egalitarian basis upon which the government was based. He taunted members across the aisle, asking if they expected southerners to "discredit the fame of our sires, dishonor ourselves, degrade our posterity . . . all for the sake of Union? Must we agree to live under the ban of our own Government?"[9] The answer was obvious.

Secessionists were quick to point out that the Republican victory did not result from a temporary derangement of otherwise rational northerners. "The history of the past shows that the aggressions of northern people have increased and multiplied with their strength," the *Arkansas True Democrat* told its subscribers. "To expect or hope that they will now stop in their victorious career, just when they have achieved the power and the means, is to hope in the face of past experience." Fire-eaters and their supporters claimed that behind the madness lay a purpose. Experience had shown that opponents of democracy had succeeded only "through some forced enthusiasm." In the most recent instance, Republicans "have carried their ends by appealing to the worst passions and prejudices of the people." No southerner thought the task had been particularly difficult. One Mississippian complained, "The character of the Northern people in public and private, collectively and individually is marked by dishonesty, injustice, rapacity & greed of gain & power." The Republican persuasion, therefore, represented the triumph of passion over reason, of moral abstractions over political realities. Southerners proclaimed themselves "aggrieved & outraged," subjected as they were "to the canting moral review & condemnation of New England bigotry."[10]

The verdict rendered in 1860 was clear. It indicated "the terms upon which [the northern people] are willing to remain in the Union." Southerners were "bound, therefore, to consider it a settled, earnest, determined purpose of the Northern states to administer this government entirely according to their own views, purposes and prejudices." They gave their answer neither "in any blindness" nor "in a sudden heat of passion and resentment." Quite the opposite, disunionists held: "It is the deliberate and mature conclusion of years." Lincoln's election evinced not only "incontrovertible proof of a diseased and dangerous public opinion all over the North," it also inaugurated "further and more atrocious aggression." A Memphis editor alleged that, having secured the spoils of victory, some Republicans gladly would stay the progress of fanaticism at the North. Plundering a whole country, after all, was more profitable than pillaging one half. "But they are unable to direct the whirlwind of their own creating," he seethed. "The conservative class of the North is cowed, dumb, and terror-stricken before the wild beast that strides over the land." Whirlwind or beast, traditional constitutional safeguards could thwart neither. If, for example, the Senate should stand in its way, then "the numerical majority will reform it." Likewise, they would transform the Supreme Court. Lincoln had been elected "because he represented an idea which [has] become part of themselves." Far from checking antislavery sentiment, Lincoln would give it a "tremendous onward impulse" through, but not limited to, "Executive patronage." [11]

As southerners understood it, "The Union, as it was adopted and formed by the fathers, and the Constitution of the United States are one and the same. To sustain the one you must maintain the other." Constitutional guarantees necessary to the safety of minorities became unsafe, "worthless," where "they are to be observed and executed by the majority only." Governor John Ellis insisted to the North Carolina legislature that Republicans, especially the higher-law types, had utterly refused to honor or be bound by the Constitution. They "now hold it up to us, as a bond to secure us from defending our property and lives against their oppressions." To thus deny southern states their "perfect equality in the territories," the *Richmond Enquirer* contended, prostituted the government "from its original spirit, even though the *forms* of the Constitution have been observed." A Tennessee disunionist proclaimed without guile that southerners "love the Union . . . revered its memories . . . were devoted to its traditions . . . and clung to its greatness." But "its very greatness appalls them when used as an instrumentality for crushing their peculiar institutions." [12]

Radicals reminded slaveholders and nonslaveholders alike that the North had succeeded in organizing a wholly sectional party that had seized the machinery of government. It was now determined to destroy the limitations and conditions under which constitutional government operated. Much of their agenda was clear: deny the equality of the citizens of the slave states; bar their access to the commonly owned territories; and condemn them as morally unfit and politically subordinate. Kenneth Rayner put it directly: "The election of Lincoln has placed *our* necks under *their* heels." In Rayner's North Carolina, the *Wilmington Daily Journal* averred that under Republican rule "ours is to be an antislavery *government* in policy and principle, and this policy and principle is [*sic*] to be permanent." Even the blind could envision the result. Republicans would "subvert [the South's] entire social & political system, reduce her to a state worse a thousand times than . . . death & seek to turn the whole into a [G]olgatha." [13]

Moving beyond the specifics of Republican rule, R. M. T. Hunter claimed that the Lincoln administration proposed to implement a system of governance "to ends and purposes not only different from, but hostile to, those for which this political organism was created[;] they [will] destroy the Union as it was framed by the fathers, and seek to substitute another for it." James Guthrie, himself no fire-eater, believed that the Republican ascendancy had produced the settled conviction in southerners' minds that there was no longer any security for them and their rights under the Constitution and within the Union. As the states of the Lower South began to secede in 1861, practically every slave-state senator agreed with Guthrie. David Yulee of Florida, for example, asserted that the cotton states "have decided that their social tranquillity and civil security are jeopardized by a longer continuance of Union . . . from the consequences, as they conceive, of an unjust exercise of the powers conferred, and a persistent disregard of the spirit of fraternity and equality in which it was founded."[14]

Of course, one could maintain (as Republicans and historians do) that the public elected Lincoln constitutionally; he was not yet inaugurated; the Constitution circumscribed his power; and Republicans had anything but absolute control over the legislature. Yet taking southern radicals at their word — the yeomanry certainly did — the real issues of secession were independence, equality, and self-government. Lincoln, they contended, did not represent the choice of the electorate, but only a portion of it. Aha! moderates and compromisers replied, that ought to make him less dangerous and less obnoxious to the South. A Tennessee editor responded that Lincoln's obscurity and sweep of the North were precisely the point. That Lincoln, a dim, seemingly uninvolved figure to the South throughout the campaign, should command a majority of votes "exhibits the political power of the party that elected him." The *Wilmington Daily Journal* remarked, "With no prestige of high ability to recommend him, with no record of important success in the legislative halls of his country — with no achievement on the battlefield — his name linked with no great measure — no forward movement, no scientific discovery, Abraham Lincoln is President of the United States." That such a nonentity could win every free state proved to secessionists that northern voters had not cast their ballots for Lincoln but for the single idea that he represented: slavery restriction. "There in lies the bitterness commended to our lips," the *Nashville Union and American* explained, "that the chief chosen by the northern sectionalists could not command one electoral vote in the Southern States by reason of this determined and avowed hostility to our institutions." Inasmuch as the idea of self-government lay at the basis of our political system, Hunter mused after Lincoln's election, "How is that principle to be maintained?"[15]

Democracy, it appeared to secessionists, had failed. "For the first time since the union was formed we have seen a President of the United States nominated and elected . . . by a sectional party . . . founded in hostility to the institution of African slavery, which exists in nearly half the States of the Union," Hunter pointed out. James Henry Hammond alleged "that party has crushed, apparently forever, all our allies in the North." A candidate not placed before the Lower South and enjoying scant support in the Upper South would rule over the slave states. As Governor Ellis put it, "A clearer case of foreign domination as to us could not well be presented." A Mississippi editor claimed that "the domination of Black Republicanism is wholly inconsistent with every idea of a free or beneficent government." He wondered, "Can a man be said to be constitutionally elected President, the very object of whose election is to *destroy* the Constitution?" To submit to "Lincolnism," he concluded, "would betray the spirit of a slave."[16]

Resolving that Lincoln's election both repudiated the equality of the slave states and their inhabitants and denied them their fundamental right to self-government, southern rights extremists determined to secure this revolutionary inheritance outside the Union. Long before Lincoln's emergence, the *Richmond Enquirer* warned that although the slave states revered and valued the Union, "to perpetuate the principles upon which it rests, if necessary, they would destroy it." Howell Cobb proclaimed in December 1860 that southern equality and safety were at an end. He logically concluded that "it only remains to be seen whether our manhood is equal to the task of asserting and maintaining independence out of it." The splenetic Alfred Iverson of Georgia scolded northern senators that it was precisely because southern people cherished a warm and sincere attachment to the principles of the American political system that they decided to secede. "Nothing but a stern conviction of the necessity and propriety of leaving it, and forming a safer and more perfect Union, would have driven them to the alternative of separation from it," he stormed. As Florida's two senators prepared to take their leave, they gave voice to the fears and hopes of their constituents. David Yulee informed his former colleagues that upon Lincoln's election Florida's voters saw "fast rising above all others the great issue of the right of the people of the States to sovereignty and self-government within their respective territorial boundaries." They decided to secure that right by leaving the Union. Stephen Mallory refused, however, to admit that secession proved the great experiment of self-government a failure. "I maintain, on the contrary, that passing events should inspire in the hearts of the patriot and statesman, not only hope but confidence."[17]

Northerners, most of them, and southern Unionists charged that disunionists were seditious traitors. Southern rights extremists saw their actions in a very different light. "I say that our purpose was not to dissolve the Union," Louis Wigfall of Texas shot back; "but the dire necessity has been put upon us. The question is whether we shall live longer in a Union in which a party hostile to us in every respect has the power of Congress, in the executive department, and in the electoral colleges? . . . We think it is not safe." Unwilling to place the form of constitutional government before the preservation of the liberties and rights of southerners, the *Daily South Carolinian* claimed, "Our conservatism tells us it is destruction to breathe longer the dangerous atmosphere." Another South Carolinian claimed that he had ever urged "conservative doctrines on my people & taught patience, liberality and forbearance." His efforts, he complained, were rewarded with "treason, insurrection & murder . . . upon quiet, unoffending fellow citizens because they have defended and sustained [their] rights and institutions." He proclaimed himself now convinced "for the *first time* that [southern rights] can no longer be preserved in this *Union*."[18]

As disunionists framed their argument, history proved instructive and prescriptive. On election day, the *Louisville Daily Courier* predicted that should Republican doctrines prevail, it "will as certainly overthrow this Government as did the oppression of Great Britain precipitate the American Revolution." Later, John Ellis admitted that indeed Lincoln had been elected according to the forms of the Constitution. "It is equally true," he added with a sneer, "that George the Third was the rightful occupant of the British throne, yet our fathers submitted not to his authority." Jefferson Davis drew a direct line from colonial affairs in 1776 to the South's position in 1861. "It is the old case over again," he observed, adding "Senators of the North, you are reenacting the blunders which statesmen in Great Britain committed." Regarding the equality of the South in the Union "lost," a North Carolina disunionist deduced that should the slave states acquiesce in Republican rule, their position "will essentially be that of a colonial dependency, or of *such* an integral part of the great Northern Empire."[19]

Secession implied no inherent defect in the American political system, Davis claimed. It sprung from a perversion of that system. Nor did the failure of the constitutional Union mean the failure of self-government. Representative liberty would remain and flourish in the seceded states much as it remained in the colonies after their separation from Great Britain. Responding to Senate Republicans' charge that he and other disunionists were "revolutionaries," he proclaimed that when the fathers "spoke of revolution, they spoke of an inalienable right . . . of the people to abrogate and modify their form of government whenever it did not meet the ends for which it was established." Picking up on Davis's cue, another secessionist proclaimed, "That the spirit of brave liberty, that abhorrence of a *foreign* tyrant" which had animated the revolutionary generation "is again abroad, & proclaims in tones of thunder, that the South will not submit to the government of a foreign and hostile people."[20]

Southern Unionists disagreed with the analogy. Thinking of the series of crises that culminated in revolution in 1776, they argued that Lincoln was not even inaugurated. Republicans had not yet made an open assault on the slave states. Secessionists responded that "there is really no necessity for any '*overt act*' in order to accomplish all the purposes of the Black Republicans." Antislavery Supreme Court justices could be appointed. Hostile postmasters and incendiary materials could be distributed through the South. Executive patronage could deploy Republican agitators to the slave states. None were overt acts; all would "annoy, distract, harass and cripple the South . . . excite apprehension . . . awaken feelings of insecurity which will disarrange the whole workings of our social system." Nor was this the end. To retain power, Republicans "must continue to cater to the antislavery sentiment of the people. . . . Hence we expect to see no concessions made to the just demands of the South." The *Vicksburg Sun* therefore concluded that submission would both make the triumph of abolitionists complete and give them the means to destroy the South. Arguing that an " 'overt act' must, sooner or later, come," a Florida disunionist asked the state's citizens, "Shall we be better prepared than now to meet it?"[21] Of course not.

A New Orleans editor put the case for secession in terms that every southerner well understood. South Carolina could not consent to remain in the Union "upon sufferance[,] the mere vassal and thrall of a party which aims at her ruin and degradation. . . . Practical servitude and submission, where all sense of equality would be lost, and where we should be placed at the relentless mercy of a master, would necessarily become perfectly intolerable." Senator Clement Claiborne Clay told the Senate that "the people who live under governments appointed against their consent . . . will not long enjoy the blessings of liberty, or have the courage to claim them." As if in response, one of Clay's constituents wrote him, "Far better to die a free man than live a slave to *Black Republicanism*."[22]

Northerners, Republican congressmen, historians, and modern-day partisans have all expended a great deal of energy parsing and refuting the constitutional logic of secession. They have defined the sectional struggle and secession as a conflict between states' rights and an indivisible Union. This, secessionists would tell you, is to mistake the process for substance. Secession, like nullification before it, was, of course, seen as a right. But whereas nullification was a remedy for constitutional wrongs in the Union, southerners viewed secession as a means to protect the essence of equality and self-government secured by the Constitution and once embraced in the Union. Secession, in other words, was not a remedy for past wrongs but a guarantee for future greatness. Secession is true and right, a North Carolinian wrote, but it "must be resorted to as a means to success, not as an end to political combinations." Viewed from this perspective, a Florida editor maintained that secession was a conservative remedy to preserve American liberties. Let southerners remember, another disunionist wrote, that the practical spirit of conservatism prompted the Founding Fathers to sever the bonds that united them to the mother country. "They then asserted self-government as necessary to a conservation of their rights," he proclaimed, "and we are now invoked by the same spirit of conservation to dissolve our present political Union, in order to retain that inheritance of self-government." Secessionists not only intended to preserve these rights for themselves, Alabama's Clay observed, but were determined "to transmit to their posterity, the freedom they received from their ancestors, or perish in the attempt." [23]

Northerners would certainly agree with fire-eaters that the meaning and future of American liberties and democracy were at stake in the secession crisis. The pretense for disunion, an incredulous Republican wrote, was "that an election by a majority of the States and people is against the *spirit* of the Constitution, because the majority who made the election live north of the 39th parallel of latitude." Not for the last time Henry Wilson lashed out at secessionist-minded senators, pointing out that the four parties clearly made their cases during the 1860 canvass, the American people fully comprehended the issues, and accordingly they had voted "against the recognition and protection of slavery in the Territories, by positive law." Now fairly beaten, he observed, "the slave propagandists rush into rebellion [and] threaten the subversion of the Government." At the same time, on the other side of the Capitol, Charles Francis Adams pointed out to the House that for the nineteenth time the citizens of the several states had been asked to select their chief executive. All responded, no complaint of fraud was heard, and their verdict was clear. Now, Adams exclaimed, the South "without intervention of a single new disturbing cause, suddenly broke out into violent remonstrance, and dashed into immediate efforts to annul their obligations to the Constitution." Such behavior, Adams protested, "had never before been taken in any quarter." The slave states' reaction to Lincoln's victory proved clearly to one Ohio party member that "the South are seeking pretexts not reasons for secession." [24]

Without irony, Republicans countered the secessionist argument for self-determination by embracing and defending self-government. The history of the nation testified and paid tribute to the principle of the democratic process and majority rule, they claimed. Lincoln was chosen, the *Albany Evening Journal* asserted, "as WASHINGTON was, by the friends of FREEDOM—as JEFFERSON and MADISON were, by REPUBLICANS, as MONROE, JOHN QUINCY ADAMS, JACKSON, HARRISON and TAYLOR WERE, by the PEOPLE." Representative Daniel W. Gooch reminded his southern colleagues that Republicans and Democrats had raised the same issues involving the territories in 1856. Upon losing, Republicans acquiesced. Had we instead followed your lead, he told slave-state congressmen, "You would have answered us with scorn and contempt if we had come here and demanded that the principles which we advocated, and the people had rejected, should be incorporated into the Constitution." Writing from Cincinnati, a party member asked Senator

Benjamin Wade if the American public, in the free states at any rate, had become so "debauched and demoralized" that it would allow a minority to dictate the terms upon which a "lawfully elected Administration" might assume its duties. If so, another Ohio Republican chimed to Wade, it "would be to confess ourselves dastards and unworthy of the name *free men*." [25]

The supposed crime, the offense of Lincoln's supporters, was their determination to follow the policies of the Founding Fathers. Henry Wilson, for one, was flabbergasted. "We Republicans are arraigned by Senators for having embodied in our platform of principles the sublime creed of the Declaration of Independence," he sputtered. "The Republican party, we are told, is a dangerous political organization, its success a cause of offense, justifying secession and rebellion, and the formation of a southern confederacy." The mind boggled at the notion. Rebuking southern rights men for their calumnies, Ohio's Benjamin Stanton pledged in the House, "The Republican party claims and maintains no principle, and proposes to carry into practice no policy, that has not been sanctioned by the fathers of the Republic, and practiced by every Administration from George Washington to General Harrison." Stanton's decision to stop in 1841 manifested no mental lapse. Implicit in his claim was that, beyond abandoning constitutional democracy upon Lincoln's election, secessionists also set themselves against the expressed mandate of the majority to change the proslavery administration of public affairs that had begun under Tyler and with Texas. By purging and purifying the whole political machinery of government, New York's John Bigelow stated, "we bring federal government once more into harmony with federal will." [26]

Operating from the assumption that their principles embodied and continued those established by Washington, Jefferson, and others, Republicans concluded, not unreasonably, that their position on slavery was "the policy of the founders of the Government—nothing more, nothing less." Conveniently ignoring the Missouri crisis, Ohio's James Ashley twitted his southern opponents, claiming that Jeffersonian Democrats first articulated the Republicans' insistence on free territories and free states. Putting slavery in a longer historical context, Stanton returned to his own, somewhat altered, chronology of public affairs. "When this Republican Administration comes into power," he declared, "the Government will be administered, so far as the slavery issue is concerned, precisely as it was by all the best Administrations of the Government [pregnant pause, no doubt] until within the last twelve years." A rank-and-file Republican warned John Sherman that while Lincoln's election had been carried by a sectional vote, "the policy adopted must be *national*, not sectional." [27]

From these interrelated series of assertions and deductions, party members quite reasonably maintained that contrary to secessionists' claims, disunionists could not point to a single instance of Republican aggression or usurpation. "Has any aggression been committed against any of the seceding States by the General Government?" Representative Harrison G. Blake asked. Why, "no man pretends it." Somewhat myopically perhaps, James Wilson proclaimed that when Congress convened in December 1860, "we were stronger, happier, richer, more honored, and more envied, than ever before in our national existence." Even "higher-law" Seward backpedaled, talking of constitutional guarantees and repeal of personal liberty laws, a Maine Republican pointed out. "The Southern *politicians* who are making all the trouble, understand perfectly well that the Republicans claimed no right to interfere with slavery in the *States*," he snapped. Disunionists may satisfy themselves with their deceitful arguments, Ashley sniffed, "but they cannot justify their conduct to an intelligent people."[28]

Closing the circle, a California Republican wrote, "As the clamor raised at all comes from the extreme South . . . it is evident that the only real cause for discontent &. agitation is the election of a Republican president." Seceders and their accomplices, another party member claimed, "not only [wanted] to tie the hands of the Republican Party before it gets into power, but also to kill it off by destroying its moral influence." A correspondent of Wade reduced southern complaints, or more precisely fears, to their lowest common denominator: "Lincoln has *constitutionally* been elected . . . and . . . Republicans are determined *constitutionally* to exclude slavery from the U.S. territories forever if they can." Oh, spare me the cant about equality and self-government, an Illinois Republican begged; "the slaveholders see plainly that government will be transferred from them into the hands that will at least represent in part the interests of Free Labor."[29]

Believing as they did that the disunionists had no just cause for complaint, then or in the future, Republicans in the winter of 1860–61 resolved that the essence of the South's demand was, "We must control! We must govern the North—the North must obey! The minority must govern the majority!" Therefore, the issue presented to Congress and the American public was "whether they will allow a small faction of malcontents or the majority acting lawfully to govern." Pennsylvania representative Edward Morris claimed that however wary the founders were of consolidation of power in the federal government, never in their wildest nightmares did they dream that it could be reduced to such a "helpless condition," subject to the dictation of the states. Minority dictation, he cried, amounted to the overthrow of democracy and constitutional government—"an act of political insanity without parallel."[30]

Morris's colleague James Ashley noticed that secessionists were the same men who had ruled the national government for the past twenty-five years, dictated its policy, controlled its legislation, and run roughshod over the Democratic Party. Another House member, James McKean, added that the disfranchised still governed the Senate and the House while maintaining the fealty of legions of appointed government officials. Ohio's Sidney Edgerton sputtered that the South had made "every department intensely sectional. No man could hold office under it for one hour unless he was pro-slavery." The fact is, one Republican observed, "the South has become accustomed to rule . . . and whenever we wished to have things according to our mind . . . at once they raise the cry of disunion." To talk now of minor concessions—repealing state laws, turning over forts, divvying up property and the national debt—to placate the South was useless and beside the point. "The champions of slavery feel that all the forces of American civilization are against them," the *Boston Daily Journal* ventured, "and that the political grasp which . . . they have so long held upon the country is now loosening, and can never be regained. It is the death of a dynasty inflicted by the mere progress of civilization."[31]

Secessionist threats in late 1860 were one thing; after South Carolina's adieu, disunion became something else altogether. Long used to southerners' dark harangues on constitutional obligations, Republicans, down to December 20 at least, considered their threats so much bluster and bluff—though with a point. Wade dismissed them as so much "humbug." "They will howl and rave like so many devils, tormented before their time," he predicted. "Their only object is to obtain some compromise or some exhibition of weakness from the incoming Administration." Senator William Pitt Fessenden of Maine stopped short of characterizing Jefferson Davis's secessionist threats as outright lies; he did consider them disingenuous, though. "His object and hope are to demoralize the Republican party," he claimed, "by destroying the confidence of our people in our capacity and principles." Having heard this disunionist dirge many, many times before, an Illinois Republican advised Lyman Trumbull "to listen, patiently, to the music of the secessionists." He and others feared that humbug threats would maneuver Republicans into a fraudulent compromise "whereby the North will be cheated."[32]

Disunionist threats were by now old hat. And the frenzy in the slave states led more than a few Republicans to wonder if all southerners were "lunatics." One asked, "In the name of Heaven what evil spirit has taken possession of our Southern Brethren[?] Have they become so demented, or are they really crazy, or have they determined to push their treasonable schemes to the bitter end[?]" The Antichrist, South Carolina, soon provided the answer. Its secession persuaded Republicans that slavery had made the South more antidemocratic than ever imagined. Surely it was the institution that lessened the southern regard for equal rights, Senator Wilson exclaimed; worse, it "destroyed that reverence for liberty which is the vital principle of a Republic." Secession in and of itself, another party member maintained, finally revealed to the nation "the barbarism of slavery." The *Philadelphia Daily News* condemned South Carolina's secessionists as "monarchists," while a Portsmouth editor denounced the nonslaveholding whites who supported them as "ignorant and dependent." One Republican succinctly commented, "The entire southern population are mad."[33]

For all their alarm, Republicans agreed with fire-eaters that, of itself, secession implied no defect in republican government. It did prove to northerners that self-government in the slave states was an utter failure. A Pennsylvanian argued that slaveholders "insolently defy the popular will. . . . They set themselves above the people. . . . They believe that government, being instituted for the many, should be sanctioned by their approval." Frank Blair Jr. wrote to his brother Montgomery that in the wake of Lincoln's election affairs in the South had reached such an extreme that either the North must accept the South as its master or dispute the point with the slavocracy on the field of battle. "The country will prosper from their overthrow and the more complete the better," he predicted.[34]

The initial reaction to disunion South Carolina–style was a total refutation of the constitutional logic of secession. The Constitution was no mere "compact, subject to the caprice of any State or section, but a fundamental law, solemnly ratified by the *people* of the Union," a New Jersey editor held. The idea of an indivisible Union stretched back to the "united colonies." It was meant to be perpetual. The government established by the Constitution did not contemplate its own destruction. Thus the citizens of the several states owed their primary allegiance to the Union of the states. The "right" of secession, in other words, was "a sham of shams, a humbug of humbugs, a gross delusion as political insanity ever conjured up." If a state secedes, wrote the *New York Evening Post*, "it is revolution, and the seceders are traitors."[35]

Love for a perpetual Union and hatred for a treacherous enemy do not fully comprehend the reaction to disunion, however. For the North, just as for the South, the essence and survival of liberty and democracy lay at the heart of the secession crisis. As the struggle took shape in the minds of Republicans, its dynamics both were and were not like those of the American Revolution. "We have it in our power to prove to the world that there are two Independence days in the history of our country," James McKean informed the House, "—the one July 4, 1776; the other November 6, 1860." From Milwaukee, one Republican saw in the struggle against disunion "the same fundamental principles at stake that have been at bottom of all the world's strifes. . . . It is . . . whether *all* men have rights, or whether a few only have rights." Our fathers pledged their lives, fortunes, and sacred honor for the liberties we have inherited, a Connecticut party member wrote to John Sherman. To compromise now, he declared, would forfeit that heritage and in the bargain admit "that we are slaves to the slaveholders." An Ohio farmer wrote Benjamin Wade that his father and grandfather had fought in the Revolution to secure the liberty that he and his family enjoyed. "I have one son an able bodied man who is willing to enlist if need be to achieve a second independence and I could do some service myself," he promised. "Sir, no more slavery in the territories and no more slave states must be our motto."[36]

Secessionists' claims to the revolutionary mantle were "odious to all friends of free Government." The fathers had genuine grievances; those of the seceders were "*imaginary*." The fathers drew the sword to defend freedom; seceders threw down the gauntlet for slavery. The fathers struggled to overthrow a despotic government; seceders "would destroy the best Government on earth and . . . establish a despotic Government 'based upon the solid substratum of African Slavery.'" Representative James Wilson observed that the colonies rebelled "against the oppressions of an arbitrary Government, in which they had no part, and by which they were hopelessly crushed. This is a revolution against itself, against its own chosen Government, against its own Administration, against its own legislation, against its own supreme Judiciary, and against its own national legislature." Put simply, Senator Henry Wilson sneered, it was a rebellion against imagined future dangers. Whether the object of the revolution was a southern confederacy or the reconstruction of the Constitution on a slaveholding basis constituted a distinction without a difference. "Rebellion is 'secession,'" an Ohio Republican maintained. "Traitors are 'secessionists.'"[37]

Believing that the decree of the November election was that "the tendency of this Government after the 4th of March shall be towards liberty not slavery," Republicans reduced the secession crisis to a simple but ominous proposition. "We are fighting to preserve our republican institutions in their purity," a Philadelphia editor told his readers, "to establish the authority of the Constitution and laws over violence and anarchy; to secure popular rights against aristocratic assumption." An Illinois Republican denied that the issue was simply one of union or disunion, the restriction or extension of slavery, or the extent of territorial limits. At stake, he claimed, was "the very existence of liberty itself—the continuance or disastrous overthrow, of the great principles of popular rights, Constitutional authority, and genuine liberty." The intent of Republicans, therefore, was not to depose, destroy, conquer but to restore, build up, liberate. On the one side, an Ohio restrictionist claimed, was government resting on the will of the people and a free constitution; on the other was usurpation, disorganization, and obnoxious innovation. "On the one side the struggle is unequivocally one for the rights of the people," he exclaimed; "on the other, it is just as plainly for the supremacy of a slave propaganda." Yield and "we are enslaved forever." If my party should quail, compromise, or cede one inch of territory, an Illinois Republican declared, "I would no longer consider myself a . . . free citizen of the United States."[38]

As the secession crisis deepened, northern Democrats and many of Douglas's supporters in the slave states again positioned themselves between extremists North and South. In the free states they attempted to alert the public that Republicans were whistling past the dangers of disunion and press upon them the possibility that fire-eaters might have legitimate grievances. Following Lincoln's election, the *Hartford Times* claimed that secessionists were neither crackpots nor sore losers. Political defeat, they claimed, southerners could abide. But when the victors represented the power and antislavery prejudice of one section, southern rights activists might reasonably conclude that they were "in the hands of foes." A Michigan Democrat similarly maintained that the fact of Lincoln's election was less alarming than the reality of Republicans' "connection with previous aggressions and violations of vested rights, nullification of the Constitution, and departures from good faith and honor." The *Rochester Daily Union and Advertiser* urged its readers for a moment to consider the matter from the South's point of view. Taking measure of the Republican platform, it claimed that a plausible case could be made that the Lincoln administration intended "to *nullify the Constitution* . . . to rob the South of its equal rights in the Territories . . . and consequently to destroy utterly and irrevocably every Constitutional guaranty designed to protect the institutions, rights and interests of the minority." The editor did not insist that such was the case, but "we do say that its action, taken in its entirety, is susceptible to this construction."[39]

In the Upper South, Democrats scorned those "crazy people," who seemed bent on proving to the free states that the South was incapable of sustaining self-government. The *Louisville Democrat* predicted on the eve of the election, "We are soon to bring ourselves below the level of [Mexico], whose staple and annual production is revolution." In December with events daily providing proof it was correct, the paper threatened nonslaveholders, "The white man loses his liberty at last in an insane quarrel about the negro, who is incapable of freedom." They continued to blast secessionists as antirepublican and antidemocratic. Southern moderates rebuked those who would "servilely *submit* to the dictation of speculative and ambitious *party leaders*." They asked southern voters if secessionists, who had neither the wisdom nor the statesmanship to preserve this Union, had the intelligence or will "to invent institutions and frame a Union out of a part in the midst of all these embarrassments and trouble."[40]

Picking up on this observation, free-state Douglas Democrats made clear the limits of their sympathies. For all their commitment to a federal government and states' rights, party members declared that "the different Commonwealths of our Union are not now and *never were* sovereign." Secession, therefore, was "rebellion" and "treason." Peaceful secession was an oxymoron: "Language, habits, customs and the very enactments of nature forbid it." The Founding Fathers "declared their purpose to be 'to form a more perfect Union,'" the *Providence Daily Post* observed. "If any state can secede at pleasure, our government is but a rope of sand." Acknowledging that "the right of revolution is inherent in every people," a Detroit compromiser insisted that revolt "may not be rightly undertaken until such a time as the existing government has committed grievous wrongs." Distinguishing between the excesses of a party and the wickedness of an administration, a Cleveland Democrat agreed that until the corruption of a Lincoln White House made "the evils of [the] existing government . . . greater than would be the evils of revolution" then "secession will be *inexcusable rebellion*." "Unless all remain in the Union as it now exists," the *Pittsburgh Daily Post* believed, "there is no safety for the North or South."[41]

Breckinridge Democrats in the North, too, warned outgoing Buchanan administration officials that secession was "unpopular" with the party and northern masses generally. All would recognize the right "if recurred to as a last resort against the oppression of the General Government or of a majority of the States." They apprised administration officials that reckless action in the South would "give political strength to her opponents" while at once "driving many of their best friends from [it]." Following South Carolina's departure, former slave-state allies in the North excoriated its "*stubborn blind . . . ignorant pertinacity*" and condemned its policy as "suicidal." One ruefully noted that secession had "succeeded in uniting Bell men, Douglas men & Breckinridge men with Lincoln men at the North in one unbroken phalanx . . . against the Southern cause."[42]

Unionist sentiment commingled with fulminations against hasty southern action only heightened the apparent ambiguity of the Democracy's position during the winter crisis. While they railed against fire-eater treachery, northern Democrats also believed, "Public opinion can hold this confederacy together with strong ties. But bayonets cannot pin it together." Although New York's legislature resolved to commit men and arms to put down rebellion in the Lower South, one state Democrat sounded a word of caution. "I represent a family, Sir, who furnished two men during the Revolution, one (my own Father) in 1813 and one during the Mexican War," he wrote Buchanan. "Am I to stand here and see this Glorious Union broken up—What am I to do sir— can I take up arms against my own country men. No sir never never never." Although the president was the last person to guide this poor soul out of his dilemma, this farmer's quandary neatly sums up the moderates' dilemma as well as their insight. Benjamin Hallett complained to Buchanan that Republican hard-liners continued to draw a false analogy between the nullification crisis and secession. Then, he observed, South Carolina was isolated, Unionist sympathies ran deep in the slave states, and Congress and President Jackson were resolute. Assuming that the president took no offense at this latter observation, he read on. Now, Hallett argued, the South Carolina "republic" enjoyed widespread if not unanimous support among the slave states. With some foresight he accordingly predicted, "The first blood shed on her soil by the troops of the United States would be like the first blood shed at Lexington, [and] rally all those States in her defense as it did all the Colonies in the defense of Massachusetts." If the North through coercion should produce "civil war," the *Burlington Weekly Sentinel* maintained that the struggle would end "in slaughter, rapine, destitution and untold distress." Not surprisingly, then, a Democratic convention in Monroe County, Michigan, resolved, "We look upon the voluntary and friendly Union of the States as highly necessary to the preservation of liberty and self-government on this continent."[43]

Douglas Democrats found themselves in this quandary not because they lacked a spine but on account of their long-standing ideological convictions, especially their commitment to popular sovereignty. "Our government is Democratic," the *Daily Eastern Argus* averred. "It lives in the free consent of the people. . . . To set federal power (force) upon [the South] will involve defeat and the ultimate destruction of free government, because it will be indirect war with its spirit." In the Indiana House, Democratic representatives professed, "This Government 'derives its just powers from the consent of the governed,' and it would become subversive of the very spirit of liberty and natural right to attempt . . . to coerce or compel the people of any State or States to remain an integral part of a Government they desire to separate from." If coercion should be pursued, they warned, "the free citizen of Indiana would have no guarantee of his liberties worth the name." In neighboring Ohio, a party manager maintained, "Force will do with some people, but not ours." Applying the logic of their territorial policy to the secession crisis, Democrats declared unqualifiedly, "The great truth of the sovereignty of the people must be comprehended and acknowledged."[44]

Northern Democrats understood the secession crisis in precisely the same terms that they viewed the territorial issue: the American Revolution. Republicans, so they argued, pursued the policies of Lord North and Parliament "who claimed to have abstract right on their side. . . . And for a mere theory of no utility, they lost England her brightest colonial jewel." Democrats cast themselves as "Pitt, and Barry, and Burke," warning Republicans that "the present position of the southern Cotton States was not without a close analogy to our fathers of the revolution." A Detroit editor informed Michigan Democrats that just as "our fathers fought for . . . their own cause — their own rights," fealty to that legacy "consists in devotion to our own liberty." He reminded his readers that the people of the South, too, were "animated by the same spirit which fired the hearts of the patriots of the Revolution." In the Indiana House, Representative John H. Stotsenberg ventured that the commitment to personal independence perhaps burned a bit brighter in the South. Wherever slavery existed, he observed, "those who are free are by far the most proud and zealous of their freedom. Freedom to them is not only an enjoyment, but a kind of rank and privilege. . . . In such a people the haughtiness of domination combines with the spirit of freedom, fortifies it and renders it invincible." [45]

With an eye toward their stiff-necked opponents in both sections, moderates concluded, "Barbarism and tyranny eschew compromise as much as possible." Believing that concessions produced the Constitution, which itself gave expression to and defended American liberties, they maintained that "this glorious Union of States . . . can only be continued by an observance of the same spirit." A Chicago acquaintance wrote Stephen Douglas that Illinois Democrats "are for the Union, and are in favor of giving to the South all the rights they are entitled to by virtue of the Constitution." In Philadelphia, a party member suggested to Buchanan that the surest way to guarantee relief to the South was "in the proper administration of the principles upon which the confederacy was established." Determined no less than their Republican opponents to preserve the Union and liberties bequeathed to them, Democrats feared the worst if a middle ground could not be found. "If we are broken up the dial of the world's progress will have gone backwards a hundred years," a New Hampshire Democrat claimed. "Monarchy and absolutism will have all the field for a century to come. What nation struggling for its rights will wish to repeat the experiment of republicanism after we have failed?" [46]

Southern Unionists joined compromise-minded Democrats calling for forbearance and a negotiated settlement to the secession crisis. Their analysis of sectional politics had changed little since the canvass. "Hackneyed office holders and hat brained politicians" in the South had rushed the public into rebellion. By constant agitation and "daily telegraphs & other means" fire-eaters "blind and madden their people, and thus plunge them into war." In the North, meanwhile, congressional Republicans "play the game of boys and say if I put a chip on my shoulder will you knock it off[?]" Extremists in both sections "have made politics a trade — they have fomented agitation . . . they have rode into power upon the slavery issue." [47]

Now was the time to unseat them from their hobby. As it had been during the campaign, Unionists believed that their only hope was to go around the politicians "to get the question *to the people* not only South but at the North." Repudiating Alabama extremists for their apparent belief that "*the masses are incapable of self-government*," a Tuscaloosa Unionist insisted that "the people have a right to be heard, and being heard, to be obeyed." Northern Unionists predicted that the Republican rank and file favored compromise, and in view of the sectional crisis brought about by Lincoln's election, "could they tomorrow, they would recall their votes." A Pennsylvania conservative wrote John Crittenden that in Erie County, "The universal voice of all men in all parties is—'Down with Treason and Traitors!'" Only if and when the American people were seduced by "the political orgies" that surrounded them would Unionists "confess that republicanism is a failure, and that the people are not capable of self-government." A hopeful William Cabell Rives, speaking for all compromise-minded Americans, asserted, "We owe it to ourselves and our posterity, no less than to the mercy of our fathers that every proper and reasonable expedient should be tried before we determine upon the last and melancholy resort of dissolution of the noblest fabric of political wisdom which the world has ever seen."[48]

Republicans were not immune to this appeal. Those inclined to respond fell generally into two categories: compromisers and temporizers. Fearing for the Union and their own political lives should the party be blamed for its destruction, compromise-minded Republicans joined with Democrats and Unionists to counsel conciliation and magnanimity. While these peacemakers would draw the line at a compromise on the right of secession, they advanced conciliatory alternatives, ranging from soothing words to repeal of free-state personal liberty laws to restoration of the Missouri Compromise line. Lower South secession made this line of argument difficult to sustain, however. Republican moderates concluded that "it would be disgraceful to make any attempt whatever to conciliate [secessionists]." And though some waffled to the end, it was largely for partisan appearances and in the hope that the Upper South might be persuaded to remain in the Union.[49]

A smaller number of Republicans disdained the idea of capitulation to fire-eaters' terms and believed that in any case "nothing that could be said or done by or from the North can do any good what ever." While denying "that any man, any neighborhood, town, county, or even State, may break up this Union," in the next breath they conceded that it "was cemented by voluntary suffrage, and . . . cannot by the genius of our polity be maintained by force." Rather than forfeit Republican principles in concessions, they recommended, "Why then let them *go!*" Future president Rutherford B. Hayes was in this camp. He favored enforcing the laws but opposed a policy of conquest. How one was to be achieved without incurring the other, he did not know. But, he maintained, a war to subdue the seceded states "would have us loaded with debt and would certainly fail us of its object."[50]

As a party, Republicans pursued neither of these alternatives. Peaceable disunion they considered "simply absurd." "No nation ever *peaceably* fell to pieces," one House member scoffed; "no nation ever will. The sentiment of *nationality* and *patriotism* is the master sentiment of our people." Some hinted that, like William Lloyd Garrison, peaceful disunionists "carry their *moral* views on slavery so far that they wish to get it out of the Union." Concede the principle of disunion, they predicted, and neither nations nor citizens would place their confidence in the fag end that remained. Congressional Republicans heaped abuse on a supposed peaceable remedy "which sunders a great nation . . . strikes down a free constitution . . . extinguishes the rights of thirty million Americans . . . [and] blots a great people from the face of the earth." Representative John Bingham jeered, "You might as well talk about a peaceable earthquake."[51]

To those in the party who advocated compromise or passivity, the intransigent suggested that the history of the Whigs and Democrats was instructive. Each "had one set of measures to go into an election upon, but another to act upon when the election was secured." And now, like the woolly mammoth, each was extinct. Our party made it clear to the public in 1860 that it intended to focus upon the territorial question and to solve it, they reminded the weak-kneed. We rejected further compromise and condemned northern Democrats for truckling to southern extremists. To crawfish from that position now "would be the destruction of our present party organization with all its power for good." War, a Hoosier admonished, would be preferable "than to degrade ourselves by yielding one iota of our principles." Throughout the free states constituents exhorted congressional Republicans to avoid "ignoble compromise" and to "Stand up!" We ask nothing more, one wrote, "then wat we hangered for in the Shigago *platform*." Yield one point, another party member claimed, and "we are conquered and our hard one victory is a cheat—a delusion."[52]

Rank-and-file Republicans told their congressmen "that this struggle is not merely the triumph of any party as such but the great principle of Freedom for Supremacy in this government." They maintained that the sectional contest for the right to control the national government began in earnest after the Mexican War when the issue of slavery extension was "evaded both by the people and their representatives in Congress either by disregarding it [1848] or attempting to smother it down by compromises [1850]." Benjamin Wade believed that in 1860 northern voters declared, "The day of compromise is past." One of Wade's correspondents cautioned him that "one retrograde step taken by the Republican party . . . would encourage secessionists in their arrogant demands." Another Ohioan expressed grave reservations "whether a surrender of *vital principle* for an apparent prospect of temporary tranquillity, would secure the *transient* object of the great sacrifice." With, as they had it, "*right* and *truth* & eternal *justice*" hanging in the balance, the question of compromise was "not only of *present* importance, but involves interests of future weal or woe of far greater magnitude."[53]

Because secession had transformed the sectional conflict over the territories into an ominous controversy over the preservation of the Union, Republicans refused to sustain the latter by conceding their principles on the former. As they viewed it, the issue in 1860–61 was "not union or disunion; but new guarantees to slavery or disunion." Concessions to terms dictated by Yancey and others would "have then made slavery a governmental institution and have yielded all that the most elevated slave-holder has desired, for this peculiar property." Any amendment that ensured slaveholders' rights in any part of the common territories would both relinquish the right of the government to control the question and commit Republicans "to an acknowledgment of the right to property in slaves." The implications ran deep. "If we buy the right to administer the Government now," Daniel Gooch told the House, "we recognize the right of secession in every State, and every law enacted by this Government will receive its force and vitality, not from the Federal Government, but from the acquiescence of each one of the States."[54] That is, the government established by the Constitution would be a nullity; the substance if not the form of the Confederation government would be put in its stead.

By 1861, the promise of compromise, concession, and give-and-take had long since proven false. Republicans maintained that "the whole history of these compromises should teach us that this slavepower will leap over all barriers in its clamorous and insatiable demands." Starting with the obvious, they cited, somewhat anachronistically, the repeal of the Missouri Compromise. "When the South thought they could rob us of Kansas," a Pennsylvania party member contended, "they repealed it against the remonstrances and votes of Republicans. We can trust them therefore in no future compromise." Claiming that the party's principles were based "on the Declaration of Independence, the Constitution and the teachings of the Fathers," Republicans denied that there was anything about their platform they should—or could—compromise. The absolutes of liberty and democracy were halves of a monism that could be neither diminished nor divided. "Fundamental principles of civil government are not proper subjects of either concessions or compromise," an Ohio restrictionist claimed. Charles J. Ingersoll exclaimed, "I do not see why we should not have *Liberty* as well as the *Southerners* do *slavery*. . . .

I value the Union *as the fathers made it.*" Lyman Trumbull added with disdain, "Why, sir, any people can have peace at the price of degradation."[55]

Clearly the most fundamental issue at stake among those such as Trumbull who opposed compromise was "the existence of constitutional government." If Congress chose to *"purchase* peace" in 1861, Michigan's Francis Kellogg predicted that similar demands would be made four years later when "the defeated party, encouraged by their success now, [will] rise again in rebellion, and *demand* the substitution of *their policy* for *ours* in the administration of the Government." The *Providence Daily Journal* maintained that to accept the principle as well as the conditions of concession to minority demands, "We not only sap the foundations of our present government, but render it impossible to establish and perpetuate any liberal and stable government hereafter." If the government in Washington could not enforce obedience to its laws, one Illinois Republican ventured, "we do not think it worth preserving." And a Union that could be altered or struck down "by disaffected and turbulent men," Representative Edward Wade grimly concluded, "is no Union at all."[56]

America, as Lincoln later put it, was the last best hope of humankind. Now, in the face of secession, the *New York Daily Tribune* demanded, "It is really of the greatest and most enduring consequence to know whether the nation called the United States of America is a sham, a humbug, a myth, or not." We have put to shame the despotisms of the Old World, Representative Harrison Blake exclaimed. Americans had vindicated the right of the people to govern themselves; citizens could be governed and remain free. The party's duty in this crisis was "preserving the Union and perpetuating its blessings [as it] was transmitted to us by Patriots and Statesmen who knew its value. . . . Are we unworthy of such an inheritance?" If the ideals of liberty and equality that underlie our government are destroyed, the *Philadelphia Public Ledger* would later warn, then the principles that give "vitality to our democratic representative government [are] gone also, and with it the faith of mankind in popular government." Northerners such as Francis Kellogg insisted, "We owe it to the heroes of the Revolution; to the founders of our Government — we owe to liberty, to civilization, and humanity, and to all who are struggling against tyranny throughout the world, *to maintain this Government and preserve the Union to the last, let the consequences to ourselves be what they may.*"[57]

Ironically, in the end northerners agreed with secessionists that there was nothing intrinsically wrong with the Constitution or the government that it created. Ours was "the best system of national Government ever devised by human wisdom" claimed Representative Morris. His colleague from Illinois, John Farnsworth, similarly declared, "The Constitution which Washington, Madison, and the wise men who formed it, made for us, is good enough for me." In short, Republicans, no less than southern disunionists, were determined to keep the American experiment alive. To one farmer who claimed to have worked his whole life "to save what I have from the jaws of greedy creditors," the secession crisis resolved itself into a simple proposition: "Is the majority or minority to rule?" As he prepared for Lincoln's inauguration, a fellow Illinois Republican wrote that the success of his administration would determine "whether the principles of our Declaration [of Independence] are to prevail, or fall. Whether our country is to remain on the basis of our fathers, or is to be changed into a semi-despotism of a few." For him, shadows obscured the future. One thing was certain, however: "The irrepressible conflict is more and more manifest between slavery and freedom."[58]

And so the war came. This study maintains that the territorial issue contributed to the coming of the Civil War. But it does not claim that it caused the Civil War. In fact, a curious anomaly should have occurred to the careful reader. If access to the territories was the principal demand of the South, why did the slave states secede from the Union? If, however, the primary object of the Republican Party and the North was to keep slavery out of the territories, why did it not acquiesce in secession? Clearly, the relationship between expansion, slavery extension, and disunion is complex. Territorial expansion raised the issue of slavery extension; this, in turn, produced the election of Lincoln; his election led to the secession crisis, which in turn led to the calling of troops. That is, the territorial question sectionalized American politics and resulted in the election of a sectional president. The election of a sectional president produced disunion.

The unique force of expansion gave rise to and shaped the events of the 1840s and 1850s. The urbanization and industrialization of these decades, so often noted by historians, symbolized to anxious Jacksonian Americans the closing in of society upon their way of life. With the vague sense that opportunities in the East were no longer there, many Americans fled to freedom in the great desert of the West, and many more held the possibility of doing so in reserve, in case the course of their lives required it. The desire to maintain and expand personal freedom and liberation constituted the ideological rationale and driving force of territorial aggrandizement. Expansion, therefore, had a resonance with the basic premises of Jacksonian America. Ultimately, because it was such an intense force, expansionism meant that the political source of the Civil War would come to be anchored in the meaning of national growth.

Northerners and southerners viewed the events of these years — Texas, the Mexican-American War, the Wilmot Proviso, the Mexican cession, the Compromise of 1850, the Kansas-Nebraska Act, "Bloody Kansas," the Lecompton struggle, *Dred Scott*, Harpers Ferry, the Charleston convention, Lincoln's election, and secession—through the same prism: the American Revolution. The meaning of that experience, understood in terms of independence, freedom, and self-government, defined what was American. The Revolution also constituted a common past and provided a common identity for a diverse, highly mobile population. The random factor that made consensus ultimately impossible was slavery. At each step, from Texas annexation to Fort Sumter, the nation had to deal with the Americanness of slavery.

Slavery had always been the central symbol of American political ideology. As an institution and, no less importantly as a trope, slavery negated liberty, contradicted equality, and precluded self-determination. Put in reductive terms, freedom as a symbol existed because the symbol of slavery existed. The conflict between slavery and freedom reflected fears of encroaching power usurping liberty. In the early republic the lines of battle were drawn between the power of the national government and the rights of states and the liberties of their citizens.

With the ascendancy of Jacksonian democracy, the balance of power shifted in the direction of states. The concomitant growth of a market economy further reconfigured these tensions and political configurations. Social and cultural dissimilarities within sections and class-based conflicts over economic agendas issued in a national polity in which the lines of tension were urban and rural, East and West. The debate over Texas reflected these political parameters. Democrats, most of whom favored annexation, apprehended that economic dependency and wage slavery increasingly jeopardized personal independence. Whigs, fearing the economic bondage of a widely dispersed population and the limiting conditions of a subsistence economy, opposed rapid western expansion.

Wilmot's proviso marked the beginning of the transformation of established national party lines. Down to 1846, citizens' loyalties were to family and community. Their revolutionary past gave Americans a national identity. Reverence for the Union forged a common allegiance. Conflict over economic issues engendered national political loyalties. The axis of political conflict and the locus of loyalty began to shift after the introduction of the proviso. Political conflict between the periphery and center over the shape and power of the national government was replaced by a sectional conflict to shape the character of the territories and thus to control the national government. The territorial issue, therefore, became for Americans of the 1840s and 1850s what the bank issue was for the Jacksonians: a way of identifying and destroying the subversive elements in American democracy. As soon as slavery was taken up by American politics in the territorial question, the tragedy was foretold. For unlike the bank divisions that were inter-party, the territorial (or slavery extension) issue divided Americans along sectional lines.

Beginning with Wilmot's proviso, politicians agitating the territorial question eventually engendered the conviction that each section had become the negation of what the other side stood for. Northerners saw slavery and what they saw as the civilization that it had produced as un-American, not following from revolutionary principles. Southerners believed that what they saw as the capitalist urban society of the North did not represent the true America. Northern values were not harmonious with the national character as shaped by the Revolution. Considered from the voters' perspective, the sectional conflict was not North versus South. It was America versus the South, or America versus the North. The ideals and standards of the Revolution shaped the perceptions and actions of both sides. The meaning of freedom and democracy was at stake in this battle over the essence of the American character.

The long-standing, inherent tension between liberty and equality and freedom and democracy defined, made salient, and exacerbated the territorial issue. Free-soilers insisted on the primacy of individual freedom. Southerners demanded their equal rights in the territories and under the Constitution. The North came to believe that an imperious minority of slaveholders was intent on frustrating the will of a majority that favored restriction. Southerners insisted that they had the liberty to take their property and their institutions to the commonly owned territories. They came to fear that an overweening majority intended to enslave and degrade them.

By 1860, free-soil northerners and states'-rights southerners believed each other to be engaged in a plot or conspiracy to control America and to deny the other a role or participation in the national government. Because the burdens of freedom were so great, because the success of America would determine the success of all republican institutions, the apparent failure of democracy forced each side to search out and destroy the forces undermining the form of government. The crisis of American democracy came to a head with the election of Lincoln. As the choice of a clear majority of an alien electorate, Lincoln loomed as a foreign tyrant in the South's future. He would rule over an entire section now relegated to second-class citizenship. His election was the failure of democracy. To preserve the republican essence of the Constitution and the Union, the South seceded. Northerners believed that the slave states, now debauched beyond anyone's imagination, were unwilling to accept the popular choice of the electoral process. By seceding, an aristocratic South repudiated the fundamental premises and principles of republican government. The North resisted secession to preserve the Union and the natural operation of constitutional democracy. The North and the South each fought to keep the American experiment alive. Lincoln had it right—or half right—at Gettysburg. The Civil War was understood to be a test of whether any nation conceived in liberty and dedicated to equality could long endure. So it did. So it has.

Notes

Introduction

1. Stevenson to Reed, Oct. 13, 1859, Box 2, Thomas B. Stevenson Papers, Cincinnati Historical Society, Cincinnati, Ohio.

2. Charles W. Ramsdell, "Changing Interpretations of the Civil War," *Journal of Southern History* 3 (1937): 3.

3. Henry Wilson, *The History of the Rise and Fall of the Slavepower in America* (Boston, 1877), 127.

4. Alexander H. Stephens, *A Constitutional View of the Late War between the States: Its Causes, Character, Conduct and Results, Presented in a Series of Colloquies at Liberty Hall*, 2 vols. (1868–70; rpt. New York, 1970), 1:130.

5. Edward Channing, *History of the United States*, 6 vols. (New York, 1905–25), 6:3; James Ford Rhodes, *A History of the United States from the Compromise of 1850 to the Final Restoration of Home Rule at the South in 1877*, 7 vols. (1893–1906; rpt. New York, 1919), 3:148.

6. Charles A. Beard and Mary R. Beard, *The Rise of American Civilization*, 2 vols. (New York, 1927), 2:6–7, 51.

7. J. G. Randall, "The Blundering Generation," *Mississippi Valley Historical Review* 27 (1940): 7.

8. Arthur M. Schlesinger Jr., "The Causes of the American Civil War: A Note on Historical Sentimentalism," *Partisan Review* 16 (1949): 976, 978.

9. Eric Foner, *Free Soil, Free Labor, Free Men: The Ideology of the Republican Party before the Civil War* (New York, 1970).

10. For an informed assessment of this literature, see Joel H. Silbey, "The Civil

War Synthesis in American Political History," *Civil War History* 10 (1964): 130–40; and Silbey, "The Surge of Republican Power: Partisan Apathy, American Social Conflict, and the Coming of the Civil War," in *Essays on American Antebellum Politics, 1840–1860,* ed. Stephen E. Maizlish and John J. Kushma (College Station, 1982), esp. 227–29.

11. Michael F. Holt, *The Political Crisis of the 1850s* (New York, 1978), is the definitive study.

12. *Pittsburgh Morning Post,* Apr. 25, 1857; Carville Earle and Changyong Cao, "Frontier Closure and the Involution of American Society, 1840–1890," *Journal of the Early Republic* 13 (1993): 163–69. A recent study suggests that in addition to the migration from east to west there was also a significant south-to-north stream. This may have had the effect of heightening the importance of, and intensifying the conflict in, the territories. See Peter D. McClelland and Richard J. Zeckhauser, *Demographic Dimensions of the New Republic: American Interregional Migration, Vital Statistics, and Manumissions* (Cambridge, Eng., 1982), 6–7.

13. *Historical Statistics of the United States: Colonial Times to 1970,* 2 vols. (Washington, D.C., 1975), 1:22–37.

14. Recent literature on the frontier is vast. For an insightful overview that has informed my own work, see Lacy K. Ford Jr., "Frontier Democracy: The Turner Thesis Revisited," *Journal of the Early Republic* 13 (1993): 150–55.

15. Jacob E. Cooke, ed., *The Federalist* (Middletown, 1961), 64.

16. Ibid.; J. Mills Thornton III, "Comment," in *The Civil Rights Movement in America,* ed. Charles W. Eagles (Jackson, 1986), 151–52.

17. Nahum Capen, *Plain Facts and Considerations: Addressed to the People of the United States, without Distinction of Party, in Favor of James Buchanan, of Pennsylvania, for President, and John C. Breckinridge, of Kentucky, for Vice President. By an American Citizen* (Boston, 1856), 27.

18. Robert H. Wiebe, *The Opening of American Society: From the Adoption of the Constitution to the Eve of Disunion* (New York, 1984), 354.

19. Holt, *Political Crisis*; J. Mills Thornton III, *Politics and Power in a Slave Society: Alabama, 1800–1860* (Baton Rouge, 1978); William E. Gienapp, *The Origins of the Republican Party, 1852–1856* (New York, 1987); Lacy K. Ford Jr., *Origins of Southern Radicalism: The South Carolina Upcountry, 1800–1860* (New York, 1988).

20. *New York Daily Tribune,* Nov. 27, 1860; *Memphis Daily Avalanche,* Apr. 15, 1861.

21. Gene Wise, "Political 'Reality' in Recent American Scholarship versus Symbolists," *American Quarterly* 19 (1967): 303–28.

22. Thornton, "Comment," 154; Nancy F. Cott, "Feminist Theory and Feminist Movements: The Past before Us," in *What Is Feminism: A Re-examination,* ed. Juliet Mitchell and Ann Oakley (New York, 1986), 49–50. See also Mary P. Ryan, *Women in Public: Between Banners and Ballots, 1825–1880* (Baltimore, 1990), 130–41; and Elizabeth R. Varon, "Tippecanoe and the Ladies, Too: White Women and Party Politics in Antebellum Virginia," *Journal of American History* 82 (1995–96): 494–521.

Chapter One

1. Ralph Waldo Emerson, *Journals and Miscellaneous Notebooks*, ed. William H. Gilman et al., 16 vols. (Cambridge, Mass., 1960–82), 9:74–75.

2. John R. Pease to Levi Woodbury, May 18, 1844, Ser. II, Vol. 22, Levi Woodbury Papers, Library of Congress; James A. Campbell to John C. Calhoun, May 14, 1844, in Chauncey S. Boucher and Robert P. Brooks, eds., "Correspondence Addressed to John C. Calhoun, 1837–1849," *Annual Report of the American Historical Association for the Year 1929* (Washington, D.C., 1930), 227.

3. See John Higham, *From Boundlessness to Consolidation: The Transformation of American Culture, 1848–1860* (Ann Arbor, 1969); Major L. Wilson, *Space, Time, and Freedom: The Quest for Nationality and the Irrepressible Conflict, 1815–1861* (Westport, 1974), 108–19; and David M. Potter, *The Impending Crisis, 1848–1861* (New York, 1976), 17.

4. Robert V. Remini, *Andrew Jackson and the Course of American Democracy, 1833–1845* (New York, 1984), 357–60, 367–68; John M. Belohlavek, *"Let The Eagle Soar!": The Foreign Policy of Andrew Jackson* (Lincoln, 1985), 218–38.

5. John Niven, *Martin Van Buren: The Romantic Age of American Politics* (New York, 1983), 444–46; Major L. Wilson, *The Presidency of Martin Van Buren* (Lawrence, 1984), 148–52.

6. *Savannah Daily Republican*, Apr. 6, 1844. For Texas on and off stage, see Elgin Williams, *The Animating Pursuit of Speculation: Land Traffic in the Annexation of Texas* (New York, 1949); Holman Hamilton, "Texas Bonds and Northern Profits: A Study in Compromise, Investment, and Lobby Influence," *Mississippi Valley Historical Review* 43 (1957): 579–94; Ephraim D. Adams, *British Interests and Activities in Texas, 1838–1846* (Baltimore, 1910); Lelia M. Roeckell, "British Interests in Texas, 1825–1846" (Ph.D. diss., St. Peter's College, University of Oxford, 1993); Noel M. Loomis, *The Texas–Santa Fé Pioneers* (Norman, 1958); David M. Pletcher, *The Diplomacy of Annexation: Texas, Oregon, and the Mexican War* (Columbia, 1973), 84–87; William H. Goetzmann, *When the Eagle Screamed: The Romantic Horizon in American Diplomacy, 1800–1860* (New York, 1966), 34–36; and Thomas R. Hietala, *Manifest Design: Anxious Aggrandizement in Late Jacksonian America* (Ithaca, 1985), 17–26, 217–20. Justin Smith sees little evidence of American interest down to 1845 (*The Annexation of Texas* [1911; rpt. New York, 1941], 71–75).

7. Tyler's prediction in 1832 in Robert Seager II, *And Tyler, Too: A Biography of John and Julia Gardiner Tyler* (New York, 1963), 210; James D. Richardson, comp., *A Compilation of the Messages and Papers of the Presidents, 1789–1897*, 10 vols. (Washington, D.C., 1896–99), 4:258, 336.

8. John Quincy Adams, *Memoirs of John Quincy Adams, Comprising Portions of His Diary from 1795 to 1848*, ed. Charles Francis Adams, 12 vols. (Philadelphia, 1874–77), 11:167; Tyler to Col. John S. Cunningham, Nov. 4, 1855, in Lyon G. Tyler, *The Letters and Times of the Tylers*, 3 vols. (1884–86; rpt. New York, 1970), 2:262; Oliver Perry Chitwood, *John Tyler, Champion of the Old South* (New York, 1939), 332.

9. Henry A. Wise, *Seven Decades of the Union: The Humanities and Materialism, Illustrated by a Memoir of John Tyler, with Reminiscences of Some of His Great Contemporaries* (Philadelphia, 1872), 181–82; Tyler to Webster, Oct. 11, 1841, in *The Letters of Daniel Webster, from Documents Owned Principally by the New Hampshire Historical Society*, ed.

Claude H. Van Tyne (New York, 1902), 239–40. On the Tyler-Clay feud see Chitwood, *Tyler*, 217–51; George Rawlings Poage, *Henry Clay and the Whig Party* (1936; rpt. Gloucester, 1965), 66–106; Glyndon G. Van Deusen, *The Life of Henry Clay* (Boston, 1937), 337–57; David Krueger, "The Clay-Tyler Feud, 1841–1842," *Filson Club History Quarterly* 42 (1968): 162–77; and Richard A. Gantz, "Henry Clay and the Harvest of Bitter Fruit: The Struggle with John Tyler, 1841–1842" (Ph.D. diss., Indiana University, 1986). On Tyler's cautious diplomacy see Chitwood, *Tyler*, 342–47; and Pletcher, *Diplomacy of Annexation*, 113–38.

10. Quoted in Lawrence F. Kohl, *The Politics of Individualism: Parties and the American Character in the Jacksonian Era* (New York, 1989), 140, 142.

11. First quotation in John Ashworth, *'Agrarians' and 'Aristocrats': Party Political Ideology in the United States, 1837–1846* (London, 1983), 22; "NEW TERRITORY versus NO TERRITORY," *United States Magazine and Democratic Review* 21 (1847): 292.

12. "Demagoguism," *Brownson's Quarterly Review* 1 (1844): 85; *Philadelphia Public Ledger and Daily Transcript*, Feb. 2, 1846; Bancroft to B. F. Hallett et al., Aug. 15, 1844, published in *Richmond Enquirer*, Aug. 27, 1844.

13. Mirabeau Buonaparte Lamar, *Letter of Gen. Mirabeau B. Lamar, ex-President of Texas, on the Subject of Annexation, Addressed to Several Citizens of Macon, Geo.* (Savannah, 1844), 25–26, 24; *Congressional Globe*, 28th Cong., 2d sess., 249; *Mississippian* (Jackson), Oct. 30, 1844.

14. Levi Woodbury to J. H. Reid et al., May 11, 1844, published in *Richmond Enquirer*, May 24, 1844; Samuel A. Cartwright to Robert J. Walker, Nov. 30, 1845, Vol. H-3, 209, Robert J. Walker Papers, Library of Congress; "Memorial of a Number of Merchants and Traders, Citizens of New York, Praying for the Ratification of a Treaty of Commerce and Navigation between the United States and Texas, February 22, 1844," *Senate Documents*, 28th Cong., 1st sess., no. 139; *Mississippian*, Apr. 3, 1844.

15. *Daily Madisonian* (Washington, D.C.), Mar. 22, 1844; "Address by William Wilkins to the People of the 21st Congressional District of Pennsylvania," Apr. 14, 1844, published in *Harrisburg Democratic Union*, Apr. 20, 1844; Ellis quoted in Hietala, *Manifest Design*, 185; *Congressional Globe*, 28th Cong., 1st sess., Appendix, 543.

16. *Daily Madisonian*, Apr. 2, 1844; *Congressional Globe*, 28th Cong., 1st sess., Appendix, 721; Fauquier County address published in *Richmond Enquirer*, May 28, 1844.

17. "The March of Our Republic," *Merchants' Magazine and Commercial Review* 13 (1845): 549; *Congressional Globe*, 28th Cong., 1st sess., Appendix, 350; David Davis to Julian Rockwell, May 14, 1844, Box 3, Folder 12, David Davis Papers, Chicago Historical Society, Chicago, Ill.

18. *New Orleans Daily Picayune*, Mar. 26, 1844; Henry Clay to John J. Crittenden, Dec. 5, 1843, in Ann M. B. Coleman, ed., *The Life of John J. Crittenden, with Selections from His Correspondence and Speeches*, 2 vols. (Philadelphia, 1871), 1:207.

19. Clay to the editors of the *Daily National Intelligencer*, Apr. 17, 1844, in Calvin Colton, ed., *The Life, Correspondence, and Speeches of Henry Clay*, 6 vols. (New York, 1857), 3:29. On Clay's philosophical position, see Clay to Crittenden, Apr. 17, 19, 1844, John J. Crittenden Papers, Perkins Library, Duke University, Durham, N.C.; Thomas Brown, *Politics and Statesmanship: Essays on the American Whig Party* (New York, 1985), 145; and Thomas B. Jones, "Henry Clay and Continental Expansion, 1820–

1844," *Register of the Kentucky Historical Society* 72 (1975): 260–61. Assessments critical of Clay's Raleigh letter may be found in Poage, *Clay*, 134–35, 139, 141; and Robert Seager II, "Henry Clay and the Politics of Compromise and Non-Compromise," *Register of the Kentucky Historical Society* 85 (1987–88): 24.

20. "Foreign Miscellany," *American Review: A Whig Journal of Politics, Literature, Art, and Science* 1 (1845): 327; Clay to Jacob Gibson, July 25, 1842, in Henry Clay, *Private Correspondence of Henry Clay*, ed. Calvin Colton (1855; rpt. Freeport, 1971), 466. On the Whigs' whiggish sense of history, see Daniel Walker Howe, *The Political Culture of the American Whigs* (Chicago, 1979), 74–77.

21. David Francis Bacon, *Progressive Democracy. A Discourse, on the History, Philosophy and Tendency of American Politics, Delivered in National Hall, New York City, before a Large Mass-Meeting of Whigs and Young Men, by D. Francis Bacon* (New York, 1844), 12; Charles Sumner, "The True Grandeur of Nations," in *Memoirs and Letters of Charles Sumner*, ed. Edward L. Pierce, 4 vols. (Boston, 1877–93), 1:347.

22. Bacon, *Progressive Democracy*, 11, 12; "The Spirit of Liberty," *American Review* 2 (1845): 614; *Raleigh Register and North Carolina Gazette*, May 15, 1846. See also [William Robinson Watson], *An Address to the People of Rhode Island, Published in the Providence Journal, in a Series of Articles during the Months of September and October, 1844* (Providence, 1844), 4; and Howe, *Political Culture*, 74, 76.

23. Daniel Webster, *Speech Delivered at the Dinner Given to Mr. Webster by the Merchants of Baltimore on Thursday, May 18, 1843* (New York, 1843), 6; Lawrence to Rives, Jan. 7, 1846, in Abbott Lawrence, *Letters from the Hon. Abbott Lawrence to the Hon. William C. Rives, of Virginia* (Boston, 1846), 6; *Jonesborough* (Tenn.) *Whig and Independent Journal*, May 8, 1844.

24. Webster to Mr. [John] Bigelow et al., Jan. 23, 1844, Vol. 10, Daniel Webster Letterbooks, New Hampshire Historical Society, Concord, N.H. See also Nolan Fowler, "Territorial Expansion—A Threat to the Republic?," *Pacific Northwest Quarterly* 52 (1962): 36.

25. Everett quoted in Rush Welter, *The Mind of America, 1820-1860* (New York, 1975), 47; *Congressional Globe*, 28th Cong., 2d sess., Appendix, 393. Still the best treatment of Whigs and time is Wilson, *Space, Time, and Freedom*, esp. 111.

26. *Congressional Globe*, 28th Cong., 1st sess., Appendix, 688; *Daily National Intelligencer* (Washington, D.C.), Mar. 16, 1844; "Our Foreign Relations," *American Review* 2 (1845): 431.

27. Clay to Crittenden, Dec. 5, 1843, in Coleman, ed., *Life of Crittenden*, 1:208; *New York Daily Tribune*, May 11, 1844; [Calvin Colton], *Annexation of Texas* (New York, 1844), 19.

28. *House Journal*, 28th Cong., 2d sess., 258–59; Charles H. Atherton to Charles G. Atherton, Mar. 21, 1844, Box 1, Folder 8, Atherton Family Papers, New Hampshire Historical Society, Concord, N.H.

29. [Watson], *Address to Rhode Island*, 5.

30. William G. Brownlow, *A Political Register, Setting Forth the Principles of the Whig and Locofoco Parties in the United States, with the Life and Public Services of Henry Clay* (Jonesborough, 1844), 121; *Congressional Globe*, 28th Cong., 2d sess., Appendix, 392, 403.

31. S. C. Charles, "New England Emigration," *American Agriculturalist* 4 (1845): 145–46; *Congressional Globe*, 28th Cong., 2d sess., Appendix, 351.

32. *Congressional Globe*, 28th Cong., 1st sess., Appendix, 688; *Columbus* (Ga.) *Enquirer*, May 29, 1844.

33. *Congressional Globe*, 28th Cong., 2d sess., 360; Seward to E. A. Stansbury, Sept. 2, 1844, Folder 938, William Henry Seward Papers, Rush Rhees Library, University of Rochester, Rochester, N.Y.; Stephens to James Thomas, May 17, 1844, in Ulrich B. Phillips, ed., "The Correspondence of Robert Toombs, Alexander H. Stephens and Howell Cobb," *Annual Report of the American Historical Association for the Year 1911*, 2 vols. (Washington, D.C., 1913), 2:57–58. On antislavery Whigs, see Nolan Fowler, "The Anti-Expansionist Argument in the United States Prior to the Civil War" (Ph.D. diss., University of Kentucky, 1955), esp. 605; Kinley J. Brauer, *Cotton versus Conscience: Massachusetts Whig Politics and Southwestern Expansion, 1843-1848* (Lexington, 1967), 30–35, 49–76; and Stephen E. Maizlish, *The Triumph of Sectionalism: The Transformation of Ohio Politics, 1844-1856* (Kent, 1983), 38–39.

34. *Congressional Globe*, 28th Cong., 2d sess., Appendix, 271, 393; J. Mills Thornton III, *Politics and Power in a Slave Society: Alabama, 1800-1860* (Baton Rouge, 1978), 167–68. One southern Whig predicted that annexation would not strengthen slavery but "would only be a transfer of population from the southern States to Texas, to the utter ruin of South Carolina, Georgia, Alabama, part of Tennessee, if not Mississippi and Louisiana" (Colonel Charles Perrow to William Cabell Rives, June 26, 1844, Box 70, William Cabell Rives Papers, Library of Congress).

35. "Mr. Clay—The Texas Question," *American Review* 1 (1845): 76.

36. Clay to Rives, Aug. 19, 1844, Box 71, Rives Papers; *Congressional Globe*, 28th Cong., 1st sess., 354.

37. Henry C. Carey, *Principles of Social Science*, 3 vols. (Philadelphia, 1858–59), 3:230, 214, 101. See also Rodney C. Morrison, "Henry C. Carey and Economic Development," *Explorations in Entrepreneurial History* 2d ser., 5 (1968): 135–36; and Fowler, "Territorial Expansion," 39. For the roots of this argument see Peter S. Onuf, "Liberty, Development, and Union: Visions of the West in the 1780s," *William and Mary Quarterly* 3d ser., 43 (1968): 189–202; and Andrew R. L. Cayton, *The Frontier Republic: Ideology and Politics in the Ohio Country, 1780-1825* (Kent, 1986), 21–24.

38. *Congressional Globe*, 28th Cong., 1st sess., 652. Every Whig senator except John Henderson of Mississippi voted against the treaty.

39. James K. Polk to Andrew Jackson Donelson, Oct. 19, 1843, in St. George L. Sioussat, ed., "Letters of James K. Polk to Andrew J. Donelson, 1843-1848," *Tennessee Historical Magazine* 3 (1917): 53; A. Vandapell to Martin Van Buren, Apr. 13, 1844, Vol. 49, Martin Van Buren Papers, Library of Congress; *State Capitol Gazette* (Harrisburg, Pa.), Feb. 14, 1843; *Albany Daily Argus*, Mar. 1, 1844; *Mobile Register and Journal*, Sept. 14, 1843; *New York Evening Post* reprinted in *Washington Daily Globe*, Oct. 10, 1843.

40. James C. N. Paul, *Rift in the Democracy* (1951; rpt. New York, 1961), chaps. 2–3.

41. On Jacksonian fiscal policies and politics, see Bray Hammond, *Banks and Politics in America: From the Revolution to the Civil War* (1957; rpt. Princeton, 1985), chap. 19; James Roger Sharp, *The Jacksonians versus the Banks: Politics in the States after the Panic of 1837* (New York, 1970); Herbert Ershkowitz and William G. Shade, "Consensus or Conflict? Political Behavior in the State Legislatures during the Jacksonian Era," *Journal of American History* 58 (1971): 591–621; John M. McFaul, *The Politics of Jack-*

sonian Finance (Ithaca, 1972); William G. Shade, *Banks or No Banks: The Money Issue in Western Politics, 1832–1865* (Detroit, 1972); Charles G. Sellers, *The Market Revolution: Jacksonian America, 1815–1846* (New York, 1991), esp. 333–48, 355–59; and Maizlish, *Triumph of Sectionalism*, 29–33. On western disdain for New York Democrats' maneuvers on the tariff, see Amos Kendall to Van Buren, Apr. 19, 1844, and Cave Johnson to Van Buren, Apr. 20, 1844, both in Vol. 49, Van Buren Papers; and *Washington Daily Globe*, May 10, 1844. For southern discontent with equivocating free-state Democrats on the tariff, see Armistead Burt to Nathan L. Green, Jan. 10, 1844, in Milledge L. Bonham Jr., ed., "A Carolina Democrat on Party Prospects in 1844," *American Historical Review* 42 (1936): 79–82; and a series of editorials in the pro–Van Buren *Mobile Register and Journal*, Oct. 31, Nov. 9, 1843, Jan. 8, 1844.

42. Johnson to Polk, Apr. 30, 1844, James K. Polk Papers, Library of Congress; William J. Brown to Van Buren, Apr. 29, 1844, Vol. 50, Van Buren Papers; Ritchie to Howell Cobb, May 6, 1844, in Phillips, ed., "Correspondence of Toombs, Stephens, and Cobb," 56; Preston King to Van Buren, May 7, 1844, Vol. 50, Van Buren Papers.

43. Wright to Polk, Feb. 27, 1844, Johnson to Polk, Apr. 10, May 12 (quotation), 1844, Polk Papers.

44. Hugh Legaré quoted in Michael O'Brien, *A Character of Hugh Legaré* (Knoxville, 1985), 277; *Washington Daily Globe*, Sept. 9, 1843.

45. *Washington Daily Globe*, July 27, 1843.

46. J. S. Kimball to Polk, May 8, 1844, Polk Papers; Letcher to Crittenden, Jan. 18, 1844, in Coleman, ed., *Life of Crittenden*, 1:213; Mangum to Paul C. Cameron, Feb. 10, 1844, in *The Papers of Willie Person Mangum*, ed. Henry Thomas Shanks, 5 vols. (Raleigh, 1950–56), 4:42.

47. *Washington Daily Globe*, Apr. 27, 1844.

48. Fairfield to Anna Fairfield, Apr. 28, 1844, in *The Letters of John Fairfield*, ed. Arthur G. Staples (Lewiston, 1922), 335; F. P. Moore to Frank Blair Sr., May 13, 1844, Box 14, Blair Family Papers, Library of Congress; William J. Brown to Van Buren, Apr. 29, 1844, Vol. 50, Van Buren Papers.

49. A[ndrew] Stevenson to Salmon P. Chase et al., Apr. 24, 1844, printed in *Richmond Enquirer*, May 21, 1844; Solomon W. Downs, *Speech of S. W. Downs before a Public Meeting of the People of the Parish of Union, on the Annexation of Texas, Delivered at Farmersville, on the 19th June 1844* (New Orleans, [1844]), 55; Gilmer quoted in Gerald Douglas Saxon, "The Politics of Expansion: Texas as an Issue in National Politics, 1819–1845" (Ph.D. diss., North Texas State University, 1979), 110; *Harrisburg Democratic Union*, May 8, 1844.

50. Jackson to Frank Blair Sr., May 7, 1844, typescript, Box 1, Blair Family Papers, Jackson-Blair Correspondence, Library of Congress; Williamson Smith to Polk, Apr. 29, 1844, Edwin Polk to Polk, May 11, 1844, both in Polk Papers; Lucius Elmore to Peter D. Vroom, May 15, 1844, Peter D. Vroom Papers, Butler Library, Columbia University, New York; Augustus Dodge to Van Buren, Apr. 30, 1844, Vol. 50, Van Buren Papers.

51. Kendall to Van Buren, May 13, 1844, Vol. 50, Van Buren Papers; Johnson to Polk, May 5, 1844, Polk Papers; Alfred Balch to Van Buren, May 22, 1844, W[illiam] A. Roane to Van Buren, Apr. 30, 1844, both in Vol. 50, Van Buren Papers.

52. Niven, *Van Buren*, 526–27; Charles G. Sellers, *James K. Polk: Continentalist, 1843–1846* (Princeton, 1966), chap. 3; Edwin A. Miles, "'Fifty Four Forty or Fight'—An American Political Legend," *Mississippi Valley Historical Review* 44 (1957): 291–309.

53. Alexander Anderson, *The Letter of Alexander Anderson, of Tennessee, in Reply to the Committee of Invitation to Attend a Dinner Given by the Democracy of Maury, Tennessee, on the 13th July to the Delegation from That State to the National Convention* (N.p., 1844), 3; Bancroft to Robert J. Walker, June 19, 1844, Folder 1836–46, Robert J. Walker Papers, New-York Historical Society, New York.

54. "The Annexation of Texas," *Southern Quarterly Review* 6 (1844): 498; *Richmond Enquirer*, June 28, 1844.

55. *Congressional Globe*, 28th Cong., 1st sess., Appendix, 766–67, 532. For a concise argument for the nationality of annexation, see Robert J. Walker to the Democratic Party of Mississippi, June 1844, Robert J. Walker Letterbook, Darlington Memorial Library, University of Pittsburgh, Pittsburgh, Pa.

56. Dixon H. Lewis to John C. Calhoun, Mar. 6, 1844, in J. Franklin Jameson, ed., "Correspondence of John C. Calhoun," *Annual Report of the American Historical Association for the Year 1899*, 2 vols. (Washington, D.C., 1900), 2:936; *Congressional Globe*, 36th Cong., 1st sess., Appendix, 532.

57. *Congressional Globe*, 28th Cong., 1st sess., Appendix, 240; Pletcher, *Diplomacy of Annexation*, 214–17.

58. *Congressional Globe*, 28th Cong., 1st sess., Appendix, 623; "Petitions of a Number of Citizens of Ohio Praying for the Adoption of a Measure for the Occupation and Settlement of the Territory of Oregon," *Senate Documents*, 28th Cong., 1st sess., no. 56, 2. See also Norman A. Graebner, *Empire on the Pacific: A Study in American Continental Expansion* (New York, 1955), 36–39, 63–64; Robert G. Cleland, "Asiatic Trade and the American Occupation of the Pacific Coast," *Annual Report of the American Historical Association for the Year 1914*, 2 vols. (Washington, D.C., 1916), 1:283–89. Democrats, unlike Whigs, were much less inclined to stress the civilizing effect of commercial growth, and they opposed an activist federal government promoting what historian Jean H. Baker has called "state-directed favoritism." Whereas Whigs looked to government to foster economic growth and to create institutional arrangements that were a necessary adjunct to a market economy, Democrats advocated release from public and private restraints to foster a gradual expansion of economic opportunities. See Jean H. Baker, *Affairs of Party: The Political Culture of Northern Democrats in the Mid-Nineteenth Century* (Ithaca, 1983), 143–48.

59. Pickens to Calhoun, Apr. 22, 1844, in Boucher and Brooks, eds., "Correspondence Addressed to Calhoun," 222; *Philadelphia Public Ledger and Daily Transcript*, Dec. 4, 1843; M. A. Goodfellow to William Allen, Jan. 20, 1845, Vol. 6, William Allen Papers, Library of Congress.

60. *Washington Daily Globe*, June 13, 1844.

61. Quoted in Wilson, *Space, Time, and Freedom*, 111.

62. *Savannah Daily Republican*, May 6, 1844; *Vicksburg* (Miss.) *Weekly Whig*, Aug. 5, 1844; Winthrop to John H. Clifford, Mar. 3, 1844, Robert C. Winthrop Papers, Massachusetts Historical Society, Boston.

63. William Hale to John C. Calhoun, May 18, 1844, in Boucher and Brooks,

eds., "Correspondence Addressed to Calhoun," 231; William Parry to William Allen, Mar. 29, 1844, Vol. 4, Allen Papers.

64. *Ohio State Journal* (Columbus), Aug. 29, 1844; *Albany Evening Journal*, Mar. 18, 1844. The antislavery argument also produced tensions within northern whiggery. See Brauer, *Cotton versus Conscience*, 56, 62–63, 70, 75–76; and Maizlish, *Triumph of Sectionalism*, 36–38.

65. [Miller] Grieve and [Richard H.] Orme to John M. Berrien, June 30, 1844, Box 1, John McPherson Berrien Papers, Southern Historical Collection, University of North Carolina, Chapel Hill; James F. Strother to Rives, May 28, 1844, Box 70, Rives Papers.

66. J. C. Wright to Clay, Sept. 5, 1844, in Clay, *Private Correspondence*, 493; Payne to Rives, May 3, 1844, Box 70, Rives Papers; Mississippi Whig quoted in James E. Winston, "The Annexation of Texas and the Mississippi Democrats," *Southwestern Historical Review* 25 (1921): 5.

67. Everett to Charles J. Ingersoll, Box 3, Folder 9, Charles J. Ingersoll Papers, Historical Society of Pennsylvania, Philadelphia; W. Dean Burnham, *Presidential Ballots, 1836–1892* (Baltimore, 1955), 27–33, 246, 248, 250, 252, 254, 887.

68. See Michael A. Morrison, "Martin Van Buren, the Democracy, and the Partisan Politics of Texas Annexation," *Journal of Southern History* 61 (1995): 722–23n.

69. Ibid.

70. Poage, *Clay*, 150–51; Van Deusen, *Life of Clay*, 375–76; Sellers, *Polk*, 157–61. Although the Whigs ran competitively throughout the Union, the percentage of Clay's votes as compared with William Henry Harrison's in 1840 declined in every single state. In the South it fell by an average of 5.8 percent, in the North by 5.5 percent. Nonetheless, in the seven free states that Clay lost (Maine, New Hampshire, Pennsylvania, New York, Illinois, Indiana, and Michigan), if the entire Liberty vote is added to the Whig total, Clay would have won but two—New York and Michigan. Indeed, Clay's anti-Texas stand did much to blunt the growth of the political antislavery movement. See Richard H. Sewell, *Ballots for Freedom: Antislavery Politics in the United States, 1837–1860* (New York, 1976), 110; Michael F. Holt, *The Political Crisis of the 1850s* (New York, 1978), 40–44; and James Brewer Stewart, "Abolitionists, Insurgents, and Third Parties: Sectionalism and Partisan Politics in Northern Whiggery, 1836–1844," in *Crusaders and Compromisers: Essays on the Political Relationship of the Antislavery Struggle to the Antebellum Party System*, ed. Alan M. Kraut (Westport, 1983), 33–36.

71. E. Pettigrew to Clay, Jan. 1, 1845, in Clay, *Private Correspondence*, 518; H. M. Cunningham to Stephens, Dec. 21, 1844, Vol. 1, Alexander H. Stephens Papers, Library of Congress; Prentice quoted in Betty Congleton, "Texas Annexation and the War with Mexico—A Kentucky Editor's Analysis," *Filson Club Historical Quarterly* 41 (1967): 144; Arthur Campbell to David Campbell, Nov. 21, 1844, Campbell Family Papers, Perkins Library, Duke University.

72. *Vicksburg Weekly Whig*, Nov. 18, 1844; *Arkansas State Gazette* (Little Rock), Jan. 27, 1845; Peyton to David Campbell, Feb. 16, 1845, Campbell Family Papers; Henry F. French to Benjamin B. French, Jan. 19, 1845, Box 2, Benjamin B. and Henry F. French Correspondence, New Hampshire Historical Society, Concord, N.H. For Tyler's message, see Richardson, comp., *Messages and Papers of the Presidents*, 4:345.

73. *Congressional Globe*, 28th Cong., 2d sess., 194. A Washington observer suggested that Brown proposed his resolution to save his career in the face of intense public enthusiasm at home for annexation in Texas (Arthur Campbell to David Campbell, Jan. 30, 1845, Campbell Family Papers). Only eight southern Whigs joined fifty-three free-state Democrats and fifty-nine slave-state Democrats in passing Brown's resolution. They were Milton Brown, James [Joseph] H. Peyton, William T. Senter and John B. Ashe of Tennessee, Alexander H. Stephens and Duncan L. Clinch of Georgia, James Dellet of Alabama, and Willoughby Newton of Virginia. The three Whig senators who voted for Walker's amendment were William D. Merrick of Maryland, John Henderson of Mississippi, and Henry Johnson of Louisiana. Every House Whig except Dellet of Alabama opposed Walker's amendment. Every House Democrat except Richard D. Davis of New York and John P. Hale of New Hampshire voted for it. Seven House Democrats and six House Whigs were absent. See Cole, *Whig Party in the South*, 117–18; Smith, *Annexation of Texas*, 333, 345–47.

74. *Congressional Globe*, 28th Cong., 2d sess., 362, 372; Smith, *Annexation of Texas*, 327–37; Pletcher, *Diplomacy of Annexation*, 180–82.

75. Chitwood, *Tyler*, 334; Smith, *Annexation of Texas*, 352–54; Pletcher, *Diplomacy of Annexation*, 183.

76. Jackson to Frank P. Blair Sr., Apr. 10, 1845, Box 1, Blair Family Papers, Jackson-Blair Correspondence; *Vicksburg Sentinel*, Mar. 11, 1845; *New Orleans Daily Picayune*, Mar. 8, 1845; Benjamin B. French to Henry F. French, Jan. 27, 1845, Box 2, French Correspondence.

Chapter Two

1. James D. Richardson, comp., *A Compilation of the Messages and Papers of the Presidents, 1789–1897*, 10 vols. (Washington, D.C., 1896–99), 4:459.

2. James K. Polk, *The Diary of James K. Polk during His Presidency, 1845 to 1849*, ed. Milo M. Quaife, 4 vols. (Chicago, 1910), 1:34–35 (Sept. 16, 1845), 68–72 (quotation at 71) (Oct. 24, 1845), 398, 397 (May 13, 1846), 438 (May 30, 1846), 2:56–57 (July 31, 1846). See also Charles G. Sellers, *James K. Polk: Continentalist, 1843–1846* (Princeton, 1966), 231–32, 262, 265–66.

3. *Congressional Globe*, 29th Cong., 1st sess., 1211–13; David M. Potter, *The Impending Crisis, 1848–1861* (New York, 1976), 18–19.

4. *Congressional Globe*, 29th Cong., 1st sess., 1217; Potter, *Impending Crisis*, 19.

5. *Congressional Globe*, 29th Cong., 1st sess., 1213–14. For reluctant Whig support, see John H. Clifford to Robert C. Winthrop, May 18, 1846, Robert C. Winthrop Papers, Massachusetts Historical Society, Boston; David L. Paulhaus, "Rhode Island and the Mexican War," *Rhode Island History* 37 (1978): 89–96; and John H. Schroeder, *Mr. Polk's War: American Opposition and Dissent, 1846–1848* (Madison, 1973), 40–41.

6. *Congressional Globe*, 29th Cong., 1st sess., 1214, 1217; *Boston Whig* quoted in Potter, *Impending Crisis*, 23. See also Charles Buxton Going, *David Wilmot, Free Soiler: A Biography of the Great Advocate of the Wilmot Proviso* (New York, 1924), 84–98; and Chaplain W. Morrison, *Democratic Politics and Sectionalism: The Wilmot Proviso Controversy* (Chapel Hill, 1967), 18. On Wilmot's authorship, see Richard Stenberg, "The Mo-

tivation of the Wilmot Proviso," *Mississippi Valley Historical Review* 18 (1932): 535–41. A Hamilton County, Ohio, Democratic convention anticipated Wilmot's adaptation of the Northwest Ordinance when it earlier resolved that the ordinance be extended "over our Pacific Empire present and future" (quoted in Sellers, *Polk*, 479).

7. *Congressional Globe*, 29th Cong., 1st sess., 1214–17.

8. Ibid., 1220–21; Going, *Wilmot*, 101–2.

9. Polk, *Diary*, 2:75–76 (Oct. 10, 1846). On the South see Charles S. Sydnor, *The Development of Southern Sectionalism, 1819-1848* (Baton Rouge, 1948), 329; William J. Cooper Jr., *The South and the Politics of Slavery, 1828-1856* (Baton Rouge, 1978), 233–34; and William W. Freehling, *The Road to Disunion: Secessionists at Bay, 1776-1854* (New York, 1990), 461–62.

10. Niles quoted in Richard H. Sewell, *Ballots for Freedom: Antislavery Politics in the United States, 1837-1860* (New York, 1976), 143. On Democratic factionalism, see Potter, *Impending Crisis*, 19–20, 23–27; and Morrison, *Democratic Politics*, 4–15.

11. First *Cleveland Plain Dealer* quotation in Stephen E. Maizlish, *The Triumph of Sectionalism: The Transformation of Ohio Politics, 1844-1856* (Kent, 1983), 60–61; *Cleveland Plain Dealer*, June 22, 1846. On the alleged Van Buren betrayal, see Morgan Dix, comp., *The Memoirs of John Adams Dix*, 2 vols. (New York, 1883), 2:192; Thomas Hart Benton, *Thirty Years' View; or, A History of the Working of the American Government for Thirty Years, from 1820 to 1850*, 2 vols. (New York, 1854–56), 2:591–96; and Benjamin Tappan to Lewis Tappan, Feb. 16, 1847, Box 1, Folder 21, Benjamin Tappan Papers, Ohio Historical Society, Columbus. On Oregon's effect on Democratic comity, see William Ballard Preston to William Cabell Rives, Feb. [28], 1847, Box 76, William Cabell Rives Papers, Library of Congress; Russell Jarvis to William Allen, Mar. 9, 1846, Vol. 12, Willam Allen Papers, Library of Congress; Carl E. Persinger, "The 'Bargain of 1844' as the Origin of the Wilmot Proviso," *Annual Report of the American Historical Association for the Year 1911*, 2 vols. (Washington, D.C., 1913), 1:189–95; Potter, *Impending Crisis*, 25–26; Sellers, *Polk*, 236–37; and Maizlish, *Triumph of Sectionalism*, 54, 60–61.

12. Eric Foner, "The Wilmot Proviso Revisited," *Journal of American History* 56 (1969): 267–79; *Ohio Statesman* quoted in Maizlish, *Triumph of Sectionalism*, 62. Also see Major L. Wilson, *Space, Time, and Freedom: The Quest for Nationality and the Irrepressible Conflict, 1815-1861* (Westport, 1974), 122–23; and Morrison, *Democratic Politics*, 25–26.

13. William Hale to John C. Calhoun, May 18, 1844, in Chauncey S. Boucher and Robert P. Brooks, eds., "Correspondence Addressed to John C. Calhoun, 1837–1849," *Annual Report of the American Historical Association for the Year 1929* (Washington, D.C., 1930), 231.

14. Major Wilson's penetrating *Space, Time, and Freedom* (especially chapters 2 and 6) has informed this argument. For the sake of clarity, the analysis of the Missouri crisis will not include the congressional reaction in 1821 to the Missouri constitution, which restricted the immigration of free blacks into the state. Although the 1821 debate dredged up all the old arguments and added a few new ones, the issue of slavery restriction had been resolved (for the time being) by the Compromise of 1820.

15. *Annals of Congress*, 15th Cong., 2d sess., 273–79, 418, 422, 1166, 1170, 1214–17, 1433–35, 1438. See also Glover Moore, *The Missouri Controversy, 1819-1821* (1953; rpt. Lexington, 1966), 33–35, 53–63.

16. John Quincy Adams, *Memoirs of John Quincy Adams, Comprising Portions of His*

Diary from 1795 to 1848, ed. Charles Francis Adams, 12 vols. (Philadelphia, 1874–77), 4:529–30 (Feb. 23, 1820); Ronald C. Woolsey, "The West Becomes a Problem: The Missouri Controversy and Slavery Expansion as the Southern Dilemma," *Missouri Historical Review* 77 (1983): 410.

17. *Annals of Congress*, 16th Cong., 1st sess., 245.

18. Ibid., 124–25; Homer C. Hockett, "Rufus King and the Missouri Compromise," *Missouri Historical Review* 2 (1908): 214; Rufus King, *The Life and Correspondence of Rufus King, Comprising His Letters, Private and Official, His Public Documents, and His Speeches*, ed. Charles R. King, 6 vols. (New York, 1894–1900), 6:701.

19. Shaw quoted in Wilson, *Space, Time, and Freedom*, 25; *Annals of Congress*, 16th Cong., 1st sess., 183. A similar argument may be found in Joseph Blunt, *An Examination of the Expediency and the Constitutionality of Prohibiting Slavery in the State of Missouri* (New York, 1819), 19.

20. *Annals of Congress*, 15th Cong., 2d sess., 1173, 1172.

21. Ibid., 1178; ibid., 16th Cong., 1st sess., 254; Blunt, *Examination*, 7–9. On King, see Joseph L. Arbena, "Politics or Principle? Rufus King and the Opposition to Slavery, 1785–1825," *Essex Institute Historical Collection* 101 (1965): 56–77; and Robert Ernst, *Rufus King, American Federalist* (Chapel Hill, 1968), 369.

22. King, *Life*, 6:700; *Annals of Congress*, 16th Cong., 1st sess., 184. Other views on the problematic three-fifths compromise include *A Caveat; or Considerations Against the Admission of Missouri, with Slavery, into the Union* (New Haven, 1820), 22; Arbena, "Politics or Principle," 66–77; Albert F. Simpson, "The Political Significance of Slave Representation, 1787–1821," *Journal of Southern History* 7 (1941): 315–41; Richard H. Brown, "The Missouri Crisis, Slavery, and the Politics of Jacksonianism," *South Atlantic Quarterly* 65 (1966): 62; and Zed H. Burns, "Sectional Controversy and the Missouri Compromise," *Southern Quarterly* 5 (1967): 335–45.

23. King, *Life*, 6:702; *Annals of Congress*, 15th Cong., 2d sess., 1170.

24. Plumer to William Plumer Sr., Feb. 25, 1821, in Everett Somerville Brown, ed., *The Missouri Compromises and Presidential Politics, 1820–1825, from the Letters of William Plumer, Junior, Representative from New Hampshire* (St. Louis, 1926), 41.

25. *Annals of Congress*, 16th Cong., 1st sess., 408, 397.

26. Ibid., 397, 104, 399.

27. Ibid., 107, 175; *Missouri Gazette* quoted in Floyd C. Shoemaker, *Missouri's Struggle for Statehood, 1804–1821* (Jefferson City, 1916), 101. Similarly, Montgomery County, Missouri, citizens resolved "that the restriction attempted to be imposed on the people of this Territory as a condition of their admission into the Union is a daring stretch of power [and] an usurpation of our sacred rights" (quoted in Frank Heywood Hodder, "Side Lights on the Missouri Compromise," *Annual Report of the American Historical Association for the Year 1909* [Washington, D.C., 1911], 153).

28. Madison to Robert Walsh, Nov. 27, 1819, Madison to Monroe, Feb. 20, 1820, James Madison Papers, Library of Congress; *Annals of Congress*, 16th Cong., 1st sess., 396, 309. The imagery of the Revolution invoked by southern Republicans during the Missouri debates is striking. It was not only effective and resonant but also reveals their understanding of the inherent danger of power unrestrained. For example, William Pinkney clearly connected the usurpation of power by the federal govern-

ment in the Missouri crisis with the excesses of British colonial control in the eighteenth century. "That such an irresponsible power [of Congress over states and territories] is not likely to be abused, who will undertake to assert? If it is not, 'experience is a cheat, and fact a liar.' The power which England claimed over the colonies was such a power, and it was abused; and hence the Revolution. Such a power is always perilous to those who wield it, as well as to those on whom it is exerted. Oppression is but another name for irresponsible power, if history is to be trusted." In a like vein, Nicholas Van Dyke of Delaware claimed that "a British statesman may boast of the omnipotence of a British Parliament, but an American statesman will never claim the attribute of omnipotence for an American Congress" (*Annals of Congress*, 16th Cong., 1st sess., 396, 304). Major Wilson has emphasized the use made by Republican restrictionists of revolutionary imagery when they referred to the animating principles of the Declaration of Independence. The rhetoric of southern Republicans, however, was also cast to draw upon the "lessons of 1776" (Wilson, *Space, Time, and Freedom*, 35–42). For insights into the South's attitude toward Great Britain, see Philip F. Detweiler, "Congressional Debate on Slavery and the Declaration of Independence, 1819–1821," *American Historical Review* 63 (1958): 598–616; and Kenneth S. Greenberg, *Masters and Statesmen: The Political Culture of American Slavery* (Baltimore, 1985), 107–23.

29. Wilson, *Space, Time, and Freedom*, 35–42.

30. Pinckney quoted in Hockett, "Rufus King," 217–18; John Glendy to John C. Calhoun, Feb. 22, 1820, in John C. Calhoun, *The Papers of John C. Calhoun*, ed. Robert L. Meriwether, W. Edwin Hemphill, and Clyde N. Wilson, 22 vols. (Columbia, 1959–95), 4:678; Jefferson to Albert Gallatin, Dec. 26, 1820, Thomas Jefferson Papers, Library of Congress.

31. Clay quoted in George Dangerfield, *The Awakening of American Nationalism, 1815–1828* (New York, 1965), 112; *Annals of Congress*, 16th Cong., 1st sess., 85–100, 418–24, 467–69, 471–72, 1572–73, 1586–87. The Maine and Missouri bills were united by a vote of 23 to 21 with 4 northern Republicans voting in the majority. The vote to strike slavery restriction from the final Missouri bill was 90 to 87 and carried with the votes of 14 free-state representatives and 4 free-state abstentions.

32. Clay to Henry Marie Brackenridge, Mar. 7, 1820, Henry Marie Brackenridge Letterbook, Historical Society of Western Pennsylvania, Pittsburgh, Pa.; Calhoun to Virgil Maxcy, Aug. 12, 1820, in Calhoun, *Papers*, 5:327.

33. Polk, *Diary*, 2:289–92 (Dec. 23, 1846), 349–50 (Jan. 23, 1847); James Buchanan to Andrew Jackson Donelson, Jan. 29, 1847, Vol. 11, Andrew Jackson Donelson Papers, Library of Congress; Richardson, comp., *Messages and Papers of the Presidents*, 4:495; *Congressional Globe*, 29th Cong., 2d sess., 105.

34. Welles to John Cochran, July 12, 1848, Vol. 35, Gideon Welles Papers, Library of Congress; restrictionist Democrat quoted in Morrison, *Democratic Politics*, 61. On latent northern antislavery as it pertained to the West, see Potter, *Impending Crisis*, 46, 48–49; Rush Welter, "The Frontier West as Image of American Society: Conservative Attitudes before the Civil War," *Mississippi Valley Historical Review* 46 (1960): 593–614; Welter, "The Frontier West at Image of American Society, 1776–1860," *Pacific Northwest Quarterly* 52 (1961): 1–6; and Henry E. Fritz, "Nationalistic Response to Frontier Expansion," *Mid-America* 51 (1969): 228, 232–33, 239.

35. *Congressional Globe*, 29th Cong., 2d sess., Appendix, 438, 315; first Chase quote in Frederick J. Blue, *Salmon P. Chase: A Life in Politics* (Kent, 1987), 51; Chase to Lewis Tappan, Mar. 18, 1847, Box 7, Salmon P. Chase Papers, Library of Congress.

36. Wright to John Dix, Jan. 19, 1847, John A. Dix Papers, Butler Library, Columbia University, New York; Leonard Marsh, *A Bake-Pan for the Dough Faces. By One of Them. . . . Try It* (Burlington, 1854), 45.

37. Garrison to Elihu Burritt, July 16, 1845, in William Lloyd Garrison, *The Letters of William Lloyd Garrison*, ed. Walter M. Merrill and Louis Ruchames, 8 vols. (Cambridge, Mass., 1971–81), 3:299, 301; Russel B. Nye, *William Lloyd Garrison and the Humanitarian Reformers* (Boston, 1955), 142; "Address to the Friends of Freedom and Emancipation in the United States," in George M. Fredrickson, ed., *William Lloyd Garrison* (Englewood Cliffs, 1968), 123; Garrison to the *Liberator*, Jan. 8, 1844, in Garrison, *Letters*, 3:245; Garrison to Samuel May, Dec. 2, 1848, ibid., 604. Garrison, of course, did not speak for all abolitionists. Some of them, like the free-soilers, saw the Constitution as basically antislavery. Still other abolitionists saw the document as neutral on the issue of slavery and thought abolition a moral, not a constitutional, question.

38. *Congressional Globe*, 29th Cong., 2d sess., 548, 466, 372; Erastus Dean Culver to Thurlow Weed, Dec. 19, 1846, Thurlow Weed Papers, Rush Rhees Library, University of Rochester, Rochester, N.Y. (first quotation). See also John McLean to William Cabell Rives, Feb. 27, 1847, Box 76, Rives Papers; Robert C. Winthrop Jr., *A Memoir of Robert C. Winthrop* (Boston, 1897), 62–63; and Wilson, *Space, Time, and Freedom*, 125.

39. Salmon P. Chase and Charles D. Cleveland, *Anti-Slavery Addresses of 1844 and 1845* (Philadelphia, 1867), 77, 79; "Marcellus" to the editor of the *American Citizen*, Apr. 4, 1845, Salmon P. Chase Papers, Outgoing Correspondence Folder, Historical Society of Pennsylvania, Philadelphia.

40. Chase and Cleveland, *Anti-Slavery Addresses*, 76, 17.

41. *Brooklyn Eagle*, Apr. 22, 1847, in Cleveland Rogers and John Black, eds., *The Gathering of the Forces*, 2 vols. (New York, 1970), 1:201, 202; Smith to John Thompson Mason, Nov. 18, 1846, Gerrit Smith Letterbook, Vol. 2, Gerrit Smith Papers, Syracuse University, Syracuse, N.Y.

42. Henry S. Wilde to Caleb Cushing, Nov. 9, 1847, Box 54, Caleb Cushing Papers, Library of Congress; *Congressional Globe*, 29th Cong., 2d sess., Appendix, 345. See also Benjamin B. French to Henry F. French, Nov. 1846, Box 2, Benjamin B. and Henry F. French Correspondence (typescript of originals in the Library of Congress), New Hampshire Historical Society, Concord, N.H.

43. Calhoun to Lewis S. Coryell, Nov. 7, 1846, in J. Franklin Jameson, ed., "Correspondence of John C. Calhoun," *Annual Report of the American Historical Association for the Year 1899*, 2 vols. (Washington, D.C., 1900), 2:710; *Congressional Globe*, 29th Cong., 2d sess., 187–88, 455.

44. J[ames] H. Hammond, *Two Letters on Slavery in the United States, Addressed to Thomas Clarkson, Esq.* (Columbia, 1845), 48.

45. *Congressional Globe*, 29th Cong., 2d sess., Appendix, 245, 137 (quotation).

46. Resolutions of the Virginia Legislature, Mar. 8, 1847, in Herman V. Ames, ed., *State Documents on Federal Relations*, no. 4, *Slavery and the Union, 1845–1861* (Philadel-

phia, 1906), 246; *Congressional Globe*, 29th Cong., 2d sess., Appendix, 163; *Mississippian* (Jackson), Apr. 16, 1847. Looking to a less manifest future, the Texas legislature resolved, "The 'Proviso' if submitted to, would prevent the slaveholding sates from enjoying the full benefits of any territory which may be hereafter acquired" (Joint Resolution of the Texas Legislature, Mar. 18, 1848, MSS 2, Governors' Papers, Ohio Historical Society).

47. Daniel quoted in Morrison, *Democratic Politics*, 65; Montgomery editor quoted in James Crawford King Jr., "'Content with Being': Nineteenth Century Southern Attitudes toward Economic Expansion" (Ph.D. diss., University of Alabama, 1985), 220; "Notes for Article on the Wilmot Proviso," Vol. 6, Franklin Harper Elmore Papers, Library of Congress; James Hamilton to Calhoun, Feb. 7, 1847, in Boucher and Brooks, eds., "Correspondence to Calhoun," 366–67.

48. *Congressional Globe*, 29th Cong., 2d sess., Appendix, 76–77. On African American slavery and white southerners, see Edmund S. Morgan, "Slavery and Freedom: The American Paradox," *Journal of American History* 59 (1972): 5–29.

49. *Congressional Globe*, 29th Cong., 2d sess., 361, 388; David Johnson to Calhoun, Oct. 26, 1847, Box 16, John C. Calhoun Papers, South Caroliniana Library, University of South Carolina, Columbia; "Remarks of General Waddy Thompson at the Wilmot Proviso Meeting Held at the Greenville Courthouse, South Carolina," published in *Daily National Intelligencer* (Washington, D.C.), Oct. 21, 1847.

50. *Congressional Globe*, 29th Cong., 2d sess., Appendix, 246, 112; Calhoun quoted in Morrison, *Democratic Politics*, 59–60. See also J. William Harris, "Last of the Classical Republicans: An Interpretation of John C. Calhoun," *Civil War History* 30 (1984): 262.

51. *Illinois State Register* (Springfield), Aug. 21, 1846; *Congressional Globe*, 29th Cong., 2d sess., Appendix, 113.

52. See J. Mills Thornton III, "Comment," in *The Civil Rights Movement in America*, ed. Charles W. Eagles (Jackson, 1986), 153.

53. *Congressional Globe*, 29th Cong., 2d sess., Appendix, 151; *Brooklyn Daily Eagle*, Sept. 1, 1847, in Rogers and Black, eds., *Gathering of Forces*, 1:211; *New Orleans Daily Picayune*, Jan. 14, 1848.

54. Polk, *Diary*, 2:305–6 (Jan. 4, 1847), 458–59 (Apr. 5, 1847); *Harrisburg Democratic Union*, Jan. 30, 1847.

55. Robert D. Buckley Jr., "A Democrat and Slavery: Robert Rantoul, Jr.," *Essex Institute Historical Collection* 110 (1974): 216–38; *Congressional Globe*, 29th Cong., 2d sess., 210, Appendix, 322–23.

56. Davis to Charles S. Searles, Sept. 19, 1847, in Jefferson Davis, *The Papers of Jefferson Davis*, ed. Haskell M. Monroe Jr., James T. McIntosh, and Lynda Lasswell Crist, 8 vols. (Baton Rouge, 1971–95), 3:225–26; *Mississippian*, Sept. 17, 1847; *Congressional Globe*, 29th Cong., 2d sess., 370.

57. *Congressional Globe*, 29th Cong., 2d sess., 517 (quotation), 555, 556, 573. The Senate vote was one slave-state senator and twenty free-state senators for the proviso, twenty-six slave- and five free-state against. In the House, seventy-nine slave-state representatives and twenty-three free-state representatives voted to remove the proviso, while one slave-state and ninety-five free-state representatives voted to keep it.

58. James G. Blaine, *Twenty Years of Congress: From Lincoln to Garfield; with a Review*

of the Events Which Led to the Political Revolution of 1860, 2 vols. (Norwich, 1884), 1:67; Calhoun to Thomas G. Clemson, July 8, 1847, in Jameson, ed., "Correspondence of Calhoun," 735.

Chapter Three

1. Thomas Wortham, *James Russell Lowell's Bigelow Papers* (DeKalb, 1977), 62–63. On the war, see K. Jack Bauer, *The Mexican War, 1846–1848* (New York, 1974), 32–253, 259–74, 297–301, 306, 323; David M. Pletcher, *The Diplomacy of Annexation: Texas, Oregon, and the Mexican War* (Columbia, 1973), 465–66, 481–83, 488–89, 494–98, 511–21, 530–32; Allan Nevins, *Ordeal of the Union*, 2 vols. (New York, 1947), 1:3–6; John D. P. Fuller, *The Movement for the Acquisition of All Mexico, 1846–1848* (Baltimore, 1936), 79–111; and Edward G. Bourne, "The Proposed Absorption of Mexico in 1847–48," *Annual Report of the American Historical Association for the Year 1899*, 2 vols. (Washington, D.C., 1902), 1:157–69.

2. James K. Polk, *The Diary of James K. Polk during his Presidency, 1845 to 1849*, ed. Milo M. Quaife, 4 vols. (Chicago, 1901), 3:189–90 (Oct. 12, 1847), 216–17 (Nov. 9, 1847), 229 (Nov. 23, 1847); James D. Richardson, comp., *A Compilation of the Messages and Papers of the Presidents, 1789–1897*, 10 vols. (Washington, D.C., 1896–99), 4:545.

3. Polk, *Diary*, 3:185 (Oct. 4, 1847); Trist to James Buchanan, Dec. 6, 1847, *Senate Executive Documents*, 30th Cong., 1st sess. (Serial 509), No. 52, 231–66; Pletcher, *Diplomacy*, 528–29, 538–39.

4. Kent to Daniel Webster, Oct. 13, 1847, in Daniel Webster, *The Papers of Daniel Webster*, Ser. 1, *Correspondence*, ed. Charles M. Wiltse and Harold D. Moser, 6 vols. (Hanover, 1974–84), 6:242; *Daily National Intelligencer* (Washington, D.C.), Sept. 14, 1847; *Congressional Globe*, 30th Cong., 1st sess., 61–62, 64, 93. See also Nevins, *Ordeal*, 1:13–19; and John H. Schroeder, *Mr. Polk's War: American Opposition and Dissent, 1846–1848* (Madison, 1973), 145, 154. Polk fumed that Trist's letter "was arrogant, impudent, and very insulting to his Government, and even personally offensive to his President." As for the writer, he was "destitute of honour and principle . . . a very base man" (Polk, *Diary*, 3:300–301 [Jan. 15, 1848]).

5. Polk, *Diary*, 3:323–24 (Feb. 2, 1848); Jesse S. Reeves, "The Treaty of Guadalupe Hidalgo," *American Historical Review* 10 (1904–5): 309–24; Charles I. Bevans, comp., *Treaties and Other International Agreements of the United States of America, 1776–1949*, 12 vols. (Concord, 1968–74), 9:791–806; Trist to Buchanan, Feb. 2, 1848, in William R. Manning, ed., *Diplomatic Correspondence of the United States: Inter-American Affairs, 1831–1860*, 12 vols. (Washington, D.C., 1932–39), 8:1059–60; Pletcher, *Diplomacy*, 549. Trist may have been an "impudent scoundrel," but he had a delicious sense of the ironic. Waxing eloquent over the choice of Guadalupe Hidalgo, Trist observed that the village was "a spot which, agreeably to the creed of this country, is the most sacred on earth, as being a scene of the miraculous appearance of the Virgin, for the purpose of declaring that Mexico was taken under her special protection" (quoted in Jesse S. Reeves, *American Diplomacy under Tyler and Polk* [Baltimore, 1907], 325–26).

6. Norman A. Graebner, *Empire on the Pacific: A Study in American Continental Expansion* (New York, 1955), 1; Polk, *Diary*, 3:345 (Feb. 19, 1848), 346–47 (Feb. 20, 1848);

Fuller, *Movement for Acquisition*, 145, 154. Polk's dilemma was known to others. See, for example, Sim Boyd to Norvin Green, Feb. 23, 1848, File 4, Norvin Green Papers, Filson Club, Louisville, Ky.; Daniel M. Berringer to John W. Ellis, Mar. 2, 1848, Box 1, Folder 3, John Willis Ellis Papers, Southern Historical Collection, University of North Carolina, Chapel Hill; David Outlaw to Emily B. Outlaw, Mar. 6, 1848, David Outlaw Papers, Southern Historical Collection.

7. Polk, *Diary*, 3:347–50 (Feb. 21, 1848).

8. Richardson, comp., *Messages and Papers of the Presidents*, 4:442; *Congressional Globe*, 29th Cong., 1st sess., 791–95, 796–804; Clayton and John Davis voted against the bill, Crittenden and William Upham voted "ay, except the preamble" (*Congressional Globe*, 29th Cong., 1st sess., 804).

9. *Congressional Globe*, 29th Cong., 2d sess., 481; McLean to John Teasdale, Apr. 6, 1847, Collection 39, Box 1, Folder 2, John M. McLean Papers, Ohio Historical Society, Columbus.

10. Daniel D. Barnard, "War with Mexico," *American Review* 3 (1846): 579; James Graham to William A. Graham, Jan. 10, 1847, in William A. Graham, *The Papers of William Alexander Graham*, ed. J. G. deRoulhac Hamilton and Max R. Williams, 7 vols. (Raleigh, 1957–84), 3:171–72; Webster to Fletcher Webster, May 20, 1846, Vol. 10, Daniel Webster Letterbooks, New Hampshire Historical Society, Concord, N.H.

11. Erastus Dean Culver to Thurlow Weed, June 3, 1846, Thurlow Weed Papers, Rush Rhees Library, University of Rochester, Rochester, N.Y.; *Congressional Globe*, 29th Cong., 2d sess., Appendix, 155; ibid., 29th Cong., 1st sess., Appendix, 763–67.

12. *Congressional Globe*, 29th Cong., 2d sess., Appendix, 104; ibid., 30th Cong., 1st sess., Appendix, 399; *Daily National Intelligencer*, Dec. 15, 1846.

13. *Congressional Globe*, 29th Cong., 2d sess., 60, 327. One Ohio newspaper provided its readers with a history lesson that bore on the war and its origins. "The Whigs of the United States are satisfied with their name, because, as in England, it truly represents the principles of the party. The name was borrowed from England, and was adopted in the revolution of '76. The Whigs then were the champions of Liberty, of Free Representative Government, of Equal Laws and Equal Taxation, and they were also for a written Constitution and a Government of Limited Powers. The Tories . . . were for trusting all power in the hands of the king and his ministers. After the Revolution they were for a strong government, throwing as much power into the hands of the chief Executive as possible. . . . The Tory principles of Mr. Polk and his coadjutors stand out in every act. It is POWER they are aiming at—POWER at the expense of the People, in contempt of the Constitution . . . and the power which seeks to *enslave*, becomes the object of attack and opposition of *Liberty*. No alternative will be left us. And then will be renewed in the fiercest form, the old struggles of *Whig* and *Tory* for Freedom and Free Government" (*Ohio State Journal* [Columbus], Dec. 23, 1846).

14. "California," *American Review* 3 (1846): 85–86; *Daily National Intelligencer*, May 13, 1848; Rives to Crittenden, Feb. 8, 1847, Crittenden to Rives, Feb. 28, 1847, Box 76, William Cabell Rives Papers, Library of Congress; *Congressional Globe*, 29th Cong., 2d sess., Appendix, 270, 437; Ernest N. Paolino, *The Foundations of the American Empire: William H. Seward and U.S. Foreign Policy* (Ithaca, 1973), 6–14; Thomas E. Schott, *Alexander H. Stephens of Georgia: A Biography* (Baton Rouge, 1988), 59–60, 68, 71; Graebner, *Empire on the Pacific*, 100–101, 159–61, 219–20, 224–26.

15. *Congressional Globe*, 29th Cong., 2d sess., Appendix, 228; Daniel Walker Howe, *The Political Culture of the American Whigs* (Chicago, 1979), 138, 141, 145–46.

16. Rives to David Campbell, Sept. 13, 1847, Campbell Family Papers, William R. Perkins Library, Duke University, Durham, N.C.; *Congressional Globe*, 29th Cong., 2d sess., 345; *Arkansas State Gazette* (Little Rock), June 1, 1846. The extent to which Whigs tended to extrapolate public lessons from personal behavior may be seen in the observation of a Pennsylvania Whig on the consequences of the war. "The spirit of conquests in a nation is identical with that of acquisition in an individual," he commented, "& like jealousy it grows on what it feeds—it is an appetite that has no surfeit" (William H. Morrell to Willie P. Mangum, Jan. 1, 1847, in Willie P. Mangum, *The Papers of Willie Person Mangum*, ed. Henry Thomas Shanks, 5 vols. [Raleigh, 1950–55], 5:1–2).

17. *Jonesborough* (Tenn.) *Whig*, June 10, 1846; *Daily National Intelligencer*, Dec. 15, 1846; *Congressional Globe*, 29th Cong., 2d sess., Appendix, 436.

18. David Campbell to William B. Campbell, Dec. 24, 1846, Campbell Family Papers; *Savannah Daily Republican*, Feb. 25, 1848; Professor M. Stuart to Daniel Webster, June 15, 1846, Vol. 11, Webster Papers; *Congressional Globe*, 29th Cong., 2d sess., Appendix, 353.

19. *Congressional Globe*, 29th Cong., 2d sess., Appendix, 301, 353; ibid., 30th Cong., 1st sess., 300.

20. *Congressional Globe*, 29th Cong., 2d sess., Appendix, 237.

21. Ibid., 236, 133; William H. Morrell to Willie P. Mangum, Jan. 1, 1847, in Mangum, *Papers*, 5:1–2; *Congressional Globe*, 30th Cong., 1st sess., Appendix, 300; David Outlaw to Emily Outlaw, Feb. 3, 1848, Outlaw Papers.

22. Webster quoted in Howe, *Political Culture*, 143; *Congressional Globe*, 29th Cong., 2d sess., Appendix, 436, 132.

23. *Congressional Globe*, 29th Cong., 2d sess., Appendix, 372; John H. Sanders to McLean, Dec. 29, 1846, Vol. 12, John McLean Papers, Library of Congress; John H. Clifford to Robert C. Winthrop, Jan. 7, 1847, Robert C. Winthrop Papers, Massachusetts Historical Society, Boston.

24. *Congressional Globe*, 29th Cong., 2d sess., Appendix, 365, 372; Robert C. Winthrop Jr., ed., *A Memoir of Robert C. Winthrop* (Boston, 1897), 63.

25. *Congressional Globe*, 29th Cong., 2d sess., 548.

26. Ibid., Appendix, 284; John L. Carey, *Slavery and the Wilmot Proviso; with Some Suggestions for a Compromise* (Baltimore, 1847), 18; *Ohio State Journal*, Jan. 13, 1847.

27. *Vicksburg* (Miss.) *Triweekly Whig*, Sept. 25, 1847; *Raleigh Standard* quoted in Marc W. Kruman, *Parties and Politics in North Carolina, 1836-1865* (Baton Rouge, 1983), 115.

28. *Congressional Globe*, 29th Cong., 2d sess., 330, 326. Alexander Stephens offered a similar resolution in the House.

29. Rives to Crittenden, Feb. 5, 1847, Vol. 10, John J. Crittenden Papers, Library of Congress; *Congressional Globe*, 29th Cong., 2d sess., Appendix, 61.

30. *Congressional Globe*, 29th Cong., 2d sess., 345, 338, Appendix, 61.

31. "Speech of Thomas Corwin," Feb. 11, 1847, Robert C. Schenck Papers (microfilm), University of Miami, Oxford, Ohio. See also Edgar Allen Holt, "Party Politics in Ohio, 1848–1850," *Ohio Archeological and Historical Publications* 38 (1929): 143–44.

32. Corwin quoted in Stephen E. Maizlish, *The Triumph of Sectionalism: The Transformation of Ohio Politics, 1844-1856* (Kent, 1983), 89; Corwin to Stevenson, Sept. 23, 1847, Box 1, Thomas B. Stevenson Papers, Cincinnati Historical Society, Cincinnati, Ohio. On the reaction to Corwin, see George C. Fogg to John L. Carlton, July 18, 1847, Box 1, Folder 1, George G. Fogg Papers, New Hampshire Historical Society, Concord, N.H.; Nevins, *Ordeal*, 1:11; Norman E. Tutorow, *Texas Annexation and the Mexican War: A Political Study of the Old Northwest* (Palo Alto, 1978), 177; Norman A. Graebner, "Thomas Corwin and the Election of 1848: A Study in Conservative Politics," *Journal of Southern History* 17 (1951): 164-65; and Holt, "Party Politics," 156-57.

33. *Sciotto Gazette* reprinted in *Ohio State Journal*, Aug. 18, 1847; *Congressional Globe*, 29th Cong., 2d sess., Appendix, 233. See also Hal W. Bochin, "Caleb B. Smith's Opposition of the Mexican War," *Indiana Magazine of History* 69 (1973): 95-114; and Joel H. Silbey, "The Slavery-Extension Controversy and Illinois Congressmen, 1846-50," *Illinois State Historical Society Journal* 58 (1965): 379, 389-93.

34. *Congressional Globe*, 29th Cong., 2d sess., 545, 555, 556. Twenty-eight Democrats voted against Berrien's resolutions, none for it. The Senate vote on the Wilmot Proviso showed fourteen northern Whigs for the amendment and ten—all from the South—against. Only Simon Cameron, Democratic senator from Pennsylvania, voted against the $3 million bill. In the House Stephens's no-territory resolution was defeated in a procedural vote, 76-88. No Whig opposed it (ibid., 240).

35. *Nashville Union* quoted in Fuller, *Movement for Acquisition*, 50; *Philadelphia Public Ledger*, May 18, 1847; "NEW TERRITORY versus NO TERRITORY," *United States Magazine and Democratic Review* 21 (1847): 291; Robert J. Walker to John W. Forney, June 27, 1847, Robert J. Walker Letterbook, Darlington Memorial Library, University of Pittsburgh, Pittsburgh, Pa.

36. Richardson, comp., *Messages and Papers of the Presidents*, 4:538, 544; *Congressional Globe*, 30th Cong., 1st sess., 321, 300, Appendix, 95.

37. *Congressional Globe*, 30th Cong., 1st sess., 484, Appendix, 316, 217; *Boston Courier*, Jan. 20, 1848.

38. *Senate Executive Documents*, 30th Cong., 1st sess. (Serial 509), No. 52, 4, 9; Daniel Berringer to James W. Ellis, Mar. 2, 1848, Box 1, Folder 3, Ellis Papers; *New York Daily Tribune*, Mar. 1, 1848.

39. *Senate Executive Documents*, 30th Cong., 1st sess. (Serial 509), No. 52, 18, 24, 86; Andrew S. Fulton to [David Campbell], Mar. 5, 1848, Campbell Family Papers. On the Whig dilemma, see Thomas B. Stevenson to Smith, Mar. 6, 1848, Vol. 1, Caleb B. Smith Papers, Library of Congress.

40. *Congressional Globe*, 29th Cong., 1st sess., 1217; Polk, *Diary*, 2:309 (Jan. 5, 1847), 335 (Jan. 16, 1847); Potter, *Impending Crisis*, 56-57; Milo Milton Quaife, *The Doctrine of Non-Intervention with Slavery in the Territories* (Chicago, 1910), 42-43.

41. Cass to Nicholson, Dec. 24, 1847, printed in *Washington Daily Union*, Dec. 30, 1847. See also Quaife, *Non-Intervention*, 51-59; Potter, *Impending Crisis*, 57-58; Allen Johnson, "Genesis of Popular Sovereignty," *Iowa Journal of History and Politics* 3 (1905): 3-19; and Willard Carl Klunder, "Lewis Cass and Slavery Expansion: 'The Father of Popular Sovereignty' and Ideological Infanticide," *Civil War History* 32 (1986): 293-98.

42. "Remarks by Robert C. Schenck . . . August 1, 1848, the Oregon Bill Being

Under Consideration," Schenck Papers (microfilm); *Congressional Globe*, 30th Cong., 1st sess., Appendix, 1047.

43. *Congressional Globe*, 30th Cong., 1st sess., 883, Appendix, 701; Stephens to the Editor of the *Federal Union*, Aug. 30, 1848, in Ulrich B. Phillips, ed., "The Correspondence of Robert Toombs, Alexander H. Stephens, and Howell Cobb," *Annual Report of the American Historical Association for the Year 1911*, 2 vols. (Washington, D.C., 1913), 2:118; *Congressional Globe*, 30th Cong., 1st sess., 1001, 883; *Vicksburg Triweekly Whig*, Aug. 29, 1848. For one southerner the choice was simple: "All freemen must feel that 'death is preferable to acknowledged inferiority' " (Jabez L. M. Curry to James H. Joiner, July 19, 1847, Ser. 1, Vol. 1, Jabez Lamar Monroe Curry Papers, Library of Congress).

44. J. White to McLean, July 17, 1848, Vol. 15, McLean Papers; David to Emily Outlaw, July 28, 1848, Outlaw Papers.

45. *Baltimore American and Commercial Daily Advertiser*, May 27, 1848; *Sciotto Gazette* (Chillicothe, Ohio), Oct. 25, 1848; *Columbus* (Ga.) *Enquirer*, Sept. 19, June 20, June 6, 1848; *Nashville Republican Banner*, July 31, Sept. 15, 1848; *Columbus Enquirer*, Oct. 24, 1848.

46. Philip Hone, *The Diary of Philip Hone, 1828-1851*, ed. Allan Nevins, 2 vols. (1927; rpt. New York, 1970), 2:856 (Nov. 7, 1848); David Davis to Julius Rockwell, July 6, 1848, Box 1, Rockwell-Walker Correspondence, New-York Historical Society, New York; Thomas Bragg to John W. Ellis, Nov. 13, 1847, Box 1, Folder 2, Ellis Papers; *Daily Missouri Republican* (St. Louis), July 7, 1848.

47. Clay to Stevenson, Aug. 14, 1848, Box 3, Thomas B. Stevenson Papers in the William H. Smith Collection [uncataloged], Indiana Historical Society, Indianapolis; Cabell quoted in Herbert Doherty Jr., "The Whigs of Florida, 1845-1851," *University of Florida Monographs: Social Sciences*, No. 1 (Gainesville, 1959), 22, 23.

48. *Savannah Daily Republican*, Apr. 8, 1847; Lt. John James Peck quoted in Richard F. Pourade, *The Sign of the Eagle* (San Diego, 1970), 157; Joseph Glover Baldwin to George B. Sanders, June 12, 1848, in Malcolm C. McMillan, ed., "Joseph Glover Baldwin Reports on the Whig National Convention of 1848," *Journal of Southern History* 25 (1959): 376-77; *Baltimore American and Commercial Daily Advertiser*, Oct. 28, 1848; Edward J. Harden to Howell Cobb, May 3, 1847, in Phillips, ed., "Correspondence of Toombs, Stephens, and Cobb," 87-88; *Columbia Enquirer*, Nov. 1, 1848; Thomas Dowling to John Dowling, Aug. 21, 1847, Box 1, John Dowling Papers, Indiana Historical Society, Indianapolis; James W. Osborne to William A. Graham, Oct. 11, 1848, in Graham, *Papers*, 3:246; Lincoln to Thomas S. Flournoy, Feb. 17, 1848, in Abraham Lincoln, *The Collected Works of Abraham Lincoln*, ed. Roy P. Basler, 8 vols. (New Brunswick, 1953-55), 1:452. See also Michael F. Holt, "Winding Roads to Recovery: The Whig Party from 1844 to 1848," in *Essays on American Antebellum Politics, 1840-1860*, ed. Stephen E. Maizlish and John J. Kushma (College Station, 1982), 161-62.

49. Clay supporter quoted in McMillan, ed., "Baldwin Reports," 373; *Columbia Enquirer*, Aug. 29, 1848; *Arkansas State Gazette*, Aug. 26 ("our fathers"), July 27 ("Cincinnatus," "Marcus Curtis"), 1848; *Sciotto Gazette*, Jan. 19, 1848; *Sangamo Journal* (Springfield, Ill.), June 15, 1848.

50. *Congressional Globe*, 30th Cong., 1st sess., Appendix, 825, 842; *Nashville Repub-*

lican Banner, Mar. 13, 1848; *Arkansas State Gazette*, Aug. 12, 1847; *Florida State Sentinel* (Tallahassee), July 13, 1848; Lawrence to William Cabell Rives, June 22, 1848, Box 78, Rives Papers. Perhaps the best analyst of Taylor's nomination observed:

> another pint thet influences the minds o' sober jedges
> Is that the Gin'ral hez n't gut tied hand an' foot with pledges;
> he hez n't told ye wut he is, an' so there aint no knowin'
> but wut he may turn out to be the best there is agoin'.

Wortham, *Bigelow Papers*, 136.

51. George McDuffie to James H. Hammond, Aug. 21, 1848, Vol. 15, James Henry Hammond Papers, Library of Congress; Winthrop, ed., *Memoir of Winthrop*, 86.

52. Fred Somkin, *Unquiet Eagle: Memory and Desire in the Idea of American Freedom, 1815–1860* (Ithaca, 1967), 151; *Arkansas State Gazette*, June 29, 1848; *Sciotto Gazette*, Dec. 15, 1847; Joseph P. Taylor to Zachary Taylor, Sept. 8, 1847, Zachary Taylor Papers, Library of Congress; Dallas C. Dickey, *Seargent S. Prentiss, Whig Orator of the Old South* (Baton Rouge, 1945), 329; *Congressional Globe*, 30th Cong., 1st sess., 898–99, Appendix, 943.

53. Baldwin to Sanders, June 12, 1848, in McMillan, ed., "Baldwin Reports," 374; "Speech of Seargent S. Prentiss to the Louisiana Whig State Convention," printed in *Weekly Raleigh Register and North Carolina Gazette*, Apr. 12, 1848; *Baltimore American and Commercial Daily Advertiser*, May 5, Sept. 4, 1848; *Weekly Raleigh Register and North Carolina Gazette*, June 14, 1848.

54. "Southron," in *Florida State Sentinel*, Aug. 8, 1848; *Arkansas State Gazette*, Aug. 12, 1847, Sept. 28, 1848; "Mass Meeting of Baltimore Citizens for Zachary Taylor," in *Weekly Raleigh Register and North Carolina Gazette*, Mar. 29, 1848.

55. *Sangamo Journal*, Sept. 30, Aug. 8, 1847.

56. Smith to John Sherman, Sept. 12, 1848, Box 1a, John Sherman Papers, Library of Congress; Thomas Ewing to Members of the Carthage Convention, June 30, 1848, Box 51, Thomas Ewing Papers, Library of Congress; Hunt to Thurlow Weed, Jan. 1, 1848, in Thurlow Weed Barnes, ed., *Memoir of Thurlow Weed* (Boston, 1884), 165; Gentry to [William B. Campbell], June 18, 1848, Campbell Family Papers.

57. *Congressional Globe*, 30th Cong., 1st sess., 1091, Appendix, 779, 780; *Vicksburg Triweekly Whig*, Aug. 3, 1848. On Whigs and governance, see Howe, *Political Culture*, 87–90.

58. *Congressional Globe*, 30th Cong., 1st sess., Appendix, 1041, 1019.

59. Ibid., 842, 846.

60. Ibid., 1091, 1076, 845, 665. The position that control over the territories was a responsibility of the federal legislature led southerners like Stephens to vote against the Clayton Compromise that would have left the decision on slavery restriction ultimately in the hands of the courts. See Stephens to General David L. Clinch, Oct. 7, 1848, Alexander H. Stephens Papers, Duke University, Durham, N.C.; Stephens to the Editor of the *Federal Union*, Aug. 30, 1848, in Phillips, ed., "Correspondence of Toombs, Stephens, and Cobb," 118.

61. *Congressional Globe*, 30th Cong., 1st sess., Appendix, 844, 695.

62. James Wilson Jr. to [Harley F. Smith], Sept. 20, 1848, Box 1, Folder 6, James Wilson Jr. Papers, New Hampshire Historical Society, Concord, N.H.; *Congressional*

Globe, 30th Cong., 1st sess., Appendix, 845–47; *Facts for Those Who Will Understand Them. Gen. Cass's Position on the Slavery Question Defined by Himself and His Friends. Also, a Brief Notice of Southern Objections to Millard Fillmore, the Whig Vice Presidential Candidate* (Washington, [1848]), 3–5; Rives to William B. Preston, May 27, 1848, Preston Family Papers, Virginia Historical Society, Richmond.

63. W. Dean Burnham, *Presidential Ballots, 1836-1892* (Baltimore, 1955), 35–42. Also see John Vollmer Mering, *The Whig Party in Missouri* (Columbia, 1967), 151–53; Brian G. Walton, "The Elections for the Thirtieth Congress and the Presidential Candidacy of Zachary Taylor," *Journal of Southern History* 35 (1969): 186–202; Randolph Campbell, "The Whig Party of Texas in the Elections of 1848 and 1852," *Southwestern Historical Quarterly* 73 (1969–70): 17–25; M. J. Heale, *The Presidential Quest: Candidates and Images in American Political Culture, 1787-1852* (New York, 1982), 124–27; Joel H. Silbey, *The American Political Nation, 1838-1893* (Stanford, 1991), 97–98, 113–14; Peter B. Knupfer, *The Union as It Is: Constitutional Unionism and Sectional Compromise, 1787-1861* (Chapel Hill, 1991), 175–76; James Brewer Stewart, "Abolitionists, Insurgents, and Third Parties: Sectionalism and Partisan Politics in Northern Whiggery, 1836–1844," in *Crusaders and Compromisers: Essays on the Relationship of the Antislavery Struggle to the Antebellum Party System*, ed. Alan M. Kraut (Westport, 1983), 37; Doherty, "The Whigs of Florida," 28; Kruman, *Parties and Politics*, 119–21; Maizlish, *Triumph of Sectionalism*, 117; and Holt, "Party Politics," 316.

64. Taylor to Jefferson Davis, July 10, 1848, Taylor Papers; *Illinois State Register* (Springfield), Nov. 17, 1848.

Chapter Four

1. Julian Dana, *Sutter of California: A Biography* (1934; rpt. Westport, 1974), 296–97; Hubert Howe Bancroft, *History of California*, 7 vols. (San Francisco, 1884–90), 6:32–38; Richard Dillon, *Fool's Gold: The Decline and Fall of Captain John Sutter of California* (New York, 1967), 277–79 (quotations at 278, 279).

2. Bancroft, *California*, 6:39n; *House Executive Documents*, 30th Cong., 2d sess., No. 1 (Serial 537), 58, 51–52, 55; Ralph P. Bieber, "California Gold Mania," *Mississippi Valley Historical Review* 35 (1948–49): 7–11.

3. Bancroft, *California*, 6:110–25; J. Peter Zollinger, *Sutter: The Man and His Empire* (1939; rpt. Gloucester, 1967), 282; Bieber, "Gold Mania," 16–28 (quotation at 21–22); Holman Hamilton, *Zachary Taylor: Soldier in the White House* (Indianapolis, 1951), 176–77.

4. *House Executive Documents*, 30th Cong., 2d sess., No. 1 (Serial 537), 65; James K. Polk, *The Diary of James K. Polk*, ed. Milo M. Quaife, 4 vols. (Chicago, 1910), 4:135–38 (Sept. 30, 1848), 146–50 (Oct. 7, 1848); Polk to George Bancroft, Jan. 5, 1849, George Bancroft Papers, Massachusetts Historical Society, Boston; James Buchanan to William H. Voorhies, Oct. 7, 1848, in James Buchanan, *The Works of James Buchanan, Comprising His Speeches, State Papers, and Private Correspondence*, ed. John Bassett Moore, 12 vols. (Philadelphia, 1908–11), 8:211–14 (quotations).

5. James D. Richardson, comp., *A Compilation of the Messages and Papers of the Presidents, 1789-1897*, 10 vols. (Washington, D.C., 1896–99), 4:639–42. As late as the fall,

Polk still favored the extension of the Missouri Compromise line as the preferred mode of settlement. In fact, it was not until a week before Congress met that Polk modified his message to emphasize noninterference as "the true course." Now, the Missouri line became merely a compromise to which Polk "was willing to accede" (Polk, *Diary*, 4:207 [Nov. 23, 1848]).

6. *Congressional Globe*, 30th Cong., 2d sess., 1, 21.

7. Polk, *Diary*, 2:231–32 (Dec. 12, 1848), 254–55 (Dec. 23, 1848), 308–9 (Jan. 25, 1849); Giddings and antislavery northerner quoted in Robert W. Johannsen, *Stephen A. Douglas* (New York, 1973), 242; "matter of little importance" quoted in William J. Cooper Jr., " 'The Only Door': The Territorial Issue, the Preston Bill, and the Southern Whigs," in *A Master's Due: Essays in Honor of David Herbert Donald*, ed. William J. Cooper Jr., Michael F. Holt, and John McCardell (Baton Rouge, 1985), 70; Hopkins Holsey to Howell Cobb, Feb. 13, 1849, in Ulrich B. Phillips, ed., "The Correspondence of Robert Toombs, Alexander H. Stephens, and Howell Cobb," *Annual Report of the American Historical Association for the Year 1911*, 2 vols. (Washington, D.C., 1913), 2:149. There were other Democrats who opposed Douglas's proposed settlement on more pragmatic grounds. Polk's vice-president, George M. Dallas, wanted Congress "to try hard to do nothing—leaving all unsettled questions and especially the free soil one, to harrass [*sic*] Genl. Taylor next winter." Similarly, Representative John L. Robinson advised Polk to withdraw his support from the statehood solution and "to throw the responsibility of settling the slavery question on General Taylor's administration." Polk was unpersuaded. The president believed that "if no Government be provided for *California*, there is imminent danger that rich and fine country will be lost to the Union." Dallas quoted in Cooper, " 'The Only Door,' " 67; Robinson quoted in Polk, *Diary*, 4:293 (Jan. 18, 1849); Polk to Lewis Cass, Dec. 15, 1848, Vol. 12, Lewis Cass Papers, William L. Clements Library, University of Michigan, Ann Arbor.

8. Caleb B. Smith to Thomas B. Stevenson, Jan. 4, 1849, Box 2, Thomas B. Stevenson Papers, Cincinnati Historical Society, Cincinnati, Ohio; Toombs to John J. Crittenden, [Jan. 3, 1849], in Phillips, ed., "Correspondence of Toombs, Stephens, and Cobb," 139. A Georgia Whig concluded that if the party members followed Calhoun's course, they "would be false to our party, false to ourselves, false to our country, and false to our creator." A satisfied New Orleans editor predicted, "The South will have none of Mr. Calhoun's desperate remedies." In the end, forty-six of forty-eight congressional Whigs turned their backs on Calhoun's united-front strategy (*Savannah Daily Republican*, Apr. 5, 1849; *New Orleans Bee* quoted in Arthur C. Cole, *The Whig Party in the South* [1914; rpt. Gloucester, 1962], 142). Calhoun was not all that popular with the Democracy either. Dallas thought him "teeming with revolution, or rather disunion." Southern Democrats, too, flagged in their support. Just forty-six of seventy-three southern Democrats signed Calhoun's address. Cobb, like Toombs, was concerned about the effect Calhoun's movement would have on the integrity of the two-party system. He wrote James Buchanan that the issue that he made with Calhoun (whom he called an "old reprobate") was his desire to organize a sectional, southern party to overthrow the Democratic Party in the South. "Such I have no doubt is his purpose, and for that object he prepared [the address] and *designedly* failed to make any distinction between Northern Democrats, Whigs and Abolitionists" (Dallas to Sophie Dallas, Dec. 16, 1848, Box 13, George M. Dallas Papers,

Historical Society of Pennsylvania, Philadelphia; Cobb to Buchanan, June 17, 1849, in Phillips, ed., "Correspondence of Toombs, Stephens, and Cobb," 164; David M. Potter, *The Impending Crisis, 1848-1861* [New York, 1976], 85, 86).

9. Alexander Stephens to [George W. Crawford], Dec. 27, 1848, in Phillips, ed., "Correspondence of Toombs, Stephens, and Cobb," 139; *Congressional Globe*, 30th Cong., 2d sess., 477, 478, 381; Cooper, "'The Only Door,'" 79. By the time Preston introduced his bill in the House, Douglas, at Polk's urging, had modified his own original proposal so as to create two states, California and New Mexico. Polk, *Diary*, 4:233 (Dec. 13, 1848), 236-37 (Dec. 14, 1848), 235-37 (Dec. 23, 1848), 251-56.

10. Crittenden to Clayton, Jan. 7, 1849, Vol. 2, John M. Clayton Papers, Library of Congress; *Congressional Globe*, 30th Cong., 2d sess., Appendix, 247, 213.

11. *Congressional Globe*, 30th Cong., 2d sess., Appendix, 121; Holsey to Howell Cobb, Feb. 13, 24, 1849, in Phillips, ed., "Correspondence of Toombs, Stephens, and Cobb," 150, 154.

12. *Congressional Globe*, 30th Cong. 2d sess., 607; Cooper, "'The Only Door,'" 84.

13. Ibid., 552, 553; Allan Nevins, *Ordeal of the Union*, 2 vols. (New York, 1947), 1:226; Henry S. Foote, *Letter from Hon. H. S. Foote, of Mississippi, to Hon. Henry A. Wise* (N.p., [1849]), 1. Douglas's bill was never voted on. John Bell, a Tennessee Whig, tried to amend Robert J. Walker's amendment to the civil and diplomatic appropriations bill to admit the entire cession as a state. Shouted down by Whigs and Democrats as inappropriate, it received all of four votes (*Congressional Globe*, 30th Cong., 2d sess., 560-66, 573).

14. Richardson, comp., *Messages and Papers of the Presidents*, 5:5, 6; snide assessment quoted in K. Jack Bauer, *Zachary Taylor: Soldier, Planter, Statesman of the Old Southwest* (Baton Rouge, 1985), 257; William H. Haywood to Francis Preston Blair Sr., May 16, 1849, Ser. 2, Box 12, Folder 10, Blair-Lee Papers, Firestone Library, Princeton University, Princeton, N.J.; Whig journalist quoted in Nevins, *Ordeal*, 1:244.

15. John H. Payne to William L. Marcy, Apr. 22, 1849, Vol. 16, William L. Marcy Papers, Library of Congress; Crittenden to Clayton, Apr. 11, 1849, Vol. 4, Clayton Papers.

16. Hamilton, *Taylor*, 178; Bauer, *Taylor*, 291; Edward M. Steel Jr., *T. Butler King of Georgia* (Athens, 1964), 71-73.

17. Clayton quoted in Steel, *King*, 72; King to Anna M. King, June 28, 1849, Ser. A, Box 5, Thomas Butler King Papers, Southern Historical Collection, University of North Carolina, Chapel Hill; King to Clayton, June 20, 1849, Vol. 5, Clayton Papers; Bancroft, *California*, 6:281-84, 290-302.

18. Bauer, *Taylor*, 292-94; William Campbell Binkley, "The Question of Texan Jurisdiction in New Mexico under the United States, 1848-1850," *Southwestern Historical Quarterly* 26 (1920-21): 13-17; Robert W. Larson, *New Mexico's Quest for Statehood, 1846-1912* (Albuquerque, 1968), 14-15, 18-19; Loomis Morton Ganaway, *New Mexico and the Sectional Controversy, 1846-1861* (1944; rpt. Philadelphia, 1976), 26; Thomas S. Edrington, "Military Influence on the Texas–New Mexico Boundary Settlement," *New Mexico Historical Review* 59 (1987): 381.

19. Nevins, *Ordeal*, 1:252n; northern Whig quoted in Holman Hamilton, *Prologue to Conflict: The Crisis and Compromise of 1850* (Lexington, 1964), 41; *Congressional Globe*, 31st Cong., 1st sess., 66-67.

20. Richardson, comp., *Messages and Papers of the Presidents*, 5:19 (quotation), 27–29.

21. Winthrop to John H. Clifford, Feb. 10, 1850, Robert C. Winthrop Papers, Massachusetts Historical Society, Boston; Colfax to William H. Seward, Mar. 26, 1850, Folder 1290, William Henry Seward Papers, Rush Rhees Library, University of Rochester, Rochester, N.Y.; Corwin to James A. Briggs, Mar. 20, 1850, Vertical File Manuscripts (VFM) No. 1397, Ohio Historical Society, Columbus. For southern reactions see, for example, William Campbell to David Campbell, Jan. 9, 1850, Campbell Family Papers, William R. Perkins Library, Duke University, Durham, N.C.; James Graham to William A. Graham, Apr. 21, 1850, in William A. Graham, *The Papers of William Alexander Graham*, ed. J. G. de Roulhac Hamilton and Max R. Williams, 7 vols. (Raleigh, 1957–84), 3:320–21; *New Orleans Daily Picayune*, Dec. 8, 1849; and *Vicksburg* (Miss.) *Triweekly Whig*, Jan. 16, 1850.

22. George N. Briggs to Horace Mann, Mar. 22, 1850, Horace Mann Papers, Massachusetts Historical Society, Boston; *Congressional Globe*, 31st Cong., 1st sess., Appendix, 454, 880; Julius Rockwell to David Davis, Jan. 26, 1850, Box 4, Folder 27, David Davis Papers, Chicago Historical Society, Chicago, Ill. (copies of originals held at the Illinois State Historical Library). See also Colfax to Caleb B. Smith, Feb. 18, 1850, Vol. 8, Caleb B. Smith Papers, Library of Congress; and *Address and Resolutions, Adopted at the Whig State Convention, Worcester, October 3, 1849, Together with the Speeches of Hon. John Davis, George S. Hilliard, Esq., Hon. Josiah Quincy, Jr., Hon. S. G. Goodrich, and Hon. Linus Child* (Boston, 1849), 3, 8.

23. Toombs quoted in Robert C. Winthrop Jr., ed., *A Memoir of Robert C. Winthrop* (Boston, 1897), 100; *Congressional Globe*, 31st Cong., 1st sess., 201, 203; David Outlaw to Emily Outlaw, May 31, 1850, David Outlaw Papers, Box 1, Folder 9, Southern Historical Collection, University of North Carolina, Chapel Hill.

24. Yulee to John C. Calhoun, July 10, 1849, in Chauncey S. Boucher and Robert P. Brooks, eds., "Correspondence Addressed to John C. Calhoun, 1837–1849," *Annual Report of the American Historical Association for the Year 1929* (Washington, D.C., 1930), 515; Calhoun to James H. Hammond, Jan. 4, 1850, in J. Franklin Jameson, ed., "Correspondence of John C. Calhoun," *Annual Report of the American Historical Association for the Year 1899*, 2 vols. (Washington, D.C., 1900), 2:779; *Floridian and Journal* (Tallahassee), Feb. 9, 1850.

25. Winthrop to Nathan Appleton, Jan. 6, 1850, Winthrop Papers; *Congressional Globe*, 31st Cong., 1st sess., 207, 205; John F. Henry to David Davis, Jan. 22, 1850, Ser. I, Folder A-16, David Davis Papers, Illinois State Historical Library, Springfield, Ill.; "calm, collected" quoted in George Rawlings Poage, *Henry Clay and the Whig Party* (1936; rpt. Gloucester, 1965), 205; "New England farmer" quoted in Nevins, *Ordeal*, 1:260.

26. *Congressional Globe*, 31st Cong., 1st sess., 244–49, 251, 252.

27. Hugh O'Neal to Henry Smith Lane, Mar. 7, 1850, Box 3, Henry Smith Lane Papers, Indiana Historical Society, Indianapolis; Outlaw to Emily Outlaw, Apr. 20, 1850, Box 1, Folder 8, Outlaw Papers; Everett to Winthrop, Feb. 1, 1850, Winthrop Papers; *Columbus* (Ga.) *Enquirer*, Feb. 5, 1850.

28. *Congressional Globe*, 31st Cong., 1st sess., Appendix, 229, 525, 882; Amos Tuck to John Gorham Palfrey, Apr. 13, 1850, Folder 925, Palfrey Family Papers, Houghton Library, Harvard University, Cambridge, Mass.

29. *Congressional Globe*, 31st Cong., 1st sess., Appendix, 885, 306, 142, 181; *Pennsylvania Telegraph* (Harrisburg), Apr. 18, 1849; Daniel Goodloe, *The South and the North: Being a Reply to a Lecture on the North and the South, by Ellwood Fisher, Delivered before the Young Men's Mercantile Library Association of Cincinnati, January 16, 1849. By a Carolinian* (Washington, D.C., 1849), 5.

30. *Keystone* (Harrisburg, Pa.), Dec. 11, 1849; Goodloe, *South and North*, 27; *Congressional Globe*, 31st Cong., 1st sess., Appendix, 518, 142, 609; George W. Julian, *Speeches on Political Questions, 1850-1868* (New York, 1872), 68; A. G. Zabriskie to Hamilton Fish, Dec. 6, 1851, Box 339, Hamilton Fish Papers, Library of Congress; *Address of the Free Soil Association of the District of Columbia to the People of the United States, together with a Memorial to Congress, of 1060 Inhabitants of the District of Columbia, Praying for the Gradual Abolition of Slavery* (Washington, D.C., 1849), 3; John M. Read, *Speech of Hon. John M. Read, at the Democratic Town Meeting in Favor of the Union and California, held in the Hall of the Chinese Museum, on Wednesday the 13th March, 1850* ([Philadelphia, 1850]), 11.

31. *Congressional Globe*, 31st Cong., 1st sess., Appendix, 231; Montgomery Blair et al., *Address to the Democracy of Missouri* ([St. Louis, 1850]), 11-12; William R. Watson, *The Great American Question* (Providence, 1848), 15-16; *American Farmer* n.s., 3 (1847): 116.

32. "Remarks on the Resolutions and Manifesto of the Southern Caucus," *American Review* 15 (1849): 226; Julian, *Speeches*, 67-68; *Congressional Globe*, 31st Cong., 1st sess., Appendix, 609, 641, 694; Blair et al., *Address*, 12-13, 4. A disillusioned Ohio Democrat wailed, "We labored long and faithfully to separate the Government from the monopoly and monied interests of the North, and ultimately succeeded—succeeded, too, mainly by the aid of southern statesmen, who would now claim for the slave interest, what they so manfully struggled against when the Bank of the United States, with all its hired minions, was in the field" (*Congressional Globe*, 31st Cong., 1st sess., Appendix, 663).

33. *Congressional Globe*, 31st Cong., 1st sess., Appendix, 511, 255, 564; "Speech at Charleston, Massachusetts, August 27, 1849," Box 31, Salmon P. Chase Papers, Library of Congress.

34. *Congressional Globe*, 31st Cong., 1st sess., Appendix, 754, 641, 512; "Speech at Charleston," Box 31, Chase Papers; John Parker Hale to John G. Palfrey, Dec. 10, 1849, Folder 394, Palfrey Papers.

35. *Congressional Globe*, 31st Cong., 1st sess., Appendix, 515; "cosmopolitan habits" quoted in Richard H. Sewell, *Ballots for Freedom: Antislavery Politics in the United States, 1837-1860* (New York, 1976), 192; William Kephart to Chase, Mar. 27, 1851, Box 9, Chase Papers; Adam Klippel to Chase, Sept. 14, 1849, in S. H. Dodson, comp., "Diary and Correspondence of Salmon P. Chase," *Annual Report of the American Historical Association for the Year 1902*, 2 vols. (Washington, D.C., 1903), 2:473-74; Chase to E. S. Hamlin, Jan. 15, 1851, Box 9, Chase Papers; J. W. Schuckers, *The Life and Public Services of Salmon Portland Chase, United States Senator and Governor of Ohio; Secretary of the Treasury, and Chief Justice of the United States* (New York, 1874), 116.

36. *Congressional Globe*, 31st Cong., 1st sess., Appendix, 511, 565, 512, 595; Colfax to Caleb B. Smith, Feb. 18, 1850, Vol. 8, Smith Papers; "Speech at Charleston," Chase Papers.

37. *Congressional Globe*, 31st Cong., 1st sess., Appendix, 254, 178, 359, 304; Sackett

and Bingham quoted in Major L. Wilson, *Space, Time, and Freedom: The Quest for Nationality and the Irrepressible Conflict, 1815–1861* (Westport, 1974), 166, 161.

38. *Congressional Globe*, 31st Cong., 1st sess., 246, Appendix, 778, 708; John Y. Mason to Charles Mason, May 8, 1850, Section 24, Box 10, Folder 5, Mason Family Papers, Virginia Historical Society, Richmond.

39. Benjamin C. Yancey to [?], Apr. 20, 1850 [draft], Box 2, Benjamin C. Yancey Papers, Southern Historical Collection, University of North Carolina, Chapel Hill; *Congressional Globe*, 31st Cong., 1st sess., Appendix, 1167, 949; Mirabeau Bonaparte Lamar, *Gen. Mirabeau B. Lamar's Letter to the People of Georgia* (N.p., [1850]), 7.

40. *Congressional Globe*, 31st Cong., 1st sess., Appendix, 947, 948, 648, 467–68.

41. Ibid., 394, 426, 704, 241. Other discussions of slavery and white equality include [James Henry Hammond], *The North and the South: A Review of the Lecture on the Same Subject, Delivered by Mr. Elwood Fisher, before the Young Men's Mercantile Association of Cincinnati, Ohio* (Charleston, 1849), 8, 25; and [Augustus Baldwin Longstreet], *A Voice from the South: Comprising Letters from Georgia to Massachusetts, and to the Southern States. With an Appendix containing an Article from the Charleston Mercury on the Wilmot Proviso* (Baltimore, 1847), 48–53.

42. *Congressional Globe*, 31st Cong., 1st sess., Appendix, 425, 686, 947, 394; Joseph Finklin to William L. Marcy, Feb. 19, 1851, Vol. 19, Marcy Papers; Colquhoun to John Y. Mason, May 10, 1851, Section 24, Box 6, Mason Family Papers.

43. James K. Paulding to Robert J. Dillon et al., Mar. 14, 1850, in James Kirke Paulding, *The Letters of James Kirke Paulding*, ed. Ralph M. Aderman (Madison, 1962), 511; Davis to Samuel A. Cartwright, June 10, 1849, Davis to Malcolm D. Haynes, Aug. 18, 1849, in Jefferson Davis, *The Papers of Jefferson Davis*, ed. Haskell M. Monroe Jr., James T. McIntosh, and Lynda Lasswell Crist, 8 vols. (Baton Rouge, 1971–95), 4:27, 30; James B. Thornton to Daniel Webster, Apr. 28, 1850, Vol. 9, Daniel Webster Papers, Library of Congress; *Congressional Globe*, 31st Cong., 1st sess., Appendix, 1065, 1252, 545.

44. Davis to Haynes, Aug. 18, 1849, in Davis, *Papers*, 4:41; Yancey to [?], Mar. 20, 1850 [draft], Box 2, Folder 15, Yancey Papers; Berrien to Charles J. Jenkins, Jan. 7, 1850, Box 2, John MacPherson Berrien Papers, Southern Historical Collection, University of North Carolina, Chapel Hill; *Congressional Globe*, 31st Cong., 1st sess., Appendix, 947. See also J. Mills Thornton III, *Politics and Power in a Slave Society: Alabama, 1800–1860* (Baton Rouge, 1978), 213–18.

45. "Speech of W. L. Sharkey, President of the Southern States' Convention, October 6, 1849," printed in *Mississippian* (Jackson), Oct. 12, 1849; *Congressional Globe*, 31st Cong., 1st sess., Appendix, 363, 703; Thomas L. Clingman, *Letter of T. L. Clingman* (Washington, D.C., [1850]), 2; Lowndes to King, June 6, 1850, John A. King Papers, New-York Historical Society, New York.

46. *Congressional Globe*, 31st Cong., 1st sess., 531, Appendix, 702, 378, 430, 1084, 1083.

47. Potter, *Impending Crisis*, 97–108; Michael F. Holt, *The Political Crisis of the 1850s* (New York, 1978), 76–85.

48. Marcy Diary, Nov. 8, 1849, Vol. 85, Marcy Papers; *Congressional Globe*, 31st Cong., 1st sess., Appendix, 837.

49. Brackenridge to Crittenden, Jan. 11, 1849, Vol. 13, Crittenden Papers; *Congressional Globe*, 31st Cong., 1st sess., Appendix, 320, 840, 663, 302.

50. "Popular Sovereignty and States Rights," *United States Magazine and Democratic Review* 25 (1849): 3; *Congressional Globe*, 31st Cong., 1st sess., 841, 560.

51. "Popular Sovereignty and States Rights," 4; *Pittsburgh Morning Post*, Oct. 2, 1849. See also Johannsen, *Douglas*, 240, 249, 256.

52. *Congressional Globe*, 31st Cong., 1st sess., Appendix, 663, 841, 424, 302, 841.

53. "Speech of the Hon. D. S. Dickinson at the Great Public Dinner, in Honor of Him, at Tammany Hall, June 17, 1850," *United States Magazine and Democratic Review* 27 (1850): 112; *Congressional Globe*, 31st Cong., 1st sess., Appendix, 560, 301, 663.

54. *Congressional Globe*, 31st Cong., 1st sess., Appendix, 841, 675, 841; Bancroft quoted in John Ashworth, *'Agrarians' and 'Aristocrats': Party Political Ideology in the United States, 1837-1846* (London, 1983), 10; *Detroit Free Press*, Feb. 4, 1850; *Congressional Globe*, 31st Cong., 1st sess., Appendix, 841.

55. Hiram Gray to Marcy, Aug. 6, 1849, Vol. 16, Marcy Papers; *Congressional Globe*, 31st Cong., 1st sess., Appendix, 65.

56. *Keystone*, May 8, 1849; Read, *Speech in Favor of the Union*, 11. See also Bruce Collins, "The Ideology of Antebellum Northern Democrats," *Journal of American Studies* 11 (1977): 117–18.

57. *Congressional Globe*, 31st Cong., 1st sess., 402, Appendix, 154.

58. Johannsen, *Douglas*, 294–98; Hamilton, *Prologue to Conflict*, 102–3, 144–46; Holt, *Crisis of the 1850s*, 85–86; Potter, *Impending Crisis*, 107–8; F[rank] H. Hodder, "The Authorship of the Compromise of 1850," *Mississippi Valley Historical Review* 22 (1936): 525–36; Robert R. Russel, "What Was the Compromise of 1850?," *Journal of Southern History* 22 (1956): 292–309. Speaking for many, Pierre Soulé of Louisiana commented on the popular sovereignty provision of the territorial bills: "We all know that we do not understand this section alike. We know that its import in different minds amounts to absolute antagonism. If we are not deceiving one another, we are deceiving our constituents" (quoted in Potter, *Impending Crisis*, 117n).

59. Robert J. Rayback, *Millard Fillmore: Biography of a President* (Buffalo, 1959), 224–27; Potter, *Impending Crisis*, 108–12; Hamilton, *Prologue to Conflict*, 131–42, 156–61; George D. Harmon, "Douglas and the Compromise of 1850," *Illinois State Historical Society Journal* 21 (1929): 453–99; Holman Hamilton, "Democratic Senate Leadership and the Compromise of 1850," *Mississippi Valley Historical Review* 41 (1954): 403–18; Don E. Fehrenbacher, *The South and Three Sectional Crises: Friends, Foes, and Reforms* (Baton Rouge, 1980), 43. One of the defeated who was not silent was Salmon P. Chase, who growled, "The question of slavery in the territories has been avoided. It has not been settled" (quoted in Potter, *Impending Crisis*, 116).

60. Potter, *Impending Crisis*, 112–14, 116 (Douglas and Toombs quotes); Holt, *Crisis of the 1850s*, 87–88; Hamilton, *Prologue to Conflict*, 140–41, 143–44, 161–64. In the Senate eleven northern Democrats and thirteen southern Democrats voted for the Utah bill (July 31, 1850); they were joined by eight southern Whigs. No northern Whig voted for it; three northern Democrats opposed, and five southern Democrats did not vote. In the House thirty northern Democrats and thirty-two southern Democrats voted for the Utah bill (September 7, 1850); they were joined by twenty-two

southern Whigs. Ten northern Whigs voted for it, forty-two against. Thirteen north-ern Democrats, fourteen southern Democrats, and two southern Whigs opposed it. On Texas (August 9), northern Democrats in the Senate voted eleven to two in favor, the southern Democrats were split, six to ten against. On New Mexico (August 15), Senate party unity returned with ten northern Democrats being joined by nine south-ern Democrats in support. One northern Whig voted for it, as did seven southern Whigs. Three northern Democrats voted nay, no southern Democrat voted against (although nine did not vote), no southern Whig opposed (but five abstained). The Texas and New Mexico bills were joined in a "Little Omnibus" in the House. Here the Democratic Party was split, fifty-eight yeas to forty-one nays (northern Democrats: thirty-two yeas, thirteen nays, and four abstentions; southern Democrats: twenty-six yeas, twenty-eight nays, and three abstentions) as were the Whigs, forty-eight yeas to forty-six nays (northern Whigs: twenty-three yeas, forty-four nays, and seven absten-tions; southern Whigs: twenty-five yeas, two nays, and two abstentions). If Douglas was troubled by the split in his own party, he was undoubtedly cheered by the issue that he thus made with northern Whigs with regard to territorial organization and the voting pattern of southern Whigs in both houses. Parenthetically, California split the Democratic Party in the Senate (northern Democrats: fifteen yeas and no nays; southern Democrats: two yeas and fourteen nays) and the House (northern Demo-crats: forty-six yeas, no nays, and three abstentions; southern Democrats: ten yeas, forty-four nays, and three abstentions). Given the position of the sections on this issue as far back as the Douglas-Preston initiatives in the Thirtieth Congress, this division was not surprising; looking ahead to Kansas and remembering the various positions, it was, however, ominous. Statistics gleaned from roll call tabulations in Hamilton, *Prologue to Conflict*, 191–200; and Mark J. Stegmaier, "The U.S. Senate in the Sectional Crisis, 1846–1861: A Roll-Call Voting Analysis" (Ph.D. diss., Univer-sity of California, Santa Barbara, 1975), chap. 5.

61. *Illinois State Register* (Springfield), Sept. 13, 1850; Marcy Diary, May 13, 1851, Vol. 85, Marcy Papers; Douglas to Francis B. Cutting et al., May 3, 1851, in Stephen A. Douglas, *The Letters of Stephen A. Douglas*, ed. Robert W. Johannsen (Urbana, 1961), 217; Arkansas Democrat quoted in Nevins, *Ordeal*, 2:7n.

Chapter Five

1. Benjamin F. Pierce to Jane Pierce, June 11, 1852, Franklin Pierce Papers, New Hampshire Historical Society, Concord; W. Dean Burnham, *Presidential Ballots, 1836–1892* (Baltimore, 1955), 47–48.

2. Reports of *Boston Courier*, *Boston Post*, and *New York Herald* reprinted in *Washing-ton Daily Globe*, Jan. 9, 11, 1853.

3. Allan Nevins, *Ordeal of the Union*, 2 vols. (New York, 1947), 2:45; Roy Franklin Nichols, *Franklin Pierce: Young Hickory of the Granite Hills* (Philadelphia, 1958), 203, 224–26, 234–36; Lary Gara, *The Presidency of Franklin Pierce* (Lawrence, 1991), 32, 47–49.

4. T. L. Willis to Daniel M. Barringer, Oct. 7, 1850, Box 2, Folder 19, Daniel M. Barringer Papers, Southern Historical Collection, University of North Carolina,

Chapel Hill; William A. Graham to James Graham, Jan. 6, 1851, in William A. Graham, *The Papers of William Alexander Graham*, ed. J. G. deRoulhac Hamilton and Max R. Williams, 7 vols. (Raleigh, 1957–84), 4:3.

5. Marcy Diary, Oct. 1, 1850, Vol. 85, William L. Marcy Papers, Library of Congress; "Draft of a Statement by William L. Marcy on his Position on the Compromise Measures of 1850," [Mar. 29, 1852], Vol. 24, ibid.

6. James D. Richardson, comp., *A Compilation of the Messages and Papers of the Presidents, 1789-1897*, 10 vols. (Washington, D.C., 1896–99), 5:93; "to walk away" quoted in Michael F. Holt, *The Political Crisis of the 1850s* (New York, 1978), 96; Horace Mann to Mary Tyler Mann, Aug. 18, 1850, Horace Mann Papers, Massachusetts Historical Society, Boston; Hamilton Fish to Henry J. Raymond, Feb. 6, 1851, Box 339, Hamilton Fish Papers, Library of Congress.

7. Vermont free-soiler quoted in Richard H. Sewell, *Ballots for Freedom: Antislavery Politics in the United States, 1837-1860* (New York, 1976), 232; Mann to Samuel Downer, Dec. 22, 1850, Mann Papers.

8. Edward Everett to Charles Sumner, Dec. 6, 1850, Charles Sumner Papers, Houghton Library, Harvard University, Cambridge, Mass.; A. G. Zabriskie to Hamilton Fish, Dec. 6, 1851, Box 339, Fish Papers; Philip Hone, *The Diary of Philip Hone, 1828-1851*, ed. Allan Nevins, 2 vols. (1927; rpt. New York, 1970), 2:910 (Dec. 31, 1850); Daniel Webster, *An Address Delivered before the New York Historical Society, February 23, 1852, by Daniel Webster* (New York, 1852), 49, 48; William Hooper to William Schouler, [Dec. 1850], William Schouler Papers, Massachusetts Historical Society, Boston.

9. Rives to Joseph Gales, Sept. 30, 1850, Box 81, William Cabell Rives Papers, Library of Congress. See also Arthur C. Cole, *The Whig Party in the South* (1914; rpt. Gloucester, 1962), 173, 195; and J. Mills Thornton III, *Politics and Power in a Slave Society: Alabama, 1800-1860* (Baton Rouge, 1978), 186–87.

10. Toombs to Absalom H. Chappell and others, Feb. 15, 1851, in Ulrich B. Phillips, ed., "The Correspondence of Robert Toombs, Alexander H. Stephens, and Howell Cobb," *Annual Report of the American Historical Association for the Year 1911*, 2 vols. (Washington, D.C., 1913), 2:228; "Speech of Henry W. Miller, Esq. at Oxford, Nov. 5th, 1850 in Reply to the Hon. A. W. Venable," printed in *Weekly Raleigh Register and North Carolina Gazette*, Nov. 27, 1850.

11. Thornton, *Politics and Power*, 187; William A. Graham to James Graham, Jan. 6, 1851, in Graham, *Papers*, 4:3–4; Stephens to Linton Stephens, Dec. 10, 1851, in Phillips, ed., "Correspondence of Toombs, Stephens, and Cobb," 273.

12. Richard K. Meade to Andrew Jackson Donelson, May 7, 1851, Vol. 16, Andrew Jackson Donelson Papers, Library of Congress; John R. Tucker to Moscoe Garnett, Dec. 5, 1850, Garnett-Mercer-Hunter Papers, Library of Virginia, Richmond; "Speech of Hon. Albert Gallatin Brown Delivered at Elwood Springs . . . on the 2d Day of November, 1850," printed in *Mississippian* (Jackson), Nov. 15, 1850.

13. Benjamin F. Perry Journal, Sept. 14, 1850, Benjamin F. Perry Papers, Southern Historical Collection, University of North Carolina, Chapel Hill; Langdon Cheves, *Speech of Hon. Langdon Cheves, in the Southern Convention, at Nashville, Tennessee, November 14, 1850* ([Nashville], 1850), 4; Jefferson Davis, "Speech at Fayette, July 11, 1851," in Jefferson Davis, *The Papers of Jefferson Davis*, ed. Haskell M. Monroe Jr., James T.

McIntosh, and Lynda Lasswell Crist, 8 vols. (Baton Rouge, 1971–95), 4:203; Tucker to Garnett, Dec. 5, 1850, Garnett-Mercer-Hunter Papers. See also Robert R. Russel, "What Was the Compromise of 1850?," *Journal of Southern History* 22 (1956): 292–309; and Don E. Fehrenbacher, *The South and Three Sectional Crises: Friends, Foes, and Reforms* (Baton Rouge, 1980), 43.

14. E. F. Gurney to Oren Bryant, Nov. 22, 1850, Vertical File Manuscript (VFM) 755, Ohio Historical Society, Columbus; Cobb to Absalom H. Chappell and others, Feb. 7, 1851, in Phillips, ed., "Correspondence of Toombs, Stephens, and Cobb," 225; Buchanan to Andrew Jackson Donelson, Mar. 20, 1851, Vol. 16, Donelson Papers.

15. *Arkansas State Gazette and Democrat* (Little Rock), Oct. 3, 1851. For a more detailed account of López and administration policy, see Michael A. Morrison, "The Eclipse of Manifest Destiny: The Ideology of American Expansion, 1844–1860" (Ph.D. diss., University of Michigan, 1989), 203–7.

16. *Knoxville* (Tenn.) *Whig*, June 1, 1850; *Philadelphia Public Ledger*, Apr. 28, 1851, May 27, 1850.

17. *Ohio Statesman* quoted in Philip Foner, *A History of Cuba and Its Relations with the United States*, 2 vols. (New York, 1962–63), 2:39; *Columbus* (Ga.) *Enquirer*, June 4, 1850. See also John Higham, *From Boundlessness to Consolidation: The Transformation of American Culture, 1848–1860* (Ann Arbor, 1969), 15–19; and Rush Welter, *The Mind of America, 1820–1860* (New York, 1975), 54–61.

18. "Antiquated foundations" quoted in Higham, *Boundlessness to Consolidation*, 18; George Ticknor to George S. Hillard, July 17, 1848, in George Ticknor, *Life, Letters, and Journals of George Ticknor*, ed. George S. Hillard, 2 vols. (London, 1876), 2:234; James K. Paulding to Martin Van Buren, Apr. 16, 1848, in James Kirke Paulding, *The Letters of James Kirke Paulding*, ed. Ralph M. Aderman (Madison, 1962), 479.

19. *Congressional Globe*, 32d Cong., 1st sess., Appendix, 441, 318.

20. Joseph Hall to John Y. Mason, Apr. 26, 1852, Section 24, Box 8, Mason Family Papers, Virginia Historical Society, Richmond; *Columbus Enquirer*, May 4, 1852; *Savannah Daily Republican*, Feb. 10, 1852.

21. *Knoxville Whig*, Jan. 31, 1852; *Congressional Globe*, 32d Cong., 1st sess., 22; "Magic chain" quoted in Higham, *Boundlessness to Consolidation*, 17.

22. *Congressional Globe*, 32d Cong., 1st sess., Appendix, 68.

23. John C. Darby to J. Warren Grigsby, Feb. 14, 1852, File 258, John Warren Grigsby Papers, Filson Club, Louisville, Ky.; Holt, *Political Crisis*, 97–98; Thornton, *Politics and Power*, 225, 262–66; David M. Potter, *The Impending Crisis, 1848-1861* (New York, 1976), 126–30; Avery O. Craven, *The Growth of Southern Nationalism, 1848-1861* (Baton Rouge, 1953), 120–21; Roy Franklin Nichols, "The Democratic Machine, 1850–1854," *Columbia University Studies in History, Economics and Public Law* 111, no. 248 (1923), 94.

24. *Congressional Globe*, 32d Cong., 1st sess., Appendix, 65, 68, 591.

25. Ibid., 593; Douglas to Francis B. Cutting et al., May 3, 1851, in Stephen A. Douglas, *The Letters of Stephen A. Douglas*, ed. Robert W. Johannsen (Urbana, 1961), 217; *Floridian and Journal* (Tallahassee), June 14, 1851; *Arkansas State Gazette and Democrat*, Mar. 21, 1851; *Congressional Globe*, 32d Cong., 1st sess., Appendix, 317.

26. *Congressional Globe*, 32d Cong., 1st sess., Appendix, 321, 317; Bagby quoted in Thornton, *Politics and Power*, 237.

27. D. Solomon to Marcy, Oct. 22, 1851, and Marcy to Prosper Wetmore, Sept. 9, 1851, Vol. 20, Marcy Papers.

28. Linn Boyd to Norvin Green, Apr. 30, 1852, File 8, Norvin Green Papers, Filson Club, Louisville, Ky.; "Andrew Jackson Donelson's Speech at the Jackson Democratic Association Banquet, January 8, 1852," Jackson Democratic Association, *Proceedings at the Banquet of the Jackson Democratic Association, Washington, Eighth of January, 1852* (Washington, D.C., 1852), 12; W. W. Holder to John W. Ellis, Jan. 8, 1852, Box 1, Folder 6, John W. Ellis Papers, Southern Historical Collection, University of North Carolina, Chapel Hill.

29. "Lewis Cass' speech at the Jackson Democratic Association Banquet," Jackson Democratic Association, *Proceedings*, 8; "Stephen Douglas' Speech at the Jackson Democratic Association Banquet," ibid., 16; "Speech by Nathaniel P. Banks before a Committee of Delegates from the Thirteen Original States in Independence Hall, Philadelphia, July 5, 1852," Box 81, Nathaniel P. Banks Papers, Library of Congress.

30. *Congressional Globe*, 32d Cong., 1st sess., Appendix, 677, 464.

31. *Knoxville Whig*, Apr. 26, 1851; *Congressional Globe*, 32d Cong., 1st sess., Appendix, 373. See also Potter, *Impending Crisis*, 232–33; Holt, *Political Crisis*, 96–97, 123; and William E. Gienapp, *The Origins of the Republican Party, 1852-1856* (New York, 1987), 16–17.

32. *Congressional Globe*, 32d Cong., 1st sess., Appendix, 876, 629; Millard Fillmore to Oran Follett, May 3, 1852, Box 2, Oran Follett Papers, Cincinnati Historical Society, Cincinnati, Ohio.

33. Smith to David Barringer, May 1, 1852, Box 3, Folder 27, Barringer Papers; Benjamin F. Wade to Caroline M. Wade, Feb. 8, 1852, Vol. 1, Benjamin F. Wade Papers, Library of Congress; Lewis D. Campbell to John Sherman, Apr. 5, 1852, Vol. 1A, John Sherman Papers, Library of Congress; Davis to Robert C. Winthrop, Apr. 4, 1852, Robert C. Winthrop Papers, Massachusetts Historical Society, Boston.

34. Hamilton Fish to C. T. Crosby, Jan. 12, 1852, Fish Letterbook, Vol. 194, Fish Papers; *Savannah Daily Republican*, July 19, 1852. On the convention and its aftermath, see Gienapp, *Origins of the Republican Party*, 16–19; Holt, *Political Crisis*, 97; Cole, *Whig Party*, 245–59, 262–69; Potter, *Impending Crisis*, 232–34; Sewell, *Ballots for Freedom*, 152–69; Roy Nichols and Jeannette Nichols, "Election of 1852," in *History of American Presidential Elections, 1789-1968*, ed. Arthur M. Schlesinger Jr., 2 vols. (New York, 1971), 2:943–45; and Charles R. Schultz, "The Last Great Conclave of the Whigs," *Maryland Historical Magazine* 63 (1968): 379–400.

35. Nichols, *Pierce*, 201–3; Potter, *Impending Crisis*, 141–42; Gara, *Presidency of Pierce*, 32–35.

36. Congressional Quarterly, Inc., *Presidential Elections since 1789* (Washington, D.C., 1979), 5; Nichols and Nichols, "Election of 1852," 946–47; Gienapp, *Origins of the Republican Party*, 20–27; Holt, *Political Crisis*, 102–26.

37. Burnham, *Presidential Ballots*, 47–48; Gienapp, *Origins of the Republican Party*, 27–31; Nichols and Nichols, "Election of 1852," 948–49; Holt, *Political Crisis*, 127–30.

38. George W. Jones to Cobb, May 19, 1853, in Phillips, ed., "Correspondence of Toombs, Stephens, and Cobb," 327; Colin M. Ingersoll to Cobb, Jan. 20, 1854, ibid.,

339–40; "we lack for issues" and "real grounds of difference" quoted in Gienapp, *Origins of the Republican Party*, 35.

39. Douglas to [Charles H. Lamphier], Nov. 11, 1853, in Douglas, *Letters*, 267; Samuel Treat to Douglas, Dec. 18, 1853, Box 1, Folder 38, Stephen A. Douglas Papers, Joseph Regenstein Library, University of Chicago.

40. *Congressional Globe*, 33d Cong., 1st sess., 1, 44, 115.

41. *Senate Reports*, 33d Cong., 1st sess., No. 15 (Serial 706). For other motives or explanations of Douglas's actions see Robert W. Johannsen, *Stephen A. Douglas* (New York, 1973), 386–400; Frank H. Hodder, "The Railroad Background of the Kansas-Nebraska Act," *Mississippi Valley Historical Review* 12 (1925): 3–22; P. Orman Ray, "The Genesis of the Kansas-Nebraska Act," *Annual Report of the American Historical Association for the Year 1914*, 2 vols. (Washington, D.C., 1915), 1:259–80; and Gerald M. Capers, *Stephen A. Douglas: Defender of the Union* (Boston, 1959), 87, 90.

42. *Illinois State Register* (Springfield), July 26, 1854; *Daily Missouri Republican* (St. Louis), Feb. 7, 1854.

43. Augustus Caesar Dodge, *Letter from A. C. Dodge, to His Constituents, Respecting the Kansas-Nebraska Bill* (N.p., 1854), 1; *Congressional Globe*, 33d Cong., 1st sess., Appendix, 1023; *Cleveland Plain Dealer*, Feb. 16, 1854.

44. *Congressional Globe*, 33d Cong., 1st sess., Appendix, 607, 249.

45. Ibid., 818, 355; *Cleveland Plain Dealer*, Feb. 3, 1854.

46. Burke to Douglas, Jan. 9, 1854, Box 1, Folder 39, Douglas Papers; *Washington Daily Union*, Jan. 22, 1854; *Richmond Enquirer*, Jan. 27, 1854.

47. *Illinois State Register*, July 1, 1854; *Congressional Globe*, 33d Cong., 1st sess., Appendix, 743, 441; Robert Johannsen, "The Kansas Nebraska Act and Territorial Government in the United States," in *Territorial Kansas: Studies Commemorating the Centennial* (Lawrence, 1954), 22–23. For the "truce" view, see Potter, *Impending Crisis*, chap. 5; for the finality argument, see Fehrenbacher, *Three Sectional Crises*, 51.

48. *Congressional Globe*, 31st Cong., 1st sess., Appendix, 699, 720.

49. William Fuller to John G. Davis, Mar. 2, 1854, Box 2, John G. Davis Papers, Indiana Historical Society, Indianapolis; *Congressional Globe*, 31st Cong., 1st sess., Appendix, 720.

50. *Washington Daily Union*, Jan. 24, 1854; *Congressional Globe*, 33d Cong., 1st sess., Appendix, 143; Henry M. Breckinridge to John C. Breckinridge, Apr. 24, 1854, Vol. 167, Breckinridge Family Papers, Library of Congress.

51. *Congressional Globe*, 33d Cong., 1st sess., Appendix, 907, 501; *Charleston Mercury*, Oct. 5, 1854.

52. *Congressional Globe*, 33d Cong., 1st sess., Appendix, 1132.

53. Stephen A. Douglas, *Letter of Senator Douglas, Vindicating His Character and His Position on the Nebraska Bill Against the Assaults Contained in the Proceedings of a Public Meeting Composed of Twenty-Five Clergymen of Chicago* (Washington, D.C., 1854), 14; *Congressional Globe*, 33d Cong., 1st sess., Appendix, 514, 531, 536, 196.

54. Douglas, *Letter of Douglas*, 14; *Congressional Globe*, 33d Cong., 1st sess., Appendix, 466; "Draft of a Speech accepting the Democratic Nomination for Representative," [1854], Box 7, Folder 2, William H. English Papers, Indiana Historical Society, Indianapolis.

55. William Franklin to John G. Davis, Feb. 21, 1854, Box 2, Davis Papers; Cobb to Douglas, Feb. 5, 1854, Box 1, Folder 40, Douglas Papers; *Mississippian*, Apr. 21, 1854; *Congressional Globe*, 31st Cong., 1st sess., Appendix, 609; Herman J. Redfield to Douglas, Feb. 27, 1854, Box 1, Folder 40, Douglas Papers.

56. *Congressional Globe*, 31st Cong., 1st sess., Appendix, 458; Treat to Caleb Cushing, Feb. 23, 1854, Box 68, Caleb Cushing Papers, Library of Congress; *Pittsburgh Morning Post*, Feb. 11, 1854; *Congressional Globe*, 33d Cong., 1st sess., Appendix, 514.

57. Horace K. E. Miller to John C. Breckinridge, Jan. 26, 1854, Vol. 163, Breckinridge Family Papers.

58. *Congressional Globe*, 33d Cong., 1st sess., Appendix, 1002.

59. Ibid., 476; James O. Putnam, *The Missouri Compromise: Sketch of the Remarks of James O. Putnam upon the Nebraska Resolutions, in Senate of the State of N. York, February 3, 1854* (Albany, 1854), 3; Dix to James C. Curtis, Feb. 25, 1854, in Morgan Dix, comp., *Memoirs of John Adams Dix*, 2 vols. (New York, 1883), 1:284; *New York Daily Times*, Jan. 24, 1854.

60. "A Democrat," [draft of a letter], Mar. 1854, Vol. 38, Gideon Welles Papers, Library of Congress; *Congressional Globe*, 33d Cong., 1st sess., Appendix, 713; *Albany Evening Journal*, July 25, 1854.

61. Dr. Francis Wayland, *Dr. Wayland on the Moral and Religious Aspects of the Nebraska Bill. Speech at Providence, R.I., March 7* (Rochester, 1854), 1; *Congressional Globe*, 33d Cong., 1st sess., Appendix, 159, 737, 843. See also John W. Andrews, *The Nebraska Bill: Speech of John W. Andrews, esq., at a Meeting of Citizens of Columbus, Ohio, Held February 14th, A.D. 1854* (Columbus, 1854), 12.

62. *Indianapolis Daily Journal*, May 5, 1854; *Illinois State Journal* (Springfield), Jan. 21, 1854; *Albany Evening Journal*, Mar. 3, 1854; King to Francis Preston Blair Sr., Aug. 29, 1854, Ser. 2, Box 15, Folder 2, Blair-Lee Papers, Firestone Library, Princeton University, Princeton, N.J.; Blair to John A. Dix, [Jan. 1854], in Dix, comp., *Memoirs of John A. Dix*, 1:283.

63. C[harles] H. A. Bulkley, *Removal of Ancient Landmarks: or, The Causes and Consequences of Slavery Extension. A Discourse Preached to the Second Congregational Church of West Winsted, Ct., March 5th, 1854* (Hartford, 1854), 18; *New York Daily Times*, Feb. 18, 1854; Hon. A. Lovering to John G. Davis, May 18, 1854, Box 5, Davis Papers; Gideon Welles to [?], May 1854, Box 3, Gideon Welles Papers, Connecticut Historical Society, Hartford.

64. "Appeal of the Independent Democrats to the People of the United States. Shall Slavery Be Permitted in Nebraska?," Jan. 19, 1854, Box 31, Salmon P. Chase Papers, Library of Congress; Hamilton Fish to Sidney Lawrence, May 26, 1854, Fish Letterbook, Vol. 196, Fish Papers; Thomas Ewing to John Teasdale, Apr. 17, 1854, Roll 2, Frame 536, Thomas Ewing Sr. Papers, University of Notre Dame Archives, South Bend, Ind. (microfilm); *Congressional Globe*, 33d Cong., 1st sess., Appendix, 612.

65. *Congressional Globe*, 33d Cong., 1st sess., Appendix, 591, 494; Blair quoted in Elbert B. Smith, *Francis Preston Blair* (New York, 1980), 222.

66. *Congressional Globe*, 33d Cong., 1st sess., Appendix, 737; J. P. Jones to William Marcy, Mar. 21, 1854, Vol. 49, Marcy Papers.

67. George W. Hack to Alexander St. Clair Boys, June 26, 1854, Box 1, Folder 4, Alexander St. Clair Boys Papers, Ohio Historical Society; *Congressional Globe*, 33d

Cong., 1st sess., Appendix, 155; Heman Humphrey, *The Missouri Compromise: An Address Delivered before the Citizens of Pittsfield by Rev. Heman Humphrey, D.D. in the Baptist Church on Sabbath Evening, Feb. 26, 1854* (Pittsfield, 1854), 29.

68. Augustus Lincoln to Abraham Lincoln, Dec. 17, 1854, Ser. 1, Roll 2, Robert Todd Lincoln Collection, Library of Congress (microfilm); H. P. Cutting, *The Crisis — Slavery or Freedom. A Discourse Preached in Williston and Hinesburgh, on Sundays, June 25th, and July 2d, 1854* (Burlington, 1854), 6.

69. *Congressional Globe*, 33d Cong., 1st sess., Appendix, 609, 249; Thomas C. Reynolds to Caleb Cushing, May 16, 1854, Box 69, Cushing Papers; *Pittsburgh Morning Post*, June 27, May 31, 1854; Stephen A. Douglas, *Letter of Senator Douglas in Reply to the Editor of the State Capitol Reporter, Concord, N.H.* (Washington, D.C., 1854), 6.

70. Potter, *Impending Crisis*, 160-67; Nevins, *Ordeal of the Union*, 2:136-45, 154-57 (quotation at 156); Roy F. Nichols, *Blue Prints for Leviathan: American Style* (New York, 1963), 95-121.

71. *Albany Evening Journal*, May 23, 1854; Cutting, *The Crisis — Slavery or Freedom*, 13; *Indianapolis Daily Journal*, Oct. 26, 1854.

72. Douglas to Cobb, Apr. 2, 1854, in Phillips, ed., "Correspondence of Toombs, Stephens, and Cobb," 343.

73. Nevins, *Ordeal of the Union*, 2:341-45; Potter, *Impending Crisis*, 175.

74. Johannsen, *Douglas*, 461.

Chapter Six

1. *Congressional Globe*, 34th Cong., 1st sess., 1486, Appendix, 724, 727.

2. Alexander H. Stephens, *Recollections of Alexander H. Stephens; His Diary Kept When a Prisoner at Fort Warren, Boston Harbour, 1865; Giving Incidents and Reflections of His Prison Life and Some Letters and Reminiscences*, ed. Myrta Lockett Avary (1910; rpt. New York, 1971), 248-56, 280-84, 462-65; Alexander H. Stephens, *A Constitutional View of the Late War between the States: Its Causes, Character, Conduct, and Results, Presented in a Series of Colloquies at Liberty Hall*, 2 vols. (1868-70; rpt. New York, 1970), 2:58-59. Also see Edmund Wilson, *Patriotic Gore: Studies in the Literature of the American Civil War* (New York, 1962), 395-401.

3. Stephens, *Constitutional View*, 1:32, 2:252, 258, 130; Wilson, *Patriotic Gore*, 401-2.

4. *House Reports*, 34th Cong., 1st sess., No. 200 (Serial 869), 1, 2.

5. Ibid., 84.

6. Ibid., 3, 30-33, 72-100, 607-60, 874, 934, 936. Also see Paul Wallace Gates, *Fifty Million Acres: Conflicts over Kansas Land Policy, 1854-1890* (Ithaca, 1954), 19-22, 48-71; Samuel A. Johnson, *The Battle Cry of Freedom: The New England Emigrant Aid Company in the Kansas Crusade* (Lawrence, 1954), 16-17, 25; Mary J. Klem, "Missouri in the Kansas Struggle," Mississippi Valley Historical Association, *Proceedings* 9 (1917-18): 400; David M. Potter, *The Impending Crisis, 1848-1861* (New York, 1976), 204; and James C. Malin, "The Topeka Statehood Movement Reconsidered: Origins," in *Territorial Kansas: Studies Commemorating the Centennial* (Lawrence, 1954), 33-69.

7. Johnson, *Battle Cry*, 104-65; W. H. Isely, "The Sharps Rifle Episode in Kansas History," *American Historical Review* 12 (1907): 546-66; Potter, *Impending Crisis*, 206-9,

211–14; Allan Nevins, *Ordeal of the Union*, 2 vols. (New York, 1947), 2:432–37, 472–75; James C. Malin, *John Brown and the Legend of Fifty-Six* (Philadelphia, 1942), 52–59, 94–116, 560–92.

8. Pierce quoted in Roy Franklin Nichols, *Franklin Pierce: Young Hickory of the Granite Hills* (1931; rpt. Philadelphia, 1958), 442; Potter, *Impending Crisis*, 207–8.

9. *Congressional Globe*, 34th Cong., 1st sess., Appendix, 749–805, 844; William E. Gienapp, "The Crime against Sumner: The Caning of Charles Sumner and the Rise of the Republican Party," *Civil War History* 25 (1979): 218–45.

10. *Congressional Globe*, 34th Cong., 1st sess., Appendix, 872; McLean to John Teasdale, Nov. 2, 1855, Box 1, Folder 3, John McLean Papers, Ohio Historical Society, Columbus; *Cleveland Plain Dealer*, May 5, 1855.

11. *Cleveland Plain Dealer*, Jan. 11, 1855; *Pittsburgh Morning Post*, June 3, 1856; *Illinois State Register* (Springfield), Feb. 1, 1856.

12. Chilton Allan to Horace Greeley, Dec. 28, 1856, Box 6, Horace Greeley Papers, Library of Congress; *Congressional Globe*, 34th Cong., 1st sess., Appendix, 844; *Illinois State Register*, July 18, 1855.

13. Benjamin F. Hallett, *Speech of the Hon. B. F. Hallett at the Democratic Ratification Meeting in Waltham, Massachusetts, Friday Evening, November 2, 1855* ([Boston, 1855]), 6; *Cleveland Plain Dealer*, Dec. 8, 1855.

14. *Congressional Globe*, 34th Cong., 1st sess., Appendix, 859; Howell Cobb, *Speech of Hon. Howell Cobb, of Georgia, Delivered in Concord, N.H., at a Mass Meeting of the Democratic Party of Merrimac County* (N.p., [1855]), 4, 5.

15. Hallett, *Speech*, 9; Cobb, *Speech Delivered in Concord*, 5, 6.

16. *Congressional Globe*, 34th Cong., 1st sess., Appendix, 841, 762, 755.

17. *Albany Evening Journal*, Apr. 22, 1856; *Congressional Globe*, 34th Cong., 1st sess., Appendix, 854; Eliot quoted in Bernard Bailyn, *The Ideological Origins of the American Revolution* (Cambridge, Mass., 1967), 93; *New York Daily Times*, Sept. 11, 1855.

18. *Daily Illinois State Journal* (Springfield), Feb. 27, 1856; *Albany Evening Journal*, Apr. 23, 1855; *Congressional Globe*, 33d Cong., 2d sess., Appendix, 250.

19. *New York Daily Times*, May 4, 1855; *Free Soil, Free Speech, Free Men. Proceedings of the Democratic Republican State Convention, at Syracuse, July 24, 1856* (Albany, 1856), 6; *Congressional Globe*, 33d Cong., 2d sess., Appendix, 751.

20. *Cincinnati Gazette* quoted in Stephen E. Maizlish, *The Triumph of Sectionalism: The Transformation of Ohio Politics, 1844-1856* (Kent, 1983), 229; Sumner to Raymond, Mar. 2, 1856, Box 1, Henry J. Raymond Papers, New York Public Library, New York; *Free Soil, Free Speech, Free Men*, 6.

21. Day to Friedrich Hassaurek, May 30, 1856, Box 2, Folder 3, Friedrich Hassaurek Papers, Ohio Historical Society, Columbus; *New York Daily Times*, Nov. 18, 1856; *Albany Evening Journal*, May 17, 1854. On revolutionary charges, see Bailyn, *Ideological Origins*, 124–25.

22. Charles Eliot Norton to Francis J. Child, Mar. 15, 1855, Norton to James Russell Lowell, Apr. 6, 1855, in Charles Eliot Norton, *The Letters of Charles Eliot Norton, with Biographical Comment*, ed. Sarah Norton and M. A. DeWolfe Howe, 2 vols. (Boston, 1913), 1:121–22, 126–27; [Mrs. L. J. Barker], "Influence of Slavery upon the White Population," in *Anti Slavery Tracts* (New York, 1855–56), No. 9, 5.

23. *New York Daily Times*, June 10, 1856; [John Bloomfield Jervis], *Letters Addressed*

to the Friends of Freedom and the Union, by "Hampden." Originally Published in the New York Evening Post (New York, 1856), 4; "capital and against men" quoted in Fred H. Harrington, Fighting Politician: Major General N. P. Banks (Philadelphia, 1948), 19.

24. E[phraim] G[eorge] Squier, Lecture on the Condition and True Interests of the Laboring Class of America (New York, 1843), 3; Mayhew quoted in Bailyn, Ideological Origins, 57n.

25. Forbes to J. Hamilton Cowper, Dec. 4, 1856, in John Murray Forbes, Letters and Recollections of John Murray Forbes, ed. Sarah Forbes Hughes, 2 vols. (Boston, 1899), 1:157; Edwin H. Chapin, The American Idea, and What Grows Out of It. An Oration, Delivered in the New York Crystal Palace, July 4, 1854 (Boston, 1854), 10.

26. Gideon Welles, "Sound Principles as Against Epithets—Free Soilers and Abolitionists are Names Only—the Principles behind them are vital," Mar. 1855, Vol. 39, Gideon Welles Papers, Library of Congress; Welles to Preston King, Apr. 23, 1855, ibid.; Albany Evening Journal, Sept. 14, 1855; Forbes to William Nassau Senior, July 3, 1855, in Forbes, Letters and Recollections, 1:144.

27. New York Daily Times, Sept. 12, 1856; Albany Evening Journal, July 28, 1857.

28. Forbes to Nassau, July 3, 1855, in Forbes, Letters and Recollections, 1:144; Cassius Marcellus Clay, The Life of Cassius Marcellus Clay. Memoirs, Writings, and Speeches Showing His Conduct in the Overthrow of American Slavery, the Salvation of the Union, and the Restoration of the Autonomy of the States (Cincinnati, 1886), 214, 239; Forbes to Cowper, Dec. 4, 1856, in Forbes, Letters and Recollections, 1:153–58.

29. "Draft of Speech, November 1856," Box 1, Richard Yates Papers, Illinois State Historical Library, Springfield. On conspiracy paradigms, see Daniel Walker Howe, The Political Culture of the American Whigs (Chicago, 1979), 79; and Bailyn, Ideological Origins, 138.

30. Pike quoted in Robert Franklin Durden, James Shepherd Pike: Republicanism and the American Negro, 1850-1882 (Durham, 1957), 25; Congressional Globe, 34th Cong., 1st sess., Appendix, 793; Harrisburg Telegraph, May 23, 1856; Salmon P. Chase, Speech of Hon. Salmon P. Chase, Delivered at the Republican Mass Meeting in Cincinnati, August 21, 1855; Together with Extracts from His Speeches in the Senate on Kindred Subjects (Columbus, 1855), 11.

31. Congressional Globe, 34th Cong., 1st sess., Appendix, 751. The most informed and sometimes withering attacks on republicanism include Joyce Appleby, "Republicanism in Old and New Contexts," William and Mary Quarterly 43 (1986): 20–34; Isaac Kramnick, "Republican Revisionism Revisited," American Historical Review 87 (1982): 629–64; John P. Diggins, The Lost Soul of American Politics: Virtue, Self-Interest, and the Foundations of Liberalism (Chicago, 1984); and Daniel T. Rodgers, "Republicanism: The Career of a Concept," Journal of American History 79 (1992): 11–38.

32. Charles Sumner, The Slave Oligarchy and Its Usurpations. Speech of Hon. Charles Sumner, November 2, 1855, in Faneuil Hall, Boston (Washington, D.C., [1855]), 15–16.

33. Congressional Globe, 33d Cong., 2d sess., Appendix, 252; ibid., 34th Cong., 1st sess., Appendix, 790; William H. Bissell to Joseph Gillespie, Feb. 17, 1856, Joseph Gillespie Papers, Illinois State Historical Library, Springfield.

34. Albany Evening Journal, Dec. 1, 1855; Wade to Oran Follett, Apr. 13, 1856, Box 2, Oran Follett Papers, Cincinnati Historical Society, Cincinnati; Charles Miner to John A. King, Mar. 2, 1856, John A. King Papers, New-York Historical Society, New

York; Parke Godwin, *A Biography of William Cullen Bryant with Extracts from His Private Correspondence*, 2 vols. (New York, 1883), 2:89.

35. *New York Daily Times*, July 9, 1855; William G. Coffin to John Dowling, Nov. 6, 1855, Box 2, John Dowling Papers, Indiana Historical Society, Indianapolis; Fish to Robert A. West, Oct. 22, 1855, Vol. 196, Hamilton Fish Papers, Library of Congress; Chase to Sumner, Dec. 13, 1856, in S. H. Dodson, comp., "Diary and Correspondence of Salmon P. Chase," *Annual Report of the American Historical Association for the Year 1902*, 2 vols. (Washington, D.C., 1903), 2:275.

36. *Congressional Globe*, 34th Cong., 1st sess., Appendix, 775; *Illinois State Journal*, Sept. 18, 1856. Also see John A. Wilstach, *The Imperial Period of National Greatness. A Lecture on the Destiny of the West, by John A. Wilstach, before the Western Literary Union, at Farmers' Institute, Vicinity of Lafayette, Indiana, 12th of First Month, 1855* (Lafayette, 1855), 21.

37. *Daily Missouri Republican* (St. Louis), May 1, Aug. 28, 1855; James Kirke Paulding to Clayton, Apr. 12, 1856, in James Kirke Paulding, *Letters of James Kirke Paulding*, ed. Ralph M. Aderman (Madison, 1962), 569, 570.

38. *Mobile Daily Register*, Apr. 1, 1856, Nov. 6, 1855; *Richmond Daily Enquirer*, Dec. 21, 1855; *Charleston Mercury*, Dec. 18, 1855. Another reason why the emigrant aid movement seemed to mark a new phase in the war against the South's peculiar institution is that it demonstrated the willingness of a state to legislate against slavery. See *Address to the People of the United States, Together with the Proceedings and Resolutions of the Pro-Slavery Convention of Missouri, Held at Lexington, July, 1855* (St. Louis, 1855), 22–23.

39. *Congressional Globe*, 34th Cong., 1st sess., Appendix, 793, 759; "Draft of a Speech Given at Tippecanoe, Indiana, September, 1856," Vol. 187, Breckinridge Family Papers, Library of Congress.

40. Lamar to B. S. Rozell, Mar. 8, 1858, in Edward Mayes, *Lucius Q. C. Lamar: His Life, Times, and Speeches, 1825-1893* (Nashville, 1896), 73–74.

41. *Richmond Daily Enquirer*, Mar. 18, 1856; *Charleston Mercury*, July 13, 1857.

42. Edmund Ruffin, *African Colonization Unveiled* (Washington, D.C., [1859]), 1, in Section 4, Box 6, Edmund Ruffin Papers, Virginia Historical Society, Richmond; Hammond quoted in Wilfred Carsel, "The Slaveholders' Indictment of Northern Wage Slavery," *Journal of Southern History* 6 (1940): 513; "Andrew Johnson's Address to the State of Tennessee held in the Representatives Hall, January 8, 1856," quoted in *Nashville Union and American*, Jan. 13, 1856; *Richmond Daily Enquirer*, Aug. 18, 1855.

43. Keitt to Susanna Sparks, June 19, 1856, Lawrence M. Keitt Papers, William R. Perkins Library, Duke University, Durham, N.C.; Edmund Ruffin, *"The Political [!] Economy of Slavery," or, the Institution Considered in Regard to Its Influence on Public Wealth and the General Welfare* ([Washington, D.C., 1857]), 26, in Section 4, Box 6, Ruffin Papers.

44. Johnson to the Editor of the *North American and Gazette*, Oct. 6, 1856, Hershel V. Johnson Papers, William R. Perkins Library, Duke University, Durham, N.C.; *Richmond Daily Enquirer*, Jan. 29, 1855; Brown quoted in Steven Hahn, *The Roots of Southern Populism: Yeomen Farmers and the Transformation of the Georgia Upcountry, 1850-1890* (New York, 1983), 86.

45. Platte County Self-Defense Association, *Negro Slavery, No Evil; or, The North and the South. The Effects of Negro Slavery, as Exhibited in the Census, by a Comparison of the Condition of the Slaveholding and Non-slaveholding States, Considered in a Report Made to the*

Platte County Self-Defense Association, by a Committee, Through B. F. Stringfellow, Chairman (St. Louis, 1854), 30; *Charleston Mercury*, Oct. 22, 1856.

46. W. B. Davis to Clement Claiborne Clay, May 11, 1856, Box 4, Clement Claiborne Clay Papers, William R. Perkins Library, Duke University, Durham, N.C.; *Charleston Mercury*, July 5, 1858.

47. Levi P. Ruerr to Quitman, Dec. 30, 1850, Box 2, John A. Quitman Papers, Houghton Library, Harvard University, Cambridge, Mass.; "Speech Given at Tippecanoe," Vol. 187, Breckinridge Papers.

48. Wise to William F. Sanford, John H. Thomas, Christopher Davis et al., Aug. 23, [1855], in James P. Hambleton, *A Biographical Sketch of Henry A. Wise, with a History of the Political Campaign in Virginia in 1855* (Richmond, 1856), 438; *Richmond Daily Enquirer*, Apr. 14, 1856; *Congressional Globe*, 34th Cong., 1st sess., Appendix, 770.

49. Roy Franklin Nichols, *The Disruption of American Democracy* (1948; rpt. New York, 1967), 22–32; Robert W. Johannsen, *Stephen A. Douglas* (New York, 1973), 505–20; Nevins, *Ordeal*, 2:457–60; Robert E. May, *John A. Quitman: Old South Crusader* (Baton Rouge, 1985), 314–15, 318–20; William B. Hesseltine and Rex G. Fisher, eds., *Trimmers, Trucklers and Temporizers: Notes of Murat Halstead from the Political Conventions of 1856* (Madison, 1961), 35–40. One imaginative party publicist made the following stretcher: "Like Washington, Madison, and Jackson, Mr. Buchanan is childless. God has denied these benefactors children, 'that the nation might call them father' " (*The Agitation of Slavery: Who Commenced! and Who Can End It!! Buchanan and Fillmore Compared from the Record* [Washington, D.C., 1856], 32).

50. "General Jos. Lane's Speech in Phoenix Hall," in *Speeches of Messrs. Weller, Orr, Lane, and Cobb Delivered in Phoenix and Depot Halls, Concord, N.H., at a Mass Meeting of the Democratic Party of Merrimac County* ([Concord, 1856]), 19–20; Vallandigham quoted in Maizlish, *Triumph of Sectionalism*, 231–32.

51. *Cleveland Plain Dealer*, Oct. 26, Aug. 9, 1855; Robert J. Walker, *An Appeal for the Union. Letter from the Hon. Robert J. Walker. New York, Tuesday, Sept. 30, 1856. Hon. Charles Shaler and Others, Democratic Committee, Pittsburgh, Pennsylvania* (New York, [1856]), 10.

52. *Cleveland Plain Dealer*, Jan. 31, 1854; *Richmond Daily Enquirer*, Sept. 15, 1855.

53. *Illinois State Register*, Feb. 14, 1855; *New Orleans Daily Picayune*, June 22, 1856; Rives to William M. Burwell, Mar. 19, 1855, Box 2, Burwell Family Papers, Alderman Library, University of Virginia, Charlottesville.

54. *Floridian and Journal* (Tallahassee), Oct. 11, 1856; Stevenson quoted in Francis F. Wayland, *Andrew Stevenson: Democrat and Diplomat, 1785–1857* (Philadelphia, 1949), 232; *New Orleans Daily Picayune*, Oct. 7, 1856; Marcy to John Y. Mason, Sept. 11, [1856], Section 24, Box 10, Mason Family Papers, Virginia Historical Society, Richmond.

55. "To elevate the African race" quoted in Michael F. Holt, *The Political Crisis of the 1850s* (New York, 1978), 187; *Cleveland Plain Dealer*, Aug. 30, 1855; *The Issue Fairly Presented. The Senate Bill for the Admission of Kansas as a State. Democracy, Law, Order, and the Will of the Majority of the Whole People of the Territory, Against Black Republicanism, Usurpation, Revolution, Anarchy, and the Will of a Meagre Minority* (Washington, D.C., 1856), 5.

56. Walker, *An Appeal for the Union*, 6; *Cleveland Plain Dealer*, Oct. 1, 1855; James C. Zabriskie, *Speech of Col. Jas. C. Zabriskie, on the Subject of Slavery and in Reply to the Address of the Pittsburgh Convention, and Geo. C. Bates, esq. Delivered at Sacramento, Cal., on the 10th Day of May, A.D. 1856* (Sacramento, 1856), 13; Barringer to W. A. Houck, Aug. 6,

1856, Box 3, Folder 36, Daniel M. Barringer Papers, Southern Historical Collection, University of North Carolina, Chapel Hill.

57. *Nashville Daily Union and American*, Dec. 13, 1855; "Senator Weller's Speech at Phoenix Hall," in *Speeches of Weller, Orr, Lane, and Cobb*, 7.

58. "No enthusiasm" quoted in Holt, *Political Crisis*, 175–76; *Illinois State Journal*, Apr. 26, 1856.

59. Hesseltine and Fisher, eds., *Trimmers, Travelers and Temporizers*, 87–93; William E. Gienapp, *The Origins of the Republican Party, 1852-1856* (New York, 1987), 316–46.

60. Republican Party, National Committee, *Philadelphia National Convention. Circular of the National Committee of the Pittsburgh Convention, Appointed February 22, 1856* (Washington, D.C., 1856), 4; "Hannibal Hamlin on the State of the Nation and the Democracy, June 1856," in Charles Eugene Hamlin, ed., *The Life and Times of Hannibal Hamlin*, 2 vols. (1899; rpt. Port Washington, N.Y., 1971), 2:286; *New York Daily Times*, June 17, 1856; *Indianapolis Daily Journal*, July 25, 1856.

61. *Illinois State Journal*, Aug. 20, 1856; Lincoln to George Robertson, Aug. 15, 1855, in Abraham Lincoln, *The Collected Works of Abraham Lincoln*, ed. Roy P. Basler, 8 vols. (New Brunswick, 1953–55), 2:318; Quincy to Samuel Hoar, May 27, 1856, in F[ranklin] B[enjamin] Sanborn, *Recollections of Seventy Years*, 2 vols. (Boston, 1909), 1:50.

62. Pike quoted in Durden, *Pike*, 23; "Speech by Hannibal Hamlin to a Republican Meeting at Faneuil Hall, June 23, 1856," in Hamlin, ed., *Life of Hamlin*, 2:299; Thomas F. Hicks to Wade, [June 19, 1856], Vol. 2, Benjamin F. Wade Papers, Library of Congress; Greeley to William M. Chase, Samuel Peckham, and Wingate Hayes, May 9, 1856, Box 1, Folder 12, Horace Greeley Papers, New York Public Library.

63. *Ohio State Journal* quoted in Maizlish, *Triumph of Sectionalism*, 230; Republican Party National Convention, *Proceedings of the First Three Republican National Conventions of 1856, 1860 and 1864, including Proceedings of the Antecedent National Convention Held at Pittsburgh, in February, 1856, as Reported by Horace Greeley* (Minneapolis, [1893]), 31; *Albany Evening Journal*, June 21, 1856. On nativism in the 1856 canvass, see Potter, *Impending Crisis*, 258; Holt, *Political Crisis*, 180–81, 189; and Tyler Anbinder, *Nativism and Slavery: The Northern Know Nothings and the Politics of the 1850s* (New York, 1992), chap. 9. On ethnocultural conflict in this period generally, see Ronald P. Formisano, *The Birth of Mass Political Parties: Michigan, 1827-1861* (Princeton, 1971), 102–3, 110, 138, 160–64; Paul J. Kleppner, *The Cross of Culture: Social Analysis of Midwestern Politics, 1850-1900* (New York, 1970), 59–61; Kleppner, *The Third Electoral System, 1853-1892: Parties, Voters, and Political Cultures* (Chapel Hill, 1979), 143–97; Joel H. Silbey, "The Surge of Republican Power: Partisan Antipathy, American Social Conflict, and the Coming of the Civil War," in Stephen E. Maizlish and John J. Kushma, eds., *Essays on American Antebellum Politics, 1840-1860* (College Station, 1982), 227–29; Silbey, *The American Political Nation, 1838-1893* (Stanford, 1991), esp. 171–75; Michael F. Holt, *Forging a Majority: The Formation of the Republican Party in Pittsburgh, 1848-1860* (New Haven, 1969); Holt, *Political Crisis*, 154–79; and Gienapp, *Origins of the Republican Party*, esp. 60, 65, 66–67, 81–82, 88–89, 99–100, 160–65, 179–86. For state studies that emphasize the destructive (or halfway house) nature of Know-Nothingism in the North see Maizlish, *Triumph of Sectionalism*, 204–9, 211–16; Dale Baum, *The Civil War Party System: The Case of Massachusetts, 1848-1876* (Chapel Hill, 1984), 25–43; and Hendrik Booraem,

The Formation of the Republican Party in New York: Politics and Conscience in the Antebellum North (New York, 1983), 68–70, 75. For a telling critique of ethnocultural interpretation of the sectional crisis, see Don E. Fehrenbacher, "The New Political History and the Coming of the Civil War," *Pacific Historical Review* 54 (1985): 117–42.

64. John Trible to Lyman Trumbull, Jan. 25, 1856, Vol. 1, Lyman Trumbull Papers, Library of Congress; Hannibal Hamlin speech at Bangor, Maine, June 27, 1856, in Hamlin, ed., *Life of Hamlin*, 2:302; *Albany Evening Journal*, Nov. 27, 1855; "Letter of Cassius M. Clay to the Republican Association of Boston," Feb. 8, 1856, File 12, Cassius M. Clay Papers, Filson Club, Louisville, Ky. Although William Gienapp has demonstrated that Republicans had to tread warily around the nativist issue, men such as William Seward asserted that "the question of the day is not about natives and foreigners, not about Protestants and Roman Catholics, but about free men and slaves. . . . The issue raised by the Know Nothings is an immaterial, irrelevant, and false issue." In the South, the challenge of slave-state Know-Nothings actually heightened the salience of the Kansas issue. In some places (Alabama, for example) it made the Democracy more sensitive to the territorial question. In many slave states (for example, Alabama, Mississippi, and Georgia), southern rights men dismissed nativism as a distracting issue that prevented regional unity on the territorial question. See William H. Seward, *The Parties of the Day. Speech of William H. Seward, at Auburn, October 21, 1856* (Washington, D.C., 1857), 6. On the South, see Marc W. Kruman, *Parties and Politics in North Carolina, 1836–1865* (Baton Rouge, 1983), 174–75; W. Darrell Overdyke, *The Know-Nothing Party in the South* (Baton Rouge, 1950), 80–81, 139–43, 209; Thornton, *Politics and Power*, 355–57; and May, *Quitman*, 296–305.

65. *Richmond Daily Enquirer*, Oct. 6, Sept. 26, 1856; *Nashville Union and American*, Oct. 3, 1856; *Charleston Mercury*, Sept. 16, 1856.

66. R. M. T. Hunter, *Speech of Hon. R. M. T. Hunter, of Virginia, before the Democratic Mass Meeting, at Poughkeepsie, on October 1, 1856* (New York, 1856), 4; *Weekly North Carolina Standard*, Sept. 17, 1856; Barringer to H. Gleisening, A. Eugene Smith, and R. R. Fulerswider, Nov. 11, 1856, Box 3, Folder 36, Barringer Papers.

67. Hershel V. Johnson to the Editor of the *North American and Gazette*, Oct. 6, 1856, Johnson Papers.

68. *Mobile Daily Register*, Nov. 17, 1855; *Richmond Daily Enquirer*, Mar. 25, 1857.

69. Clement Claiborne Clay to Clement Comer Clay, June 7, 1856, Box 4, Clay Papers; *Richmond Daily Enquirer*, July 15, 1855, Oct. 1, 1856; *Floridian and Journal*, Aug. 30, May 24, 1856.

70. Buchanan to Mason, Aug. 15, 1856, Section 24, Box 5, Mason Family Papers; Roy F. Nichols and Philip S. Klein, "Election of 1856," in *History of American Presidential Elections, 1789–1968*, ed. Arthur M. Schlesinger Jr., 4 vols. (New York, 1971), 2:1094; Nichols, *Disruption of American Democracy*, 60; Potter, *Impending Crisis*, 264–65n.

71. Johnson to Sam Milligan, Nov. 23, 1856, in Andrew Johnson, *The Papers of Andrew Johnson*, ed. LeRoy P. Graf and Ralph W. Haskins, 12 vols. (Knoxville, 1967–95), 2:452; Marcy to Bancroft, Dec. 23, 1856, George Bancroft Papers, Massachusetts Historical Society, Boston; Guy M. Bryan to Rutherford B. Hayes, Jan. 1, 1857, typescript, Hayes-Bryan Correspondence, Rutherford B. Hayes Memorial Library, Fremont, Ohio; Shubal York to Lyman Trumbull, Dec. 6, 1858, Vol. 15, Lyman Trumbull Papers, Library of Congress.

72. Philip Shriver Klein, *President James Buchanan: A Biography* (University Park, 1962), 271–72; James D. Richardson, comp., *A Compilation of the Messages and Papers of the Presidents, 1789–1897*, 10 vols. (Washington, D.C., 1896–99), 5:431–32.

Chapter Seven

1. Elbert B. Smith, *The Presidency of James Buchanan* (Lawrence, 1975), 27; Allan Nevins, *The Emergence of Lincoln*, 2 vols. (New York, 1950), 1:91–92, 101; Bernard C. Steiner, *The Life of Roger Brooke Taney, Chief Justice of the United States* (1922; rpt. Westport, 1970), 343–55; Carl Brent Swisher, *Roger B. Taney* (New York, 1935), 485–511. In the record of the case, John A. Sanford's name was misspelled by the clerk as Sandford.

2. Smith, *Presidency of Buchanan*, 24–29; Nevins, *Emergence of Lincoln*, 2:473–77; Don E. Fehrenbacher, *The Dred Scott Case: Its Significance in American Law and Politics* (New York, 1978), 305–14; David M. Potter, *The Impending Crisis, 1848–1861* (New York, 1976), 270–72; F[rank] H. Hodder, "Some Phases of the Dred Scott Case," *Mississippi Valley Historical Review* 16 (1929): 3–22; Philip G. Auchampaugh, "James Buchanan, the Court, and the Dred Scott Case," *Tennessee Historical Magazine* 11 (1926): 231–40; Philip Shriver Klein, *President James Buchanan: A Biography* (University Park, 1962), 271–72.

3. *New York Journal of Commerce*, Mar. 11, 1857; Fehrenbacher, *Dred Scott*, 456–57.

4. James A. Hamilton to Joseph Holt, Jan. 1, 1860, Vol. 22, Joseph Holt Papers, Library of Congress; *Cleveland Daily National Democrat*, Apr. 18, 1860.

5. *Albany Evening Journal*, Mar. 11, 1857; *Congressional Globe*, 35th Congress, 1st sess., 941; *Ohio State Journal* (Columbus), Mar. 11, 1857.

6. *Congressional Globe*, 35th Cong., 1st sess., 1004, 620.

7. James A. Hamilton to John A. King, Mar. 10, 1857, John A. King Papers, New-York Historical Society, New York; *Ohio State Journal*, May 11, 1858; Bryant quoted in Nevins, *Emergence of Lincoln*, 1:96.

8. Abraham Lincoln, *The Collected Works of Abraham Lincoln*, ed. Roy P. Basler, 8 vols. (New Brunswick, 1953–55), 2:465–66; *Harrisburg Telegraph* quoted in Richard H. Sewell, *A House Divided: Sectionalism and Civil War, 1848–1865* (Baltimore, 1988), 60. Lincoln's analysis may be compared to Thomas Jefferson's analysis of British machinations in 1774. Jefferson stated that though "single acts of tyranny may be ascribed to the accidental opinion of a day . . . a series of oppressions, begun at a distinguished period and pursued unalterably through every change of ministers, too plainly prove a deliberate and systematic plan of reducing us to slavery" (quoted in Bernard Bailyn, *The Ideological Origins of the American Revolution* [Cambridge, Mass., 1967], 119–20).

9. Welles to [?], Mar. 15, 1858, Box 4, Gideon Welles Papers, Connecticut Historical Society, Hartford; Doolittle quoted in Fehrenbacher, *Dred Scott*, 452.

10. *Illinois State Journal* (Springfield), Mar. 20, June 19, 1857; *New York Daily Times*, Mar. 7, 1857; *Ohio State Journal*, May 11, 1858.

11. *Illinois State Register* (Springfield), Mar. 19, 1857; *Nashville Union and American*, Mar. 15, 1857; *Keystone* (Harrisburg, Pa.), Sept. 30, 1857.

12. *Pittsburgh Morning Post*, Mar. 14, 1857; *Louisville Daily Journal*, Mar. 14, 1857.

13. *Mobile Daily Register*, June 14, 1857; [William S. Winder] to Hershel V. Johnson, Mar. 4, 1858, Hershel V. Johnson Papers, William R. Perkins Library, Duke University, Durham, N.C.

14. *Nashville Union and American*, Mar. 17, 1857; *Charleston Mercury*, Mar. 17, 1857.

15. *Richmond Daily Enquirer*, Mar. 10, 1857; *Cleveland Plain Dealer*, Mar. 24, 1857; "Speech of William Bigler at Clarion, Pennsylvania," printed in *Keystone*, Sept. 23, 1857; *New Orleans Daily Picayune*, Mar. 20, 1857.

16. *Illinois State Register*, Mar. 19, 1857; *New Orleans Daily Picayune*, Mar. 20, 1857; *Nashville Union and American*, Mar. 17, 1857; *Louisville Daily Journal*, Mar. 31, 1857.

17. Douglas and *Washington Union* quoted in Fehrenbacher, *Dred Scott*, 456–57.

18. *Weekly North Carolina Standard* (Raleigh), June 24, 1857; *Charleston Mercury*, Apr. 20, 3, 1857; *Nashville Union and American*, Mar. 17, 1857.

19. Potter, *Impending Crisis*, 297–300; Smith, *Presidency of Buchanan*, 39–46; Klein, *Buchanan*, 296–312; James P. Shenton, *Robert John Walker: A Politician from Jackson to Lincoln* (New York, 1961), 150–55.

20. Thomas W. Thomas to Alexander H. Stephens, June 15, 1857, in Ulrich B. Phillips, ed., "The Correspondence of Robert Toombs, Alexander H. Stephens, and Howell Cobb," *Annual Report of the American Historical Association for the Year 1911*, 2 vols. (Washington, D.C., 1913), 2:400, 401; Toombs to W. W. Burwell, July 11, 1857, ibid., 403; Keitt to William Porcher Miles, June 15, 1857, Box 1, Folder 9, William Porcher Miles Papers, Southern Historical Collection, University of North Carolina, Chapel Hill.

21. Potter, *Impending Crisis*, 300, 305–14.

22. James D. Richardson, comp., *A Compilation of the Messages and Papers of the Presidents, 1789-1897*, 10 vols. (Washington, D.C., 1896–99), 5:450–53 (quotation at 453); Klein, *Buchanan*, 301, 304–5, 308; Potter, *Impending Crisis*, 318.

23. *Congressional Globe*, 35th Cong., 1st sess., 14–18.

24. Lucius Q. C. Lamar to Howell Cobb, July 17, 1857, in Phillips, ed., "Correspondence of Toombs, Stephens, and Cobb," 406; *Congressional Globe*, 35th Cong., 1st sess., 1033, 1095; *Mobile Daily Register*, Dec. 1, 1857.

25. Andrew G. Magrath to William Porcher Miles, Feb. 18, 1858, Box 1, Folder 13, Miles Papers; "Alexander H. Stephens to the Voters of the Eighth Congressional District of Georgia," Aug. 14, 1857, in Phillips, ed., "Correspondence of Toombs, Stephens, and Cobb," 417.

26. *Nashville Union and American*, July 7, 1857; R. M. T. Hunter to Hon. Shelton F. Leake, Oct. 16, 1857, in Charles Henry Ambler, ed., "Correspondence of Robert M. T. Hunter, 1826-1876," *Annual Report of the American Historical Association for the Year 1916*, 2 vols. (Washington, D.C., 1918), 2:240; *Louisville Daily Courier*, Mar. 6, 1858.

27. *Congressional Globe*, 35th Cong., 1st sess., 1064, 572, 548; "Stephens to the Voters of the Eighth Congressional District of Georgia," Aug. 14, 1857, in Phillips, ed., "Correspondence of Toombs, Stephens, and Cobb," 411.

28. *Mobile Daily Register*, Dec. 1, 1857; *Congressional Globe*, 35th Cong., 1st sess., 1029; Hunter to Leake, [1857?], in Ambler, ed., "Correspondence of Hunter," 260.

29. J. B. Norman to William H. English, Dec. 30, 1857, Box 2, Folder 6, William H. English Papers, Indiana Historical Society, Indianapolis; *Cleveland Plain Dealer*, Jan. 25, 1858; *Congressional Globe*, 35th Cong., 1st sess., Appendix, 309; Samuel A. Hall

to John G. Davis, Feb. 13, 1858, Box 4, John G. Davis Papers, Indiana Historical Society, Indianapolis.

30. *Cleveland Plain Dealer*, Apr. 7, 1858; *Congressional Globe*, 35th Cong., 1st sess., 309; Douglas to John W. Forney et al., Feb. 6, 1858, in Stephen A. Douglas, *The Letters of Stephen A. Douglas*, ed. Robert W. Johannsen (Urbana, 1961), 409–10.

31. Welles to Douglas, Dec. 12, 1857, Box 4, Folder 10, Stephen A. Douglas Papers, Joseph Regenstein Library, University of Chicago; *Congressional Globe*, 35th Cong., 1st sess., 1443, 570.

32. A. B. Florer to Davis, Dec. 1857, Box 3, Davis Papers; *Harrisburg Daily Telegraph*, Feb. 13, 1858; Jerry Smith to John G. Davis, Jan. 1, 1858, and A. B. Conduitt to Davis, Feb. 1, 1858, Box 4, Davis Papers.

33. *Mobile Daily Register*, Jan. 27, 1858.

34. *Louisville Daily Courier*, Jan. 23, 1858; *Congressional Globe*, 35th Cong., 1st sess., 960, 572; *Weekly Register* (Raleigh, N.C.), Feb. 10, 1858.

35. *Charleston Mercury*, Apr. 5, 1858; *Congressional Globe*, 35th Cong., 1st sess., 1096.

36. *Congressional Globe*, 35th Cong., 1st sess., 1066; *Richmond Daily Enquirer*, Jan. 30, 1858.

37. *Nashville Union and American*, June 24, 1858; *Louisville Daily Courier*, Mar. 22, 1858; *Mobile Daily Register*, Dec. 31, 1857.

38. *Pittsburgh Morning Post*, Feb. 24, 1858; *Illinois State Register*, Feb. 1, 1858.

39. *Illinois State Journal*, Jan. 7, 1858; *Congressional Globe*, 35th Cong., 1st sess., 615, 1092, 523; *Harrisburg Daily Telegraph*, Feb. 17, 1858.

40. *Congressional Globe*, 35th Cong., 1st sess., 1136, 574, 548, 1896.

41. *Harrisburg Daily Telegraph*, Feb. 11, 1858; Mark W. Summers, *The Plundering Generation: Corruption and the Crisis of the Union, 1849–1861* (New York, 1987), 249–54, 271–79; Roy F. Nichols, *The Disruption of American Democracy* (1948; rpt. New York, 1967), 165. The undercard was fought the previous afternoon in the congressional lobby. Two House members from Maryland and Pennsylvania squared off for an hour and seventeen minutes by the clock (or sixty-four rounds by other accounts). Though the Pennsylvania representative got the worst of it, both combatants were badly beaten.

42. *Washington Union*, July 12, 1858; Nichols, *Disruption of Democracy*, 176–180; Potter, *Impending Crisis*, 323–25.

43. *Illinois State Journal*, Apr. 27, 1858; *Congressional Globe*, 35th Cong., 1st sess., 1821, 1823, 1895.

44. *Congressional Globe*, 35th Cong., 1st sess., 1869, 1846, 1844; *Illinois State Register*, Apr. 28, 1858. Douglas's determined stand was preceded by some fancy footwork. On the Saturday before his anti-English speech in the Senate, Douglas, after intense lobbying by the administration, agreed reluctantly to go for the compromise. When he informed other irreconcilable anti-Lecompton Democrats, including Stuart, of his decision, to a man they urged him not to yield. Senator David Broderick of California railed, "I can't understand you, sir. You will be crushed between the Administration and the Republicans. I shall denounce you, sir. You had better go into the street and blow out your brains!" Faced with those unpleasant prospects, Douglas reversed field. Broderick quoted in Nevins, *Emergence of Lincoln*, 1:300.

45. Joseph E. Brown to Alexander H. Stephens, May 7, 1858, in Phillips, ed., "Correspondence of Toombs, Stephens, and Cobb," 434; Samford quoted in J. Mills

Thornton III, *Politics and Power in a Slave Society: Alabama, 1800–1860* (Baton Rouge, 1978), 368–69; Potter, *Impending Crisis*, 324. In August 1858, the people of Kansas rejected the Lecompton Constitution (or, strictly speaking, insisted upon receiving the larger land grant) by a better than ten to one margin.

46. Samford quoted in Thornton, *Politics and Power*, 369.

47. Lincoln, *Collected Works*, 3:51, 114–15; Johannsen, *Douglas*, 672.

48. Lincoln, *Collected Works*, 3:121, 117, 279, 316.

49. Ibid., 181, 312.

50. Stevenson to Thomas B. Stevenson, Jan. 27, 1860, Box 2, Thomas B. Stevenson Papers, Cincinnati Historical Society, Cincinnati, Ohio; *Louisville Daily Courier*, Mar. 5, 1860; *Floridian and Journal* (Tallahassee), Apr. 21, 1860.

51. *Senate Reports*, 36th Cong., 1st sess., No. 278 (Serial 1040), 18; *Floridian and Journal*, Oct. 29, 1859; *Congressional Globe*, 36th Cong., 1st sess., 37.

52. *Senate Reports*, No. 278, 13; *Mississippian*, Oct. 25, 1859.

53. Rutherfoord quoted in Henry T. Shanks, *The Secession Movement in Virginia, 1847–1861* (Richmond, 1934), 100.

54. First quote (William Barnwell Rhett) in Steven A. Channing, *Crisis of Fear: Secession in South Carolina* (New York, 1970), 92; *Congressional Globe*, 36th Cong., 1st sess., 29; Taylor quoted in Channing, *Crisis of Fear*, 93. Although northern Democrats saw the origin of Brown's raid in the same light as their slave-state colleagues, they sharply disagreed with them on its effect. Southerners despaired over the deranged state of northern public opinion and its harmful impact on the Democracy there. Free-state Locos predicted that reaction to Brown's excesses and Republican complicity with him would "injure Seward and the Republican party." (They were half right.) But, they went on, this would happen only if the South observed "an indignant silence. . . . The less they say—the more will be *said* and *done* in [the North] to the entire break up of that rascally fanaticism which dares to assume the name party." See John D. Andrews to Caleb Cushing, Oct. 22, 1859, Box 85, Caleb Cushing Papers, Library of Congress; C[harles] A. Davis to Buchanan, Oct. 24, 1859, James Buchanan Papers, Historical Society of Pennsylvania, Philadelphia.

55. *Louisville Daily Courier*, Jan. 24, 1860; *Mississippian*, Dec. 23, 1859; *Memphis Daily Avalanche*, Jan. 6, 1860; *Houston Telegraph* reprinted in *San Antonio Ledger and Texan*, Feb. 11, 1860.

56. *Congressional Globe*, 36th Cong., 1st sess., 125, 30, 15.

57. *Baltimore Sun* quoted in Jules Abels, *Man on Fire: John Brown and the Cause of Liberty* (New York, 1971), 315; *Weekly North Carolina Standard*, Nov. 5, 1859; *Richmond Daily Enquirer*, Oct. 25, 1859.

58. *Richmond Whig* quoted in Shanks, *Secession Movement in Virginia*, 9; editor quoted in Avery O. Craven, *The Growth of Southern Nationalism, 1848–1861* (Baton Rouge, 1953), 308.

59. William Porcher Miles to Christopher C. Memminger, Jan. 10, 1860, Christopher C. Memminger Papers, Southern Historical Collection, University of North Carolina, Chapel Hill; Williams to Clay, Dec. 5, 1859, Box 6, Clement Claiborne Clay Papers, William R. Perkins Library, Duke University, Durham, N.C.; [Speed] to Henry Smith Lane, Aug. 2, 1859, Box 4, Henry Smith Lane Papers, Indiana Historical Society, Indianapolis.

60. *Congressional Globe*, 36th Cong., 1st sess., 37, 128; farmer quoted in Craven, *Growth of Southern Nationalism*, 311.

61. *Congressional Globe*, 36th Cong., 1st sess., 658. For a fuller discussion of Davis's proposals (that were rendered nugatory by a set of contingencies) and similar demands by Albert Gallatin Brown (that were not), see Fehrenbacher, *Dred Scott*, 508–9, 531–33.

62. *Congressional Globe*, 36th Cong., 1st sess., 1058, 776, 1006.

63. *Congressional Globe*, 35th Cong., 2d sess., 1242.

64. Ibid., 1251.

65. *Congressional Globe*, 36th Cong., 1st sess., 2271; John Williams to Clement Claiborne Clay, Dec. 5, 1859, Box 6, Clay Papers. For the fealty argument, see Potter, *Impending Crisis*, 403. On the perversion of states' rights, see Arthur Bestor, "State Sovereignty and Slavery: A Reinterpretation of Proslavery Constitutional Doctrine, 1846–1860," *Journal of the Illinois State Historical Society* 54 (1961): 117–80.

66. *Congressional Globe*, 36th Cong., 1st sess., 1941, 1060.

67. Ibid., Appendix, 309, 314; ibid., 35th Cong., 2d sess., 1261.

68. *Congressional Globe*, 35th Cong., 2d sess., 1246, 1261; ibid., 36th Cong., 1st sess., Appendix, 314.

69. *Nashville Union and American*, May 15, 1860; *Congressional Globe*, 36th Cong., 1st sess., 1967, 2121, 2143.

70. Fehrenbacher, *Dred Scott*, 531; Potter, *Impending Crisis*, 403–4; Nichols, *Disruption of the Democracy*, 298–303.

71. *Washington States and Union*, Mar. 20, 1860; *Columbia City* (Ind.) *Weekly News*, Feb. 23, 1860; *Petersburg Press* reprinted in *Washington States and Union*, Mar. 1, 1860; *Louisville Daily Democrat*, Feb. 21, 1860 (quotation).

72. *Mississippian*, Feb. 28, 1860; *Memphis Daily Avalanche*, Feb. 22, 1860; *New York Daily News*, Feb. 28, 1860; *Mississippian*, Mar. 16, 1860.

73. Floyd to Buchanan, Sept. 5, 1859, Buchanan Papers; *Vicksburg Weekly Sun*, Nov. 4, 1859; *Louisville Daily Courier*, Apr. 25, 1860.

74. Appleton to James Buchanan, [Sept.] 1859, T. W. Bartley to Buchanan, Dec. 5, 1859, Cook to Buchanan, Jan. 14, 1860, all in Buchanan Papers; *Bangor Daily Union*, Mar. 7, 1860.

75. *Louisville Daily Courier*, Mar. 5, 1860; *Memphis Daily Avalanche*, Mar. 27, 1860; *Wilmington* (N.C.) *Daily Journal*, Feb. 23, 1860.

76. *Louisville Daily Courier*, Jan. 28, 1860; Sam Milligan to Andrew Johnson, Jan. 18, 1860, in Andrew Johnson, *The Papers of Andrew Johnson*, ed. Leroy P. Graf, Ralph W. Haskins, and Paul Bergeron, 12 vols. (Knoxville, 1967–95), 3:386.

77. *Cincinnati Daily Enquirer*, Mar. 24, 1860; *Providence Daily Post*, Nov. 28, 1859; *New Hampshire State Gazette* (Concord), Mar. 21, 1859; D. P. Rhodes to Douglas, Oct. 23, 1859, Box 26, Folder 1, Douglas Papers; *Columbia City Weekly News*, Jan. 12, 1860.

78. Pierce to Jefferson Davis, Jan. 6, 1860, Box 3, Benjamin F. Butler Papers, Library of Congress; J. A. Cravens to Douglas, Jan. 20, 1860, Box 28, Folder 8, Douglas Papers; Cain to George C. Patterson, May 19, 1860, Box 28, Folder 18, ibid.

79. Enoch P. Sloan to Logan, Jan. 18, 1860, Box 1, John A. Logan Papers, Library of Congress; "pointless," "fatal" from *Louisville Daily Democrat*, Jan. 8, 1860; John Taylor to John G. Davis, May 19, 1860, Box 6, Davis Papers.

80. Thomas L. Drew to Douglas, Jan. 7, 1860, Box 27, Folder 41, Douglas Papers; *Cleveland Plain Dealer*, Jan. 20, 1860; *Louisville Daily Democrat*, Jan. 24, 1860; Wick to Hunter, May 6, 1860, in Ambler, ed., "Correspondence of Hunter," 323; Smith Jones to Davis, Nov. 22, 1859, Box 5, Davis Papers.

81. *Trenton Daily True American*, Jan. 23, 1860; *Cleveland Plain Dealer*, Jan. 24, 1860; Douglas to [James W. Singleton], Mar. 31, 1859, in Douglas, *Letters*, 439; John W. Miller to Davis, May 12, 1860, Box 6, Davis Papers.

82. *Cleveland Plain Dealer*, Apr. 10, 1860; *Charleston Mercury*, Apr. 16, 1860.

Chapter Eight

1. *New York Evening Post*, Apr. 19, 1860; *New York Daily Tribune*, Apr. 19, 1860; Irving Katz, *August Belmont: A Political Biography* (New York, 1968), 67–68; Roy Franklin Nichols, *The Disruption of American Democracy* (1948; rpt. New York, 1967), 292.

2. Nichols, *Disruption of Democracy*, 291. On Yancey, see J. Mills Thornton III, *Politics and Power in a Slave Society: Alabama, 1820-1860* (Baton Rouge, 1978), 382–84. Thornton's interpretation, which I share, may be compared with harsher assessments of Yancey and his cohorts in Nichols, *Disruption of Democracy*, 282, 295; Allan Nevins, *The Emergence of Lincoln*, 2 vols. (New York, 1950), 2:205, 207; Avery O. Craven, *The Growth of Southern Nationalism, 1848-1861* (Baton Rouge, 1953), 326–27; and Damon Wells, *Stephen Douglas: The Last Years, 1857-1861* (Austin, 1971), 208–10.

3. "Address of A. G. Brown to the Mississippi Legislature," printed in *Mississippian* (Jackson), Nov. 16, 1859; *New York Daily News*, Feb. 17, 24, 1860; *Memphis Daily Avalanche*, Feb. 27, 1860.

4. *New Orleans Daily Crescent*, July 28, 31, 1859; "Speech of Hon. L. M. Stone of Pickens in the Alabama Senate," printed in *Montgomery Daily Confederacy*, Dec. 20, 1859.

5. *Proceedings of the National Democratic Convention, Convened at Charleston, South Carolina, April 23, 1860* (Washington, D.C., 1860), 19–21.

6. *Proceedings of the National Convention at Charleston and Baltimore. Pub. by Order of the National Democratic Convention, (Maryland Institute, Baltimore,) under the Supervision of the National Democratic Executive Committee* (Washington, D.C., 1860), 48, 62.

7. Ibid., 69, 68, 60. On the disappointments of the Pierce and Buchanan administrations, see Edmund Ruffin, "The True Policy for the Southern States," [1860], Section 4, Box 6, Edmund Ruffin Papers, Virginia Historical Society, Richmond.

8. *Proceedings at Charleston and Baltimore*, 82, 52, 55 (quotation).

9. Ibid., 121, 127.

10. Nichols, *Disruption of Democracy*, 307–18; Robert W. Johannsen, *Stephen A. Douglas* (New York, 1973), 758–59, 762–63, 767–72.

11. *Providence Daily Post*, May 9, June 14, 1860; *Point Coupee* (La.) *Echo*, reprinted in *Washington States and Union*, May 14, 1860; *St. Joseph* (Mo.) *South* reprinted ibid., May 12, 1860.

12. *Philadelphia Press*, Apr. 30, 1860; *Memphis Daily Appeal*, May 11, 1860.

13. *Albany Atlas and Argus*, May 12, 1860; *Indiana Daily State Sentinel* (Indianapolis), May 14, 1860; *Memphis Daily Appeal*, May 9, 1860; *Mobile Daily Register*, May 4, 1860.

14. Hershel V. Johnson to the editor of the *Albany* (Ga.) *Patriot*, May 28, 1860, Hershel V. Johnson Papers, William R. Perkins Library, Duke University, Durham, N.C.; Foster to Douglas, May 7, 1860, Box 32, Folder 8, Stephen A. Douglas Papers, Joseph Regenstein Library, University of Chicago; R. A. Baker to the editor of the *Montgomery Daily Confederate*, June 4, 1860.

15. *Indiana Daily State Sentinel*, May 12, 1860; *Cincinnati Daily Enquirer*, June 1, 1860.

16. *Boston Herald*, June 26, 1860; Nichols, *Disruption of Democracy*, 307–18; Johannsen, *Douglas*, 758–59, 762–63, 767–72.

17. W. E. Arthur to John W. Stevenson, June 8, 1860, Vol. 28, John W. Stevenson Papers, Library of Congress; Robert Toombs to Alexander H. Stephens, June 9, 1860, in Ulrich B. Phillips, ed., "Correspondence of Robert Toombs, Alexander H. Stephens, and Howell Cobb," *Annual Report of the American Historical Association for the Year 1911*, 2 vols. (Washington, D.C., 1913), 2:481; *Address to the Democracy and the People of the United States, by the National Democratic Executive Committee* (Washington, D.C., 1860), 4; Johnson to Stevenson, May 16, 1860, Vol. 27, Stevenson Papers. A somewhat more sympathetic northern Democrat, noting Douglas's determination to go to the people with his cause, observed that it occurred to him that "the 'Little Giant' rather likes to be in hot water—and is never more pleased than when to use one of his own expressions he is 'assailed.' There is after all a pluck and pet about him that captivates—and here I think is the secret of his strength" (C. M. Ingersoll to Stevenson, June 4, 1860, Vol. 28, Stevenson Papers).

18. Toombs to Stephens, June 9, 1860, in Phillips, ed., "Correspondence of Toombs, Stephens, and Cobb," 481; *Mississippian*, May 4, 1860; *Cleveland Daily National Democrat*, May 14, 1860.

19. *Wilmington* (N.C.) *Daily Journal*, May 1, 1860; *New York Daily News*, May 12, 1860; *Daily South Carolinian*, May 6, 1860, in Dwight L. Dumond, ed., *Southern Editorials on Secession* (1931; rpt. Gloucester, 1964), 73; *Newark* (N.J.) *Evening Journal*, May 3, 1860.

20. *Memphis Daily Avalanche*, May 10, 1860; *Newark Evening Journal*, May 3, 1860.

21. *Nashville Union and American*, June 28, 1860; *Louisville Daily Courier*, May 7, 1860; Potter, *Impending Crisis*, 412–13; Nichols, *Disruption of Democracy*, 310–13, 317–18.

22. *Louisville Daily Courier*, July 19, 1860.

23. *Boston Daily Journal*, Apr. 25, 1860; *Newark Daily Advertiser*, June 25, 1860; *New York Daily Tribune*, Apr. 30, 1860; *Indianapolis Daily Journal*, May 4, 1860; *Sciotto Gazette* (Chillicothe, Ohio), May 22, 1860.

24. *New York Evening Post*, May 12, 1860; *Indianapolis Daily Journal*, May 10, 1860. See also William McKee Dunn, *The Republican Party and the Republican Candidate for the Presidency. Speech of Hon. W. McKee Dunn, of Indiana, Delivered in Independence Square, Philadelphia, May 26, 1860, before a Mass Meeting, Held to Ratify the Nominations of Abraham Lincoln and Hannibal Hamlin for the Presidency and Vice Presidency of the United States* (Washington, D.C., 1860), 2.

25. *Providence Daily Journal*, Jan. 10, 1860; *Philadelphia Daily News*, Feb. 24, 1860. These sentiments were linked invariably to the territorial question. Orville Hickman Browning insisted that rather than extend the area of freedom, Democrats were employing all means fair and foul "to acquire territory for the growth of slavery alone." If allowed to shape the character of the western territories, another Republican

added, "the National Government shall promote the extension of a system which enslaves the husbandman and makes the mechanic chattel." In 1844, Whigs had insisted that rapid expansion would lead to degradation. In 1860, Republicans said the same—with a significant twist: slavery, not the conditions of frontier life, would be the means of debasement. The difference is instructive. See Browning, *Speech of Hon. O. H. Browning, Delivered at the Republican Mass-Meeting, Springfield, Ill., August 8th, 1860* (Quincy, 1860), 4; William T. Coggeshall, *The Issue of the November Election. An Address to Young Men: By William T. Coggeshall, Ohio State Librarian. Delivered before the Wide-Awakes of Tiffin, Ohio, Oct. 18, 1860* (Columbus, 1860), 4.

26. *New York Evening Post*, Feb. 15, 1860; *Wisconsin State Journal* (Milwaukee), May 24, 1860; John W. Bell to Simon Cameron, Aug. 22, 1859, Box 4, Simon Cameron Papers, Historical Society of Dauphin County, Harrisburg, Pa.; *Boston Daily Journal*, Nov. 6, 1860.

27. *New Hampshire Statesman* (Concord), Mar. 31, 1861; Browning, *Speech at Springfield*, 14; *Delaware Republican* (Wilmington), July 19, 1860; *Illinois State Journal*, Aug. 8, 14, 1860. The definitive analysis of free-labor ideology is still Eric Foner, *Free Soil, Free Labor, Free Men: The Ideology of the Republican Party before the Civil War* (New York, 1970).

28. *Connecticut Courant* (Hartford), Mar. 17, 1860; *Albany Evening Journal*, Mar. 24, 1860; *Providence Daily Journal*, Apr. 30, 1860. See also John Johnson, *A Defense of Republicanism by John Johnson, Esq., (ex-mayor of Kansas City). An Address Delivered before the Kansas City Republican Club, on the 15th day of September, 1860* (Kansas City, 1860), 3.

29. Potter, *Impending Crisis*, 418–29; Richard H. Sewell, *A House Divided: Sectionalism and Civil War, 1848–1865* (Baltimore, 1988), 74–75; Don E. Fehrenbacher, *Prelude to Greatness: Lincoln in the 1850s* (Stanford, 1962), 143–61. A measure of Republican intransigence on the slavery issue is reflected in a Maine delegate's comment on Seward's waffling that "he ought to consider that the day for compromises has long gone by" (quoted in Sewell, *House Divided*, 75).

30. *Nashville Republican Banner*, Mar. 29, 1860, in Dumond, ed., *Southern Editorials*, 64; *Tuscaloosa Independent Monitor*, Mar. 3, 1860.

31. Everett to Rives, Dec. 12, 1859, and Rives to Hiram Ketchum, June 29, 1859, Box 90, Rives Papers, William Cabell Rives Papers, Library of Congress; *Daily National Intelligencer*, Apr. 26, 1860.

32. Everett to C. C. Lothrop, Edward C. Beecher, and Fred W. Grayson, Feb. 1, 1860, Edward Everett Papers, Massachusetts Historical Society, Boston; *Augusta Daily Chronicle and Sentinel*, Nov. 7, 1860; *Southern Watchman*, reprinted ibid., Oct. 13, 1860; *Nashville Daily Patriot*, July 25, 1860, in Dumond, ed., *Southern Editorials*, 150; Jere Clemens to Richard F. Inge, Mar. 18, 1860, reprinted in *Southern Recorder* (Milledgeville, Ga.), Apr. 24, 1860.

33. Joseph Howard Parks, *John Bell of Tennessee* (Baton Rouge, 1950), 348–49, 352; Nevins, *Emergence of Lincoln*, 2:261–62; Albert D. Kirwan, *John J. Crittenden: The Struggle for the Union* (Lexington, 1962), 336–65. Bell's rivals were Winfield Scott, age seventy-four, Sam Houston, sixty-seven, and Edward Bates, sixty-seven. Bell was seventy-four, Everett, sixty-seven (Potter, *Impending Crisis*, 417). Peter B. Knupfer has recently suggested that despite the age of the party's leaders, it effectively reached a new generation of voters ("Aging Statesmen and the Statesmanship of an Earlier

Age: Generational Roots of the Constitutional Union Party, 1859–1861," paper presented at the Annual Meeting of the American Historical Association, San Francisco, Jan. 7, 1994).

34. *Cleveland Plain Dealer*, Jan. 11, 1860; *Cincinnati Daily Enquirer*, June 29, 1860; *Columbia* (Ind.) *Weekly City News*, Jan. 26, 1860; *Illinois State Register*, Feb. 10, 1860; James M. Lucas to John G. Davis, Dec. 18, 1859, Box 5, John G. Davis Papers, Indiana Historical Society, Indianapolis.

35. James H. Smith to Douglas, Oct. 29, 1859, Box 26, Folder 8, Douglas Papers; *Newport Advertiser*, Feb. 29, 1860; *Albany Atlas and Argus*, May 18, Aug. 31, 1860; *Vermont Patriot* (Burlington), July 21, 1860.

36. *Detroit Free Press*, Sept. 29, 1860.

37. *Peoria* (Ill.) *Daily Democratic Union*, Mar. 7, 1860; *Council Bluffs* (Iowa) *Weekly Bugle*, Apr. 4, 1860; *Wisconsin Patriot*, May 19, 1860; *Cleveland Plain Dealer*, Aug. 15, 1860.

38. *Detroit Free Press*, Sept. 20, 1860; *Cincinnati Daily Enquirer*, Oct. 16, 1860; *Illinois State Register* (Springfield), Sept. 28, 1860; *Peoria Daily Democratic Union*, Oct. 24, 1860.

39. J. K. Egerton to Douglas, July 11, 1860, Box 34, Folder 28, Douglas Papers; H. K. S. O'Malley to John A. Logan, Jan. 6, 1860, Box 1, John A. Logan Papers, Library of Congress; *Vermont Patriot*, Sept. 1, 1860; "Speech of Stephen A. Douglas at Petersburg, Virginia," Aug. 28, 1860, printed in *Detroit Free Press*, Sept. 6, 1860; "Speech of Stephen A. Douglas at Chicago," Oct. 5, 1860, ibid., Oct. 9, 1860.

40. *Pittsburgh Morning Post*, Oct. 10, 1860; *Peoria Daily Democratic Union*, Oct. 5, 1860; Douglas to William A. Richardson, June 20, 1860, in Stephen A. Douglas, *The Letters of Stephen A. Douglas*, ed. Robert W. Johannsen (Urbana, 1961), 492.

41. Stephen Goshen to Douglas, May 5, 1860, Box 32, Folder 4, Douglas Papers; W. B. Boldring to Douglas, Dec. 1859, Box 26, Folder 44, ibid.

42. *Louisville Daily Democrat*, June 1, Oct. 30, 1860; *Providence Daily Post*, Oct. 1, 1860; *Cleveland Plain Dealer*, Jan. 28, 1860; Thomas Oliver to Davis, Feb. 6, 1860, Box 6, Davis Papers; *Davenport* (Iowa) *Weekly Democrat and News*, June 28, 1860.

43. Douglas quoted in Emerson David Fite, *The Presidential Campaign of 1860* (New York, 1911), 150; *Pittsburgh Morning Post*, Oct. 17, 1860; William A. Richardson, *Speech of Hon. W. A. Richardson, of Illinois, Delivered in Burlington, New Jersey, Tuesday Evening, July 17, 1860* (Philadelphia, 1860), 7.

44. Toombs to Robert Collins and others, May 10, 1860, in Phillips, ed., "Correspondence of Toombs, Stephens, and Cobb," 475; *Charleston Mercury*, May 3, 1860.

45. *Louisville Daily Courier*, May 21, 24, 1860; *Memphis Daily Avalanche*, Sept. 15, May 16, 1860; *Mississippian*, July 27, 1860.

46. *San Antonio Ledger and Texan*, May 16, 1860; *Arkansas True Democrat* (Little Rock), Aug. 25, 1860; *Vicksburg Weekly Sun*, Aug. 6, 27, 1860.

47. "Floridian" in *Floridian and Journal* (Tallahassee), Feb. 18, 1860; *Richmond Daily Enquirer*, May 21, 1860; *Wilmington* (N.C.) *Daily Journal*, Oct. 23, 1860. In a breathtaking misreading of political strategy, one northern Breckinridge Democrat declared that the Republicans would avoid taking a principled stand on the territorial issue. Relying on "claptrap and humbug," "slang cries and catch words," they would revive the " 'log cabin' operations of 1840" (*Hartford Weekly Times*, May 25, 1860).

48. *Nashville Union and American*, Sept. 30, 1858; *New York Daily News*, Mar. 9, Feb. 3, 1860; *Hartford Weekly Times*, Mar. 10, 1860.

49. *San Antonio Ledger and Texan*, Aug. 18, 1860; *Arkansas True Democrat*, Mar. 14, 1860.

50. "Extract of a Speech by B. F. Hallett on the Re-Annexation of Texas, 1844," in Benjamin F. Hallett, *Three Letters of B. F. Hallett, to Col. C. G. Green, editor of the Boston Post, on the course of the Democratic Party of Massachusetts, upon Political Abolitionism, the Union, the Nationality, and the Brotherhood of the North and South* ([Boston], 1852), 7; *Indiana State Sentinel*, Apr. 11, 1844; William W. Crump to James Buchanan, Mar. 30, 1860, James Buchanan Papers, Historical Society of Pennsylvania, Philadelphia; *Richmond Semi-Weekly Examiner*, Oct. 26, 1860, in Dumond, ed., *Southern Editorials*, 193.

51. James Lyons to Caleb Cushing, June 15, 1860, Box 87, Caleb Cushing Papers, Library of Congress; *Louisville Daily Courier*, May 26, 1860; *Newport Advertiser*, Aug. 29, 1860; *Cleveland Daily National Democrat*, Sept. 8, 1860; *Louisville Daily Courier*, July 10, 1860.

52. *Memphis Daily Avalanche*, Mar. 7, 1860; *Address to the Democracy by the National Democratic Executive Committee*, 2; *Southern Aegis* (Bel Air, Md.), Sept. 29, 1860; *Richmond Daily Enquirer*, Mar. 7, 1860.

53. *Louisville Daily Courier*, Sept. 27, 1860; *Wilmington Daily Journal*, Sept. 25, 1860; John C. Breckinridge, *Speech of Hon. J. C. Breckinridge. Delivered at Ashland, Ky., September 5th* (New York, 1860), 12; *Richmond Daily Enquirer*, July 10, 1860.

54. *Nashville Union and American*, July 18, 1860; *Vicksburg Weekly Sun*, July 6, Apr. 2, 1860; *Southern Aegis*, Aug. 18, 1860.

55. *Nashville Union and American*, July 18, 1860; *Memphis Daily Avalanche*, Nov. 1, 1860; *Vicksburg Weekly Sun*, Oct. 8, 1860; Clement Claiborne Clay, *Speech on Slavery Issues delivered at Huntsville, Alabama, Sept. 5, 1859* (Huntsville, [1859?]), 2; *Richmond Daily Enquirer*, Oct. 18, 1860; *Hartford Weekly Times*, Sept. 29, 1860.

56. *Mississippian*, June 22, 1860; John Tyler to Joseph Holt, July 21, 1860, Vol. 25, Joseph Holt Papers, Library of Congress; Lane to Cushing, June 30, 1860, Box 87, Cushing Papers; Breckinridge to Cushing, July 6, 1860, File 2, Breckinridge-Marshall Papers, Filson Club, Louisville, Ky.

57. Yancey quoted in Fite, *Campaign of 1860*, 166; Miles to Bancroft, Feb. 6, 1860, George Bancroft Papers, Massachusetts Historical Society, Boston; *Vicksburg Weekly Sun*, Oct. 1, 1860.

58. John W. Bell to Simon Cameron, Aug. 22, 1859, Box 4, Cameron Papers; "Speech of Hon. Daniel Ullmann of New York at the Lincoln and Hamlin Meeting in Newark, New Jersey," June 12, 1860, Daniel Ullmann Papers, New-York Historical Society, New York; *Albany Evening Journal*, Aug. 2, July 18, 1860.

59. *New York Evening Post*, Sept. 7, 1860; John Hickman, *Democracy—The Old and the New. Speech of Hon. John Hickman, of Penn., on the Battle Ground of Brandywine, September 11, 1860* ([Philadelphia, 1860]), 3; *Harrisburg* (Pa.) *Telegraph*, Mar. 7, 1860; Coggeshall, *The Issue of the Election*, 9; *Albany Evening Journal*, Aug. 25, 1860.

60. Davis to John Fox Potter, Oct. 25, 1859, Moses M. Davis Papers, State Historical Society of Wisconsin, Madison; Howe, "To Nominate, or Not to Nominate? The Debate at the Republican State Convention," transcript copy of an article in the *Wisconsin State Journal*, Mar. 2, 1860, Box 2, Carl Schurz Collection, State Historical Society of Wisconsin, Madison; Browning, *Speech at Springfield*, 5; Wilmot quoted in Republican Party, National Convention, *Proceedings of the First Three Republican National*

Conventions of 1856, 1860, and 1864, including Proceedings of the Antecedent National Convention Held at Pittsburgh, in February, 1856 as Reported by Horace Greeley (Minneapolis, [1893]), 85; *Albany Evening Journal*, June 30, 1860.

61. Carl Schurz, "Speech on the Republican Nomination for the Presidency," transcript of an article in the *Wisconsin State Journal*, Mar. 1, 1860, Box 2, Schurz Collection; Smith D. Atkins, *Democracy and Dred Scott. Speech Delivered by Smith D. Atkins, before the Freeport Wide Awakes, at Plymouth Hall, Monday Evening, Aug. 14, 1860* ([Freeport, 1860]), 13; *Boston Daily Journal*, May 5, 1860; Coggeshall, *The Issue of the Election*, 5.

62. *Address of the Cameron and Lincoln Club of the City of Chicago, Ill., to the People of the North West* (Chicago, 1860), 1; *New York Evening Post*, Mar. 24, 1860; *Delaware Republican*, Aug. 20, 1860; Johnson, *Defense of Republicanism*, 6; *New Hampshire Statesman*, Aug. 11, 1860.

63. Atkins, *Democracy and Dred Scott*, 19; *Albany Evening Journal*, Oct. 5, 1860; Schurz, "Speech on the Republican Nomination."

64. Cyrus Woodman to Martha Osgood, Apr. 5, 1860, Vol. 97, Cyrus Woodman Letterbooks, State Historical Society of Wisconsin, Madison; Thomas Ewing, *Speech of the Hon. Thomas Ewing, at Chillicothe, Ohio, before a Republican Mass Meeting, September 29th, 1860* (Cincinnati, 1860), 13; Hiram J. Keeler to John Dowling, Jan. 10, 1860, Box 2, John Dowling Papers, Indiana Historical Society, Indianapolis.

65. William Dudley Foulke, *Life of Oliver P. Morton, Including His Important Speeches*, 2 vols. (Indianapolis, 1899), 1:69; *Newark Daily Advertiser*, Oct. 27, June 7, 1860; *Boston Daily Journal*, Aug. 8, 1860; *New York Evening Post*, May 11, 1860.

66. J. Webster to John Sherman, May 28, 1860, Vol. 14, John Sherman Papers, Library of Congress; *Connecticut Courant*, May 12, 1860; *Boston Daily Journal*, July 27, 1860. One Republican wag, mindful of the advanced age of the nominees and their dated if quaint political notions, allowed that if the western continent had stood stock-still for thirty years, if social, civil, and political institutions had remained unchanged, the Bell-Everett ticket then might have "vitality enough in it, perhaps, to outlive the first September frost" (*Worcester Palladium*, May 16, 1860).

67. *New York Evening Post*, Feb. 15, 1860; *Indianapolis Daily Journal*, Feb. 13, 1860; Lee F. Crippen, *Simon Cameron, Ante-bellum Years* (1942; rpt. New York, 1972), 181; *Connecticut Courant*, Oct. 27, 1860; *Delaware Republican*, May 7, 1860.

68. *Cincinnati Daily Commercial*, Oct. 18, 1860, in Howard C. Perkins, ed., *Northern Editorials on Secession*, 2 vols. (New York, 1942), 1:54; *Philadelphia Daily News*, Oct. 27, 1860; *Pittsburgh Daily Gazette*, Nov. 2, 1860, in Perkins, ed., *Northern Editorials*, 1:69, 70.

69. *Indianapolis Daily Journal*, May 10, 1860; Browning, *Speech at Springfield*, 3; *Portsmouth Journal of Literature and Politics*, Aug. 18, 1860.

70. *Knoxville Whig*, Mar. 10, May 5, 1860; *Augusta Daily Chronicle and Sentinel*, May 5, 6, 1860.

71. *Augusta Daily Chronicle and Sentinel*, Mar. 13, 7, 1860; *Knoxville Whig*, Mar. 10, 1860.

72. Rives to Crittenden, May 4, 1860, Box 91, Rives Papers; Everett to G. S. Hillard, May 1, 1860, Everett Papers; *Southern Recorder*, May 15, 1860; *New Orleans Daily Crescent*, July 18, 9, 1860.

73. Daniel D. Barnard to Chauncy W. Moore, Chester Driggs, and others, Feb. 2, 1860, Letterbook: 1853–61, Daniel D. Barnard Papers, New York State Library, Albany; *Augusta Daily Chronicle and Sentinel*, Sept. 27, 1860; "Resolutions of the State

Convention of the Constitutional Union Party of Massachusetts," printed in *Daily National Intelligencer*, Apr. 3, 1860; *Columbus* (Ga.) *Daily Enquirer*, May 10, 1860; John A. Gilmer to C. W. Littell, Mar. 2, 1860, printed in *Daily National Intelligencer*, Apr. 29, 1860.

74. *Weekly North Carolina Standard* (Raleigh), June 13, 1860; Bell to William A. Graham, Sept. 6, 1860, in William A. Graham, *Papers of William Alexander Graham*, ed. J. G. de Roulhac Hamilton and Max R. Williams, 7 vols. (Raleigh, 1957–84), 5:174; "Speech by John J. Crittenden to Whigs and Bell Men of Illinois," Oct. 30, 1860, printed in *Illinois State Register*, Oct. 31, 1860; *Knoxville Whig*, Aug. 18, 1860; *Nashville Republican Banner*, Mar. 29, 1860, in Dumond, ed., *Southern Editorials*, 64.

75. *Knoxville Whig*, June 23, Apr. 14, 1860; *Augusta Daily Chronicle and Sentinel*, Apr. 11, Feb. 13, 1860; John J. Crittenden, "To the People of the United States," printed in *Daily National Intelligencer*, Feb. 25, 1860.

76. *Southern Watchman* reprinted in *Augusta Daily Chronicle and Sentinel*, Oct. 13, 1860; "Resolutions of the National Union Party Convention of New Jersey," Feb. 22, 1860, printed in *Daily National Intelligencer*, Feb. 28, 1860; Everett to Hilliard, June 1, 1860, Everett Papers; "Proceedings of the State Convention of the Kentucky Opposition Party," printed in *Daily National Intelligencer*, Feb. 28, 1860; *Tuscaloosa Independent Monitor*, Mar. 3, 1860.

77. Everett to Hunt, July 21, 1860, Everett Papers.

78. *Augusta Daily Chronicle and Sentinel*, Oct. 10, May 15, 1860; *Augusta Daily Chronicle and Sentinel* reprinted in *Southern Recorder*, Apr. 24, 1860; *North Carolina Whig*, Apr. 27, 1860; *Savannah Republican* reprinted in *Augusta Daily Chronicle and Sentinel*, Feb. 3, 1860. See also John V. Mering, "The Slave State Constitutional Unionists and the Politics of Consensus," *Journal of Southern History* 43 (1977): 395–410.

79. *Vicksburg Whig*, Dec. 19, 1859. Edward Bates noted in his diary that "to say only that they go for the Constitution and the enforcement of the laws, is only what every other party says" (quoted in Parks, *Bell*, 356).

80. Belmont to Douglas, July 28, 1860, Box 34, Folder 48, Douglas Papers; Taylor to Douglas, Aug. 13, 1860, Box 35, Folder 11, ibid.; Austin Brown to Douglas, Sept. 2, 1860, Box 35, Folder 18, ibid.; *Cincinnati Daily Enquirer*, Sept. 20, 1860.

81. *Arkansas True Democrat*, Oct. 20, 1860; *Memphis Daily Avalanche*, Oct. 11, 1860; *Augusta Daily Constitutionalist*, Oct. 23, 1860; *Louisville Daily Democrat*, Oct. 21, 1860.

82. W. Dean Burnham, *Presidential Ballots, 1836-1892* (Baltimore, 1955), 77, 246–56; Potter, *Impending Crisis*, 438–39, 442–47.

83. Trumbull to Wade, Nov. 9, 1860, Vol. 4, Benjamin F. Wade Papers, Library of Congress; *Richmond Semi-Weekly Examiner*, Nov. 9, 1860, in Dumond, ed., *Southern Editorials*, 223.

Conclusion

1. Allan Nevins, *The Emergence of Lincoln*, 2 vols. (New York, 1950), 2:375–79 (quotation at 379); Roy Franklin Nichols, *The Disruption of American Democracy* (1948; rpt. New York, 1967), 423–27; Kenneth M. Stampp, *And the War Came: The North and the Secession Crisis, 1860-1861* (1950; rpt. Baton Rouge, 1970), 75–79.

2. T. A. Marshall to Holt, Dec. 29, 1860, Vol. 26, Joseph Holt Papers, Library of Congress; Victor Davoust to Buchanan, Jan. 1, 1861, James Buchanan Papers, Historical Society of Pennsylvania, Philadelphia.

3. *Providence Daily Journal*, Jan. 1, 1861; R. S. Rutherford to Trumbull, Jan. 1, 1861, Vol. 28, Lyman Trumbull Papers, Library of Congress; *Providence Daily Post*, Jan. 1, 1861.

4. David M. Potter, *The Impending Crisis, 1848-1861* (New York, 1976), chap. 18; Nevins, *Emergence of Lincoln*, 2:chap. 18; Nichols, *Disruption of Democracy*, chap. 24; Daniel W. Crofts, *Reluctant Confederates: Upper South Unionists in the Secession Crisis* (Chapel Hill, 1989), esp. chaps. 5-7.

5. The best and most recent interpretation of the fire-eater mentality is Eric H. Walther, *The Fire-Eaters* (Baton Rouge, 1992).

6. The classic studies are J. Mills Thornton III, *Politics and Power in a Slave Society: Alabama, 1800-1860* (Baton Rouge, 1978); and Lacy K. Ford Jr., *Origins of Southern Radicalism: The South Carolina Upcountry, 1800-1860* (New York, 1988).

7. See, for example, William W. Freehling and Craig M. Simpson, eds., *Secession Debated: Georgia's Showdown in 1860* (New York, 1992).

8. Cobb to the People of Georgia, Dec. 8, 1860, in Ulrich B. Phillips, ed., "Correspondence of Robert Toombs, Alexander H. Stephens, and Howell Cobb," *Annual Report of the American Historical Association for the Year 1911*, 2 vols. (Washington, D.C., 1913), 2:514; William H. Sutton to John Covode, Dec. 18, 1860, Box 1, Political Correspondence, 1860 Folder, John Covode Papers, Historical Society of Western Pennsylvania, Pittsburgh; *Congressional Globe*, 36th Cong., 2d sess., Appendix, 311.

9. Hammond, "Draft of a Letter to the South Carolina Legislature," [Dec.] 1860, Box H, James Henry Hammond Papers, South Caroliniana Library, University of South Carolina, Columbia; *Congressional Globe*, 36th Cong., 2d sess., Appendix, 487, 486.

10. *Arkansas True Democrat* (Little Rock), Dec. 15, 1860; *Republican Farmer* (Bridgeport, Conn.), Nov. 9, 1860; Robert S. Holt to Joseph Holt, Nov. 20, 1860, Vol. 26, Holt Papers; Rufus Wheeler Peckham to [Wheeler Hazard Peckham], Jan. 4, 1861, Box 1, Rufus Wheeler Peckham Family Papers, Library of Congress.

11. *Floridian and Journal* (Tallahassee), Nov. 24, 1860; *New Orleans Bee*, Dec. 5, 1860, in Dwight L. Dumond, ed., *Southern Editorials on Secession* (1931; rpt. Gloucester, 1964), 306; *Memphis Daily Avalanche*, Nov. 29, 1860; Robert Holt to Joseph Holt, Nov. 9, 1860, Vol. 26, Holt Papers; *Louisville Daily Courier*, Dec. 19, 1860; *Augusta Daily Constitutionalist*, Nov. 16, 1860, in Dumond, ed., *Southern Editorials*, 244. A Louisiana secessionist had no faith that Lincoln could preserve the South's constitutional rights inasmuch as Democratic presidents, "elected to preserve the Constitution and Slavery," had basely allowed northern legislatures to pass personal liberty laws and generally "to nullify & trample underfoot the Constitution & Laws to protect the rights of the South" (Maunsel White to James D. B. De Bow, Dec. 10, 1860, Box 3, James D. B. De Bow Papers, William R. Perkins Library, Duke University, Durham, N.C.).

12. R. M. T. Hunter to James R. Micou, Thomas Croxton, and Others Signing the Call, Dec. 10, 1860, in Charles H. Ambler, ed., "Correspondence of R. M. T. Hunter, 1826-1876," *Annual Report of the American Historical Association for the Year 1916*, 2 vols. (Washington, D.C., 1918), 2:343; "Message of Governor John W. Ellis," printed in

North Carolina Whig (Raleigh), Nov. 27, 1860; *Richmond Daily Enquirer*, Nov. 26, 1860; *Nashville Union and American*, Nov. 20, 1860.

13. Rayner to Caleb Cushing, Dec. 9, 1860, Box 88, Caleb Cushing Papers, Library of Congress; *Wilmington* (N.C.) *Daily Journal*, Nov. 13, 1860; Robert Holt to Joseph Holt, Nov. 20, 1860, Box 26, Holt Papers.

14. Hunter to Micou, Dec. 10, 1860, in Ambler, ed., "Correspondence of Hunter," 344; Guthrie to Paul G. Washington, Dec. 9, 1860, Folder 1, James Guthrie Papers, Southern Historical Collection, University of North Carolina, Chapel Hill; *Congressional Globe*, 36th Cong., 2d sess., 484.

15. *Nashville Union and American*, Dec. 1, 1860; *Wilmington Daily Journal*, Nov. 13, 1860; Hunter to the Citizens of Essex County, Nov. 24, 1860, Box 32, Hunter-Garnett Collection, Alderman Library, University of Virginia, Charlottesville.

16. Hunter to Micou, Dec. 10, 1860, in Ambler, ed., "Correspondence of Hunter," 338; Hammond, Draft of a Letter, [Dec.] 1860, Box H, Hammond Papers; "Message of Ellis," printed in *North Carolina Whig*, Nov. 27, 1860; *Vicksburg Weekly Sun*, Nov. 19, 5, 1860. Lincoln received 23 percent of the vote in Delaware, 10 percent in Missouri, and no more than 3 percent in any other slave state. South of Virginia, Missouri, and Kentucky, he was not on the ballot.

17. *Richmond Daily Enquirer*, Jan. 19, 1858; Cobb to the People of Georgia, Dec. 6, 1860, in Phillips, ed., "Correspondence of Toombs, Stephens, and Cobb," 515; *Congressional Globe*, 36th Cong., 2d sess., 589, 485.

18. *Congressional Globe*, 36th Cong., 2d sess., 788; *Daily South Carolinian*, Dec. 2, 1860, in Dumond, ed., *Southern Editorials*, 289; J. D. Ashmun to Horatio King, Nov. 5, 1860, Vol. 3, Horatio King Papers, Library of Congress.

19. *Louisville Daily Courier*, Nov. 6, 1860; "Message of Ellis," in *North Carolina Whig*, Nov. 27, 1860; *Congressional Globe*, 36th Cong., 2d sess., 311; *Wilmington Daily Journal*, Nov. 16, 1860.

20. *Congressional Globe*, 36th Cong., 2d sess., 310, 309; Thomas S. Mitchie to James D. Davidson, Dec. 11, 1860, Ser. 1AH, Box 27, James D. Davidson Papers, State Historical Society of Wisconsin, Madison.

21. *Floridian and Journal*, Nov. 10, Dec. 1, 1860; *Louisville Daily Courier*, Dec. 19, 1860; *Vicksburg Weekly Sun*, Nov. 12, 1860.

22. *New Orleans Bee*, Nov. 19, 1860, in Dumond, ed., *Southern Editorials*, 248; *Congressional Globe*, 36th Cong., 2d sess., 486; David Clapton to Clay, Dec. 13, 1860, Box 6, Clement Claiborne Clay Papers, Perkins Library, Duke University, Durham, N.C.

23. [C. B.] Harrison to Lawrence O'Brien Branch, Dec. 2, 1860, Branch Family Papers, Perkins Library, Duke University, Durham, N.C.; *Floridian and Journal*, Nov. 24, 1860; *Daily South Carolinian*, Dec. 2, 1860, in Dumond, ed., *Southern Editorials*, 290; *Congressional Globe*, 36th Cong., 2d sess., 486.

24. "Sectionalism—Votes on the Presidency," [1861], Box 2, Vol. 2, Scrapbook 6, Edward D. Mansfield Papers, Ohio Historical Society, Columbus; *Congressional Globe*, 36th Cong., 2d sess., 1092, 124; D. Cadwell to Benjamin F. Wade, Dec. 25, 1860, Vol. 4, Benjamin F. Wade Papers, Library of Congress.

25. *Albany Evening Journal*, Nov. 7, 1860; *Congressional Globe*, 36th Cong., 2d sess., 262; Aaron F. Perry to Wade, Dec. 25, 1860, and J. D. Cox to Wade, Dec. 21, 1860, Vol. 4, Wade Papers.

26. *Congressional Globe*, 36th Cong., 2d sess., 1091, 57; Bigelow to William Hargreaves, Nov. 10, 1860, Box 1, John Bigelow Papers, New York Public Library, New York.

27. *Congressional Globe*, 36th Cong., 2d sess., 1089, 63, 61; Simon Rush to John Sherman, Dec. 3, 1860, Vol. 17, John Sherman Papers, Library of Congress.

28. *Congressional Globe*, 36th Cong., 2d sess., Appendix, 223, 129, 63; Woodbury Davis to William Pitt Fessenden, Jan. 14, 1861, Vol. 1, William Pitt Fessenden Papers, Library of Congress.

29. Edward Harte to Trumbull, Dec. 20, 1860, Vol. 27, Trumbull Papers; William Reynold to Edward McPherson, Feb. 12, 1861, Box 48, Edward McPherson Papers, Library of Congress; "Justice" to Wade, Dec. 24, 1860, Vol. 4, Wade Papers; E. Chamberlin to Elihu B. Washburne, Dec. 21, 1860, Vol. 12, Elihu B. Washburne Papers, Library of Congress.

30. *Congressional Globe*, 36th Cong., 2d sess., Appendix, 42, 215; *Providence Daily Journal*, Nov. 10, 1860.

31. *Congressional Globe*, 36th Cong., 2d sess., Appendix, 69, 221, 128; James Davis to Covode, Dec. 17, 1860, Box 1, Political Correspondence, 1860 Folder, Covode Papers; *Boston Daily Journal*, Nov. 19, 1860 (morning edition).

32. Wade to Trumbull, Nov. 14, 1860, Vol. 25, Trumbull Papers; Fessenden to Hamilton Fish, Dec. 15, 1860, Vol. 47, Hamilton Fish Papers, Library of Congress; F. Dainese to Trumbull, Nov. 9, 1860, Vol. 24, Trumbull Papers; J. W. Griffin to Sherman, Dec. 25, 1860, Vol. 18, Sherman Papers.

33. W. H. Bradley to Thomas Ewing, Nov. 22, 1860, Box 64, Ewing Family Papers, Library of Congress; A. J. Botts to Washburne, Nov. 24, 1860, Vol. 11, Washburne Papers; *Congressional Globe*, 36th Cong., 2d sess., 1092; Simon Rush to Wade, Dec. 24, 1860, Vol. 4, Wade Papers; *Portsmouth* (N.H.) *Journal of Letters and Politics*, Dec. 22, 1860; James W. Beckman to Horace Greeley, Jan. 17, 1861, Box 6, Horace Greeley Papers, Library of Congress.

34. *Congressional Globe*, 36th Cong., 2d sess., Appendix, 216; Blair to Blair, Nov. 23, 1860, Box 7, Folder 5, Blair-Lee Papers, Firestone Library, Princeton University, Princeton, N.J.

35. *Newark* (N.J.) *Daily Advertiser*, Dec. 21, 1860; *Illinois State Journal* (Springfield), Jan. 22, 1861; *Trenton Daily State Gazette and Republican*, Dec. 6, 1860, in Howard C. Perkins, ed., *Northern Editorials on Secession*, 2 vols. (New York, 1942), 1:194; *New York Evening Post*, Dec. 12, 1860.

36. *Congressional Globe*, 36th Cong., 2d sess., Appendix, 222; *Milwaukee Daily Sentinel*, Jan. 17, 1861; Silas H. Mead to Sherman, Feb. 5, 1861, Vol. 21, Sherman Papers; Jonathan Ward to Wade, Jan. 12, 1861, Vol. 4, Wade Papers.

37. *Illinois State Journal*, Jan. 21, 1861; *Congressional Globe*, 36th Cong., 2d sess., Appendix, 130; J. R. Swan to Sherman, Dec. 17, 1860, Vol. 18, Sherman Papers.

38. Alfred E. Hale to Washburne, Jan. 5, 1861, Vol. 12, Washburne Papers; *Philadelphia Public Ledger*, June 7, 1861; *Chicago Daily Journal*, Apr. 17, 1861, in Perkins, ed., *Northern Editorials*, 2:808; *Cincinnati Daily Commercial*, May 6, 1861; *New York Evening Post*, Dec. 5, 1860; John Olney to Trumbull, Dec. 21, 1860, Vol. 27, Trumbull Papers.

39. *Hartford Weekly Times*, Nov. 17, 1860; *Detroit Free Press*, Nov. 9, 1860; *Rochester Daily Union and Advertiser*, Jan. 29, 1861.

40. *Louisville Daily Democrat*, Nov. 1, Dec. 9, 11, 1860; *Memphis Daily Appeal*, Nov. 14, 1860.

41. *Philadelphia Press*, Jan. 1, 1861; *Illinois State Register*, Nov. 7, 1860; *Wisconsin Patriot* (Milwaukee), Feb. 9, 1861; *Providence Daily Post*, Nov. 19, 1860; *Detroit Free Press*, Nov. 8, 1860; *Cleveland Plain Dealer*, Nov. 9, 1860; *Pittsburgh Morning Post*, Dec. 17, 1860.

42. George M. Wharton to Buchanan, Nov. 16, 1860, Charles Davis to Buchanan, Nov. 10, 1860, George Taylor to Buchanan, Dec. 17, 1860, Davis to Buchanan, Jan. 7, 1861, all in Buchanan Papers; Howard Crosby to Holt, Dec. 31, 1860, Vol. 26, Holt Papers.

43. *Hartford Weekly Times*, Mar. 2, 1861; William H. Ranson to Buchanan, Jan. 12, 1861, Hallett to Buchanan, Dec. 27, 1860, both in Buchanan Papers; *Burlington Weekly Sentinel*, Dec. 21, 1860; "Resolutions of the Democratic Convention of Monroe County, Michigan," Feb. 2, 1861, printed in *Detroit Free Press*, Feb. 7, 1861.

44. *Daily Eastern Argus* (Portland, Maine), Dec. 14, 1860; "Minority Report on Federal Relations," printed in *Indiana Daily State Sentinel* (Indianapolis), Feb. 4, 1861; *Cincinnati Daily Enquirer*, Dec. 8, 1860; *Illinois State Register*, Nov. 16, 1860.

45. "Remarks of John H. Stotsenberg, Democratic Representative, Floyd County, Indiana, in the Indiana House of Representatives," Jan. 31, 1861, printed in *Indiana Daily State Sentinel*, Feb. 4, 1861; "Remarks of M. Jenkenson, Democratic Representative, Allen County, Indiana, in the Indiana House of Representatives," ibid.; *Detroit Free Press*, Jan. 15, 19, 1861.

46. *Cincinnati Daily Enquirer*, Dec. 8, 1860; J. W. Sheahan to Stephen A. Douglas, Dec. 12, 1860, Box 35, Folder 51, Stephen A. Douglas Papers, Joseph Regenstein Library, University of Chicago; D. Solomon to Buchanan, Nov. 18, 1860, Buchanan Papers; Henry E. Parker to Clement Claiborne Clay, Jan. 21, 1861, Box 6, Clay Papers.

47. *New Orleans Daily Crescent*, Nov. 9, 1860; Alexander H. Arthur to Holt, Jan. 11, 1861, Vol. 26, Holt Papers; James A. Hamilton to E. D. Morgan, Dec. 17, 1860, in James A. Hamilton, *Reminiscences of James A. Hamilton; or, Men and Events, at Home and Abroad, during Three Quarters of a Century* (New York, 1869), 456; Gov. [Thomas] Hick to John J. Crittenden, Jan. 25, 1861, Vol. 25, John J. Crittenden Papers, Library of Congress; *Brownlow's Knoxville Whig*, Nov. 17, 1860.

48. James S. Thayer to Crittenden, Dec. 25, 1860, Vol. 23, Crittenden Papers; *Tuscaloosa Independent Monitor*, Feb. 15, 1861, Nov. 16, 1860; Washington Murray to Crittenden, Dec. 24, 1861, Vol. 23, Crittenden Papers; S. E. Woodruff to Crittenden, Jan. 2, 1861, Vol. 24, ibid.; Rives to John H. Bibb et al., Jan. 23, 1861, Box 91, William Cabell Rives Papers, Library of Congress.

49. *Philadelphia Daily News*, Jan. 14, 1861. For other examples of Republicans urging compromise, see Hamilton Fish to Fessenden, Dec. 11, 1860, Vol. 1, Fessenden Papers; W. S. Gilman to Trumbull, Dec. 11, 1860, Vol. 27, Trumbull Papers; J. Dille to Sherman, Jan. 8, 1861, George G. Baker to Sherman, Jan. 8, 1861, both in Vol. 19, Sherman Papers; William S. McCormick to Jonathan Churchman, Feb. 6, 1861, Ser. 1A, Box 16, McCormick Collection, State Historical Society of Wisconsin, Madison; *Newark Daily Advertiser*, Nov. 30, Dec. 8, 13, 1860, Jan. 22, 1861; *New York Daily Tribune*, Dec. 12, 1860; *Hartford Evening Press*, Dec. 3, 1860, in Perkins, ed., *Northern Editorials*, 1:112; and *Connecticut Courant* (Hartford), Mar. 2, 1861.

50. *New York Daily Tribune*, Nov. 21, 19, 1860; *Newark Daily Advertiser*, Dec. 6, 1860; F. E. Patrick to Henry L. Dawes, Dec. 13, 1860, Box 17, Henry L. Dawes Papers, Library of Congress; Hayes to Birchard, [Jan. 12, 1861], typescript, Hayes-Sardis Birchard Correspondence, Rutherford B. Hayes Memorial Library, Fremont, Ohio. As the conflicting (vacillating, really) positions taken by the *New York Daily Tribune* and *Newark Daily Advertiser* suggest, moderate Republicans were ambivalent about the justness (or possibility) of compromise and the wisdom (or likelihood) of peaceful secession. Greeley, for one, was all over the map: now suggesting compromise, now peaceful secession, now taking a hard line.

51. Fessenden to Fish, Dec. 15, 1860, Vol. 47, Fish Papers; George G. Fogg to Henry Dana, Dec. 18, 1860, Box 6, Greeley Papers; Rush to Sherman, Dec. 3, 1860, Vol. 17, Sherman Papers; *Congressional Globe*, 36th Cong., 2d sess., Appendix, 81.

52. William G. Arnold to James F. Simmons, Jan. 17, 1861, Box 24, James F. Simmons Papers, Library of Congress; J. D. Cox to Wade, Dec. 21, 1860, Vol. 4, Wade Papers; William H. Brisbane to George W. Julian, Jan. 31, 1861, Vol. 4, Joshua Giddings–George Julian Correspondence, Library of Congress; G. O. Poseden to Trumbull, Dec. 23, 1860, Vol. 27, Trumbull Papers; [L. S. Abbott] to Sherman, Feb. 8, 1861, Vol. 11 (misfiled), Sherman Papers; John Oldham to Sherman, Jan. 29, 1861, Vol. 21, ibid.; E. Stafford to Trumbull, Dec. 20, 1860, Vol. 27, Trumbull Papers.

53. E. Chamberlin to Washburne, Feb. 19, 1861, Vol. 14, Washburne Papers; Joseph B. Lemen to Trumbull, Dec. 24, 1860, Vol. 28, Trumbull Papers; Wade to Trumbull, Nov. 14, 1860, Vol. 25, ibid.; [?] to Wade, Dec. 23, 1860, Vol. 4, Wade Papers; Milton Sutcliff to Fessenden, Feb. 15, 1861, Vol. 1, Fessenden Papers; A. J. Botts to Washburne, Dec. 31, 1860, Vol. 12, Washburne Papers.

54. *Congressional Globe*, 36th Cong., 2d sess., Appendix, 250, 264; Peleg Bunker to Sherman, Jan. 12, 1861, George B. Nay to Sherman, Jan. 26, 1861, both in Vol. 20, Sherman Papers.

55. *Congressional Globe*, 36th Cong., 2d sess., Appendix, 85; V. L. Moswell to Sherman, Dec. 8, 1860, Vol. 17, Sherman Papers; John Montelius to Washburne, Dec. 5, 1860, Vol. 11, Washburne Papers; F. D. Parish to Sherman, Nov. 23, 1860, Vol. 17, Sherman Papers; Ingersoll to Dawes, Feb. 16, 1861, Box 18, Dawes Papers; *Congressional Globe*, 36th Cong., 2d sess., 313.

56. *Congressional Globe*, 36th Cong., 2d sess., 313, Appendix, 270, 228; *Providence Daily Journal*, Dec. 18, 1860; George B. Nay to Sherman, Jan. 19, 1861, Vol. 20, Sherman Papers.

57. *New York Daily Tribune*, Jan. 16, 1861; *Congressional Globe*, 36th Cong., 2d sess., Appendix, 223; *Albany Evening Journal*, Dec. 13, 1860; *Philadelphia Public Ledger*, June 7, 1861; *Congressional Globe*, 36th Cong., 2d sess., Appendix, 272.

58. *Congressional Globe*, 36th Cong., 2d sess., Appendix, 215, 120; G. H. Bowen to Washburne, Dec. 21, 1860, O. M. Cooley to Washburne, Jan. 2, 1861, both in Vol. 12, Washburne Papers.

Select Bibliography

Primary Sources

Manuscript Collections

Bowdoin College, Brunswick, Maine.
   Fessenden Family Papers
   Nathaniel Hawthorne Papers
   James S. Pike–Charles A. Dana Correspondence [microfilm]
   James S. Pike–William P. Fessenden Correspondence [microfilm]
Chicago Historical Society, Chicago, Illinois.
   Newton Arnold Papers
   David Davis Papers
   Zebina Eastman Papers
   Joseph Gillespie Papers
   Charles Gunther Autograph Collection
   Hardin Family Papers
   John Wentworth Papers
Cincinnati Historical Society, Cincinnati, Ohio.
   Warner M. Bateman Papers
   Oran Follett Papers
   William Greene Papers
   William Greene Scrapbook
   Murat Halstead Papers
   Alexander Long Papers
   Thomas B. Stevenson Papers

Timothy Walker Papers
Columbia University, Butler Library, New York, New York.
  John A. Dix Papers
  Hamilton Fish Papers
  Rufus King Papers
  Peter D. Vroom Papers
Connecticut Historical Society, Hartford, Connecticut.
  John M. Niles Papers
  Gideon Welles Papers
Detroit Public Library, Burton Collection, Detroit, Michigan.
  Austin Black Papers
  Lewis Cass Papers
  Alpheus Felch Papers
  Robert McClelland Papers
  William Woodbridge Papers
Duke University, William R. Perkins Library, Durham, North Carolina.
  Alexander R. Boteler Scrapbook
  Branch Family Papers
  Armistead Burt Papers
  John C. Calhoun Papers
  Campbell Family Papers
  Clement Claiborne Clay Papers
  Henry Clay Papers
  John J. Crittenden Papers
  James D. B. De Bow Papers
  George C. Dromgoole Papers
  Hemphill Family Papers
  George S. Houston Papers
  Hershel V. Johnson Papers
  Lawrence M. Keitt Papers
  George McDuffie Papers
  Appleton Oaksmith Papers
  Francis Pickens Papers
  Alexander H. Stephens Papers
Essex Institute, Salem, Massachusetts.
  George Peabody Papers
  Robert Rantoul Papers
  John Greenleaf Whittier Papers
  Henry A. Wise Papers
Filson Club, Louisville, Kentucky.
  Hew Ainslie Papers
  Breckinridge-Marshall Papers
  Orlando Brown Papers
  John B. Bruner Papers
  Cassius M. Clay Papers
  Henry Clay Papers

Norvin Green Papers
Willis Green Papers
John Warren Grigsby Papers
Guthrie-Caperton Collection
Charles Lanman Papers
David Merriwether Papers
George Miles Papers
Lemuel C. Porter Papers
Preston Family Papers: Davie Collection
Andrew Sea Scrapbook
Texas Miscellaneous Papers
Charles Stewart Todd Papers
Harvard University, Houghton Library, Cambridge, Massachusetts.
J. Preston Bigelow Papers
Abbott Lawrence Papers
Charles E. Norton Papers
Palfrey Family Papers
John A. Quitman Papers
Charles Sumner Papers
Sumner–Samuel Gridley Howe Correspondence
Rutherford B. Hayes Memorial Library, Fremont, Ohio.
Henry Clay Papers
Rutherford B. Hayes Papers
Hayes–Sardis Birchard Correspondence
Hayes–Guy M. Bryan Correspondence
Robert C. Schenck Papers [microfilm]
Historical Society of Dauphin County, Harrisburg, Pennsylvania.
Simon Cameron Papers
Historical Society of Pennsylvania, Philadelphia, Pennsylvania.
William Bigler Papers
James Buchanan Papers [microfilm]
John Cadwalader Papers
Salmon P. Chase Papers
George M. Dallas Diary
George M. Dallas Papers
Edward Carey Gardiner Collection: Henry C. Carey Papers
Henry D. Gilpin Papers: Joel R. Poinsett Collection
Gratz Collection
Charles J. Ingersoll Papers
Jonathan Roberts Papers
Historical Society of Western Pennsylvania, Pittsburgh, Pennsylvania.
Henry Marie Brackenridge Letterbook
John Covode Papers
Illinois State Historical Library, Springfield, Illinois.
Nathaniel P. Banks Papers
Sidney Breese Papers

Orville H. Browning Papers
David Davis Papers
Augustus French Papers
Joseph Gillespie Papers
Ozias Hatch Papers
Kane-Bissell Collection
Charles Lanphier Papers
John A. McClernand Papers
Jesse B. Thomas Papers
Richard S. Thomas Papers
Trumbull Family Papers
Richard Yates Papers
Indiana Historical Society Library, Indianapolis, Indiana.
Daniel Bearss Papers
John G. Davis Papers
John Dowling Papers
William H. English Papers
Fry-Rhue Papers
John L. Ketcham Papers
Elisha King Diary
Henry Smith Lane Papers
Joseph Lane Papers
William Rockhill Papers
William H. Smith Collection: Henry Clay Papers
William H. Smith Collection: Thomas B. Stevenson Papers
William H. Smith Papers
Ephraim G. Squier Papers
Milton Stapp Memoir [typescript]
Indiana State Library, Indianapolis, Indiana.
Joseph A. Wright Papers
Library of Congress, Washington, D.C.
William Allen Papers
Nathaniel P. Banks Papers
Bayard Family Papers
John Bell Papers
Jeremiah S. Black Papers
Blair Family Papers
Milledge Luke Bonham Papers
Breckinridge Family Papers
James Buchanan Papers
Anson Burlingame Papers
Benjamin F. Butler Papers
John C. Calhoun Papers
Simon Cameron Papers
Campbell-Preston-Floyd Family Papers
Zachariah Chandler Papers

Salmon P. Chase Papers
James Chesnut Papers
Henry Clay Papers
John M. Clayton Papers
Schuyler Colfax Papers
Thomas Corwin Papers
John Covode Papers
John J. Crittenden Papers
Jabez Lamar Monroe Curry Papers
Caleb Cushing Papers
Jefferson Davis Papers
Henry L. Dawes Papers
Andrew Jackson Donelson Papers
James Rood Doolittle Papers
Easby-Smith Family Papers
Franklin Harper Elmore Papers
George Eustis Papers
Edward Everett Papers
Ewing Family Papers
John Fairfield Papers
William Pitt Fessenden Papers
Hamilton Fish Papers
Joshua Giddings–George Julian Correspondence
Horace Greeley Papers
Duff Green Papers
Artemus Hale Papers
James Henry Hammond Papers
John Scott Harrison Papers
Joseph Holt Papers
Reverdy Johnson Papers
William High Keim Papers
Horatio King Papers
Robert Todd Lincoln Papers
John A. Logan Papers
Robert McClelland Papers
Louis McLane Papers
John McLean Papers
Edward McPhereson Papers
James Madison Papers
William L. Marcy Papers
James M. Mason Papers
William P. Medill Papers
James Monroe Papers
Justin Smith Morrill Papers
Nathaniel Niles Papers
Rufus Wheeler Peckham Family Papers

Philip Phillips Papers
Francis W. Pickens Papers
Pickens-Bonham Correspondence
Franklin Pierce Correspondence
James K. Polk Papers
Preston Family Papers
Thomas Ritchie Papers
William Cabell Rives Papers
John Sherman Papers
Daniel Sickles Papers
James F. Simmons Papers
Caleb B. Smith Papers
William Russel Smith Papers
Francis Elias Spinner Papers
Ephraim G. Squier Papers
Edwin M. Stanton Papers
Alexander H. Stephens Papers
Thaddeus Stevens Papers
Andrew Stevenson Papers
Stevenson Family Papers: John W. Stevenson Papers
Charles Sumner Papers
Benjamin Tappan Papers
Zachary Taylor Papers
Waddy Thompson Papers
Lyman Trumbull Papers
John Tyler Papers
Martin Van Buren Papers
Benjamin F. Wade Papers
Robert J. Walker Papers
Elihu B. Washburne Papers
Israel Washburne Papers
Israel Washburne Papers: Cadwallader C. Washburn
Daniel Webster Papers
Gideon Welles Papers
John H. Wheeler Papers
Louis Trezevant Wigfall Papers
Henry Wilson Papers
Levi Woodbury Papers
Augustus R. Wright Papers
Library of Virginia, Richmond, Virginia.
Thomas H. Bayly Papers
Garnett-Mercer-Hunter Papers
Robert M. T. Hunter Papers
Hunter-Garnett Papers
John Letcher Papers

James M. Mason Papers
Matthew F. Maury Papers
Thomas Ritchie Papers
Tazewell Family Papers
Henry A. Wise Papers
Maine Historical Society, Portland, Maine.
Charles P. Chandler Papers
Nathan Clifford Papers
Samuel Fessenden Papers
Robert Goodenow Papers
Isaac Hodson Papers
Francis O. J. Smith Papers
William Willis Papers
Maryland Historical Society, Baltimore, Maryland.
Archer Family Papers
Reverdy Johnson Papers
John P. Kennedy Papers
James A. Pearce Papers
Massachusetts Historical Society, Boston, Massachusetts.
Adams Family Papers [microfilm]
Nathan Appleton Papers
George Bancroft Papers
John H. Clifford Papers
Richard H. Dana Jr. Papers
Franklin G. Dexter Papers
Edward Everett Papers [microfilm]
C. E. French Autograph Collection
Abbott A. Lawrence Papers
Horace Mann Papers
Marcus Morton Letterbook
Norcross Autograph Collection
William H. Prescott Papers
William Schouler Papers
Robert C. Winthrop Papers [microfilm]
New Hampshire Historical Society, Concord, New Hampshire.
Atherton Family Papers
Rufus Choate Papers
George G. Fogg Papers
Benjamin B. and Henry F. French Correspondence
John P. Hale Papers
Franklin Pierce Papers
Mason Weare Tappan Papers
Daniel Webster Letterbooks
James Wilson Jr. Papers
Levi Woodbury Papers

New-York Historical Society, New York, New York.
  Aaron V. Brown Papers
  Fairchild Collection: Horatio Seymour Papers
  Albert Gallatin Papers
  John A. King Papers
  Rockwell-Walker Correspondence
  Horatio Seymour Papers
  Ephraim G. Squier Papers
  Daniel Ullmann Papers
  Robert J. Walker Papers
New York Public Library, New York, New York.
  James G. Bennett Papers
  John Bigelow Papers
  Bryant-Godwin Papers
  James R. Doolittle Papers
  Azariah C. Flagg Papers
  Horace Greeley Papers
  Henry J. Raymond Papers
  Samuel J. Tilden Papers
  Gideon Welles Papers
New York State Library, Albany, New York.
  Daniel D. Barnard Papers
  John R. Brodhead Papers
  Benjamin F. Butler Papers
  Hamilton Fish Papers
  William L. Marcy Papers
  Edwin Morgan Papers
  Horatio Seymour Papers
North Carolina State Archives, Raleigh, North Carolina.
  Lawrence O'Bryan Branch Papers
  Nancy Blount Branch Papers
  William A. Graham Papers
  Willie P. Mangum Papers
  David S. Reid Papers
Ohio Historical Society, Columbus, Ohio.
  William Bebb Papers
  Alexander St. Clair Boys Papers
  Lewis D. Campbell Papers
  James B. Clay Papers
  Thomas Ewing Sr. Papers [microfilm]
  Samuel Galloway Papers
  William T. Goggeshall Papers
  Governors' Papers [microfilm]
  Friedrich Hassaurek Papers
  John McLean Papers
  Edward D. Mansfield Papers

John Sloane Papers
Benjamin Tappan Papers
Eli Todd Tappan Papers
Allen G. Thurman Papers
Trimble Family Papers
Princeton University, Firestone Library, Princeton, New Jersey.
Blair-Lee Papers
Butler Family Papers
Silas Wright–Benjamin F. Butler Correspondence
State Historical Society of Wisconsin, Madison, Wisconsin.
Rasmus Anderson Papers
Charles Benton Papers
Edward Bragg Papers
William Brisbane Papers
Henry Cooper Papers
James D. Davidson Papers
Moses M. Davis Papers
James R. Doolittle Papers
Timothy Howe Papers
McCormick Collection
John F. Potter Papers
Carl Schurz Collection
Cadwallader Washburn Papers
Cyrus Woodman Letterbooks
Syracuse University, Syracuse, New York.
John A. Dix Papers
Hamilton Fish Papers
Gerrit Smith Papers
University of Chicago, Joseph Regenstein Library, Chicago, Illinois.
Stephen A. Douglas Papers
University of Maine, Orono, Maine.
Hannibal Hamlin Papers
University of Michigan, William L. Clements Library, Ann Arbor, Michigan.
Lewis Cass Papers
Lucius Lyons Papers
University of North Carolina, Southern Historical Collection, Chapel Hill, North
Carolina.
Daniel M. Barringer Papers
John M. Berrien Papers
John Branch Papers
David F. Caldwell Papers
Robert L. Caruthers Papers
Clingman-Puryear Family Papers
Edward Dromgoole Papers
John W. Ellis Papers
Franklin H. Elmore Papers

Duff Green Papers
James Guthrie Papers
Gustus Adophus Henry Papers
Spencer Jarnagin Papers
Thomas Butler King Papers
John Y. Mason Papers
Christopher G. Memminger Papers
William Porcher Miles Papers
Appleton Oaksmith Papers
Orr-Patterson Family Papers
David Outlaw Papers
Benjamin F. Perry Papers
Quitman Family Papers
James G. Ramsey Papers
Abraham Rencher Papers
Robert Barnwell Rhett Papers
Waddy Thompson Papers
Nicholas Trist Papers
David Valentine Diary
Abraham Venable Papers
John H. Wheeler Papers
Henry A. Wise Papers
Benjamin C. Yancey Papers
University of Pittsburgh, Darlington Memorial Library, Pittsburgh, Pennsylvania.
Robert J. Walker Letterbook
University of Rochester, Rush Rhees Library, Rochester, New York.
William Henry Seward Papers
Thurlow Weed Papers
University of South Carolina, South Caroliniana Library, Columbia, South
Carolina.
Milledge Luke Bonham Papers
John C. Calhoun Papers
Franklin Elmore Papers
James Henry Hammond Papers
Francis W. Pickens Papers
University of Virginia, Alderman Library, Charlottesville, Virginia.
Lawrence O'Bryan Branch Papers
Burwell Family Papers
Joseph C. Cabell Papers
Halsey Family Papers
Robert R. Hubard Papers
Hunter-Garnett Collection
John McCauley Papers
James McDowell Papers
New Market Democratic Association Papers
John A. Quitman Papers

William C. Rives Papers
Edmund Ruffin Papers
Alexander H. H. Stuart Papers
John R. Thompson Papers
Virginia Historical Society, Richmond, Virginia.
Barbour Family Papers
Preston Davie Papers
Hugh Blair Grigsby Papers
Mason Family Papers
Matthew F. Maury Papers
John W. Nash Papers
Preston Family Papers
William C. Rives Papers
Edmund Ruffin Papers

Published Works

OFFICIAL PAPERS

28th Congress, 1st sess., Senate Document 56.
28th Congress, 1st sess., Senate Document 82.
28th Congress, 1st sess., House Report 69.
28th Congress, 2d sess., Senate Document 22
28th Congress, 2d sess., Senate Document 56.
28th Congress, 2d sess., Senate Document 95.
29th Congress, 1st sess., Senate Document 220.
29th Congress, 1st sess., Senate Document 288.
29th Congress, 1st sess., House Executive Document 106.
30th Congress, 1st sess., Senate Executive Document 52.
30th Congress, 2d sess., House Executive Document 1.
34th Congress, 1st sess., House Report 200.
36th Congress, 1st sess., Senate Report 278.
36th Congress, 2d sess., Senate Report 288.
36th Congress, 2d sess., House Report 31.
Ames, Herman V., ed. *Senate Documents on Federal Relations*, No. 4, *Slavery and the Union, 1845-1861*. Philadelphia: Department of History of the University of Pennsylvania, 1906.
Annals of Congress, 15th Congress, 2d sess.–16th Congress, 1st sess. (1819–20).
Bevans, Charles I., comp. *Treaties and Other International Agreements of the United States of America, 1776-1949*. 12 vols. Concord: Rumford Press, 1968–74.
Congressional Globe, 28th Congress, 1st sess.–36th Congress, 2d sess. (1843–61).
Garrison, George Pierce, ed. *Diplomatic Correspondence of the Republic of Texas*. *Annual Report of the American Historical Association for the Years 1907, 1908*. 3 vols. Washington, D.C.: Government Printing Office, 1908–11.
Manning, William R., ed. *Diplomatic Correspondence of the United States: Inter-American Affairs, 1831-1860*. 12 vols. Washington, D.C.: Carnegie Endowment for International Peace, 1932–39.

Richardson, James D., comp. *A Compilation of the Messages and Papers of the Presidents, 1789–1897.* 10 vols. Washington, D.C.: Published by the Authority of Congress, 1896–99.

LETTER COLLECTIONS, DIARIES, AUTOBIOGRAPHIES, AND REMINISCENCES

Abbott, Lyman. *Reminiscences.* Boston: Houghton Mifflin, 1915.

Adams, John Quincy. *Memoirs of John Quincy Adams, Comprising Portions of His Diary from 1795 to 1848.* Edited by Charles Francis Adams. 12 vols. Philadelphia: J. B. Lippincott, 1874–77.

———. *The Writings of John Quincy Adams.* Edited by Worthington C. Ford. 7 vols. New York: Macmillan, 1913–17.

Ambler, Charles H., ed. "Correspondence of Robert M. T. Hunter, 1826–1876." *Annual Report of the American Historical Association for the Year 1916.* 2 vols. Washington, D.C.: Government Printing Office, 1918.

———. *The Life and Diary of John Floyd: Governor of Virginia, an Apostle of Secession, and the Father of the Oregon Country.* Richmond: Richmond Press, 1918.

Arnett, Benjamin W., ed. *Orations and Speeches of J. M. Ashley of Ohio.* Philadelphia: Publishing House of the A.M.E. Church, 1894.

Axley, Lowry, ed. "Letters of Henry Clay to John MacPherson Berrien." *Georgia Historical Quarterly* 29 (1945): 23–41.

Barnes, Thurlow Weed. *Memoir of Thurlow Weed.* Boston: Houghton Mifflin, 1884.

Barnwell, John, ed. "Hamlet to Hotspur: Letters of Robert Woodward Barnwell to Robert Barnwell Rhett." *South Carolina Historical Magazine* 77 (1976): 236–56.

Beale, Howard K., ed. "Diary of Edward Bates, 1859–1866." *Annual Report of the American Historical Association for the Year 1930.* Vol. 4. Washington, D.C.: Government Printing Office, 1933.

Benton, Thomas Hart. *Thirty Years' View, or A History of the Working of the American Government for Thirty Years, from 1820 to 1850.* 2 vols. New York: D. Appleton, 1854–56.

Bigelow, John. *Retrospections of an Active Life.* 5 vols. New York: Baker and Taylor, 1909–13.

Blaine, James G. *Twenty Years of Congress: From Lincoln to Garfield; with a Review of the Events Which Led to the Political Revolution of 1860.* 2 vols. Norwich, Conn.: Henry Bill Publishing Company, 1884.

Boucher, Chauncey S., and Robert P. Brooks, eds. "Correspondence Addressed to John C. Calhoun, 1837–1849." *Annual Report of the American Historical Association for the Year 1929.* Washington, D.C.: Government Printing Office, 1930.

Brown, Everett Somerville, ed. *The Missouri Compromises and Presidential Politics, 1820–1825, from the Letters of William Plumer, Junior, Representative from New Hampshire.* St. Louis: Missouri Historical Society, 1926.

Browning, Orville H. *Diary, 1850–1881.* Edited by Theodore C. Pease and James G. Randall. 2 vols. Springfield, Ill.: Trustees of the Illinois State Historical Library, 1925–33.

Buchanan, James. *The Works of James Buchanan, Comprising His Speeches, State Papers, and Private Correspondence.* Edited by John Bassett Moore. 12 vols. Philadelphia: J. B. Lippincott, 1908–11.

Butler, Benjamin F. *Autobiography and Personal Reminiscences of Major-General Benjamin F. Butler; Butler's Book*. Boston: A. M. Thayer, 1892.

Butler, William Allen. *A Retrospect of Forty Years, 1825–1865*. New York: C. Scribner's Sons, 1911.

Byers, John R., Jr., ed. "Selections from the Official Consular Dispatches of Nathaniel Hawthorne from Liverpool, August 1, 1853–December 31, 1857." *Essex Institute Historical Collections* 113 (1977): 241–322.

Calhoun, John C. *The Papers of John C. Calhoun*. Edited by Robert L. Meriwether, W. Edwin Hemphill, and Clyde N. Wilson. 22 vols. Columbia: University of South Carolina Press, 1959–95.

———. *The Works of John C. Calhoun*. Edited by Richard K. Crallé. 6 vols. New York: Appleton, 1854–55.

Carson, James Petigru. *Life, Letters and Speeches of James Louis Petigru, the Union Man of South Carolina*. Washington, D.C.: W. H. Lowdermilk, 1920.

Chittenden, L. E. *Personal Reminiscences Including Lincoln and Others, 1840–1890*. New York: Richmond, Croscup, 1893.

Claiborne, J. F. H. *Life and Correspondence of John A. Quitman, Major General, U.S.A., and Governor of the State of Mississippi*. 2 vols. New York: Harper and Brothers, 1860.

Clay, Cassius Marcellus. *The Life of Cassius Marcellus Clay: Memoirs, Writings, and Speeches Showing His Conduct in the Overthrow of American Slavery, the Salvation of the Union, and the Restoration of the Autonomy of the States*. Cincinnati: J. Fletcher Brennan, 1886.

Clay, Henry. *The Papers of Henry Clay*. Edited by James F. Hopkins, Mary W. M. Hargreaves, Robert Seager II, et al. 11 vols. Lexington: University Press of Kentucky, 1959–92.

———. *Private Correspondence of Henry Clay*. Edited by Calvin Colton. 1855. Reprint. Freeport: Books for Libraries Press, 1971.

Clingman, Thomas L. *Selections from the Speeches and Writings of Hon. Thomas L. Clingman of North Carolina with Additions and Explanatory Notes*. Raleigh: John Nichols, 1877.

Cluskey, M. W., ed. *Speeches, Messages and Other Writings of the Honorable Albert G. Brown, a Senator in Congress from the State of Mississippi*. Philadelphia: James B. Smith, 1859.

Coleman, Ann M. B., ed. *The Life of John J. Crittenden, with Selections from His Correspondence and Speeches*. 2 vols. Philadelphia: J. B. Lippincott, 1871.

"Col. M. C. Taylor's Diary in Lopez Carbena's Expedition, 1850." *Register of the Kentucky State Historical Society* 19 (1921): 79–89.

Colton, Calvin, ed. *The Life, Correspondence, and Speeches of Henry Clay*. 6 vols. New York: A. S. Barnes, 1857.

Davis, Jefferson. *The Papers of Jefferson Davis*. Edited by Haskell M. Monroe Jr., James T. McIntosh, and Lynda Lasswell Crist. 8 vols. Baton Rouge: Louisiana State University Press, 1971–95.

Dix, Morgan, comp. *The Memoirs of John Adams Dix*. 2 vols. New York: Harper and Brothers, 1883.

Dodson, S. H., comp. "Diary and Correspondence of Salmon P. Chase." *Annual*

Report of the American Historical Association for the Year 1902. Vol. 2. Washington, D.C.: Government Printing Office, 1903.

Douglas, Stephen A. *The Letters of Stephen A. Douglas.* Edited by Robert W. Johannsen. Urbana: University of Illinois Press, 1961.

Everett, Edward. *Orations and Speeches on Various Occasions.* 4 vols., 8th ed. Boston: Little, Brown, 1870-72.

Fairfield, John. *The Letters of John Fairfield.* Edited by Arthur G. Staples. Lewiston: Lewiston Journal Company, 1922.

Fillmore, Millard. "Millard Fillmore Papers." Edited by Frank H. Severance. *Publications of the Buffalo Historical Society* 10 and 11 (1907).

Foote, Henry S. *Casket of Reminiscences.* 1874. Reprint. New York: Negro Universities Press, 1968.

Forbes, John Murray. *Letters and Recollections of John Murray Forbes.* Edited by Sarah Forbes Hughes. 2 vols. Boston: Houghton Mifflin, 1899.

Forney, John W. *Anecdotes of Public Men.* New York: Harper and Brothers, 1873.

Ford, Worthington C., ed. "Van Buren-Bancroft Correspondence, 1830-1845." *Massachusetts Historical Society Proceedings, 1908-1909* 42 (1909): 381-442.

Foulke, William Dudley. *Life of Oliver P. Morton, Including His Important Speeches.* 2 vols. Indianapolis: Bowen-Merrill, 1899.

Gallatin, Albert. *The Writings of Albert Gallatin.* 1879. Reprint. Edited by Henry Adams. 3 vols. New York: Antiquarian Press, 1960.

Godwin, Parke. *A Biography of William Cullen Bryant with Extracts from His Private Correspondence.* 2 vols. New York: D. Appleton, 1883.

Graham, William A. *Papers of William Alexander Graham.* Edited by J. G. de Roulhac Hamilton and Max R. Williams. 7 vols. Raleigh: State Department of Archives and History, 1957-84.

Hamilton, James A. *Reminiscences of James A. Hamilton; or, Men and Events, at Home and Abroad, during Three Quarters of a Century.* New York: Charles Scribner, 1869.

Hamlin, Belle L., ed. "Selections from the Follett Papers, II." *Quarterly Publication of the Historical and Philosophical Society of Ohio* 9 (1914): 70-100.

——. "Selections from the Follett Papers, III." *Quarterly Publication of the Historical and Philosophical Society of Ohio* 10 (1915): 1-38.

——. "Selections from the Follett Papers, IV." *Quarterly Publication of the Historical and Philosophical Society of Ohio* 11 (1916): 1-35.

——. "Selections from the Follett Papers, V." *Quarterly Publication of the Historical and Philosophical Society of Ohio* 11 (1916): 39-78.

Hamlin, Charles Eugene. *The Life and Times of Hannibal Hamlin.* 2 vols. 1899. Reprint. Port Washington, N.Y.: Kennikat Press, 1971.

Holcombe, John W., and Hubert M. Skinner, eds. *Life and Public Services of Thomas A. Hendricks with Selected Speeches and Writings.* Indianapolis: Carlon and Ollenbeck, 1886.

Hollcroft, Temple R., ed. "A Congressman's Letters on the Speaker Election in the Thirty-Fourth Congress." *Mississippi Valley Historical Review* 43 (1956-57): 444-58.

Hone, Philip. *The Diary of Philip Hone, 1828-1851.* Edited by Allan Nevins. 2 vols. 1927. Reprint. New York: Arno Press, 1970.

Houston, Sam. *The Writings of Sam Houston.* Edited by Eugene C. Barker and Amelia W. Williams. 8 vols. Austin: University of Texas Press, 1938–43.

Howe, M. A. DeWolfe. *The Life and Letters of George Bancroft.* 2 vols. New York: Charles Scribner's Sons, 1908.

Jackson, Andrew. *Correspondence of Andrew Jackson.* Edited by John S. Bassett and James Franklin Jameson. 7 vols. Washington, D.C.: Carnegie Institute of Washington, 1926–35.

Jameson, J. Franklin, ed. "Correspondence of John C. Calhoun." *Annual Report of the American Historical Association for the Year 1899.* 2 vols. Washington, D.C.: Government Printing Office, 1900.

Johnson, Andrew. *The Papers of Andrew Johnson.* Edited by Leroy P. Graf, Ralph W. Haskins, and Paul Bergeron. 12 vols. Knoxville: University of Tennessee Press, 1967–95.

Julian, George W. *Political Recollections.* Chicago: Jansen, McClurg, 1884.

———. *Speeches on Political Questions, 1850–1868.* New York: Hurd and Houghton, 1872.

Kendall, Amos. *Autobiography of Amos Kendall.* 1872. Reprint. Edited by William Stickney. New York: Peter Smith, 1949.

King, Rufus. *Life and Correspondence of Rufus King, Comprising His Letters, Private and Official, His Public Documents, and His Speeches.* Edited by Charles R. King. 6 vols. New York: G. P. Putnam's Sons, 1894–1900.

Lamar, Mirabeau Buonaparte. *The Papers of Mirabeau Buonaparte Lamar.* Edited by Charles A. Gulick et al. 6 vols. Austin: A. C. Baldwin and Sons, 1921–27.

"Letters from John Adams Dix to Dr. George Cheyne Shattuck, 1818–1848." *Massachusetts Historical Society Proceedings, 1916–1917* 50 (1917): 135–68.

"Letters to John G. Davis, 1857–1860." *Indiana Magazine of History* 24 (1928): 201–13.

Lincoln, Abraham. *The Collected Works of Abraham Lincoln.* Edited by Roy P. Basler. 8 vols. New Brunswick: Rutgers University Press, 1953–55.

McMillan, Malcolm C., ed. "Joseph Glover Baldwin Reports on the Whig Convention of 1848." *Journal of Southern History* 25 (1959): 366–82.

McPherson, Elizabeth G., ed. "Unpublished Letters from North Carolinians to James K. Polk." *North Carolina Historical Review* 16–17 (1939–40): 54–79, 174–200, 328–57, 428–57.

———. "Unpublished Letters from North Carolinians to Martin Van Buren." *North Carolina Historical Review* 15 (1938): 53–81, 131–55.

Mangum, Willie P. *The Papers of Willie Person Mangum.* Edited by Henry Thomas Shanks. 5 vols. Raleigh: State Department of Archives and History, 1950–56.

Mayes, Edward. *Lucius Q. C. Lamar: His Life, Times, and Speeches, 1825–1893.* Nashville: Publishing House of the Methodist Episcopal Church, South, 1896.

Monroe, James. *The Writings of James Monroe.* 1898–1903. Reprint. Edited by Murray Stanislaus Hamilton. 7 vols. New York: AMS Press, 1969.

Moore, Frederick W., ed. "Calhoun as Seen by His Political Friends: Letters of Duff Green, Dixon H. Lewis, Richard Crallé during the Period from 1831 to 1848." *Publications of the Southern Historical Association* 7 (1903): 159–69, 269–91, 353–61, 419–26.

Motley, John L. *The Correspondence of John Lothrop Motley.* Edited by George W. Curtis. 2 vols. New York: Harper and Brothers, 1889.

Norton, Charles Eliot. *The Letters of Charles Eliot Norton, with Biographical Comment.* Edited by Sara Norton and M. A. DeWolfe Howe. 2 vols. Boston: Houghton Mifflin, 1913.

Palmer, George Thomas, ed. "Letters from Lyman Trumbull to John M. Palmer, 1854–1858." *Journal of the Illinois State Historical Society* 16 (1923–24): 20–41.

Parkman, Francis. *Letters of Francis Parkman.* Edited by Wilbur R. Jacobs. 2 vols. Norman: University of Oklahoma Press, 1960.

Parks, Joseph H., ed. "Polk-Nicholson Letters." *Tennessee Historical Magazine* 8 (1929): 67–80.

Paulding, James Kirke. *The Letters of James Kirke Paulding.* Edited by Ralph M. Aderman. Madison: University of Wisconsin Press, 1962.

Perry, Thomas Sergeant, ed. *The Life and Letters of Francis Lieber.* London: Trubner, 1882.

Phillips, Ulrich B., ed. "Correspondence of Robert Toombs, Alexander H. Stephens, and Howell Cobb." *Annual Report of the American Historical Association for the Year 1911.* 2 vols. Washington, D.C.: Government Printing Office, 1913.

Phillips, Wendell. *Speeches, Lectures, and Letters.* 1863. Reprint. Boston: Lee and Shepard, 1884.

Pierce, Edward L. *Memoirs and Letters of Charles Sumner.* 4 vols. Boston: Roberts Brothers, 1877–93.

Polk, James K. *The Diary of James K. Polk during His Presidency, 1845 to 1849.* Edited by Milo M. Quaife. 4 vols. Chicago: A. C. McClurg, 1901.

Quincy, Edmund. *Life of Josiah Quincy of Massachusetts.* Boston: Ticknor and Fields, 1867.

Reeves, Jesse S., ed. "Letters of Gideon J. Pillow to James K. Polk, 1844." *American Historical Review* 11 (1906): 832–43.

Ruffin, Edmund. *The Diary of Edmund Ruffin.* Edited by William K. Scarborough. 3 vols. Baton Rouge: Louisiana State University Press, 1972–89.

Sanborn, F[ranklin] B[enjamin]. *Recollections of Seventy Years.* 2 vols. Boston: Gorham Press, 1909.

Sargent, Nathan. *Public Men and Events from the Commencement of Mr. Monroe's Administration in 1817, to the Close of Mr. Fillmore's Administration in 1853.* 2 vols. 1875. Reprint. New York: Da Capo Press, 1970.

Schuckers, J. W. *The Life and Public Services of Salmon Portland Chase, United States Senator and Governor of Ohio; Secretary of the Treasury, and Chief Justice of the United States.* New York: D. Appleton, 1874.

Schurz, Carl. *The Reminiscences of Carl Schurz.* 6 vols. New York: McClure, 1907–8.

———. *Speeches, Correspondence and Political Papers of Carl Schurz.* Edited by Frederick Bancroft. 2 vols. New York: G. P. Putnam's Sons, 1913.

Seitz, Don C., ed. *Letters from Francis Parkman to E. G. Squier.* Cedar Rapids, Iowa: Torch Press, 1911.

Seward, William Henry. *Works of William H. Seward.* Edited by George E. Baker. 5 vols. New York: Redfield, 1853–54.

Sherman, John. *John Sherman's Recollections of Forty Years in the House, Senate and Cabinet.* 2 vols. Chicago: Werner, 1895.

Sioussat, St. George L., ed. "Diaries of S. H. Loughlin of Tennessee, 1840, 1843." *Tennessee Historical Magazine* 2 (1916): 43–86.

———. "Letters of James K. Polk to Andrew J. Donelson, 1843–1848." *Tennessee Magazine of History* 3 (1917): 51–74.

———. "Letters of James K. Polk to Cave Johnson, 1838–1848." *Tennessee Historical Magazine* 1 (1915): 209–56.

———. "Selected Letters, 1844–1845, from the Donelson Papers." *Tennessee Historical Magazine* 3 (1917): 134–63, 257–92.

Stanton, Henry B. *Random Recollections.* New York: Harper and Brothers, 1887.

Steiner, Bernard C., ed. "Some Letters from Correspondence of James Alfred Pearce." *Maryland Historical Magazine* 16 (1921): 150–79.

Stephens, Alexander H. *A Constitutional View of the Late War between the States: Its Causes, Character, Conduct, and Results. Presented in a Series of Colloquies at Liberty Hall.* 2 vols. 1868–70. Reprint. New York: Kraus Reprint, 1970.

———. *Recollections of Alexander H. Stephens; His Diary Kept When a Prisoner at Fort Warren, Boston Harbour, 1865; Giving Incidents and Reflections of His Prison Life and Some Letters and Reminiscences.* Edited by Myrta Lockett Avary. 1910. Reprint. New York: Da Capo Press, 1971.

Strong, George Templeton. *The Diary of George Templeton Strong.* Edited by Allan Nevins and M. H. Thomas. 4 vols. New York: Macmillan, 1952.

Ticknor, George. *Life, Letters, and Journals of George Ticknor.* Edited by George S. Hillard. 2 vols. Boston: J. R. Osgood, 1876.

Tilden, Samuel J. *The Writings and Speeches of Samuel J. Tilden.* Edited by John Bigelow. 2 vols. New York: Harper and Brothers, 1885.

Tipton, John. *The John Tipton Papers.* Edited by Nellie Armstrong Robertson and Dorothy Riker. 3 vols. Indianapolis: Indiana Historical Bureau, 1942.

Wainwright, Nicholas B., ed. *A Philadelphia Perspective: The Diary of Sidney George Fisher, Covering the Years 1834–1871.* 2 vols. Philadelphia: Historical Society of Pennsylvania, 1967.

Webster, Daniel. *The Letters of Daniel Webster, from Documents Owned Principally by the New Hampshire Historical Society.* Edited by Claude H. Van Tyne. New York: McClure, Phillips, 1902.

———. *The Papers of Daniel Webster.* Ser. 1, *Correspondence.* Edited by Charles M. Wiltse and Harold D. Moser. 6 vols. Hanover: University Press of New England, 1974–84.

———. *The Private Correspondence of Daniel Webster.* Edited by Fletcher Webster. 2 vols. Boston: Little, Brown, 1851.

Weiss, John. *Life and Correspondence of Theodore Parker.* 2 vols. 1864. Reprint. New York: Bergman, 1969.

Whitman, Walt. *The Gathering of the Forces.* Edited by Cleveland Rogers and John Black. 2 vols. New York: G. P. Putnam's Sons, 1920.

Williams, Mary W., ed. "Letters of E. George Squier to John M. Clayton, 1849–1850." *Hispanic American Historical Review* 1 (1918): 426–34.

Winthrop, Robert C., Jr., ed. *A Memoir of Robert C. Winthrop*. Boston: Little, Brown, 1897.

Wise, Henry A. *Seven Decades of the Union: The Humanities and Materialism, Illustrated by a Memoir of John Tyler, with Reminiscences of Some of His Great Contemporaries*. Philadelphia: J. B. Lippincott, 1872.

CONTEMPORARY PAMPHLETS, PARTY ADDRESSES, AND SPEECHES

Adams, Charles Francis. *Texas and the Massachusetts Resolutions*. Boston: Eastburn's Press, 1844.

———. *What Makes Slavery a Question of National Concern? A Lecture, Delivered by Invitation at New York, January 30, at Syracuse, February 1, 1855*. Boston: Little, Brown, 1855.

[Adams, John] [pseud.]. *To the Hon. John Quincy Adams, and the Other Twenty Members of Congress Who Addressed "The People of the Free States of the Union," Remonstrating Against the Annexation of Texas to the American Union*. Houston, Tex., 1843.

Adams, John Calvin. *General Taylor and the Wilmot Proviso*. Boston: Wilson and Damrell, [1848].

———. *A Northern No! Addressed to the Delegates from the Free States to the Whig National Convention at Philadelphia, 1848*. N.p., 1848.

Address Adopted by the Whig State Convention at Worcester, September 13, 1848. Together with the Resolutions and Proceedings. [Worcester, 1848].

Address and Resolutions, Adopted at the Whig State Convention, Worcester, October 3, 1849, Together with the Speeches of Hon. John Davis, George S. Hilliard, Esq., Hon. Josiah Quincy, Jr., Hon. S. G. Goodrich, and Hon. Linus Child. Boston: Eastburn's Press, 1849.

The Address of Southern Delegates in Congress, to Their Constituents. Washington, D.C.: Towers, 1848.

Address of the Cameron and Lincoln Club of the City of Chicago, Ill., to the People of the North West. Chicago, 1860.

Address of the Central National Democratic Republican Committee to the Democracy of the United States. [Washington, D.C., 1848].

Address of the Committee of the Mississippi Convention to the Southern States. [Jackson?, 1850?].

Address of the Free Soil Association of the District of Columbia to the People of the United States; together with a Memorial to Congress, of 1060 Inhabitants of the District of Columbia, Praying for the Gradual Abolition of Slavery. Washington, D.C.: Buell and Blanchard, 1849.

Address to the Democracy and the People of the United States, by the National Democratic Executive Committee. Washington, D.C.: McGill & Witherow, 1860.

Address to the People of the United States, Together with the Proceedings and Resolutions of the Pro-Slavery Convention of Missouri, Held at Lexington, July, 1855. St. Louis: Printed by the Republican Book and Job Office, 1855.

The Agitation of Slavery. Who Commenced! and Who Can End It! Buchanan and Fillmore Compared from the Record. Washington, D.C.: Printed at the Union Office, 1856.

Allen, George. *The Complaint of Mexico and Conspiracy Against Liberty*. Boston: J. W. Alden, 1843.

Allen, William. *Mr. Clay's Declaration of Principles and Measures for General Harrison's Administration.* Washington, D.C., 1842.

The American Text Book, for the Campaign of 1856. Baltimore: Bull & Tuttle, 1856.

Anderson, Alexander. *The Letter of Alexander Anderson, of Tennessee, in Reply to the Committee of Invitation to Attend a Dinner Given by the Democracy of Maury, Tennessee, on the 13th July to the Delegation from that State to the National Convention.* N.p., 1844.

Andrews, John W. *The Nebraska Bill: Speech of John W. Andrews, esq., at a Meeting of Citizens of Columbus, Ohio, Held February 14th, A.D. 1854.* Columbus: State Journal Office, 1854.

Anti-Slavery Tracts. New York: American Anti Slavery Society, 1855–56.

The Anti-Texass [sic] Legion. Protest of Some Free Men, States and Presses Against the Texass [sic] Rebellion Against the Laws of Nature and of Nations. Albany, 1845.

An Appeal to the Concerned Men of All Parties. N.p., 1860.

The Ashland Text Book, Being a Compendium of Mr. Clay's Speeches, on Various Public Measures. Boston: Redding, 1844.

Atkins, Smith D. *Democracy and Dred Scott. Speech Delivered by Smith D. Atkins, before the Freeport Wide Awakes, at Plymouth Hall, Monday Evening, Aug. 14, 1860.* [Freeport, 1860].

Austin, Arthur Williams. *Speech of Arthur W. Austin, of West Roxbury, at Charlestown, Mass., Nov. 1, 1856.* [Charlestown?, 1856?].

An Authentic Exposition of the "K.G.C.," "Knights of the Golden Circle"; or, A History of Secession from 1834 to 1861. Indianapolis: C. O. Perrine, 1861.

Bacon, David Francis. *Progressive Democracy. A Discourse, on the History, Philosophy and Tendency of American Politics, Delivered in National Hall, New York City, before a Large Mass-Meeting of Whigs and Young Men, by D. Francis Bacon.* Published by the Central Clay Committee at the Request of the Mass Meeting. New York: A. Baptist, 1844.

Bagby, Arthur P. *Letter of Arthur P. Bagby, Senator in Congress, to the People of Alabama.* Washington, D.C.: J. and G. S. Gideon, 1845.

[Barton, Seth]. *The Randolph Letter on the Slavery Question, Published in the Richmond Enquirer, April 10, 1850.* Richmond: Ritchie and Dunnavant, 1850.

[Bayard, William]. *Comments on the Nebraska Bill with Views on Slavery in Contrast with Freedom; Respectfully Addressed to the Free States, by One Acquainted with Southern Institutions.* Albany: J. Munsell, 1854.

Benton, Thomas Hart. *Speech of the Hon. Thos. H. Benton, Delivered at the Capitol at Jefferson City, May 26th, 1849.* St. Louis: Union Job Printers, 1849.

Berry, Rev. Philip. *A Review of the Bishop of Oxford's Counsel to the American Clergy, with Reference to the Institution of Slavery. Also Supplemental Remarks on the Relation of the Wilmot Proviso to the Interests of the Colored Class.* Washington, D.C.: William M. Morrison, 1848.

Black Republican Imposture Exposed! Fraud Upon the People. Frémont and His Speculations. Washington, D.C.: Polkinhorn's Steam Job Office, 1856.

Blair, Montgomery, et al. *Address to the Democracy of Missouri.* [St. Louis, 1850].

Blunt, Joseph. *An Examination of the Expediency and Constitutionality of Prohibiting Slavery in the State of Missouri.* New York: C. Wiley, 1819.

Botts, John Minor. *Letters of John Minor Botts, of Virginia, on the Nebraska Question.* Washington, D.C.: John T. and Lem. Towers, 1853.

———. *The Past, the Present, and the Future of our Country.* Washington, D.C.: Lemuel Towers, 1860.

———. *Speech of Hon. John Minor Botts, Delivered on the Occasion of a Complementary Dinner, at Newark, N.J., on the 19th of September, 1853.* Newark: Printed on the Steam Press of the Daily Mercury, 1853.

———. *Speech of John Minor Botts at a Dinner at Powhatan Courthouse, Virginia, June 15, 1850.* N.p., [1850].

[Botts, John Minor]. *To the Whigs of Virginia.* Washington, D.C.: J. and G. S. Gideon, [1848].

———. *To The Whole Whig Party of the United States.* Washington, D.C.: J. and G. S. Gideon, 1848.

Bradford, Samuel D. *Letters to the Honorable William M. Meredith, Secretary of the Treasury, on His Recent Treasury Report. The Injurious Effects of Protective and Prohibitory Duties, and the Advantages of Free Trade.* Boston: Beals and Greene, 1850.

Breckinridge, John C. *Speech of Hon. J. C. Breckinridge. Delivered at Ashland, Ky., September 5th.* New York; Van Evrie, Horton, 1860.

Brisbane, Albert. "Reform Movements Originating among the Producing Classes." *Harbinger* 2 (Jan. 24, 1846): 111–12.

Broadside for the Times; by E PLURIBUS UNUM. New York: James O. Noyes, 1861.

Brown, Aaron V. *Texas and Oregon. Letters and Speeches of the Hon. A. V. Brown, of Tennessee, in Reply to the Hon. John Quincy Adams, on the Annexation of Texas, and on the Bill for the Organization of a Territorial Government over Oregon.* Washington, D.C.: Blair and Rives, 1845.

Browne, Peter A. *A Lecture on the Oregon Territory.* Philadelphia: United States Book and Job Printing Office, 1843.

Browning, Orville Hickman. *Speech of Hon. O. H. Browning, Delivered at the Republican Mass-Meeting, Springfield, Ill., August 8th, 1860.* Quincy: Whig and Republican Steam Power Press Printer, 1860.

Brownlow, William G. *A Political Register, Setting Forth the Principles of the Whig and Locofoco Parties in the United States, with the Life and Public Services of Henry Clay.* Jonesborough: Office of the "Jonesborough Whig," 1844.

Bulkley, C[harles] H. A. *Removal of Ancient Landmarks: or, The Causes and Consequences of Slavery Extension. A Discourse Preached to the Second Congregational Church of West Winsted, Ct., March 5th, 1854.* Hartford: Press of Case, Tiffany, 1854.

Butler, Benjamin F. *The Candidature for the Presidency in Eight Years of Stephen A. Douglas. His Selfishness, and the Duplicity in Principle of His Followers. Speech of Gen. Benj. F. Butler, in Lowell, August 10, 1860.* Lowell: Hildreth and Hunt, 1860.

Camillus [pseud.]. *The Essays of Camillus, Addressed to the Hon. Joel Holleman, Originally Published in the Norfolk and Portsmouth Herald.* Norfolk: T. G. Braughton & Son, 1841.

Carey, Henry C. *The Past, the Present, and the Future.* Philadelphia: Carey and Hart, 1848.

———. *Principles of Social Science.* 3 vols. Philadelphia: J. B. Lippincott, 1858–59.

———. *The Prospect: Agricultural, Manufacturing, Commercial, and Financial: At the Opening of the Year 1851.* Philadelphia: J. S. Skinner, 1851.

———. *The Slave Trade, Domestic and Foreign; Why It Exists, and How It May Be Extinguished.* Philadelphia: A. Hart, late Carey and Hart, 1853.

Carey, John L. *Slavery and the Wilmot Proviso; with Some Suggestions for a Compromise.* Baltimore: Joseph N. Lewis, 1847.

A Caveat; or Considerations Against the Admission of Missouri, with Slavery into the Union. New Haven: A. H. Maltby, 1820.

Cazneau, Jane. *The King of Rivers, with a Chart of Our Slave and Free Soil Territory. By Cora Montgomery [pseud.].* New York: Charles Wood, 1850.

Channing, William Henry. "Cassius M. Clay's Appeal." *Harbinger* 1 (Oct. 25, 1845): 317–19.

———. "Labor for Wages." *Harbinger* 2 (May 30, 1846): 395–97.

Chapin, Edwin H. *The American Idea, and What Grows Out of It. An Oration, Delivered in the New York Crystal Palace, July 4, 1854.* Boston: Abel Tompkins, 1854.

———. *The Relation of the Individual to the Republic. A Sermon Delivered before His Excellency Marcus Morton, Governor, His Honor Henry H. Childs, Lieutenant Governor, the Honorable Council, and the Legislature of Massachusetts, at the Annual Election, on Wednesday, January 3, 1844.* Boston: Dutton and Wentworth, 1844.

Chase, Salmon P. *Speech of Hon. Salmon P. Chase, Delivered at the Republican Mass Meeting in Cincinnati, August 21, 1855; Together with Extracts from His Speeches in the Senate on Kindred Subjects.* Columbus: Ohio State Journal Company, 1855.

———. *Speech of Senator Chase Delivered at Toledo, May 30, 1851, before a Mass Convention of the Democracy of Northwestern Ohio.* Cincinnati: Ben Franklin Book and Job Office, [1851].

Cheves, Langdon. *Speech of Hon. Langdon Cheves, in the Southern Convention, at Nashville, Tennessee, November 14, 1850.* [Nashville]: Southern Rights Association, 1850.

Chittenden, L. E. *A Report of the Debates and Proceedings in the Secret Sessions of the Conference Convention, for Proposing Amendments to the Constitution of the United States, Held at Washington, D.C., in February, A.D. 1861.* New York: D. Appleton, 1864.

A Citizen of the United States [Benjamin Lundy]. *The war in Texas; a Review of the Facts and circumstances, showing that this contest is a crusade against Mexico, set on Foot and supported by Slaveholders, Land Speculators, &c, in order to reestablish, extend and perpetuate the System of Slavery and the Slave trade.* Philadelphia: Merridew and Gunn, 1837.

Clarke, James Freeman. *The Annexation of Texas. A Sermon, Delivered in the Masonic Temple on Fast Day.* Boston: Office of the Christian World, 1844.

Clay, Cassius M. *Speech of Cassius M. Clay, against the Annexation of Texas to the United States of America in Reply to Col. R. M. Johnson and Others in a Mass Meeting of Citizens of the Eighth Congressional District at the White Sulphur Springs, Scott County, Ky., on Saturday, Dec. 30, 1843.* Lexington: Observer and Reporter Office, 1844.

Clay, Clement Claiborne. *Speech on Slavery Issues Delivered at Huntsville, Alabama, September 5th, 1859.* Huntsville, [1859?].

Clay, Henry. *Mr. Clay's Speech, Delivered at the Mechanic's Dinner in the Appollonian Garden, Cincinnati, on the Third of August, 1830.* Baltimore: Baltimore Patriot Office, 1830.

————. *Mr. Clay's Speech, Delivered in the City of Raleigh, April 13th, 1844.* N.p., [1844].

————. *Speech of Mr. Henry Clay, of Kentucky, Delivered June 27, 1840, on the occasion of a Public Dinner, given in compliment to Him, at Taylorsville, in his native County of Hanover, in the State of Virginia.* N.p., [1840].

Clayton, John M. *Speech of the Hon. John M. Clayton Delivered at a Public Dinner Given to Him at Wilmington on the 16th November 1850, by the Whigs of Delaware.* Wilmington, Del., 1853.

Cleveland, Charles Dexter. *Anti Slavery Addresses of 1844 and 1845. By Salmon P. Chase and Charles Dexter Cleveland.* Philadelphia: J. A. Bancroft, 1867.

Cline, A. J. *Secession Unmasked, or An Appeal from the Madness of Disunion to the Sobriety of the Constitution and Common Sense.* Washington, D.C.: Henry Polkinhorn, 1861.

Clingman, Thomas L. *Letter of T. L. Clingman.* Washington, D.C.: Gideon, [1850].

Cobb, Howell. *Speech of Hon. Howell Cobb, of Georgia, Delivered in Concord, N.H., at a Mass Meeting of the Democratic Party of Merrimac County.* N.p., [1855].

Coercion of the North, as a Union Measure. Baltimore, 1860.

Coggeshall, William T. *The Issue of the November Election. An Address to Young Men: By William T. Coggeshall, Ohio State Librarian. Delivered before the Wide-Awakes of Tiffin, Ohio, Oct. 18, 1860.* Columbus, 1860.

[Colton, Calvin]. *The Junius Tracts.* New York: Greeley and McElrath, 1844.

————. *The Life and Times of Henry Clay.* New York: A. S. Barnes, 1846.

Columbia, S.C. Citizens. *Reception and Speech of P. S. Brooks. — Presentation of Mayor Arthur. — Speech of Mr. Brooks.* Boston: J. P. Jewett, 1856.

Colwell, Stephen. *The South: A Letter from a Friend in the North. With Special Reference to the Effects of Disunion Upon Slavery.* Philadelphia: C. Sherman and Son, 1856.

Considerations on the Impropriety and Inexpediency of Renewing the Missouri Question. By a Pennsylvanian. Philadelphia: M. Carey and Son, 1820.

Constitutional Union Party. *John Bell's Record, a Full Exposition of Mr. Bell's Course on the Slavery Question, from the Commencement of the Abolition-Petition in 1835 down to the Termination of His Congressional Career in 1859.* Washington, D.C.: W. H. Moore, 1860.

Correspondence of Nathan Appleton and John G. Palfrey Intended as a Supplement to Mr. Palfrey's Pamphlet on the Slave Power. Boston: Eastburn's Press, 1846.

Crowell, John. *The Wickedness of the Nebraska Bill. A Sermon Preached in the Second Presbyterian Church, Orange, N.J., February 26th, 1854.* New York: M. W. Dodd, 1854.

Curry, Jabez L. M. *Perils and Duty of the South. Substance of a Speech Delivered by Jabez L. M. Curry, in Talladega, Alabama, November 26, 1860.* Washington, D.C.: L. Towers, 1860.

Curtis, George Ticknor. *The Just Supremacy of Congress over the Territories.* Boston: A. Williams, 1859.

Cushing, Caleb. *Speech of Hon. Caleb Cushing, in Norombega Hall, Bangor, October 2, 1860, before the Democracy of Maine.* Bangor?, 1860.

Cutting, H. P. *The Crisis — Slavery or Freedom. A Discourse Preached in Williston and Hinesburgh, on Sundays, June 25th, and July 2d, 1854.* Burlington: Samuel B. Nichols, 1854.

Cutts, J. Madison. *A Brief Treatise upon Constitutional and Party Questions, and the History of Political Parties, as I Received It Orally from the Late Senator Stephen A. Douglas, of Illinois.* New York: D. Appleton, 1866.

Dahlgren, Charles Gustavus. *Letter to His Excellency Gov. Harris, of Tennessee, on State Rights and Secession, from C. G. Dahlgren.* Natchez: Daily Courier Book and Job Office, 1861.

Dana, Charles A. "Cassius M. Clay—Slavery." *Harbinger* 1 (Sept. 6, 1845): 204–5.
———. "Labor for Wages." *Harbinger* 2 (Apr. 25, 1846): 318–19.

Dana, Richard H. *Speech of Richard H. Dana, Jr., at Manchester, N.H. on Tuesday Evening, February 19, 1861.* Boston: Redding, 1861.

Dawson, John Littleton. *An Address by Hon. John L. Dawson, before the Washington and Union Societies of Washington College. Delivered on Wednesday Evening, June 18th, 1856.* Washington, Pa.: Grayson & Hart, 1856.
———. *Speech of Hon. John L. Dawson, of Pennsylvania, before the Great Democratic Mass Meeting at Waynesburg, Green County, Pennsylvania, August 21, 1856.* Washington, D.C.: Congressional Globe, 1867.

De Bow, J. D. B. *The Interest in Slavery of the Southern Non-Slaveholder. The Right of Peaceful Secession. Slavery in the Bible.* Charleston: Presses of Evans & Cogswell, 1860.

The Democratic Party and Its Fruits. Washington, D.C.: Published under the Authority of the National and Jackson Democratic Association Committee, 1848.

Demund, Isaac S. *Liberty Defended.* New York: John A. Gray, 1851.

Dewey, Orville. *A Discourse on Slavery and the Annexation of Texas.* New York: Charles S. Francis, 1844.

Dodge, Augustus Caesar. *Letter from A. C. Dodge, to His Constituents, Respecting the Kansas-Nebraska Bill.* N.p., 1854.

Dodge, Robert. *Secession: A Book for Every Soldier's Knapsack. Tracts for the War. The Remedy and Result.* New York: James Miller, 1861.

Dorsey, John L. *The Spirit of Modern Democracy Explained.* St. Louis: Press of the Missouri Saturday News, 1840.

Douglas' Doctrine of Popular Sovereignty in the Territories; Its Counterpart. By a Missourian. St. Louis: R. V. Kennedy, 1860.

Douglas, Stephen A. *Address of the Hon. Stephen A. Douglas, at the Annual Fair of the New York State Agricultural Society, Held at Rochester, September, 1851.* Albany: C. Van Benthuysen, 1851.
———. *An American Continental Commercial Union or Alliance.* Edited by J. Madison Cutts. Washington, D.C.: T. McGill, 1889.
———. *Letter of Senator Douglas in Reply to the Editor of the State Capitol Reporter, Concord, N.H.* Washington, D.C.: Sentinel Office, 1854.
———. *Letter of Senator Douglas, Vindicating His Character and His Position on the Nebraska Bill Against the Assaults Contained in the Proceedings of a Public Meeting Composed of Twenty-Five Clergymen of Chicago.* Washington, D.C.: Sentinel Office, 1854.
———. *Remarks of the Hon. Stephen A. Douglas, on Kansas, Utah, and the Dred Scott Decision. Delivered at Springfield, Illinois, June 12, 1857.* Chicago: Daily Times Book & Job Office, 1857.
———. *Speeches of Senator S. A. Douglas, on the Occasion of His Public Receptions by*

the Citizens of New Orleans, Philadelphia, & Baltimore. Washington, D.C.: Lemuel Towers, 1859.

Downs, Solomon W. *Speech of S. W. Downs, before a Public Meeting of the People of the Parish of Union on the Annexation of Texas, Delivered at Farmersville, on the 19th June 1844.* New Orleans: J. A. Noble, [1844].

Dunn, William McKee. *The Republican Party and the Republican Candidate for the Presidency. Speech of Hon. W. McKee Dunn, of Indiana, Delivered in Independence Square, Philadelphia, May 26, 1860, before a Mass Meeting, Held to Ratify the Nominations of Abraham Lincoln and Hannibal Hamlin for the Presidency and Vice Presidency of the United States.* Washington, D.C.: Republican Congressional Committee, 1860.

Dunne, Henry C. *Democracy Versus Know-Nothingism and Republicanism: Letter from Henry C. Dunne to John H. Jones and John Given.* Philadelphia, 1858.

Dwight, John S. "Democracy Versus Social Reform." *Harbinger* 5 (Oct. 16, 1847): 300–302.

Eldridge, James, comp. *John Brown, His Men and Friends. Harpers Ferry Slave Insurrection.* N.p., n.d.

[Ellis, George Edward.] *Letters upon the Annexation of Texas addressed to John Quincy Adams, as originally published in the Boston Atlas under the signature Lisle.* Boston: White, Lewis and Potter, 1845.

Ely, Alfred. *The Revolutionary Movement.* Washington, D.C., 1861.

English, William H. *Address of W. H. E. Delivered at Livonia, Indiana, before the Washington and Orange District Agricultural Society, October 15, 1857.* Washington, D.C.: Congressional Globe Office, 1858.

Everett, Edward. *An Oration Delivered at Charlestown on the Seventy-Fifth Anniversary of the Battle of Bunker Hill, June 17, 1850.* Boston: Redding, 1850.

Ewing, Thomas. *Speech of the Hon. Thomas Ewing, at Chillicothe, Ohio, before a Republican Mass Meeting, September 29th, 1860.* Cincinnati: Rickey, Mallory, 1860.

Fabius. *Common Sense.* Nashville: Republican Banner Office, 1860.

Facts for the Present Crisis, Containing: I. a Letter of Hon Wiley P. Harris to Col. J. F. H. Claiborne. II. Portions of the Late Address of the State Central Democratic Committee of Virginia on the Know-Nothing Issues. III. Resolutions of the Democratic Convention Held at Baltimore, June, 1852. New Orleans: Office of Louisiana Courier, 1855.

Facts for Those Who Will Understand Them. Gen. Cass's Position on the Slavery Question. Defined by Himself and His Friends. Also, a Brief Notice of Southern Objections to Millard Fillmore, the Whig Vice-Presidential Candidate. Washington, D.C.: J. and G. S. Gideon, [1848].

Faulkner, Charles James. *National Politics. Speech of Hon. Chas Jas. Faulkner, of Virginia, at Reading, Pennsylvania, September 4, 1852.* Washington, D.C.: A. O. P. Nicholson, 1853.

Field, David Dudley. *The Danger of Throwing the Election of President into Congress. Speech of David Dudley Field, Delivered at Philadelphia, August 20, 1860.* Washington, D.C., 1860.

Foot, Solomon. *Address to the People of the United States.* Washington, D.C.: Buell and Blanchard, 1854.

Foote, Henry S. *Letter from Hon. H. S. Foote, of Mississippi, to Hon. Henry A. Wise.* N.p., [1849].

Forney, John Wien. *Address on Religious Intolerance and Political Proscription. Delivered at Lancaster, Pa., on the Evening of the 24th of September.* Washington, D.C., 1855.

Forsyth, John. *Letters of Hon. John Forsyth, of Alabama, Late Minister to Mexico, to Wm. F. Samford, Esq., in Defense of Stephen A. Douglas.* Washington, D.C.: L. Towers, 1859.

Free Soil, Free Speech, Free Men. Proceedings of the Democratic Republican State Convention, at Syracuse, July 24, 1856. Albany: J. D. Parsons, 1856.

[Galt, John M.]. *Political Essays.* N.p., [1852?].

Garland, Hugh A. *The Second War of Revolution; or The Great Principles Involved in the Present Controversy between Parties.* Washington, D.C.: Office of Democratic Review, 1839.

Gayarré, Charles. *Address to the People of Louisiana on the State of Parties.* New Orleans: Sherman & Wharton, 1855.

General Cass and the Quintuple Treaty. Washington, D.C.: Published under the Authority of the National and Jackson Democratic Association Committee, 1848.

Gentry, Meredith P. *Speech of M. P. Gentry, of Tennessee, Vindicating His Course in the Late Presidential Election. Delivered to His Constituents at Franklin, Tennessee, November 20, 1852.* Washington, D.C.: Congressional Globe Office, 1853.

———. *Speech of the Hon. M. P. Gentry, Delivered before the Whig State Convention of Nashville, March 20th, 1851.* Nashville: W. F. Bang, 1851.

George, John Hatch. *Speech of John H. George, esq., of Concord, at the Mass Convention of the Democracy of New Hampshire in Honor of the Nomination of General Franklin Pierce, Held at Concord, N.H., June 10, 1852.* N.p.: C. Alexander, [1852?].

Gilbert, John. *The Curious Adventures, Painful Experience, and Laughable Difficulties of a Man of Letters, While Travelling as a Peddler in the South during the Late Harper's Ferry Excitement.* Baltimore: J. Gilbert, 1860.

Godwin, Parke. "Free Trade, Free Soil, Free Labor, and Free Speech." *Harbinger* 6 (Nov. 13, 1847): 12.

Goodloe, Daniel R. *The South and the North: Being a Reply to a Lecture on the North and the South, by Elwood Fisher, Delivered before the Young Men's Mercantile Library Association of Cincinnati, January 16, 1849. By a Carolinian.* Washington, D.C.: Buell and Blanchard, 1849.

Great Union Meeting, Philadelphia, December 7, 1859. Philadelphia: Crissy & Markley, 1859.

[Greenwood, Alfred B.] *Letter of Hon. Alfred B. Greenwood, of Arkansas, to His Constituents.* Washington, D.C.: Congressional Globe Office, 1856.

Hallett, Benjamin Franklin. *The Remedy for Kansas — Equality of all the States in all the Territories. Address of Hon. B. F. Hallett to the Democrats of Cheshire County, at Keene, New Hampshire, Fourth of July, 1856.* Boston: Office of Boston Post, 1856.

———. *Speech of the Hon. B. F. Hallett at the Democratic Ratification Meeting in Waltham, Massachusetts, Friday Evening, November 2, 1855.* [Boston]: Office of the Boston Post, [1855].

———. *Three Letters of B. F. Hallett, to Col. C. G. Greene, editor of the Boston Post, on the course of the Democratic Party of Massachusetts, upon Political Abolitionism, the Union, the Nationality, and the Brotherhood of the North and South.* [Boston], 1852.

Hambleton, James P. *A Biographical Sketch of Henry A. Wise, with a History of the Political Campaign in Virginia in 1855*. Richmond: J. W. Randolph, 1856.

Hamilton, Laurentine. *The Nebraska Offence, A sermon, preached in the Presbyterian Church, Ovid, June 4, 1854*. Ovid, N.Y.: Corydon Fairchild, 1854.

Hammond, Jabez Delano. *Letter to the Hon. John C. Calhoun on the Annexation of Texas*. Cooperstown: H. and E. Phinney, 1844.

[Hammond, James H.] *The North and the South: A Review of the Lecture on the Same Subject, Delivered by Mr. Elwood Fisher, before the Young Men's Mercantile Association of Cincinnati, Ohio*. Charleston: James S. Burges, 1849.

———. *Two Letters on Slavery in the United States, Addressed to Thomas Clarkson, Esq.* Columbia: Allen, McCarter, 1845.

Hayes, John L. *Remarks made at a Democratic meeting in Portsmouth on the 7th of Jan. 1845, in the defence of the course of John P. Hale, in relation to the annexation of Texas*. N.p., [1845].

———. *A Reminiscence of the Free Soil Movement in New Hampshire, 1845*. Cambridge, Mass.: J. Wilson and Son, 1885.

Hempstead, Samuel H. *Speech of Samuel H. Hempstead, esq., on the Mexican War, Delivered in the Democratic State Convention, at Little Rock, Jan. 3, 1848*. Little Rock: Reardon and Garritt, 1848.

[Hickman, George H.] *The Democratic Text Book, Being a Compendium of the Principles of the Democratic Party*. New York: Burgess, Stringer, 1848.

Hickman, John. *Democracy—The Old and the New. Speech of Hon. John Hickman, of Penn., on the Battle Ground of Brandywine, September 11, 1860*. [Washington, D.C., 1860].

———. *Political Issues and Presidential Candidates. Speech of Hon. John Hickman, at Concert Hall, Philadelphia, Tuesday Evening, July 24th, 1860*. [Philadelphia, 1860].

Humphrey, Heman. *The Missouri Compromise: An Address Delivered before the Citizens of Pittsfield, by Rev. Heman Humphrey, D.D., in the Baptist Church, on Sabbath evening, Feb. 26, 1854*. Pittsfield: Reed, Hull and Peirson, 1854.

Hunter, R. M. T. *Speech of Hon. R. M. T. Hunter, of Virginia, before the Democratic Mass Meeting, at Poughkeepsie on October 1, 1856*. New York: J. W. Bell, 1856.

Inducements for the Annexation of Texas to the United States and the Pledges Made by that Government to Texas, fully shown by letters from Cols. Guy M. Bryan and Ashbel Smith. Galveston, Tex.: "News" Steam Book and Job Office, 1876.

The Issue Fairly Presented. The Senate Bill for the Admission of Kansas as a State. Democracy, Law, Order, and the Will of the Majority of the Whole People of the Territory, Against Black Republicanism, Usurpation, Revolution, Anarchy, and the Will of a Meagre Minority. Washington, D.C.: Union Office, 1856.

Jackson Democratic Association. *Jackson Banquet at Washington City, January 8, 1854. Resolutions—Regular and volunteer toasts—Speeches of Mr. Latham, Webster, Col. Forney, and Mr. McNerbany*. Washington, D.C., 1854.

———. *Proceedings at the Banquet of the Jackson Democratic Association, Washington, Eighth of January, 1852*. Washington, D.C.: Congressional Globe Office, 1852.

Jagger, William. *To the People of Suffolk, of All Parties*. New York: Craighead & Allen, 1838.

Jay, John. *America Free, or America Slave. An Address on the State of the Country. Delivered* by *John Jay, esq. at Bedford, Westchester County, New York. October 8th, 1856.* New York: Office of the New York Tribune, [1856].

[Jervis, John Bloomfield]. *Letters Addressed to the Friends of Freedom and the Union, by "Hampden." Originally Published in the New York Evening Post.* New York: W. C. Bryant, 1856.

Johnson, John. *A Defense of Republicanism by John Johnson, Esq., (ex-mayor of Kansas City). An Address Delivered before the Kansas City Republican Club, on the 15th day of September, 1860.* Kansas City: Free State Republican Office, 1860.

Johnston, James. *The Contemplated Secession from the Federal Republic of North America by the Southern States.* Detroit?, 1861.

Johnston, William. *An Address on the Aspect of National Affairs and the Right of Secession. Delivered before the Literary Club of Cincinnati. Saturday Evening, March 16, 1861.* Cincinnati: Rickey & Carroll, 1861.

Kennedy, John Pendleton. *Defence of the Whigs.* New York: Harper and Brothers, 1844.

King, John W. *Federalism: or, The Question of Exclusive Power, the True Issue in the Present Monetary and Political Discussion in the United States.* Cincinnati: Shepard & Stearns, 1840.

Lamar, Mirabeau Buonaparte. *Gen. Mirabeau B. Lamar's Letter to the People of Georgia.* N.p., [1850].

———. *Letter of Gen. Mirabeau B. Lamar, ex-President of Texas, on the Subject of Annexation, Addressed to Several Citizens of Macon, Geo.* Savannah: Thomas Purse, 1844.

Lawrence, Abbott. *Letters from the Hon. Abbott Lawrence to the Hon. William C. Rives, of Virginia.* Boston: Eastburn's Press, 1846.

———. *Remarks of Hon. Abbott Lawrence before the Convention of Manufacturers, Dealers and Operatives, in the Shoe and Leather Trade, Held in the Marlboro' Chapel, Boston, March 2, 1842.* Boston?, 1842.

The Life, Speeches, and Public Service, of John Bell, Together with a Sketch of the Life of Edward Everett. Union Candidates for the Offices of President and Vice-President of the United States. New York: Rudd and Carleton, 1860.

[Longstreet, Augustus Baldwin]. *A Voice from the South: Comprising Letters from Georgia to Massachusetts and to the Southern States. With an Appendix Containing an Article from the Charleston Mercury on the Wilmot Proviso.* Baltimore: Western Continent Press, 1847.

Mallory, Stephen R. *Views of Mr. Mallory, of Florida, on the Relations of the United States with Cuba.* Washington, D.C.: Towers, 1857.

Mann, Horace. *Horace Mann's Letters on the Extension of Slavery into California and New Mexico; and on the Duty of Congress to provide the trial by Jury for alleged fugitive slaves.* Washington, D.C.: Buell and Blanchard, [1850].

[Mann, Jesse.] *The Two Tariffs [1842-46] compared and both found wanting in the element of protection for American Labor.* Boston: Redding, 1846.

Marsh, Leonard. *A Bake-Pan for the Dough-Faces. By One of Them. . . . Try It.* Burlington, Vt.: C. Goodrich, 1854.

Marshall, Thomas F. *Speech of Hon. Thos. F. Marshall, in Opposition to the Principles of the Know-Nothing Organization.* N.p., [1855].

Maryland. General Assembly. House of Delegates. Committee on Federal Relations. *Report of the Committee on Federal Relations, to Which Was Referred That Portion of
the Governor's Message Which Relates to the Controversy Now Existing between the United
States and Great Britain, in Reference to the Oregon Territory.* [Annapolis], 1846.

Massachusetts State Anti-Texas Committee. *Report of the Massachusetts Committee to
Prevent the Admission of Texas as a Slave State.* N.p., [1845].

Massachusetts State Texas Committee. *How to Settle the Texas Question.* [Boston?:
E. Wright?, 1845].

McClure, Alexander K. *Fusion in Pennsylvania.* Philadelphia, 1860.

McHenry, George. *The African Race in America, North and South. Being a Correspondence
on That Subject between Two Pennsylvanians. With an Appendix Containing Extracts in
Reference to the Right of Secession.* London, 1861.

McKnight, Robert. *Mission of Republicans — Sectionalism of Modern Democracy; Speech
of Robert McKnight, of Penn. Delivered in the House of Representatives, April 24, 1860.*
Washington, D.C.: Republican Executive Congressional Committee, 1860.

McRoberts, Samuel. *To the Members of the General Assembly of Illinois.* N.p., 1840.

Nahum, Capen. *Plain Facts and Considerations: Addressed to the People of the United States,
without Distinction of Party, in Favor of James Buchanan, of Pennsylvania, for President,
and John C. Breckinridge, for Vice President. By an American Citizen.* Boston: Brown,
Bazin, 1856.

New York Democratic Vigilant Association. *The Rise and Progress of the Bloody Outbreak
at Harper's Ferry.* New York: John F. Trow, 1859.

New York (State) Legislature. Assembly. *United States Senatorial Question. Speeches De-
livered in the Assembly of the State of New-York by Honorables C. C. Leigh, C. P. Johnson,
J. W. Stebbins, D. C. Littlejohn, A. W. Hull, S. B. Cole and Others, in Exposition of the
Oaths, Obligations and Rituals of the Know-Nothings.* Albany: Weed, Parsons, 1855.

*North and South: Letters Addressed to George P. Marsh, Signed: A Northern Man with Southern
Citizenship.* N.p., [1845].

Nott, Samuel. *Slavery, and the remedy; or Principles and suggestions for a remedial code.*
Boston: Crocker and Brewster, 1856.

*Official Proceedings of the National Democratic Convention, Held in Cincinnati, June 2-6,
1856.* Cincinnati: Enquirer Company Steam Printing Establishment, 1856.

*Official Report of the Great Union Meeting Held at the Academy of Music, New York,
December 19th, 1859.* New York: Dawes and Kent, 1859.

Ohio Coon Catcher [Columbus] 1–11 (Aug. 17, 1844–Oct. 26, 1844).

One Idea. N.p., [1848].

Orr, James L. *The Cincinnati Convention. Letter from James L. Orr, of South Carolina,
to Hon. C. W. Dudley, on the Prospect of Having the State of South Carolina Represented
in the Democratic National Convention to Be Held in Cincinnati.* Washington, D.C.:
H. Polkinhorn's, 1855.

Owens, James B. *The Right, Causes and Necessity for Secession. Argument of the Hon.
James B. Owens, Delegate to the State Convention of Florida on the Secession Resolutions.*
[Apalachicola, Fla., 1861].

Papers for the People. Nos. 1–18, June 26[?]–Oct. 23, 1852. New York: Jefferson Union,
1852.

Parker, Joel. *The True Issue and the Duty of the Whigs. An Address before the Citizens of Cambridge, October 1, 1856.* Cambridge, Mass.: James Munroe, 1856.

Parker, Theodore. *The Nebraska Question. Some Thoughts on the New Assault upon Freedom in America, and the General State of the Country in relation thereto, set forth in a discourse preached at the Music Hall, in Boston, on Monday, Feb. 12, 1854.* Boston: Benjamin B. Mussey, 1854.

Pearce, James Alfred. *Old Line Whigs for Buchanan and Breckinridge. Letters from Hon. James Alfred Pearce and Hon. Thomas G. Pratt to the Whigs of Maryland.* N.p., [1856].

Pendleton, John. *To the Whig Party of Virginia.* Washington, D.C.: J. and G. S. Gideon, 1848.

Phillips, Stephen C. *An Address on the Annexation of Texas, and the Aspect of Slavery in the United States, in Connection Therewith. Delivered in Boston, November 14 and 18, 1845.* Boston: William Crosby and H. P. Nichols, 1845.

Platte County Self-Defense Association. *Negro Slavery, No Evil; or The North and the South. The Effects of Negro Slavery, as Exhibited in the Census, by a Comparison of the Condition of the Slaveholding and Non-slaveholding States, Considered in a Report Made to the Platte County Self-Defense Association, by a Committee, through B. F. Stringfellow, Chairman.* St. Louis: M. Niedner, 1854.

Popular Sovereignty in the Territories. The Democratic Record. Baltimore: Murphy, 1860.

Popular Sovereignty in the Territories: The Dividing Line between Federal and Local Authority. New York: Harper and Brothers, 1859.

Powell, Cuthbert. *Letter of Mr. Cuthbert Powell to the People of the Fourteenth Congressional District of Virginia.* Washington, D.C., 1842.

Pratt, Thomas George. *An Appeal for the Union! Letters of the Hon. Thomas G. Pratt and Hon. James Alfred Pearce, United States Senators, to Their Constituents, the People of Maryland; and a Speech of James B. Clay, Esq., on the Duty of Old-Line Whigs in the Presidential Election.* Washington, D.C.: Union Office, 1856.

Precept and Practice: How They Differ. Washington, D.C., 1860.

Proceedings and Speeches at the Whig Ratification Meeting Held in Washington City on Monday Evening, June 28, 1852. Washington, D.C.: Gideon, 1852.

Proceedings of a Convention of Delegates, Chosen by the People of Massachusetts, without distinction of Party, and Assembled at Faneuil Hall, in the City of Boston, on Wednesday, the 29th Day of January, 1845, to take into consideration the proposed annexation of Texas to the United States. Boston: Eastburn's Press, 1845.

Proceedings of a Public Meeting of the Citizens of Providence Held in the Beneficent Congregational Church, March 7, 1854, to Protest Against Slavery in Nebraska; with the Addresses of the Speakers. Providence: Knowles, Anthony, 1854.

Proceedings of the Democratic National Convention, Held at Baltimore, May 22, 1848. Washington, D.C.: Printed at the Office of Blair and Reeves, 1848.

Proceedings of the Democratic National Convention, Held at Baltimore, June 1–5, 1852, for the Nomination of Candidates for President and Vice President of the United States. Washington, D.C.: Printed by Robert Armstrong, 1852.

Proceedings of the First Three Republican National Conventions of 1856, 1860 and 1864, including Proceedings of the Antecedent National Convention Held at Pittsburg, in February, 1856, as reported by Horace Greeley. Minneapolis: Charles W. Johnson, 1893.

Proceedings of the National Convention at Charleston and Baltimore. Pub. by Order of the National Democratic Convention, (Maryland Institute, Baltimore,) under the Supervision of the National Democratic Executive Committee. Washington, D.C., 1860.

Proceedings of the National Democratic Convention, Convened at Charleston, South Carolina, April 23, 1860. Washington, D.C.: Thomas McGill, 1860.

Proceedings of the Whig State Convention Held at Springfield, Massachusetts, September 10, 1851. [Springfield, 1851].

Proceedings of the Whig State Convention Held at Worcester, Oct. 2d, 1855. With the Official Report of the Speeches of Dr. Luther V. Boll, J. T. Stevenson, Saml. H. Walley, Geo. S. Hillard, Wm C. Fowler, Otis P. Lord, and Letters of Rufus Choate and Robert C. Winthrop. Boston: Published at Office of the Boston Courier, 1855.

Putnam, James O. *The Missouri Compromise: Sketch of the Remarks of James O. Putnam upon the Nebraska Resolutions, in the Senate of State of N. York, Feb. 3, 1854.* Albany: Albany Register Office, 1854.

Randall, Josiah. *Speech of Josiah Randall, esq., of Philadelphia, Delivered at Chambersburg, August 6, 1856, at the Request of the Democratic State Convention, of Pennsylvania.* N.p., [1856].

Raymond, Henry J. *The Slavery Question in New York.* [Albany?, 1850].

Read, John M. *Speech of Hon. John M. Read, at the Democratic Town Meeting in Favor of the Union and California, held in the Hall of the Chinese Museum on Wednesday the 13th March, 1850.* [Philadelphia, 1850].

Reed, Henry. *The Secession of the Whole South an Existing Fact. A Peaceable Separation, the True Course. Its Effect on Peace and Trade between the Sections.* Cincinnati: Henry Reed, 1861.

Reflections and Suggestions on the Present State of Parties. By an Old Clay Whig. Nashville: G. C. Torbett, 1856.

Rencher, Abraham. *Circular Address of Abraham Rencher, of North Carolina, to His Constituents.* Washington, D.C., 1843.

Report of the Discussion at Pottsville—August 10, 1844. Between J. G. Clarkson and F. W. Hughes on the Course of Henry Clay and James K. Polk, Relative to the Protective System, etc. Philadelphia, 1844.

Report of the Union Meeting, Held in Brewster's Hall, New Haven, Connecticut, Wednesday, December 14, 1859. New Haven: Thomas J. Stafford, 1860.

Republican Congressional Committee. *The Ruin of the Democratic Party.* [Washington, D.C.: Republican National Committee, 1860].

[Republican Party]. *Philadelphia National Convention. Circular of the National Committee of the Pittsburgh Convention, Appointed February 22, 1856.* Washington, D.C.: Buell and Blanchard, 1856.

A Review of the Defence of General Cass's Course on the Wilmot Proviso. Washington, D.C.: Towers, 1847.

Richardson, William A. *Speech of Hon. W. A. Richardson, of Illinois, Delivered in Burlington, New Jersey, Tuesday Evening, July 17, 1860.* Philadelphia: Ringwalt & Brown, 1860.

Ripley, George. "The Tendencies of Modern Civilization." *Harbinger* 1 (June 28, 1845): 33–35.

Rives, William C. *Letter from the Hon. William C. Rives to a Friend, on the Important Questions of the Day*. Richmond: Whig Book and Job Office, 1860.

Ruffin, Edmund. *African Colonization Unveiled*. Washington, D.C.: Towers, [1859].

———. *"The Political [!] Economy of Slavery": or, the Institution Considered in Regard to Its Influence on Public Wealth and the General Welfare*. [Washington, D.C.]: Towers, [1857].

Saunders, Romulus. *An Address of R. M. Saunders to the People of North Carolina*. Washington, D.C., 1843.

Schurz, Carl. *Speech of Carl Schurz, of Wisconsin, in Hampden Hall, Springfield, Mass., January 4, 1860*. Washington, D.C.: Buell & Blanchard, 1860.

Sebastian, William K. *Substance of the Speech of Hon. W. K. Sebastian, Made before the Democratic Mass Meeting, at Helena, November 23, 1855*. Washington, D.C.: Congressional Globe Office, 1855.

Sedgwick, Theodore. *Thoughts on the Proposed Annexation of Texas to the United States*. New York: D. Fanshaw, 1844.

Segar, Joseph. *Speech of Mr. Joseph Segar, (of Elizabeth City and Warwick) on the Wilmot Proviso. Delivered in the House of Delegates, January 19, 1849*. Richmond: Shepherd and Colin, 1849.

A Series of Articles on the Cuban Question. Published by the Editors of "La Verdad." New York: Printed at the Office of "La Verdad," 1849.

Seward, William H. *The Destiny of America. Speech of William H. Seward at the Dedication of Capital University, at Columbus, Ohio. September 14, 1853*. Albany: Weed, Parsons, 1853.

———. *Oration by William H. Seward, at Plymouth, December 21, 1855*. Albany: Weed, Parsons, 1856.

———. *The Parties of the Day. Speech of William H. Seward, at Auburn, October 21, 1856*. Washington, D.C.: Republican Association of Washington, 1857.

———. *The True Basis of American Independence: A Lecture before the American Institute, New York, Oct. 20, 1853, in the Broadway Tabernacle*. New York: Fowlers and Wells, 1853.

———. *The True Greatness of Our Country. A Discourse before the Young Catholic Friends' Society at Baltimore, December 22, 1848*. Washington, D.C.: J. and G. S. Gideon, 1848.

Short Answers to Reckless Fabrications, Against the Democratic Candidate for President, James Buchanan. Philadelphia: William Rice, 1856.

[Smith, Seth]. *The National Clay Almanack, 1845*. Philadelphia: Desilver and Muir, 1845.

Smith, Truman. *Remarks of Mr. Truman Smith, of Conn., on the Imputations of N. B. Blunt, Esq., of the City of New York, on His course as a Delegate to the Recent Whig National Convention, together with an exposition of the benefits which will result to the country from the elevation of Gen. Zachary Taylor to the presidency of the United States*. Washington, D.C.: J. and G. S. Gideon, 1848.

The South, in the Union or Out of it. [Washington?, D.C., 1860].

Southern State Rights, Free Trade and Anti-Abolition Tract No. 1. Charleston: Walker and Burke, 1844.

Spaulding, Elbridge G. *The Republican Platform. Revised Speech of Hon. E. G. Spauld-ing, of New York, Delivered at Buffalo and Washington, at Meetings Held to Ratify the Nomination of Abraham Lincoln and Hannibal Hamlin for President and Vice President.* Washington?, D.C., 1860.

Speeches of Messrs. Weller, Orr, Lane, and Cobb Delivered in Phoenix and Depot Halls, Con-cord, N.H., at a Mass Meeting of the Democratic Party of Merrimac County. [Concord, 1856].

Squier, E. G. *"Is Cotton 'King'? A Letter Addressed to Hon. H. B. Anthony, U.S.S."* N.p., [1861].

———. *Lecture on the Condition and True Interests of the Laboring Class of America.* New York, 1843.

———. *Letter to Hon. H. S. Foote.* N.p., [1850].

Stephens, Alexander H. *Extracts from the Speech of the Hon. Alex. H. Stephens, Delivered at Appling, (Ga.) on the 11th July 1855.* New Orleans: Office of Louisiana Courier, 1855.

Straight, A. D. *The Crisis of Eighteen Hundred and Sixty-One in the Government of the United States. Its Cause, and How It Should Be Met.* Indianapolis, 1861.

Stuart, Alexander H. H. *Anniversary Address before the American Institute of the City of New York, at the Broadway Tabernacle, October 18, 1844, during the Seventeenth Annual Fair.* New York: James Van Norden, 1844.

Sumner, Charles. *The Law of Human Progress: An Oration before the Phi Beta Kappa Society of Union College, Schenectady. July 25th, 1848.* Boston: William D. Ticknor, 1849.

———. *The Republican Party; Its Origin, Necessity and Permanence. Speech of Hon. Charles Sumner, before the Young Men's Republican Union of New York, July 11th, 1860.* New York: J. A. H. Hasbrouck, 1860.

———. *The Slave Oligarchy and Its Usurpations. Speech of Hon. Charles Sumner, Novem-ber 2, 1855, in Faneuil Hall, Boston.* Washington, D.C.: Buell and Blanchard, [1855].

Taylor Whiggery Exposed. Washington, D.C.: Published under Authority of National and Jackson Democratic Association Committee, 1848.

The Texas Question, Reviewed by an Adopted Citizen, Having Twenty-One Years of Residence in the United States. New York, 1844.

Thompson, John Burton. *Circular of J. B. Thompson, of Ky., to His Constituents.* Washington, D.C.: J. and G. S. Gideon, [1843].

Thompson, Richard W. *Speech of R. W. Thompson, upon the political aspects of the Slavery question, made at a public meeting of the People, Terre-Haute, Indiana, on the 11th day of August, 1855.* Terre Haute: Express Power Press, 1855.

[Townsend, John]. *The Southern States, Their present peril and their certain remedy. Why do they not right themselves? And so fulfill their Glorious Destiny.* Charleston: Edward C. Councell, 1850.

Trescot, William H. *The Position and Course of the South.* Charleston: Walker and James, 1850.

The True Whig Sentiment of Massachusetts. N.p., [1846?].

The United States Government has injured the Liberty of the people of Cuba. The People of Cuba Demand Justice of the people of America. New York: Impr de "La Verdad," 1849.

Walker, Robert J. *An Appeal for the Union. Letter from the Hon. Robert J. Walker. New York, Tuesday, Sept. 30, 1856. Hon. Charles Shaler and Others, Democratic Committee, Pittsburgh, Pennsylvania.* New York: John F. Trow, [1856].

[Watson, William Robinson]. *An Address to the People of Rhode Island, Published in the Providence Journal, in a Series of Articles during the Months of September and October, 1844.* Providence: Knowles and Vose, 1844.

————. *The Great American Question.* Providence: Knowles and Vose, 1848.

————. *The Whig Party; its objects — its principles — its candidates — its duties — and its prospects. An Address to the people of Rhode Island, Published in the Providence Journal, in a Series of Articles during the months of September and October, 1844. By Hamilton [pseudonym].* Providence: Knowles and Vose, 1844.

Wayland, Dr. Francis. *Dr. Wayland on the Moral and Religious Aspects of the Nebraska Bill. Speech at Providence, R.I., March 7.* Rochester, N.Y.: William N. Sage, 1854.

Webster, Daniel. *An Address Delivered before the New York Historical Society, February 23, 1852, by Daniel Webster.* New York: Press of the Historical Society, 1852.

————. *Correspondence between Mr. Webster and His New Hampshire Neighbors.* Washington, D.C.: Gideon, 1850.

————. *Mr. Webster's Address at the Laying of the Cornerstone of the Addition to the Capitol; July 4th, 1851.* Washington, D.C.: Gideon, 1851.

————. *Mr. Webster's Speeches at Buffalo, Syracuse, and Albany, May, 1851.* New York: Mirror Office, 1851.

————. *Reception of Mr. Webster at Boston, September 30, 1842. With His Speech, Delivered in Faneuil Hall on That Occasion.* Boston: Samuel N. Dickinson, 1842.

————. *Speech Delivered at the Dinner Given to Mr. Webster by the Merchants of Baltimore on Thursday, May 18, 1843.* New York: John S. Taylor, 1843.

————. *Speech Delivered September 1, 1848 at Marshfield, Massachusetts.* Boston: T. R. Marvin, 1848.

————. *Speech of Hon. Daniel Webster, at Abington, October 9, 1848.* N.p., [1848].

————. *Speech of the Hon. Daniel Webster of Massachusetts, at the Dinner Given to Him by the Merchants and Other Citizens of Philadelphia, December 2, 1846.* Washington, D.C.: J. and G. S. Gideon, 1847.

————. *Speeches of Hon. Daniel Webster of Massachusetts, Delivered at the Festival of the Sons of New Hampshire, in Boston, Nov. 7th, 1849.* Boston: James French, 1849.

————. *Speeches of Mr. Webster at Capon Springs, Virginia Together with Those of Sir H. L. Bulwer and Wm. L. Clarke, esq., June 28, 1851.* Washington, D.C.: Gideon, [1851].

Whig Congressional Committee. *Prospect before Us, or Loco Foco Impositions Exposed. To the People of the United States.* Washington, D.C.: Gideon's Office, [1844].

————. *To the Whigs and Conservatives of the United States.* Washington, D.C., 1840.

————. *Whig Textbook, or Democracy Unmasked. To the People of the United States.* Washington, D.C.: Gideon's Office, [1844].

Wickliffe, Robert. *Speech of R. Wickliffe, Jr., . . . Delivered in the National Convention of the Whig Young Men of the United States, Assembled at Baltimore, May 4th & 5th, 1840.* Lexington: Observer & Reporter, 1842.

Will There Be War? Analysis of the Elements Which Constitute, Respectively, the Power of England and the United States . . . by an Adopted Citizen. New York: William Taylor, 1846.

Wilson, John M. *Remarks of Mister John M. Wilson, on the Present and Future Prospects of Cuba: Delivered before the Phoenix Lyceum, in Washington City on Monday Evening, July 3, 1854.* Washington, D.C.: C. Alexander, 1854.

Wilson, William. *The Great American Question, democracy vs. doulocracy; or, Free Soil, free Labor, free Men, and free Speech, against the extension and domination of the slave holding interest. A letter addressed to each freeman of the United States, with special reference to his duty at the approaching election.* Cincinnati: E. Shepard's Steam Press, 1848.

Wilstach, John A. *The Imperial Period of National Greatness. A Lecture on the Destiny of the West, by John A. Wilstach, before the Western Literary Union, at Farmers' Institute, Vicinity of Lafayette, Indiana, 12th of First Month, 1855.* Lafayette: Howe, 1855.

Words of Counsel to Men of Business, by a Man of Business. N.p., [1856].

Yates, Richard. *Governor's Message.* N.p., 1861.

———. *Speech of Hon. Richard Yates, Delivered at the Republican Ratification Meeting, of the Citizens of Sangamon County, in the Hall of the House of Representatives, Springfield, June 7th, 1860.* Springfield?, 1860.

Zabriskie, James C. *Speech of Col. Jas. C. Zabriskie, on the Subject of Slavery, and in Reply to the Address of the Pittsburgh Convention, and Geo. C. Bates, esq. Delivered at Sacramento, Cal., on the 10th Day of May, A.D. 1856.* Sacramento: Democratic State Journal Office, 1856.

NEWSPAPERS

Alabama
Daily Confederacy (Montgomery)
Independent Monitor (Tuscaloosa)
Register and Journal (Mobile)

Arkansas
Arkansas State Gazette (Little Rock)
Arkansas True Democrat (Little Rock)

Connecticut
Connecticut Courant (Hartford)
Daily Times (Hartford)
Republican Farmer (Bridgeport)
Weekly Times (Hartford)

District of Columbia
Constitution
Daily Madisonian
Globe
Madisonian
National Intelligencer
States and Union
Union

Delaware
Daily Republican (Wilmington)
Delaware Gazette (Wilmington)
Delaware Republican (Wilmington)

Florida
Florida Sentinel (Tallahassee)
Floridian and Journal (Tallahassee)
Georgia
Daily Chronicle and Sentinel (Augusta)
Daily Constitutionalist (Augusta)
Daily Enquirer (Columbus)
Daily Republican (Savannah)
Southern Recorder (Milledgeville)
Iowa
Weekly Bugle (Council Bluffs)
Weekly Democrat and News (Davenport)
Illinois
Daily Democratic Register (Peoria)
Illinois State Journal (Springfield)
Illinois State Register (Springfield)
Tribune (Chicago)
Indiana
Daily Journal (Indianapolis)
Indiana Daily State Sentinel (Indianapolis)
Palladium (Richmond)
Weekly City News (Columbia)
Western Sun and General Advertiser (Vincennes)
Kentucky
Daily Courier (Louisville)
Daily Democrat (Louisville)
Daily Journal (Louisville)
Kentucky Whig (Lexington)
Weekly Kentucky Yeoman (Frankfort)
Louisiana
Daily Crescent (New Orleans)
Daily Picayune (New Orleans)
True Delta (New Orleans)
Maine
Daily Eastern Argus (Portland)
Daily Union (Bangor)
Maryland
American and Commercial Daily Advertiser (Baltimore)
Democratic Alleganian (Cumberland)
Southern Aegis (Bel Air)
True Union (Baltimore)
Massachusetts
Daily Atlas and Bee (Boston)
Daily Journal (Boston)
Daily Morning Journal (Boston)

  Herald (Boston)
  Palladium (Worcester)
  Post (Boston)
  Sun (Pittsfield)
Michigan
  Daily Free Press (Detroit)
Mississippi
  Daily Sentinel (Vicksburg)
  Daily Whig (Vicksburg)
  Mississippian (Jackson)
  Southern Banner (Holly Springs)
  Weekly Sun (Vicksburg)
  Weekly Whig (Vicksburg)
Missouri
  Missouri Republican (St. Louis)
New Hampshire
  Journal (Portsmouth)
  Journal of Letters and Politics (Portsmouth)
  New Hampshire Patriot and State Gazette (Concord)
  New Hampshire Sentinel (Concord)
  New Hampshire Statesman (Concord)
  Rough and Ready (Concord)
  Union Democrat (Manchester)
New Jersey
  Daily Advertiser (Newark)
  Evening Journal (Newark)
  New Jersey True American (Trenton)
New York
  Atlas and Argus (Albany)
  Daily News (New York)
  Daily Tribune (New York)
  Daily Union and Advertiser (Rochester)
  Evening Journal (Albany)
  Evening Post (New York)
  Herald (New York)
  Journal of Commerce (New York)
  Morning Courier and New York Enquirer (New York)
  Times (New York)
  Union and Advertiser (Rochester)
North Carolina
  Daily Journal (Wilmington)
  North Carolina Standard (Raleigh)
  North Carolina Whig (Raleigh)
  Register and North Carolina Gazette (Raleigh)
  Semi-Weekly Standard (Raleigh)

Ohio
Commercial (Cincinnati)
Daily Enquirer (Cincinnati)
Daily National Democrat (Cleveland)
Ohio State Journal (Columbus)
Plain Dealer (Cleveland)
Sciotto Gazette (Chillicothe)
Pennsylvania
Daily News (Philadelphia)
Democratic Union (Harrisburg)
Keystone (Harrisburg)
Morning Pennsylvanian (Philadelphia)
Morning Post (Pittsburgh)
North American and U.S. Gazette (Philadelphia)
Old Warrior (Harrisburg)
Pennsylvania Telegraph (Harrisburg)
Press (Philadelphia)
Public Ledger and Daily Transcript (Philadelphia)
State Capitol Gazette (Harrisburg)
Telegraph (Harrisburg)
United States Gazette (Philadelphia)
Rhode Island
Advertiser (Newport)
Daily Journal (Providence)
Daily Post (Providence)
South Carolina
Mercury (Charleston)
Tennessee
Daily Appeal (Memphis)
Daily Avalanche (Memphis)
Republican Banner (Nashville)
Star Spangled Banner (Nashville)
Union and American (Nashville)
Whig (Jonesborough)
Whig (Knoxville)
Texas
Ledger and Texan (San Antonio)
Vermont
Patriot and Gazette (Montpelier)
Vermont Patriot (Burlington)
Weekly Sentinel (Burlington)
Virginia
Daily Enquirer (Richmond)
Semi-Weekly Examiner (Richmond)
Whig (Richmond)

Wisconsin
Daily Patriot (Madison)
Daily Sentinel (Milwaukee)
Wisconsin Patriot (Milwaukee)
Wisconsin State Journal (Milwaukee)

MAGAZINES, WEEKLY JOURNALS, AND PERIODICALS

American Agriculturalist
American Farmer
American Review
Brownson's Quarterly Review
De Bow's Review
Harbinger
Merchants' Magazine and Commercial Review
Monthly Journal of Agriculture
Niles' National Register
Plough, the Loom and the Anvil
Prairie Farmer
Southern Agriculturist
Southern Quarterly Review
Subterranean and Working Man's Advocate
United States Magazine and Democratic Review
Western Journal and Civilian

Secondary Sources

Books and Articles

Abernathy, Thomas P. "Democracy on the Southern Frontier." *Journal of Southern History* 4 (1938): 3–13.

Alexander, Thomas B. *Sectional Stress and Party Strength: A Study of Roll Call Voting Patterns in the United States House of Representatives, 1836–1860.* Nashville: Vanderbilt University Press, 1967.

Anbinder, Tyler. *Nativism and Slavery: The Northern Know Nothings and the Politics of the 1850s.* New York: Oxford University Press, 1992.

Arieli, Yehoshua. *Individualism and Nationalism in American Ideology.* 1964. Reprint. Baltimore: Penguin, 1966.

Ashworth, John. *'Agrarians' and 'Aristocrats': Party Political Ideology in the United States, 1837–1846.* London: Royal Historical Society, 1983.

Bailyn, Bernard. *The Ideological Origins of the American Revolution.* Cambridge, Mass.: Harvard University Press, 1967.

Baker, Jean H. *Affairs of Party: The Political Culture of Northern Democrats in the Mid-Nineteenth Century.* Ithaca: Cornell University Press, 1983.

Barney, William. *The Road to Secession: A New Perspective on the Old South.* New York: Praeger, 1972.

————. *The Secession Impulse: Alabama and Mississippi in 1860*. Princeton: Princeton University Press, 1974.

Bateman, Fred, and Thomas Weis. "Comparative Regional Development in Antebellum Manufacturing." *Journal of Economic History* 35 (1975): 182–208.

Bauer, K. Jack. *The Mexican War, 1846-1848*. New York: Macmillan, 1974.

————. *Zachary Taylor: Soldier, Planter, Statesman of the Old Southwest*. Baton Rouge: Louisiana State University Press, 1985.

Baum, Dale. "Know-Nothingism and the Republican Majority in Massachusetts: The Political Realignment of the 1850s." *Journal of American History* 64 (1977–78): 959–86.

Beard, Charles A., and Mary R. Beard. *The Rise of American Civilization*. 2 vols. New York: Macmillan, 1927.

Belohlavek, John M. *"Let the Eagle Soar!": The Foreign Policy of Andrew Jackson*. Lincoln: University of Nebraska Press, 1985.

Benson, Lee. *The Concept of Jacksonian Democracy: New York as a Test Case*. Princeton: Princeton University Press, 1961.

Berwanger, Eugene H. *The Frontier against Slavery: Western Anti-Negro Prejudice and the Slavery Extension Controversy*. Urbana: University of Illinois Press, 1967.

Bestor, Arthur. "State Sovereignty and Slavery: A Reinterpretation of Proslavery Constitutional Doctrine, 1846-1860." *Journal of the Illinois State Historical Society* 54 (1961): 117–80.

Blue, Frederick J. *The Free Soilers: Third Party Politics, 1848-54*. Urbana: University of Illinois Press, 1973.

————. *Salmon P. Chase: A Life in Politics*. Kent: Kent State University Press, 1987.

Bonner, James C. "Profile of a Late Antebellum Community." *American Historical Review* 49 (1943–44): 663–80.

Boucher, Chauncey S. "*In Re* That Aggressive Slavocracy." *Mississippi Valley Historical Review* 8 (1921): 13–79.

Bourne, Edward G. "The Proposed Absorption of Mexico in 1847–48." *Annual Report of the American Historical Association for the Year 1899*, 1:157–69. Washington, D.C.: Government Printing Office, 1902.

Brauer, Kinley J. *Cotton versus Conscience: Massachusetts Whig Politics and Southwestern Expansion, 1843-1848*. Lexington: University of Kentucky Press, 1967.

Brown, Richard D. *Modernization: The Transformation of American Life, 1600-1865*. New York: Hill and Wang, 1976.

Brown, Richard H. "The Missouri Crisis, Slavery, and the Politics of Jacksonianism." *Southern Atlantic Quarterly* 65 (1966): 55–72.

Brown, Thomas. *Politics and Statesmanship: Essays on the American Whig Party*. New York: Columbia University Press, 1985.

————. "The Southern Whigs and Economic Development." *Southern Studies* 20 (1981): 20–38.

Burnham, W. Dean. *Presidential Ballots, 1836-1892*. Baltimore: Johns Hopkins University Press, 1955.

Bury, J. B. *The Idea of Progress: An Inquiry into Its Origins and Growth*. London: Macmillan, 1920.

Carpenter, Jesse T. *The South as a Conscious Minority, 1789-1861: A Study in Political Thought.* New York: New York University Press, 1930.

Carsel, Wilfred. "The Slaveholders' Indictment of Northern Wage Slavery." *Journal of Southern History* 6 (1940): 504-20.

Carwardine, Richard. *Evangelicals and Politics in Antebellum America.* New Haven: Yale University Press, 1993.

Cash, W. J. *The Mind of the South.* New York: Knopf, 1941.

Channing, Steven A. *Crisis of Fear: Secession in South Carolina.* New York: Simon and Schuster, 1970.

Chitwood, Oliver Perry. *John Tyler, Champion of the Old South.* New York: D. Appleton-Century, 1939.

Cole, Arthur C. *The Irrepressible Conflict, 1850-1865.* New York: Macmillan, 1934.

———. *The Whig Party in the South.* 1914. Reprint. Gloucester: Peter Smith, 1962.

Collins, B. W. "Community and Consensus in Ante-Bellum America." *Historical Journal* 19 (1976): 635-63.

Collins, Bruce. "The Ideology of the Antebellum Northern Democrats." *Journal of American Studies* 11 (1977): 103-23.

Collins, Herbert. "Southern Industrial Gospel before 1860." *Journal of Southern History* 12 (1946): 386-402.

Cooper, William J., Jr. *Liberty and Slavery: Southern Politics to 1860.* New York: Knopf, 1983.

———. *The South and the Politics of Slavery, 1828-1856.* Baton Rouge: Louisiana University Press, 1978.

Cooper, William J., Jr., Michael F. Holt, and John McCardell, eds. *A Master's Due: Essays in Honor of David Herbert Donald.* Baton Rouge: Louisiana State University Press, 1985.

Craven, Avery O. *The Coming of the Civil War.* New York: Charles Scribner's Sons, 1942.

———. *The Growth of Southern Nationalism, 1848-1861.* Baton Rouge: Louisiana State University Press, 1953.

———. "Poor Whites and Negroes in the Antebellum South." *Journal of Negro History* 15 (1930): 14-25.

———. *The Repressible Conflict, 1830-1861.* Baton Rouge: Louisiana State University Press, 1939.

Crofts, Daniel W. *Reluctant Confederates: Upper South Unionists in the Secession Crisis.* Chapel Hill: University of North Carolina Press, 1989.

Curti, Merle E. "The Impact of the Revolutions of 1848 on American Thought." *Proceedings of the American Philosophical Society* 93 (1949): 209-15.

———. "Young America." *American Historical Review* 32 (1926-27): 34-55.

Danbom, David B. "The Young America Movement." *Journal of the Illinois State Historical Society* 67 (1974): 294-306.

Davis, David Brion. "The Emergence of Immediatism in British and American Antislavery Thought." *Mississippi Valley Historical Review* 49 (1962-63): 209-30.

———. *The Problem of Slavery in Western Culture.* Ithaca: Cornell University Press, 1966.

———. *The Slave Power Conspiracy and the Paranoid Style*. Baton Rouge: Louisiana State University Press, 1969.

———. "Some Ideological Functions of Prejudice in Antebellum America." *American Quarterly* 15 (1963): 115–25.

Dawson, Jan C. "The Puritan and Cavalier: The South's Perception of Contrasting Traditions." *Journal of Southern History* 44 (1978): 597–614.

Donald, David. "American Historians and the Causes of the Civil War." *South Atlantic Quarterly* 59 (1960): 351–55.

———. *Charles Sumner and the Coming of the Civil War*. New York: Knopf, 1960.

Dumond, Dwight Lowell. *Antislavery: The Crusade for Freedom in America*. Ann Arbor: University of Michigan Press, 1961.

———. *The Secession Movement, 1860-1861*. New York: Macmillan, 1931.

———, ed. *Southern Editorials on Secession*. 1931. Reprint. Gloucester: Peter Smith, 1964.

Eaton, Clement. *The Mind of the Old South*. Baton Rouge: Louisiana State University Press, 1964.

Ekirch, Arthur A. *The Idea of Progress in America, 1815-1860*. New York: Columbia University Press, 1944.

Elkins, Stanley M. *Slavery: A Problem in American Institutional and Intellectual Life*. Chicago: University of Chicago Press, 1968.

Ershkowitz, Herbert, and William G. Shade. "Consensus or Conflict? Political Behavior in the State Legislatures during the Jacksonian Era." *Journal of American History* 58 (1971): 591–621.

Faust, Drew Gilpin. *James Henry Hammond and the Old South: A Design for Mastery*. Baton Rouge: Louisiana State University Press, 1982.

———. *A Sacred Circle: The Dilemma of the Intellectual in the Old South, 1840-1860*. Baltimore: Johns Hopkins University Press, 1977.

———. "A Southern Stewardship: The Intellectual and Proslavery Argument." *American Quarterly* 31 (1979): 63–80.

Fehrenbacher, Don E. *Chicago Giant: A Biography of "Long John" Wentworth*. New York: American Book–Stratford Press, 1957.

———. *The Dred Scott Case: Its Significance in American Law and Politics*. New York: Oxford University Press, 1978.

———. "The New Political History and the Coming of the Civil War." *Pacific Historical Quarterly* 54 (1985): 117–42.

———. *Prelude to Greatness: Lincoln in the 1850s*. Stanford: Stanford University Press, 1962.

———. *The South and Three Sectional Crises: Friends, Foes, and Reforms*. Baton Rouge: Louisiana State University Press, 1980.

Filler, Louis. *The Crusade against Slavery, 1830-1860*. New York: Harper & Row, 1960.

Fite, Emerson David. *The Presidential Campaign of 1860*. New York: Macmillan, 1911.

Foner, Eric. "The Causes of the American Civil War: Recent Interpretations and New Directions." *Civil War History* 20 (1974): 197–214.

———. *Free Soil, Free Labor, Free Men: The Ideology of the Republican Party before the Civil War*. New York: Oxford University Press, 1970.

———. "The Wilmot Proviso Revisited." *Journal of American History* 56 (1969): 267–79.

Ford, Lacy K., Jr. "Frontier Democracy: The Turner Thesis Revisited." *Journal of the Early Republic* 13 (1993): 144–63.

———. "Inventing the Concurrent Majority: Madison, Calhoun, and the Problem of Majoritarianism in American Politics." *Journal of Southern History* 60 (1994): 19–58.

———. *Origins of Southern Radicalism: The South Carolina Upcountry, 1800-1860.* New York: Oxford University Press, 1988.

Forgie, George B. *Patricide in the House Divided: A Psychological Interpretation of Lincoln and His Age.* New York: Norton, 1979.

Formisano, Ronald P. *The Birth of Mass Political Parties: Michigan, 1827-1861.* Princeton: Princeton University Press, 1971.

Foust, James D. *The Yeoman Farmer and Westward Expansion of U.S. Cotton Production.* New York: Arno Press, 1975.

Freehling, William W. *The Reintegration of American History: Slavery and the Civil War.* New York: Oxford University Press, 1994.

———. *The Road to Disunion: Secessionists at Bay, 1776-1854.* New York: Oxford University Press, 1990.

Freehling, William W., and Craig M. Simpson, eds. *Secession Debated: Georgia's Showdown in 1860.* New York: Oxford University Press, 1992.

Fuller, John D. P. *The Movement for the Acquisition of All Mexico, 1846-1848.* Baltimore: Johns Hopkins University Press, 1936.

Gara, Larry. "Slavery and the Slave Power: A Crucial Distinction." *Civil War History* 15 (1969): 5–18.

Gates, Paul Wallace. *Fifty Million Acres: Conflicts over Kansas Land Policy, 1854-1890.* Ithaca: Cornell University Press, 1954.

Genovese, Eugene D. *Political Economy of Slavery: Studies in the Economy and Society of the Slave South.* New York: Pantheon Books, 1965.

Geyl, Pieter. "The American Civil War and the Problem of Inevitability." *New England Quarterly* 24 (1951): 147–68.

Gienapp, William E. "The Crime against Sumner: The Caning of Charles Sumner and the Rise of the Republican Party." *Civil War History* 25 (1979): 218–45.

———. "Nativism and the Creation of a Republican Majority in the North before the Civil War." *Journal of American History* 72 (1985–86): 541–57.

———. *The Origins of the Republican Party, 1852-1856.* New York: Oxford University Press, 1987.

———. "The Whig Party, the Compromise of 1850, and the Nomination of Winfield Scott." *Presidential Studies Quarterly* 14 (1984): 399–415.

Goetzmann, William H. *When the Eagle Screamed: The Romantic Horizon in American Diplomacy, 1800-1860.* New York: Wiley, 1966.

Going, Charles Buxton. *David Wilmot, Free Soiler: A Biography of the Great Advocate of the Wilmot Proviso.* New York: D. Appleton, 1924.

Govan, Thomas P. "Was the Old South Different?" *Journal of Southern History* 21 (1955): 447–55.

Graebner, Norman A. "1848: Southern Politics at the Crossroads." *Historian* 25 (1962): 14–35.

———. *Empire on the Pacific: A Study in American Continental Expansion*. New York: Ronald Press, 1955.

———. "Lessons of the Mexican War." *Pacific Historical Review* 47 (1978): 325–42.

———. "Maritime Factors in the Oregon Compromise." *Pacific Historical Review* 20 (1951): 331–45.

———. "The Mexican War: A Study in Causation." *Pacific Historical Review* 49 (1980): 405–26.

———. "Politics and the Oregon Compromise." *Pacific Northwest Quarterly* 52 (1961): 7–14.

Green, Fletcher M. "Democracy in the Old South." *Journal of Southern History* 12 (1946): 3–23.

Greenberg, Kenneth S. *Masters and Statesmen: The Political Culture of American Slavery*. Baltimore: Johns Hopkins University Press, 1985.

———. "Revolutionary Ideology of the Proslavery Argument: The Abolition of Slavery in Antebellum South Carolina." *Journal of Southern History* 42 (1976): 365–84.

Gunderson, Gerald. "The Origin of the American Civil War." *Journal of Economic History* 34 (1974): 915–50.

Hahn, Steven. *The Roots of Southern Populism: Yeomen Farmers and the Transformation of the Georgia Upcountry, 1850-1890*. New York: Oxford University Press, 1983.

Hamilton, Holman. *Prologue to Conflict: The Crisis and Compromise of 1850*. Lexington: University of Kentucky Press, 1964.

———. *Zachary Taylor: Soldier in the White House*. Indianapolis: Bobbs-Merrill, 1951.

Hanley, Mark Y. *Beyond a Christian Commonwealth: The Protestant Quarrel with the American Republic, 1830-1860*. Chapel Hill: University of North Carolina Press, 1994.

Harris, J. William. "Last of the Classical Republicans: An Interpretation of John C. Calhoun." *Civil War History* 30 (1984): 254–67.

Harris, Neal. *Humbug: The Art of P. T. Barnum*. Chicago: University of Chicago Press, 1981.

Hart, Charles. "The Natural Limits of Slavery Expansion: Kansas-Nebraska, 1854." *Kansas Historical Quarterly* 34 (1968): 32–50.

Hesseltine, William B. "Some New Aspects of the Pro-Slavery Argument." *Journal of Negro History* 21 (1936): 1–14.

Hesseltine, William B., and Rex G. Fisher, eds. *Trimmers, Trucklers and Temporizers: Notes of Murat Halstead from the Political Conventions of 1856*. Madison: State Historical Society of Wisconsin, 1961.

Hietala, Thomas R. *Manifest Design: Anxious Aggrandizement in Late Jacksonian America*. Ithaca: Cornell University Press, 1985.

Higham, John. *From Boundlessness to Consolidation: The Transformation of American Culture, 1848-1860*. Ann Arbor: William L. Clements Library, 1969.

Hodder, F[rank] H. "The Authorship of the Compromise of 1850." *Mississippi Valley Historical Review* 22 (1936): 525–36.

————. "The Railroad Background of the Kansas-Nebraska Act." *Mississippi Valley Historical Review* 12 (1925): 3–22.

Holt, Michael F. *Forging a Majority: The Formation of the Republican Party in Pittsburgh, 1848-1860.* New Haven: Yale University Press, 1969.

————. *The Political Crisis of the 1850s.* New York: Wiley, 1978.

————. *Political Parties and American Political Development: From the Age of Jackson to the Age of Lincoln.* Baton Rouge: Louisiana State University Press, 1992.

————. "The Politics of Impatience: The Origins of Know Nothingism." *Journal of American History* 60 (1973–74): 309–31.

Horsman, Reginald. *Race and Manifest Destiny: The Origins of American Racial Anglo-Saxonism.* Cambridge, Mass.: Harvard University Press, 1981.

Howe, Daniel Walker. *The Political Culture of the American Whigs.* Chicago: University of Chicago Press, 1979.

Johannsen, Robert W. "The Kansas Nebraska Act and Territorial Government in the United States." In *Territorial Kansas: Studies Commemorating the Centennial,* 17–32. Lawrence: University of Kansas Publications, Social Science Studies, 1954.

————. *Stephen A. Douglas.* New York: Oxford University Press, 1973.

————. "Stephen A. Douglas, Popular Sovereignty, and the Territories." *Historian* 22 (1960): 378–95.

————. *To the Halls of the Montezumas: The Mexican War in American Imagination.* New York: Oxford University Press, 1985.

Johnson, Allen. "Genesis of Popular Sovereignty." *Iowa Journal of History and Politics* 3 (1905): 3–19.

Kleppner, Paul J. *The Cross of Culture: A Social Analysis of Midwestern Politics, 1850-1900.* New York: Free Press, 1970.

————. *The Third Electoral System, 1853-1892: Parties, Voters, and Political Cultures.* Chapel Hill: University of North Carolina Press, 1979.

Knupfer, Peter B. *The Union as It Is: Constitutional Unionism and Sectional Compromise, 1787-1861.* Chapel Hill: University of North Carolina Press, 1991.

Kohl, Lawrence F. *The Politics of Individualism: Parties and the American Character in the Jacksonian Era.* New York: Oxford University Press, 1989.

Kraut, Alan M., ed. *Crusaders and Compromisers: Essays on the Relationship of the Antislavery Struggle to the Antebellum Party System.* Westport: Greenwood Press, 1983.

Kruman, Marc W. *Parties and Politics in North Carolina, 1836-1865.* Baton Rouge: Louisiana State University Press, 1983.

Lee, Susan Previant. *The Westward Movement of the Cotton Industry, 1840-1860: Perceived Interests and Economic Realities.* New York: Arno Press, 1977.

Litwack, Leon F. *North of Slavery: The Negro in the Free States, 1790-1860.* Chicago: University of Chicago Press, 1961.

Luraghi, Raimondo. "The Civil War and the Modernization of American Society: Social Structure and Industrial Revolution in the Old South before and during the War." *Civil War History* 18 (1972): 230–50.

Lynch, William O. "Antislavery Tendencies of the Democratic Party in the Northwest, 1848-1850." *Mississippi Valley Historical Review* 11 (1924–25): 319–31.

Maizlish, Stephen E. *The Triumph of Sectionalism: The Transformation of Ohio Politics, 1844-1856.* Kent: Kent State University Press, 1983.

Maizlish, Stephen E., and John J. Kushma, eds. *Essays on American Antebellum Politics, 1840-1860*. College Station: Texas A & M University Press, 1982.

Malin, James C. *John Brown and the Legend of Fifty-Six*. Philadelphia: American Philosophical Society, 1942.

————. *The Nebraska Question, 1852-1854*. Lawrence: University Press of Kansas, 1953.

————. "The Topeka Statehood Movement Reconsidered: Origins." In *Territorial Kansas: Studies Commemorating the Centennial*, 33-69. Lawrence: University of Kansas Publications, Social Science Studies, 1954.

May, Robert E. *John A. Quitman: Old South Crusader*. Baton Rouge: Louisiana State University Press, 1985.

————. *The Southern Dream of a Caribbean Empire, 1854-1861*. Baton Rouge: Louisiana State University Press, 1973.

McCardell, John. *The Idea of a Southern Nation: Southern Nationalists and Southern Nationalism, 1830-1860*. New York: Norton, 1979.

McMillan, Malcolm C. "Joseph Glover Baldwin Reports on the Whig National Convention of 1848." *Journal of Southern History* 25 (1959): 366-82.

McPherson, James M. "Antebellum Southern Exceptionalism: A New Look at an Old Question." *Civil War History* 29 (1983): 230-44.

————. *Battle Cry of Freedom: The Civil War Era*. New York: Oxford University Press, 1988.

————. *What They Fought For, 1861-1865*. Baton Rouge: Louisiana State University Press, 1994.

McWhiney, Grady. "Were the Whigs a Class Party in Alabama?" *Journal of Southern History* 23 (1957): 510-22.

Merk, Frederick. *Slavery and the Annexation of Texas*. New York: Knopf, 1972.

Merk, Frederick, and Lois Bannister Merk. *Manifest Destiny and Mission in American History: A Reinterpretation*. New York: Knopf, 1963.

Meyers, Marvin. *The Jacksonian Persuasion: Politics and Belief*. Stanford: Stanford University Press, 1957.

Morgan, Edmund S. "Slavery and Freedom: The American Paradox." *Journal of American History* 59 (1972): 5-29.

Morgan, Robert J. *A Whig Embattled: The Presidency under John Tyler*. Lincoln: University of Nebraska Press, 1954.

Morrison, Chaplain W. *Democratic Politics and Sectionalism: The Wilmot Proviso Controversy*. Chapel Hill: University of North Carolina Press, 1967.

Nagel, Paul C. *One Nation Indivisible: The Union in American Thought, 1776-1861*. New York: Oxford University Press, 1964.

Nevins, Allan. *The Emergence of Lincoln*. 2 vols. New York: Charles Scribner's Sons, 1950.

————. *Ordeal of the Union*. 2 vols. New York: Charles Scribner's Sons, 1947.

Nichols, Alice. *Bleeding Kansas*. New York: Oxford University Press, 1954.

Nichols, Roy Franklin. *The Democratic Machine, 1850-1854*. New York: Columbia University Press, 1923.

————. *The Disruption of American Democracy*. 1948. Reprint. New York: Free Press, 1967.

————. *Franklin Pierce, Young Hickory of the Granite Hills*. 1931. 2d ed. Philadelphia: University of Pennsylvania Press, 1958.

————. "The Kansas Nebraska Act: A Century of Historiography." *Mississippi Valley Historical Review* 43 (1956–57): 187–212.

Niven, John. *Gideon Welles: Lincoln's Secretary of the Navy*. New York: Oxford University Press, 1973.

————. *John C. Calhoun and the Price of Union: A Biography*. Baton Rouge: Louisiana State University Press, 1988.

————. *Martin Van Buren: The Romantic Age of American Politics*. New York: Oxford University Press, 1983.

Osterweis, Rollin G. *Romanticism and Nationalism in the Old South*. New Haven: Yale University Press, 1949.

Overdyke, W. Darrell. *The Know-Nothing Party in the South*. Baton Rouge: Louisiana State University Press, 1950.

Owsley, Frank Lawrence, and Harriet C. Owsley. "The Economic Basis of Society in the Late Antebellum South." *Journal of Southern History* 6 (1940): 24–45.

Paul, James C. N. *Rift in the Democracy*. 1951. Reprint. New York: A. S. Barnes, 1961.

Pease, William H., and Jane H. Pease. "Anti-Slavery Ambivalence: Immediatism, Expediency, Race." *American Quarterly* 17 (1965): 682–95.

Perkins, Bradford. *The Creation of a Republican Empire, 1776-1865*. Cambridge, Eng.: Cambridge University Press, 1993.

Perkins, Howard C., ed. *Northern Editorials on Secession*. 2 vols. New York: D. Appleton-Century, 1942.

Phillips, Ulrich Bonnell. *Life and Labor in the Old South*. Boston: Little, Brown, 1929.

Pletcher, David M. *The Diplomacy of Annexation: Texas, Oregon, and the Mexican War*. Columbia: University of Missouri Press, 1973.

Poage, George Rawlings. *Henry Clay and the Whig Party*. 1936. Reprint. Gloucester: Peter Smith, 1965.

Potter, David M. "The Historian's Use of Nationalism and Vice Versa." *American Historical Review* 67 (1961–62): 924–50.

————. *The Impending Crisis, 1848-1861*. New York: Harper & Row, 1976.

————. *Lincoln and His Party in the Secession Crisis*. New Haven: Yale University Press, 1942.

Pressly, Thomas J. *Americans Interpret Their Civil War*. Princeton: Princeton University Press, 1954.

Quaife, Milo Milton. *The Doctrine of Non-Intervention with Slavery in the Territories*. Chicago: Mac C. Chamberline, 1910.

Ramsdell, Charles W. "The Natural Limits of Slavery Expansion." *Mississippi Valley Historical Review* 16 (1929): 151–71.

Randall, J. G. "The Blundering Generation." *Mississippi Valley Historical Review* 27 (1940): 3–28.

Randall, James G., and David Donald. *The Civil War and Reconstruction*. 1953. Reprint. Boston: D. C. Heath, 1961.

Rawley, James A. *Race and Politics: "Bleeding Kansas" and the Coming of the Civil War*. Philadelphia: Lippincott, 1969.

Rayback, Joseph G. *Free Soil: The Election of 1848*. Lexington: University Press of Kentucky, 1970.

Rayback, Robert J. *Millard Fillmore: Biography of a President*. Buffalo: Published for the Buffalo Historical Society by H. Stewart, 1959.

Remini, Robert V. *Andrew Jackson and the Course of American Diplomacy, 1833-1845*. New York: Harper & Row, 1984.

Russel, Robert R. *Economic Aspects of Southern Sectionalism, 1840-1861*. Urbana: University of Illinois Press, 1924.

———. "The Effects of Slavery Upon Non-slaveholders in the Antebellum South." *Agricultural History* 15 (1941): 112–26.

Schlesinger, Arthur M., Jr. "The Causes of the American Civil War: A Note on Historical Sentimentalism." *Partisan Review* 16 (1949): 967–81.

Schott, Thomas E. *Alexander Stephens of Georgia: A Biography*. Baton Rouge: Louisiana State University Press, 1988.

Schroeder, John H. *Mr. Polk's War: American Opposition and Dissent, 1846-1848*. Madison: University of Wisconsin Press, 1973.

Sellers, Charles G. *James K. Polk: Continentalist, 1843-1846*. Princeton: Princeton University Press, 1966.

———. *The Market Revolution: Jacksonian America, 1815-1846*. New York: Oxford University Press, 1991.

———. "Who Were the Southern Whigs." *American Historical Review* 59 (1953–54): 335–46.

Sewell, Richard H. *Ballots for Freedom: Antislavery Politics in the United States, 1837-1860*. New York: Oxford University Press, 1976.

———. *A House Divided: Sectionalism and Civil War, 1848-1865*. Baltimore: Johns Hopkins University Press, 1988.

Shalhope, Robert E. "Thomas Jefferson's Republicanism and Antebellum Southern Thought." *Journal of Southern History* 42 (1976): 529–56.

Silbey, Joel H. *The American Political Nation, 1838-1893*. Stanford: Stanford University Press, 1991.

———. *The Shrine of Party: Congressional Voting Behavior, 1841-1852*. Pittsburgh: University of Pittsburgh Press, 1967.

———. "The Slavery-Extension Controversy and Illinois Congressmen, 1846-50." *Journal of the Illinois State Historical Society* 58 (1965): 378–95.

———. "The Southern National Democrats, 1845-1861." *Mid-America* 47 (1965): 176–90.

Simpson, Craig M. *A Good Southerner: The Life of Henry A. Wise of Virginia*. Chapel Hill: University of North Carolina Press, 1985.

Somkin, Fred. *Unquiet Eagle: Memory and Desire in the Idea of American Freedom, 1815-1860*. Ithaca: Cornell University Press, 1967.

Stampp, Kenneth M. *And the War Came: The North and the Secession Crisis, 1860-1861*. 1950. Reprint. Baton Rouge: Louisiana State University Press, 1970.

Stanley, Gerald. "Racism and the Early Republican Party: The 1856 Presidential Election in California." *Pacific Historical Review* 43 (1974): 171–87.

Stegmaier, Mark J. "Zachary Taylor versus the South." *Civil War History* 33 (1987): 218–41.

Summers, Mark W. *The Plundering Generation: Corruption and the Crisis of the Union, 1849-1861.* New York: Oxford University Press, 1987.

Swisher, Carl Brent. *Roger B. Taney.* New York: Macmillan, 1935.

Taylor, William R. *Cavalier and Yankee: The Old South and the American National Character.* New York: G. Braziller, 1961.

Thomas, John L. "Romantic Reform in America, 1815-1865." *American Quarterly* 17 (1965): 656-81.

Thornton, J. Mills, III. *Politics and Power in a Slave Society: Alabama, 1800-1860.* Baton Rouge: Louisiana State University Press, 1978.

Tuveson, Ernest L. *Redeemer Nation: The Idea of America's Millennial Role.* Chicago: University of Chicago Press, 1968.

Van Alstyne, Richard W. "American Nationalism and Its Mythology." *Queens Quarterly* 65 (1958): 423-36.

———. *The Rising American Empire.* 1960. Reprint. Chicago: Quadrangle Books, 1965.

Van Deusen, Glydon G. *The Life of Henry Clay.* Boston: Little, Brown, 1937.

———. "Some Aspects of Whig Thought and Theory in the Jacksonian Period." *American Historical Review* 63 (1957-58): 305-22.

———. *Thurlow Weed, Wizard of the Lobby.* Boston: Little, Brown, 1947.

———. *William Henry Seward.* New York: Oxford University Press, 1967.

Varon, Elizabeth R. "Tippecanoe and the Ladies Too: White Women and Party Politics in Antebellum Virginia." *Journal of American History* 82 (1995-96): 494-521.

Vevier, Charles. "American Continentalism: An Idea of Expansion, 1845-1910." *American Historical Review* 65 (1959-60): 323-35.

Weinberg, Albert K. *Manifest Destiny: A Study of Nationalist Expansionism in American History.* Baltimore: Johns Hopkins University Press, 1935.

Weir, Robert M. "'The Harmony We Were Famous For': An Interpretation of Pre-Revolutionary South Carolina Politics." *William and Mary Quarterly* 26 (1969): 473-501.

Welter, Rush. "The Frontier West as Image of American Society, 1776-1860." *Pacific Northwest Quarterly* 52 (1961): 1-6.

———. "The Frontier West as Image of American Society: Conservative Attitudes before the Civil War." *Mississippi Valley Historical Review* 46 (1960): 593-614.

———. *The Mind of America, 1820-1860.* New York: Columbia University Press, 1975.

Wiebe, Robert H. *The Opening of American Society: From the Adoption of the Constitution to the Eve of Disunion.* New York: Vintage Books, 1984.

Williams, William Appleman. *The Roots of the Modern American Empire: A Study in the Growth and Shaping of Social Consciousness in a Marketplace Society.* New York: Random House, 1969.

Wilson, Major L. "Manifest Destiny and Free Soil: The Triumph of Negative Liberalism in the 1840s." *Historian* 31 (1968): 36-56.

———. *The Presidency of Martin Van Buren.* Lawrence: University Press of Kansas, 1984.

————. *Space, Time, and Freedom: The Quest for Nationality and the Irrepressible Conflict, 1815–1861*. Westport: Greenwood Press, 1974.

Wood, Gordon S. *The Creation of the American Republic, 1776–1787*. Chapel Hill: University of North Carolina Press, 1969.

————. *The Radicalism of the American Revolution*. New York: Knopf, 1992.

Woodward, C. Vann. "The Anti Slavery Myth." *American Scholar* 31 (1961–62): 312–28.

————. "The Search for Southern Identity." *Virginia Quarterly Review* 34 (1958): 321–38.

Wright, Gavin. *The Political Economy of the South: Households, Markets, and Wealth in the Nineteenth Century*. New York: Norton, 1978.

Dissertations

Atkins, Jonathan M. "'A combat for liberty': Politics and Parties in Jackson's Tennessee, 1832–1851." Ph.D. diss., University of Michigan, 1991.

Barker, Robin Edward. "Class and Party: Voting Behavior in the Late Antebellum South." Ph.D. diss., Texas A & M University, 1989.

Byrne, John Edward. "The News from Harpers Ferry: The Press as Lens and Prism for John Brown's Raid." Ph.D. diss., George Washington University, 1987.

Fowler, Nolan. "The Anti-Expansionist Argument in the United States Prior to the Civil War." Ph.D. diss., University of Kentucky, 1955.

Hart, Charles Ralph Desmond. "Congressmen and the Expansion of Slavery into the Territories: A Study in Attitudes, 1846–1861." Ph.D. diss., University of Washington, Seattle, 1965.

Jenkins, Robert Louis. "The Gadsden Treaty and Sectionalism: A Nation Reacts." Ph.D. diss., Mississippi State University, 1978.

King, James Crawford, Jr. "'Content with Being': Nineteenth Century Southern Attitudes toward Economic Development." Ph.D. diss., University of Alabama, 1985.

Lampton, John E. "The Kansas-Nebraska Act Reconsidered: An Analysis of Men, Methods, and Motives." Ph.D. diss., Illinois State University, 1979.

Ley, Douglas Arthur. "Expansionists All? Southern Senators and American Foreign Policy, 1841–1860." Ph.D. diss., University of Wisconsin, 1990.

Michael, Steven Bruce. "Ohio and the Mexican War: Public Response to the 1846–1848 Crisis." Ph.D. diss., Ohio State University, 1985.

Ndukwa, Maurice Dickson. "Antislavery in Michigan: A Study of Its Origin, Development, and Expression from the Territorial Period to 1860." Ph.D. diss., Michigan State University, 1979.

Phillips, Adrienne Cole. "Responses in Mississippi to John Brown's Raid." Ph.D. diss., University of Mississippi, 1983.

Roeckell, Lelia M. "British Interests in Texas, 1838–1846." Ph.D. diss., St. Peter's College, University of Oxford, 1993.

Saxon, Gerald Douglas. "The Politics of Expansion: Texas as an Issue in National Politics, 1819–1845." Ph.D. diss., North Texas State University, 1979.

Stegmaier, Mark J. "The U.S. Senate in the Sectional Crisis, 1846–1861: A Roll-Call Voting Analysis." Ph.D. diss., University of California, Santa Barbara, 1975.

Stevens, Walter William. "A Study of Lewis Cass and His United States Senate Speeches on Popular Sovereignty." Ph.D. diss., University of Michigan, 1959.

Index

Dawson, William C., 134

Day, Timothy C., 166

Dayton, William, 181

Democratic Party: idea of liberty, 16–17; and territorial expansion, 16–17, 81, 138, 140; and Texas annexation, 16–19, 29–32; and commercial growth, 17–18; and nature of Union, 18; election of 1844, 26–33; and Oregon, 32–33, 43; and Wilmot Proviso, 41–44, 56–62; internal divisions (1843–44), 42–43; and popular sovereignty, 84, 99, 119–23, 136–37; and 1848 election, 86, 95; and Compromise of 1850, 127–28, 131–32, 135–37, 144–45, 206; internal divisions (1850–52), 131–32, 140–41; election of 1852, 140–41; and Kansas turmoil, 162–64; election of 1856, 177–81; and racism, 180; sectional rift in, 189–90, 197–99, 201–3, 205, 214–18, 221–22, 228; and *Dred Scott*, 193–96; and Lecompton constitution, 196–203, 205–6

Dickinson, Daniel S., 84, 121

Disney, David T., 120

Dix, John A., 149

Dixon, Archibald, 146

Dixon, James, 77

Dodge, Augustus C., 142, 143

Donelson, Andrew Jaskson, 38

Doolittle, James R., 192

Douglas, Stephen A., 84, 100, 101, 102, 103, 120, 124, 125, 135, 136, 178, 218, 234; and Kansas-Nebraska Act, 128, 142–43, 154, 155; and American Revolution, 146–47; views on Kansas turmoil, 163; and *Dred Scott*, 195; and Lecompton constitution, 197–98, 200, 205; and Freeport doctrine, 206–7, 212; debates with Lincoln, 206–8; southern rights Democrats views on, 215–16, 236; nomination, 226

Douglas Democrats: and Lecompton constitution, 200–201, 205–6; and southern rights Democrats, 203,

216–22, 224–51; opposition to slave code, 213, 235; and Charleston convention (1860), 220, 222–24; and Baltimore convention (1860), 226; in 1860 campaign, 232–36; and Republican Party, 233–34; and American Revolution, 235–36

Dred Scott, 188–89; Republican Party and, 189, 190–93; Democratic Party and, 189–90, 193–96; and 1860 campaign, 220, 222. *See also* Slavepower

Duer, William, 82, 105

Dunham, Cyrus L., 120, 121, 122, 146

Edmundson, Henry A., 154

Ellis, John W., 257, 258–59, 260

English, William H., 143, 153

Everett, Alexander H., 35

Everett, Edward, 21, 35, 109, 129, 150, 231, 232, 246, 248, 249

Fairfield, John, 29

Farnsworth, John, 275–76

Federalist Number 10, 5, 18

Federal slave code, 211–15, 222, 223, 227–28, 234

Fessenden, William Pitt, 191, 203, 265

Fillmore, Millard, 124, 132, 139

Fish, Hamilton, 129, 172

Fitch, Graham N., 225

Fitzpatrick, Benjamin, 226

Flournoy, Thomas S., 93, 94

Floyd, John B., 136, 215, 252, 253

Foner, Eric, 43

Foote, Henry S., 103, 124

Forbes, John Murray, 168, 169

Ford, Lacy K., Jr., 7

Forney, John J., 224

Foster, J. L., 225

Free labor: northern views on, 109–10; southern views on, 115–16, 256–57

Freeport doctrine, 206–7

Free-Soil Party, 95, 140, 141

Frémont, John C., 181

Fulton, Andrew S., 83

Preston, William B., 101–2
Pugh, George, 213, 223

Quincy, Josiah, 182
Quitman, John A., 177, 178

Raleigh letter (Clay), 19
Randall, James G., 3
Rantoul, Robert, 63
Raymond, Henry, 181
Rayner, Kenneth, 140, 257
Reeder, Andrew, 161
Reid, David S., 173
Republican Party: and popular sovereignty, 164–65, 192–93, 241; and slavepower, 165–69, 182–83, 191–92, 204, 238, 243, 264–66; and southern society, 168–69; and American Revolution, 169–71, 182–83, 242, 263, 266–68; southern fears of, 174, 183–85, 257–58, 260–61; 1856 election, 181–83; and *Dred Scott*, 189, 190–93; and Lecompton constitution, 203–4, 205; in 1860 campaign, 229–30, 241–46; and racism, 230; and Constitutional Union Party, 244; and secession crisis, 253, 262–68, 272–76, 278–79
Rhett, Robert Barnwell, 59
Richardson, William A., 121, 236
Richmond convention (1860), 227–28
Riley, Bennet, 104
Ritchie, Thomas, 27
Rives, William Cabell, 21, 25, 35, 73, 78, 94, 130, 179, 231, 246, 272
Roberts, Jonathan, 46
Ruffin, Edmund, 174, 175
Rush, Richard, 27
Rutherfoord, John C., 209

Samford, William, 206
Savage, John H., 121
Schlesinger, Arthur M., Jr., 3
Scott, Winfield, 66, 81, 139, 140
Sebastian, William K., 198
Secession, 253–54; Republicans and, 252, 262–68, 272–76; northern Democrats and, 253, 254, 268–71; southern Unionists and, 254, 260, 268, 271–72; territorial issue and, 255, 262; southern argument for, 255–62, 278; and self-government, 258–59, 262, 269–70; and legacy of American Revolution, 259–62, 263, 266–68, 270–71, 274–76; and states' rights, 261–62, 266
"Secret Six," 208–9
Seddon, James, 60
Severance, Luther, 77
Seward, William Henry, 108, 152, 162, 171, 191, 204, 230, 264
Shannon, Wilson, 161
Shaw, Lemuel, 47
Slavepower: anti-Nebraska sentiment, 150–51, 152–53; Republican views on, 165–69, 182–83, 243; and secession, 228–29, 264–66. See also *Dred Scott*
Slavery: restrictionists' views on, 98, 110–11, 166–67; southern views on, 98–99, 114–16, 175–76
Slavery extension: and Texas annexation, 24–25, 31–32, 34, 44; in Missouri statehood debate, 47–49; free-soil opposition to, 53–58; Mexican cession and, 98–99, 102, 107, 110–11, 112–13, 116–17, 123; and Kansas-Nebraska Act, 148–53; in Kansas, 168–69, 176–77; in 1860 campaign, 229–30, 231, 232, 233–34, 239, 243
Smith, Caleb Blood, 89
Smith, Gerrit, 57
Smith, Persifor, 104
Smith, Samuel, 195
Smith, Truman, 91, 139
Southern rights Democrats: and Kansas, 172–73, 177; and Republican Party, 173–74, 183–84, 200, 237–38; social ideology of, 174–76; and restriction of slavery, 176–77, 190, 202, 227, 237–40; 1856 election, 178, 183–85; prospect of Republican rule, 183–85, 257–58, 260–61; views of Union, 184–85, 239, 257–58, 259–60; and *Dred Scott*, 189–

76, 78–81; 1844 campaign, 33–35; and
slavery extension, 34, 44, 55–56, 87;
and Mexican War, 40–41, 66–68,
70–81; and Wilmot Proviso, 55–56, 73,
76–78, 92–93; and racism, 75; sectional strains in, 77–78, 85–86, 106–7,
129–31, 138–40; and Treaty of Guadalupe Hidalgo, 83; 1848 election,
86–95; and popular sovereignty,
92–94; and Mexican cession, 101–2,
106–7; and Compromise of 1850,
129–31; 1852 campaign, 138–40, 141
White, Hugh, 41
Wick, William W., 84, 217–18
Wigfall, Louis T., 212
Wilkins, William, 18
Williams, Christopher, 139
Williams, John, 210
Wilmot, David, 41, 43, 113, 242
Wilmot Proviso: introduction, 41; free-
soil Democrats and, 43–44, 53–58, 98;

Whigs and, 55–56, 69, 76–78, 92–93;
southern' rights Democrats and,
58–62, 98–99, 116–17; in 1848 elec-
tion, 90; moderate Democrats and,
99, 119–20
Wilson, Henry, 165, 170, 172, 173, 189,
262, 263, 265–66, 267
Wilson, James, 267
Wilson, Major L., 56, 61
Winthrop, Robert C., 41, 77, 89, 106, 108
Wise, Henry A., 177
Wood, Fernando, 220
Woodbury, Levi, 17, 27, 31
Wright, Silas, 28

Yancey, Benjamin, 117
Yancey, William Lowndes, 220, 223, 241,
274
Yates, Richard, 165, 169, 171
Young America, 35, 140, 141
Yulee, David, 107, 114, 258, 259

CPSIA information can be obtained at www.ICGtesting.com
Printed in the USA
BVOW012321290112

281557BV00002B/6/A

9 780807 847961